The Age of Deficits

The Age of Deficits

PRESIDENTS AND UNBALANCED BUDGETS
FROM JIMMY CARTER TO GEORGE W. BUSH

Iwan Morgan

University Press of Kansas

© 2009 by the University Press of Kansas
All rights reserved

Published by the University Press of Kansas (Lawrence, Kansas 66045), which was organized
by the Kansas Board of Regents and is operated and funded by Emporia State University, Fort
Hays State University, Kansas State University, Pittsburg State University, the University of
Kansas, and Wichita State University

Library of Congress Cataloging-in-Publication Data

Morgan, Iwan W.
  The age of deficits : presidents and unbalanced budgets from Jimmy
Carter to George W. Bush / Iwan Morgan.
    p. cm.
  Includes bibliographical references and index.
  ISBN 978-0-7006-1685-5 (cloth : alk. paper)
  1. Budget deficits—United States—History—20th century. 2. Budget deficits—United
States—History—21st century. 3. Presidents—United States—History—20th century.
4. Presidents—United States—History—21st century. 5. Political parties—United
States—History. 6. Finance, Public—United States—History—1933– 7. Fiscal policy—
United States—History—20th century. 8. Fiscal policy—United States—History—21st
century. 9. United States—Economic policy—20th century 10. United States—Economic
policy—2001– I. Title.
  HJ2051.M653 2009
  339.5'23097309045—dc22   2009025059

British Library Cataloguing-in-Publication Data is available.

Printed in the United States of America

10 9 8 7 6 5 4 3 2 1

The paper used in this publication is recycled and contains 30 percent postconsumer waste.
It is acid free and meets the minimum requirements of the American National Standard for
Permanence of Paper for Printed Library Materials Z39.48-1992.

To Theresa, Humphrey, and Eleanor

Contents

Preface

This book is a political history of how presidents from Jimmy Carter to George W. Bush shaped federal budget policy in what can be termed the age of deficits. The U.S. government only balanced its budget in four of the thirty-two years of their combined occupancy of the White House. Unbalanced budgets were nothing new in American history, of course, but the scale and chronic nature of deficits in the late twentieth and early twenty-first centuries were unprecedented. It was also paradoxical that this loss of budgetary control occurred when American politics had broadly shifted rightwards. In the mid-twentieth century, deficits had been the fiscal instrument for liberal ends, but they were bigger and more frequent in the conservative era that followed.

The four presidents who held office from 1977 to 2001 were unanimous in portraying the budget deficit as a threat to the national interest. George W. Bush did not follow suit, but he could not ignore the renewed descent of federal finances into the red on his watch. At the end of his first term, he promised to halve the budget deficit by the time he left office, a pledge he failed ultimately to fulfill.

Apart from Bill Clinton, the presidents who depicted the deficit as a threat had no more success than Bush in achieving their aims of either substantially reducing it or eliminating it altogether. The almost annual ritual of American politics since the late 1970s involved the president setting a budget plan that prioritized deficit control and Congress setting a budget resolution agreeing that action to this end was needed. When the budget-making process had run its course, however, the gap between outlays and revenues tended to remain dauntingly large. It is said that the only certainties in life are death and taxes, but the modern American experience suggests that unbalanced federal budgets could be added to the list.

In contrast to works by political scientists, historical studies of modern U.S. budget policy are relatively thin on the ground. At one level, this paucity of interest on the part of historians is understandable. Budgeting is hardly a heroic field for study. An arcane, inside-the-beltway domain of public policy that appears all too susceptible to special interest lobbying, it operates in a different political universe from the morally uplifting social movements whose struggles to expand rights and equality shaped modern America. It is an endlessly repetitive process, the annual political equivalent of the ever-lasting Groundhog Day with no prospect of closure or final victory for the good cause—even if there could be agreement on what that was. It even has its own time frame—the Fiscal Year (October 1 to September 30 since 1976)—that enhances its Parallel Earth separateness from the experience of ordinary people who live in "real" time. Moreover, it appears to make little difference whether the budget is balanced or not. Perpetual deficits have not yet produced a day of reckoning in the form of a crisis of public finance. This may well happen in time, but historians have a natural preference to explain the past rather than to predict the future.

In spite of this, historians neglect budget policy at their peril. Esoteric, elitist, and endless it may be, but analysis of it over time tells us much about issues that have been central to American politics since the inception of the republic. The federal budget's allocation of funds to public programs is the principal determinant of the size and scope of national government. Its revenue-raising element determines how much money will be transferred from the private-sector economy to pay for national programs and which groups in society will bear the costs of this. Finally, its operation of a deficit determines how much of the present costs of government will be transferred to the future.

The budget is the main statement of the national government's priorities in a particular year. More importantly, trends over time in federal spending, taxation, and borrowing are a significant index of America's political course and its prevailing views on the role of government. In this regard, the budget has long been at the center of political debate and conflict within and between not only the institutions of national government that are responsible for formulating it but also the political parties that seek to control them and the broader constituencies that these represent.

In focusing on presidential leadership on the deficit issue, this study seeks to put budget policy at the center of America's recent political history. Its emphasis on the occupant of the White House does not preclude recognition that Congress has the ultimate power of the purse but is premised on the president's widely recognized authority to set the terms of national budget debate and to determine the fiscal agenda on which the legislature deliberates. My fundamental argument is that each of the presidents under review approached budget issues as a political leader rather than the nation's accountant-in-chief. However trenchantly they defined the deficit as a threat, their solutions for it reflected their political values and their assessment of how to reconcile deficit reduction with the other elements of their governing agenda. Accordingly, a particular president's stand on the deficit was an intensely political reflection of his views on the legitimate purpose of government, the priorities of government spending, and the proper scope of taxation.

In essence, budget trends constitute a vital indicator not only of governmental activism but also of the outcome of political struggles over this. Examination of presidential budget policy and response to the deficit problem can therefore illuminate the broader politics of conservatism's advance and liberalism's adaptation to this in late twentieth and early twenty-first century America. It also offers an important policy domain for evaluation of the leadership and significance of the five presidents under review within this wider political context.

Jimmy Carter's presidency signaled the transition from the Keynesian era when deficits were considered a positive instrument of public purpose to a new fiscal era when they were deemed a threat. The first wave of Carter historiography interpreted his administration's significance chiefly as a symbol of liberalism's collapse because of its apparent uncertainty of purpose, priority, and direction in the difficult economic circumstances of the late 1970s. By contrast, a new revisionism presents the thirty-ninth president as straddling the Roosevelt-Johnson legacy of social reform and rights expansion and the market-oriented conservatism of the late twentieth century. This study's examination of Carter's budget policy is largely supportive of this latter perspective, even if its explanation of his failure to bring about a workable synthesis of these two traditions tends to confirm conventional criticism of his leadership skills. In its assessment, his presidency marked the first step in the Democrats' late twentieth-century embrace of deficit control as the instrument to deliver their social mission within a framework of business prosperity and noninflationary economic growth.

For Ronald Reagan, the budget was the primary instrument to deliver his conservative agenda of low taxes, reduced government, and defense expansion, but this came at the cost of unprecedented peacetime deficits. This volume is in accord with recent historical assessment that Reagan was a pragmatic ideologue who demonstrated shrewd leadership in operating through a combination of strategic clarity and tactical flexibility. In contrast to claims that the Reagan deficits were an intentional instrument to shackle the liberal state, however, it argues instead that they limited the scope of conservative change in the 1980s by necessitating budgetary compromises to effect their reduction. Although the fortieth president's achievements fell well short of being a "Reagan Revolution," he still pushed through enough of his fiscal agenda to shift public policy from the liberal course of the New Deal order in the direction of a new antistatism. A number of historians have conjectured the existence of an "Age of Reagan" on grounds that his legacy continued to set the tone of politics and public policy in the twenty years after he left office. Insofar as the budget is concerned, this is certainly the case. Reagan's successors had to work out the implications of the fiscal changes that he initiated, including the deficits that were their most problematic consequence, in a conservative era that he had done much to bring about.

In marked contrast to generally favorable evaluations of his foreign policy leadership, George H. W. Bush has the historical reputation of being a failed domestic president. In terms of budget leadership, however, he merits some reinterpretation for combining policy success with political failure. The programmatic and procedural elements of Bush's 1990 bipartisan budget compromise with the congressional Democrats laid crucial foundations for the restoration of fiscal responsibility by the end of the decade. In effect, the forty-first president transcended his predecessor's legacy of large deficits at the cost of undermining his legacy of low taxes by agreeing to revenue enhancement measures as part of the deal. Envisioning this as a betrayal, conservative Republicans henceforth put the restoration and expansion of Reagan's tax agenda at the core of their political mission in the 1990s. Bush's compromise also made them determined to balance the budget through far greater domestic retrenchment than Reagan had ever envisaged in order to preempt further threats to his legacy in the name of deficit reduction.

Measured on the criterion of balancing the budget, Bill Clinton was the most successful fiscal president since the 1920s. More significantly, despite his reputation for slipperiness and expediency, he consistently took political risks to achieve deficit reduction that he deemed essential for the long-term expansion of prosperity within the market economy. The combination of the Clinton administration's fiscal restraint and the Federal Reserve's monetary relaxation, the reverse of the economic policy mix of the 1980s, was instrumental in bringing about the strongest economic growth in thirty years in the second half of the 1990s. For some liberal-left critics, Clinton's appropriation of the traditional Republican cause of balanced budgets perpetuated the Reagan Revolution in constraining government activism to spread the fruits of prosperity. In contrast, this study interprets his success in reducing and eventually eliminating the deficit at a high level of revenue as a political achievement of historic significance for the defense of the liberal state. This enabled Clinton to preserve the bulk of New Deal–Great Society social provision from the efforts of Reagan's heirs in Congress to emasculate it in the name of achieving fiscal equilibrium at a low level of revenue. Nevertheless, Clinton's presidency also constituted a lost opportunity for investing the second-term budget surpluses to guarantee the long-term solvency of Social Security and Medicare. Failure to achieve entitlement reform denied him a legacy of preparing America to meet the fiscal challenges of the twenty-first century.

Whatever the future holds for estimations of George W. Bush's presidential reputation, it is difficult to anticipate a favorable revisionism of his budget policy. Notwithstanding problems of objectivity in assessing the recent past, this study is broadly critical that he sacrificed the fiscal discipline of the 1990s in pursuit of a governing agenda of tax reduction, defense expansion, and big government conservatism. As a budget leader, Bush was successful in achieving most of his core objectives, but his policies had problematic consequences. A series of tax cuts skewed toward the wealthy renewed the impetus of Reaganism, but the revenue costs were instrumental in the return of large and chronic deficits. Unwilling to choose between guns and butter, Bush was the first president ever to cut taxes in wartime and only the second since 1950 to expand both the defense and domestic budgets. Last but not least, he left America's entitlement state in a much worse financial condition than when he took office. Instead of seeking a bipartisan fix to ensure its long-term solvency, he promoted a hugely expensive prescription drug benefit for partisan gain and botched Social Security reform by insisting on private investment accounts in line with his Republican vision of an "ownership society."

Assessment of the historical significance of ongoing developments must be made with caution, but Bush may well have been the last president of the Age of Reagan. Budget politics took a new turn in response to the economic crisis that blighted his final year in office and showed no signs of ending as he left the White House. Contrary to the free-market ethos of recent times, Barack Obama engaged in a level of fiscal activism unmatched since the Great Depression to counteract this catastrophe. Deficit spending once more became the instrument to revitalize the private economy that it had been in the Age of Keynes. At the same time, however, projections of rising health-care and pension program costs indicated that timely reform of the entitlement state was needed to avert a crisis of fiscal sustainability in the long term. Accordingly, this study offers a preliminary assessment of the complex budget issues facing the forty-fourth president.

In analyzing presidential budget leadership within the framework of the budget's political relevance in the age of deficits, this study poses the following questions: What part did presidents play in the development of the deficit problem in the late 1970s and 1980s, its reduction in the 1990s, and its resurrection in the following decade? How did the political values and personal backgrounds of each president under review shape their cognitive understanding of the causes of the deficit problem and their ideas for resolving it? How did presidents in their approach to the deficit affect their relations with the opposition party and their own party in Congress? Why were Republican presidents generally more tolerant of deficits than Democratic ones? Why did Democratic presidents Jimmy Carter and Bill Clinton seek to reduce or eliminate the deficit at a high level of revenue, whereas Republicans Ronald Reagan and George W. Bush looked to do so at a low level of revenue? Why did Ronald Reagan and George H. W. Bush press for constitutional change prohibiting unbalanced budgets despite the expansion of the deficit on their watch, and why did Jimmy Carter and Bill Clinton trenchantly oppose a constitutional amendment to this end despite their prioritization of deficit reduction? Finally, what relevance did the fiscal experience of the five presidents under review have for understanding the budget leadership challenges facing Barack Obama?

In addressing these issues, this work has drawn on material in the relevant presidential archives and other collections of private papers with regard to the budgetary policy of Jimmy Carter, Ronald Reagan, and George H. W. Bush. Such primary documentation was not yet available for analysis of budgeting during the presidencies of Bill Clinton and George W. Bush. Nevertheless, presidential statements, official published documents, think tank and budget watchdog reports, the writings of political actors, press articles, and a host of political science studies provided a substantial body of evidence for historical analysis of the most recent presidents and to supplement evaluation of earlier ones. Budget statistics were also an essential source, but these are kept to a reasonable minimum in the main body of the text. Readers wishing a more detailed statistical profile of the fiscal histories of the presidencies under review can find additional information in tabular form in the Appendices.

Acknowledgments

I have acquired many debts of gratitude to people who helped me bring this project to completion. Fortunately these are more pleasurable to acknowledge than are the debts of public finance that are the subject of my study.

I should begin by thanking Fred Woodward of the University Press of Kansas for his support for and belief in this project from beginning to end. It has also been a pleasure to work with the press from the proposal review stage through to the final editing stage. I thank everyone involved in this process, not least the reviewers who helped to improve and sharpen my thinking about my subject.

My thanks go to the Institute for the Study of the Americas of the University of London's School of Advanced Study for financial support to carry out research for this volume. In addition, I am grateful to my ISA colleagues, both academic and administrative, for making it a wonderful place to engage in study of not only the United States but also the Americas in their entirety. In this regard I should particularly record my gratitude to James Dunkerley and Maxine Molyneux, respectively former and current ISA directors.

This book could not have been written without the assistance of a small army of archivists and librarians who have helped me find my way to relevant budget materials and documents. In the United States these include the staff of the Jimmy Carter Presidential Library, the Ronald Reagan Presidential Library, the George H. W. Bush Presidential Library, the National Archives, the Special Collections (James Wright Papers) at Texas Christian University, the Robert J. Dole Institute of Politics, and the Minnesota State Historical Society. My thanks go also to the staff responsible for the fine research collections on the United States in the University of London Library (particularly Shereen Colvin).

I am pleased to record my gratitude for the opportunity to present parts of my argument to scholarly audiences, whose feedback greatly helped me to improve it. Tony Badger twice asked me to speak to his American history seminar at Cambridge University. Gareth Davies and Cheryl Hudson invited me to present at the Oxford University Rothermere American Institute's conference on America in the 1980s. Thanks to Jonathan Bell, I was able to try out my ideas about Jimmy Carter to the Reading University history seminar.

Most significantly, I am grateful to my colleagues at the University of London U.S. history seminar for providing such a lively and enriching forum to explore American history from colonial times to the present. Regular presentations to the UK American Politics Group also kept me abreast of how my political science colleagues viewed budget issues.

David Keating, Roger Porter, and Laura Tyson took time out of their busy schedules to enlighten me on budgetary affairs with which they were closely involved. A number of colleagues and friends also helped me in different ways at various stages of this project, notably Philip Davies, John Dumbrell, George Edwards, Michael Heale, Tim Lynch, Robert Mason, Jim Pfiffner, Andy Rudalevige, Diego Sanchez-Ancochea, Adam Smith, and Neil Wynn.

Two friends read the draft manuscript in its entirety. Dennis Ippolito of Southern Methodist University gave me the benefit of his immense knowledge of budget politics, policy, and process from the establishment of the Constitution to the present. Jeffrey Weinberg, a Fulbright Visiting Fellow at the Institute for the Study of the Americas in 2007, also subjected my analysis to a thorough and insightful review. Both helped me to improve the clarity of my argument, avoid errors of interpretation and fact (those that remain are entirely my responsibility), and reduce the size of the manuscript for the benefit of readers.

Finally, I acknowledge the huge debt I owe to my family for sustaining my spirits during this venture. My wife, Theresa, has had to put up with my deficit of attention to family matters but has (almost always) done so cheerfully and (always) borne more than her fair share of responsibility for dealing with them. In the time that it has taken me to write this book, my son and daughter, Humphrey and Eleanor, have taken their important steps in the journey from youth to young adulthood in a manner that has made them a source of great pride to their parents. I hope that I was of some help to both on their way in spite of my scholarly obsessions. My dedication of this book to my wife and children is a small token of my love for and gratitude to them.

CHAPTER 1

Presidents and
the Other Red Peril

"Now we are living in the era of the budget," wrote two scholars in the late 1980s. "The budget has been to our era what civil rights, communism, the depression, industrialization, and slavery were at other times."[1] This historical comparison may have strained the boundaries of hyperbole, but it signaled that the budget deficit had become America's greatest domestic problem in the late twentieth century. In the words of Senator Daniel Patrick Moynihan (D-NY), it was now "the first fact of national government."[2] The deficit had become the other red peril at the very moment that America's confrontation with the original one of communism was coming to a successful conclusion.

THE OTHER RED PERIL

The flood of budgetary red ink that has defined America's recent fiscal history is unprecedented. In the quarter century after World War II, only one in three annual budgets had been balanced, but deficits were small and controllable. The two largest deficits in this period—in recession-hit fiscal year (FY) 1959 and Vietnam-affected FY1968—were both followed immediately by balanced budgets. By contrast, the budget was never out of the red from FY1970 through FY1997, the longest sequence of deficits in American history. After a brief cycle of surplus budgets in FY1998–FY2001 died in infancy, deficits returned with a vengeance in the first decade of the new century.

As well as being chronic, annual deficits were of a scale unthinkable in the recent past (see Table1.1). In FY1976, a deficit of $73.8 billion was unprecedented in peacetime. In FY2009, the budget looked to be heading some $1.7 trillion into the red. Measured in constant dollars, the escalation was smaller than these unadjusted numbers but was still vast. Of course, the true measure of the deficit in the late twentieth century and beyond was not its dollar size but its size in relation to the gross domestic product (GDP). Even on this index, it habitually dwarfed any budgetary imbalance that the federal government had hitherto operated in peacetime other than in the exceptional and finite circumstances of the Great Depression in the 1930s.

Deficits of such size and frequency were primarily structural rather than cyclical in nature. In other words, they resulted more from policy makers'

Table 1.1. The Budget Deficit: Annual Average in Presidential Administrations
FY1962–2008°

Fiscal Years	Current-Dollar Deficit (billions)	FY2000 Constant-Dollar Deficit (billions)	Deficit-GDP Size (percent)
1962–1968			
(Kennedy-Johnson)	8.1	40.6	1.1
1970–1977			
(Nixon-Ford)	31.4	94.9	2.1
1978–1981			
(Carter)	63.2	129.9	2.4
1982–1989			
(Reagan)	176.5	260.3	4.3
1990–1993			
(G.H.W. Bush)	259.0	310.4	4.3
1994–1997			
(Clinton)	124.2	136.6	1.7
2002–2008			
(G.W. Bush)	305.0	266.6	2.5

° Excluding surplus budgets of FY1969, FY1998–FY2001.
Source: Office of Management and Budget, Budget of the United States Government Fiscal Year 2009: Historical Tables, table 6.1.

budgetary decisions rather than the economy's performance. It was evident by the late 1970s that America's fiscal situation had changed for the worse. In contrast to the pattern that followed past conflicts, U.S. withdrawal from the Vietnam War did not lead to restoration of balanced budgets. Moreover, economic recovery from the sharp recession of 1974–1975 only brought the deficit down in the late 1970s to a GDP level comparable with its occasional high points in the postwar quarter century. The mushrooming of the gap between outlays and revenues in the early 1980s confirmed that a new fiscal era had dawned. The United States has been living ever since in what can be termed the *age of deficits*.

The presidents of the late twentieth century regularly decried deficits as a threat to the national interest when calling for action to repair federal finances. In October 1978, Jimmy Carter warned, "We must face a time of national austerity. Hard choices are necessary if we want to avoid consequences that are even worse."[3] Ronald Reagan proclaimed the deficit "a clear and present danger to the basic health of our Republic" in his 1983 State of the Union address.[4] In uncharacteristically dramatic rhetoric for him, George H. W. Bush explicitly compared it with America's enemy in the Persian Gulf war. "Our nation is standing firm against Saddam Hussein's aggression," he declared in October 1990, "but here at home there's another threat, a cancer gnawing away at our nation's health. That cancer is the budget deficit."[5]

Finally, Bill Clinton portrayed the deficit as a threat to the American Dream. Its reduction was essential, he asserted in February 1993, "so that our children will be able to buy a home, so that our companies can invest in the future . . . so that our Government can make the kind of investments we need to be a stronger and smarter and safer nation."[6]

George W. Bush did not pronounce the deficit a threat when it returned on his watch. Instead, he justified it as necessary to fund the war on terror and provide for tax cuts that would restore the vitality of an economy buffeted by recession and the shock of the attacks of September 11, 2001. Nevertheless Bush could not buck recent history for long. In his 2004 State of the Union address, he implicitly signaled that the deficit was a danger in calling for its reduction by half within five years.[7] However, the financial crisis and severe recession that blighted Bush's final year in office eradicated all hope of fiscal improvement and plunged the budget deeper into the red than at any time since World War II. The urgent need to address the worst economic crisis since the 1930s overrode deficit concerns, but some policy makers warned of the problematic legacy bequeathed to the newly elected Barack Obama. "The next president will inherit a fiscal and economic mess of historic proportions," warned Senate Budget Committee chair Kent Conrad (D-ND). "It will take years to dig our way out."[8]

THE PRESIDENT AS BUDGET LEADER

In calling for eradication of the deficit threat, modern presidents exercised their primary role as budget leaders to set the national government's fiscal agenda. As budget expert Allen Schick put it, "The White House is a budget pulpit; from the Oval Office, the president has the capacity to define the terms of the budget debate. He decides which issues will be on the table, whether to seek changes in revenues and entitlements, and whether to demand program initiatives. His budget is the trigger for congressional action on these and other matters."[9]

The president's principal instrument for budget leadership is his responsibility to submit an annual budget plan providing Congress with estimates of expenditures and revenues necessary in his judgment to support the operations of government. According to one analyst, this is both "the number-one *political* document of the country . . . [and] the chief *priorities* document." The Budget and Accounting Act of 1921, which established the legal requirement for a presidential budget, marked the birth of the modern presidency. As political scientist James Sundquist observed, "Before 1921, a president did not have to propose a fiscal policy for the government, and many did not; after 1921, every chief executive had to have a fiscal policy, every year. The act made the president a leader, a policy and program initiator, and a manager, whether he wished to be or not."[10]

This legislation also created the Bureau of the Budget (BoB), whose expert staff undertook the complex and laborious business of budget plan development and oversaw the executive's implementation of the eventual budget agreed on by Congress. Initially located in the Department of the Treasury, this agency became part of the new Executive Office of the Presidency in 1939 in recognition of its fundamental significance to the modern presidency. Another BoB overhaul in 1970 resulted in its redevelopment as the Office of Management and Budget (OMB) with enhanced powers over executive budget policymaking in service of the president's goals. Its mission consequently shifted from a primarily administrative function to a political one. Every OMB director has acted as the political spokesperson and promoter of the president's budget plan. As a result the agency became identified "more as a member of the President's own political family and less a broker supplying an independent analytic service to every President."[11]

In setting their fiscal agenda, presidents exercise what can be termed their "power to recommend."[12] They rely on their "power to persuade" to win congressional approval of their budget goals. This is dependent on a number of variables, notably the president's status as party leader and whether his party controls Congress, his political skills, his ability to organize his staff and get the most out of them, his capacity to link his budget policy to his broader vision, and the ultimate threat of his veto power. Potentially the greatest source of presidential influence is public support. This does not enable the president to dominate Congress but can provide leverage to gain acceptance of his priorities. Without it, he has little prospect of achieving his agenda. Popular approval or its absence effectively sets the limits of what Congress will do for or to the president.[13] Modern presidents have consequently used public rhetoric to inform, educate, and persuade Americans about the merits of their programmatic goals.[14] Reflecting this, the deficit became a more regular topic of presidential remarks as budget problems grew in scope.[15]

The president can propose a budget but lacks the constitutional power of the purse. Only the legislature can give substance to federal accounts through enactment of legislation to raise revenue and spend it. The relative power of the two branches in the domain of budget policy has changed significantly over time.[16] Congress dominated the haphazard and decentralized process of budgeting that operated from 1789 to 1921. The establishment of a presidential budget ushered in a half century of presidential ascendancy. In broad terms the two branches recognized their fiscal domains as distinct under the new system. Congress accepted the president's strategic budgetary leadership and generally sought only adjustments to his specific program requests. In Louis Fisher's words, "The president took responsibility for the aggregates, and congress lived within the totals while rearranging the priorities. In short, each branch did what it was well suited for."[17]

The Congressional Budget and Impoundment Control Act of 1974 aimed to readjust the institutional balance of power in the belief that enhanced congressional authority would bring about better budgeting. Hitherto the legislative budget was the accumulation of decisions by individual committees with jurisdiction over specific programs. In reaction to the budget controversies between the Nixon administration and the Democrat-led Congress, the 1974 reform established a congressional budget process to coordinate fiscal actions in accordance with the legislature's priorities. It created the House and Senate Budget Committees to recommend a budget to Congress. Once approved through a concurrent resolution, the Budget Committees were to set targets for other standing committees to meet the overall totals and monitor their observance of these. To give Congress more time to complete the work of appropriations, the start of the fiscal year was moved back from July 1 to October 1. The measure also created the Congressional Budget Office (CBO) to provide the Budget Committees with the kind of staff expertise that the OMB gave the president. The CBO was mandated to provide independent assessment of the presidential budget's economic and fiscal projections. Congress relied on its scorekeeping of the budgetary costs of legislation under consideration if different from the OMB estimate.[18]

Ultimately, however, the new system of congressional budgeting exacerbated the lack of coordination that it was meant to overcome. The growing problem of deficit control highlighted its shortcomings in this regard. Whatever its virtues in theory, a budget process involving 535 individual political actors, two political parties, and two chambers with differing institutional cultures was unwieldy and incohesive in practice. The reformed system was complex, time-consuming, and seemingly incapable of effective focus on aggregate issues pertaining to revenue and outlay levels. Agenda setting by congressional party leaders, the incidence of economic problems, and majority party change could intermittently counter the centrifugal tendencies within the legislature to focus attention on deficit reduction. For the most part, however, the majority of legislators were less interested in the budget as a whole than in the separate parts that engaged their partisan or constituency concerns. Over time, therefore, the intrinsic congressional bias toward programs meant that the president was the prime mover in the cause of deficit control.[19]

By any measure, the unitary and hierarchical nature of presidential budgeting was more efficient in establishing broad fiscal priorities than the multidimensional and collegial congressional system. Operating in the president's name and supported by his active involvement in the final stages, OMB staff regulated executive spending requests that went into the annual budget plan through negotiations with department heads. Though lengthy and often fractious, this top-down process of budgeting was capable of elevating aggregate objectives over program allocations and always delivered a budget plan on time.

In setting its budget resolution, the legislature generally adopted fiscal aggregates in accord with the president's budget but engaged in prolonged squabbling over program allocations.[20] Approval of this blueprint only prefaced further wrangling in the standing committees that had jurisdiction over taxation and spending programs. These bodies had to report out reconciliation bills if the budget totals they eventually fixed upon required changes in revenue levels or entitlement spending. Meanwhile those committees responsible for discretionary programs needed their spending authorizations obligated by the Appropriations Committees. The resultant legislation then had to be agreed to by both chambers of Congress. The habitual failure of the legislature to complete its work by the start of the fiscal year necessitated enactment of a continuing resolution to fund government operations until the unfinished parts of the budget could be agreed on. It was small wonder, therefore, that the cumbersome system of congressional budgeting could neither define nor focus upon deficit-control priorities with the same clarity as the president.

THE POLITICS OF THE DEFICIT

If the president was best equipped in institutional terms for the leadership role in the war on deficits, political consensus in support of his battle plan was rare. Budgetary disputes recurred throughout American history but reached new intensity in the late twentieth century. As the deficit grew, the options for dealing with it narrowed. Political leaders still had choices, but none were easy or attractive. The combination of divided party control of government and the changing composition of the budget increased the difficulty of promoting solutions to the budget problem. As a consequence, presidents became locked in conflict with opposition-led congresses over how to make progress toward fiscal equilibrium without damage to their differing programmatic priorities.

Unified party control of government existed for all but eight years between 1932 and 1968, but only for ten years from 1969 to 2008. Jimmy Carter was the solitary president in this later era never to experience divided government. Bill Clinton had the benefit of Democratic control of both houses of Congress only in 1993–1994, and George W. Bush operated with a Republican-led Congress briefly in 2001 and for a longer period in 2003–2006. Otherwise, presidents faced opposition majorities in one or both chambers of the legislature during their time in office. The most disadvantaged White House occupants in this regard were George H. W. Bush and Bill Clinton. The former dealt with a Congress entirely controlled by the opposition party during his single term in office, and the latter did so for six years, longer than any other president in the age of deficits.

Because the budget was the most important statement of the federal role in the nation's life, the means of deficit reduction cut across broader issues of party ideology regarding the appropriate size and purpose of national government. The divergent values of Democrats and Republicans on this score made it difficult for presidents and congresses to develop common solutions for fiscal problems in circumstances of divided government. Despite occasional consensus, presidential-congressional interactions on the deficit were more usually marked by partisan disagreement over whether domestic or defense programs should bear the brunt of economy drives, whether entitlements should be preserved or reformed, and whether taxes should be raised or reduced.

Significant changes in budget composition widened the deficit-reduction fissures generated by divided government. In the twenty years following World War II, Cold War defense spending was the principal driver of expenditure growth. From the late 1960s onward, however, social program outlays increasingly outstripped military spending as a result of new commitments undertaken in the belief that the high economic growth rates of the postwar era would continue generating the tax revenues to fund them. This domestic expansion had become firmly entrenched by the time that the economy ran into problems in the second half of the 1970s. Fundamental to its development was the growth in entitlement programs that made automatic payments to individuals as fixed by law (see Table 1.2).

In FY2000 entitlements accounted for 59.8 percent of the total budget, compared with 26.2 percent forty years previously. At the start of the 1960s, these programs mainly consisted of Social Security, veterans' benefits, and Aid to Families with Dependent Children. The Great Society added others, notably Medicare, Medicaid, and food stamps, and expanded existing programs. In the 1970s the indexation of benefits to inflation in over twenty entitlement programs, including Social Security, and the quasi-indexation of others, particularly Medicare and Medicaid, through built-in adjustments for rising service costs enhanced the uncontrollability of outlays. Some programs, like Medicare, were periodically subject to legislative adjustments of costs, but others escaped restraint. Among the latter was the largest entitlement, Social Security, whose outlays grew by over 250 percent in real terms even though recipients only increased in number by 70 percent between FY1970 and FY2000.[21]

The expansion of mandatory spending on entitlements was driven by past

Table 1.2. Outlays-GDP (in Percent) by Major Spending Categories,
FY1962–FY2005

Fiscal Year	Discretionary			Mandatory		Offsetting Receipts	Outlays
	Defense	International	Domestic	Entitlements	Net Interest		
1962	9.2	1.0	2.5	6.1	1.2	−1.2	18.8
1965	7.4	0.7	3.2	5.8	1.2	−1.1	17.2
1970	8.1	0.4	3.4	7.2	1.4	−1.2	19.3
1975	5.6	0.5	4.0	10.9	1.5	−1.1	21.3
1980	4.9	0.5	4.7	10.7	1.9	−1.1	21.6
1985	6.1	0.4	3.5	10.8	3.1	−1.1	22.9
1990	5.2	0.3	3.2	10.9	3.2	−1.0	21.8
1995	3.7	0.3	3.4	11.2	3.2	−1.1	20.7
2000	3.0	0.2	3.1	10.6	2.3	−0.8	18.4
2005	4.0	0.3	3.6	11.8	1.5	−1.0	20.2

Source: Congressional Budget Office, *The Budget and Economic Outlook: Fiscal Years 2008 to 2017*, tables E6 and E8.

decisions rather than assessment of present and future needs. As one analyst put it in understated fashion, "current budget processes are not allocating the national output well."[22] The loss of fiscal suppleness as a result of automatic expenditure growth enhanced the difficulties of deficit reduction. Policy makers increasingly looked to make savings in outlays on defense, international, and domestic programs that were more controllable through the congressional appropriations process. The combined share of the federal budget allocated to these discretionary programs shrank from 61.5 percent in FY1970 to 40 percent in FY1990. However, the parallel decline in their aggregate outlays, from 11.9 percent GDP to 8.7 percent GDP, was exceeded by entitlement program growth from 7.2 percent GDP to 10.9 percent GDP.

Driven by entitlement expansion, outlays rose much faster than receipts for most of the second half of the twentieth century. Annual expenditure averaged 22.2 percent GDP in FY1980–FY1989, compared with 17.6 percent GDP in FY1950–FY1959. The parallel figures for revenues were 18.3 percent GDP and 17.2 percent GDP. As with expenditure, compositional changes made it difficult to achieve deficit control through the taxation side of the budget ledger. Individual income taxes and social insurance taxes (primarily payroll taxes for Social Security) provided over four-fifths of receipts by FY1990, compared with only half in FY1950. In mid-century, business taxes had accounted for over a quarter of all federal receipts and indirect excise taxes for another fifth (see Table 1.3). This shift meant that revenue enhancement for deficit-reduction purposes necessarily required increases in direct taxes paid by individuals, the most politically sensitive form of taxation.

Table 1.3. Federal Receipts: Composition by Source and GDP Size,
FY1950–FY2000 (Percentages)

Fiscal Year	Individual Income Taxes	Corporation Income Taxes	Social Insurance and Retirement Receipts	Excise Taxes	Other	Receipts–GDP
1950	39.9	26.5	11.0	19.1	3.4	14.4
1960	44.0	23.2	15.9	12.6	4.2	17.8
1970	46.9	17.0	23.0	8.1	4.9	19.0
1980	47.2	12.5	30.5	4.7	5.1	19.0
1985	45.6	8.4	36.1	4.9	5.1	17.7
1990	45.2	9.1	36.8	3.4	5.4	18.0
1995	43.7	11.6	35.8	4.3	4.6	18.5
2000	49.6	10.2	32.2	3.4	4.5	20.9

Source: Office of Management and Budget, Budget of the United States Government Fiscal Year 2009: Historical Tables, table 2.3.

Failure to control the deficit precipitated significant expansion in another element of automatic spending that accelerated the budget's plunge into the red. As a result of massive borrowing to pay for World War II, the government debt held by the public equaled 108.6 percent GDP in FY1946. This declined steadily thereafter to stand at 26.1 percent GDP in FY1980, approximately what it had been a century earlier in the wake of post–Civil War debt reduction. Sharply reversing this trend, the huge deficits incurred in the 1980s and early 1990s thrust up the debt-GDP ratio to a late twentieth century peak of 49.4 percent by the end of FY1993, with significant consequences for interest costs. The budget share of net annual interest payments on government borrowing had declined steadily from a postwar peak of 14.6 percent in FY1948 to a postwar low of 6.2 percent in FY1968, but steady incidence of sizeable deficits thereafter drove it back up to 8.9 percent in FY1980. It then escalated rapidly to 14.8 percent by FY1989, making debt obligation the fastest growing part of the budget during this decade of very large deficits (see Table 1.4).

In the face of political and ideological disputes that made the deficit problem increasingly intractable, presidents claimed the moral high ground as the champions of the fiscal good. Taking advantage of what political scientist Clinton Rossiter termed their "voice of the people" function, White House occupants trumpeted their solutions to the budget problem as the embodiment of the public interest.[23] In this regard, the application of the threat concept to the deficit implicitly appropriated the president's commander-in-chief responsibility for the nation's security against external enemies to meet an internal challenge to its well-being. The common presidential imagery portrayed massive fiscal imbalances as a danger in both substantive and symbolic terms. In an era when inflation had replaced unemployment

Table 1.4. Public Debt and Net Interest 1950–2008°

Fiscal Years	Public Debt–GDP	Net Interest–GDP	Net Interest Share of Budget
1950–1959	58.2	1.3	7.6
1960–1969	38.5	1.3	6.9
1970–1979	26.7	1.5	7.4
1980–1989	34.6	2.6	12.5
1990–1999	46.1	3.0	14.6
2000–2008	36.4	1.7	8.8

° Figures are average annual percentages.
Source: Office of Management and Budget, *Budget of the United States Government Fiscal Year 2009: Historical Tables,* tables 6.1 and 7.1.

as the principal economic problem, presidents warned that unbalanced budgets were harbingers of high interest rates and inflationary psychology. They also decried failure to control the deficit as a symbol of politicians' inability to subordinate partisan interests to the greater cause of governance in the nation's best interests. Finally, linking substance and symbolism, presidents cautioned that ongoing fiscal problems placed a cloud over the future in terms of the build-up of unsustainable public debt and the erosion of the American Dream.

In the presidential narrative, the obstacle to resolving the deficit in the manner beneficial to the nation tended to be the opposition-led Congress that was motivated by partisanship, ideology, or constituency special interests. Typical of this was Ronald Reagan's rhetoric in support of his 1985 budget plan to reduce the deficit by $300 billion over three years and end the federal government's "dangerous addiction to deficit spending." This is "no time for partisanship," he warned. "Our future is too precious to permit this crucial effort to be picked apart piece by piece by the special interest groups. We've got to put the public interest first." When the Democrat-controlled House of Representatives approved a budget resolution that put the onus for deficit reduction on defense rather than on domestic retrenchment as he had recommended, the president expressed outrage on the public's behalf. "It is, frankly, unacceptable—unacceptable to me and to the American people," he declared. Reagan later contrasted the fiscal virtue of the presidency with the fiscal vice of Congress in his memoirs to explain the durability of the deficit. "Presidents don't create deficits," he fulminated, "Congress does. Presidents can't appropriate a dollar of taxpayers' money; only congressmen can—and Congress is susceptible to all sorts of influences that have nothing to do with good government."[24]

A Democratic president was just as capable of condemning a Republican-controlled legislature for fiscal partisanship. In 1995 the first GOP Congress in forty years approved a budget resolution proposing a seven-year plan of deficit elimination that combined massive domestic retrenchment with huge tax cuts. In response, Bill Clinton produced a ten-year plan that he claimed would "balance the budget without hurting our future." Effectively damning the congressional proposal as the product of Republican ideology, he declared that the debate over fiscal responsibility "must go beyond partisanship. It must be about what's good for America." The failure of the White House and Congress to agree on a budget eventually resulted in two shutdowns of government. Explaining his brinkmanship in this duel, Clinton later declared, "I didn't want to be president if the price of doing so was meaner streets, weaker health care, fewer educational opportunities, dirtier air and more poverty. I was betting that the American people didn't want those things either."[25]

Congress seemingly validated presidential criticism of its particularism by enacting new rules that reduced its own budget prerogatives even as it fought the White House over programmatic fiscal issues. In supporting these procedural reforms, senior figures in both parties effectively put the blame for deficits on the legislature's failure to subordinate its constituency-representation function to its public-interest policymaking function. Commending the fiscal controls of the Budget Enforcement Act of 1990, Senate Majority Leader George Mitchell (D-ME) declared, "In a legislative body, in a representative democracy, nobody likes to vote to raise taxes . . . [or] to cut popular spending programs. But we all know that the reality we confront is that a budget deficit can be closed by one or both of two ways. We must either raise revenues or reduce spending, or do both." Defending the significant transfer of budgetary power to the president in the Line-Item Veto Act of 1996, future Senate Majority Leader Trent Lott (R-MS) asserted, "We can only have one Commander in Chief at a time. He is the ultimate authority. He should have the ability to . . . knock out things that are not justified, that have not been sufficiently considered, that cost too much—whatever reason—without having to veto the whole bill."[26]

Notwithstanding occasional bouts of congressional self-flagellation, the notion that the president was the embodiment of the public interest in fiscal matters had no basis in reality. In the first place, presidential claims to be the voice of the people on deficit control obscured the public's contradictory perspective on the issue. Popular belief that balanced budgets should be the norm was deeply ingrained in America's political culture, but public opinion was more complex beneath the surface veneer of belief in fiscal responsibility as an abstract principle. Polls asking "How important do you think it is to balance the federal budget—very important, fairly important or not so important?" regularly drew the answer "very important" from 70 percent or more of respondents during the 1980s and 1990s. There was also substantial public support for a balanced-budget constitutional amendment. In January 1979, 73 percent of respondents to a CBS–*New York Times* poll expressed approval of this, a level that remained more or less constant for the next two decades.[27] However, many Americans believed that deficit elimination was largely a matter of ridding government of waste.[28] When it came to making real sacrifices to balance the budget, polls showed that most people were unwilling to pay higher taxes and wanted spending for many programs maintained or expanded.[29] Typifying popular ambiguity, one survey taken in 1995 found that 61 percent of respondents favored cutting entitlements but 66 percent opposed doing so in the case of the three most expensive ones—Social Security, Medicare, and Medicaid.[30]

More significantly, presidents engaged in the struggle against the other red peril were not politically neutral actors. However large the deficits they faced, none of the White House occupants from Jimmy Carter to George W. Bush saw his job as being the chief accountant of American government. All these presidents explicitly or implicitly regarded the deficit as a threat to the national interest, but their proposals for addressing it conformed to the programmatic goals of their governing agenda. In other words, deficit reduction complemented rather than took precedence over their political priorities. Accordingly, presidential strategies for fiscal improvement varied in accordance with each president's view of the proper size and scope of government and the reach of taxation to fund this. In recognition of this, some legislators battled in vain against congressional surrender of budget prerogatives to the White House. Such abdication of power, warned Senator Mark Hatfield (R-OR), "does not make us more responsive to the will of the people, it makes us more responsive to one person: the President."[31]

Alexander Hamilton foresaw more than two hundred years ago that the budget could not be a neutral tool of public finance because the power of the purse had such immense significance for what government did. As he asserted in the *Federalist Papers* (No. 30), "Money is, with propriety, considered as the vital principle of the body politic; as that which sustains its life and motion and enables it to perform its most essential functions."[32] The budget is a natural battleground for political actors holding different views about what the federal government should do and who should pay for it. In the words of Aaron Wildavsky, "If politics is regarded in part as conflict over whose preferences shall prevail in the determination of national policy, then the budget records the outcome of this struggle."[33]

Political dispute over the budget in the age of deficits fundamentally centered on whether deficit reduction should be achieved at high or low levels of revenue, which had significant implications for taxation and spending. This was why Ronald Reagan once observed that "all balanced budgets aren't created equal." On another occasion, the fortieth president commented that "the cost of government, not just necessarily the deficit, was the problem." Elaborating on this, he approvingly cited the opinion of conservative economist Milton Friedman that an unbalanced budget with an expenditure level of $200 billion was preferable to a balanced budget with outlays of $400 billion.[34] The means of restoring fiscal responsibility was inseparable from the end in the calculations of the nation's leaders. Accordingly, presidents endowed their antideficit strategies with meanings that reflected their own political agenda.

For Jimmy Carter and Bill Clinton, the restoration of fiscal discipline signified that governmental activism was still possible within a balanced budget. For Reagan, deficit reduction was the agency for shrinking the federal government in conjunction with cutting taxes. In a variation of this theme, George W. Bush saw it as justification for his agenda of big-government conservatism that combined low taxes with selective expansion of federal activism. The exception that proved the rule, George H. W. Bush split his party because his major antideficit initiative was not embedded within a broader political rationale.

Presidential politics regarding the deficit from Jimmy Carter to George W. Bush underlined the perennial importance of the role of government to debate over the budget. Balanced budgets had always represented far more in American history than mere equilibrium between federal income and outlays. They had been invested with powerful symbolism about the legitimate purpose of national government since the early days of the republic. Nevertheless, what balanced budgets signified in terms of federal activism would undergo a number of transformations from the small-government era of the early nineteenth century to the Keynesian era of the mid-twentieth century. A review of this protean development is therefore necessary to put late twentieth and early twenty-first century political debate over deficits in historical perspective.

CHAPTER 2

Presidents and Balanced Budgets: A Historical Perspective

Ideas have always had particular importance in American politics in shaping the way that issues are defined and contested, but their meanings are anything but static. As political scientist Michael Foley observes, "In the United States ideas are nothing if not promiscuous. Their advocates are equally eclectic in the manner in which they fashion ideas into ever more adaptable mutations."[1] Changes over time in what balanced budgets and deficits signified offer a perfect illustration of this. Despite lacking formal budgetary powers until the early twentieth century, presidents have always been important actors in shaping the different meanings invested in these supposedly immutable terms.

At first sight America's fiscal history appears to be divided into three eras. From the 1790s to the 1920s, balanced budgets were the norm except in war or recession. Belief that government had an obligation to balance its outlays and income was so strong in this era that it constituted an unwritten rule of budget policy.[2] From the 1930s to the early 1970s, in contrast, deficits were regularly utilized as an instrument of economic management in accordance with what can broadly be termed Keynesian principles. Since the late 1970s, however, the federal government has operated chronic and huge budget deficits regardless of circumstance and usually without economic rationale for their necessity.[3]

Nevertheless, the changing political and economic meaning of balanced and unbalanced budgets was a good deal more complex than this tripartite division of fiscal history suggests. Over the course of the nineteenth and early twentieth centuries balanced budgets were transformed from the hallmark of limited government to the agency of government expansion. What deficit budgets symbolized also underwent significant adjustments in the Keynesian era in line with their increasing use to manage the economy.

BALANCED BUDGETS AND LIMITED GOVERNMENT: THE 1790S TO THE CIVIL WAR

Observance of the balanced-budget rule by early American government was a case of achieving "coordinated outcomes without coordinated controls."

Endowed with the constitutional power of the purse as a restraint on executive authority, Congress operated a haphazard process of budgeting that lacked control and planning mechanisms. In theory, the initial concentration of responsibility for revenue, expenditure, and other financial bills in the House Ways and Means Committee and the Senate Finance Committee provided oversight capacity. In practice, the legislature set tariff levels, the main source of receipts, more to protect domestic industry than to raise desired levels of revenue. The Secretary of the Treasury's annual submission of executive spending requests in the Book of Estimates provided some element of expenditure control, but Congress often considered separate requests from individual departments. Despite the shortcomings of this system of budgeting, balanced budgets became the norm in the early republic because the federal government had few domestic responsibilities, limited military needs, and a predictable flow of revenues from tariffs.[4]

Congressional ascendancy in budgeting did not prevent the nineteenth-century presidency from forging an institutional role as the moral guardian of the public purse. Thomas Jefferson, dubbed "the first 'economy' president" by one scholar, was initially responsible for this.[5] More than any other individual he saddled deficits with a negative image as the agency of federal aggrandizement. In the Jeffersonian canon, balanced budgets signified "popular willingness and ability to limit the purpose and size of American government, to restrain its influence in the economy, to protect states' rights, to maintain the Constitution's balance of powers, and to protect republican virtue."[6] Jefferson's animus against deficits emanated from his political battles with Alexander Hamilton when both were members of George Washington's administration. The fundamental dialectic between their different visions and efforts to synthesize them became a recurrent feature of American budgetary politics over the next two centuries and beyond.

The intellectual champion of the Federalist Party's program, Hamilton idealized a strong national government that employed its fiscal powers to promote America's commercial and industrial development. At the heart of his vision was an instrumental assessment of the utility of the national debt that the fledgling republic had incurred to fund its war for independence but faced difficulty in repaying. Issued in his capacity as secretary of the Treasury Department, Hamilton's *First Report on Public Credit* advocated conversion of the interest arrears on the national debt into principle, full redemption of the total debt as now calculated, and federal assumption of the individual states' war debts. Approved by Congress in 1791, this eased the immediate problem of interest repayment, ensured the federal government's creditworthiness in case it needed to borrow to meet future exigencies, and asserted the fiscal supremacy of the national government over the states.[7]

In stark opposition to the Hamiltonian vision, Jefferson avowed, "I place economy among the first and most important of republican virtues, and public debt as the greatest of dangers to be feared."[8] The champion of agrarian democracy, he reviled deficits and public debt as a threat to America's exceptionalism as a nation of small farmers. In his credo unbalanced budgets were the agency of excessive federal power, the harbingers of political and economic inequality, and the patronage instruments of executive authority to corrupt the legislature into acceptance of measures beneficial to financial, commercial, and industrial elites.[9]

Jefferson's canonization by late-twentieth-century conservatives as the patron saint of balanced budgets obscured the complexity of his presidential record. His initial insistence on economy in executive spending helped to reduce outlays for purposes other than debt retirement by some 20 percent during his first two years in office. In the first significant use of presidential impoundment power, he also refused in 1803 to expend congressional appropriations for gunboats on grounds that the emergency necessitating their approval had passed. Nevertheless, smaller interest payments on the shrinking debt and buoyant tariff revenues created the margin for military and civilian outlays to increase by nearly 50 percent over the entire course of his presidency without running a deficit. Jefferson also relaxed his own strictures against federal debt in taking out a long-term loan of $11.2 million at 6 percent to cover most of the $15 million cost of purchasing the Louisiana Territory from France in 1804. In his estimate, the acquisition of the new land would perpetuate the agrarian nature of the American republic, thereby justifying the addition to the public debt. This made the Louisiana Purchase historically significant in budgetary terms as the first presidential trade-off of fiscal restraint to achieve a political end.[10]

In the half century after Jefferson left office, his successors sustained his ideals of economy in government; some even proved themselves more Jeffersonian than their role model. The financial consequences of the War of 1812 returned the debt issue to the center of the political agenda. Over the next twenty years presidents preached the imperative of total redemption through fiscal discipline. As this ideal drew near to fulfillment, Andrew Jackson anticipated that America would soon present "the rare example of a great nation, abounding in all the means of happiness and security, altogether free from debt."[11]

Two recessions and the Mexican War set back hopes of debt extinction, but presidents continued to struggle for economy in these adverse conditions. Martin Van Buren and John Tyler carefully reviewed and reduced departmental spending estimates with an eye to deficit control amid the economic problems that flowed from the panic of 1837. James Buchanan followed their example during the economic downturn of the late 1850s, but Congress ignored his special message on finance calling for measures to

increase revenues. Earlier, James Polk had rooted out waste in military estimates while preparing for war with Mexico.[12]

Presidential advocacy of fiscal responsibility embodied the early American understanding of balanced budgets as symbols of limited federal government. All political parties represented in Congress during the first half of the
nineteenth century shared this belief. Although federal spending increased
steadily over this period and did so rapidly in the 1850s, this primarily resulted from the growth of America's territory and population rather than
from program innovation.

SURPLUS BUDGETS AND REPUBLICAN BIG GOVERNMENT:
THE LATE NINETEENTH CENTURY

In an inversion of Jeffersonian tradition, congressional Republicans transformed the balanced-budget rule into the instrument of government growth
after the Civil War. To justify high tariffs that protected northern industrial
development, they used surplus revenues to expand outlays on a host of programs.[13] In continuing to advocate economy as the paramount national interest, the presidents of this era consolidated the reputation of their office as
the principal guardian of the public purse.

The initial budgetary priority after the Civil War was to reduce a public debt that had grown more than fortyfold during the conflict. Between
FY1866 and FY1893 the longest-ever sequence of surplus budgets diminished federal indebtedness from $2.75 billion to $961 million. By the late
1870s, however, the consumption tax regime inherited from the Civil War—
in which high protective tariffs and excises on tobacco and alcohol furnished
the bulk of revenues—delivered surpluses that exceeded debt scheduled for
redemption. Even the heavy premiums paid to purchase unmatured debt on
the open market did not exhaust Treasury resources.[14]

The burgeoning surplus became the focus of partisan conflict in the way
that deficits had once been in the Jeffersonian era. Voicing the anger of the
agrarian South and West that high tariffs were an unfair subsidy to monopoly trusts, the Democrats demanded their reduction to meet revenue needs
only. In response, congressional Republicans increased expenditure on public works, internal improvements, railroad promotion, army and navy expansion, and, in particular, generous pension provision for Union veterans of
the Civil War to run down the surpluses produced by taxes beneficial to the
North. Despite fluctuating party control of the House and Senate in the late
1870s and 1880s, the multisectional benefits of many of these programs secured their approval by Congress.[15]

The fragmentation of budgetary authority in the legislature facilitated spending expansion. Because the Ways and Means and Finance Committees had experienced difficulty coping with Civil War budgeting, the House and Senate had created new Appropriations Committees to handle all spending bills in 1865 and 1867 respectively. Bipartisan resentment of spending control quickly undermined the authority of these new committees. Capitalizing on this, other committees wrested power from them to determine expenditure in program areas over which they had jurisdiction. This decentralization occurred in the House between 1877 and 1884. It did not reach full flow in the Senate until later but culminated in dismantlement of its Appropriations Committee in 1899.[16]

The drive for surplus reduction transformed the composition of the federal budget. Between FY1870 and FY1890, interest payments declined from 41.7 percent to 11.7 percent, and veterans' pensions rose from 9.1 percent to 33.6 percent of total outlays. Federal spending for purposes other than defense or debt reduction more than doubled over the same period. Expenditure grew steadily in the 1880s but exploded when the Republicans enjoyed the rare advantage of unified control of the legislature and the White House. Thanks to the largesse of the so-called Billion Dollar Congress of 1889–1891, federal expenditure ran to nearly $366 million in FY1891, compared with the annual average of $237 million in the 1880s.[17]

Rutherford B. Hayes and Benjamin Harrison excepted, post–Civil War presidents acted as champions of fiscal restraint in the face of congressional prodigality. In the most significant case of impoundment since Jefferson, Ulysses S. Grant withheld funds appropriated for river and harbor works in 1876 on grounds that these served a purely private or local interest. Fellow Republican Chester Alan Arthur broke party ranks to veto the Rivers and Harbors Act of 1882 as an unconstitutional and unwarranted expense, but Congress quickly overrode him. Grover Cleveland completed the consecration of the late-nineteenth-century presidency as the enemy of extravagance. In his first term, the Democrat undertook a fruitless campaign against high tariffs as the root of spending excess and issued nearly three times as many vetoes as all previous presidents in total, four-fifths of them against pension bills. His consequent unpopularity with Grand Army of the Republic veterans contributed to his election defeat in 1888.[18]

Though irregular, desultory, and often ineffective, such interventions established the presidency as the disinterested paragon of economy in the public mind. A contrasting image took hold of a spendthrift legislature susceptible to manipulation by special interests, notably pension agents, railroad companies, and big business. This dichotomy undoubtedly influenced the belief of early twentieth-century reformers that fiscal responsibility could be better achieved by expanding presidential authority over the budget.[19]

THE PROGRESSIVE CONCEPT OF BALANCED BUDGETS:
THE EARLY TWENTIETH CENTURY

The surplus controversy lost relevance when the record cycle of balanced budgets gave way to a spate of deficits at the end of the nineteenth century and the beginning of the twentieth century. Far from inspiring a Jeffersonian reaction against Republican distortion of balanced-budget symbolism, this development generated debate about how government could discharge its expanded responsibilities without incurring deficits. The balanced-budget rule now came to reflect the contemporary concerns of the Progressive movement with efficiency and equity in government. In this evolutionary stage it stood for professionalism, orderliness, and discipline in the administration of federal expenditure and a new element of fairness in taxes that required the wealthy to bear a greater share of the increased costs of government. Early twentieth-century presidents played a leading role in this transformation, and their office was eventually endowed with new budget powers to deliver the Progressive vision.

There were fourteen unbalanced budgets from FY1894 through FY1915, compared with twenty-nine from FY1789 through FY1893. These deficits mainly resulted from the kind of cyclical and external factors that had produced unbalanced budgets in the past. The United States experienced a major economic slump in the 1890s, fought a war with Spain in 1898, and suffered a sharp recession following the Banker's Panic of 1907. Federal finances were hardly in chaos—the public debt only grew by $75 million, some 7 percent, in this period—but the regular imbalances provoked increasing concern.

Despite criticism of congressional spending, the finger of blame for the deficits could hardly be directed at government extravagance. Outlays doubled in current-dollar terms from FY1894 through FY1915 but declined as a share of national income from FY1900 onward. Moreover, spending composition changed to reflect America's rise to world power. In FY1890 military expenditure accounted for one-fifth of the budget and domestic programs for two-thirds, but their portions had drawn equal by FY1915.[20] More problematic was the lack of elasticity and predictability in revenues at a time when need for funds was growing. America's diminished demand for imported manufactures as a result of its own industrialization meant that tariffs could no longer underwrite ever higher spending.

Early twentieth-century presidents did not follow their predecessors' example of advocating fiscal restraint to eliminate deficits. They recognized that America's geopolitical interests as a world power carried permanently higher budgetary costs and occasionally exceptional ones. Theodore Roosevelt considered his decision to construct the Panama Canal the most important of his presidency. Initial outlays on this project tipped the budget into deficit in FY1904–FY1905. The total twelve-year cost of $400 million, one-third from borrowing, made it by far the most expensive public works project in American history to date. Nevertheless, Roosevelt deemed the expense an entirely justifiable investment in strategic expansion.[21]

Nor did Roosevelt and his successors look to make savings from the domestic budget. Their outlook reflected the influence of the Progressive movement and its Populist predecessor, which legitimized new federal activism and fostered acceptance that this would not come cheap. William Howard Taft and Woodrow Wilson, in particular, equated economy in budgeting with efficiency rather than retrenchment. Taft warned in 1910, "A reduction in the total of the annual appropriations is not in itself a proof of economy, since it is often accompanied by a decrease in efficiency."[22] Wilson similarly avowed in 1914, "The American people are not jealous of the amount their Government costs if they are sure they get what they need and desire for the outlay, that the money is being spent for objects of which they approve, and that it is being applied with good business sense and management."[23]

Opposed to rash economizing, Progressive-era presidents were drawn inexorably to the conclusion that deficits had to be addressed from the revenue side of the budget. Embarrassed by the large imbalances that followed the 1907 financial panic, Roosevelt voiced support for direct taxation of income to supplement protective tariff receipts. With congressional Republicans divided on the issue, Taft proposed a compromise that led to enactment of an excise tax on corporate income and a proposed constitutional amendment to legitimize direct taxation of income without apportionment among the states.[24]

Woodrow Wilson and his party were initially more interested in the social justice of income taxes than their revenue-raising potential. Following ratification of the Sixteenth Amendment to the Constitution in early 1913, the newly ascendant Democrats introduced taxes on personal and corporate income and reduced tariffs with the intent of achieving a modest redistribution of wealth from the very rich and big business. Set at low rates and with high levels of exemption that excused the middle classes from payment, income taxes initially yielded meager revenues and left the budget in deficit.[25]

The shared determination of the Wilson administration and Democratic congressional leaders that the costs of America's participation in the Great War should be borne as far as possible by direct taxation eventually necessitated better exploitation of the income tax. Thanks to a series of tax hikes and exemption reductions, income taxes accounted for 59 percent of total revenues of $5.1 billion by FY1919, compared with just 16 percent of $783 million three years earlier. Corporate taxes accounted for two-thirds of this expansion in reflection of Democratic concern to tax monopoly power and excessive profits. The corollary belief that a mass-based tax was a betrayal of party principles persuaded the Wilson administration to maintain the elite character of the personal income tax, which limited its revenue benefit. Americans paying this levy increased in number more than twelvefold in four years but only constituted 14 percent of the workforce in FY1920.[26]

The financial consequences of World War I also led to institutional budgetary reform. The professional ethos of administration fostered by the corporate private sector, the Progressive movement's advocacy of executive-centered administrative reform, and the frequency of deficits had all contributed to the growing sense that this was needed. When the conjunction of flat revenues and the extraordinary outlay of $50 million for the Panama Canal right-of-way produced a deficit in FY1904, Roosevelt appointed the Keep Commission to investigate how the executive could improve financial management in light of modern business practices. Following the large deficits of FY1908–FY1909, Taft created the Commission on Economy and Efficiency to produce a blueprint for presidential budget planning, but its proposals fell afoul of congressional Democratic concern about executive centralization. The need for surplus budgets to ensure rapid debt reduction after the war tipped the scales in favor of reform. Despite the new income taxes, fully 70 percent of war costs were financed from borrowing, with the result that public debt had ballooned from $1.2 billion in FY1916 to $25.4 billion in FY1919.[27]

The Budget and Accounting Act of 1921 transformed the president from the chief lobbyist for the balanced-budget rule into the coordinator-in-chief of the process intended to ensure its better implementation. The parallel decisions of both the House of Representatives and the Senate to restore jurisdiction over all spending bills to their Appropriations Committees further aided the cause of budgetary control. The new system delivered balanced budgets aplenty in the hands of the Republican administrations and congresses of the 1920s. Eleven consecutive surpluses, the second-longest sequence in American history, allowed for more than a third of the public debt to be redeemed by FY1930.

Calvin Coolidge's inaugural address declaration—"Economy is idealism in its most practical form"—perfectly encapsulated the fiscal ethos of 1920s Republicanism. Trumpeting this usually overlooked president as a personal hero for delivering debt-reducing surpluses at reduced rates of taxation, Ronald Reagan later hung a portrait of him in the White House cabinet room.[28] The Republican presidents of the 1920s had good cause in addition to debt-reducing imperatives to prioritize expenditure control. Before the Great War, the growth of federal spending had been funded from high tariffs that were helpful to the business community. In the future the costs of state building would come mainly from direct taxation that fell heaviest on this GOP constituency and wealthy individuals associated with it. Nevertheless, Republican economy did not signify a return to Jeffersonian small-government values as latter-day conservatives fondly imagined. What made the 1920s significant in terms of fiscal history was the federal government's success in operating balanced budgets in accordance with the Progressive understanding of what they constituted.

Notwithstanding the economy rhetoric of the time, the budgetary statistics of the 1920s put Republican fiscal "normalcy" in true light. Annual spending for purposes other than debt obligations averaged some $2 billion, far higher than in prewar budgets. Enhanced services and benefits for World War I veterans and high military outlays largely accounted for this. Domestic expenditure was held down until the declining cost of debt retirement allowed for some expansion in the late 1920s, mainly for public works and farm programs. The need for plentiful revenue to fund debt reduction and higher spending militated against restoration of the consumption tax regime. Corporate and personal income tax rates underwent reduction in line with the new trickle-down theory that the resultant availability of greater funds for private investment would enhance general prosperity, but these continued to furnish over half of annual receipts. Although the Fordney-McCumber tariff of 1922 doubled import duties, the revenues it produced only compensated for the decline in excises, particularly the Prohibition-imposed loss of alcohol duties.[29]

FROM EMERGENCY DEFICITS TO FISCAL POLICY: THE NEW DEAL ERA

The United States operated an unprecedented sequence of large deficits from FY1931 through FY1946 in the crisis conditions of economic depression and global war. Contradicting Progressive expectations that the president would be the guardian of fiscal responsibility, Franklin D. Roosevelt engaged in deficit spending in support of his New Deal program, but he was hesitant to validate it as a positive instrument of economic policy. What finally endowed deficits with substantive and symbolic legitimacy was their contribution to the spectacular success of the economy during World War II in verification of novel Keynesian theory.

Though Roosevelt was the first Keynesian president, the New Deal was "Keynesian only by occasional coincidence" prior to 1938.[30] The emergency justification for deficit spending that FDR initially propounded was similar to Herbert Hoover's rationale before his misguided reversion to budget-balancing orthodoxy. The deficit had ballooned from an already unprecedented peacetime level of $462 million (0.6 percent GDP) in FY1931 to a staggering $2.7 billion (4.0 percent GDP) in FY1932. Fearful that massive government borrowing would crowd out business from already tight credit markets, Hoover sought to balance the FY1933 budget through enactment of the largest tax increases in peacetime history. The higher taxes mainly served to depress purchasing power in an already devastated economy with the consequence that their meager revenue yield reduced the deficit to just $2.6 billion (4.5 percent GDP).[31] Roosevelt's more flexible concept of sound finance enabled him to pursue a fiscal course that was better suited to the economic conditions.

The early New Deal's priority was to restore business confidence through institutional and regulatory reforms that eliminated stock market malpractice, strengthened banking and real estate finance, and created a more orderly market economy. In Roosevelt's assessment, continuously large budget deficits might harm this cause by arousing concern that government would finance its huge borrowing through an inflationary expansion of the money supply. To forestall this danger, the president distinguished between "ordinary" government expenditure, which he kept flat, and "emergency" outlays on programs like unemployment relief, public works, and farm assistance, which rose annually from $1 billion to $4.4 billion over the course of his first term.[32] This signified that the regular costs of government were still subject to balanced-budget discipline in line with Progressive ideals and held out the prospect that deficit-producing abnormal expenditure would decline and eventually disappear as the economy improved.

True to the logic of this fiscal dichotomy, Roosevelt retrenched emergency outlays in his FY1938 budget in the mistaken belief that the economic depression was drawing to an end. In combination with the Federal Reserve's parallel tightening of monetary policy to throttle the build-up of inflationary pressures expected to accompany recovery, the removal of fiscal stimulus was instrumental in precipitating a new recession in the second half of 1937. It was in response to this downturn that the New Deal took a Keynesian turn. A battle ensued for the president's ear between advisers urging perseverance with his balanced-budget inclinations as the only way to revive business confidence and those advocating deficit spending to stimulate the economy in accordance with the prescriptions of British economist John Maynard Keynes. Eventually heeding the latter, Roosevelt sent Congress in the spring of 1938 a new spending and credit program that he justified as necessary to boost the nation's purchasing power. Fiscal policy in the form of deficit spending was now the core of his economic strategy.[33]

Far from showing a convert's zeal, Roosevelt was at best half-hearted in his acceptance of unbalanced budgets as an economic good. A pragmatist to his core, the president was inherently skeptical of any theory. As one biographer noted, "A Keynesian solution . . . involved an absolute commitment, and Roosevelt was not one to commit himself absolutely to any political or economic method."[34] FDR was reluctant to endorse deficits as a long-term approach to full recovery rather than a temporary necessity. His jaw was set even more firmly against the contention of some Keynesians that unbalanced budgets were a permanent necessity to compensate for the intrinsic stagnation of America's economy in its mature stage of development in succession to dynamic nineteenth-century growth.

Seeking a middle-way rationale between fiscal orthodoxy and full-blooded Keynesianism, FDR in his 1939 budget message once more distinguished between ordinary and extraordinary government spending but now accepted that the latter would be a permanent feature of the budget. In this iteration, extraordinary expenditures—generally for government loans, capital outlays, and relief of need—represented "the relationship between fiscal policy and the economic welfare of the country" and were "of such a flexible character as to provide, through their contraction and expansion, a partial offset for the rise and fall of national income."[35]

Roosevelt's coyness about the value of deficits contrasted with the increasingly trenchant denunciation of them by his political opponents. The New Deal's expansion of national government made conservatives in both Republican and Democratic congressional ranks increasingly fearful that it threatened the constitutional order. Although the state-building that offended them was as much regulatory as budgetary in form, the deficit became a powerful symbol of excessive federal power in their eyes. In essence, the conservatives of the 1930s resurrected the Jeffersonian understanding of balanced budgets that had fallen into abeyance after the Civil War to challenge the validity of the New Deal.

The steady improvement in economic conditions initially deterred these critics from open rebellion, but the recession deprived Roosevelt of this shield. Reinforcing political concerns about deficits as a threat to founding values, the downturn persuaded congressional conservatives that they were also harmful to business confidence. An informal bipartisan coalition formed in opposition to the New Deal early in FDR's second term. Its numbers boosted by Republican gains in the midterm elections of 1938, this bloc prevented enactment of the president's spending-lending economic stimulus bill in 1939.[36]

The legitimacy of deficit spending was under significant challenge by the end of the 1930s. Hated by the New Deal's enemies, unbalanced budgets hardly had a place in the hearts of its supporters. The political conflicts of the Great Depression decade marked the emergence of an ideological divide over the economic activism of the state that gave new meaning to contemporary liberalism and conservatism. In Roosevelt's own words, liberalism had become "plain English for a changed concept of the duty and responsibility of government toward economic life." Determined to preserve the free market as both an economic and political entity, conservatives saw the deficit as the principal instrument of an activist state, but this exaggerated its significance for their liberal adversaries. Roosevelt's ambivalence aside, many New Dealers regarded the recession of the late 1930s as proof that the maldistribution of wealth was the principal obstacle to a consumption-led economic recovery. They regarded planning, regulatory, and antimonopoly initiatives as a more effective solution than compensatory deficits for this.[37]

True believers in Keynesian doctrine were a small band in the community of Washington policy makers. It would remain an esoteric doctrine as long as the economic utility of unbalanced budgets remained unproven. The New Deal's record by 1940 hardly offered encouraging evidence of their expansionary benefits. Despite eight years of deficits that were unprecedented in dollar size and in relationship to GDP, unemployment had only been reduced from 25 percent to 15 percent of the labor force, and economic output had not recovered to its 1929 level.

From the Keynesian perspective, the simple explanation for the New Deal's failure to restore prosperity was that it never implemented the Keynesian prescription. According to the most eminent American exponent of this doctrine, Harvard economist Alvin Hansen, "For the most part the federal government engaged in a salvaging program and not in a program of positive expansion."[38] In Keynesian theory, deficit spending on relief, public works, credit, and other programs would put money in peoples' pockets; the recipients would then spend it on their needs; and those paid it would spend it in their turn. This multiplier effect would lead to a doubling or more of the economic value of the government's original outlay. The consequent boost to consumption would in turn generate increased production, rising employment, and the restoration of business confidence. The ultimate goal for Keynesians was the revival of capital investment that they deemed essential to raise productivity, the fundamental requirement for economic growth. In their view it was the expectation of profits that generated new investment, and the key to business profitability was a high consumption–full employment economy, which could be achieved through deficit spending of sufficiently ambitious scale.

In Keynesian eyes, the New Deal deficits were utterly insufficient for this purpose. Measured in terms of how far these resulted from the fiscal actions of government rather than cyclical factors, only the FY1934 and FY1936 deficits (respectively 5.9 percent and 5.5 percent GDP) were significantly more expansionary than those operated by Hoover in FY1932–FY1933. Paradoxically, Roosevelt's Keynesian deficits of FY1939–FY1940 averaged only 3.1 percent GDP, making them less expansionary than his predecessor's unbalanced budgets. By this juncture, the president's effective loss of control of Congress ruled out a bigger stimulus.[39]

The inadequacy of New Deal spending only partly explained its fiscal policy limitations. The increase in tax revenues at a rate far exceeding expenditure growth acted as a drag on the economy. Receipts and outlays respectively equated to 7.1 percent and 10.3 percent GDP in FY1939, compared with 3.5 and 8.0 percent GDP in FY1933. The bulk of revenue expansion resulted from economic recovery, but a goodly portion was attributable to higher taxes. The Roosevelt administration repeatedly secured the extension of excise taxes that Hoover had raised in 1932, levied new duties on alcohol after repeal of Prohibition, and raised taxes on business in pursuit of deficit-controlling revenues. The new payroll taxes mandated by the Social Security Act of 1935 to fund old-age pensions became the largest single source of receipts in FY1938–FY1940. The reduction of purchasing power resulting from their initial collection was an instrumental factor in precipitating recession in 1937.[40]

Nevertheless, New Deal deficits were large enough to deter the revival of corporate confidence that was necessary for economic recovery. In combination with higher taxes and increased regulation, they made business nervous that its freedoms and profits were imperiled by an incipient socialism. Without evidence that the Keynesian elixir worked, business leaders regarded unbalanced budgets as an economic and political threat rather than an asset in the quest to renew prosperity. Exemplifying this, the Chamber of Commerce attacked deficit spending, in one historian's words, as "the single greatest obstacle to faith in the free-enterprise system and recovery from the Depression." Alongside other business organizations, it became an enthusiastic supporter of the congressional conservative challenge to the New Deal in the late 1930s.[41]

The metamorphosis from scarcity to abundance in World War II finally offered proof of the Keynesian pudding not served on the New Deal menu. Massive federal spending on defense ended the depression and energized the economy in a way that Roosevelt's hesitant civilian initiatives never could. Of a magnitude that dwarfed those of the 1930s, wartime deficits equated to 14.2 percent GDP in FY1942, 30.3 percent GDP in FY1943, 22.7 GDP in FY1944, and 21.5 percent GDP in FY1945. The stimulus they provided brought about full employment by 1943 and boosted GDP from $96.8 billion in 1940 to $221.4 billion in 1945. In these circumstances policy makers readjusted their focus from dealing with the scarcity of the 1930s to maximizing the abundance that was the promise of postwar America.[42]

BALANCING THE BUSINESS CYCLE: THE EARLY
POSTWAR ERA

The wartime experience engendered belief that government had an obligation to ensure the economy's continued well-being in peacetime. This produced a new understanding of the balanced-budget rule that budgets should be balanced over the course of the business cycle rather than in a particular year. As a result deficits enjoyed far greater legitimacy as instruments to manage postwar prosperity than as means to alleviate unemployment during the Great Depression.

Congressional debate over the Employment Act of 1946 reflected both the extent and limits of economic consensus at the end of the war. An early version of the bill produced by liberal Democrats mandated federal responsibility to ensure full employment through consumption-boosting compensatory spending on public works and social programs. Fearing that this would become a smokescreen for social activism funded by permanent deficits or higher taxes, bipartisan conservatives and their business allies pressed successfully for adoption of a more modest measure. This established a vaguely worded commitment that government would "promote maximum employment, production, and purchasing power." It also created the Council of Economic Advisers (CEA), located in the Executive Office of the Presidency, to provide the president with expert advice on the economy and prepare an annual report in his name assessing the state of the economy.[43]

Despite liberal dissatisfaction with its terms, the Employment Act was a landmark in economic policy as both an extension of and a departure from the New Deal. It institutionalized federal responsibility to maintain high employment and economic stability amid general prosperity rather than just during bad times. In creating the CEA, it established professional economic advice for the executive that contrasted with the ad hoc arrangements of the 1930s. Finally, it confirmed the president as the chief manager of prosperity in providing him with a new advisory system and endowing him with responsibility for reporting on the economy. This necessarily affirmed the primacy of fiscal policy, the principal tool of economic management at presidential disposal.

The development of fiscal policy under the Employment Act's mandate entailed a bipartisan trade-off. Most Republicans accepted unbalanced budgets as an effective tool of economic stabilization. Holdouts on the right of the party discovered the dangers of being outside the political mainstream when Barry Goldwater's antistatist campaign for president in 1964 went down to landslide defeat. Democrats in turn accepted that government's role was to ensure stability and high employment within the private economy rather than to redistribute wealth. Keynesian-influenced postwar fiscal policy was perfectly suited to this end because it aimed to correct business cycle fluctuations rather than alter the structure of capitalism in the manner of New Deal institutional reforms. In this sense public-sector deficits came to be seen as the guarantors of private-sector well-being rather than a threat to business and democracy that conservatives had imagined in the 1930s.[44]

This did not signify acceptance that unbalanced budgets should be the norm. Both Harry Truman and Dwight Eisenhower, the Democratic and Republican occupants of the White House in the early postwar era, worried that running deficits during prosperity would aggravate inflationary pressures.[45] This economic concern reinforced their political preference for fiscal responsibility. A moderate liberal who had made his name as chair of a senatorial committee investigating waste in the wartime defense program, Truman considered balanced budgets a symbol of efficiency and economy in government. As he put it, "There is nothing sacred about the pay-as-you-go idea so far as I am concerned except that it represents the soundest principle of financing that I know."[46] A moderate conservative, Eisenhower wanted to control deficit spending partly out of concern that its utilization by the New Deal had launched the nation along "the kind of road that if followed forever will lead to socialism." More immediately, he feared that the inflationary consequences of unbalanced budgets could undermine America's capacity to wage the Cold War.[47]

Nevertheless, both presidents recognized the utility of deficits to counter downswings in the business cycle. Facing the first postwar recession in 1949, Truman declared, "We cannot expect to achieve a budget surplus in a declining economy. There are economic and social deficits that would be far more serious than a temporary deficit in the federal budget." Eisenhower put a Republican seal of approval on compensatory fiscal policy by running deficits to combat the recessions of 1953–1954 and 1957–1958. Recognizing that fiscal responsibility was sometimes in conflict with economic stabilization, he told one associate, "If conditions require, we shall not hesitate to subordinate the first . . . for the second."[48]

Accordingly, the most salient feature of postwar fiscal policy was equilibrium over time. Truman operated a deficit in recession-hit FY1950, and Eisenhower followed suit in FY1954–FY1955, FY1958–FY1959, and FY1961. Otherwise, the only unbalanced budgets of the period occurred in conformity with wartime norms in Korea-affected FY1952–FY1953. Conversely, the two presidents ran a comparable number of surpluses during prosperity in FY1947–FY1949, FY1951, FY1956–FY1957, and FY1960. Furthermore, absent the abnormally large surplus of FY1948 (4.6 percent GDP) and the unusually large deficit of FY1959 (2.6 percent GDP), deficits and surpluses more or less balanced out on yearly average at 1.6 percent GDP and 1.5 percent GDP, respectively, in the Truman-Eisenhower budgets.

If this outcome was not the result of precise fiscal engineering, neither was it accidental. In effect both Truman and Eisenhower amended the balanced-budget rule to signify achievement of fiscal balance over the course of the business cycle. This idea found initial expression as "stabilizing budget policy" in a statement issued in 1947 by the Committee for Economic Development, a business group interested in developing a cooperative relationship between corporations and the state. According to Herbert Stein, the organization's research director and later CEA chair during Richard Nixon's presidency, this became "the standard approach to fiscal policy" in the postwar era.[49]

The stabilizing budget rationale substituted the traditionally negative symbolism of deficits with a positive understanding of them as a public good provided they were small and temporary. As Eisenhower put it in 1953, "Balancing the budget will always remain a goal of any administration. . . . That does not mean you can pick any specific date and say, 'Here all things must give way before a balanced budget.' It is a question of where the importance of a balanced budget comes in." Six years later, his Cabinet Committee on Economic Growth and Price Stability declared that running surpluses at high employment and deficits in recession was "consistent with the goal of a balanced budget, but the periods within which balance would be attained would correspond with cycles in American economic activity rather than with cycles in the calendar."[50]

The new significance of automatic fiscal stabilizers facilitated the attainment of cyclical balance. Rising joblessness in a recession produced parallel growth in federal spending because of increased demand for unemployment insurance, a contributory program created by the Social Security Act of 1935 and steadily expanded after World War II. Far more significant was the stabilizing effect of the broad-based personal tax system created during the war. Whereas only 5 percent of families at most had paid individual income taxes in any year during the 1930s, 74 percent did so in FY1945 as a result of wartime expansion of tax eligibility. In FY1940 federal income taxation, including corporation taxes, constituted only 16 percent of taxes collected by all levels of government, but ten years later it accounted for over 51 percent.[51] The automatic decline in tax receipts in postwar recessions therefore became the principal driver of counter-cyclical deficits. Their automatic growth in recovery periods conversely generated cyclical balance and countered inflationary pressures from the revival of consumer demand.[52]

The salve of economic growth ensured that taxes were not the bone of contention that they became in the later age of deficits. Surging profits and income effectively reconciled business leaders and most Republicans to corporate tax rates and marginal rates of personal taxes for high earners considered punitive in the recent past. Meanwhile, the Democrats steadily abandoned redistributive tax goals to focus on pro-growth strategies as the best way to raise the standard of living of nonaffluent Americans. Importantly, too, the mass of taxpayers accepted the new rates, largely thanks to postwar prosperity but also because wartime propaganda that income tax payment was an obligation of citizenship had shaped a new taxpaying culture. The use of "tax expenditures"—special preferences in the form of exclusions, deductions, and credits—also sugared the pill for middle-class families. The most expensive was the deduction for mortgage interest that had been in the tax code since 1913 but increased in significance with the postwar expansion of homeownership.[53]

Bountiful revenues from prosperity also funded massive expansion of federal spending within a balanced budget. In FY1940, outlays of $9.5 billion ($108.8 billion in FY2000 dollars) and revenues of $6.5 billion ($75.3 billion) respectively equaled 9.8 percent and 6.8 percent GDP. In FY1960, outlays of $92.2 billion ($526.8 billion in FY2000 dollars) and receipts of $92.5 billion ($528.5 billion) each constituted 17.8 percent GDP. The bulk of spending in the 1950s supported the militarization and globalization of Cold War containment. The national defense share (including nonmilitary components) of the post–Korean War budgets of FY1955–FY1961 averaged 56.4 percent. By contrast, postwar trends in domestic spending were less clear-cut. Outlays were significantly higher in constant-dollar terms in FY1960 compared with FY1940 but remained flat in relation to economic output (at 6.5 percent and 6.7 percent GDP, respectively) and constituted a much smaller share of the total budget (37.1 percent compared to 68.1 percent).[54]

The scale of defense outlays reflected broad agreement across the political spectrum that the Soviet Union and its allies posed a significant threat to America's security. Domestic spending, in contrast, manifested the limits of consensus on the state's role outside the realm of economic management. Truman's surprise reelection in 1948 demonstrated lack of popular support for New Deal rollback but did not provide a mandate for new program development. Second-term initiatives with a budgetary dimension that fell afoul of the conservative coalition in Congress included a national health insurance plan, federal aid to education, and the Brannan plan to combine increased support for farm income and lower food prices for consumers. Sensing that the GOP would never regain power if it continued to attack the New Deal, Eisenhower developed a middle-way approach that accepted the basic structure of Roosevelt's legacy but held the line against its expansion into new areas of state activism. Significantly, the domestic program that experienced the biggest growth in outlays—from negligible levels in FY1940 to 2.2 percent GDP twenty years later—was Social Security. This was a consequence not only of more contributors reaching retirement age but also of expansion in program coverage and benefits promoted by the Truman and Eisenhower administrations.[55]

Both postwar presidents also strove to maintain the nexus between spending and taxation in order to deliver their business-cycle adaptation of the balanced-budget rule. Truman fought the tax-cutting initiatives of the GOP-controlled Eightieth Congress of 1947–1948 to safeguard revenues and suppress inflationary pressures. Determined to rescind the $5 billion tax cut enacted over his veto on the third time of trying in 1948, he pressed for a $4 billion increase in corporation, top-band personal income, and estate taxes in 1949 until recession persuaded him to desist. The Korean War renewed his prioritization of revenue enhancement. On the president's recommendation, Congress enacted in late 1950 temporary increases in corporate and personal tax rates and a new excess profits tax that helped to balance the FY1951 budget. The follow-up Revenue Act of 1951 only gave Truman half the $10 billion additional revenues that he wanted. Nevertheless, the surge in receipts from wartime economic growth kept the budget close to aggregate balance over the course of the conflict.[56]

Despite his belief that high taxes were an economic disincentive, Eisenhower showed similar determination to protect revenues. Tax cuts amounting to $7.4 billion in calendar year 1954, the largest single-year reduction hitherto, seemingly belied this, but $5 billion resulted from the scheduled expiry of temporary Korean War taxes. The remaining $2.4 billion, coming from tax cuts contained in the administration's tax reform program and excise reductions, amounted to less than 4 percent of general revenues. The anti-inflation requirements of cyclical balance inhibited Eisenhower from supporting further tax relief. As his departure from office drew near, he looked to prevent his successor straying from fiscal righteousness on this score. Forecasting a surplus of $4.2 billion for FY1961, Eisenhower declared, "Personally I do not believe that any amount can be properly called a 'Surplus' as long as our nation is in debt. I prefer to think of such an item as a reduction on our children's 'inherited mortgage.'" In his view, only when payments to scale back the public debt were "normal practice" should taxes be cut.[57]

By now, however, the main threat to Eisenhower's fiscal objectives came from the spending side of the budget. The former army general feared that continuous growth of Cold War defense spending would either bankrupt the nation or produce a garrison state. In his first term, he achieved significant military economies not only through post-Korea retrenchment but also prioritization of air-atomic power as a more cost-effective instrument of containment than conventional force expansion. However, the Soviet launch of Sputnik in late 1957 generated widespread concern that America was falling behind in rocket technology. Charging that Eisenhower's penny-pinching had endangered national security, congressional Democrats agitated for a significant expansion of defense expenditure. Their parallel demands for greater domestic spending to counter the 1957–1958 recession also came into conflict with the president's insistence on budgetary restraint.[58]

Worrying signs that foreigners would lose confidence in the dollar if the administration did not show commitment to control inflation enhanced Eisenhower's determination to balance the FY1960 budget. Under the terms of the Bretton Woods agreement of 1944, the dollar had a fixed convertibility rate into gold as the world's principal reserve currency. Huge outflows of dollars for economic aid, military outlays, loans, and investments resulted in the United States almost continuously operating an international balance-of-payments deficit after World War II. This provided liquidity to facilitate the recovery of the international economy. Industrial nations engaged in post-war reconstruction could accumulate dollars to compensate for the weakness of their own currencies. With their economies largely rebuilt by the late 1950s, however, their need for greenbacks had diminished. Foreign central bankers consequently urged the Eisenhower administration to balance the budget lest the inflationary consequences of fiscal deficits compelled devaluation of the dollar. If this appeared imminent, they feared that foreign dollar-holders would launch a preemptive run on U.S. gold, thereby undermining America's reserve position and throwing the international financial system into chaos.[59]

Eisenhower appeared in a weak position to resist new spending pressures after the 1958 midterm elections produced large Democratic majorities in Congress. Using the presidential bully pulpit and his veto, however, he energized a coalition of Republicans and conservative Democrats, by now a largely Southern bloc, to hold the line against the ambitious spending plans of his Democratic opponents. Opinion polls showed that he was also successful in convincing the public that deficit spending would seriously exacerbate inflationary pressures. As the *New Republic*'s liberal columnist Richard Strout lamented, the president turned the tables on his adversaries "with the bogey words 'inflation,' 'spenders' and 'deficits.'"[60]

The FY1960 budget eventually ended up with a small surplus equal to 0.1 percent GDP. However, the rapid shift from the relatively large FY1959 deficit of 2.6 percent GDP undermined recovery from the recession. Denied adequate stimulus, the economy experienced another downturn in late 1960. This worked to Democratic advantage in the close-fought presidential election between John F. Kennedy and Richard Nixon. The recession also discredited stabilizing budget policy as a tool of economic management. The economy evidently needed a stronger dose of fiscal adrenaline to counter its chronic slack. GDP growth in 1956–1960 was barely half the Truman era rate and fell below that achieved in Western Europe, Japan, and the Soviet Union. Average annual unemployment of 5.1 percent in this period compared to 3.7 percent in 1951–1955 also posed the question whether Eisenhower had fulfilled his obligations under the Employment Act.[61]

In light of these shortcomings, liberal economists grew increasingly dismissive of what they dubbed the "cyclical mentality" of postwar fiscal orthodoxy. In their credo, the solution to the economy's problems lay not in stabilizing cyclical fluctuations but in accelerating the rate of economic growth around which cyclical fluctuations occurred. This idea found its way into the Democratic agenda as the 1960 presidential election drew near. Within a few years of Kennedy's victory the fiscal revolution that had started in the 1930s would reach its culmination.

BALANCING THE ECONOMY: FROM THE 1960S
TO THE GREAT RECESSION

The "new economics" of the 1960s advocated that fiscal policy should be based on an assessment of the economy's needs in a particular year rather than over the course of the business cycle. It promoted a new understanding of the balanced-budget rule as balancing the economy. Described by one proponent as "Keynes-*cum*-growth," this doctrine advocated continuous expansion of productive output and closure of the gap between actual output and the economy's expanding potential. The Kennedy CEA, the champion of the new thinking, estimated that there was a performance gap of almost $50 billion, equal to nearly 10 percent of current GDP, between actual output and potential output at full-employment level in the economy inherited from Eisenhower. Its instrument to close this and keep it shut was the "full-employment budget." Guided by their economic advisers, Kennedy and his successor, Lyndon B. Johnson, looked to balance actual outlays against the hypothetical level of receipts if the economy were operating at full employment.[62]

This approach automatically factored economic growth into budget policy. Full employment, conventionally defined as a jobless rate of 4 percent or less, was a moving target because the labor force was continuously expanding and productivity improvements were constantly replacing jobs with technology. Accordingly, the full-employment budget provided a more accurate measure as to whether fiscal policy was expansionary or not. A full-employment deficit indicated a stimulative budget, a full-employment surplus the reverse. Measured on this basis, the actual deficit of $3.3 billion in FY1961—the recession had torpedoed Eisenhower's original balanced-budget projection—turned into a restrictive hypothetical surplus of $10 billion. The new economics also drew inspiration from the "Phillips curve" theory of British-based economist A. W. Phillips that there was an inverse relationship between inflation and unemployment whereby one fell as the other rose. Through use of fiscal stimuli, its practitioners looked to fine-tune the economy to achieve a trade-off of their target unemployment rate against inflation of around 2 percent.[63]

The full-employment label safeguarded the new fiscal policy against association of deficits with inflation. It provided a normative justification for the functional Keynesian linkage of the budget to the state of the economy.

Exemplifying this, Kennedy's final *Economic Report* proclaimed, "Recession and slack generate deficits; prosperity and growth balance budgets." As Walter Heller later remarked, "The power of Keynesian ideas could not be harnessed to the nation's lagging economy without putting them in forms and terms . . . fitting the vocabulary and the values of the public. At the same time, men's minds had to be conditioned to accept new thinking, new symbols, and new and broader concepts of the public interest."[64]

Taking its cue from Keynes, the Kennedy CEA regarded consumption as the agency of economic growth. From its perspective, the built-in flexibility of the automatic stabilizers that had underpinned postwar fiscal policy was holding back the economy. Whereas the decline of tax receipts counteracted recession, their rise during recovery acted as drag on the growth of private income. The consequent retardation of economic expansion was the main cause of the performance gap between actual and potential GDP. As a corrective, the new economists recommended an injection of fiscal stimulus in the form of tax cuts that would be faster acting than increased spending. They also reasoned that congressional conservatives and foreign financiers would be more tolerant of deficits resulting from tax reduction than expenditure expansion.[65]

Kennedy had campaigned for the White House on the theme of getting the country moving again after the Eisenhower years. Economic growth was the chain that linked his vision of what America needed to do at home, abroad, and in space, but he did not immediately embrace full-employment budget theory as its agency. With the economy emerging from the shallow recession of 1960, Kennedy proposed a balanced budget for FY1962 to reassure business that inflation would be checked. However, sluggish recovery and the need for supplemental military appropriations amid escalating Cold War tensions combined to produce an actual deficit double that of recession-hit FY1961 in both dollar and GDP terms. As a consequence Kennedy converted to the new economics faith in pro-growth tax reduction.[66]

The centerpiece of the Kennedy tax program was a three-year cut in income taxes, which was enacted in amended form early in Lyndon B. Johnson's presidency. Despite compromises to secure congressional approval—notably the elimination of tax-reform proposals for business loophole closures—the Revenue Act of 1964 was the most significant change in tax policy since World War II. Unlike the tax cuts of the 1920s, 1948, and 1954, it was not intended to provide relief from high wartime taxes and was approved when the budget was in deficit and expenditure was growing. The measure provided $11.5 billion in tax savings over two years, $9 billion of which went to individuals. Signifying that the aim was economic growth, not wealth redistribution, rate reductions were broadly similar for taxpayers in the $5,000–$50,000 income range that accounted for 80 percent of tax liabilities.[67]

The expansionary results confirmed the new economists' most optimistic predictions. According to CEA member Arthur Okun, the multiplier effect produced $1.82 in increased consumer spending for every $1 of tax relief in calendar year 1964–1965. He calculated that the resultant economic growth generated an increase in federal revenues at an annual rate of $10 billion for FY1966. Yale economist James Tobin, formerly of the Kennedy CEA, estimated that the increase in the economy's productive capacity was responsible for 75 percent of its growth in 1961–1965, with the remainder coming from cyclical recovery. Significantly, the FY1965–FY1966 budget deficits—respectively $1.4 billion (0.2 percent GDP) and $3.7 billion (0.5 percent GDP)—were the smallest of the Kennedy-Johnson presidencies.[68]

To allay concerns that tax reduction would necessitate permanent deficits, Kennedy had undertaken a campaign to educate both business elites and the mass public that it was a fiscally responsible and politically neutral agency of economic growth. In his best-known address, he declared, "What is at stake in our economic decisions today is not some grand warfare of rival ideologies which will sweep the country with passion but the practical management of the modern economy."[69] Nevertheless, the tax cut was instrumental in loosening control over spending in pursuit of liberal objectives. Outlays rose from a yearly average of 18.6 percent GDP in Kennedy's presidency to 19.3 percent GDP in FY1966–FY1970.

The revenue harvest from tax reduction convinced the Johnson administration and its congressional allies that economic growth would be everlasting because the proper policies were now available to ensure it. Headily confident of an endless fiscal dividend, they did not foresee a time when revenue increments would be insufficient to finance rising program costs. The success of the new economics in relating the budget to the economy also had unforeseen consequences. Utilization of deficits in slack conditions made them more likely when growth was strong. Thanks to the hypothecated full-employment budget's removal of tight constraints over real aggregates, spending levels rose to accommodate political judgment about the benefits of program expansion and innovation.[70]

After his landslide reelection in 1964, LBJ launched the Great Society at home while waging war in Southeast Asia. In the greatest outburst of state building since the 1930s, he massively increased social welfare provision, particularly through expansion of entitlements. In contrast to fiscal trends during previous conflicts, the domestic share of the budget not only grew but also did so at a faster rate than did defense in the Vietnam war era. By FY1969 expenditure for national defense and human resource programs respectively amounted to 8.7 percent and 7 percent GDP, compared with 7.4 percent and 5.3 percent in FY1965.

Johnson's grandiose agenda turned the budget into an engine of inflation.

The increase in spending to pay for the Great Society and the war in Vietnam outstripped the fiscal dividend from economic growth. The budget deficit ratcheted upwards to $8.6 billion (1.1 percent GDP) in FY1967 and ballooned to a postwar record of $25.2 billion (2.9 percent GDP) in FY1968. This constituted a breach of the administration's own full-employment budget rule because it provided too much stimulus for an economy already operating at or near its full potential. The average unemployment rate was beneath the effective full-employment level at 3.7 percent in 1966–1968, compared with 5.5 percent in 1961–1965. The effect of aggregate demand rising faster than production was to bid up prices. The consumer price index (CPI) inflation rate, which had grown at an annual rate of just over 1 percent in 1961–1965, consequently rose to 4.2 percent in 1968.[71]

In late 1965 Johnson rejected CEA advice to raise taxes to fund the Vietnam conflict and throttle inflationary pressures out of concern that congressional conservatives would instead demand cuts in Great Society programs. Projections that the FY1968 budget could run a deficit over three times greater than the original estimate of $8 billion eventually necessitated this remedy. On August 3, 1967, the president sent Congress a special message requesting a 10 percent temporary surcharge on personal and corporate income taxes with immediate effect. Looking to shock the legislature into compliance, he employed rhetoric that would become commonplace from his successors. "A deficit of that size," LBJ warned, "poses a clear and present danger to America's security and economic health." Unmoved by this, House Ways and Means Committee chair Wilbur Mills (D-AR) set aside consideration of a tax bill until agreement was reached to reduce domestic outlays.[72]

Initially determined to resist calls for retrenchment, Johnson beat a retreat in the face of a new gold crisis. Britain's devaluation of its inflation-weakened pound in late 1967 made foreign dollar-holders fearful that America would follow suit to rescue its own currency. This sparked a run on its gold holdings that reached alarming proportions in early 1968. Under pressure to reassure foreigners of America's determination to control inflation, Johnson accepted Mills's demand for cuts of $6 billion in domestic programs as the price for his committee's approval of the tax surcharge. Although Congress was unable to produce savings of anything like this scale, the Revenue and Expenditure Control Act of 1968 underwrote a $3.2 billion surplus in FY1969, making this the last balanced budget until FY1998.[73]

Despite the Johnson administration's deviation from the new economics script, its authors remained confident that their prescription was adaptable to changing economic conditions. Acknowledging that the "task of combining prosperity with price stability now stands as the major unsolved problem of aggregative economic performance," Arthur Okun predicted that a "satisfactory compromise" between these two ends would be found in the 1970s.[74]

Instead, the economy suffered from rising unemployment and inflation, an unprecedented combination that came to be labeled *stagflation*. The CPI rose 6.1 percent on annual average in 1969–1976, peaking at 11 percent under pressure of spiraling energy costs in 1974. The cost-push effect of wage hikes tied to rising prices and a slowdown in productivity growth also fueled inflation. Meanwhile, unemployment averaged 5.9 percent, peaking at 8.5 percent in recession-hit 1975. The 1960s assumption that 4 percent unemployment was the effective full-employment rate was no longer applicable to a labor market experiencing huge influx of baby-boomers and women, groups with a higher jobless rate than adult white males.[75]

In these circumstances, the notion that the budget should balance the economy became unsustainable. As historian Allen Matusow observed, Richard Nixon's Republican administration ended up "fiscally lost" after vainly trying every known path to exit the stagflation maze. Its strategy was consistent only in its inconsistency: a real surplus in 1969; a balanced full-employment budget in 1970; an implicit full-employment deficit in 1971; an explicit full-employment deficit in 1972; a balanced full-employment budget in 1973; and finally a real balanced budget in 1974.[76] This zigzagging between expansionary and anti-inflationary priorities reflected the difficulty of addressing one side of stagflation without aggravating the other.

With his reelection in mind, Nixon operated relatively large deficits of $23 billion (2.1 percent GDP) in FY1971 and $23.4 billion (2 percent GDP) in FY1972 to boost recovery from the mild recession of 1970. To preempt the corollary danger of another foreign run on gold and boost exports, he abruptly suspended the fixed-convertibility of the dollar in 1971 as a prelude to managed devaluation and later allowed the greenback to float on the world money markets from 1973 onward. Despite the brutal fashion of its implementation, the termination of the Bretton Woods system acknowledged the reality that the dollar was overvalued in the context of the changing international economy. It relieved Nixon and his successors of the gold outflow pressures that had plagued Eisenhower and Johnson when they ran large budget deficits. However, dollar devaluation also increased the cost of imports at a time when the United States was not only growing more dependent on imported oil but also purchasing an increasing volume of foreign manufactures. As a result, the greenback's decline accounted for about a quarter of the inflation rate in 1973.[77]

Stagflation undermined the utility of fiscal policy and its attendant budget rules for economic management. This had a twofold legacy for budgeting in the age of deficits. The first element of this was what Herbert Stein referred to as "the disintegration of fiscal policy."[78] All the different meanings of balanced budgets, including the Keynesian variants, had rested on aggregate-based rules. Although there had always been tension between the two, budget aggregates had hitherto taken precedence over the component parts of the budget. This changed when it became evident that the full-employment budget was inoperable in the economic conditions of the 1970s. Thereafter, presidents continued to be interested in budget aggregates but based on adaptation to taxation and spending levels rather than any rule pertaining to the appropriate size of surplus or deficit.

Early signs of this were evident in the budgetary confrontations between Nixon and the Democrat-controlled Congress. Despite agreeing to expand entitlement benefits and indexing some to inflation, they clashed over discretionary spending. The president increasingly resorted to his veto against what he considered excessive domestic allocations, particularly for education and physical resource programs. In addition, he refused to spend some $12 billion that Congress appropriated for domestic purposes in FY1973. Conversely, Nixon wanted higher funding for defense, whereas many Democrats wanted to cut its appropriations in order to restrain American militarism in the wake of Vietnam. The outcome was broadly a compromise that served each side's programmatic preferences over its aggregate ones. The president accepted higher domestic spending than he wanted, and the congressional Democrats did the same with regard to defense, with the result that overall spending levels were higher than both wanted.[79]

The second consequence of fiscal policy's decline as an instrument of economic management was monetary policy's emergence as an alternative. In his 1967 presidential address to the American Economics Association, monetarist economist Milton Friedman had delivered the most significant critique of Keynesianism since it became the new orthodoxy in the 1940s. His case boiled down to three fundamental arguments: First, there was a "natural rate of unemployment" that reflected the basic structure of the labor market at any given time, so full-employment initiatives only generated inflation that ultimately cost jobs. This contradicted the Phillips curve rationale of the new economics that a trade-off between the two was possible. Second, expansionary fiscal policy based on government borrowing "crowded out" private investment from credit markets, which counterbalanced public stimulus. Finally, the only sure formula for sustainable growth was to keep the money supply steady at a rate consistent with price stability.[80]

Though not agreeing with Friedman that only money mattered in economic management, Nixon's economic advisers endorsed his view that monetary policy should follow a steady course in contrast to the stop-go lurches of the 1960s. However, the independent Federal Reserve continued to react to economic circumstances to the detriment of one or another element of stagflation. Excessive tightening to control inflation slowed the economy in 1969–1970, excessive easing to counter recession in 1971–1972 then fueled inflation, and a steep rise in interest rates to cure the Great Inflation of

1973–1974 precipitated the Great Recession of 1974–1975.[81] Monetarism consequently had no more legitimacy than Keynesianism by the end of Nixon's presidency. Nevertheless, its strictures against an inflation-unemployment trade-off would eventually underwrite monetary policy's establishment as the principal instrument of economic management when inflation became the paramount concern of economic stabilization in the late 1970s.

In the meantime, Keynesianism appeared to make a comeback in the worst recession since the 1930s. The budget deficits of $53.2 billion (3.4 percent GDP) in FY1975 and $73.7 billion (4.2 percent GDP) in FY1976 were the largest in peacetime since FDR's first term. However, recession politics demonstrated that the postwar consensus on compensatory fiscal policy was fraying. Newly installed as president following Nixon's resignation over his Watergate wrongdoings, Gerald Ford insisted that deficit spending should not aggravate inflation that rose at an annual rate of 9.1 percent in recession-hit 1975. In essence, his administration treated unemployment as a short-term problem and inflation as the long-term one. According to CEA chair Alan Greenspan, the aim was "to simmer down the deficit, the rate of inflation, and eventually get to a stable, balanced economy. . . . I thought that if the short-term policy became expansive at this stage, it would eventually prove counterproductive."[82]

The Ford administration advocated temporary personal tax cuts and tax credits for business to stimulate the private economy in conjunction with expenditure restraint to curb inflationary pressures. In contrast, the congressional Democrats, their numbers swollen by midterm election success in 1974, called for even bigger tax cuts and a huge spending program to reduce unemployment as quickly as possible. Ford's dogged use of the veto thwarted their most expansive proposals, but discretionary domestic outlays still rose from 3.6 percent GDP in FY1974 to 4.5 percent GDP in FY1976. Decrying the president's resistance to antirecession spending as a throwback to do-nothing Hooverism, Senate Budget Committee chair Edmund Muskie (D-ME) avowed, "We must reject those of timid vision who counsel us to go back. We cannot give up. And we will not."[83]

Far from going back, the United States was entering a new era when large deficits became the norm. As the budget lost effectiveness as an economic tool, political calculation pertaining to its programmatic composition increasingly shaped its aggregates. Presidents railed against huge deficits, but the needs of their broader agenda generally determined their solutions to them. George H. W. Bush paid the political price for being the exception to this rule. Nevertheless, the patterns of the past were discernible in the budget strategies of other presidents. In seeking to prove that activist government was compatible with fiscal discipline, Jimmy Carter and Bill Clinton harked back to the Progressive concept of balanced budgets. Ronald

Reagan's focus on tax reduction and spending retrenchment resurrected the Jeffersonian understanding of balanced budgets. In cutting income taxes to run down the surplus, George W. Bush was the heir of late-nineteenth-century Republicans, whose inverse concept of balanced budgets underwrote high tariffs. In the past, however, balanced budgets had substance as well as symbolic importance. In contrast, large deficits were an intractable reality in the late twentieth and early twenty-first centuries. Budgetary symbolism was no substitute for substantive fiscal actions needed to deal with them.

CHAPTER 3

Jimmy Carter: Confronting the Deficit

Of all the presidents in the age of deficits, Jimmy Carter was the most dedicated to budgetary restraint. Robert Gates, a national security official in five Cold War administrations, adjudged him "the most fiscally conservative president I ever served."[1] Carter was ahead of his time because he sought to tackle the nation's fiscal problems before many in Washington recognized their gravity. As House Speaker Thomas (Tip) P. O'Neill (D-MA) remarked, he "alerted the country to the problems of the federal deficit back when it was only a fraction of what it grew to be under Reagan."[2]

In Carter's credo, balanced budgets were the hallmark of efficiency and economy in government, a concept that traced its lineage to early-twentieth-century Progressivism. Substantive economic rationale reinforced his understanding of their significance before his presidency was a year old. Initially willing to give the economy an employment-boosting dose of fiscal stimulus, he changed course in recognition that "my major economic battle would be against inflation, and I would stay on the side of fiscal prudence, restricted budgets, and lower deficits."[3] Although Carter ultimately failed to balance the budget and conquer inflation, his presidency had immense significance for partisan fiscal governance. It marked the first step in the Democrats' transition from their mid-twentieth-century acceptance of deficits as a Keynesian instrument of economic growth to their late-twentieth-century belief that deficit control was necessary for prosperity and social activism.

SOUTHERN MAN

Born on October 1, 1924, Jimmy Carter grew up in the hamlet of Archery, southwest Georgia, where his father owned a large and thriving farm. Throughout youth and adulthood he strove for self-improvement through hard work and acquisition of knowledge. A star student, he completed high school at age sixteen, studied a year at Georgia Tech, and entered the U.S. Navy Academy in 1943, where he excelled in engineering. Carter spent seven years as a navy officer, the last of them in the nuclear submarine program. Abandoning this promising career to run the family farm and associated businesses upon his father's death in 1953, he expanded the enterprise into a thriving agribusiness that grossed more than $2 million a year by 1976.

In politics, Carter displayed all the ambition and drive that he had shown in his previous careers. Three years after election to the Georgia Senate in 1962, he was ranked among the most influential legislators in one newspaper poll. In 1966 he entered a crowded Democratic gubernatorial primary, running a creditable third despite his lack of statewide reputation. Unaccustomed to failure, he fell into depression, but he found solace in a born-again religious experience of intense spirituality. Elected governor on his second attempt in 1970, Carter forged a strong record in office as an exemplar of the racially moderate "New South." This gave him the platform to run for president in 1976. Though he was largely unknown outside Georgia, his outsider status proved a positive advantage because of the anti-establishment national mood generated by Watergate.[4]

The commitment to budgetary restraint that marked Carter's presidency was the product of his personality, background, and values. The influence of his father was particularly strong in this regard. Earl Carter's economic success amidst rural hard times was built on hard work, thrift, and avoidance of debt. In contrast, Lillian Carter, a qualified nurse imbued with voluntary ideals, rendered free medical care to impoverished local families of both races. During their son's presidency, observed confidante and professional psychiatrist Peter Bourne, "the aspects of his personality acquired from his mother—his general commitment to the interests of blacks, women, and the poor—were eclipsed by the cost-conscious business orientation that was his legacy from Mr. Earl."[5] As a problem solver, Carter was logical, methodical, and punctual, rather than creative, traits that his training as a naval engineer reinforced. According to political ally Bert Lance, this professional background impelled him to put "a deadline on everything he does—and everything you do."[6] This was reflected in his promise to balance the budget by the end of his first term. Carter's religiosity also inclined him to view politics as a struggle for justice in a sinful world. In budgetary terms, this caused him to identify his deficit-control aims as the embodiment of the public good and demands for higher spending as driven by special-interest selfishness.[7]

Important as these influences were in shaping Carter's fiscal outlook, his status as the first president from the South since the Civil War was its mainspring. Throughout his career in politics, he refused to be tagged with conventional labels. When he began addressing audiences outside Georgia in the early 1970s, he described himself as a "benevolent conservative" to signify commitment to compassion and economy, but this phrase never caught on. Running for president, he declared himself "a fiscal conservative but quite liberal on such issues as civil rights, environmental quality, and helping people overcome handicaps to lead fruitful lives."[8] This put him at odds with the liberal orthodoxy that more federal spending was necessary to uplift the disadvantaged. Disillusioned with Carter's efforts to control social program outlays, Arthur Schlesinger Jr. contended that the thirty-ninth president was "not a Democrat—at least in anything more recent than the Grover Cleveland sense of the word."[9] Historian Stephen Gillon similarly characterized the Georgian as "a Democrat who thought like a Republican."[10]

A different kind of Democrat Carter may have been on the national scene, but he was a familiar one in the South. The Georgian belonged to the first substantial cohort of the Southern upper-middle class, its ranks swollen by the region's postwar economic renaissance. In sociologist John Shelton Reed's assessment, one reason why Carter was so little understood outside the South was because the regional class he came from was "effectively invisible" in the national consciousness that stereotyped white Southern males as either rednecks or good old boys. As another commentator observed, Carter was "a fairly typical representative of the new breed of entrepreneurs and managers" that proliferated in the New South. He was ambitious, hard working, dedicated to efficiency, practical rather than philosophical in outlook, and careful with money because optimism about the good times was tempered by memories of the South's dismal economic past.[11] As a politician Carter manifested the values of his class. According to historian Robert McMath, his governorship of Georgia from 1971 to 1975 was "squarely within the tradition of southern business progressivism" that habitually drew support from the regional upper-middle class.[12]

Carter had much in common with other Democrats elected to the South's state houses in the 1970s. They combined modern acceptance of the civil rights revolution with emphasis on economy and efficiency in government in the tradition of business-oriented reform governors whose regional lineage stretched back to the 1920s. Among them were Reuben Askew in Florida, Dale Bumpers in Arkansas, Edwin Edwards in Louisiana, James Hunt in North Carolina, and William Winter in Mississippi. Like their Progressive forbears, the New South governors undertook to make state government work better through businesslike management, better planning, and reliance on expert advice.[13] They preferred to spend money on infrastructure programs like education, roads, and high-tech development that attracted new industries to their states than on social programs. Although federal aid had largely been responsible for the postwar development of the New South, Carter and his colleagues pinned their hopes for the future on the expansion of private enterprise.[14] Accordingly, they tended to be more conservative on fiscal issues than that other breed of Southern governor, the segregationist with populist sympathies.

Carter displayed his business Progressivism in implementing Georgia's first executive reorganization plan since 1931. Produced by a study group that included business leaders, academics and public officials, this reduced the plethora of often overlapping state bureaus, boards, commissions, and departments from 300 to 22. Carter claimed that reorganization delivered $55 million savings for the state government in FY1973, but this was fanciful. A state auditor later failed to identify any economies that were directly attributable to it. In a moment of candor during the presidential campaign, Carter press secretary Jody Powell told a reporter, "No one really knows how much it saved or cost. It depends on how you calculate it."[15]

Despite Carter's emphasis on economy, Georgia's budget underwent substantial expansion during his governorship. Far from retrenching state government, he sought to ensure that its growth was disciplined and cost-effective. In line with this, his State of the State address of 1972 announced the introduction of zero-based budgeting to encourage "the search for more efficient ways to do the job." Drawing on the business model pioneered by the Texas Instruments Corporation, this required departments annually to justify their budgets and prioritize spending requirements. However, it was not the surefire solution to reducing waste that Carter claimed. Department heads could manipulate the process by placing low priority on a needed program and high priority on a pet project of lesser utility. The system's dependence on accurate revenue forecasts was also problematic. Because priority rankings changed under different funding levels, Carter asked for entirely new budget submissions for FY1974 (when revenues exceeded forecasts) and FY 1975 (when the reverse occurred). In practice, zero-based budgeting had little impact on departmental spending. Only two of thirteen department heads responding to one survey agreed that it "may have led" to resource reallocation.[16]

As president, Carter found it difficult to reconcile his efficiency orientation with the uncertain outcomes of macroeconomic decision making. Wanting to approach fiscal policy as a technocratic problem-solver, he was uncomfortable with the menu of choices and trade-offs before him. His business Progressive outlook made him skeptical of the utility of deficit spending. Carter had particular trouble with Keynesianism's multiplier dictum that "'wasteful' loan expenditures may nevertheless enrich the community." According to Council of Economic Advisers (CEA) chair Charles Schultze, he was resistant to "the idea that however wrong it was to spend money inefficiently, that in doing an economic forecast the inefficient expenditure of money, at least in the short run, was nevertheless employment creating."[17] The inexactitude of economic forecasting was another frustration, causing him to snap at one cabinet meeting, "There's a mystic down in Smithsville who's got as good a batting average as my economic advisers."[18]

Carter's fiscal conservatism in relation to the expenditure side of the budget did not make him a conservative tax-cutter on its revenue side. Instead, his Progressive instincts, reinforced by his faith-based antipathy to special interests, endowed him with concern for tax equity. As governor, he rejected a proposal to fund property tax cuts by slashing the state education budget. Seeing better schools as vital to Georgia's development, he asserted, "There are some things more important than a tax reduction." Carter also resisted another initiative to finance property tax relief through sales tax increases. "There are many public officials in this state panting for the opportunity to load the poor with more sales tax and take off from the rich their property burden," he told Atlanta mayor Maynard Jackson.[19] Running for president, Carter trained his guns on the inequities of the federal tax structure as a "disgrace to this country." He promised comprehensive reform of tax expenditures and allowances that were "a welfare program for the rich."[20]

Carter preferred to appeal to middle-class voters as a budget-balancer rather than a tax-cutter. He continually trumpeted business Progressive ideals of fiscal efficiency throughout his long campaign for president. In his first address to a Washington audience at the National Press Club, on February 9, 1973, he advocated zero-based budgeting in the federal executive in combination with congressional adoption of spending limits to balance the federal budget. In his campaign autobiography, he avowed, "Government at all levels can be competent, economical and efficient." One journalist noted that he spoke from the heart on the stump about his practical experience of keeping outlays in line with income. At a time of record federal deficits, Carter proudly told audiences, "I have never known an unbalanced budget in my business or my farm or as Governor of Georgia."[21]

Commitment to fiscal responsibility fitted with the trust-in-government theme that was Carter's main campaign issue to win the Democratic presidential nomination in the post-Watergate environment of 1976. Nevertheless, he found it more difficult to sustain his image as a budgetary white knight once he attained that prize. As he later commented, "All of a sudden, whether I wanted it or not, I inherited the Democratic party." His legacy included a national party platform supporting national health insurance, welfare reform, and other commitments that were bound to increase government costs. The only area where the Democratic manifesto looked to save money was defense, but the projected savings of $5 billion to $7 billion nowhere near offset expensive domestic promises.[22] Carter's endorsement of the platform, albeit only in broad outline, exposed him to Republican charges that he was just another big-government Democrat.

In response, Carter grew more assertive in avowing dedication to balancing the budget. The principal economics position paper that he issued during the primary campaign had recognized the short-term utility of deficits to combat recession but in the manner of Truman-Eisenhower stabilizing budget strategy rather than of Kennedy-Johnson new economics. It asserted, "Social needs and the need for economic stabilization may require from time to time unbalancing of the budget. . . . The surplus years should balance the deficits."[23] In the general election, however, Carter engaged in blanket condemnation of unbalanced budgets to attack the record deficits of "the Nixon-Ford years." The Republicans, he declared, were guilty of "the worst fiscal mismanagement in our history." This charge made no allowance for the effect of recession on federal finances or the disposition of the Democrat-controlled Congress to run even larger deficits but for Gerald Ford's veto.[24]

Carter's counterattack did not wholly repair his frugal image because Ford hung the Democratic platform like an albatross round his neck. In their first debate, the president warned that it meant "more spending, bigger deficits, more inflation, and more taxes." Carter pollster Pat Caddell found that this attack hit home more than any other. Thereafter Ford held a significant lead in his opinion surveys on control of spending and cutting taxes. "The cautious, 'cheap' Jimmy Carter of the primaries," Caddell observed, "was to some extent transformed into a typical 'expensive' Democrat." In one scholar's assessment, Carter could well have lost what became a very close election had his fiscal conservatism not "somewhat offset" Ford's insistence that Democratic budget-busting policies were a recipe for inflation.[25]

In the wake of recession, Carter focused on jobs as his main line of attack against Ford. "Under this Republican administration," he declared when launching his campaign, "the unemployment rate has been the highest since the Hoover depression." Consistent with his anti-inflation priority, the president refused to stimulate the economy in time for the election, but this ultimately worked to his disadvantage. The pace of recovery slowed in the second half of 1976, pushing unemployment back up from 7.3 percent in May to 8 percent in November. Accordingly, Carter benefited from the kind of economic alignment that traditionally favored Democratic presidential candidates but had virtually disappeared in 1972. Seven of every eight voters whose main issue-concern was unemployment cast their ballots for him. The bedrock of his support came from lower-middle-income households, blue-collar workers, African Americans, low-income whites, and urban dwellers.[26]

Despite the economic conditions favoring him, Carter squeezed home with a popular-vote majority of 50.1–48 percent over Ford. His opponent ran well with college-educated voters, professionals, independents, and suburban dwellers, whose numbers were growing in significance within the electorate. Although Carter carried more Southern states than any Democratic presidential candidate since 1944, his support came mainly from newly enfranchised African Americans and fellow Baptist rural and small-town whites rather than residents of Sunbelt growth hotspots. Ford also ran well ahead of him nationwide among voters more concerned about inflation than unemployment.[27]

In a memorandum for the new president, Pat Caddell warned that the

Democrats could no longer depend on the "coalition of economic division" that had kept them in power since the New Deal because economic growth had produced more "haves" than "have nots." The traditional base was a "fragile coalition" that could "no longer provide the margin of victory." The lesson of 1976 was that Carter's reelection required support from voters who did not speak the "old language of American politics." This meant appealing to the "younger, white collar, college-educated, middle income suburban group that is rapidly becoming the majority of America." Accordingly, Caddell advised Carter to "devise a context that [was] neither traditionally liberal nor traditionally conservative" but instead transcended "traditional ideology." He particularly warned his client to tackle inflation because of Ford's success in convincing the public that budget deficits were the cause of this. Deeming Caddell's analysis "excellent," Carter instructed all his advisers to read it and made it in effect the political blueprint for his administration.[28]

Carter's value system as a product of the New South upper-middle class and his awareness of the Sunbelt transformation of his region made him particularly receptive to the message that New Deal liberalism was outdated as an electoral force. He was one of the first Democrats to understand the demographic changes that underlay what historian Matthew Lassitter described as "the process of regional convergence marked by the parallel suburbanization of southern and American politics."[29] Northern liberals still cast blue-collar workers as the heroes of their political economy. Carter, in contrast, identified more with the white-collar and professional middle classes that made their homes in the expanding suburbs of Atlanta and other Southern cities. They were racially moderate but opposed to compulsory integration, believers in free-market meritocracy but beneficiaries of middle-class entitlements, and fiscally conservative but insistent on good public services. They were also more concerned about inflation than unemployment because it made mortgages dearer, increased college tuition costs, and reduced the value of their earnings that were not protected by cost-of-living adjustments as were written into unionized workers' contracts. In all this the suburban middle classes of the South were fundamentally similar in outlook to those of the Southwest and the North. Together they formed a new and volatile center in American politics, whose fluctuating partisan loyalties were a fundamental determinant of national electoral power in the late twentieth century and beyond.[30]

The 1976 vote offered some evidence that Carter was on the right track to expand his appeal. He ran better than the Democratic presidential candidates of 1968 and 1972 with the groups Caddell identified as critical to his reelection. "We won not just because we held together the [New Deal] coalition," Jody Powell reflected. "In fact, if we had only done that, we would have lost. We won because we were able to do better than a Democrat normally does in areas that are nominally Republican."[31] Carter himself was convinced that his pledge "to bring fiscal responsibility to the federal government" had been crucial to this. He aimed to make it the linchpin of a governance strategy designed to appeal to the changing American electorate. As Powell commented, "The balanced budget came to symbolize that." Opinion polls in early 1977 showing that the Democrats were better trusted under Carter than the Republicans to manage national finances responsibly enhanced his determination "for us to live up to our new reputation." Powell recalled Carter saying that if his administration could "establish that point, and I think he meant . . . more than just fiscal responsibility [but] a whole range of things that fall around it, we will assure the Democratic party is the only party in this country for the rest of our lives."[32]

In looking to broaden his appeal, Carter had to guard against alienating the Democratic base. The crux of the problem was to reach beyond the New Deal coalition "without creating such chaos in your rear that you've got to turn round and deal with that before you can do more ahead."[33] Carter's Progressive ethos of balanced budgets as the essence of good government appeared to provide the answer. It validated activist government in the interests of traditional constituencies within a framework of fiscal responsibility that appealed to new ones. This signified abandonment of his Democratic predecessors' Keynesian-inspired efforts to justify deficits as instruments of cyclical balance or full-employment balance in the cause of economic growth. Instead, Carter reverted to the early-twentieth-century understanding of deficits as indicators of undisciplined, inefficient, and wasteful public spending.

The new president avowed his commitment to balance the FY1981 budget in his first message to Congress.[34] What was unclear was how he proposed to achieve this. A decade and a half later, another Southern Democrat rang the alarm bells of national emergency to justify a deficit-reduction program of tax increases and spending cuts. This was not an option open to Carter. First, there was not yet a perception that the deficit posed a threat to the nation's well-being, as there would be by the early 1990s. Moreover, political, international, and economic conditions were not conducive to the kind of deficit-reducing measures promoted by Bill Clinton. In essence, therefore, Carter's hope for a balanced budget rested on curbing the growth of spending and reaping a revenue harvest from economic recovery, but stagflation would put it beyond reach.

FISCAL CONSERVATISM AND THE LIBERAL STATE

Carter had a fractious relationship with the congressional wing of his party on budgetary issues from the outset of his presidency. Most Democratic legislators considered deficit reduction secondary to the cause of boosting employment and improving the living standards of Americans in the lower half of the income distribution during the difficult economic circumstances of the 1970s. In their view, vice-presidential aide Richard Moe later remarked, "the Nixon years were just an interruption of the normal—the standard way of doing things, which were the Kennedy/Johnson years." Of like mind, the party's basic constituencies—organized labor, African Americans, and urban organizations—thought they were owed for getting the president elected.[35]

Liberals inside and outside Congress were especially optimistic of expanding governmental activism now that a Democrat was back in the White House and the party held majorities of 292–143 in the House of Representatives and 62–38 in the Senate that were comparable in scale to the mid-1960s. Their counterparts on the right of the party, mostly Southerners, did not share this enthusiasm. In terms of numbers, conservative Democrats were a distinct minority within the congressional party and were proportionally more significant in the Senate than the House. Their real power lay within the standing committees that considered legislation with a budgetary dimension. Though not blind to conservative influence, liberals were optimistic of overcoming it with Carter on their side. The president's determination to fight the different battle of fiscal restraint left them increasingly disillusioned. Less than a year after Carter took office, Senator George McGovern (D-SD), the 1972 presidential candidate, lamented, "It sometimes seems difficult to remember who won last fall."[36] Championing the liberal cause, Senator Edward Kennedy (D-MA) ran against Carter for president in 1980 in a bid to restore jobs and economic growth as the core concerns of Democratic political economy.

Tip O'Neill, newly installed as Speaker, tried in vain to develop a more cooperative relationship between the new president and the congressional Democrats. A member of Congress for a working-class Boston district since 1953, this Irish American politician had a traditional Democratic commitment to social programs that helped the disadvantaged. In his biographer's words, "He believed that government was the means by which a people came together to address their community's ills, to right wrongs and craft a just society." O'Neill thought that Carter shared these values but soon realized that he translated them into different policy goals. An admirer of the president's human rights foreign policy, the Speaker was disappointed to find that "on economic issues he was a lot more conservative than I was."[37]

For his part, Carter delighted in lecturing congressional leaders on the paramount importance of fiscal responsibility. In a post-presidential interview, he recalled their "stricken expression" when he affirmed his balanced-budget goal at an early meeting. This "was anathema to them. . . . It wasn't something a Democratic President was supposed to do."[38] Taking their cue from him, some White House aides disdained O'Neill and his colleagues as captives of what one called "special forces," meaning the core Democratic constituencies.[39] In a particularly insensitive move, Carter invited Federal Reserve chair Arthur Burns to address cabinet heads and congressional leaders at a White House meeting on May 2, 1977. The message from this Republican partisan, whom many Democrats considered their sworn enemy, was that inflation-free economic growth depended on business confidence in sustained progress toward balancing the budget in FY1981. His words reinforced the president's own sermon on the need "to restrain the budget" in conditions of economic recovery.[40]

The following day, O'Neill and senior Democrats tried to persuade Carter that the party had more important goals. "I can read this Congress," the Speaker warned. "If there is no move to serve those who need compassion, we'll run into a bag of troubles." The most forthright criticism came from Senator Hubert Humphrey (D-MN). Ill with the cancer that would soon kill him, this longtime champion of governmental activism was concerned that the liberal state he had spent a political lifetime helping to build would stagnate as a result of fiscal restraint. "Not to spend, that's not the answer," he told one confidante, "that's just political bunkum." Now he informed Carter in no uncertain terms that his first duty was to reduce cyclical unemployment and develop programs to help the rapidly growing and predominantly black underclass trapped in poverty and seemingly permanent joblessness. If the president could balance the budget in addition to addressing these problems, Humphrey declared, he deserved "a special chapter in the Good Book."[41]

However, the opening shots over the budget were fired over pork, not poverty. Without consulting congressional leaders, Carter announced that nineteen water projects would be eliminated from the FY1978 budget inherited from the outgoing Ford administration. This initiative was taken on Domestic Policy Staff (DPS) advice that it would remove environmentally harmful projects, save $500 million of the $2 billion allocated to water projects, and signal the administration's intent to eradicate unnecessary spending in its drive to balance the budget.[42] As Interior Secretary Cecil Andrus had warned, the proposed retrenchment outraged legislators accustomed to consider pork-barrel spending as their right. The president's standing never recovered in western states that were major beneficiaries of water projects. OMB director Bert Lance adjudged it Carter's "worst political mistake" because it doomed any hope of a cooperative relationship with Congress.[43]

In retaliation the House enacted a public works bill with all but one project restored. Support from fiscal conservatives and members of the large freshman cohorts of 1974 and 1976, most of whom had no electoral interest in environmentally suspect dams, would have sustained a veto, but Carter accepted a compromise brokered by O'Neill to eliminate only half the projects. In time, he came to believe that this deal "was accurately interpreted as a sign of weakness on my part and I came to regret it as much as any budget decision I made as President."[44] A year later, he did not shrink from vetoing the FY1979 public works bill that provided funding for twenty-seven water projects not approved by the administration.[45]

Carter's refusal to give the sluggish economy a big stimulus also angered many congressional Democrats. By early 1977, economic growth was less than half the norm for recovery periods following previous postwar recessions, industrial production had barely recovered to its 1973 level, and business investment in plant and equipment was still well below its pre-recession volume. In the judgment of the transition team, the prospects of employment growth were "not high" unless compensatory measures were undertaken.[46] The president recognized that stronger recovery was essential to generate revenues for deficit elimination but wanted to ensure that the stimulus program did not entail permanent commitments that would hinder this.

On January 31, 1977, Carter sent Congress a $31 billion program of tax and job-creation initiatives that he claimed "would pave the way for a balanced Federal budget by fiscal year 1981." Spread equally over FY1977–FY1978, the budget costs amounted to less than 1 percent GDP in each year. The resultant acceleration of economic recovery was forecast to produce offsetting savings of $11 billion from enhanced tax revenues and reduced unemployment insurance payouts. The bulk of the program would expire as economic recovery strengthened. The most expensive item, costing $8.2 billion, was a $50 rebate for all income tax payers, Social Security recipients, and earned income credit beneficiaries.[47] Whereas some business leaders advocated permanent tax reduction, Carter's advisers preferred a rebate because it was quick acting and safeguarded future revenues. They also recognized that it would be easier to provide additional stimulus if required than to rescind a tax cut if inflationary pressures worsened.[48]

The administration plan found little favor with liberals and the main Democratic constituencies. Keynesian economists called upon to advise the transition team were taken aback to find Carter so bullish that unemployment would fall quickly without large-scale intervention. Lawrence Klein advocated a somewhat larger tax rebate of about $10 billion and a temporary expansion of public works spending targeted at areas of high unemployment. Walter Heller endorsed the rebate as a fast-acting stimulant and a means to "get the biggest deficits behind us" but recommended a more comprehensive jobs program to sustain the later stages of recovery.[49] Wanting a $30 billion public works program in 1977 alone, the AFL-CIO decried Carter's proposal as a retreat from his campaign promises to boost employment, and the United States Conference of Mayors deemed it of little benefit to the cities. Sensitive to their preferences, Tip O'Neill advised Carter to forget the rebate and put the money saved into the jobs program.[50]

In mid-April the president went halfway to following the Speaker's counsel by withdrawing the rebate without transferring the benefits elsewhere. With the Senate holding up the measure in retaliation for his retrenchment of water projects, signs of faster-than-expected economic recovery prompted an administration rethink. Carter's more conservative economic advisers, notably Treasury Secretary Michael Blumenthal and Bert Lance, persuaded him that the $50 giveaway would fuel inflation and damage his image of fiscal prudence. Legislators who had gone out to bat for the rebate, notably Senate Budget Committee chair Edmund Muskie (D-ME), were left looking foolish.[51] As finally enacted, the stimulus contained tax benefits that the administration had not recommended, including a $4 billion permanent tax cut in the form of an increased standard deduction, but the fiscal effects were small enough for the Treasury Department and the OMB to recommend approval. At this juncture Carter appeared to have had the best of both worlds. The rebate elimination reduced net stimulus costs to $23 billion, of which $17 billion would be incurred in FY1978, and the economic indicators prompting it offered hope that the budget would be balanced on schedule.[52]

Modest though it was, the stimulus program made Carter wary of supporting further initiatives. At a cabinet meeting in February, he declared that "other major additions to the budget are not feasible." Congressional leaders heard the same message shortly afterward, with the additional admonishment that the Democrats had to "remove the stigma of unjustified spending." Soon thereafter, Carter wrote to Senate Appropriations Committee chair John McClellan (D-AR) urging a tight rein on spending bills.[53] The president was determined to set a good example in this regard even if it meant retreating from his campaign promises.

To win labor's endorsement of his candidacy, Carter had reluctantly supported introduction of a comprehensive national health insurance (NHI) plan that addressed the plight of the 40 million Americans without adequate medical coverage—mainly the working poor, the unemployed, and their families. According to Peter Bourne, the "compassionate side of his personality was never so at odds with the hard-nosed, penny-pinching facet" as on this issue because memory of his mother's charitable nursing activities convinced him that voluntarism was adequate.[54] In office, he vainly sought to reconcile NHI enactment with fiscal responsibility, but his support for the program weakened as inflation rose. Even DPS chief Stuart Eizenstat, normally an enthusiast for liberal initiatives, counseled the president that he would look inconsistent by "talking about inflation and budget restraint one day and proposing what will be seen as an inflationary budget-busting scheme the next."[55]

To contain NHI costs, Carter called for gradual implementation of a "workable" program within a framework of progress toward a balanced budget. He also insisted on prior enactment of legislation to limit hospital costs, currently spiraling at an annual rate of 15 percent, to yield savings in public medical payments of $22 billion in FY1980–FY1984.[56] This approach came under immediate fire from other actors in the healthcare debate. The labor unions and their chief ally, Senator Edward Kennedy, accepted the need for hospital cost containment but wanted immediate introduction of mandatory health benefits for all Americans financed from payroll taxes and general revenues. Conversely, profit-making hospitals, the American Medical Association, and other healthcare industry groups mounted a well-funded and ultimately successful campaign against cost-containment. Meanwhile, key Democratic legislators outside the liberal spectrum, notably House Ways and Means Committee chair Al Ullman (D-OR) and Senate Finance Committee chair Russell Long (D-LA), thought the administration's NHI proposal too expensive.[57]

With consumer price inflation rising at an annual rate of 6.8 percent, Carter announced in late 1977 that an NHI bill would have to be deferred until 1979. Under pressure from Kennedy and the unions, he relented to a new deadline for enactment by the end of 1978. However, months of negotiations between them yielded no compromise on program details, even though it was evident that Kennedy's plan had no chance of congressional approval. Accordingly, Carter issued a general statement of NHI principles and deferred introduction of phase-in legislation until it had wider support. Hopes of enlisting Kennedy's backing for this approach were doomed to disappointment. At a White House meeting on July 28, 1978, the Massachusetts senator accepted NHI phasing-in but continued to insist on administration endorsement of a comprehensive plan regardless of economic or budgetary circumstances in return. Angered by Carter's refusal to countenance this, Kennedy signaled their open break by telling reporters that his "failure of leadership" had undermined NHI.[58]

A final act was played out before the issue departed the center stage of American politics for more than a decade. In May 1979 Kennedy introduced a bill for comprehensive health insurance that carried estimated first-year federal costs of $29 billion. Although this had no prospect of enactment, it highlighted White House inaction on NHI. Hoping to pacify Kennedy and his allies, Carter proposed a first-phase plan to provide only catastrophic coverage. Even this entailed substantial budgetary compromise, because it was introduced without prior enactment of hospital cost-control and required $18.2 billion in new federal outlays for initial implementation in FY1983. Similar to a plan proposed by Russell Long, the administration bill stood reasonable chance of passage with liberal and labor support. Preferring a cause to a compromise, Kennedy denounced it as a perpetuation of the nation's "separate and unequal" health care system. With moderate Democrats like

Al Ullman expressing contrary concern that it was too costly, the bill never got out of committee.[59]

Budgetary concerns also restrained Carter's commitment to enact welfare reform in the interests of greater efficiency and equity. The nation's welfare system was widely perceived as an overly complex maze of programs, many of which had different eligibility requirements and benefit levels from state to state. Delegated to devise a reform plan, Health, Education, and Welfare (HEW) Secretary Joseph Califano and Labor Secretary Ray Marshall became deadlocked in a bureaucratic wrangle over their respective departmental preferences for improvement of income maintenance programs and a jobs program to employ welfare recipients. The common feature of both options was higher welfare costs, but Carter would have none of this. The president told the disputants, "I want you to take all the money that is now being spent on welfare programs and redesign the whole system using the same amount of money."[60]

Carter eventually allowed a limited amount of new spending in recognition that the no-additional-cost stricture was impractical. Given some scope for maneuver, Califano and Marshall produced a compromise plan known as the Program for Better Jobs and Income (PBJI), a title the president personally devised. This envisaged replacing Aid for Families with Dependent Children (AFDC), food stamps, and Supplemental Security Income with uniform cash benefits. It also enhanced tax credits for the working poor, reduced the nonfederal share of public assistance costs, and created 1.4 million government jobs. The resultant annual increases in federal welfare costs were initially estimated at a modest $2.8 billion in spending and some $3 billion in earned income credits.[61] The fundamental rationale of PBJI was that cash transfers were the most effective way of helping the poor. Comprehensive reform would also yield savings on in-kind welfare programs, notably Medicaid, housing assistance, and food stamps, currently undergoing uncoordinated growth.[62]

The administration plan came under fire from both sides of the political divide. Liberal Democrats and pro-welfare constituencies complained that it set benefit levels too low, gave inadequate fiscal help for hard-pressed northern states and cities, and provided insufficient and poorly paid public jobs without day care support. Republicans and conservative Democrats charged that it encouraged welfare dependency, lacked sufficient work obligations, and was hugely expensive—a fear seemingly legitimized by a Congressional Budget Office estimate that annual costs would run to $14 billion. Skirmishing over PBJI continued until mid-1978, but its prospects receded when California voters approved Proposition 13 limiting state property taxes. The antitax sentiment this set off persuaded the congressional leadership to shelve the controversial welfare measure until after the midterm elections.[63]

PBJI exemplified Carter's difficulty in reconciling his fiscal conservatism and social liberalism. Though sincere in wanting to help the poor, he put a higher priority on controlling welfare costs. When first briefed by Califano that reform required additional spending, Carter responded, "As you've explained it, we should just leave the system as it is. We don't have $5 billion to $10 billion to put in a new system. Why don't we just say, the hell with it!" Despite relenting on extra costs, he made little effort to persuade congressional critics of their necessity, particularly after the OMB confirmed that the administration had underestimated the additional expense. Califano later claimed that Proposition 13 made Carter "determined to regain his frugal, budget-balancing image" to reassure voters that federal tax dollars were not being wasted.[64]

Whether this assessment was accurate or just sour grapes, the president offered only perfunctory support for more modest initiatives thereafter. In May 1979 he accepted a HEW proposal to establish a national minimum for AFDC benefits at 65 percent of the poverty line, which carried a price of $5.7 billion a year. Carter scrawled a fitting expression of his ambivalence on a DPS memorandum assessing program costs: "Do not ask me to approve a higher figure in the future."[65] The House passed a modified version in November, but Russell Long's implacable hostility to raising welfare benefits ensured that the measure never got out of the Senate Finance Committee.

While political leaders dithered over welfare reform, many liberals contended that jobs were the best way of lifting people out of poverty. In 1975 Hubert Humphrey had teamed up with Representative Augustus Hawkins (D-CA) to propose updating the Employment Act of 1946 in order to broaden federal responsibility for full employment in the face of stagflation. Their legislative initiative, as initially conceived, underestimated the inflationary consequences of setting a full-employment rate below 4 percent joblessness and making government the employer of last resort via provision of public service jobs. It also put too much faith in government's ability to fine-tune a national economy that was increasingly interdependent with global developments and subject to rapid technological change. With black America in economic crisis, however, supporters of the Humphrey-Hawkins bill saw it as the best hope to eradicate long-term black unemployment, uplift black youth from entrapment in permanent joblessness, and strengthen the social stability of black communities.[66]

During his presidential campaign Carter had initially adjudged a full-employment guarantee "too expensive," but he later issued a guarded endorsement. As with NHI, his conversion reflected pragmatism, not principle, for he needed to solidify black support after ill-judged remarks casting doubt on his commitment to open housing. Nevertheless, his top economic and budgetary aides remained hostile to the Humphrey-Hawkins bill. Charles

Schultze urged Carter to submit an alternative measure that proclaimed a broad commitment to full employment without requiring actions that would cost money and aggravate inflation. Rather than strain his already difficult relations with liberals, Carter agreed with Stuart Eizenstat that it was politically wiser to seek compromise with Humphrey-Hawkins supporters. Nevertheless, as Bert Lance acknowledged, there was no viable middle ground that would satisfy each side's economic concerns.[67]

Prolonged and tortuous negotiations over the course of 1977 produced some agreement but left key issues unresolved. Hoping in vain to see the bill enacted before his death, Humphrey wrote from his sickbed to his cosponsor, "A balanced budget at the expense of a frustrated and unbalanced America is no answer to our problems." Nevertheless, both conceded the president authority to modify their bill's employment goals to control inflation in return for his acceptance of a 4 percent unemployment target within a five-year time frame. Even so, it took another year before the bill was enacted as the Full Employment and Balanced Growth Act of 1978.[68] Under its terms, the president had almost total discretion to modify the employment-inflation goals according to economic circumstances and his own budget priorities. Augustus Hawkins called it "a modern-day Magna Carta of economic rights" that directly provided more than 600,000 jobs and had "more than $11 billion in it" for that purpose. In reality the measure was all symbol and no substance insofar as budgetary commitment to full employment was concerned. It soon became clear that the administration was prepared to tolerate rising unemployment in its battle for price stability.[69]

While the Carter administration was holding the line against expensive new commitments, it faced a funding shortfall in the oldest and largest entitlement program. The retirement and disability trust funds were approaching deficit owing to the rising costs of benefit improvements and cost-of-living adjustments enacted in the early 1970s. In consultation with congressional leaders, Carter decided that payroll tax hikes were necessary to preserve program solvency and benefit levels. The Social Security Amendments of 1977 instituted the largest peacetime tax increases to date in American history. Though far from enthusiastic about this, Carter forthrightly defended it as "absolutely mandatory" to avoid trust fund deficits. When a nervous House Democratic caucus, with its eye on the approaching elections, voted in March 1978 by nearly three to one to rescind the tax hikes, the president threatened to veto any rollback.[70]

The 1977 amendment helped alleviate Social Security's immediate crisis but fell short of ensuring long-term solvency. It provided for increases in payroll taxes in four stages from 1979 to 1990 to generate $227 billion in additional revenue over ten years. In 1979, however, the three Social Security trust funds needed reserves of over $4 trillion to cover obligations to existing workers but held less than $30 billion. Carter aides warned of another fund-ing shortfall in the early 1980s without preventive action. In Joseph Cali-fano's estimate, the only way to insure Social Security's actuarial well-being was to run it more tightly without hurting those in most need. In December 1978 he proposed a package of reforms that, among other things, taxed the portion of Social Security benefits exceeding the individual's contributions, tightened eligibility for disability benefits, raised the eligibility age for retire-ment benefits from 62 to 65, terminated payments for post-secondary school students who were beneficiaries of survivors, and eliminated the lump-sum death benefit for burial.[71]

Califano's initiative provoked a counterattack from a venerable trio of Social Security champions—Robert Ball, Wilbur Cohen, and Nelson Cruik-shank—that it represented the first step toward sweeping program retrench-ment. Cruikshank's testimony before the congressional Special Committee on Aging was especially controversial because he was the president's Coun-selor on Aging. However Carter did not sack him for fear that he would orga-nize senior citizens to campaign against the administration. As a concession, Califano modified the plan to exclude the tax increase and the change of eli-gibility age. With OMB's support, he persuaded a reluctant Carter to include his other proposals in the FY1980 budget plan, but they received little else in the way of presidential support and got nowhere in Congress.[72]

Understandable though it was in political terms, Carter's disinclination to tackle Social Security reform entailed capitulation to a special interest and contradicted his Progressive ideals of efficiency, effectiveness, and economy in government. As Califano told Wilbur Cohen in 1978, public officials had a duty "to educate the American people about . . . [Social Security's] problems as well as its benefits . . . and to make it clear that with so many unsatisfied needs, government should target help where it's most needed."[73] Federal benefits to people living above poverty rose from 24 percent to 40 percent of the budget between 1965 and 1980 whereas those targeted at the poor in-creased from 4 percent to 9 percent. In other words, social welfare expansion had primarily transferred income "to middle-income people—mainly old— from other middle-income people—mainly working age." Without reform, Social Security and Medicare outlays would continue growing in indiscrimi-nate fashion because of increased demand from an aging population and the inexorable growth of health care costs.[74]

Shortly after the enactment of payroll tax increases, the administra-tion sent Congress another tax measure that embodied Carter's campaign promise of tax reform. Its provisions included tax relief for lower-income families that was partially offset by closing tax loopholes beneficial to upper-income groups and business. The net annual revenue loss was estimated at $25 billion. Carter had sided with Vice President Walter Mondale and Stuart

Eizenstat, both of whom were anxious to find common cause with the administration's liberal critics, against Treasury preference for a smaller bill with fewer progressive features. A grateful Edward Kennedy congratulated the White House on "a fine tax package."[75] In contrast, conservative Democrats and many moderates criticized the proposal as inflationary. They rallied behind an entirely different initiative from Representative William Steiger (R-WI), a hitherto obscure member of the Ways and Means Committee. Strongly supported by an army of corporate lobbyists, this formed the basis for the Revenue Act of 1978 that gained a place in conservative lore as the harbinger of the supply-side revolution.[76]

The final bill reduced the capital gains tax to the benefit of upper-income taxpayers, omitted virtually all Carter's reforms, and raised the tax exemption level from $750 to $1,000 to the benefit of all taxpayers in place of the administration's proposal to target a $240 credit toward lower-income families. The annual revenue loss was $19 billion. Only presidential lobbying of Al Ullman and Russell Long persuaded them to scale back the Senate Finance Committee's preference for an even larger capital gains tax cut and broader tax relief than the Ways and Means Committee had originally approved.[77] Angry liberals urged Carter to veto what Kennedy dubbed the most regressive tax measure since the trickle-down Mellon-Coolidge Revenue Act of 1926. On the advice of aides, however, the president signed the measure to deny the Republicans an issue in the forthcoming midterm elections and to give the economy a boost that the CEA incorrectly thought it needed.[78] The end result was that he further damaged his relationship with liberals over an issue that he originally hoped would improve it.

AUSTERITY, ARMS, AND AMENDMENT POLITICS

At the outset of his presidency Jimmy Carter regarded a balanced budget as the symbol of new Democratic appeal to the middle classes. Before long, however, it also acquired substantive significance as his administration's principal instrument to control inflation. The FY1980 budget plan, described by aides as "the most constrained budget in years," marked the administration's intent to make war on inflation rather than seek a trade-off between employment growth and price stability as it had done for much of its first two years.[79] Meanwhile, a deteriorating international situation necessitated higher defense spending, which intensified the pressure on the domestic budget. Paradoxically, just as Carter placed greater emphasis on substantive retrenchment, he risked compromising its budgetary symbolism because of his administration's role in thwarting a grassroots campaign for a balanced-budget constitutional amendment.

Economic recovery brought renewed inflationary pressures in its wake. In late 1977 the CEA warned that preemptive action was necessary to prevent a "significant acceleration" of price instability that would "pose a serious threat to the continuation of healthy expansion." However, anti-inflation policy only evolved incrementally and uncertainly thereafter. In mid-1978 Carter's two principal economic advisers, Treasury Secretary Michael Blumenthal and CEA chair Charles Schultze, acknowledged that the administration lacked "a coherent long range strategy" for dealing with the problem.[80] It was not until later in the year that the semblance of one was devised.

The administration's economic policymaking process was better suited to producing bureaucratic compromises than strategic clarity. Intended to be an inter-departmental steering agency, its Economic Policy Group instead became a forum for conflicting departmental views. The Treasury and OMB had wanted a balanced budget in FY1979 to throttle inflation, even at cost of slowing down recovery. In their assessment, shock fiscal therapy would restore price stability and permit employment growth in time for Carter's reelection. Aligned against them were the heads of the government departments mainly responsible for domestic program provision, notably HEW, Housing and Urban Development (HUD), and Labor, whose commitment to jobs and social spending was broadly supported by Walter Mondale. A third group that included the CEA and the DPS held the balance of power. It wanted to restrain inflation without economic contraction but eventually accepted the need for stronger measures to attain price stability.[81]

The CEA underwent the most significant change of position of all these actors. Charles Schultze, fellow of the Brookings Institution and formerly budget director in the Johnson administration, was initially the voice of Keynesianism within the administration. In July 1977 he urged Carter to pursue "a balanced high-employment budget strategy . . . [by which] the fiscal dials are set to produce a balanced budget in 1981 only if the economy returns to high employment—that is a 4 and ¾ percent unemployment rate."[82] Schultze attributed inflation to demand shocks, namely the Vietnam war and Richard Nixon's excessive stimulation of the economy to win reelection, and oil-price shocks that he mistakenly assumed would not recur. The CEA only belatedly recognized that the marked slowing of productivity growth to the point of turning negative in 1979 was a more serious source of inflation.

Failure to gauge this slowdown until it was well advanced led to crucial policy errors. The CEA overestimated the economy's potential and consequently its level of slack, which determined how much it could be stimulated before inflation grew. What finally alerted it to this miscalculation was that unemployment actually fell faster than economic growth warranted because more workers were needed to increase output. In May 1978, Schultze advised the president that the productivity slowdown necessitated "considering strategies to reduce the FY1979 and 1980 budget deficits." Underlining these words on the memorandum, Carter penned in the margin, "a new convert?"[83] Nevertheless, the CEA continued to underestimate the extent of the slow-down, so its assessment of the fiscal restraint needed to curb inflation remained faulty. Not until late 1979 did Schultze appreciate the true severity of the problem. At this juncture, he advised Carter that a significant reduction of deficit spending to free up credit resources for private investment would be "the most important single thing we can do to help restore productivity growth."[84]

The anti-inflation program unveiled in October 1978 reflected the changing balance of economic opinion within the administration. Its success was dependent on winning business and labor compliance for new wage-price guidelines. Considerable store was also placed on controlling expenditure in FY1980 to reduce the deficit and set an example of restraint to business, workers, and the rest of the country.[85] This went against the recent trend of fiscal policy disintegration, but it only represented a half-way restoration at best. It was politically impossible for Carter to adapt his budget policy to achieve an aggregate economic target in the manner of the 1960s new economics. His FY1980 deficit projection was shaped more by political considerations than by calculation of the level most effective for inflation control.

The president's FY1979 plan had forecast a deficit of $61 billion. With the media increasingly blaming high inflation on excessive federal spending, he proposed to halve the projected deficit to $29 billion in FY1980 as a demonstration of his commitment to control costs. This decision represented a victory for Treasury and OMB over DPS concerns that it would alienate the core Democratic constituencies and CEA advice that a deficit target of $32–35 billion was more realistic.[86] In fact, the Treasury had advocated an even lower deficit, but Carter restored $2 billion of social program cuts in response to Eizenstat's lobbying that interest payment estimates could be scaled back in anticipation of lower inflation. To achieve its deficit target, the administration proposed outlays of $532 billion, a 7.7 percent increase over FY1979 estimates that barely kept pace with projected inflation. However, the budget also contained a real 3 percent increase in defense spending and automatic cost-of-living increases in some programs, notably Social Security, so there was compensatory retrenchment in discretionary domestic programs, such as school lunches, social services, urban aid, and education.[87]

The new restraint occasioned considerable dissension within the administration. The preliminary FY1980 plan provoked trenchant criticism from some department heads as being akin to a "Nixon-Ford budget" and "totally inappropriate for a Democratic president." Joseph Califano's campaign against HEW cuts confirmed his reputation for independence that eventually led to his firing in August 1979. Obliged to defend publicly administration policies that he fought against in private, Walter Mondale grew so disillusioned that he briefly considered not seeking another term as vice president.[88]

There was even greater anger within the broader Democratic party and its core constituencies. The Congressional Black Caucus denounced the president's budget as "unjust and immoral," and Vernon Jordan of the National Urban League brought a delegation of urban black leaders to the White House to protest cuts in aid to the cities. At the Democratic midterm convention, held in Memphis, Tennessee, in December 1978, United Automobile Workers president Douglas Fraser's resolution criticizing the Carter budget won support from 40 percent of the delegates. Edward Kennedy also electrified this gathering with a damning critique of administration fiscal priorities. Sounding increasingly like a contender for the 1980 nomination, he warned, "The party that tore itself apart over Vietnam in the 1960s cannot afford to tear itself apart today over budget cuts in basic social programs."[89]

The inclusion of defense expansion in an austerity budget that retrenched social expenditure was a huge political risk. Despite initial reservations about aiming for a $29 billion deficit, Stuart Eizenstat accepted that Carter would "get an enormous amount of public credit" for meeting this commitment, but he remained unhappy about spending allocations. Fearing that "the defense vs. domestic budget debate has the potential to split the party," he vainly advocated capping the military expansion at around 2 to 2.5 percent and shifting the balance of funds earmarked for defense into social programs.[90] Nevertheless, Carter was determined to honor his pledge to NATO allies that the United States would increase defense spending by 3 percent in real terms in response to the Soviet Union's expansion of its European theater force levels.

The FY1980 budget initiated a new cycle of national security expansion that would have dramatic impact on the deficit over the next decade. Hitherto Carter had engaged in a budgetary trade-off that favored domestic over defense programs without ever supporting the scale of military retrenchment envisaged by the 1976 Democratic platform. This involved him in regular dogfights with congressional defense expansionists over specific weapons development, notably the B-1 bomber, Minuteman missiles, and the Nimitz-class aircraft carrier. By the end of 1978, however, the debate on defense spending increasingly focused on the need for across-the-board increases as a result of growing concern that America was losing ground in the Cold War. The numerous critics of détente—the Republican right, Cold War Democrats led by Senator Henry Jackson (D-WA), and the Committee on the Present Danger—charged that it had provided cover for the Soviets to establish superiority in military capability. They seized on relative defense spending as the key indicator of this development, a view given credence by a number of influential government reports.[91]

A Congressional Research Service study commissioned by the Senate Armed Services Committee identified serious imbalances in the superpowers' relative nuclear and conventional strength. It concluded that budgetary projections "point to a bleak picture" with regard to rebuilding force levels and quality. Similarly, a Central Intelligence Agency (CIA) report claimed that Soviet defense spending had moved ahead of America's in 1971 to take a 40 percent lead by 1975. Though the CIA admitted in 1984 to having overestimated Soviet capability, its report was accepted as gospel at the time. In 1979 the Pentagon itself conceded that the Soviets had a lead of 25 to 45 percent in relative defense spending, which it regarded as "the best single crude measure of relative military capabilities."[92]

Carter's plan for defense expansion would reduce the perceived gap in Soviet-U.S. outlays but not close it. His determination to eliminate the deficit precluded more substantial fiscal commitment to rebuild America's power. Unwilling to make the same trade-off, Senate hawks shifted the debate over the Strategic Arms Limitation Treaty to consideration of the superpowers' relative military capabilities. Democrats among them made their support for its ratification conditional on administration approval of higher defense spending. Unable to wrest concessions from the White House, they joined with Republicans to approve a budget resolution that projected real defense increases of 5 percent in both FY1980 and FY1981.[93]

Cross-party cooperation did not extend to domestic programs. The House of Representatives, where liberal Democrats were relatively stronger, approved a budget resolution that set domestic spending ceilings higher than Carter wanted but cut his defense estimate. Unlike their Republican allies, pro-defense Democrats were prepared to buy off liberal opposition to higher military spending by acceding to social program expansion. The deal was engineered in the conference committee charged with reconciling the different House and Senate budget resolutions. Accordingly, Congress set spending levels some $15 billion above the president's estimate but kept its deficit projection below $30 billion by forecasting higher revenues from inflation. There was little expectation that this target would be met, particularly as the economy was showing signs of slowdown. House Budget Committee chair Robert Giaimo (D-CT) admitted, "We're going to have a crisis in the spring, I'm afraid, unless we do something . . . to save money." Disenchanted House Republicans proposed a floor amendment demanding a 2 percent across-the-board cut in spending that was easily defeated. Speaking for them, Delbert L. Latta (R-OH) complained, "By no stretch of the imagination can this be called restraint."[94]

The FY1980 budget resolution was the first in a long series of smoke-and-mirror forecasts projecting the illusion that the budget was under control when the opposite was true. Outlays eventually totaled $591 billion, far higher than Carter's estimate of $532 billion and the congressional target of $547.6 billion. Entitlement increases driven by inflation and recession accounted for the largest portion of this excess, but supplementary appropriations for defense in the wake of the Soviet invasion of Afghanistan in late 1979 and for domestic programs to help mitigate the effects of economic decline were also substantial. In conditions of renewed Cold War, Carter resisted DPS counsel to deny the Pentagon's supplemental requests because it was spending FY1980 funds at a faster rate than authorized. This made it impossible in an election year to refuse additional funds for social programs that were running out of money. In real terms, national defense and domestic discretionary spending ended up respectively 3.9 percent and 4.3 percent higher in the FY1980 "austerity budget" than in FY1979.[95]

The growth in spending was largely responsible for the deficit's expansion to $73.8 billion in FY1980, more than double the administration's estimate. Change on the revenue side of the budget also played a part. The combination of rising employment levels, the "bracket creep" effect of inflation-linked wage increases putting workers in higher tax brackets, and bigger Social Security revenues boosted federal coffers in the late 1970s. Receipts rose in real terms by 12.6 percent between FY1977 and FY1979, double the real growth in outlays. In FY1979 revenue totaled $23 billion more than the president's estimate of $440 billion and expenditure was only marginally higher than projected. As a result, the deficit fell to $40.7 billion, a third less than Carter had estimated. In FY1980, however, recession eroded inflation's tax dividend. Revenue totaled only $14 billion more than Carter's projection of $503 billion. This constituted a real increase of 1 percent over FY1979 compared to real outlay growth of 6.1 percent.[96]

While Carter battled for his austerity budget, he was engaged in blocking moves for a constitutional ban on deficits orchestrated by the National Taxpayers Union (NTU). This Washington-based conservative group had been engaged since 1975 in a low-profile campaign for a constitutional convention to propose a balanced-budget amendment. Congressional authorization for this hitherto untested method of changing the Constitution required two-thirds of the states to request it. By early 1979 the number to have done so reached twenty-nine, just five short of the thirty-four needed. The NTU campaign expressed popular frustration with chronic federal deficits and the public's sense that the national government should be constitutionally barred from operating unbalanced budgets like the states. Anxious not to provoke a counter-campaign, it maneuvered behind closed doors to win state petitions without attracting publicity. As Common Cause president David Cohen complained, many convention resolutions were "passed at midnight when nobody was paying attention." Only six of the first twenty-one state legislatures to petition Congress held hearings to debate the merits of the case. In

January 1979, however, the announcement by Governor Edmund G. "Jerry" Brown Jr. (D-CA) that he would actively support the convention drive, a ploy that signaled his intent to challenge Carter for the 1980 presidential nomination, brought NTU operations a blaze of unwanted attention.[97]

Once alerted to the danger, the White House looked for ways to halt the NTU drive. Even though Carter had operated under constitutional prohibition of unbalanced budgets as governor of Georgia, which joined the ranks of convention petitioners in 1976, he was firmly opposed to applying the same restraint at the national level. The president's business Progressive mindset made him receptive to the expert view not only of his own economic advisers and the broader network of Keynesian luminaries but also of many eminent conservative economists that a ban on deficits was utter folly. Among the latter, Alan Greenspan warned, "Balancing the budget year in, year out . . . is technically infeasible. I do not really know any responsible economist who would see it otherwise." The untried convention method of constitutional reform also filled Carter with foreboding because of the widely expressed concerns of legal experts that it was uncontrollable and could end up rewriting the nation's supreme law wholesale. "Spinechilling" was his terse comment after reading a memorandum by Harvard law professor Lawrence Tribe about the lack of procedural constraints to prevent this outcome.[98]

Carter's responsibilities as party leader, often in conflict with his Progressive values, reinforced his opposition to the convention movement. African American groups, labor, and urban organizations feared that constitutionally mandated balanced budgets would result in massive retrenchment of social programs. Typifying their concern, AFL-CIO boss George Meany dubbed the convention movement "a very dangerous right-wing legislative threat." At the same time, these groups were in dispute with the administration over its FY1980 budget. Carter could therefore go some way to mending fences by making common cause with them against the NTU campaign. As his senior staff observed, "There will be few other opportunities in the coming year when we will be able to work in union with the basic Democratic constituencies *without spending money*." In effect, Carter could engage in a symbolic form of Keynesianism while pursuing a political economy that was substantively the reverse of this.[99]

Opposition to the convention campaign was not risk-free, however. Many pundits considered the movement unstoppable. If a convention were called or Congress preempted this by itself proposing a constitutional amendment, Carter would be regarded as having suffered a serious personal defeat that would limit his influence in the debate over the measure. Either outcome would also enhance Brown's credibility as a presidential rival. Moreover, whether a convention was held or not, open confrontation with its supporters could harm Carter's reputation for fiscal prudence with the public.[100]

A task group of senior advisers produced a plan of action to avoid these pitfalls. In accordance with this, the White House emphasized the president's commitment to balance the budget without constitutional gimmickry and created an external organization to take on the convention movement at state level. This surrogate group was to be led by Thomas P. O'Neill III, the speaker's son and lieutenant governor of Massachusetts. The Citizens for the Constitution, as it was named, included representatives from state and local governments, business, labor, women's groups, and racial minority organizations.[101]

While this group was being established, the administration received an unexpected fillip from the California Assembly's rejection of a convention petition, an outcome engineered by Speaker Leo McCarthy in his power struggle with Jerry Brown for leadership of the state Democrats. Commencing operations shortly afterward, Citizens for the Constitution built on this first success for the anticonvention cause. Over the next three months the legislatures of Massachusetts, Minnesota, Missouri, Montana, Ohio, and West Virginia all rejected convention resolutions. The NTU's sole success came in New Hampshire, the last state in the Carter era and the thirtieth in all to petition for a convention to write a balanced-budget amendment. The well-financed and efficient counter-campaign played on fears of an uncontrollable convention and warned state politicians that a balanced-budget amendment would inevitably mean large retrenchment of federal grants. The increased media attention it generated also ensured that state legislatures now had to conduct proper hearings on convention resolutions.[102]

Democratic congressional leaders joined in the battle to defeat the convention movement. Tip O'Neill delegated Representative Dave Obey (D-WI) to inform all fifty governors of the financial consequences for their state if an amendment were approved. In a speech at the National Press Club, copies of which were mailed to 7,500 state legislators, Senator Edmund Muskie affirmed that federal grants would bear the brunt of budget-balancing economies. "That's not a threat," he declared, "it's a matter of arithmetic. We could save $31 billion—$2 billion more than President Carter's projected deficit—simply by killing revenue sharing, educational grants, sewer construction, block grants and the jobs program."[103]

Though other actors made important contributions, the Carter administration undoubtedly played the most significant role in halting the seemingly unstoppable drive for a constitutional convention to propose a balanced-budget amendment. Following the White House game plan to the letter, the Citizens for the Constitution was as effective in resisting the convention campaign as the NTU had once been in promoting it. As a senior aide acknowledged, the group had succeeded "beyond our expectations" and against the odds. Carter himself kept a low profile throughout the counter-campaign, even refusing to deliver a speech in California to help anticonvention forces in Brown's home state. Instead, his public involvement was confined to press conference remarks emphasizing the dangers of a runaway convention and an open letter on the same theme to Ohio Assembly Speaker Vern Riffe urging Buckeye state legislators to reject a convention resolution.[104] Carter could therefore savor the success of having stalled the convention juggernaut and torpedoed Brown's hopes of piggybacking his presidential ambitions on this cause, all without compromising his antideficit image. However, this was to be his last victory of any note on budget issues.

THE BALANCED-BUDGET POLITICS OF 1980

For Jimmy Carter, the budgetary politics of 1980 were an unmitigated disaster that contributed significantly to his election defeat by Ronald Reagan. This denouement was directly attributable to his insistence from the moment he became president that a balanced budget was essential. Carter's blanket condemnation of unbalanced budgets, initially as the antithesis of Progressive efficiency and ultimately as a source of inflation, made no distinction between cyclical deficits produced by recession and structural ones resulting from budgetary actions. Accordingly, he was caught in a conceptual trap of his own making when double-digit inflation and recession hit the economy in 1980. Carter could not deploy the traditional Democratic argument that a budget deficit in time of economic downturn would preserve jobs and boost recovery. Meanwhile, the impossibility of balancing the budget during a recession invalidated his credentials as an inflation-fighter. In his desperation to spring his own trap, Carter zigzagged through three different phases of budget policy in his final year in office. As a result, he lost control over the fiscal agenda and undermined his credibility as a budget leader.

As originally conceived, the FY1981 budget plan was not the centerpiece of the administration's anti-inflation strategy. By this juncture, monetary policy had become the main instrument of economic restraint. A rise of 11.3 percent in consumer prices in 1979, albeit exacerbated by Organization of Petroleum Exporting Countries oil-price hikes after the Iranian revolution disrupted supplies from that country, signified that the administration had no solution for inflation.[105] The fate of the austerity FY1980 budget underlined the difficulty of trying to combat it through fiscal means. Almost by default, therefore, primary responsibility for inflation control passed to the monetary authorities. This effectively signaled the Federal Reserve chair's replacement of the president as the chief manager of prosperity in an era when price stability had supplanted full employment as the principal indicator of economic well-being.

The baton of economic leadership passed with Carter's appointment of Paul Volcker to head the Federal Reserve in August 1979. Hitherto president of the New York Federal Reserve, the new chair was an inflation hawk held in high esteem by financiers at home and abroad because he rejected the possibility of any trade-off between price stability and unemployment. Before accepting the job, Volcker made plain to Carter his convictions about "the importance of an independent central bank and the need for tighter money." Under his lead, the Fed promptly adopted monetary targeting to control the aggregate quantity of money and reserves, a robust but painful method of inflation control. When interest rates consequently went through the ceiling, Carter continued to voice support for Volcker's castor-oil cure—even though he worried in private about the effect on jobs and his reelection.[106]

Despite the new significance of monetary policy, Carter remained committed to budgetary restraint in order to demonstrate that the deficit was under control. Any other course of action, warned presidential inflation adviser Alfred Kahn, "could so intensify inflationary expectations as to make the tendencies even more difficult to root out than they are now."[107] In effect, deficit reduction was now intended to give the public psychological reassurance that inflation could be beaten. Nevertheless, Edward Kennedy's declaration of his presidential candidacy made the White House circumspect about retrenching programs that served important Democratic constituencies.

The administration planned the FY1981 budget while it still believed that the FY1980 deficit would be close to the level forecast. On this basis, it estimated that the fiscal gap would continue to narrow to $15.8 billion. Carter reluctantly accepted that he could not propose a balanced budget as promised at the outset of his presidency because tight-money policy was expected to slow the economy. In anticipation of this, Charles Schultze initially advocated a deficit target of $26 billion, but he was persuaded to accept the OMB's more optimistic revenue forecasts.[108] The White House also found additional money for public assistance, education, and training programs to help low-income groups squeezed by recession and inflation. The AFL-CIO, whose support for Carter's renomination was in doubt, had lobbied strongly for more generous social provision. "We can't buy 100% labor endorsement of our budget," the president told aides, but he was more heedful of its concerns than a year earlier. In contrast, he stuck to the planned increases of 3 percent and 5 percent respectively in defense outlays and authorizations despite pressure from congressional hawks for bigger increases.[109]

The budget plan produced the first cracks in Carter's reputation for consistency in pursuit of fiscal restraint. If he had not faced Kennedy's challenge, he might have pursued a different course, but the need to shore up his left flank unquestionably weakened his resolve. The print media was critical of the budget's political calculations and the optimistic revenue forecasts on which deficit reduction depended. A *New York Times* editorial declared, "The nation should be at war against inflation. The President is still toying with a peashooter." Carter's plan also provided grist to Republican accusations that he was just another liberal big-spender. Senator William Roth (R-DE) charged that "to call this budget 'restrained' is like calling the Ayatollah [Iran's leader] a 'moderate.'" Meanwhile, Democrats bickered over whether it struck the right balance between defense and domestic programs.[110]

Most damaging to Carter, however, was the financial community's reaction. He learned too late the importance of the umbilical link between price stability and bond market confidence. The major source of investment funds, bonds are promises to pay interest at a fixed rate over the long term, so their value depends on the ratio of interest paid to the inflation rate. As borrowers, bond-sellers benefit from inflation, which reduces the real value of their repayment obligations. As investors, bondholders require a higher interest rate for their money if they expect high inflation. Although long-term bond rates had been rising in tandem with bank rates since the Federal Reserve's introduction of monetary targeting in late 1979, the markets endured what one analyst called "a prolonged buyers' strike" in reaction to accelerating inflation. Meanwhile, an estimated $400 billion was wiped off existing portfolios between early October and late February as jittery bondholders sold off their inflation-devalued assets.[111]

The announcement that wholesale prices had risen in January at an annual rate of 19.2 percent induced a sense of panic on Wall Street. Investment guru Henry Kaufman, speaking before the American Bankers Association, called for the declaration of national emergency to tackle the inflation crisis. In these circumstances financial leaders and influential segments of the media came to see a balanced FY1981 budget as vital to reassure the bond market that inflation was controllable. "The budget has raised inflationary expectations more than anything," declared Citybank's Leif Olsen, "so cutting Federal spending is exactly what we need to do to restore confidence and cut those higher expectations." Paul Volcker added his influential voice to the chorus singing the imperatives of fiscal responsibility.[112]

In response, Carter took the unprecedented step of recalling his budget plan to effect changes that would eliminate the projected deficit. This fiscal revision was undertaken without any belief that it would produce a significant diminution of prices in the short term. Authoritative sources were generally agreed that a balanced budget would reduce the core inflation rate by less than 1 percent. It was also a self-defeating exercise because the slowing down of the economy ruled out deficit elimination. As Stuart Eizenstat admitted, "We are proposing a budget program which is unachievable as well as undesirable in the present recessionary climate."[113]

Despite the impossible odds against a balanced budget, the president was convinced that a display of determination to achieve one was essential. In transmitting his revisions to Congress, he insisted that deficit elimination was an essential element in a comprehensive anti-inflation program even if it was not a "cure-all" in itself. Victory over inflation was impossible "until the Federal Government has demonstrated to the American people that it will discipline its own spending and its own borrowing—not just for one year or two, but as a long-term policy." As one aide acknowledged, a balanced budget plan would not lower prices for consumers but would have "a positive psychological impact on . . . the 'attentive' audience—the bond markets, etc."[114]

Carter's new budget had even less authority than the old one that he had pronounced essential to the nation's well-being. The product of intensive negotiations between White House officials and Democratic congressional leaders, it projected a surplus of $16.5 billion predominantly on the basis of revenue-enhancing measures like loophole closures and reduced deductions, and with only minimal expenditure savings. The only proposal requiring widespread sacrifice was an oil-import fee that would raise gasoline prices. Initially advocated by congressional negotiators, this won White House approval as a guaranteed means of increasing receipts regardless of how the economy performed. Seen as another political compromise, the new budget only encouraged different groups in Congress to press for their own agenda. The administration consequently found itself relegated to the sidelines during the legislature's complex maneuvering to adopt a budget resolution. "At some point, the line must be drawn in the sand if we are ever to be taken seriously in the [congressional] budget process," Stuart Eizenstat warned his boss. "We are increasingly a minor player."[115]

The intensification of Cold War hostility following the Soviet invasion of Afghanistan made it impossible to hold the line on military outlays. In defiance of party leaders, moderate Democrats on the House Budget Committee brokered a compromise with moderate Republicans regarding the scale of defense increases in a bid to preempt even higher demands from the more hawkish Senate. After prolonged maneuvering, Congress finally approved a budget resolution that raised the president's defense estimate by some 2 percent. An early casualty of efforts to find offsetting economies for the military increases was a $500 million initiative to help financially hard-up cities, which critics scornfully dubbed "the Jimmy Carter New York primary amendment." To the administration's dismay, Congress also approved a reconciliation procedure making the budget resolution binding rather than advisory because it had fallen so far behind schedule in finalizing agreement on one. With little prospect of effecting changes, White House aides feared that the FY1981 budget settlement would "redefine the Nation's priorities" and make it even more difficult to maintain expenditure discipline.[116]

Carter suffered an even greater rebuff over the oil import surcharge.

Never enthusiastic about its imposition, rank-and-file Democratic legislators increasingly turned against the measure in the face of hostile lobbying by oil companies. To Carter's disgust, congressional party leaders, who had urged its inclusion in the revised budget, surrendered without a fight. In his view, the episode represented "a new low in performance for the Congress since I've been in office." On June 4, the legislature approved by veto-proof margins a joint resolution killing the surcharge. Carter issued a quixotic veto on grounds that it was "a matter of principle" to honor party commitments to tackle inflation. As a result, he became the first president since Harry Truman to suffer the ignominy of being overridden by a Congress that his party controlled.[117]

Even worse, Carter found it progressively more difficult to keep his balanced-budget values at the center of the wider debate about the national fiscal agenda in the 1980 presidential election. He effectively secured the Democratic nomination by dint of winning two-thirds of delegates from states using the convention or caucus method of selection and performing well in early primaries when foreign policy was the dominant issue. In the second quarter of the year, however, the economy underwent a sharp downturn, rather than the mild slowdown that the administration had anticipated, under the combined impact of tight monetary policy and other credit restraints. As unemployment grew more significant as a campaign issue, Kennedy won impressive primary victories in industrial states like Connecticut, New York, New Jersey, Michigan, Pennsylvania, and California, where voters were receptive to his calls for government to do more to safeguard jobs. This success persuaded the Massachusetts senator that the nomination could still be his if the Democrats adopted an open-convention rule that released delegates to vote for any candidate. Hoping to rally the party's core constituencies to his cause, he called for the inclusion of a $12 billion job-creation program in the Democratic platform.[118]

The president's solicitude for the bond market ruled out adoption of an explicit strategy of deficit spending to boost recovery. Carter remained deaf to Eizenstat's counsel that he should offer a compromise job-creation proposal costing $4 billion in the interests of "a genuine and enthusiastic reconciliation" with the liberal wing of the party.[119] The president's allies on the platform committee defeated adoption of the $12 billion stimulus, but Kennedy supporters announced their intention to continue the fight into the convention itself. Despite Eizenstat's warnings that the outcome of a public debate was less predictable, Carter remained confident that the party would support him on this issue.[120]

This obduracy proved a political miscalculation because the national party signaled its enduring support for the New Deal tradition. Although Kennedy's hopes for an open convention got nowhere, he breathed new life into the flagging Democratic commitment to liberal economic activism. On August 12 his stirring oration in support of the jobs program transformed a hitherto muted convention into the political equivalent of a hot gospel meeting. It was now evident that the administration would lose any roll call on the economic platform. Accordingly, Carter lieutenants accepted a deal that met Kennedy's demands for economic stimulus and a commitment that the next Democratic administration would not take any action that significantly increased unemployment in return for him abandoning commitment to wage-price controls to fight inflation. The next day Carter grudgingly avowed support for the spirit of the agreement but clearly balked at the price tag. "The amounts needed to achieve our goals," he asserted, "will necessarily depend upon economic conditions, what can effectively be applied over time, and the appropriate concurrence by Congress."[121]

At the same time as Kennedy challenged Carter from the left, Republican adherence to a tax-cutting strategy of economic revitalization squeezed him from the right. GOP presidential candidate Ronald Reagan had endorsed the bill proposed by Representative Jack Kemp (R-NY) and Senator William Roth for a three-year, 30 percent across-the-board reduction in personal income taxes. This embodied new thinking that the solution to stagflation was to boost productivity through supply-side incentives rather than manipulation of demand. With Reagan's support, Senate Republicans announced on June 25 that they would seek to enact a 10 percent income tax cut effective January 1, 1981, an initiative implicitly intended to provide the first installment of Kemp-Roth. Democratic ranks held firm against the proposal, but only after Senate leader Robert Byrd (D-WA) personally lobbied wavering conservatives to keep them loyal to the president's fiscal priorities. Despite its legislative defeat, the ploy affirmed the GOP's identity as the party of low taxes. In response, Carter denounced "Reagan-Kemp-Roth" as "perhaps the most inflationary piece of legislation" ever to receive serious congressional consideration because of its consequences for the deficit.[122]

Notwithstanding such defiance, the president and his closest advisers recognized that a more positive economic policy alternative than anti-inflation balanced budgets was required to counter the appeal of Reagan's tax-cutting strategy for economic growth. This produced yet another election-year turn in Carter's stance on budgetary policy. A White House task force spent the summer months developing an economic recovery program in consultation with labor leaders and friendly bankers. The Carter plan fell well short of what liberals, unions, and segments of the business community hoped would be a new industrial policy. One analyst later dismissed it as a vacuous proposal "larded with the lingo of . . . structural, long-term partnership" between government and business but woefully short of specifics.[123] Nevertheless, the blueprint signaled the way ahead for Democratic economics in its transition from demand-side to supply-side emphasis, which found ultimate expression in Bill Clinton's economic program. In essence it put faith in government's capacity to promote long-term improvement in productivity as a strategic alternative to Reagan's free-market ethos.

To distinguish his plan from Keynesianism and Reaganomics, Carter declared that it was "neither a traditional stimulus program nor a general tax cut proposal." The fiscal components clearly manifested supply-side thinking, albeit in less than bold fashion. These included multi-year tax cuts for business in the form of enhanced depreciation allowances, an investment tax credit to help new business start-ups and ailing firms, and a tax credit to offset the payroll tax increase due in 1981. The program also envisaged increased public investment expenditure for research and development, transportation, energy-saving initiatives, countercyclical assistance for cities to maintain services necessary for local economic development, and job retraining. In addition, it provided assistance to hard-pressed Americans until the supply-side measures took effect. The jobless received a temporary extension of the duration of unemployment compensation. Those in employment got income tax relief to offset the Social Security tax increase, enhancement of the earned income tax credit, and a more generous allowance for families with two workers to help offset the "marriage penalty."[124]

The projected cost ran to $30 billion in its first year of operation (calendar year 1981) and some $222 billion over five years, all but $8 billion from revenue measures. As such, the Carter program would have had far greater budgetary impact than Kennedy's stimulus. Abandoning all pretense that the FY1981 budget could be balanced, the White House acknowledged that the recovery plan would add $5.7 billion to a deficit now projected at $30 billion. It estimated that the remaining costs of the program would be increasingly recouped through economic growth that would eventually restore balanced budgets.[125] Perhaps fortunately for Carter's historical reputation as a true believer in fiscal responsibility gospel, he never got the chance to test whether his plan worked in this regard. The record of later Republican presidents suggests that the most predictable result of supply-side tax reduction is loss of revenue rather than the reverse.

Devising a program was one thing; selling it to the American public was quite another. It needed a more effective salesman than Carter to do the job. This entailed more a failure of conviction on his part than of rhetorical skill. The president never seemed able to reconcile himself to the inevitability of short-term deficits in his new plan. Had he not boxed himself so comprehensively into the balanced-budget trap, he might have been able to sell the program as an ambitious investment in America's economic future. As it was, he was far more enthusiastic about bashing Reagan's tax program as a sure recipe for huge deficits. Carter never engaged with the more difficult challenge of educating the public as to why the deficits that would result from his program were more acceptable than those produced by his opponent's tax cuts. Listening to the president giving an economic policy address two weeks before the election, journalist Elizabeth Drew commented, "He does have a program to revitalize the economy—not a very exciting one, but a program—and he talked about it in the speech, but he doesn't seem able to implant it in the national consciousness. He doesn't even seem to have tried to."[126]

Even if Carter had been more successful in the task of convincing Americans of the merits of his economic plan, it is unlikely that he could have won a second term. Having relaxed monetary policy in midyear to counter the economic downturn, Volcker's Fed reversed course once more in October out of fear that the third-quarter recovery would exacerbate inflation. By November, interest rates were close to 20 percent, inflation was running at 13 percent, and unemployment was in excess of 7 percent. No president had faced the voters with worse economic indicators since Herbert Hoover in 1932. Carter duly became the first elected incumbent since the Great Engineer to be rejected by voters.

THE CARTER LEGACY

Jimmy Carter's ambitions of balancing the budget and building a new electoral majority on the foundations of fiscal responsibility went up in smoke in 1980. The rationale that drove him to pursue these ends was a highly dubious one. His demonization of the deficit not only exaggerated the threat that it posed but also put him in a lose-lose situation rather than the win-win one that he anticipated. Carter's spurious insistence that a balanced budget was essential to conquer inflation meant that his failure to achieve one exposed him to blame for price instability. Conversely, his futile quest to get federal finances out of the red prevented him from taking the kind of fiscal action against unemployment that Democratic constituencies expected from a Democratic president.

Even allowing for the miscalculations pertaining to declining productivity, the linkage between budget deficits and inflation in the Carter era was unclear. Oil-price hikes, the declining value of the dollar, wage settlements for labor, and higher interest rates contributed far more to price instability in this period. The balanced-budget panic sparked by the bond market decline in early 1980 was a particularly ludicrous exaggeration of the deficit's culpability for double-digit inflation. In reality the $15 billion imbalance projected in Carter's original FY1981 plan could make no difference whatsoever to price stability. Nor was the actual deficit of $79 billion finally run up in this budget a potent source of inflation. Owing to the state of the economy, the imbalance measured only $13 billion in full-employment terms, equivalent to 0.4 percent of GDP. Even on a real rather than a hypothetical index, the FY1981 deficit was no bigger at 2.6 percent GDP than the "Eisenhower deficit" of FY1959 and was significantly smaller than the "Ford deficit" of 4.2 percent GDP in FY1976.

Carter's Progressive concept of balanced budgets as the ethos of good government might have become an electoral asset to his presidency because it accorded with long-standing popular belief in fiscal responsibility. However, the anti-inflationary imperative that came to define his fiscal agenda was all pain for no gain. Carter never tied his budgetary equivalent of root-canal surgery to an alluring vision of a healthier economic future. In May 1980 Stuart Eizenstat warned him, "We are now in a balanced budget box." Administration policy was "viewed solely as one of austerity, pain and sacrifice, with few positive aspects." Carter was incapable of depicting the economic uplands to which he wanted to lead Americans. Bill Clinton would not repeat the same mistake when he pursued deficit reduction in 1993. After hearing one of Carter's salvationless jeremiads, the then Arkansas governor commented that the president sounded more like a "17th century New England Puritan than a 20th century Southern Baptist."[127]

Carter paid the price at the ballot box in 1980 for setting the impossible goal of balancing the budget in the cause of inflation control. In response to an exit poll asking voters what were the two issues most important in determining their ballot choice, 21 percent specified government failure to balance the budget. Of these, 65 percent voted for Reagan, 27 percent for Carter, and 6 percent for independent candidate John Anderson. Only inflation and the economy (33 percent) and jobs and unemployment (24 percent) ranked higher among voter concerns, both of which were interconnected with budgetary issues. Reagan's support among inflation-worried voters was similar in dimension to that he had gained from those with balanced-budget concerns (61 percent to 28 percent for Carter and 9 percent for Anderson). He also ran very close with the president on the traditional Democratic issue of jobs—48 percent of voters specifying this as a concern supported Carter, compared with 42 percent for Reagan and 7 percent for Anderson.[128]

Thanks in large part to his failure on inflation, Carter could not build on his promising showing with middle-class occupational groups in 1976. He won only 40 percent of voters in white-collar jobs and 33 percent of professionals in 1980, compared with 50 and 42 percent previously. At the same time, his appeal to the traditional Democratic constituency underwent significant decline. He won just 48 percent of voters in manual occupations and only 50 percent of those from labor-union families, compared with 58 percent and 63 percent in 1976. Just as damaging to him was the lowest turnout in any presidential election since 1948. Some four-fifths of nonvoters were from socioeconomic groups that were habitually Democratic. Reagan held no appeal for them, but neither did Carter. This prompted one historian to claim that "much of Carter's difficulty on Election Day came from being so little in the image of FDR that millions in the Roosevelt coalition . . . did not go to the polls."[129]

Whether prescient or premature in his abandonment of the New Deal tradition, Carter had not provided an alternative to it that was viable in contemporary circumstances. Nevertheless, he had pointed the way to the future, even if he was himself unable to effect the transition. Whereas liberal Democrats condemned him as "Jimmy Hoover" for his refusal to employ deficit spending to reverse economic decline, he should more accurately be seen as "Jimmy Clinton."[130] Whatever their differences in detail, Carter's economic program and Clinton's shared common principles. These included greater reliance on the market economy and less dependence on government to achieve prosperity, prioritization of the inflation problem over unemployment, elevation of monetary policy over fiscal policy as the instrument of economic management, emphasis on supply-side measures to enhance long-term productivity over short-term economic stimulus, and the need for deficit elimination as psychological reassurance for the bond market.

Far from being the precursor of Reaganite antistatism, Carter's budgetary conservatism was an attempt to adapt liberalism to postliberal conditions that required government to be more cost-conscious. The thirty-ninth president failed to persuade his fellow Democrats that the best hope of sustaining their traditional mission lay in recasting the activist state within the mold of fiscal responsibility. It required the huge deficits of the Reagan era to convert them into the antideficit party. The fiscal numbers did not support belief that the budget was out of control before then. As Tip O'Neill tartly commented, the Carter deficits were "practically a balanced budget" by the standards of what followed.[131] In reaction to the experience of the 1980s, another Southerner would have more success in leading the Democrats out of the fiscal wilderness into the milk-and-honey land of balanced budgets to which Jimmy Carter had tried in vain to take them.

CHAPTER 4

Ronald Reagan:
Coexisting with the Deficit

In the 1980 election, Ronald Reagan vowed to achieve three fiscal goals as president. "We must balance the budget, reduce tax rates and restore our defenses," he declared. "I know we can do these things, and I know that we will."[1] He was spectacularly successful in achieving two of these aims and spectacularly unsuccessful regarding the third. Reagan promoted the largest tax cut in U.S. history and set in train the greatest defense expansion since the Korean War, but at cost of unprecedented deficits that tripled the dollar size of the public debt on his watch.

In Reagan's credo, deficits were the agency of liberal big government that he held responsible for America's problems in the 1970s. This outlook had its antecedents in conservative Republican opposition to the New Deal and the ideology of the postwar GOP right. In contrast to Republican orthodoxy, however, Reagan regarded balanced budgets as the outcome of, not the prerequisite for, his antistatist agenda of lower taxes and smaller government. This outlook saved Reagan from becoming snared in the same fiscal trap as Jimmy Carter. It enabled him to coexist with huge deficits if they did not threaten the new course that he charted for the nation. Adapting his political strategy to their development, Reagan continued to rail against deficits as the symbol of big government while doing everything in his power to preserve the tax cuts and defense expansion that were their substantive cause. Typifying this, he proclaimed in 1983, "The deficits we face are not rooted in defense spending . . . [or] in tax cuts. . . . The fact is, our deficits come from the uncontrolled growth of the budget for domestic spending."[2]

FREEDOM'S TRIBUNE

Born on February 6, 1911, in Tampico, Illinois, to a family of modest means, Ronald Reagan grew up from age nine in the nearby small town of Dixon. His father, Jack, who never found success as a shoe salesman, had a drinking problem, and the adult Reagan manifested personality traits common in children of alcoholics—discomfort with personal conflict, remoteness in personal relationships, and an inclination to put a rosy gloss on unpleasant reality. However, Reagan's mother, Nelle, infused him with her indefatigable optimism and strong religious belief that were more significant in shaping his outlook. Despite his humble origins, Reagan rose ever higher in a succession of careers in adult life, experiencing only a few setbacks on the way. He would entitle his presidential memoirs *An American Life* to signify that his personal story validated his country's unique promise as the land of freedom and individual opportunity.

Scrimping and saving to pay his way through Eureka College, a small liberal arts establishment, the future president was the first in his family to attain a college degree. Graduating as an economics major when the Great Depression was near its worst, he quickly got a well-paid job as a radio sportscaster, but he hankered to be an actor. In 1937 he took a screen test that launched him on a movie career with Warner Brothers. Reagan progressed from B-movies to more prestigious roles in a career spanning fifty-three film appearances, even if he never established himself as a top star. Meanwhile, he was increasingly active in the Screen Actors Guild (SAG), which he helped preserve from communist control during Hollywood's postwar labor battles, serving as its president in 1947–1952 and again in 1959–1960. When his movie career hit the skids, salvation came in the form of television work. From 1954 to 1962 he hosted *General Electric Theater*, a popular drama series, and served the show's sponsor in a public relations role that required him to make speaking tours of its various plants.

During the 1950s Reagan's politics underwent a fundamental transformation from liberalism to conservatism. Originally an admirer of the New Deal, he voted Democrat in every presidential election from 1932 to 1948 in gratitude for Franklin D. Roosevelt's inspirational leadership during the depression and war. In the new context of Cold War and prosperity, however, Reagan came to see the growth of communist power abroad and government at home as twin threats to America's liberties. This outlook turned him into a Republican long before he formally registered as one in 1962. Two years later, the success of his nationally televised fundraising appeal for the doomed presidential candidacy of Barry Goldwater made him a prominent figure in the emerging conservative movement. Reagan's ability to articulate the antigovernment message in persuasive and optimistic fashion induced a group of businessmen to bankroll his run for California governor in 1966.

Reagan's victory over incumbent Pat Brown made him not only chief executive of America's largest state but also the nation's foremost conservative. After leaving the governorship, he spent five years in pursuit of the presidency, all the while promoting his views through syndicated newspaper columns and radio messages. In 1976 his challenge to Gerald Ford for the Republican nomination ended in narrow defeat. Four years later Reagan easily won the race to become the GOP nominee and inflicted a heavy defeat on Jimmy Carter to become president.[3]

Reagan's life experience shaped the political values that made him the most ideological president of modern times. The optimism that marked his view of America's future was a legacy from his mother's teaching and his own rise from humble origins. Reagan's Hollywood experience also made a profound impression on him. His involvement in SAG alerted him to the threat of communism's expansionist proclivities. The pain of finding himself in "the 94 percent tax bracket" as a well-paid star after World War II convinced him that high taxes were a disincentive to individual enterprise. Finally, the tales of bureaucratic red tape he heard when touring GE plants persuaded him that government was encroaching on liberty.[4]

Many liberals made the mistake of dismissing Reagan as a shallow peddler of anecdotal homilies that blended America's past with his own. As one scoffed, "What he recollected was not really history but fable. His wisdom was not illuminated by a precise memory or erudition, but by archetypal stories in which he always placed himself."[5] In contrast, close reading of Reagan's written and spoken words from the 1950s through the 1970s has convinced revisionist scholars that he was not just a storyteller but a deeper thinker than liberal critics allowed. In their view, the fortieth president had developed a philosophy of history that constituted a speculative rather than analytic set of claims about the meaning of America's existence and what could be made of its past to shape the possibilities of the future. The essence of his belief system was that America's progress depended on its eternal return to the values of freedom as conceived by the founders, namely limited government, constitutionalism, individual rights against the encroachments of the state, and a moral social order.[6] Articulating this creed in his inaugural address as California governor, Reagan warned, "Freedom is a fragile thing. . . . It must be fought for and defended constantly by each generation, for it comes only once to a people."[7]

In Reagan's interpretation of the past, FDR had never intended activist government to be more than a temporary response to the Great Depression. The permanent growth of the bureaucratic state promoted by the Democrats since World War II was a corruption of his hero's legacy that put America "along the path to a silent form of socialism" and finally brought it to crisis in the 1970s. Accepting the Republican presidential nomination, Reagan damned the opposition party for believing that "our nation has passed its zenith" and avowed that Americans would achieve a better future through renewing trust in "our legacy as a free people."[8]

Insofar as budget policy was concerned, Reagan rarely lived up to his pristine beliefs as governor. Instead, he bowed to the political realities of running a large state with modern social responsibilities in cooperation with a Democrat-controlled legislature. According to one historian, his record in Sacramento made a "shambles of his ideology." In his first year in office,

Reagan signed into law the largest tax increase in California's history to stay within its constitutional balanced-budget requirement and thereafter presided over a steady expansion in state spending. Although he provided taxpayers with rebates totaling $5.7 billion during the remainder of his governorship, the margin to do so came from his tax increases and federal revenue-sharing funds. His greatest achievement was welfare reform developed in cooperation with Democratic Assembly Speaker Robert Moretti and enacted in 1971. This reduced welfare costs by tightening eligibility requirements but increased benefits for legitimate recipients. Although Reagan claimed the credit, the 300,000 decline in California's welfare population during his subsequent time in Sacramento owed far more to the improvement in the state's economy.[9]

A failed venture provided the most significant gubernatorial precedent for Reagan's fiscal approach as president. The core belief of his conservative philosophy was that high taxes constituted the lifeblood of big government. As he put it in 1973, the taxpayer had "become the pawn in a deadly game of government monopoly whose only purpose is to serve the confiscatory appetites of runaway government spending."[10] Frustrated at having to raise taxes to support higher spending, Reagan looked for a way to control the revenue supply that fueled government's growth. In 1972 he established a committee to write a tax-limitation amendment to the state constitution. This body drew up a proposal to limit future California taxes to a fixed percentage of total personal income and require a two-thirds supermajority in both houses of the legislature for any tax increase.

When the Democrat-controlled legislature refused to put this proposal to a popular vote, Reagan promoted it instead as a ballot initiative, Proposition 1. Campaigning for this, he declared, "We think it is time to limit government's allowance—to put a limit on the amount of money they can take from the people in taxes. This is the only way we will ever bring government spending under control." Voters rejected Proposition 1 by 54 to 46 percent in late 1973. Most simply found its complex terms that ran to 5,700 words incomprehensibly dense, and some feared it would result in higher local taxes to support spending. Nevertheless, Proposition 1 pioneered the state tax-limitation movement that achieved success in California and elsewhere in the late 1970s. It also signified Reagan's understanding that the size-of-government issue could be addressed from the tax side of the budget.[11]

Claiming a mandate to lead America out of crisis, Reagan intended bolder action to restore founding principles as president and made the budget the instrument of this agenda. Tax reduction, military expansion, and domestic retrenchment were fundamental to his project of renewing America's dedication to freedom. In Reagan's original conception, deficit elimination was an equally significant and interdependent element in this task. Balanced budgets were the means for "bringing to heel a federal establishment that has taken too much power from the States, too much liberty with the Constitution and too much money from the people."[12]

Reagan blamed a selfish iron triangle of pork-minded legislators, empire-building bureaucrats, and liberal special interests for the perpetuation of deficit spending.[13] In addition to reducing domestic outlays, he looked to break its power through transferring program responsibility from the national government to the states in reaffirmation of American federalism's original principles. Reagan first proposed this reallocation in a September 1975 speech intended to lay the foundations for his presidential challenge to Gerald Ford. He claimed that resultant savings of $90 billion would make it possible "to balance the Federal budget, make an initial five-billion-dollar payment on the national debt, and cut the Federal personal income tax burden of every American by an average of 23 percent." However, Reagan's failure to explain how the states would pay for their new responsibilities enabled the Ford campaign to question his credibility. Despite this setback, program transfer remained fundamental to his vision of constitutional renewal when he became president.[14]

The corollary to Reagan's belief in self-perpetuating big government was that raising taxes did nothing to get federal finances out of the red because the extra revenue simply funded more spending. As proof of this, he claimed that tax revenues had doubled between FY1976 and FY1981 while the deficit "grew and grew." Receipts did indeed rise from $298 billion to $599 billion in current-dollar terms, but their constant-dollar growth was less than a third. In FY1981, moreover, the deficit was hardly any bigger in current dollars than in FY1976 and was significantly smaller in constant dollars and as a percentage of GDP. Never one to let statistical complexity blur the clarity of his message, Reagan held one truth to be self-evident in the budgetary experience of the 1970s: "The more Congress taxed, the more it spent, and the more it went further and further into the red."[15]

As inflation rose and federal deficits grew, Reagan triangulated these developments with the upward curve of the tax burden as mutually reinforcing elements in the nation's economic crisis. In his assessment, government was both the engine of inflation and its chief beneficiary. Like many conservatives, Reagan believed that government had fueled inflation by expanding the money supply to ease its borrowing costs. "It was this roller-coasting of money," he declared, "that, in large part, coupled with high government spending, got us in our present fix." In reality, the deficits of the 1970s—*and* the 1980s—were financed from public borrowing rather than Federal Reserve purchase of Treasury securities.[16]

Erroneous though it was, the debt monetization theory was inextricably linked in Reagan's thought process to the sounder proposition that inflation pumped up federal revenues. "Government profits by inflation," he charged, "and as cost of living pay rises move workers into higher surtax brackets the government will get that much undeserved income." The extra revenue then encouraged higher federal spending that led inexorably to bigger deficits, which fed the inflationary spiral anew. The only way to break this cycle, Reagan proclaimed in the 1980 presidential debate, was by reducing federal expenditure "to the place that we have balanced budgets and are no longer grinding out printing press money, flooding the market with it."[17]

The decline in the defense share of spending as deficits grew in the 1970s added grist to Reagan's conviction that domestic extravagance caused unbalanced budgets. He warned that military penny-pinching had weakened America and put it in retreat everywhere in the world.[18] In his worldview, détente was a sham because the Cold War was a struggle between freedom and tyranny that could only end in victory for one or the other. Reagan was confident that America could transcend the threat of communism through massive rebuilding of its military power, which the Soviets could not match without destroying their economy. An arms race, he declared in 1980, "is the last thing they want from us . . . because they are already running as fast as they can and we haven't started running." Conversely, he feared that America was vulnerable to a surrender-or-perish ultimatum should the enemy gain nuclear superiority.[19] Accordingly, Reagan established a basic rule that governed his fiscal approach as president. "The defense budget," he told aides, "cannot be determined by other programs; what we spend on defense is what we spend to maintain our national security, and how much we spend depends largely on what the Soviet Union does."[20]

Despite his concern that America was losing ground in the Cold War, Reagan regarded the economy as the most urgent problem he faced on becoming president. "Without a recovery," he later declared, "we couldn't afford to do the things necessary to make the country strong again. . . . Nothing was possible unless we made the economy sound again."[21] The economic strategy that Reagan followed in office was based on "Policy Memorandum No. 1," a summary of his ideas for renewing prosperity authored by domestic aide Martin Anderson in August 1979. This blamed runaway inflation on "the massive, continuing budget deficit of the federal government." To revive the economy, it advocated across-the-board tax cuts spread over three years and indexation to eliminate inflationary bracket creep, reduction in the rate of increase of federal spending—partly by transferring responsibility for certain social programs to the states, balanced budgets, vigorous deregulation, and a consistent monetary policy. The Anderson blueprint also recommended an Economic Bill of Rights constitutional amendment—featuring a limitation on federal spending, a presidential line-item veto, and a balanced-budget requirement—to safeguard the freedoms necessary for the proper functioning

of the economy. This economic plan was perfectly attuned to Reagan's antistatist political agenda because its formula for renewed growth required
smaller government.[22]

The emergence of complementary economic ideas facilitated the promotion of Reaganomics. Initially developed in academia and popularized
in the conservative print media, supply-side doctrine emphasized the importance of productivity growth over consumer demand and regarded individuals and businesses rather than aggregate behavior as the keystone of
economic growth. According to its dictum, the maximization of output and
wealth creation required reduction of taxes, especially of high marginal rates,
to enhance incentive to work, produce, save, and invest.[23] A small group of
congressional Republicans was responsible for supply-side ideas finding their
way into the political arena. In 1977 Representative Jack Kemp (R-NY) and
Senator William Roth (R-DE) cosponsored a bill to cut income taxes across
the board by 30 percent in three annual installments, but almost universal
Republican support in the House could not save it from repeated defeat by
the Democrats. Initially fearful of its consequences for the deficit, GOP Senate leaders came round to supporting Kemp-Roth during the budget battle
of 1980 with the Carter administration. The measure had previously received
Reagan's formal endorsement as part of a deal to win Kemp's support for
his candidacy instead of running for president himself. In essence, Kemp-
Roth was the catalyst that transformed Reagan's personal crusade against
high taxes into a party cause.[24]

The supply-side ethos confirmed rather than inspired Reagan's convictions. As close aide Ed Meese remarked, Reagan had been "a 'supply-sider'
long before the term was invented."[25] There was also a major difference between Reaganomics and its partner doctrine over the consequences of tax
reduction for the spending side of the fiscal ledger. Supply-side enthusiasts
had no qualms that their prescription would produce a short-term rise in
the deficit, which they expected to disappear eventually as a consequence
of economic growth. Their priority was to get the economy moving again by
cutting taxes, but they had no inclination to cut spending to pay for this. As
Jack Kemp put it, "A prosperous private economy can easily afford a strong
safety net of public services. A stifled, smothering economy can't. . . . Private
affluence does not mean public squalor."[26] For Reagan, however, Kemp-Roth
was both an agency of economic growth and a continuation of his Proposition
1 strategy of constraining government through limitation of its tax revenue.
As such, he always prefaced advocacy of it "with the declaration that we must
start immediately to reduce the size and cost of our federal government to
bring it down to a lesser percentage of our gross national product."[27]

A number of Reagan's economic advisers, notably Milton Friedman, Alan
Greenspan, Paul McCracken, and Herbert Stein, reinforced his conviction
on this score. In their view the growth of the public sector was both damaging

to productivity and a source of inflation. Though skeptical that Kemp-Roth could deliver massive economic growth, they valued its utility as an instrument of spending control. According to former Nixon CEA chair Paul McCracken, "The primary case for Kemp-Roth is a growing conviction that Government has been allocating too much of the national income to itself, and that the time has come to change this."[28]

Reagan, however, was far more confident than his advisers that Kemp-Roth would not blow a big hole in federal finances. The rationale for this belief was the "Laffer curve" theory, developed by supply-side pioneer Arthur Laffer of the University of Southern California, that revenue would "reflow" to government from the economic growth generated by tax reduction. This beguiling idea did not provide empirical guidance regarding the point between 100 and 0 percent taxation of income at which reflow would occur nor about the proportion of revenues that would be recouped.[29] Even so, Reagan swallowed it hook, line, and sinker as economic justification for his political conviction that high taxes undermined founding principles. So great was his enthusiasm for this concept that he went much further in his claims for it than its author. In a 1977 radio address he asserted that Kemp-Roth "would reduce the deficit which causes inflation because the tax base would be *broadened* by increased prosperity." Within weeks of becoming president, he voiced the same belief: "A cut in tax rates can very often be reflected in an increase in government revenues because of the broadening of the base of the economy."[30]

The economic advisers helping Reagan's 1980 campaign set far greater store on capital-income tax cuts than across-the-board personal tax cuts to revitalize the economy. With their support, business lobbyists persuaded the Republican platform committee to adopt a proposal for significant liberalization of business depreciation allowances on buildings, machinery, and vehicles, known as "10-5-3." Over the objections of Jack Kemp, the group's solitary supply-sider, the advisory team consequently met with Reagan to recommend lengthening the Kemp-Roth schedule as insurance against deficit growth putting 10-5-3 at risk. Alan Greenspan, in particular, counseled that it would be much easier to balance the budget if the personal tax cuts were stretched out over five years rather than three. Fortified by Laffer-curve belief, Reagan bullishly rejected such pleas for greater caution.[31] The magnitude of his gamble on the reflow benefits of tax reduction would soon become apparent.

ROSY SCENARIO AND RED REALITY

Reagan's first fiscal challenge was to convert the lame-duck Carter budget for FY1982 into a vehicle for his priorities. With the budget's growth in scope and complexity since World War II, incoming presidents had confined themselves to making incremental adjustments in the executive plan inherited from the outgoing one. Reagan challenged conventional wisdom that it was impossible to transform in a matter of weeks a budget that had taken a year to prepare.

Office of Management and Budget (OMB) director David Stockman worked a punishing schedule and drove his staff hard to convert Reagan's strategic vision into the reality of a new budget. Described by journalist Lou Cannon as "a man of restless intellect and swiftly changing visions," he had journeyed from conservatism in youth to student radicalism and back again to the right as a two-term Republican congressman for a southern Michigan district in 1977–1981. The thirty-four-year-old Stockman straddled the new and old varieties of Republicanism in his devotion to supply-side tax reduction and his fervent commitment to dismantling the welfare state. He brought immense conviction and energy but also overconfidence to the task of budget revision. Stockman's prodigious labors enabled the president to deliver what was effectively a new plan to Congress on March 10, 1981—just forty-nine days after taking office. This success established him for a heady moment as the chief engineer of the Reagan Revolution, but he would go down in history as its chief miscalculator.[32]

The revised plan embodied Reagan's agenda for tax reduction, defense expansion, and domestic rollback. In the months that followed, White House aides met almost daily in the Legislative Strategy Group (LSG) to review its implementation and find ways of outmaneuvering opposition to it. The administration eventually emerged victorious from the hard-fought battle to convert the main elements of its budget into legislation. According to political scientist James Pfiffner, this success demonstrated how a new president could impose his will on the national agenda through "advanced planning, singleness of purpose, and speed of execution."[33]

The Omnibus Budget and Reconciliation Act (OBRA) of 1981, signed into law on August 13, retrenched over 200 domestic programs at projected savings of $35.2 billion in FY1982 and $140 billion over three years. Thanks to accounting gimmicks and other backdoor escapes written into the bill by Congress, the real cutbacks turned out to be significantly smaller and almost impossible to compute accurately. Nevertheless, OBRA still constituted the largest-ever single-year retrenchment of nonmilitary spending. The ax fell mainly on public assistance and jobs programs that helped low-income Americans. Under cover of routine appropriations, Congress also granted Reagan's request for $26 billion in additional defense outlays in FY1982, a real increase of 9 percent. Equally important, its increase of budgetary authority by 8 percent over Carter administration projections guaranteed a multiyear peacetime defense expansion of unprecedented magnitude.[34]

Meanwhile, the Economic Recovery Tax Act (ERTA) of 1981, also signed on August 13, incorporated a one-step reduction from 70 percent to 50 percent in the top marginal rate of personal income tax, a modified 5-10-10 version of Kemp-Roth for other bands, and the 10-5-3 depreciation allowance. To secure its passage, the administration accepted congressional add-ons from both parties that turned the bill into a Christmas tree of benefits for special interests. These included large cuts in business, estate, and gift taxes; oil tax reductions; a capital gains tax cut; and a host of smaller tax breaks.[35] However, the most significant amendment both in terms of cost and implications was the indexation of personal income tax rates to inflation that benefited all taxpayers. Its sponsor, Senator William Armstrong (R-CO), wanted to control spending by eliminating the automatic increase in revenues generated by bracket creep.[36]

There was a design fault in the Reagan fiscal juggernaut that prevented it from reaching the balanced-budget terminus. While the FY1982 budget was being revised, a team of administration economists worked on formulating a statement of economic strategy. In essence, *America's New Beginning: A Program for Economic Recovery*, presented to Congress on February 18, put the flesh of detail on the bones of principle embodied in "Policy Memorandum No. 1." It forecast that the combination of economic growth from tax reduction, spending control, and steady lowering of inflation would yield a balanced budget at around 19 percent GDP from FY1984 onward. This was dependent on the economy achieving average growth of 4.4 percent from 1982 through 1986 and on the inflation rate declining steadily from 8.3 percent to 4.2 percent over the same period.[37]

The so-called rosy scenario of economic growth fell victim to the Federal Reserve's determination to conquer inflation immediately rather than incrementally. Draconian tightening of monetary policy in early 1981 precipitated the deepest recession since the 1930s. In consequence, economic output contracted by 2 percent instead of growing by 4 percent as anticipated. This dose of monetary castor oil finally cured the inflation problem. The consumer price index rose by a mere 3.8 percent on average in 1982–1986. However this success also had dire consequences for the fiscal calculations of Reaganomics. By FY1984, actual money GDP (real GDP and inflation) was some $400 billion less than the rosy scenario estimate. This served to depress revenue-GDP share and had the reverse effect on outlay-GDP share. Instead of being balanced at 19 percent GDP, receipts and spending respectively totaled 17.3 percent and 22.1 percent GDP to produce a massive deficit of 4.8 percent GDP.[38]

Analysts disagree whether tax cuts or expenditure growth fueled deficit growth. Those of broadly liberal outlook contend that ERTA was primarily to blame. Once it became operative, the real value of receipts did not surpass the FY1981 level until FY1985. If allowance is made for the effect of recession and for the contribution of tax reduction to recovery, total loss of revenue resulting from ERTA in FY1982–FY1986 amounted to $643 billion. This computation suggests that it was responsible for some two-thirds of the cumulative deficit.[39]

The conservative interpretation attributes the deficits of the 1980s more to increased spending on New Deal–Great Society entitlements than anything Reagan did. Its adherents also insist that ERTA's benefits to economic growth ultimately produced a greater real increase in receipts over the entire course of Reagan's presidency than in the tax-happy 1970s. In their estimate this was responsible for the decline of the deficit in Reagan's second term to the point that it only constituted 2.8 percent GDP in FY1989, more or less where it had been in FY1981.[40]

The basic fiscal numbers do not favor the conservative case. Spending and revenue respectively averaged 22.9 percent and 17.9 percent GDP in Reagan's first term budgets, compared with 21.2 percent and 18.8 percent GDP under Jimmy Carter. In other words, expenditure growth equated to two-thirds of the deficit's growth by 2.6 percent GDP. However, domestic outlays (human resources and physical resources combined) declined from 13.7 percent GDP in FY1978–FY1981 to 13.2 percent GDP in FY1982–FY1985. The drivers of expenditure growth in Reagan's first term were national defense—which averaged 5.9 percent GDP, compared with 4.8 percent GDP under Carter—and net interest payments on a mushrooming public debt, which averaged 2.8 percent GDP, compared with 1.8 percent GDP under his predecessor.

The relative improvement in federal finances during Reagan's second term owed much to the decline of annual domestic outlays to 12 percent GDP in FY1986–FY1989. Tax revenues increased by a fifth in real terms over the course of Reagan's presidency, but how much this was due to ERTA is unclear. Social insurance taxes, raised in 1983, constituted the principal source of revenue expansion in the Reagan era. Receipts from this source grew from 6 percent GDP in FY1981 to 6.7 percent GDP in FY1989 while those from personal income taxes correspondingly declined from 9.3 percent GDP to 8.3 percent GDP.[41]

Nevertheless, a purely fiscal explanation for the growth of the deficit ignores the fundamental significance of presidential leadership. Had Reagan not demonstrated such boldness, determination, and skill in pursuit of his agenda, the 1980s would not have gone down in history as an era of huge deficits. Others in the administration undertook the spadework of budget revision and the bulk of legislative maneuvering in its support, but the president called the important fiscal shots.

Republican electoral success in 1980 put Reagan in a much stronger position than his recent GOP predecessors. His landslide victory over an incumbent president endowed him with a mandate to govern that was strengthened by the seven-seat majority won by his party in the Senate, its first since 1953–1954. Meanwhile, the opposition majority in the House of Representatives had been slashed from 119 seats to 51. Despite this, Democratic leaders were confident of teaching Reagan a lesson in the reality of divided government, but they seriously underestimated him. After the budget battles of 1981, Majority Leader James Wright (D-TX) admitted, "We really haven't laid a glove on him. . . . Appalled by what seems to me a lack of depth, I stand nevertheless in awe of his political skill. I am not sure that I have seen its equal." Speaker Tip O'Neill (D-MA) found one crumb of comfort in being bested by a rival he had considered a political novice. "I guess the monkey is off the Democrats' back," he reflected. "The deficit is Reagan's deficit."[42]

The key to Reagan's victory in the House of Representatives lay in building a bipartisan coalition of Republicans, including the moderate "gypsy moths" from northern districts that benefited from federal spending, and conservative southern Democrats, nicknamed the "boll weevils." A combination of appeals for party loyalty to the new president, astute concessions to constituency interests, and the surge in Reagan's approval ratings after he was seriously wounded by a would-be assassin on March 30 enabled the administration to win its first test. On May 7, the House approved the Stockman-crafted budget resolution, named after its cosponsors, Delbert Latta (R-OH) and Phil Gramm (D-TX), to emphasize its bipartisan nature.[43]

The danger remained that the various House committees would mark up spending in defiance of Gramm-Latta limits. To circumvent this, Reagan aides recommended adoption of a reconciliation substitute for the work of seven committees that had jurisdiction over programs targeted for retrenchment. As two analysts commented, "If Reagan was proposing a revolution in spending priorities, reconciliation was a revolution in our form of governance." The Gramm-Latta II reconciliation required the largest-ever program cutbacks without allowing for deliberative assessment within the committee system. To outraged Democrats this represented as great a threat to congressional budget sovereignty as Richard Nixon's impoundment actions. Even boll weevils were suspicious of the procedural radicalism. LSG coordinator Richard Darman warned the president that the strategy was risky. If successful, "The perception of your leadership and commitment will be strengthened," but failure "will play as a major administration loss."[44]

Reagan took the gamble that determined the success of his budget strategy. Desperate to halt the president's momentum, Democratic leaders offered an alternative five-part package that purported to concede most of what he wanted but insisted on separate votes for each element in the hope of defeating some cuts. In response, Reagan lobbied members of Congress personally to support the omnibus package, approved further exemptions of constituency-oriented spending from retrenchment, and promised not to campaign in 1982 against Democrats who backed him. His reward was a seven-vote defeat of the Speaker's procedural motion supporting separate votes on budget cuts and consequent approval of Gramm-Latta II. This triumph was less than it appeared, however. The conference committee charged with harmonizing the House and Senate reconciliation bills found ways of reducing the savings below their projections. This restoration of conventional politics signaled that both the Democratic House and the Republican Senate would be more resistant in the future to administration manipulation of the substance and process of the budget.[45]

Reagan showed comparable determination in support of the Conable-Hance tax reduction bill, based on Kemp-Roth but named in another demonstration of bipartisanship after its cosponsors, Representatives Barber Conable (R-NY) and Kent Hance (D-TX). In a rare concession, the president agreed to scale back the first installment of across-the-board personal tax cuts to 5 percent in deference to the deficit concerns of boll weevils. Conversely, he refused to countenance Tip O'Neill's proposal to defer the third installment until the deficit declined. White House aides disagreed among themselves about the need for compromise, but their boss harbored no doubts. "I can win this," Murray Weidenbaum recalled him saying. The CEA chair also wondered whether "we would have had those remaining triple-digit budget deficits if he had compromised."[46]

In addition to personally lobbying legislators for their vote Reagan made a powerful prime-time national appeal on behalf of his tax program on July 27. By common consent, this was his best television performance to date. Rejecting Democratic charges that his plan was skewed toward the rich and risked deficit explosion, he promoted it as a return of the people's money that Congress wanted "to spend and spend and spend." The resultant blitz of telephone calls from the public helped to turn the expected close vote into a solid majority for the administration's tax bill.[47]

Of course, the OBRA cuts nowhere near matched the scale of revenue loss from ERTA. Owing to the almost impossibly tight deadline for its submission, Stockman's budget plan contained a so-called magic asterisk of unspecified future savings of $44 billion a year needed to balance the budget by FY1984. He anticipated going back to Congress to secure a further round of "cats and dogs" cuts worth about $10 billion a year before going after the big-ticket entitlements, but neither of these economy drives came to pass. The fiscal ledger was thrown further out of kilter by the mammoth expansion of defense spending. As Murray Weidenbaum later admitted, "On balance we really haven't cut the budget. Instead the much publicized reductions in nonmilitary programs the President has won from Congress have been fully offset by the unprecedented growth in military spending sought by Reagan. When you add that to the big tax cuts, you get horrendous deficits."[48]

Far from undertaking a hard-nosed assessment of military needs, the Reagan administration built its long-term defense strategy on the assumption that the sheer size of the Pentagon budget was the primary index of America's power. It determined the specific enhancement of military capabilities only after the expansion of defense spending was agreed. As Defense Secretary Casper Weinberger later commented, there had been no time for "lengthy conceptual debate" because the overriding priority was to invest "roughly as much in our defenses as our primary competitor invests in its forces."[49]

Accordingly, the Reagan administration continued its predecessor's weapons programs but greatly accelerated procurement and development, notably in modernization of strategic forces, and targeted significantly higher force levels, particularly a 600-ship navy. Its main innovation was the Strategic Defense Initiative (SDI), a space-based antimissile system embodying the president's commitment to comprehensive defense. Funded to the tune of $3–4 billion a year, this program became a significant bargaining chip in second-term arms negotiations with the Soviets. Where Reagan mainly differed from Carter was not in new weapons development but in providing much greater budgetary support to ensure both qualitative and quantitative strengthening of force levels. In addition, his first two budgets aimed to lock in authorization for military investments that would drive budget growth in future years. Investment spending on procurement, research and development, and military construction consequently increased from 36 percent of the defense budget in FY1980 to 46 percent in FY1983.[50]

Reagan had pledged to spend at least 5 percent a year more than Carter on defense. Although his predecessor's lame-duck budget already provided for an increase of this magnitude, Stockman and Pentagon officials quickly agreed to a five-year program of 7 percent real increases over the FY1982 baseline with its "get well" additions. Once the OMB director comprehended his unintended largess, he was horrified to discover that he had approved a defense plan costing $1.46 trillion. The consequence, Stockman admitted to journalist Laurence Barrett, was a "total disjunction" between national security outlays and budgetary control. To hold on to what it now had, the Pentagon immediately produced a long-term plan committing every cent of its vast allocation. Weinberger henceforth argued that any retreat from the established growth target would send the Soviets the wrong signal. Although Congress scaled back defense estimates from 1982 onward, outlays rose in every Reagan budget. The defense expansion slowed significantly after FY1986, but spending averaged $390 billion in FY2000 dollars in Reagan's second-term budgets, compared with the Carter average of $264 billion. This was a level exceeded since 1945 only in the Korean War budgets of FY1952–FY1953 and the Vietnam War budgets of FY1968–FY1969.[51]

Stockman's last hope of turning things around on defense was the so-called fall offensive to promote a new round of retrenchment. Even before ERTA and OBRA became law, he understood that a perfect storm of massive deficits was on its way. The OMB director maneuvered to convert the president's senior aides and Treasury Secretary Donald Regan one by one to the need for budgetary correction by scaling back the defense estimates. He finally conveyed the bad news to the president himself at a White House meeting on August 3, but to no avail. Reagan steadfastly refused to reduce his military expansion. In a "choice between defense and deficits," he told aides, national security had to come first, a stand that he was sure had the overwhelming support of the American public.[52]

Thwarted over defense retrenchment, Stockman looked instead to cut entitlements, including Social Security, but this proposal was a masterpiece of mistiming. The OMB director had already blown his best chance of achieving these savings. In February he had advised Reagan to reject a bipartisan Senate Budget Committee initiative for a freeze in Social Security cost-of-living-adjustments (COLAs) in the mistaken belief that this was an attempt to preempt bigger economies. In his quest for "magic asterisk" savings, Stockman obtained presidential approval instead for a proposed one-third cut in pension benefits for early retirees, effective from January 1, 1982. Outraged at not being consulted over such a controversial measure, Senate Republicans joined with the Democrats to reject it in a vote of 96–0 on May 20. With some justification, the CEA's William Niskanen later characterized this as "the major domestic policy mistake of the Reagan administration."[53]

Reagan was willing to try again in the fall, but Chief of Staff James Baker combined forces with GOP congressional leaders to persuade him that it was futile. With his options narrowing, Stockman played his last card at an Oval Office meeting on September 22. He now recommended that the administration defer the second and third installments of the ERTA personal tax cuts by one year and place Social Security reform in the hands of a bipartisan commission in return for congressional acceptance of further reductions in discretionary domestic spending. The proposal stood no chance of presidential approval. "Delay would be a total retreat," Reagan fumed. "We would be admitting that we were wrong."[54]

With no hope for a substantial offensive on the deficit, Stockman tried for smaller economies. However, the publication of an *Atlantic Monthly* article based on his indiscreet conversations with journalist William Greider irreparably weakened his authority. Its revelations that he had harbored doubts from the outset about his budget forecasts undermined his reputation for mastery of fiscal detail. Republican legislators became loath to support politically risky spending cuts advocated by a budget director who was now damaged goods.[55]

In Stockman's assessment, failure to take unpopular actions against the deficit was the triumph of politics over the Reagan Revolution. His bitter memoirs were especially damning in judgment of the president: "He was a consensus politician, not an ideologue. He had no business trying to make a revolution because it wasn't in his bones."[56] This assessment belied the reality that Reagan achieved most of what he had set out to do. It also manifested supreme misunderstanding of what the Reagan Revolution entailed in the eyes of its founder.

A full-bore ideologue, Stockman was willing to pay for tax cuts through a "substantial and politically painful shrinkage of the American welfare state . . . [that] would have hurt millions of people in the short run."[57] However, the rosy future that Reagan promised was supposed to be pain free for everyone except big-spending liberals, bureaucrats, and special interests. Moreover, he well understood that a frontal assault on entitlement programs with huge middle-class constituencies would have put his entire legacy at risk by making him in all likelihood a one-term president. Milton Friedman once remarked of him, "You want a principled man, which Reagan is. But he is not rigidly principled, which you don't want." In practice, Reagan was willing to settle for the half-loaf of slowing down the growth of domestic spending. "A compromise," he later remarked, "is never to anyone's liking—it's just the best you can get and contains enough of what you want to justify what you give up."[58]

Frustrated in his hope of radical governance, the OMB director was willing to balance the budget by modifying the elements of the Reagan project that were most important to the president. Proposing to delay the second and third installments of ERTA's personal tax cuts indicated that the economic benefits of one-step top-band tax reduction and the business tax cuts had paramount importance for Stockman. As he notoriously admitted to William Greider, "Kemp-Roth was always a Trojan horse to bring down the top rate. . . . The supply-side formula was the only way to get a tax policy that was really trickle down."[59] For Reagan, by contrast, across-the-board tax cuts were fundamental to his vision of individual freedom and constrained government. Stockman's belief that the defense expansion could be scaled down without ill effect for the rebuilding of American power was also at variance with the president's conviction that the dollar size of the budget was critical to persuading the Soviets of their inferiority in the arms race.

DÉTENTE WITH THE DEFICIT

As the reality of huge deficits became evident, Reagan increasingly signaled his toleration of them. This pragmatism should not have been the surprise that many found it to be. As Senate Majority Leader Howard Baker (R-TN) later observed, "The president is easy to predict. . . . He's extraordinarily analytical to test options against his philosophy."[60] In Reagan's original schema, balanced budgets were the corollary product of his agenda of tax cuts, defense expansion, and smaller government. He had now achieved two of these ends and made some progress toward the third despite the growth of the deficit. It therefore made no sense to sacrifice his core objectives on tax and defense for the sake of something no longer essential to restoration of founding principles.

Taken aback by Reagan's volte-face, many Democrats saw it as proof that he had deliberately created the fiscal crisis to de-fund the welfare state. Senator Daniel Patrick Moynihan (D-NY) started out believing that the president had mistakenly gambled on ERTA-induced deficits forcing congressional acceptance of domestic retrenchment to eliminate them. He ended up convinced that Reagan's toleration of them was based on a Machiavellian realization that they were "doing the job that had been expected from the tax cuts."[61] Other Democrats shared this suspicion about their adversary's political strategy. In James Wright's assessment, Reagan believed that "the most important thing to do is starve the government so that we can shrink it and that we will never shrink it unless we can starve it." Reflecting on the huge fiscal gap in the promised zero-deficit year of 1984, Senator Ernest Hollings (D-SC) complained, "[Reagan] knows what he's doing. He's not amnesiac. He's intentional. He not only cuts the programs but he likes the fact that deficits will keep us Democrats from ever even discussing new programs."[62]

"Starve-the-beast" theories about Reagan's deficits are not persuasive. True, he reversed Republican orthodoxy that tax reduction should await a balanced budget in the belief that it would compel the congressional Democrats and Republican moderates to swallow domestic retrenchment in preference to operating large deficits. Replicating his Proposition 1 rhetoric, Reagan declared in his first address to the nation as president, "There were always those who told us that taxes couldn't be cut until spending was reduced. Well, you know we can lecture our children about extravagance until we run out of voice and breath. Or we can cut their extravagance simply by reducing their allowance."[63] These words did not signify deliberate intent to plunge the budget deep into the red. Reagan wanted the threat rather than the reality of huge deficits to spur domestic retrenchment.

Given the president's theorizing on the ill effects of deficits in the 1970s and his sincere belief in the Laffer curve, the huge budget shortfalls constituted an unwelcome surprise for him rather than an instrument of policy. Until the fiscal results of economic recovery proved him wrong, he believed that the imbalances would disappear once his economic program had a chance to work. According to Martin Feldstein, Reagan's second CEA chair, he continued to hope in the face of increasingly grim budgetary projections that higher growth "would come to his rescue." Despite falling out with the president over the need for tax increases to close the fiscal gap, this eminent Harvard economist was adamant that nobody in the White House "would advocate that [we] run deficits of this magnitude in order to frighten Congress into a more appropriate spending policy." In Richard Darman's similar assessment, the deficits may have restrained the growth of government into the 1990s, but "the notion that this was all a matter of conscious, conspiratorial design, back in 1981, gives too much credit (and blame) to the alleged conspirators."[64]

The all-too-predictable effect of huge deficits on the "swap and turnback" New Federalism initiative reinforced the case against their purposeful design. Unveiled in early 1982, this plan embodied Reagan's long-standing intent to reallocate federal programs to the states. It projected state assumption of full responsibility for AFDC, food stamps, and more than forty grant-in-aid programs in return for Washington doing the same for Medicaid. Transitional ten-year federal funding was supposed to enable states and localities to make "critical choices" in an orderly way about program maintenance and prioritization. Congressional Democrats charged that this was a backdoor ploy to solve the long-term deficit problem. State and local officials of both parties shared their concerns. In addition, mayors feared that governors would not pass on to them a fair share of the trust fund proceeds.[65]

Richard Williamson, the White House chief negotiator on the plan, put some of the blame for state-local resistance on Stockman's vain effort to cut revenue sharing as part of the fall offensive. The White House quickly rescinded his proposals but too late to provide reassurance of the benign fiscal intent of the New Federalism. In Williamson's opinion, these short-term penny-pinching initiatives "lost a chance for meaningful structural reforms that would have provided long-term budget savings."[66] Had the New Federalism plan come to fruition, grants-in-aid would have declined from their peak budget share of 17.4 percent in FY1978 to 3–4 percent by FY1992, the lowest level since 1933. Unable to negotiate administrative and financial terms with the National Governors Association, the White House abandoned it in April 1982. In the long term, however, the real losers were the states. Taking the deal would have spared them the escalating costs of Medicaid contributions that became a significant burden on their treasuries in the early twenty-first century.

An even more persuasive argument against the fiscal conspiracy theory is that the huge deficits put pressure on Reagan to retreat from his core agenda. Far from being an offensive strategy to curtail government spending, the president's toleration of huge imbalances was primarily a defensive response to demands that he should sacrifice his tax cuts and his defense expansion to restore budgetary solvency. As his 1982 diary entries show, he faced continuous pressure from many sources—his own advisers, Democrats, and congressional Republicans—to surrender his priorities. After a White House meeting with House Republican leaders on January 11, Reagan wrote, "Except for

Jack Kemp they are h—1 bent on new taxes and cutting the defense budget. Looks like a heavy year ahead." The entry for December 14, 1982, read, "Spent most of the afternoon in a dismal economic briefing about the deficits and the little chance we have of getting further budget cuts."[67]

Reagan could ride out pressure from aides, as he had done over the fall offensive, but he faced a more assertive Congress as his public approval rating sank alongside the economy. Tip O'Neill now reaped the benefit of being pounded in the battle over the FY1982 budget. Because the president got virtually everything he wanted, the Democrats could not be held responsible for the recession. If successful in impeding the White House plan, they would have encountered accusations that the tax cuts would have boosted the economy but for their obstructionism.

Moreover, the Social Security fiasco of May 1981 persuaded the Speaker that the "fairness" issue was the ultimate repellent to Reagan's assault on government. His adoption of "Save Social Security" as the House Democratic mantra ensured that Republican legislators had no stomach for Stockman's intended fall offensive against the program. Conceding that retrenchment was politically impossible, Reagan agreed in late 1981 to establish a bipartisan National Commission on Social Security Reform with a brief to recommend long-term solutions for program funding by the end of 1982. The Democrats consequently transferred the focus of their fairness critique to the recession. In response to the 1982 State of the Union address, they aired a prepackaged advert carrying the message that Reaganomics gave the rich tax breaks and deprived working people of their jobs. In like vein, O'Neill denounced the administration's FY1983 budget plan as a "Beverly Hills" budget that offered "billions in tax breaks for the wealthy, billions in handouts to the nation's corporations and billions for lavish new defense systems."[68]

Meanwhile, congressional Republicans were growing increasingly restive about the deficit. Despite Jack Kemp's proclamation that the GOP "no longer worships at the altar of the balanced budget," most of his colleagues still believed in the old-time religion. In the Senate, senior Republicans were in despair that their first opportunity to govern in thirty years was stained by fiscal red ink. They also feared that their majority would be short-lived if voters blamed the recession-causing high interest rates on the exploding deficit. Senate Leader Howard Baker had kept his troops remarkably united on budget votes in 1981 because of their shared belief that the new president's program should be given a chance, but he was less willing to go along with the White House once the fiscal consequences were plain. Finance Committee chair Bob Dole (R-KS) and Budget Committee chair Pete Domenici (R-NM) were also determined to do something about the deficit lest it became a political albatross around the GOP's neck.[69]

In many respects, Dole became as great a thorn as O'Neill in Reagan's side. A fiscal conservative with a prairie populist's compassion for the poor and suspicion of market forces, he drew the line against further cuts in safety-net programs. During the fall offensive negotiations, the Kansan told Reagan, "We've got a few more ideas that might fly but we've about tapped out the big dollars. Somebody is going to have to start taking a hit besides welfare recipients." His populist leanings put his fingerprints on the three tax increases that Reagan signed into law between 1982 and 1984. Though keen to preserve the ERTA cuts for ordinary taxpayers, Dole felt no compunction about closing loopholes that benefited corporations and the wealthy. This made him a traitorous pariah to younger conservatives like Representative Newt Gingrich (R-GA), who dubbed him the "tax collector for the welfare state." Dole hoped to advance his presidential ambitions by harmonizing Reaganomics with Republican balanced-budget orthodoxy, but this circle was impossible to square.[70]

The president's FY1983 budget manifested utter insensitivity to congressional concerns about fairness and fiscal responsibility. Projecting a deficit of $91.5 billion, this requested a real increase of 13 percent in defense outlays, amounting to $33.6 billion; social program cutbacks of $25.9 billion; and no overt tax increases. Its only nod to revenue enhancement were tax revisions that eliminated unintended benefits and obsolete incentives to yield $7.2 billion in FY1983 and $34.1 billion over three years. On his own admission, Stockman had "out-and-out cooked the books" to keep the deficit forecast beneath $100 billion by inventing $15 billion of utterly phony spending cuts and overestimating revenues by nearly 10 percent.[71]

The FY1983 plan initiated the practice of using unrealistic budgets as a tool of presidential power. Setting a pattern that would persist until Reagan's final year in office, it was declared "dead on arrival" on Capitol Hill. Despite White House appeals for party loyalty, a GOP congressional delegation informed the president on February 23 that his budget stood no chance of enactment. Nevertheless, the revenue and spending outcomes that resulted from the process of negotiating amendments to the budget were closer to what Reagan wanted than would have been the case had he submitted a realistic plan. As Allen Schick noted, the tactical advantages for the president came at the cost of transforming his budget from "an authoritative guide to national policy" into a "bargaining chip."[72]

With Congress intent on producing a different budget, Reagan could only influence its deliberations through negotiating with it. Budget talks held in April brought together administration officials, Senate Republican leaders, and House Democratic leaders. The Republican negotiators soon reached agreement on a three-year deficit reduction plan of $450 billion based on $3 of expenditure savings for every $1 of revenue enhancement. This provided for $115 billion in higher revenues, $66 billion savings from the defense expansion, $145 billion in domestic economies that included limiting Social Security COLAs, and $124 billion from management savings and lower debt interest payments on the declining deficit. Although the Democrats accepted the bulk of the package, they insisted on reversing the GOP targets for defense and domestic economies.[73] Reagan took the unusual step of going to Capitol Hill to negotiate in person with O'Neill but only succeeded in hardening the divide. According to James Wright, the meeting "broke apart on the rocks of philosophical agreement." Despite his confidence that the House Democrats could broker a deal with the Senate Republicans, the road to compromise was tortuous.[74]

Immediately after his unsuccessful meeting with O'Neill, Reagan informed the nation that he would press for a balanced-budget constitutional amendment. This initiative was irrelevant to the immediate deficit problem since it would not come into operation until the second fiscal year after state ratification, likely to be a lengthy process even if successful. It had no prospect of initial two-thirds approval by both houses of Congress anyway. Nevertheless, championing the amendment provided Reagan with a fig leaf of fiscal rectitude to cover the embarrassment of his record deficits.

Needing to act quickly, the administration appropriated an amendment proposal that the Senate Judiciary Committee had reported out in 1981 in spite of doubts that its terms were sufficiently flexible to allow fiscal adjustment to changing economic and international circumstances.[75] The president spoke in its support at a rally on the steps of the Capitol on July 19 and worked the telephones lobbying individual legislators for their support. This flurry of activity helped to win Senate approval of the amendment by 69 votes to 31 on August 4, two more than required. Its terms were modified by floor vote to include a freeze on the debt ceiling at time of ratification that could only be lifted by a three-fifths supermajority in both chambers. Republicans voted 47 to 7 in favor, with support from 22 Democrats (14 from southern and border states, 6 westerners, and 2 northerners). Presidential pressure also helped secure the discharge of the corresponding House bill from the Judiciary Committee. Democratic leaders brought it to the floor immediately to forestall further lobbying. The vote on October 1 produced a 236 to 187 plurality for the amendment rather than a supermajority. Among the ayes were 65 Democrats (all but 5 from southern and border states), but 20 Republicans, including Jack Kemp, were nays.[76]

Given his role in creating record deficits, Reagan's support for a balanced-budget amendment reeked of hypocrisy. As *Time* magazine commented acidly, it was akin to the nation's chief distiller coming out in favor of Prohibition. The Democrats' opposition was at least consistent with their long-standing determination to safeguard domestic programs that would likely bear the brunt of mandatory budget-balancing. However it made them vulnerable to Reagan's repeated charges that they had subverted a constitutional settlement of the deficit problem. This may have been smart politics, but it did not bring a balanced budget any closer. Nor did it help the ongoing grassroots campaign for a constitutional convention to propose a balanced-budget amendment. National Taxpayers Union (NTU) leader James Davidson complained that the president's intervention had actually hurt this cause by making it "too much of a Reagan issue when Reagan is less popular than the amendment."[77]

As the battle for constitutional reform moved toward its denouement, some of the combatants were also doing the hard, dirty, and seemingly interminable work of producing a FY1983 budget resolution. Long after the schedule for approving one had passed, the House and Senate adopted a reconciled version of their separate measures in late June. This promulgated three-year deficit reduction of $378.5 billion on an approximate spending cut-revenue increase ratio of 3:1. However, $154 billion of the expenditure savings were to come from lower interest payments and management economies that Congress had no power to guarantee and $73 billion from domestic economies that were notoriously difficult to achieve in practice.[78]

The Senate Finance Committee under Dole's leadership took the initiative for developing a tax bill to enhance revenues by $98 billion in accordance with this blueprint. This measure included technical code modifications, stricter compliance requirements, loophole closures, a 10 percent withholding provision on interest and dividend payments, and a doubling of the excise tax on cigarettes. To circumvent the constitutional requirement that revenue legislation should originate in the lower chamber, it received Senate approval on July 23 as an amendment to a minor House bill. O'Neill maneuvered to go straight to conference on the Senate amendments without House consideration of a tax hike of its own. Furious antitax Republicans vowed to oppose the bill that came back from conference. Just as the Speaker intended, this put the president in the position of having to persuade dissenters to accept the tax increase. O'Neill crowed, "I want to see him use his smiley countenance and that sweet-sounding voice and hard knuckles with his Republicans."[79]

Reagan had already arm-twisted wavering GOP senators into supporting the Dole bill. He needed to work harder to win votes in the House, where bipartisan conservative opposition to taxes was more stubborn. In addition to a telephone blitz, the president hosted White House meetings with prominent boll weevils, Republican skeptics, and GOP congressional leaders to urge support for the bill. His message to them emphasized that only 17 percent of revenue enhancement in the bill came from new taxes, some 80 percent came from plugging special interest loopholes and tougher compliance, and the resultant deficit reduction would assist economic recovery. Making the same pitch in a televised national address on August 16, Reagan also attempted to steal the fairness issue from the Democrats in claiming that the tax bill would have little effect on ordinary taxpayers but would raise revenue "from those who are not now paying their fair share." The White House, meanwhile, pursued a strategy of "divide, defuse and conquer" in recruiting business supporters of deficit-reduction to counter opposition from the Chamber of Commerce and tax lobbyists like Charls Walker.[80]

Even if this effort only turned a few votes, they all proved important to enactment of the Tax Equity and Fiscal Responsibility Act (TEFRA). The House narrowly approved its passage by 226 votes to 207. Opponents included antitax Republicans, liberal Democrats critical of entitlement cuts in the measure, and others in both parties who either objected to particular provisions like the cigarette excise or were nervous about approving the first election-year tax increase since 1932. The Democrats split down the middle with 120 for and 123 against, and the Republicans were nearly as divided, with 103 for and 87 against. In a tight Senate vote, TEFRA passed by 52 votes to 47, with support from nine Democrats led by Edward Kennedy nearly counterbalancing eleven Republican nays.[81]

According to a Treasury analysis, TEFRA's annual revenue enhancement was equivalent to 1 percent GDP, making it the largest peacetime tax increase in American history.[82] It was widely regarded as marking the end of Reagan's supply-side experiment. Representative Henry Reuss (D-WI) exulted, "Reaganomics . . . is no more. Supply-side economics has become un-Kempt." Fearing that this was the case, prominent supply-siders Paul Craig Roberts and Norman Ture had departed their Treasury posts in disillusion. Pragmatists in the White House staff celebrated the self-inflicted purge of these purists as effectively killing off supply-side influence in the administration. With Jack Kemp and William Roth on different sides in the TEFRA vote, even congressional supporters of this doctrine appeared in disarray.[83]

Both the celebrations and lamentations regarding Reagan's abandonment of supply-side economics were wide of the mark. So far as the president was concerned it had never been anything more than a convenient rationalization for his broader agenda. If its opponents saw TEFRA as a counterrevolution, he saw it as the means to preserve the fundamentals of what he had already achieved. Reagan had all along insisted that his support for the measure was conditional on preservation of the remaining installments of the ERTA tax cuts. As he noted in his diary on April 28, "The D's are playing games—they want me to rescind the 3d year of the tax cut—Not in a million years." Nevertheless, he was aware that political pressure to do so could become irresistible if revenues were not enhanced in other ways.[84]

Accordingly, TEFRA was hardly a bitter pill for Reagan. The tax breaks that it rescinded were not integral to his agenda. There was more than a grain of truth in his rationalization that TEFRA was a correction of code mistakes and tougher compliance requirements for existing taxes rather than a new tax. In this regard it was similar in principle to the tax revisions in his

FY1983 budget plan, even if the projected revenue yield was some three times greater. Indeed, Reagan's willingness to defend TEFRA as a necessary step toward a fairer tax system marked the genesis of his evolution from tax cutter to tax reformer that reached its culmination in his second term. His opposition on equity grounds to later congressional efforts to rescind TEFRA's withholding provision on interest and dividend income provided further evidence of this. In this instance, intense lobbying from banks and other financial institutions overcame the combined opposition of the White House, the House leadership, and the Senate leadership to produce large majorities in favor of repeal in July 1983.[85]

TEFRA's opponents charged that it would simply fuel higher spending rather than cut the deficit. "Quietly, without debate," a large group of House Republicans warned, "the Republican Party is in danger of making a U-turn back to its familiar role of tax collector for Democratic spending programs." In contrast, Reagan assumed that it was part of the $3 spending for $1 revenue deficit-reduction package incorporated in the congressional budget resolution. TEFRA, he told GOP critics, was the price that had to be paid for continuing the domestic retrenchment started in 1981. Far from agreeing to any deal, the majority of House Democrats had voted against the first budget resolution. White House aides did not disabuse the president of his mistaken notion lest he lose enthusiasm for the tax bill.[86]

In fact, Congress adhered quite closely in the FY1983 appropriations process to the aggregates for controllable spending set in the budget resolution but altered the spending priorities. By and large the preferences of the Republican Senate leaders prevailed over those of the president and the House Democratic leaders. Instead of being retrenched, domestic programs received small funding increases that were less generous than O'Neill wanted. In a last-minute addition to the budget, the administration itself promoted a countercyclical job-creating measure to improve transport infrastructure to be partially funded through a $3 billion gasoline tax increase. Conversely, defense was subject to larger economies than the president wanted but still received real increases of 7.7 percent for outlays and 9.1 percent for authorizations that locked in his military buildup.[87]

The mythical "$3 for $1" deal became fact in Reagan's justification of TEFRA in his postpresidential writings. In his memory the Democrats had tricked him into raising taxes and then reneged on the bargain. Ed Meese dubbed TEFRA the administration's "greatest domestic error," and Donald Regan leveled the same charge.[88] This judgment entirely overlooked the role played by Senate Republican leaders. The politics of the FY1983 budget signified their growing determination to reduce the deficit even if this meant seizing the initiative from the president. Reagan's later sense of betrayal also underplayed the reality that he gained far more than he lost from TEFRA.

Not only did it extinguish the threat to the outstanding ERTA tax cuts, but it also signaled to the Federal Reserve that the administration would not let the deficit grow indefinitely.

By mid-1982 the White House was fearful that the recession was putting its economic program and the president's reelection at risk. A year earlier Murray Weidenbaum had warned Reagan that real output could decline for one or two quarters if monetary restraint took hold before his tax cuts had a chance to boost the economy.[89] This assessment underestimated the severity of the recession that started in July 1981 and lasted for six quarters. Doubting the will of politicians to sustain a long-haul fight against inflation, Paul Volcker went for a drastic but painful cure. Four months into Reagan's presidency the Fed embarked without fanfare on an unprecedented monetary squeeze, tougher even than the one that blighted Carter's final year. M-1 money supply growth slowed to 5 percent in 1981, compared to 7.3 percent in 1980.[90]

Many Democratic legislators and a goodly number of Republicans charged that the monetary cure was too harsh, but Reagan was steadfast in support of Volcker. The Fed chair attributed this stance to the president's "strong visceral aversion to inflation."[91] In reality, Reagan had little alternative, just like Carter, but to back him. As an OMB economist counseled James Baker, "Scapegoating the Fed while we struggle with triple-digit deficits will do the administration a lot of harm." In his view, this would have no credibility with the average voter, who tended to blame inflation on the deficit rather than M-1. It was also likely to provoke Volcker into condemning the administration's fiscal program. Signaling this danger, the Fed chair testified to the Joint Economic Committee in January 1982 that Wall Street's anticipation of the economic consequences of huge deficits was a serious obstacle to recovery. Conservative economists Arthur Burns and Alan Greenspan sent Reagan the same message in private. The latter warned, "At root our problem is that the markets believe that the Federal deficit will continue to hemorrhage, inducing the Federal Reserve to create excessive money supply growth and hence inflation."[92]

Despite the administration's public support of Volcker, Donald Regan lobbied him in private to change course. The message the Treasury secretary carried back to the White House was that the Fed chair would ease money "if he could see some movement by us on the deficits." A disappointed president complained to a friend, "There's no real reason why interest rates shouldn't be coming down." If the money markets would "just show a little guts, we could speed up the recovery." There was further frustration when congressional approval of the first budget resolution did not produce an immediate drop in interest rates. Reagan confided to a supporter, "This is becoming an obsession with me, but I'll try not to picket a bank."[93]

To White House relief, the Federal Reserve eventually made the first in an incremental series of discount rate reductions on July 19, sparking an immediate rally on Wall Street. With money supply now back within the central bank's target ranges, Volcker thought that "we could ease credibly" without sparking fears of an inflationary surge. The Fed itself was increasingly anxious for economic recovery because American private banks were jittery about the security of large loans that the Mexican government was finding increasingly difficult to repay. Its eventual abandonment of monetary targets in October signaled the end of the monetarist experiment.[94]

There was no clear evidence that TEFRA was instrumental in the Fed's change of course, but Reagan was convinced that the two were directly linked.[95] Accordingly, he was concerned, as were most of his economic aides, that Volcker would again tread on the monetary brakes if the deficit continued to grow. This brought about his worst moment of uncertainty as to whether he could sustain his fiscal priorities. At the Budget Review Board on January 3, 2003, he was confronted with deficit projections in excess of $200 billion. A horrified Reagan reportedly exclaimed, "We can't live with out-year deficits. I don't care if we have to blow up the Capitol, we have to restore the economy. How can we come out with that string of figures without driving interest rates right back up? How can we put this out without creating a public panic?"[96]

Despite stock market buoyancy in the second half of 1982, unemployment remained stuck at a postwar high in excess of 10 percent into 1983. The White House took some comfort that GOP national losses in the midterms only ran to twenty-six seats in the House of Representatives, but it wanted a strong recovery in place well before the 1984 election. Signs of renewed business confidence evaporated once the new budget projections became common knowledge. On January 19, 1983, a group of 500 business, political, and academic leaders signed a public letter that the prospect of huge deficits for the remainder of the decade "are a primary cause of today's economic distress." Other business leaders, like Stock Exchange chair Arthur Leavitt, made the same point about the "expanding deficits of gargantuan proportions." Meanwhile, a New York Times/CBS poll found that 63 percent of respondents favored reducing the defense buildup to cut the deficit and 62 percent were willing to forgo the third installment of the tax cut scheduled for July.[97]

Hoping to calm these worries, Reagan used his State of the Union address to propose a four-point plan for deficit reduction. It entailed a domestic spending freeze in FY1984, unspecified entitlement cuts, $55 billion savings in defense over five years, and a standby tax placing a 1 percent surcharge on personal and corporate income and a $5 excise on a barrel of oil for up to three years. This hardly amounted to a dramatic reversal of policy.

Real defense outlays were still set to grow by 10 percent annually, and the standby taxes—which were contingent on enactment of the domestic spending economies—would not come into effect until FY1986, and then only if the projected deficit exceeded 2.5 percent of economic output. For Richard Darman, one of its authors, the plan's significance was not its content but its indication that Reagan now put deficit reduction atop his budgetary agenda. In reality, the president had experienced not a change of heart but a moment of doubt that economic recovery soon extinguished. In July 1983 he made it clear to CEA chair Martin Feldstein that he no longer regarded the standby tax as necessary.[98]

The recovery that started in February 1983 proved remarkably durable despite anxieties over budget deficits, trade deficits, the 1987 Wall Street crash, and the acceleration of America's transition from a manufacturing to an information-service economy. Its 92-month duration was more than twice the average length of previous post-1945 expansionary cycles and was exceeded only by the 106 months of uninterrupted growth from 1961 to 1969. From 1983 through 1988, annual economic growth averaged 4.2 percent, gross private investment increased in real terms by 58 percent, and the Standard and Poor index of 500 stocks went up almost 300 percent. Making allowance for two million jobs lost in the recession, aggregate civilian employment grew by 17 percent under Reagan from its 1980 base of 99 million. Meanwhile, consumer price inflation averaged only 3.5 percent a year for a combination of reasons. American corporations grew leaner and more efficient because of increased competition from abroad, a global oil-supply glut ensured lower energy costs, and the unprecedented numbers of new workers from the baby-boom generation who had entered the labor market in the 1970s were now more experienced and productive. Liking what it saw, the Federal Reserve kept its foot off the monetary brakes from the second half of 1982 to the first half of 1987 and allowed M-1 to grow by 8 percent on annual average over the course of the 1980s.[99]

Though conservative and liberal economists dispute the contribution of Reagan's tax program to this success, what was not in question was its failure to generate the increase in domestic saving that supply-siders had anticipated. Instead, the Reagan deficits of FY1983–FY1986 soaked up nearly three-quarters of U.S. private savings. The net national savings rate (private savings minus government borrowing) declined precipitously from an annual average of 7.7 percent GDP in the 1970s to 2.8 percent GDP in the 1980s. America consequently grew more dependent on inflows of foreign savings to maintain private investment. This need transformed it from being the world's largest creditor, with net foreign assets of $141 billion in 1981, to being its largest debtor, with net liabilities of $111 billion in 1985.[100]

To attract overseas capital, the Federal Reserve kept interest rates 2 percent higher on average in the mid-1980s than those of Western Europe and Japan.[101] The result was a growing trade deficit because the overvalued dollar produced by high real interest rates undermined the competitiveness of American exports and made imports cheaper. Meanwhile, other nations complained that America's absorption of foreign capital threatened their economic growth. At the Williamsburg economic summit of May 1983, leaders from Canada, Great Britain, and West Germany charged that the U.S. deficits were distorting global economic development.[102]

Arthur Burns, now ambassador to West Germany, sent Reagan a compilation of European criticisms of U.S. interest rates in an effort to persuade him to act against the deficit, but to no avail. "While I deplore the deficits and am determined to get them down," Reagan responded, "I can't accept their view that deficits are the cause of high interest rates." He noted that U.S. interest rates had fallen as the deficit had risen. It was evident from these remarks that unbalanced budgets had become economically tolerable to Reagan. He remained opposed to deficits from a Jeffersonian perspective of constraining government but was prepared to bide his time to make further progress on this front. As he told Burns, "I am convinced our problem is government spending as a percentage of our national earnings and we must cut spending further than we have so far."[103]

A conservative economist closer to home also failed to persuade Reagan that deficits posed an economic threat. In Martin Feldstein's view it was essential to close the fiscal gap in order to preserve business confidence and prevent another recession. In early 1984 he advocated timely enactment of the standby tax in readiness for FY1986, a proposal that had David Stockman's strong support. In response, Reagan lectured his two aides that no previous tax hike in U.S. history had actually raised revenue. Feldstein's demonstration that "*every* increase in tax rates [from 1917 to 1969] was followed by a rise in tax revenue" could not shake the president's conviction that he was "wrong as h—l."[104] The CEA chair's regular entreaties concerning the imperative of deficit reduction, even at cost of tax increases and defense cuts, lost him all influence in the White House. Unless something was done to repair the budget, he warned Reagan in exasperation, "you will be accused of accepting the inevitability of large deficits and of believing that they do not hurt the economy."[105]

REAGAN DEFICITS VERSUS REAGANOMICS: THE 1984 PRESIDENTIAL ELECTION

The Democrats tried to turn the 1984 presidential election into a referendum on the Reagan deficits. Their standard-bearer, Walter Mondale, advocated deficit-reducing tax increases as the centerpiece of his campaign. Reagan, in contrast, focused attention on the renewal of prosperity under the aegis of his tax program. His landslide victory effectively ensured that personal tax increases remained off the agenda of deficit reduction for the remainder of his presidency.

Mondale's campaign embodied the orthodox view of the financial community, mainline economists, and editorial writers that the deficit would eventually damage the economy. As political scientist Richard Neustadt pointed out, most presidents would have felt some sense of guilt about defying the "conventional wisdom of the day," but the Democrat had the misfortune to run up against one who did not.[106] Even allowing for this, Mondale's choice of banner issue was ill advised for two reasons. First, his message that Reagan's deficits had put America on the road to ruin negated his party's historic logic that an activist state was a public good in favor of defining government's main task as being to get its finances in order. Moreover, he sadly misjudged the public's concern about deficits amid renewed prosperity.

The champion of traditional Democratic socioeconomic activism as Jimmy Carter's vice president, Mondale had come to see Keynesian liberalism as politically bankrupt and economically outdated in the face of stagflation. Addressing a Democratic strategy group in early 1982, he contended, "In 1980 we lost the middle class. They thought we cared only about the very poor. We have to emphasize the importance of federal efforts to serve the middle class."[107] Nevertheless, deficit reduction was hardly suited for this purpose unless it could be integrated into a positive vision of change. The congressional Democrats had enjoyed their greatest success against Reagan when framing their critique of his fiscal program in terms of fairness, but Mondale failed to copy their example.

Reagan was not as vulnerable as in 1982 to charges that Social Security was not safe in his hands. The bipartisan commission delegated to find solutions for program solvency had become hopelessly deadlocked as its reporting deadline neared. Fearing that the president would incur blame for the imminent depletion of the pension trust fund, administration officials held secret meetings with commission members and negotiators representing Tip O'Neill to produce agreement on a way forward. As finally enacted in March 1983, the Social Security amendments included payroll tax adjustments that raised additional program revenues of $108 billion from 1983 to 1989. Deferment of COLAs yielded a further $40 billion, and a one-off credit to the trust fund for uncashed Social Security checks produced $18 billion. Together with the gradual raising of the retirement age from 65 to 67 by 2027, these amendments ensured the solvency of Social Security into the next century. As two analysts noted, the administration had accepted revenue enhancement because "it felt under great pressure to satisfy public expectations of system conservation—or pay the consequences in a partisan war that it was losing."[108]

Nonetheless, the fairness issue still had legs. Demonstrating this, Republican Senate leaders acquiesced to Tip O'Neill's demands that spending cuts agreed upon as part of the Deficit Reduction Act (DEFRA) of 1984 should come from reductions in Medicare doctor fees rather than programs benefiting the poor. The willingness of Congress to risk the wrath of the medical lobby in an election year signaled that the Reagan Revolution against welfare had ground to a halt. DEFRA also generated $50 billion in new revenues over three years through tax loophole closures and excise tax increases.

The expenditure cuts were sufficient to appease business groups that had signified willingness to take a tax hit in the interests of deficit reduction provided there was no TEFRA-style avoidance of corollary domestic savings. Stockman also endorsed DEFRA on grounds that it manifested bipartisan consensus for putting federal finances in order. Although Reagan protested that the expenditure economies were inadequate, he signed the bill rather than hand the Democrats campaign ammunition that he had obstructed deficit control. Combined revenue enhancement from TEFRA and DEFRA equaled 31 percent of revenue loss from ERTA in FY1984–FY1988. Mondale could have built on the progressive tax principles embodied in these measures to campaign not as a tax hiker but as a champion of tax equity. Indeed, some White House aides anticipated that he would run, in Richard Darman's words, on a "soak-the-rich-end-the-unfair-loopholes-and-hit-the-big-corporations plan."[109]

The Mondale campaign also reflected the disjunction between elite obsession and the public's elasticity regarding deficit reduction. In 1982 and for most of 1983, ordinary Americans associated the deficit with high interest rates and recession. As late as August 1983, a survey by White House pollster Richard Wirthlin found that 47 percent of respondents thought that large deficits affected the economy "a great deal," and 32 percent thought they did "somewhat." Over three-quarters of respondents thought that controlling federal deficits was an important presidential responsibility, and only one-third approved Reagan's performance on this score. As confidence in the recovery grew, however, popular concern about the deficit receded. In January 1984 a *New York Times*/CBS poll found that 72 percent of respondents were unwilling to pay higher taxes for the sake of deficit reduction.[110]

Private polls conducted on behalf of both presidential candidates confirmed the decline in public concern about the deficit.[111] Despite this, Mondale charged ahead to ring the alarm bells of future national emergency as justification for his stand on taxes. In his nomination acceptance speech, he warned, "Here's the truth about the future: We are living on borrowed time. These deficits hike interest rates, clobber exports, stunt investment, kill jobs, undermine growth, cheat our kids and shrink our future." The Democrat vowed to cut the deficit by two-thirds within four years by putting up taxes, something he claimed his opponent would also do if reelected. "Mr. Reagan will raise taxes," he declared, "and so will I. He won't tell you. I just did."[112]

Presidential aides debated whether to issue a categorical rebuttal of this charge or a more cautious statement that safeguarded second-term flexibility for a "big fix" to the deficit problem. James Baker eventually cast his decisive influence in favor of drawing a clear contrast between Reagan and Mondale. On August 12 the president duly announced, "I have no plans to raise taxes nor will I allow any plan for a tax increase." The White House also worked behind the scenes to help conservative forces marshaled by Newt Gingrich win their fight against Bob Dole's allies for inclusion of an ironclad pledge against tax increases in the Republican platform.[113]

Reagan strategists hoped to demonstrate that the deficit would have been bigger if the Carter-Mondale ticket had won reelection in 1980. This idea went down in flames when an impartial projection showed that the fiscal gap in a hypothetical Carter second term would have peaked in FY1983 and narrowed to $39 billion in FY1987, by when it was forecast to reach $248 billion under Reagan. Instead the advice to the president was to exploit the discrepancy between Mondale's tax-increase formula and poll findings that consistently showed public opinion running at over 80 percent in favor of spending cuts as the preferred method of deficit reduction. Taking this line of attack against the Democrats in his nomination acceptance address, Reagan declared, "They've spent most of their political careers creating deficits. . . . Now, however, they call for an end to deficits, calling them ours, yet at the same time the leadership of their party resists our every effort to bring Federal spending under control." He twisted the knife further in highlighting the inconsistency between Democratic insistence that the deficit posed an economic threat and refusal to support a balanced-budget constitutional amendment.[114]

When Mondale released the specifics of his tax program, he only dug a deeper grave for his antideficit campaign. The plan required tax hikes for middle-income families earning between $25,000 and $45,000 a year as well as more affluent ones to achieve the promised two-thirds reduction in the deficit. The projected transfer of $30 billion from defense and agriculture to fund social programs that served low-income Americans added grist to GOP charges that the Democrats were not interested in expenditure economies to solve the budget problem.[115] Mondale's insistence that his opponent would raise taxes even higher on ordinary families rather than hit the rich fell on increasingly deaf ears. It asked middle-income voters to trade the certainty of paying more taxes if the Democrat became president for the possibility that Reagan would renege on his repeated assertions that he would never raise personal taxes.

With attention focused on Mondale's tax increases, Reagan could turn the election into a referendum on the promise of his economic program.[116] He defined the contest as a choice between growth based on the founding values of freedom and opportunity and stagnation resulting from Mondale's agenda. In this scenario the 1981 tax cuts were not the source of future-threatening deficits but the agency that enabled ordinary people to restore America's economic strength. "All we did," Reagan declared, "was get government out of your way." Contrasting this approach with his opponent's call for higher taxes, he asked, "What has happened to the Democratic party's concern for protecting the earnings of working people and promoting economic growth?"[117]

SECOND-TERM PHONY WAR ON THE DEFICIT

Reagan's landslide reelection victory signified popular affirmation for his tax program. In the president's estimate, it also gave him a mandate for a renewed assault on domestic spending that he considered the root of the deficit problem. This illusion was dispelled within days of his second inauguration. Reagan's FY1986 budget calling for a 6 percent real increase in defense and large multiyear domestic cuts elicited widespread criticism on Capitol Hill. The Congressional Budget Office also disputed the administration's forecast that the deficit would be brought down to $100 billion within five years under its proposal as another hopelessly rosy scenario that was $86 billion off target. The budget plan therefore went the way of its predecessors in being declared "dead on arrival" in Congress.[118] Unable to promote the deficit reduction program he wanted, Reagan fell back on protecting his fiscal priorities against efforts by other political actors to resolve the budget problem. Despite continuing to denounce the deficit as the agency of big government, he only engaged in a phony war against it during his second term.

New Senate leader Bob Dole stepped into the breach of antideficit leadership. Planning to run for president in 1988, he looked to prove his credentials for national office by resolving hitherto intractable budget problems. The Kansan also considered the deficit a fundamental threat to the national interest. In early 1984 he had warned that the nation faced a "black hole" of permanently huge deficits if rosy White House predictions of revenue-enhancing economic growth proved false. In this nightmare scenario, the United States was heading toward a new era of stagflation wherein it had to chose between massive deficits that bred inflation or massive deficit reduction, whose deflationary effect would pitch the economy into prolonged recession.[119]

Dole and his main ally, Senate Budget Committee chair Pete Domenici, joined forces with David Stockman, who was resolved on a final effort to sort out the budget mess that he had helped to create. All three knew that Reagan would veto the kind of substantive tax increase that they considered essential for meaningful deficit reduction. Accordingly they hit on a strategy of getting the Senate to enact a large package of spending cuts that spared neither entitlements nor defense. It was their assumption that the House Democrats would counter with a package that included personal tax increases, which could then be worked into a compromise settlement consisting of spending economies and revenue enhancement. In the endplay of their game plan, the president would have no option but to give some ground on taxes in order to prevent the burden of deficit reduction weighing more heavily on defense.[120]

Winning Senate approval for an economy package was itself a tall order. It required every Republican vote, but many GOP senators had cause to be wary of cutting domestic programs. In 1986, twenty-two of them—including the freshmen from the 1980 cohort—would be up for reelection. In the end, anxiety about the long-term effects of deficits prevailed. After months of negotiations, Dole and Domenici narrowly won Senate approval on May 10 of a FY1986 budget resolution that contained $56 billion of expenditure cuts. All but four Republicans—Alfonse D'Amato (New York), Paula Hawkins (Florida), Charles Mathias (Maryland), and Arlen Specter (Pennsylvania)—voted in favor, and every Democrat but Edward Zorinski (Nebraska) voted against. This produced a 49–49 tie that was broken by Vice President George Bush's casting vote.

The resolution projected a much more substantial retrenchment than the OBRA cutbacks of 1981. It froze defense at the inflation-adjusted FY1985 level, reduced many domestic programs (the need to corral Republican votes derailed plans for wholesale elimination of thirteen), and imposed a one-year freeze on Social Security and other federal pension COLAs. Entitlement retrenchment was hugely significant not only for the $30 billion savings it delivered but also for the leverage it provided for economies elsewhere. As Domenici aide Steve Bell observed, "Symbolically, it was the most important thing because it was supposedly untouchable. . . . Crack that, and you crack the budget problem." With further out-year savings on defense and domestic spending and reduced interest payments, the Senate budget resolution anticipated total three-year economies on the order of $295 billion, enough to reduce the projected deficit from $171 billion in FY1986 to $104 billion in FY1988.[121]

However, the Dole-Domenici-Stockman strategy had miscast the House Democrats in the role of tax-hikers. In light of Walter Mondale's crushing defeat, Tip O'Neill was determined to make the Republicans take the initiative on this score. Freed from having to accept the Senate's COLA freeze as the price for raising taxes, he also insisted that the Democrats would not accept any retrenchment of entitlements. Accordingly, the House budget resolution matched the Senate's deficit reduction target but relied on questionable assumptions about reduced interest payments and efficiency savings to do so.

The main burden of real retrenchment fell on defense, which was subject to a freeze without adjustment for inflation.[122]

The conference to reconcile the different budget resolutions endured weeks of deadlock. Dole and Domenici ultimately looked to resolve the impasse by putting tax increases on the negotiating table, but the White House got wind of their scheme. Although prepared to accept the Senate defense freeze as the lesser evil, Reagan drew the line against any concession on taxes. To preempt his Senate lieutenants breaking ranks, he warned in a radio address on June 22, "I'll repeat it until I'm blue in the face: I will veto any tax increase the Congress sends me."[123]

Reagan eventually met with congressional leaders on the evening of July 9 to discuss the budget impasse over cocktails on the patio adjoining the Oval Office. After an angry exchange over tax increases, the president and the Speaker huddled together to make peace under a nearby oak tree. There they struck a deal to safeguard their respective priorities. As a bargaining chip, O'Neill raised the possibility of a 1968-style income tax surcharge to pay for higher defense, but he ended up promising no tax increase and agreeing to the Senate's defense figure in return for Reagan accepting full COLA adjustments.[124] Taken completely by surprise at this development, Dole complained, "There was an agreement under an oak tree and it was Dole's limb they sawed off." Republican senators up for reelection in 1986 felt betrayed that their risky support for the COLA freeze had been for naught. Many would face a Democratic advertising blitz reminding seniors of their transgression. Senator Warren Rudman (R-NH) expostulated, "People feel they flew a kamikaze mission and ended up in flames and got nothing for it."[125]

Reagan had seemingly dashed the last hope of significant deficit reduction in his presidency. This was the final straw for David Stockman, who announced his resignation on July 10. In his view there was not "a rational possibility left of dealing with the irrationality that had descended on the nation." The FY1986 budget resolution eventually approved by the House and Senate grandiosely promised to halve the deficit by FY1988, but the economies it proposed fell well short of doing so.[126] The projected defense freeze melted away because prior authorization continued to drive expenditure upward. However, military authorizations were reduced for the first time in the Reagan era in FY1986, which slowed down real outlay expansion to 1.7 percent in FY1987 and 1.5 percent in FY1988.[127]

The FY1986 budget battle once more underlined Reagan's unwillingness to sacrifice any part of his core agenda to pursue a goal no longer integral to it. As Rudman charged, the president had not shown leadership on deficit reduction because it "does not rank very high" in his priorities. Media pundits considered O'Neill the big winner in the budget skirmish, but Reagan could take at least equal satisfaction from the outcome. To protect pension COLAs, the Speaker had effectively endorsed the president's tax cuts and softened the House's defense freeze. This was hardly a costly bargain for Reagan because he no longer had designs on Social Security.[128]

Disillusion with the budget settlement was directly responsible for enactment of the Balanced Budget and Emergency Deficit Reduction Act of 1985, better known as Gramm-Rudman-Hollings (GRH) after its senatorial authors, Phil Gramm (R-TX), Warren Rudman, and Ernest Hollings. It mandated deficit reduction of $11.7 billion in FY1986 and then annual installments of $36 billion to achieve a balanced budget in FY1991 on penalty of sequestration of funds if the deficit was $10 billion over target in the out years. Described by Rudman as a "bad idea whose time had come," GRH embodied the belief that the deficit was the product of a flawed budget process that could be repaired by instituting automatic fiscal discipline. In reality, the huge fiscal imbalances stemmed from political, programmatic, and economic factors that GRH did not address.[129]

A cheap vote for fiscal prudence in advance of the midterm elections, GRH deferred tough choices and enhanced programmatic protection. Concessions made to win its enactment put some three-fifths of spending off-limits to sequestration. The Senate excluded Social Security, and the House secured the additional exemption of eight antipoverty programs and limitations on health-care retrenchment. If sequestration became necessary, the savings were to come equally from defense and discretionary domestic programs. However, the only time that Congress met the GRH schedule of deficit reduction was when reaching the modest FY1986 target. Far from improving fiscal procedure, the new system made matters worse. It encouraged not only excessively optimistic revenue forecasts to avoid sequestration but also delay in approving a budget because sequesters could not be required once the fiscal year had started on October 1.

GRH also suffered from lack of presidential support. Later deficit-reduction measures benefited from strong White House involvement in their negotiation and promotion. Reagan played virtually no part in the formulation of GRH, which was fundamentally a congressional initiative from conception to enactment. Rudman commented of his belated endorsement, "The president was Ronnie-come-lately as far as we were concerned—we'd won this victory on our own." In fact, some legislators feared that Reagan would veto GRH to protect defense spending after the Pentagon dubbed it "a message of comfort to the Soviets."[130]

Whatever Reagan's doubts about GRH, a veto was implausible. First and foremost, it would have compromised the president's rhetorical insistence that excessive spending was the source of deficits. White House aides also feared that Congress would retaliate by sidelining the administration's tax reform initiative. Furthermore, a veto ran the risk of precipitating a government shutdown because GRH was enacted as an amendment to an extension of the public debt ceiling.[131] Last but not least, it would have roiled America's G-5 partners as well as the money markets. In September 1985 new Treasury secretary James Baker and Fed chair Paul Volcker had negotiated the Plaza Accord with counterparts from France, Japan, the United Kingdom, and West Germany to bring about a fall in the dollar's value. Their intervention was intended to reduce the trade gap that had energized protectionist sentiment in Congress. As part of the agreement the United States undertook to control its fiscal deficit in order that real interest rates could also come down. Rejection of GRH would have sent out the wrong signals about the Reagan administration's commitment to do so.[132]

The president's signature on GRH did not signify intent to engage constructively in its implementation. Reagan vowed that he would neither sacrifice defense nor sign a tax increase to keep to the deficit-reduction schedule. The only proper way to do so, he declared, was "by seeing to it that government fulfills its few and legitimate functions more efficiently at the same time as we eliminate waste."[133] To safeguard his priorities, the administration joined in efforts to weaken GRH's enforcement mechanism. In a suit brought by Representative Mike Synar (D-OK) and supported by the Justice Department, a federal court ruled against the legality of the sequestration process on February 7, 1986. Five months later the Supreme Court upheld its judgment that powers allocated to the General Accounting Office comptroller to formulate and promulgate sequesters were executive responsibilities that could not be exercised by an officer removable by Congress. GRH's default option required the congressional Joint Economic Committee to approve sequestration and both chambers to pass it, but there was no penalty for noncompliance. Thus, the administration and the Democrats, now in control of both houses of Congress after the midterm elections, could indulge in prolonged bickering over the FY1988 budget.

Each side defended a budget projection that promised to keep within the GRH deficit target of $108 billion but only through unrealistic revenue forecasts and accounting gimmicks. As one analyst observed, the president and the legislature "became equal competitors for the title of 'artful dodger'" in the game of fiscal legerdemain.[134] Nevertheless, there was a kernel of real disagreement underneath the soft outer layers of their respective fantasies. The Democrats wanted to force a small revenue enhancement of $19 billion on Reagan as a way of mitigating the full scale of domestic economies otherwise needed to stay within GRH limits. The resulting stalemate was particularly frustrating to Jim Wright, newly installed as Speaker following Tip O'Neill's retirement. "This is a really terrible situation," he lamented. "It creates a petty mindedness and a mean spiritedness, scraping and fighting over the little bones that are there for distribution to the domestic programs."[135]

House Democratic leaders consequently came to see a GRH "fix" as the only way to avoid a painful sequestration. Senate Republican leaders reached the same conclusion out of concern that Reagan would pursue a "high-noon" strategy of vetoing appropriations bills to force sequestration on domestic spending.[136]

In September Congress attached a rider to yet another debt ceiling extension in the form of the Emergency Deficit Control Reaffirmation Act of 1987 that modified the GRH deficit targets to $144 billion in FY1988 and $136 billion in FY1989 (originally $108 billion and $72 billion). Thereafter, the original $36 billion annual reductions were restored to schedule a balanced budget by FY1993. With the $10 billion cushion still in place, this adjustment obviated need for further deficit reduction in Reagan's last two budgets because the imbalance was already down to $149.7 billion in FY1987. As a bonus to the partners in fiscal illusion, the measure also raised the debt ceiling from $2.1 trillion to $2.8 trillion, more than enough to keep the government going until after the 1988 elections. Reagan lambasted the bill as a threat to strong defense and low taxes instead of domestic extravagance but still signed it. According to budget expert Allen Schick, the GRH fix gave politicians—the president no less than legislators—"the best of both worlds—the appearance of doing something about the deficit and the reality of not having to do very much."[137]

Nevertheless, GRH's shortcomings did not make it a historical irrelevance. It can be seen as "the first, and perhaps necessarily painful, stage in the development of American macrobudgeting rules that eventually helped the government to balance the national budget." Its automatic procedure of deficit reduction was an unprecedented budget reform that tried to break the political stalemate preventing achievement of a goal widely agreed to be in the national interest. Politicians did effect real savings under its terms— as much as $59 billion in FY1989 according to one scholarly estimate—but deficit targets were never met because of rising entitlement costs and the sensitivity of receipts to economic circumstances. Realization that GRH's goals were unattainable encouraged increasingly creative efforts to evade its sanctions on the part of both the White House and Congress. In essence, the experiment in automatic deficit reduction ended in failure because it looked to punish politicians for falling short of deficit targets regardless of whether their policies were responsible for the deficit. The main lesson to be drawn from GRH was that procedural reform to promote deficit reduction had to set politically realistic and achievable goals.[138]

Significantly, Reagan's greatest second-term fiscal achievement had nothing to do with deficit reduction, but the deficit still shaped its terms. On James Baker's advice, he had announced in his 1984 State of the Union address that the Treasury would study tax reform and report back to him in December.

This was to neutralize the danger that the Democrats would make tax reform the centerpiece of their presidential campaign. When released in early 1985, the report received an enthusiastic reception from the press and think tanks of all hues. At this juncture, Baker and Richard Darman took over as Treasury secretary and deputy secretary, and Donald Regan became White House chief of staff. The three combined forces to persuade Reagan to make tax reform the principal domestic initiative of his second term. They also won presidential agreement that any bill had to be revenue-neutral not only to prevent opponents from using the deficit as an excuse to reject it but also to preempt the kind of congressional bidding war that had distorted ERTA.[139]

Reagan announced his tax plan for "fairness, growth and simplicity" in a nationally televised address on May 26, 1985, and barnstormed the country in its support. Having played almost no part in its formulation, he proved its most important salesman. The president framed the choice facing Congress as one of enhancing tax equity or protecting unfair tax breaks. This appropriation of liberal symbolism made it difficult for Democrats to oppose him and placed Republican objectors in the uncomfortable position of defending special interests. Even so, it took a year and a half of legislative maneuvering, with several near defeats on the way, to secure the enactment of the Tax Reform Act (TRA) of 1986.[140]

This measure was the most thoroughgoing reform of the tax system since World War II. It embodied principles of horizontal equity in providing uniform treatment to broad categories of taxpayers (in contrast to the vertical equity of progressive taxation) and of economic efficiency in lowering tax rates in exchange for a broader base. TRA simplified the personal tax code from fourteen brackets to two—28 percent for top earners and 15 percent for everyone else. It increased personal exemptions and standard deductions, thereby removing six million poorer Americans from the rolls, and expanded the earned income tax credit that benefited low-income taxpayers. Conversely, top income earners faced an increase in capital gains tax from 20 to 28 percent. TRA also eliminated or reduced seventy-two tax expenditures—mainly benefiting business and investors—but it cut the top corporate tax rate from 48 percent to 34 percent in compensation. The effect was that 60 percent of taxpayers paid slightly lower taxes, 25 percent effectively paid the same as before, and the remaining 15 percent experienced a small tax increase.

For the first time since World War II, two analysts noted, "a major piece of tax legislation picked not only winners but losers." The losers were individuals, corporations, and industries whose loss of preferences was greater than their gains from rate reductions. The net increase of $120 billion in their tax payments over the next five years funded the cuts in personal income taxes. Nevertheless, TRA contradicted the supply-side ethos of using the tax system to enhance incentives for new investment. Among other things, it eliminated the investment tax credit promoted by the Kennedy administration and reduced depreciation allowances for new assets. According to one estimate, TRA's increase in tax payments on income from new investment actually amounted to $190 billion to offset its $70 billion cut in taxes on income from business capital already in place.[141]

Bipartisan enactment of TRA begged the question why political leaders could not also work together to eradicate the deficit problem. As Joseph White and Aaron Wildavsky have persuasively argued, the answer lay in their calculations of the political benefits to be gained from each.[142] GRH did not work in practice because it did not give the partisan adversaries in budget politics anything positive. Their stake in it was entirely negative—they saw it not as helping their cause but as hurting that of their opponents. However, all involved in this minus-sum game ended up feeling like losers because there was not much that could be done to reduce the deficit without cost to their own priorities. Their response was to look for ways to circumvent the constraints of GRH to protect these. In contrast, tax reform was a positive-sum game that produced gains for the president and the congressional Democrats.

Reagan envisioned a larger benefit from tax reform that justified the loss it imposed on a segment of his constituency. This was "a tax system that better fit his ideology, one that would be much harder to modify than the one he inherited."[143] TRA draped the flag of fairness around lower rates on personal income tax at the price of wiping out the remaining tax preferences that could feasibly be removed. This not only made it more difficult to increase personal tax rates in the future but also eliminated the main source relied on for revenue enhancement in the recent past. In other words, TRA appeared to put the onus for future action against the deficit onto the spending side of the budget. Meanwhile, Democrats saw tax reform as a way to make the rich pay more in taxes. In contrast to Reagan, they also calculated that the resultant broadening of the tax base meant that more revenues could be raised from smaller rate increases, which would make it politically easier to raise taxes in the future.

FINAL SKIRMISHES

Ronald Reagan's presidency ended with a breakthrough in negotiations with the Soviet Union that signaled the winding down of the Cold War. It did not achieve similar success in the case of the other red peril. In December 1987, Reagan and new Soviet leader Mikhail Gorbachev met in Washington—the third in their series of four summits—to sign the Intermediate Nuclear

Forces Treaty, the first agreement of the Cold War era to eliminate rather than merely limit an entire class of nuclear missiles. Some weeks earlier, another Washington summit—the first between the Reagan administration and bipartisan leaders of the Democratic-led Congress—produced a far less satisfactory resolution of the impasse over the FY1988 budget after month-long negotiations. Although the president was not a participant, it was clear from the outset that his preferences constrained the scope of any deal that could be struck. The contrast with the Cold War negotiations was stark. Reagan was more willing to trust Gorbachev's desire for peace than he was to engage with the Democrats in a meaningful effort to reduce the deficit.

The budget negotiations were precipitated by the stock market crash of October 19 that produced a 22.6 percent fall (508 points) in the Dow Jones industrial average, a then unprecedented single-day decline. Overvalued stock prices, the volatility of foreign asset holders, the breakdown of international efforts to achieve economic policy coordination, and the dollar's declining value were among the factors that precipitated the collapse. Concern about the effect of the budget deficit on the economy was also part of the mix. Reflecting this, the financial media demanded the speedy restoration of fiscal responsibility to boost national saving and cut the trade deficit by reducing domestic consumption. As the *Economist* editorialized, "Either the budget deficit is slashed, or interest rates will have to rise a lot; the second path leads to recession, the first could just avoid it."[144]

The White House and the Democrats were currently locked in yet another budget deadlock. Not a single appropriations bill had been enacted in time for the commencement of FY1988. The stock market crash brought the two sides to the negotiating table, but its rapid recovery eased the pressure to make painful concessions. The Federal Reserve cut interest rates to soothe worries about recession, and heavy purchase of dollars by foreign central banks signaled their determination to put a floor under the U.S. currency.[145] The budget negotiations consequently turned into a tactical rather than strategic exercise in governance. Former senator Howard Baker, now White House chief of staff, admitted, "Everyone in the room is watching the market and if the market is good today, there is no need to agree. What we need is another market bust to force the issue."[146]

Without the incentive of economic crisis, the summit produced a "budget mouse" rather than a leonine charter for fiscal renewal. The participants agreed on deficit reduction of $30.2 billion in FY1988 and $45.8 billion in FY1989 (that mainly flowed from the first installment) and repealed the GRH sequester, which was to have started three days earlier.[147] This kept the squeeze on discretionary spending, both defense and domestic, but avoided the more severe cuts that sequestration would have produced. Also, some $9.6 billion of the first-year savings came from soft economies like asset sales, increased user fees, lower debt service, and tighter enforcement of tax laws. The summit could not achieve a real breakthrough on the deficit because the same factors that had produced stalemate in the first place spilled over into its negotiations. Accordingly, the participants settled for the least they could get away with. Their main achievement was to produce a budget truce for the remainder of Reagan's presidency. As OMB director William Miller observed, "We avoided a war. At least we agreed to an outcome by peaceful means."[148]

Congress proceeded to wrap FY1988 outlays into a huge continuing resolution bill and FY1989 targets into a reconciliation bill, both of which Reagan signed into law on December 22. However, the president could not resist one last effort to prove himself the good guy in the bad world of deficit politics. In his State of the Union address on January 25, 1988, he challenged Congress to approve rescissions of wasteful FY1988 spending that he would have eliminated with a line-item veto. He took particular exception to funding for "cranberry research, blueberry research, the study of crawfish and the commercialization of flowers." This was nothing more than a public relations stunt. The budget contained very few specific project costs, so the White House itself could only come up with proposed economies of $1.5 billion.[149]

The imminence of the presidential election was a powerful incentive to avoid prolonged budget strife. Reagan's FY1989 budget rosily projected a deficit of $129.5 billion, well within GRH limits. Congress took this as the basis for its deliberations even though the CBO estimated that revenues could be $40 billion below target. Legislators proceeded to adopt a budget resolution that accorded with the summit agreement on spending and kept to this in the appropriations process. The White House complied with its accounting gimmicks that reclassified some discretionary accounts as mandatory to keep domestic spending to keep within GRH limits.[150]

Only Reagan's veto of the defense authorization bill rippled the surface of fiscal harmony. The president objected to cuts in some weapons programs, notably SDI. However, the reductions were in line with previous budgets and did not threaten SDI's development. The Pentagon's Defense Acquisitions Board would shortly approve plans for development of a Phase 1 Strategic Defense System costing $74 billion to construct. The more likely reason for Reagan's veto was to reaffirm imagery of Democratic weakness on defense in an election year.[151]

More disappointing to Reagan than the defense cuts was his failure to promote a balanced-budget amendment as a way of controlling domestic spending under his successors. In his second inaugural address he had signaled that constitutional reform to "permanently control government's power to tax and spend" would rank high on his second-term agenda.[152] To his dismay, a balanced-budget amendment proposal failed by one vote (66 to 34) to gain supermajority approval from the Senate on March 25, 1986. The ayes included 43 Republicans and 23 Democrats, the nays 24 Democrats and 10 Republicans. Amendment supporters charged that the president had not lobbied vigorously enough to corral votes. In truth, Reagan tried hard to work his powers of persuasion on GOP dissenters, but GRH's automatic timetable for deficit elimination had enhanced doubts that constitutional reform was necessary.[153]

Accordingly, Reagan inched closer to the NTU-led campaign for a balanced-budget amendment constitutional convention. Although this movement had never regained the momentum of the late 1970s, it required the support of only two more states following adoption of convention resolutions by Alaska in 1982 and Missouri in 1983. In 1984 pollster Richard Wirthlin advised Reagan to speak in support of a convention resolution before the legislatures of holdout states to blunt likely Democratic attacks on his record deficits in the forthcoming election, but other presidential strategists did not want to give the amendment issue such prominence. Reagan himself was also wary of entrusting the consolidation of his legacy to a body that might not keep to his agenda. A convention, he declared in 1982, was "a last resort, because then once it's open, they could take up any number of things."[154]

Senate rejection of the amendment convinced Reagan that Congress would only approve it if the convention movement appeared unstoppable. In early 1987 he began sending letters to holdout state legislatures, such as Montana's, urging adoption of a resolution as a means of persuading the national legislature to act, but this bore no fruit.[155] Reagan raised the stakes in a speech delivered from the steps of the Jefferson Memorial on July 3, 1987. This called for a ten-point Economic Bill of Rights to preserve economic freedom in the same way that the original Bill of Rights had safeguarded political freedom. Its centerpiece was a balanced-budget constitutional amendment containing a tax-limitation provision. Coupled with this announcement was a warning that congressional refusal to act would leave him "no choice but to take my case directly to the States."[156]

The tactic of threatening to back the convention movement as a last resort backfired because it implicitly validated fears that such a body might be uncontrollable. A New York Times editorial took Reagan to task for "playing with matches . . . to push his pet amendment."[157] A grassroots countercampaign engaged in trying to rescind existing state resolutions grew stronger in the wake of his address. Among its supporters were liberal organizations, like Americans for Democratic Action, the American Civil Liberties Union, the AFL-CIO, and the American Jewish Congress, and conservative ones, like the John Birch Society, the Gun Owners Club of America, and Eagle Forum. The former worried that a runaway convention would rewrite the Constitution under right-wing influence, whereas the latter held the inverse

concern.[158] This unlikely coalition won its first success in the South, where
the bicentennial celebrations of the Constitution intensified concern about
its preservation. On April 28, 1988, Alabama rescinded its application after
the legislature overrode the veto issued by Republican governor Guy Hunt
at the White House's behest. Florida became the second state to overturn its
convention petition on May 25. The convention movement that had entered
the 1980s believing that victory was at hand was in retreat by its end. Unsurprisingly, a leading NTU official later derided Reagan's contribution to its
cause as "pretty pathetic."[159]

THE REAGAN LEGACY

Ronald Reagan had considerable success in transforming America's fiscal
agenda in line with his own political values. He sanctified low personal taxes
as a fundamental element of late-twentieth-century American political culture. In addition, his promotion of the largest defense buildup since the Korean War had been a significant factor in bringing the Cold War to the verge
of successful resolution by the time he left office.

Aside from the inexorable growth of the major entitlement programs,
Reagan also had considerable success in constraining the domestic budget,
even if this fell well short of his initial expectations. Only one federal program was actually eliminated during his presidency. Revenue sharing, whose
stringless formula of federal aid to the states made it less popular with legislators than categorical grants-in-aid, fell victim to the FY1986 economy drive.
However, there was no significant addition to the roster of domestic spending
programs under Reagan, in contrast to the pattern of program development
under every postwar president excepting Gerald Ford. More significantly,
discretionary domestic outlays declined from 4.5 percent GDP in FY1981 to
3.1 percent GDP in FY1989.

If the mid-twentieth century was the Age of Roosevelt, the late twentieth
century and beyond was arguably the Age of Reagan. Just like FDR, Reagan's
presidency, in the words of historian Sean Wilentz, "had a long postlude . . .
that set the tone for American politics" for a generation to come. Testifying to this, future president Barack Obama observed that "after Reagan the
lines between Republican and Democrat, liberal and conservative, would be
drawn in more sharply ideological terms." As a consequence, budgetary and
economic debate no longer focused on the trade-off between growth and
distributive justice. At issue henceforth was "tax cuts or tax hikes, small government or big government."[160]

Nevertheless, Reagan's programmatic legacy fell well short of Roosevelt's.

The fortieth president may have formulated the terms of debate that shaped American politics for a quarter-century, but he did not win the hearts and minds of his fellow Americans in his own time about the necessity for retrenchment of government. While polls in the 1980s indicated public preference for spending restraint over higher taxes as the means to balance the budget, they also revealed popular reluctance to cut specific domestic programs. After the conservative *annus mirabilis* of 1981, opinion surveys consistently indicated majority support for higher outlays on health care, education, and environmental programs in particular. Even popular belief that the government was spending too much on welfare declined significantly over the course of the Reagan presidency.[161]

Nor had Reagan bequeathed to his party a conservative economic strategy that would hold sway over future economic policy in the manner of Keynesianism in the postwar era. In Herbert Stein's opinion the 1980s demonstrated two realities for economic policy makers. First, the supply-side approach provided neither explanation nor solution for inflation. Second, government's influence on the supply-side was much smaller than on the demand-side of the economy. The Federal Reserve's conquest of inflation was proof of the former. The limited benefits of the Reagan tax program for productivity growth of output per employee was proof of the latter. Total nonfarm productivity growth annually averaged only 1.3 percent in the Reagan years, compared to 2.8 percent from 1945 through 1973. Yearly economic growth of 4.1 percent in 1983–1988 was largely due to aggregate demand catching up with potential GDP after a serious recession. Whatever else it achieved, Reaganomics did not enhance capital formation. Private investment in 1980–1992 was only 17.4 percent of GDP, compared with 18.6 percent GDP in the economically troubled 1970s. In 1989, U.S. business spent 41 percent less in real terms on net investment in new plant and equipment than in 1979.[162]

In certain regards a pragmatic tendency to compromise was more evident than conviction-driven consistency in Reagan's fiscal record. He promoted the largest antitax reform (ERTA), the largest peacetime tax increase (TEFRA), and the largest tax reform (TRA) in American history. Having promised rollback of the liberal state, he settled for restricting its growth in recognition that to do more would put his own political survival at risk. Finally, he coexisted with massive deficits despite his promise to lead the federal government back to the path of fiscal righteousness.

Despite this, Reagan was clear about his core goals and refused to compromise on these. Aside from associating deficits with high interest rates in the 1982–1983 recession, his threat concept of unbalanced budgets related primarily to the danger that they posed to his political agenda. Reagan used all the resources of his office to preserve his budgetary priorities against the efforts of congressional leaders of both parties to scale back his tax and defense programs in the name of deficit reduction. Emancipation from GOP budget-balancing orthodoxy enabled him to change America's course. As Aaron Wildavsky observed, "In the past, as the party of responsible finance, Republicans would try to cut spending and deficits; generally they were successful at neither. Under Reagan they have abandoned the tasks at which they failed in the past in favor of others that are easier to accomplish."[163]

Regardless of its benefits for his governing agenda, Reagan's fiscal record had negative consequences for the budget process that was at the heart of government. As one analyst observed, "The political bill . . . against outsized deficits is formidable." The list included the collapse of budget regularity, deceitful accounting practices, and gimmicks that produced short-term improvement but did not address structural problems. Furthermore, the massive fiscal shortfalls strained the relationship between the president and Congress, crowded out their attention to other concerns, and denied them the resources to address these.[164]

If Reagan showed the GOP the political advantages of tolerating large deficits, he had the reverse effect on the Democrats. From their perspective, the huge fiscal gap that developed in the 1980s had the dual effect of funding their adversary's agenda and constraining theirs. James Wright once observed that the president's "definition of spending is purely domestic."[165] Perceiving the deficit as a threat to programs that benefited their constituencies, congressional Democrats sought to bring it down through a combination of revenue enhancement and defense retrenchment that amounted to a reversal of the Reagan Revolution. From 1982 onward the annual budget battle became just a round in a seemingly endless struggle between political adversaries determined to protect their respective program priorities while pursuing the common end of deficit reduction.

The final Reagan budgets suggested that the deficit was in decline, but this was another illusion. Exceptional circumstances helped to reduce it from 5.0 percent GDP in FY1986 to 3.2 percent GDP in FY1987. Investors rushing to avoid the TRA's hike in capital gains taxes provided a revenue windfall, observance of the modest GRH deficit targets produced defense economies, and low inflation reduced COLA payments. The promising signs of fiscal progress quickly evaporated. At first sight, Reagan's FY1989 budget suggested that the fiscal gap had continued to narrow to 2.8 percent GDP. However, this was dependent on a healthy surplus in the off-budget Social Security trust fund, the result of payroll tax increases intended to boost national saving rather than facilitate government dissaving. In on-budget terms, the deficit was slightly higher at 3.8 percent GDP than the FY1987 level of 3.6 percent GDP. Moreover, the current-dollar deficit of $152.5 billion was well above the revised GRH target of $136 billion.

Ultimately, however, the critical question about the Reagan deficits was whether they had damaged the economy. This was the subject of much contradictory analysis in the 1980s and beyond because there was no simple answer. In the short-term, there is no clear evidence that the chronically large deficits were harmful. According to one assessment by the Federal Reserve Bank of New York, real GDP would at most have been only 3 percent higher in 1990 if the federal government had balanced its budget annually over the previous decade.[166] In the longer run, however, the economic consequences of deficits were more problematic because of their effect on national saving, the seed corn of America's future.

Historically the United States was a low-saving nation in comparison to its main economic competitors, but the public dissaving represented by the Reagan deficits offset much of the private saving that did take place. The overall rate of national saving (public and private) had declined to only 3 percent of national income in 1988–1990, compared to the average of 7.7 percent in the 1970s. The huge budget deficits were therefore instrumental in the overconsumption, underinvestment, and high degree of foreign borrowing that characterized the economy of the 1980s. In essence, America raised its standard of living in the Reagan era by consuming more than it produced. Without a correction of fiscal course to enhance national saving for the benefit of productive investment, it would eventually be faced with having to reduce its standard of living by consuming less than it produced in order to meet its debt obligations to foreigners.

In the words of economist Benjamin Friedman, the challenge facing America's political leaders in the post-Reagan era was to put the national government's finances back on "a trajectory consistent with fiscal stability, rising productivity, and international competitiveness."[167] This objective would dominate the budgetary agenda of the 1990s. However, the political fault lines created by the deficit in the 1980s would continue to cut across the policy debate on how to address the legacy of Reaganomics long after the fortieth president had left office.

CHAPTER 5

George H. W. Bush:
Compromising on the Deficit

George H. W. Bush's budget leadership was defined by his acceptance of higher taxes to achieve a deficit reduction agreement with the Democrat-controlled Congress in 1990. This compromise repudiated the pledge he had given when accepting the Republican presidential nomination. "The Congress will push me to raise taxes, and I'll say no," Bush had vowed, "and they'll push, and I'll say no, and they'll push again, and I'll say to them, 'Read my lips: no new taxes.'" The president justified this turnaround as necessary to safeguard the national interest against the consequences of a rising deficit. "There is a price to divided government," he declared, "and that means that I have to compromise on items that I feel strongly about in order to do what is best for the country, and that is to reach an agreement."[1]

The prospect of a massive sequestration of spending under the terms of the Gramm-Rudman-Hollings (GRH) deficit-reduction schedule weighed heavily with Bush and his advisers. GRH may have proved something of a damp squib to date, but it had the explosive potential of a fiscal time bomb to rip through government programs and blast the economy into recession. Continuing the Reagan-era practice of setting unrealistic deficit projections to avoid sequestration carried its own risks. As OMB director Richard Darman contended, it was imprudent to expect that inflation-conscious financial markets would tolerate this sleight of hand for long.[2]

Bush found himself having to choose between preserving Ronald Reagan's legacy of low taxes and transcending his legacy of large deficits. A problem-solver rather than an ideologue, he discarded his predecessor's symbolic association of higher taxes with big government in favor of substantive action to improve federal finances. The budget deal that the president agreed on with the congressional Democrats was devoid of phony economies, and its innovative enforcement procedures set "a new course of long-term fiscal restraint."[3] Nevertheless, it was a false dawn for fiscal bipartisanship. Bush was willing to depoliticize the budget process to find a solution to the deficit problem, but conservative Republicans regarded his compromise on taxes as a betrayal of the Reagan Revolution. Accordingly, the budgetary politics of his presidency served to intensify partisan divisions over the deficit instead of laying the foundations for new consensus.

ESTABLISHMENT MAN

Born on June 12, 1924, to a blue-blooded family that was part of America's Eastern establishment, George H. W. Bush grew up in the affluent community of Greenwich, Connecticut. His upbringing gave him many advantages in life but also instilled in him the Bush family ethos that service to one's country was a duty for the privileged. His father, Prescott Bush, made a successful career as a Wall Street investment banker before being elected Republican senator for Connecticut in 1952. After graduating from the elite private school of Andover in 1942, the future president became the youngest U.S. Navy pilot in World War II, saw active service in the Pacific, and survived his torpedo bomber plane being shot down near Chichi Jima in 1944. After the war, he attended Yale, graduating with an economics degree in 1948. He then moved to Texas to work in the oil industry, but this was not the bold break to make his way in the world that it appeared. A family friend owned the firm that employed Bush, and his father sat on its board. Backed by capital from his family and its associates, he went into partnership to form the Midland-based Zapata Petroleum Corporation in 1953. Six years later Bush gained control of its $4.5 million-a-year offshore drilling subsidiary, the Zapata Off-Shore Company, whose headquarters he moved to Houston.

True to the establishment values of his family regarding its obligations of public service, Bush followed his father into politics once he had earned sufficient wealth from his oil business to ensure his financial well-being. After an unsuccessful campaign for the Senate in 1964, he won election to the House of Representatives as West Houston's congressman two years later. This entailed a not inconsiderable sacrifice since Bush resigned his executive position in his drilling business and sold off his stock for $1.1 million, a price that he could have trebled when oil prices rose shortly afterward.

Defeat in another run for the Senate in 1970 ended Bush's career in legislative politics. Thereafter he served in the Nixon and Ford administrations in a succession of positions as ambassador to the United Nations, Republican National Committee chair, head of the U.S. Public Liaison Office in the People's Republic of China, and director of the Central Intelligence Agency. Returning to private life during the Carter presidency, he became chair of First International Bancshares, the biggest Texas bank holding company, which afforded him the opportunity to replenish his personal fortune. In 1980 he contested the Republican presidential nomination but ran a distant second behind Ronald Reagan, who eventually offered him the number-two spot on the ticket. Bush served two terms as vice president before entering the White House in his own right.[4]

The central problem of Bush's fiscal leadership as president was the clash between his personal values and his role as Reagan's legatee. His background within the political, financial, and social establishment was the shaping influence not only on his approach to budgeting but also on his entire political style. It made him an elite-oriented, problem-solving, and pragmatic leader, who lacked the common touch and too often appeared uncaring about the problems of ordinary Americans.[5] However, it was his status as heir to Ronald Reagan, the embodiment of antigovernment, people-oriented conviction politics, that got him elected to the White House.

Bush pursued the Republican nomination in 1988 as the candidate of continuity. "Who can you most trust to continue the Reagan revolution?" asked one of his television advertisements during the primaries.[6] He overcame the challenge of Senator Bob Dole (R-KS) in the New Hampshire primary in large part by promising not to raise taxes if elected. A hard-hitting campaign ad asserted, "George Bush says he won't raise taxes, period. Bob Dole straddled, and he just won't promise not to raise taxes. And you know what that means."[7]

Despite his affirmations of fealty to Reagan's legacy, Bush was not a true believer in conservative ideology. According to one biographer, he "was a Burkean conservative with the heart and soul of a moderate, a conservative moderate rather than a moderate conservative."[8] Such an outlook meant that Bush was more positive but much fuzzier than Reagan in his views about government. As president, Bush called for a cooperative relationship between the free market, a dynamic state, and the commitment of ordinary citizens "to serve another in need" as the solution to America's domestic problems, but this entailed platitudes about wanting "good government" rather than "big government." In his final year in office, he was still trying out ideas on his advisers about integrating themes of prosperity, fairness, and strengthening the family into his vision of how government could build America's future.[9]

Bush also had a history of being adaptable in his beliefs to suit his circumstances. Many on the right remembered that he first ran for office as a Goldwaterite, then moved toward the middle after the electoral fiasco of 1964, and only converted to the Reaganite agenda upon being offered the vice-presidential nomination in 1980. Conservatives remained uncertain about Bush despite his loyal support for the president over the next eight years. They also found it difficult to reconcile his promise of continuity with his 1988 primary season remarks that put a positive spin on government's capacity to mitigate the free market.

Reagan scriptwriter Peggy Noonan, who was on loan to the Bush campaign, inserted the "read my lips: no new taxes" pledge into his convention address to improve his image with the Republican base and define what was at stake in the election. As she observed, "It's not subject to misinterpretation. It means, I mean this."[10] The line she crafted became the most famous sound bite of the election. Audiences would shout it out in unison with Bush as he stumped the country. The tax pledge revitalized a campaign that had trailed in early polls. It counteracted the efforts of the Democratic candidate, Governor Michael Dukakis of Massachusetts, to frame the election as being about personal competence rather than ideology. Bush now portrayed his opponent as a tax-and-spend liberal who had raised state taxes and refused to rule out deficit-reducing federal tax hikes if elected president. Although his attacks on the Democrat's cultural liberalism were also significant in defining their differences, the tax pledge was critical in energizing the conservative base.[11] For the rest of the campaign, Bush trenchantly avowed opposition to any kind of tax increase as damaging to the nation's economy.[12]

Despite Bush's issuance of the tax pledge to define his conservative identity, he lacked visceral commitment to low personal income taxes for ordinary Americans. His background endowed him with a different perspective from Reagan's belief in their necessity to protect individual liberty and restore founding principles of limited government. As populist commentator Kevin Phillips observed, "No previous presidential family has been so wholeheartedly involved with a single economic sector over multiple generations." Its vocation over the course of the twentieth century was "essentially financial, sometimes with a flow of petroleum or a whiff of natural gas."[13] Bush himself had worked primarily on the financial rather than drilling side of the oil business and then for a holding bank while on leave from government in the late 1970s.[14] Unsurprisingly, his singular fiscal passion was to provide tax breaks to business and high earners as investment incentives, in his estimate the surest route to economic growth. One conservative commentator dubbed him "a supply-sider of sorts—a corporate supply-sider." Less flatteringly, liberal economist John Kenneth Galbraith caricatured Bush's economic philosophy in these terms: "If the horse is fed amply with oats, some will pass through to the road for the sparrows."[15]

As a congressman, Bush had defended the interests of the oil industry from his seat on the Ways and Means Committee. In response to liberal charges that the oil depletion allowance and the oil import quota constituted unfair subsidies to domestic producers, he asserted that their removal would hit jobs and economic growth.[16] Rising in national politics, he broadened his economic brief to champion the investment sector as a whole. According to *Time* correspondents Michael Duffy and Dan Goodgame, "Bush believes that in economic policy what is good for wealthy investors and business executives is good for America." In their view, he had less interest in tax relief for ordinary Americans because he regarded "the educated and monied elite . . . as the creative force in the economy."[17]

Bush's discomfort with Reagan's evolution into a tax reformer lends credence to this assessment. With the 1984 campaign in full swing, the Internal

Revenue Service presented him with a bill for $200,000 in back taxes after disallowing a tax exemption from the sale of the family home in Houston on moving into the vice-presidential residence. With the media scenting blood, Bush made a public disclosure of his 1981 tax returns to prove that he had not made undue use of tax shelters and other deductions that favored the rich.[18] Far from embracing the Tax Reform Act of 1986 with enthusiasm, his main contribution to its enactment was to work in tandem with fellow Texan, Treasury Secretary James Baker, to ensure that it left oil industry exemptions largely untouched.[19]

As president, Bush sought in vain to rescind the capital gains tax increase contained in the Reagan tax reform. His efforts to ensure that the 1990 budget deal did not include an increase in the highest marginal rate of taxation were similarly unsuccessful. When a friend, retired admiral Frederick Reeder, wrote that he did not mind paying higher taxes to get the deficit down, Bush replied, "I worry about raising rates. Today it's you, tomorrow it's Joe Six Pack." He saw no contradiction between this expression of concern for the common man and the regressive tax increases that administration negotiators had promoted in the initial budget agreement rejected by the House of Representatives. In essence, Bush's attitude about taxation was rooted in old-fashioned trickle-down thinking rather than the antistatism of the new conservatism.[20]

Bush's tax pledge was vulnerable to his problem-solving inclinations as president because it was not born of conviction that tax relief was an equal right for all. Whereas Reagan drove his administration through the power of his ideas, Bush thrived on dealing with critical issues as they arose rather than seeking predetermined outcomes in accordance with a grand plan for America's future.[21] His son, George W. Bush, once observed, "The problem with my old man is that he thinks you can solve problems one at a time. . . . Jebby [his brother] and I understand that you need ideas, principles—based on belief." Vice President Dan Quayle similarly commented that Bush Sr. was a "problem solver" who did not give his administration an ideological edge.[22] His boss regarded adjustments to changing circumstances as a virtue rather than a weakness in a leader. Bush observed to two journalists in 1990, "Having vision does not necessarily mean having a fixed blueprint. It means having a general direction and an ability to redefine strategy as events require."[23]

Bush eventually changed course over taxes to address the deficit problem. This did not represent a damascene conversion because his instincts were in tune with his party's balanced-budget tradition. Running for president in 1980, Bush had derided Reagan's tax-cut proposal as "voodoo economics" that would enlarge the deficit and fuel inflation. To emphasize his own fiscal soundness, he promised to produce a balanced-budget plan within one hundred days of taking office.[24] As vice president, Bush never so much as hinted at any concern about the Reagan deficits. He stayed true to the admonition that he had given his staff on accepting the nomination: "We're now a wholly owned subsidiary and we're going to behave as one."[25] In his vice-presidential memoir, he claimed that his "voodoo economics" critique of Reagan had been a "rhetorical distinction without a difference" because they both believed in smaller government, less bureaucracy, and lower taxation.[26] These words tried to draw a veil over the real disparity between them. If elected president in 1980, Bush would almost certainly have conformed to Republican orthodoxy that deficit-reducing expenditure retrenchment should precede large-scale tax reduction.

The strategic context of the deficit had changed significantly by the time Bush entered the White House. In 1981 Reagan had been able to market his tax reduction program as the agency of economic recovery that would bring a balanced budget in its wake. By 1989 the prolonged cycle of economic expansion that was now entering its seventh year had failed to eradicate the structural imbalance in government finances. No longer considered a residual of the economy's performance, the deficit was seen instead as a threat to its continued strength. In these circumstances, Bush's problem-solving approach to leadership meant that he could not tolerate it with the apparent insouciance of his predecessor. In his inaugural address, he called for a new engagement between the executive and legislature "to bring the federal Budget into balance."[27]

The clearest early signal of Bush's fiscal intent was his appointment of Richard Darman, a foursquare deficit hawk, as OMB director. This former Reagan aide had allied with David Stockman in a vain effort to get their boss to reverse budgetary course once the rosy scenario's miscalculations became plain. A Bush campaign aide in 1988, he had tried to get the tax pledge removed from the nomination speech because this "stupid and irresponsible" commitment, as he later called it, would limit options for dealing with the deficit.[28]

To conservative Republicans, the budget director was the prince of darkness who manipulated his ideologically frail boss into abandoning his promise to the American people in order to win Democratic support for a deficit reduction package. Representative Newt Gingrich (R-GA) accused him of forgetting that the GOP "didn't win the presidency three times in a row to cut a bad deal with the guys who didn't win."[29] Darman's immense knowledge of fiscal issues gave him considerable influence with Bush. Even White House chief of staff John Sununu, who liked to rule the roost, acknowledged, "The President needs Dick, he's the only one with a coherent [budgetary] policy." Bush himself testified that Darman "simply knows more about this [the budget] than anyone else, and he has always kept my interest in the forefront."[30] All this did not make the budget director the Svengali that conservatives imagined. He certainly guided Bush's approach to the deficit problem, but the president's disposition to solve it reflected his own political outlook.

Bush's connection with the world of finance inclined him to regard the deficit as a threat to economic growth because it drained national saving, reduced investment in future productive capacity, and made financial markets nervous about inflation. This was also the constant refrain of another businessman in his cabinet, Treasury Secretary Nicholas Brady, formerly head of the Dillon, Read investment firm.[31] Bush heard the same message from economists and business leaders at a Camp David meeting to discuss the economy early in his presidency. Most of those present were willing to trade higher taxes for the lower interest rates expected to follow.[32]

Moreover, Bush could not ignore warnings from Alan Greenspan that deficits impacted adversely on monetary policy. The Federal Reserve chair made it clear that they were not "a manana problem" in postelection testimony to the National Economic Commission (NEC). Congress had established this body after the stock market crash of 1987 to propose a bipartisan solution to the budget problem in the manner that the Social Security commission had helped fix the shortfall in pension funding. Greenspan warned, "The long run is rapidly becoming the short run. If we do not act promptly, the effects will be increasingly felt and with some immediacy." He also intimated in private to Darman that a tax increase was a worthwhile price for a serious deficit-reduction package.[33]

Worried that inflation was creeping upward, the Fed raised the federal funds rate through a series of incremental hikes in the last quarter of 1988 and the first quarter of 1989 to 9¾ percent, the highest point in four years. On March 3, 1989, CEA chair Michael Boskin warned Bush that this monetary tightening could produce a recession that would in turn send the deficit back into the fiscal stratosphere. Over the next few months administration officials privately lobbied Greenspan to change course. In response, he urged them to do something about the budgetary gap that he considered the major source of inflationary expectations.[34]

Although he was more a problem-solver than conviction politician, Bush did not abandon his tax pledge lightly. Ultimately the public service ethos that was the shaping influence of his political career inclined him to do so in the national interest, even at cost to his personal credibility. To his critics, Bush's sense of duty substituted for fixed political beliefs, thereby facilitating his shifting issue positions. For his supporters, such as White House aide James Cicconi, it engendered "an inner core of conviction that was rooted in doing what's right for the country."[35]

The public service ethos manifestly influenced Bush's political style. According to conservative *Wall Street Journal* editor Robert Bartley, he belonged to the Mugwump political tradition that prized government by the best men over the brutish instincts of the masses. This made him "elitist, pessimistic, and crabbed" in outlook in contrast to the "open, optimistic, and populist" Reagan.[36] Bush clearly valued interpersonal dynamics over partisanship as the agency of good governance. His preferred mode of operation was elite cooperation to build consensus behind closed doors. Accordingly, he was inclined to engage in what one scholar characterized as "boardroom politics and brokerage among 'proper gentlemen.'"[37]

This proved an elusive ideal even in a policy domain where it might have been expected to work. Bush had an instrumental view of monetary policy as a matter of policy makers' preferences rather than a reflection of market forces. Nicholas Brady, an investment banker of the old school, shared this misconception. According to Alan Greenspan, neither took the long-term view of monetary policy, so they always expected interest rate relaxation in return for any move toward fiscal restraint. In his opinion, this was the main reason that the Fed and the Bush White House "ended up with a terrible relationship" when the economy turned sour.[38]

Bush encountered even greater difficulty in developing a cooperative relationship with Democratic leaders on budgetary issues. He may have held a range of executive offices, but his principal function had always been to carry out the mandate of others. There was little in his background to prepare him for the task of winning bipartisan support for his own agenda. Bush's elitist preferences were also instrumental in his assumption that conservative Republicans would sacrifice their ideological preferences on his say-so. Shocked by the acrimony that the 1990 budget deal generated, he remarked in private, "I am more comfortable with foreign affairs. . . . I don't like the deficiencies of the domestic, political scene. I hate the posturing on both sides . . . [people] putting their own selves ahead of the overall good. . . . If you want a friend in Washington, get a dog."[39]

Compounding his problems in dealing with Congress, Bush lacked a mandate in the manner of his predecessor. He had won 5.4 million votes less than Reagan in 1984 and failed to carry 500 counties that had gone Republican four years earlier. With majorities of 262–173 in the House and 55–45 in the Senate, the Democrats had increased their strength in both chambers in 1988, the first time since 1956 they had managed this when losing the presidency. Signifying his lack of coattails, Bush ran behind the winners in 379 of the 435 House districts.

To make matters worse, partisan fissures had intensified in the 1980s. Having changed position many times in response to circumstances, Bush misunderstood the importance that conservative Republicans put on his tax pledge as a symbol of their party's identity. For them there could be no compromise on taxes for the sake of deficit reduction. Edward Rollins, cochair of the Republican National Congressional Campaign (RNCC), warned Bush when he first considered issuing the pledge, "You can't give it up. . . . It's the last line between us and the Democrats that anybody can identify." Conversely, the president underestimated the depth of opposition party resentment of his tax pledge. Democratic leaders wanted to make Bush eat the words that had helped to elect him as payback for his Reaganite assault on them as tax-and-spend liberals. Senate Budget Committee chair Jim Sasser (D-TN) avowed, "We ought to look at those groups who profited from the tax deficit of the 1980s to solve the budget deficit of the 1990s."[40]

To have any chance of forging a depoliticized compromise on deficit reduction, Bush needed to use the presidential bully pulpit to mold popular support for his position. However, the public service concept of leadership made him reluctant to use the resources of his office to market his policies. According to aide Constance Horner, he had "a visceral antipathy to public communication. . . . He thought poorly of it, he thought it was cheap." In a similar vein, James Cicconi suggested that the president distrusted "the power of rhetoric" because it conflicted with his model of good leadership. Bush spoke most frequently on the deficit, including his first address to the nation on the subject, in support of the budget agreement that White House and congressional negotiators concocted behind closed doors in 1990. Significantly, he did not employ rhetoric as a tool to shape the outcome he wanted from these talks.[41] As political scientist Fred Greenstein observed, Bush's reluctance to go public deprived him of the "teaching function that enabled . . . Roosevelt, Kennedy and Reagan to frame public perceptions, place their administrations in a favorable light, and buffer themselves from negative developments."[42]

NOTHING VENTURED, NOTHING GAINED

Bush told *Newsweek* journalists that devising a plan to reduce the deficit would be the top priority of his first hundred days in office.[43] To get back on the GRH schedule, it had to be shrunk to $100 billion in FY1990, $64 billion in FY1991, and $28 billion in FY1992 to reach zero in FY1993. However, Bush frittered away the political capital from his election by eschewing hard fiscal choices during his first year in office. His hesitant efforts to promote bipartisan cooperation produced a slide-by budget that transparently deferred resolution of the deficit problem. Bush also presented an image of unyielding fidelity to his election promise that encouraged conservatives to believe that it was sacrosanct. "It was just a flat pledge," he told a journalist. "We don't need a tax increase."[44]

During the campaign Bush had proposed a "flexible freeze" on spending as a way to balance the budget in four to six years. This would have tied increases in aggregate outlays to the inflation rate while relying on economic growth to deliver the revenues that would lift the budget out of the red. Bush never specified which programs should be cut to achieve the freeze, but he did promise new initiatives in areas like education, environmental protection, and the war on drugs that would require higher spending. The unspoken logic was that these measures would be funded through savings on entitlements, which were growing much faster than inflation. In Richard Darman's judgment, this posed "an inescapable dilemma" for the new administration because the congressional Democrats were certain to demand a tax increase as the price for accepting this economy.[45]

Bush did not consider using the tax pledge as a bargaining chip to win a deficit reduction deal at the outset of his presidency for fear of compromising his credibility with the public.[46] Had he grasped the nettle, he could have used the NEC as cover. Word reached the Bush camp in the transition period that this group was divided along partisan lines over the need for higher taxes. The president-elect could have employed his right to select two new members to tilt it in favor of the tax-increase option. NEC Democratic cochair Robert Strauss counseled his fellow Texan to seize this lifeline, but Bush packed it with antitax appointees instead.[47]

At a private meeting on December 6, 1988, Bush also obtained assurances that House Ways and Means chair Dan Rostenkowski (D-IL), an old friend since their days on the committee twenty years previously, would not press for tax increases during his first year in office. Nevertheless, he recognized that the issue would not go away for long. According to Darman's record of their meeting on December 21, the president-elect foresaw that he might have to bite the bullet in his second year. Bush confirmed his thinking on this score in an aide-memoir about a budget briefing on March 30, 1989. "I can't raise taxes this time round," he asserted, "and it will be very hard in the future, but I want to see the options, and I'm not going to be held up by campaign rhetoric. . . . If the facts change, I hope I'm smart enough to change, too." Ultimately, Bush hoped to get agreement on spending cuts, Social Security reform, and adequate defense if he had to surrender his pledge.[48]

The incoming administration adopted a two-step approach to deficit reduction that was more tactical than strategic. The initial goal was to win bipartisan support for a status quo FY1990 budget with no new taxes. The economic indicators did not as yet point to serious problems ahead, so there was no reason to doubt that the GRH target could be finessed through the combination of modest deficit reductions and accounting gimmicks that had served in the past. The aim was to buy time to negotiate a "big fix" in the succeeding budget even if the price for spending restraint and entitlement reform was some tax increase. As Bush's closest adviser, James Baker, had observed at an early meeting to thrash out tactics, "Once you're in negotiations, you let it play out."[49]

On February 9, 1989, the new president went before Congress to request bipartisan negotiations to keep the FY1990 budget within the GRH deficit target of $100 billion. On the same day, the administration unveiled its revisions to the Reagan lame-duck budget. In his memoirs Darman characterized the amended plan without a hint of irony as a "moderately credible budget," but this was being economic with the truth. Aping the original, it relied on one-off savings such as asset sales, overly optimistic revenue assumptions, and several instances of creative accounting to project a deficit of $94.8 billion. Far from proposing higher taxes, Bush called for a capital gains tax cut that was expected to net first-year savings of $4.8 billion by encouraging investors to cash in long-held gains. His budget also projected specific increases in spending for education, the war on drugs, the environment, housing, and Medicare, but it required unspecified cutbacks in other domestic programs to comply with the deficit limit. Only defense, targeted for a one-year freeze, was subject to real economy.[50]

There was plenty to displease the Democrats in the Bush plan. They particularly resented the proposed capital gains tax cut as a windfall for the rich that would substantially reduce revenues in the long run. The announcement of spending increases coupled with unspecified reductions also came in for condemnation. As House Budget Committee member Charles Schumer (D-NY) observed, "He picks the increases and lets us make the cuts—that's not very bipartisan." Nevertheless, Democratic leaders could hardly refuse to negotiate with a new president who had extended the hand of friendship and showed willingness to modify his predecessor's stand on defense and domestic programs—if not on taxes.[51]

The talks produced a palpably fictitious formula for deficit reduction totaling $27 billion based equally on spending cuts and revenue increases. The new deficit forecast of $99.5 billion for FY1990 relied on an optimistic economic growth projection, gimmicks like tougher enforcement of tax laws, and unspecified revenue measures. The abandonment of the flexible freeze also made the agreement suspect on the spending side. To safeguard defense, administration negotiators accepted an overall increase for domestic programs subject to annual appropriations.[52] Both sides had a vested interest in avoiding hard choices. For the White House, the agreement kept a tax increase off the agenda for the time being. Unwilling to take the lead in proposing one, the Democrats connived in agreeing to an unrealistic deficit forecast to protect their programmatic priorities.

Translating this settlement into budget legislation exposed the limits of bipartisanship. On the domestic side of the ledger, the Democrats ended up appropriating more funds than Bush wanted for education and the war on drugs.[53] Meanwhile, legislators from both parties balked at the specifics of the administration's defense savings. Abandoning his predecessor's projected 2 percent annual expansion, Bush authorized a modified four-year program for 0, 1, 1, and 2 percent real increases in military outlays. To achieve the FY1990 freeze, Defense Secretary Richard Cheney sliced $10 billion from the Reagan estimates. This entailed canceling one aircraft carrier, slowing down some weapons programs, and terminating three of these not deemed cost effective—the Navy's F-14D fighter, the Marine Corps's V-22 Osprey troop carrier, and the Army's AHIP helicopter. However, a bipartisan group representing districts affected by the proposed weapons cancellations persuaded the House to continue funding them.[54]

Cheney eventually negotiated a compromise that allowed research and development of the Osprey to continue and committed to further production of eighteen F-14D fighters and thirty-six AHIP helicopters prior to their termination. To fund this, Congress diverted $1.1 billion from the Strategic Defense Initiative estimate of $4.9 billion and made smaller economies in the B-2 Stealth bomber and the Trident II missile programs.[55] Taxpayers ended up funding weapons that were surplus to Pentagon needs in large part because White House failure to provide a coherent rationale for postcontainment defense retrenchment enabled legislators to protect constituency interests with impunity.[56]

Adding to its difficulties on the deficit, the Bush administration had to grapple with the cost of the savings and loans (S&L) industry bailout. In line with the deregulatory impulse of the Carter and Reagan years, federal oversight of this financial sector had been significantly relaxed in an effort to boost its profitability. However, a combination of reckless lending, rampant fraud, and inept government supervision brought many S&Ls to grief. By 1986 the Federal Savings and Loan Insurance Corporation (FSLIC), the industry's public insurer, had exhausted its funds on bailouts of failed thrifts. This made taxpayer involvement in eventual resolution of the crisis almost inevitable. As the Reagan presidency ended, about a third of thrifts were insolvent and another third were financially weak. Estimates of federal bailout costs ranged from $50 billion to $100 billion, but the final bill went higher.[57]

The Bush camp steadfastly denied the gravity of the problem during the election campaign for fear of the triple embarrassment it could cause. The issue cast a stain on the Reagan economic record; Texas was the epicenter of the crisis, with more failing S&Ls than any other state; and the vice-president's son Neil had until recently been a partner in Denver's Silverado S&L, which had reported heavy losses. In April 1988 Treasury Secretary James Baker told the House Appropriations Committee that a $10.8 billion recapitalization of the insolvent FSLIC would be sufficient to save the industry.[58] Shortly before the election, Bush promised to oppose any "costly government bailout," a pledge that did not survive his first month in office.[59]

Amid worsening crisis, the newly installed president proposed a plan to raise $50 billion in thirty-year government bonds to fund a bailout. This placed a substantial burden on the public purse but looked to mitigate the effect by spreading the cost over time. It projected interest payments of $126 billion over ten years (and possibly $200 billion in total), of which $60 billion would be funded from the budget and the remainder from higher insurance premiums for healthy thrifts.[60] Within a short time, however, it was evident that the number of S&Ls in danger of failing far exceeded the administration's estimate. In midyear, Bush received confidential forecasts that the bailout could cost more than $200 billion in the 1990s alone.[61]

The urgency of dealing with the escalating crisis eventually trumped deficit worries. On August 9 Congress enacted an expanded version of the Bush plan as the Financial Institutions Reform, Recovery, and Enforcement Act (FIRREA). This provided $50 billion for a new agency, the Resolution Trust Corporation (RTC), to take over thrifts that were placed into receivership over the next three years (later extended to June 30, 1995). About $20 billion was to come directly from Treasury appropriations and the remainder from long-term bonds to be issued by a new private-public partnership. Two further measures in 1991 and one in 1993 extended RTC funding to deal with the increasing volume of closures. FIRREA also abolished the insolvent FSLIC and transferred its assets, liabilities, and operations to the newly created FSLIC Resolution Fund (FRF), capitalized from Treasury appropriations.

The RTC was responsible for closing 744 thrifts with total assets of $394 billion. Estimates of the total bailout cost to the public purse varied enormously—some going as high as $500 billion by 2020—because of incomplete information, differing methodologies, and underestimates of the effect of economic recovery on asset sales. When better data was available, two Federal Deposit Insurance Corporation economists calculated that as of December 31, 1999, the net bill for the closure of insolvent thrifts from 1989 through 1995 was $152.9 billion. Some four-fifths of this ($123.8 billion) accrued to the public purse and the rest to the thrift industry itself.[62]

Continuous upward revision of the bailout costs increased the urgency of dealing with the deficit problem. It took nearly six months after enactment of FIRREA before the RTC had the working capital and the personnel to start the rescue operation in earnest. It was at this juncture that the fiscal consequences for the GRH targets fully hit home within the White House. As Darman observed with more than a hint of understatement, "This has major potential for political and financial difficulty—if not handled with great care." Only the first-year bailout costs were designated as being off-budget. The administration's preferred solution was to remove future outlays from the GRH sequester calculations without handing the Democrats any leverage by appearing "too eager" to do so. On July 30, 1990, it announced that funds for dealing with the S&L crisis were near depletion and projected that the FY1991 tab for rescuing thrifts could go as high as $100 billion.[63]

The bipartisan consensus on the S&L bailout marked an exception to the prolonged sparring between the Bush administration and the Democrats over spending in 1989. However, it was a tax issue involving a comparatively small sum of money that provoked their biggest disagreement. The two sides were at loggerheads over how to raise $5.3 billion in unspecified additional revenues that the April budget agreement had projected. Democratic leaders harbored hopes of forcing the president to renege on his tax pledge to meet this target, but Bush looked to do so through a capital gains tax cut. The dispute prevented enactment of a budget reconciliation bill in time to avoid sequestration under the GRH terms.

A rebellion by conservative Democrats on the Ways and Means Committee seemingly handed the advantage to the president. With Republican support, they outmaneuvered Dan Rostenkowski to report out a bill containing a capital gains tax cut projected to raise $4.8 billion in its first year. Aggressive White House lobbying, particularly with regard to imminent sequestration, helped to win House approval for this measure by 239 to 190 votes on September 28. The Democrats were in disarray because Speaker James Wright (D-TX) and Whip Tony Coelho (D-CA), both deeply implicated in the S&L scandal, had recently resigned from Congress because of ethical transgressions. The new leadership team, headed by Speaker Thomas Foley (D-WA), countermobilized too late to head off the defection of sixty-eight Democrats, mostly southern and western conservatives.[64]

Bush paid one of his infrequent visits to Capitol Hill on October 6 to insist on the Senate adopting the House measure. It appeared likely to do so because at least twelve Democrats supported capital gains tax relief. Even Senate Majority Leader George Mitchell (D-ME) had backed it during the debate over the Reagan tax reform in 1986. However, the fight was now about politics rather than economics. Mitchell deemed the president guilty of bad faith in pushing an issue that lay outside the terms of the bipartisan agreement reached in April. He was determined that Bush should not replicate Reagan's success in getting effective control of Congress on tax issues by combining unbroken Republican support with conservative Democratic breakaways.

The Senate leader countered with a proposal to strip the reconciliation bill of extraneous spending items conventionally added by legislators in return for exclusion of capital gains relief. Some Republicans were willing to take this deal as a way of controlling earmarks. When Bush refused to budge, Mitchell persuaded Lloyd Bentsen (D-TX), a supporter of capital gains tax reduction, to hold the party line against GOP efforts to incorporate it in the reconciliation bill produced by his Finance Committee. The majority leader then rallied other wavering Democrats to support a filibuster should the Republicans attempt to force a floor vote. The question he put them was, "Do you want to give George Bush a win?"[65]

With the imbroglio delaying approval of a reconciliation bill beyond the

GRH deadline, Bush ordered an across-the-board sequestration of $16.1 billion to meet the $100 billion GRH deficit target.[66] Neither side took comfort from this outcome. Whereas the Democrats worried about the effects of the domestic cuts on their constituencies, the Pentagon made evident its displeasure at further economies atop its zero-growth budget. The standoff also clouded White House hopes of securing bipartisan agreement for a deficit reduction agreement in 1990.[67] To end the deadlock, Bush announced on November 2 that he would accept a reconciliation bill without a capital gains tax cut if it achieved gimmick-free deficit reduction of $14 billion and was shorn of extraneous spending commitments. On November 22, Congress enacted legislation that came close to meeting these terms. This raised $6 billion in new revenue through a variety of small-scale loophole closures and accelerations and kept the sequester in place until February to achieve $4.6 billion in savings on spending. True to custom, it also featured over $3 billion of accounting gimmicks, but these were ones the White House had accepted as part of the April bipartisan agreement.[68]

At the close of the budget skirmish, Richard Darman reflected on the Bush administration's scorecard: "All things considered, we have completed the first year in relatively good shape." The no-new taxes pledge was intact, congressional appropriations broadly conformed to the terms of the bipartisan deal, and presidential enforcement of sequestration had demonstrated that "there is some trace of fiscal discipline." Having set the bar low, the White House had achieved its main objectives, but it had only papered over the fiscal cracks. As the budget director acknowledged in private, the FY1990 deficit was likely to top $134 billion because of higher entitlement spending and revenue shortfalls and would go significantly higher if the economy proved weaker than assumed.[69] There were no more soft options that could be substituted for hard choices. Darman sounded a warning for FY1991: "We're just about out of accounting gimmicks. . . . It will have to be a *genuinely radical* budget." In his estimation, this required entitlement reform, a further defense freeze, and new revenues—possibly from a 25-cent-per-gallon hike on gasoline taxes and higher "sin" taxes on alcohol and tobacco.[70]

When Darman penned these thoughts, the political context of the deficit had deteriorated just as much as the policy context. The drive for capital gains tax reduction had been a huge tactical error for an administration that wanted bipartisan support to resolve the budget problem. The issue became a test of wills between George Mitchell and the president. In offering the olive branch of compromise, Bush raised his adversary's hopes that he could be bested over his tax pledge. In a sign of hardening partisanship, the Senate leader now refused to enter talks on the FY1991 budget until the president produced a realistic deficit-reduction plan.[71]

THE BIG FIX OF 1990

The deficit dominated domestic politics during Bush's second year in office and poisoned his relations with the GOP right. Darman came tantalizingly close to negotiating the "big fix" that would enable the administration to turn its attention to other matters of public policy, but this fell afoul of bipartisan congressional opposition. "If I didn't have this budget problem hanging over my head," the president remarked in frustration, "I would be loving this job."[72]

The first act in the fiscal drama of 1990 looked like a retread of past episodes in the budget saga. Without bipartisan cover, the administration was unwilling to take sole responsibility for proposing hard choices. The FY1991 budget plan was the usual concoction of optimistic revenue estimates, interest obligations and entitlement forecasts, and equally fanciful domestic spending cuts that had little hope of enactment. Projecting a deficit of $63.1 billion, it maintained the charade that the GRH timetable was being observed. The most unusual feature of the budget lay in its presentation, not its detail. A lengthy introduction by Darman made a thinly veiled attack on Democratic leaders that would have been inappropriate coming from the president. This struck an informal tone in places, notably in comparing the deficit to the Sesame Street "Cookie Monster" because it gobbled up resources needed for private investment and future growth. More significantly, it was stingingly critical of congressional profligacy and refusal to engage in politically difficult decisions to bring the budget under control.[73]

The White House nearly lost control of the fiscal agenda at the outset. Senator Daniel Patrick Moynihan (D-NY) enthused conservative Republicans with a maverick proposal to cut payroll taxes and ringfence the Social Security trust fund so that it could no longer be raided to finance other programs. Darman and White House chief of staff John Sununu cajoled the Senate Republican Policy Committee not to endorse this initiative. Previously angered by Bush's surrender on capital gains, many on the GOP right saw this as further proof of his unreliable commitment to low taxes. Taken together, conservative White House aide Charles Kolb later charged, these actions constituted "the functional and political equivalent of unilateral disarmament followed by suicide." In reality, Bush regarded Moynihan's plan as "a disguise for increased taxes around the corner," which were likely to hit upper-income groups that he wanted to protect. Democratic chieftains conversely opposed the New Yorker's initiative out of concern that it would necessitate domestic retrenchment.[74]

This was virtually the sole point of budgetary agreement between the White House and opposition party leaders. Their main bone of contention was over defense expenditure. At issue was no longer whether to cut military spending but the extent of the economies and, more significant, what to do with the savings. The sudden collapse of the Soviet Union's satellite regimes in Eastern Europe in late 1989 raised Democratic hopes for an immediate "peace dividend" that could be invested in domestic spending. Even before the Velvet Revolution reached its peak, Darman warned, "In the absence of a tax increase, DoD [Department of Defense] has become a 'bank' for the funding of non-DoD programs." For its part, the administration was adamant that any peace dividend had to be invested in deficit reduction.[75]

Bush wanted to respond in a measured way to Soviet bloc developments because he considered their outcome unpredictable. "When it comes to the security of this country," he asserted, "I would rather be called cautious than . . . reckless."[76] On his authority, Dick Cheney ordered Pentagon chiefs to formulate proposals for slicing $180 billion from FY1992–FY1994 baseline defense authority.[77] Coming off the original plan for steady growth, the projected cutbacks were not as big as they sounded. According to a CBO analysis founded on its own baseline calculation, the military blueprint unveiled in the FY1991 budget envisaged a less ambitious retrenchment of $134 billion in authority and $96 billion in appropriations over five years. Though comparable in scale to post-Vietnam retrenchment, this still left FY1995 defense spending 13 percent higher in real terms than when relative Soviet power was at its peak in FY1980. Darman failed to win approval for deeper cuts that would accommodate "both domestic economic dictates and the radically changing nature of external threats." Despite the opportunity for new détente, the defense guidance issued to accompany the budget cited the need to remain on guard against a Soviet threat to the Third World.[78]

Angered by Darman's budget statement, the Democrats decided to produce a FY1991 budget resolution without entering negotiations with the White House, but intraparty divisions over defense cuts that could hit jobs made for slow progress. The House Budget Committee eventually reported a resolution that provided just $283 billion for Pentagon outlays—$24 billion less than Bush requested—and redistributed most of the savings on social programs. This barely won House approval on May 2 in the face of opposition from every Republican and thirty-four Democrats. On the same day, the Senate Budget Committee reported a resolution setting military spending at $289 billion.[79]

At this juncture the White House made confidential overtures to hold bipartisan talks. New projections that the FY1990 budget could be as much as $170 billion in the red exposed the charade of GRH timetable observance. According to CBO calculations, a sequestration of $100 billion might be necessary in FY1991. A bipartisan budget agreement was therefore essential not only to preempt massive retrenchment from devastating the economy but also to reassure the financial markets that the deficit could be brought under control.[80] Talks began once Bush accepted on May 9 that there should be "no preconditions" about their scope, but prospects for agreement looked bleak. Although Thomas Foley was willing to set out a Democratic blueprint for deficit reduction, George Mitchell insisted on waiting until the president made public recognition that higher taxes were necessary.[81]

The Maine senator's outwardly mild demeanor masked a fierce partisanship and liberal devotion to his party's working-class base. No doubt, too, this self-made man risen from blue-collar origins in the textile-mill town of Waterville harbored populist animosity against the blue-blooded president, whose family had a summer seaside residence in his home state at Kennebunkport. An unnamed Bush administration official said of him, "When you cut to the core of Mitchell, . . . what you get is a very, very, very tough street fighter. . . . The further down you get . . . the more anger you get." Senate Democrats elected him majority leader in 1989 because they wanted an articulate partisan to confront the new president. Mitchell fixed his sights on overturning Bush's tax pledge, which he deemed a ploy to safeguard the rich.[82]

The negotiations—sometimes involving as many as twenty-six participants from congressional and administration ranks—were effectively stalled throughout May and June. Bush remained adamant that whatever was done on taxes had to be through agreement on everyone's part rather than his initiative. For this reason, too, he refused Democratic entreaties to make a national address informing Americans about the budget problem. However, time was not on the White House's side because it would have unilateral responsibility for announcing the FY1991 sequestration after release of the mid-session budget review on July 15. As one Democratic aide commented, "We were always of the view that we should just continue to walk through the fields, day by day, grinding them down."[83]

Advised by Darman that he would have to accept higher taxes to progress the talks, Bush finally conceded this at a meeting with a small group of senior negotiators at the White House on June 26. The president then issued an agreed-upon public statement that read: "It is clear to me that both the size of the deficit problem and the need for a package that can be enacted require all of the following: entitlement and mandatory program reform; tax revenue increases; growth incentives; discretionary spending reductions; orderly reductions in defense expenditures; and budget process reform." Mitchell had insisted on the addition of the words "to me" as a way of personalizing Bush's responsibility for the decision to raise taxes.[84]

This was the moment when Bush should have deployed the public resources of his office to sell his turnaround on taxes as an act of wise leadership. Presidential Assistant for Legislative Affairs Nick Calio urged him to go on television to tell Americans that "the deficit is the problem. . . . I have to do what I think is best for the country and I hope you will come with me."

Instead, the president followed Darman's advice to keep matters low-key in the hope of facilitating the budget talks. His statement was simply tacked onto the White House pressroom bulletin board without any public relations fanfare. Although Bush made some explanatory comment at his June 29 press conference, this had little impact on the public consciousness.[85]

In contrast, Democratic leaders spun their press briefings to emphasize the president's repudiation of his tax pledge. House Campaign Committee chair Beryl Anthony (D-AR) crowed, "This is an admission that the Republican policies of the last ten years were a failure." This was the message that the media picked up, exemplified by the *New York Post* headline, "'Read My Lips . . . I Lied.'"[86] GOP conservatives consequently deluged the White House with complaints that Bush's surrender would hurt both the party and the economy. On July 18, the House Republican Conference defied Minority Leader Robert Michel (R-IL) to adopt by a two-to-one majority a nonbinding resolution opposing new taxes. Its sponsor, Dick Armey (R-TX), declared, "Today we sent a message to congressional Democrats that if they want to raise taxes, they can do it without us."[87]

Nevertheless, the White House remained confident of getting a deal that Republicans could live with. It aimed to confine tax increases to energy, gasoline, and excise taxes while leaving marginal rates on income untouched. Darman also thought that he could trump Mitchell to obtain capital gains tax reduction with help from Dan Rostenkowski and Lloyd Bentsen. On domestic spending, the administration operated on the assumption that the president's tax concession legitimized demands for entitlement reform in return. On defense, it looked for a five-year reduction in line with what it had already proposed. The Iraqi invasion of Kuwait on August 2 and the massive deployment of American forces to protect Saudi Arabia made it difficult for the Democrats to push for the scale of military economies that the House budget resolution had projected. Pressing the point home, Bush declared at his news conference on August 8, "An operation of this nature has considerable expense. . . . But whatever it is, we're going to have to pay it."[88]

Finally, the White House wanted some element of procedural reform to constrain future spending. Bush had continued the Reagan campaign for a balanced-budget constitutional amendment. Although there was no prospect that Democratic leaders would agree to this as part of any deal, it was evident that many in Congress wanted new rules to tighten budget control. On July 17 the House of Representatives fell just seven votes short of approving a balanced-budget constitutional amendment proposal, the closest it had yet come to achieving a two-thirds majority. Republicans voted overwhelmingly in favor, by 169 votes to 5, but the Democrats were more divided than usual—145 stuck with the leadership and 110 voted for, some for the first time. A chastened Thomas Foley recognized that many in his party "wanted to see something more dramatically done" about deficits.[89]

The bipartisan talks quickly produced an outline agreement for deficit reduction of $50 billion in FY1991 and $500 billion over five years, but it took months to work out the details. Deadlines came and went with monotonous regularity. Hating the acrimony, Bush willingly delegated negotiating responsibility to Darman, John Sununu, and Nicholas Brady. Nothing was agreed by the time Congress recessed in early August. The negotiators withdrew to Andrews Air Force Base, Virginia, in early September with the hope of finalizing a deal away from the hurly-burly of Washington, but they returned empty-handed after eleven days.[90]

Clashes of ego made a difficult situation worse. Congressional negotiators from both parties took offense at what they considered the lack of respect shown them by Darman and, particularly, the abrasive Sununu. However, the real fault lines were over the substantive issues of whether to increase taxes on the wealthy and how far to cut entitlements. The Democrats would likely have traded a cut in the capital gains tax for a hike in the top rate of income tax, but administration negotiators pressed for one unconditionally. Behind the scenes, business friends like Charls Walker, chair of the American Council for Capital Foundation, urged Bush to hold out for the full "15-Percent solution" to boost the economy rather than take a "weak tea" alternative.[91]

What broke the logjam was the president's warning on September 25 that he would not sign a continuing resolution spending bill for the next fiscal year. With less than twenty-four hours left and 139 days since talks had started, a summit group of eight senior negotiators finally produced an agreement that avoided a government shutdown. The settlement promised deficit reduction of $500 billion over five years to be achieved through revenue increases of $162.9 billion (offset by $29 billion of revenue loss from new tax incentives for investment), discretionary spending cuts of $182.4 billion, entitlement savings of $106.3 billion, user fee increases of $13.9 billion, and interest savings on the public debt of $64.8 billion.[92]

This outcome was a personal victory for Richard Darman, the chief administration negotiator. The Democrats surrendered demands for an increase in the top rate of income tax and a surcharge on millionaires. Only $50 billion in new revenues came from wealth taxes in the form of limitations on itemized deductions for those with over $100,000 income, corporate tax rule changes, a hike in the income level at which the Medicare tax was phased out, and higher levies on luxury goods. Some $90 billion of revenue increases came from increases in regressive taxes on energy ($57 billion), beer and tobacco ($16 billion), and payrolls (through expansion of social security/Medicare coverage to all state and local government workers—$17 billion). Darman's sole failure was not getting comprehensive capital gains tax relief, but indexing of capital gains to inflation for small-business investment was among the tax incentives he won. The focus on consumption taxes conformed to the president's supply-side preferences and CEA advice that "deficit reduction should interfere with national saving and investment as little as possible."[93]

Defense economies that accounted for over two-thirds of projected discretionary savings were in line with administration plans. As a sop to the Democrats, cuts in domestic programs were delayed until the last two years of the cycle, and discretion about where to make them was left to the annual appropriations process. Nevertheless, the summit produced entitlement savings greater than considered possible in the Reagan era, with $60 billion coming from Medicare—nearly half from higher user charges and the rest through reduced payments to providers. In addition, the agreement contained spending-control provisions that would prove more effective instruments of budgetary restraint than GRH.

The Democratic leaders had accepted a deal that hit their own constituencies. On this occasion Foley persuaded Mitchell that refusal to cooperate would allow Bush to blame them for a government shutdown and sequestration. Sheer exhaustion after a week of almost nonstop talks also played a part in wearing down Democratic negotiators. Nor was there time to run the tax provisions through the Congressional Joint Committee on Taxation computer before Bush's deadline expired. It would show that the tax burden of those earning less than $10,000 a year would go up by 7.6 percent, compared with just 1.7 percent for those earning over $200,000. Once this became known, House Majority Leader Richard Gephardt (D-MO), one of the summit negotiators, responded, "I detest it. I think it's wrong. . . . But there is nothing more that we could do. It's the least-worst alternative."[94] At this juncture it looked as if the budget deal might create a damaging split in Democratic ranks. Bush could then have defended his turnaround on taxes as a statesmanlike act that contrasted with opposition bickering over constituency concerns.

Ironically, dissident House Republicans led by Newt Gingrich came to the Democrats' rescue. The Georgia congressman was uninterested in short-term tactical gains that conflicted with his strategic goal of creating a GOP conservative majority in the House of Representatives. Early in his political career he had helped form the Conservative Opportunity Society to promote a new agenda in pursuit of this end. Gingrich disdained the minority complex that gripped senior colleagues because of their long years out of power. The maxim he lived by was "If you're not on offense, you're on defense." Ronald Reagan's brand of conviction politics inspired his belief that only through visionary conservatism could the House GOP attain majority status.[95] In Gingrich's assessment the budget agreement put that project at risk by sacrificing the issue that defined the Republicans as the party of prosperity and individual enterprise for the sake of fiscal responsibility. "There is a clear difference between those of us who believe passionately in growth incentives and those with the traditional view that reducing the deficit is more important," Gingrich declared. "It's a debate that has been going on for 15 years."[96]

To tie the GOP right into the budget deal, the White House had insisted on Gingrich, recently elected whip, and Senator Phil Gramm (R-TX), formerly the Democratic cosponsor of the Reagan tax bill of 1981, being part of the negotiating group. In parallel with the latter's acceptance of "non-incentive-crushing taxes" to avoid sequestration, Gingrich agreed to consider revenue increases if the budget deal included capital gains tax reduction, significant cuts in domestic expenditure and entitlements, and spending controls. The resulting storm of conservative protest obliged him to reassert his ideological credentials and keep his distance from the talks. In a speech to the Heritage Foundation on August 22, Gingrich called for a five-year, $134 billion program of capital gains tax reduction, savings incentives, and expanded tax credit for families that would deliver a balanced budget through economic growth. Seizing the Reaganite banner discarded by Bush, he asserted that this tax-cut program would define the GOP as the party of jobs and prosperity, in opposition to the Democrats as the party that wanted to raise taxes in support of a bureaucratic welfare state and at cost of economic decline.[97]

A condition of the agreement was that majorities of both parties should approve it in both chambers so that neither would be singled out for blame over the tax increases. Thanks to his command of the whip's resources, Gingrich was in a strong position to enlist the eighty-nine Republican votes needed to wreck the deal. The Chamber of Commerce, which feared the tax increases would hasten an economic downturn, placed its lobbying muscle behind his campaign. The Heritage Foundation also put out critical backgrounders that the agreement "will damage the economy very seriously." Hardball tactics by the White House also backfired. Sununu's warning to the Republican House Conference that Bush was prepared to speak against defectors in their constituencies only angered legislators who had not benefited from presidential coattails in 1988.[98]

Desperate to salvage the situation, Bush on this occasion followed Nick Calio's advice to get involved in marketing the deal. He addressed a meeting of business association leaders convened by Dan Quayle to counter the Chamber of Commerce. He also worked the phone and hosted droves of balking Republicans at White House meetings. At stake, Bush warned, was not just the economy's future but his own standing in the eyes of the world as international coalition leader in the Persian Gulf. Many legislators wanted stronger political cover for approving a tax increase. Accordingly, for only the fourth time since he took office, the president addressed the nation on October 2 to ask that Americans voice support for the bipartisan plan to their congressional representatives.[99]

Bush and his speechwriters hoped to parlay the nation's unity regarding the Gulf crisis into support for the budget agreement, but they failed to strike the right tone. The address opened with high-flowing rhetoric urging national solidarity to deal with fiscal problems and then descended into a nose-holding endorsement for the bipartisan deal. "Anyone of us alone," the president declared, "might have written a better plan. But it is the best agreement that can be legislated now." Such rhetoric was unlikely to inspire popular willingness to make sacrifices for the common good. The following day congressional offices were deluged with constituent calls running about six to one against the plan.[100]

This response belied opinion polls conducted on the eve of Bush's presidency showing widespread expectation that he would eventually have to raise taxes.[101] Part of the explanation for this paradox is that the president paid the price for not making earlier use of the bully pulpit to educate the public about why higher taxes were necessary at this particular time. Bush's failure to spell out the consequences of the escalating deficit for sequestration and interest rates meant that most Americans felt no sense of fiscal crisis. There was also a marked difference between the substance of his tax increases and his predecessor's. The Reagan tax hikes had mainly hit corporations and investors. The principal exception had been the 1983 payroll tax increases, but the near insolvency of the Social Security trust fund had provided justification for this. Bush was now asking ordinary taxpayers to support a solution to the budget problem that was a great deal more painful for most of them than the deficit itself appeared to be. Moreover, instead of presenting the bipartisan plan for common sacrifice as a triumph of statesmanship, he told his audience that their taxes would have to go up because their leaders could not agree on a better solution.

The president's inept management of public expectations contributed to the scale of rebellion against the budget deal. The House rejected it by 254 votes to 179 on October 5, with partisan majorities of almost equal proportions—60 percent of Republicans and 58 percent of Democrats—making up the nays. Speaking for GOP conservatives, Dick Armey declared his preference for sequestration because it "hurts government, and this package hurts the American people and their economy." Angry about the Medicare cuts and the lack of tax progressivity in the deal, liberal Democrats deserted in droves once it was evident that a majority of Republicans were voting against. The rebellion reached high into party ranks. Only fourteen of the House's twenty-seven standing committee chairs backed the proposal. Speaking for many liberals, David Obey (D-WI) called for an end to "phony bipartisanship" and urged Democratic leaders to "let people know what you stand for."[102]

An alternative plan was needed in short order to avoid the GRH sequester. On October 6 Bush precipitated a partial shutdown of government by vetoing a continuing resolution to fund government until a new agreement was reached. The president insisted that Congress had to pass either a budget plan or a continuing resolution permitting GRH sequesters to kick in. Determined to avoid sequestration, Democratic conferees from the House and Senate Budget Committees hastily devised a resolution that adopted the outline aggregates of the discarded bipartisan plan but allowed congressional committees discretion to determine how these were to be achieved. On October 7 this won approval from both houses, thereby enabling Bush to sign a continuing resolution that kept the government running for two more weeks in the hope that a budget reconciliation bill could be approved by then.[103]

Many on Capitol Hill thought that Bush would accept a hike in the top band of income tax for a cut in the capital gains rate as the first step to a new compromise. The president sent out confusing signals about his position, culminating in a flippant remark—"read my hips"—when a journalist asked for clarification during one of his jogging sessions. This predictably infuriated GOP congressional leaders engaged in trying to get a budget settlement acceptable to the White House. On October 11 a chastened Bush unambiguously rejected any trade lest it legitimize something "further to the left" than was acceptable on income taxes. The president was also wary of what one Republican warned him was "a Democratic plot to bust you twice" by getting him to agree to an income tax hike and accusing him of protecting the rich with capital gains relief.[104]

It was evident that House Democrats would press for a soak-the-rich deficit-reduction scheme. The Senate, where southern and western Democrats had more influence and institutional rules accorded the Republican minority greater powers, was more moderate in outlook. It would almost certainly have approved the bipartisan settlement rejected by the House. Accordingly, the White House focused on getting the Senate to produce a reconciliation bill similar in terms to the summit agreement in the hope of brokering an acceptable compromise in the conference negotiations, but this scenario did not work out anywhere near as well as hoped.[105]

Abetted by Gingrich's refusal to negotiate, House Democrats produced a reconciliation measure skewed toward their middle- and lower-income constituencies. This raised the top rate of income tax from 28 to 33 percent, put a 10 percent surcharge on those with annual incomes over $1 million, and suspended income tax indexing for one year to make up revenues lost by dropping the gasoline tax increase. On the spending side, it significantly reduced the entitlement cuts in the bipartisan deal. With most Senate Democrats keen to avoid sequestration, they cooperated with Republicans to produce a less progressive reconciliation measure that did not raise income taxes but limited deductions available to upper-income taxpayers.[106]

The compromise from the conference projected a deficit reduction of $42.5 billion in FY1991 and $496.2 billion for FY1991–FY1995. It retained the discretionary savings from the summit agreement but reduced entitlement cuts by $20 billion to accommodate smaller increases in Medicare costs to beneficiaries. In a clear victory for the Democrats, however, the new plan differed significantly from the original in distribution of higher taxes. Under its terms, the majority of taxpayers experienced an average increase of around 2 percent in their tax bill. However, those making under $10,000 a year and those making $10,000–$20,000 received average cuts of 2 percent and 3.2 percent, respectively, and those making more than $200,000 got an average increase of 6.3 percent.[107]

Although House negotiators surrendered the "millionaires' tax," they secured phasing out of the current personal exemption ($2,050) for individuals with taxable income above $100,000. The Senate conversely accepted an increase in the top income tax rate from 28 percent to 31 percent. Bush could take some comfort that this actually entailed a tax cut for some high-income families paying a 33 percent top rate under the existing tax bubble. As a further sop, the conference limited the top rate of tax on capital gains to 28 percent, whereas current law taxed it at the same rate as an individual's ordinary income. The wealthy were also hit with an increase in the alternative minimum tax from 21 percent to 24 percent, new limits on deductions, and a raised cap on wages subject to Medicare tax ($125,000, compared with the current $51,300). The investment incentive provisions of the summit agreement were also eliminated. In contrast, lower-income taxpayers received two-thirds of the $27.4 billion tax breaks in the package, including $13.1 billion for the earned income tax credit to help the working poor. The most regressive provision was the increase in the gasoline tax, but this preempted the need to freeze indexation of income tax.[108]

More pleasing to the administration, the conference committee also agreed on the terms of the Budget Enforcement Act (BEA) of 1990, which had formed part of the original agreement. This effectively repealed GRH's deficit limits and the sequestration penalties pertaining to these.[109] It made provision instead for elastic deficit targets that were adjustable in light of changing economic circumstances and technical assumptions. In the interests of transparency, the Social Security surplus was excluded from calculation of the deficit. Instead of trying to control the deficit in the manner of GRH, the BEA sought to discipline spending and transferred sequestration to support this end. First, it set specific caps on discretionary budget authority and outlays for the defense, international, and domestic programs. Exempted from these ceilings were emergency appropriations, including funds for military operations in the Persian Gulf and the S&L bailout. Additionally, "Pay-As-You-Go" (PAYGO) provisions instituted offset requirements for new entitlement spending not subject to annual appropriation and tax cuts. In contrast to GRH, the BEA held Congress responsible for what it controlled, namely the size of federal spending, rather than the size of the deficit, which was sensitive to economic conditions, foreign crises, and uncontrollable entitlement outlays. It also aimed to constrain the programs that caused the deficit rather than punish those that did not.

The BEA had considerable significance for institutional budgetary powers. It endowed the executive with principal responsibility for budgetary control at the expense of the majority party in the legislature. The president was given discretion to adjust the deficit target in recognition that he could do so more speedily than Congress, and the OMB was tasked with monitoring compliance. Within Congress, the new rules increased the powers of the appropriation committees at the expense of the budget committees because the spending controls diminished the significance of congressional budget resolutions. Engineered by Darman and Senate Appropriations Committee chair Robert Byrd (D-WV), the new enforcement mechanisms were intended to reward the executive agencies and the appropriations committees that had shown greater efficiency than the authorizing committees in adhering to expenditure targets agreed to in the 1989 bipartisan deal. The intracongressional transfer of power also benefited the president's strategic leadership in budgeting. Whereas the budget committees were a counterweight to this, the appropriations committees had an incremental perspective regarding presidential spending requests and were indifferent to the revenue side of the budget.[110]

The Omnibus Budget Reconciliation Act of 1990 cleared the House by 228 votes to 200 and the Senate by 55 votes to 45, but the majority of Republicans—128 and 26 in the respective chambers—voted against it. RNCC cochair Edward Rollins circulated a memorandum on October 15 advising GOP candidates in the midterm elections to distance themselves from Bush's acceptance of new taxes. "Do not hesitate," he declared, "to oppose either the president or proposals being advanced in Congress." Incandescent with rage, Bush threatened never to sign another fund-raising letter for the RNCC unless the disloyal political operative was fired. Rollins's resignation preempted his dismissal, but his intervention legitimized GOP opposition to the reconciliation bill.[111]

Bush's relationship with conservative Republicans never recovered from his reversal on taxes. In retirement, he lamented that his critics had put up with his predecessor's larger hikes without accusing him of betrayal.[112] However, conservatives forgave Reagan his transgressions because he provided visionary leadership of the change they wanted. In contrast, the GOP right regarded Bush's tax turnaround as proof that he was a pragmatic manager of government rather than a devotee to its reduction. The president's compromise also brought about a change in the attitude of Gingrich and his allies toward the deficit. In the 1980s they had prioritized opposition to tax increases in the face of its growth, but OBRA persuaded them that deficit elimination was necessary to preserve low taxes.

Vainly attempting to mend fences with his Republican critics, Bush accused the Democrats of holding him to ransom over taxes as the price for a deficit-reduction deal essential to the nation's well-being. Rather than using its power to serve "the common interest," he charged in his major address of the midterm campaign, this "arrogant majority" protected "its own prerogatives, its own perks, its own privileges, its own pet projects . . . in the name of politics and higher taxes."[113] Unfortunately for the president, this was the speech that conservatives had wanted him to give a month earlier as justification for a government shutdown.

In Newt Gingrich's opinion, Bush could have placed responsibility for this denouement on the opposition party by uttering the words, "I did my best, but the Democrats just won't talk about anything but taxes." This was the very tactic that Bill Clinton would employ against him in 1995–1996, but the circumstances were different in 1990. Presidential leadership on the budget could not be conducted without an eye to other matters of pressing national importance. Bush was keen to avoid a government shutdown, however partial, amid an international crisis. Hoist with the petard of his election pledge, he had no option but to squirm off it for a cause of greater importance. As he later acknowledged, "'Read my lips' was rhetorical overkill. When push came to shove and our troops were moving overseas, we needed a fully functioning government."[114]

No less than the GOP right, some in the Bush camp saw the reversal on taxes as the beginning of the end for his presidency. "If you want to look for a place where things first went wrong," Dan Quayle reflected, "I'd pick the 'budget summit' of 1990."[115] This was a case of hindsight having 20/20 vision. At the time, the budget settlement did not look so bad for Bush. GOP losses of eight House seats and one Senate seat in the 1990 elections were significantly less than the presidential party had suffered in recent midterms. White House tracking polls found that the budget agreement "was successful in achieving a bi-partisan public reaction." Pluralities of Republicans, ticket-splitters, and Democrats thought that it did not cut spending enough. The first two groups also believed that it increased taxes too much, and the third was evenly divided on this score. Moreover, 57 percent of those polled blamed Congress primarily for the deficit, compared to just 13 percent blaming the president.[116]

Encouraged by these findings, John Sununu audaciously informed the Conservative Leadership Conference that Bush could take a more adversarial stance against the Democratic Congress now that deficit reduction was enshrined in legislation. "There's not another single piece of legislation that needs to be passed in the next two years for this president," he asserted. "We don't need them." Moreover, the budget deal seemingly freed the president to move on to other issues, particularly foreign policy, on which to build a successful record for reelection. In apparent confirmation of this, his approval rating shot up from 52 percent in late October to 90 percent in the spring of 1991 thanks to rapid success in the Gulf War.[117]

The doomsayers were proved right in the end, however. The budget deal substituted deficit reduction for the tax pledge as the core element of Bush's domestic agenda. His success as president therefore became dependent on being able to demonstrate that this was a worthwhile trade-off. In Bush's own assessment, the compromise "would have been digested if the economy had vigorously recovered."[118] Far from exiting the national agenda, however, the deficit became the symbol of an economy in crisis and a nation on the wrong track by the time he faced reelection.

TANGLED UP IN RED

The deficit continued to rise under Bush from $221.1 billion in FY1990 to $269.3 billion in FY1991 and to $290.4 billion in FY1992 before falling to $255.1 billion in FY1993. It averaged 4.3 percent of GDP over this period, compared with 3.5 percent in the Reagan second-term budgets, and its constant-dollar average was nearly a third higher than in FY1986–FY1989. When OBRA was enacted, the CBO projected that the deficit would continue to grow for two years but thereafter decline rapidly. By the end of Bush's presidency, however, expectations that a new era of surplus budgets was in sight had given way to resignation that big deficits would stretch far into the future. In October 1991 the CBO issued a new baseline projection that a $300 billion imbalance was likely in FY2001 even with continuous economic growth.[119]

This fiscal deterioration provided conservatives with plentiful ammunition to justify their original antipathy to the budget deal. The Cato Institute dubbed it the "Crime of the Century" in charging that cumulative FY1991–FY1995 deficits would be $1.3 trillion higher than under the GRH goals because total domestic outlays were growing faster than at any time in thirty years. In the assessment of its chief fiscal analyst, Stephen Moore, this signified that the real purpose of the budget agreement for the Washington establishment had been to avoid GRH sequestration rather than reduce the deficit. The Heritage Foundation similarly complained that OBRA had transferred the peace dividend of defense cuts into higher domestic spending. Supply-siders placed more emphasis on the 2 percent real decline of revenues in FY1991 under the new tax regime compared with the 3.5 percent real annual increase over the previous five years. Seeing the Reagan-era growth as proof of Laffer curve theory, Chamber of Commerce economist Matthew Kibbe forecast that 81 percent of the revenues expected from the 1990 tax increases would fail to materialize.[120]

These diatribes were wide of the mark. The Bush administration had been left holding a number of fiscal babies not of its paternity. Federal spending averaged 22 percent GDP in Bush's four budgets, but this was not far out of line with the average of 21.6 percent GDP in Reagan's second-term budgets. The growth occurred in uncontrollable areas of the budget. Entitlement and other mandatory spending averaged 11.3 percent GDP under Bush, compared with 10.2 percent GDP in FY1986–FY1989. In contrast, discretionary outlays averaged only 8.6 percent GDP, compared with 9.5 percent GDP. The decline in defense from 5.9 percent GDP during Reagan's second term to 5 percent GDP under Bush was almost wholly responsible for this decline. The domestic budget had meanwhile absorbed the S&L bailout costs of $72 billion in FY1991–FY1993, the bulk in FY1991. If interest payments that covered past commitments were also discounted, Michael Boskin told Bush, "the Administration may be thought of as paying its own way." However, it was never able to put across this message with the clarity needed to counter its critics.[121]

Most significantly for deficit growth under Bush, the economy underwent a recession that began in the third quarter of 1990 and reached its trough in March 1991. The consequent recovery proved surprisingly anemic in its early stages. Real per capita disposable income actually declined in the second half of 1991. Total output was only 3.3 percent above its prerecession peak in the first quarter of 1993, a much smaller gain than in any previous postwar expansion except that following the 1974–1975 recession. The recovery brought only a small monthly increase of 36,000 in nonfarm jobs in its first six quarters.[122] According to CBO calculations, cyclical economic factors, which depressed tax receipts and expanded mandatory income assistance, accounted for $51 billion of the deficit in FY1991 (19 percent), $68 billion in FY1992 (23.4 percent), and $57 billion in FY1993 (22.3 percent).[123]

Notwithstanding conservative insistence that Bush's acceptance of tax increases was somehow responsible for ending the Reagan expansion, the economy was in decline by the time the budget agreement was enacted. The downturn was the product of many factors, notably Federal Reserve monetary tightening, a banking system weakened by previous bad loans to Latin America, the effect of the S&L crisis on the housing market, over-building of commercial real estate, and the effect on business confidence of oil-price volatility resulting from the Persian Gulf crisis. Although unemployment never reached the levels of the 1974–1975 and 1981–1982 downturns, it hit middle-class occupations much harder. Many of the job losses appeared permanent as corporations sought to downsize middle management in the drive to cut costs and enhance competitiveness. No less than their blue-collar counterparts, white-collar workers now worried about debt, job security, and the value of their homes. Consumer confidence sank to its lowest level in seventeen years. In December 1991, Alan Greenspan told a congressional committee, "There is a deep-seated concern out there that I must say to you I haven't seen in my lifetime."[124]

Expecting a normal recovery pattern, the Bush administration initially focused on the long-term goal of deficit control. To preserve BEA spending caps, it desisted from proposing a stimulus package lest the Democrats use this as a vehicle for their own spending proposals. Such concerns appeared justified by the Senate's consideration of a massive highway bill under guise of being a jobs program. The administration also used the PAYGO restrictions to block a Democratic initiative extending unemployment compensation for workers who had exhausted their benefits. At issue was just $5.8 billion for a measure that had received routine approval in previous recessions. When the Democrats enacted the bill with offsetting revenue increases in September 1991, Bush vetoed it, but Republican desertions nearly led to a Senate override. Amid mounting evidence of slow recovery, the president reversed his stand to sign an amended measure in November. Nevertheless, he still ruled out tax cuts to boost the economy on grounds that the enlargement of the deficit would make the financial markets nervous about inflation.[125]

Meanwhile, the White House pressed ahead with further defense cuts after the Soviet Union's disintegration in late 1991. The Base Force Plan, its new program for national security in the unipolar post–Cold War world, envisaged a four-pronged strategy of deterrence, forward presence, crisis response, and reconstitution should the threat level grow again. This projected a 25 percent reduction in armed forces and substantial spending cuts for all three military services by FY1995 in recognition of the diminished threat level. To achieve that target, Bush sought multiyear defense savings of $50 billion above those planned in earlier reviews. Although House Armed Services Committee chair Les Aspin (D-WI) charged that still greater economies were possible, most Democrats had little interest in making deeper cuts that would undermine defense employment in a weak economy.[126]

Worried that the sluggish recovery posed an electoral threat, the White House relaxed its strictures on deficit control in 1992, but its efforts at fiscal stimulus ran aground on the rocks of divided government. Bush's FY1993 budget proposed tax reduction to boost savings and investment offset with a freeze on domestic spending. Democrats countered with proposals for middle-class tax relief funded through higher taxes for upper-income earn-ers. As a compromise, they enacted a $77.5 billion measure incorporating most of the administration's proposals along with their own, only to have it vetoed by Bush as a budget-busting bill that would weaken the foundations of economic recovery. A similar measure appended to an urban aid initiative en-acted after the Los Angeles riots of April 1992 suffered the same fate. Mean-while, the Democrats complied with the domestic freeze out of concern that Bush would exploit a confrontation over spending in the election.[127]

In the absence of fiscal stimulus, the administration was wholly dependent on monetary policy to boost recovery. Aware that the economy was heading into recession as the budget deal was finalized, Bush hoped that his commit-ment to deficit reduction would produce interest-rate relaxation.[128] The Fed duly obliged with an immediate ¼ percent cut, followed by further regular reductions in 1991 that lowered the federal funds rate from 7 to 4 percent over the course of the year. However, this was a slower pace of relaxation than in previous recessions because inflation still remained a concern. The central bank continued to operate in accordance with Greenspan's admonition to the Open Market Committee on November 13, 1990. "It's very clear to me," he asserted, "that if we are perceived as responding excessively easily to all the other signs that would induce central bank ease, that the risks of the system cracking on us are much too dangerous."[129]

Dissatisfied with his caution, the White House seriously considered not reappointing Greenspan when his term as chair expired in August 1991 but relented because of his strong support within the financial community. Re-lations continued to deteriorate because of Fed reluctance to cut rates in the first half of 1992. After Nicholas Brady's efforts to arm-twist Greenspan got nowhere, Bush finally went public with a call for monetary relaxation in a newspaper interview on June 23. Only when new employment figures pointed to rising joblessness did the Fed accommodate him. Two consecutive cuts of ½ percent on July 2 and September 4 brought the federal funds rate down to 3 percent, the lowest for twenty years and effectively a zero-interest level because inflation was also running at 3 percent. By the end of the year, the economy was at last showing signs of new vigor, but too late for Bush.[130]

Compounding the problems that the recession caused Bush was the ad-ministration's premature insistence that early signs of recovery prefaced the return of prosperity. As Michael Boskin admitted, "A bad error was made in not doing a better job in explaining that even if the recession had ended, that did not mean that economic good times were here or would soon oc-cur." By October 1991 the CEA chair put chances of a double-dip recession at 30 percent. Only on threat of resignation did he get past Sununu to tell Bush that "our discussion of the economy was out of touch with reality."[131]

However, the administration's consequent change of tone failed to eradicate the damaging impression that it was out of touch with the national mood of pessimism about the nation's long-term economic decline.

The economy's disappointing recovery seemingly legitimized the doom-saying that had first developed momentum in the late 1980s. A number of influential studies, notably Yale historian Paul Kennedy's best-selling *The Rise and Fall of the Great Powers*, had warned of the economic consequences of the excessive accumulation of public debt in the 1980s. This set off a debate in the op-ed pages as to whether America's attempt to borrow its way to prosperity and power had undermined the foundations of its economic strength.[132] In the early 1990s the stream of "declinist" literature turned into a flood that inflated pessimism about the economic future.

Theories that America had hit the skids were based on three fundamental arguments. Some analysts blamed the Reagan administration's predisposition to help the rich at the expense of the blue-collar and white-collar middle classes through its tax cuts skewed to the wealthy, its facilitation of corporate America's drive to create low-wage jobs on threat of transferring operations abroad, and its erosion of federal aid for homeownership, college education, and training programs.[133] Others emphasized the failure of America's leaders to develop industrial policy initiatives that would enhance its competitiveness in the new globalized economy.[134] A third school warned that unbalanced budgets were the greatest threat to America's economic well-being. From its perspective, massive deficits kept long-term interest rates high because of investor concerns about inflation. As a consequence, expensive borrowing costs would not only discourage private investment but also constrain public investment in infrastructure and human capital needed for economic growth.[135]

The deficit theory of national decline gained increasing credence as the recession plunged federal finances ever deeper into the red. It gained something of an official imprimatur from a General Accounting Office (GAO) report forecasting that the budget gap would rise to 20 percent GDP by 2020 if allowed to grow at the same rate as under Reagan and Bush. This predicted that the United States would be reduced to Third World debtor status by 2012 unless it took corrective action. According to the GAO, even a "muddling through" approach of operating permanent deficits of around 3 percent GDP would require huge cuts in discretionary programs or large tax increases to fund interest costs on a rising national debt. In its estimate, America's best hope of fiscal and economic salvation was to accept the pain of eliminating the deficit by 2001 and reap the consequent benefits of lower interest rates for economic growth in the first two decades of the next century.[136] CEA officials criticized these findings as "derived from an extremely simplistic model of the economy with several obvious biases." However, deficit pessimists regarded the GAO's report as a realistic warning that America was in danger of becoming what one called "a fiscal Brazil."[137]

The normally unexcitable Nicholas Brady called for an administration counteroffensive against the pessimists, but this was tantamount to closing the stable door after the horse had bolted.[138] The declinist theory had already fed into the politics of the 1992 presidential election. Former Reagan aide Patrick Buchanan appropriated it to underwrite his challenge for the Republican nomination. This populist maverick accused Bush of strangling economic growth through his acceptance of higher taxes in 1990. "Thanks to White House abandonment of our principles," he charged, "the 92-month-long economic boom has been put on a fast track to Mexico." Buchanan's quest was a futile one, but it forced Bush into a tactical retreat. To safeguard his appeal to the GOP base, he admitted that the budget compromise had been the "biggest mistake" of his presidency.[139] This helped to neutralize Buchanan, but it meant that Bush could no longer brandish his deficit-reduction program as a necessary sacrifice to strengthen the foundations of economic recovery.

Meanwhile, Paul Tsongas advanced a deficit reduction plan for entitlement savings, defense cuts, and tax increases as the banner issue of his campaign for the Democratic nomination.[140] Though unsuccessful in his presidential quest, the former Massachusetts senator teamed up with retiring senator Warren Rudman (R-NH) and former Nixon administration Commerce secretary Peter Peterson to form the Concord Coalition to lobby for fiscal responsibility. Consciously rejecting politics-as-usual, this organization proclaimed that only budgetary nonpartisanship could build a stronger, richer, and fairer nation.[141] In Rudman's bleak assessment, "We are about to enter an era of annual $400 and $500 billion deficits that will truly wreck the country. . . . We will have foreign governments in a position to dictate terms and conditions of money they will loan us. And interest rates will go high. And the economy will be seriously impaired. And the standard of living will decline."[142]

However, it was Ross Perot's independent candidacy that turned the deficit into both symbol and substance of popular uncertainty about the economy in the 1992 election. In normal circumstances this Texan billionaire businessman and citizen-volunteer, who had never previously sought office and lacked any particular constituency, would not have made any electoral impact.[143] Now, however, his trenchant critique that the recession was "the result of ten years of gross excess spending and mismanagement of the country" resonated with many Americans. Perot called for common sacrifice to get the budget under control for the sake of the nation's economic future. "We allowed politicians to buy our votes," he charged, "by promising newer and grander giveaways (with money . . . they had to borrow from our children). We allowed them to rack up deficit after deficit while we reelected them time after time." His message was a clear and simple one: that only restoration of fiscal responsibility would boost competitiveness, stimulate investment, and create jobs.[144]

A genius at selling his ideas about the gravity of the deficit problem, Perot was initially less adept at presenting solutions for it. His embryonic agenda betrayed a fundamental lack of understanding about the distributional impact of domestic spending retrenchment and an excessive optimism that determined auditors could identify $180 billion of "waste, fraud and abuse" within government. An unimpressive performance in the face of tough questioning on NBC's *Meet the Press* on May 3 forced him into a rethink. He consequently hired former Carter OMB official John White to put together a credible five-year, $754 billion deficit-elimination plan to balance the budget by FY1998.[145]

The new Perot program advocated reducing discretionary spending by 15 percent to save $108 billion over five years, a third from the elimination of unnecessary or outdated programs and the remainder from an across-the-board cut for all federal departments. It also sought a more streamlined defense attuned to post–Cold War conditions to yield a minimum of $40 billion savings beyond those already targeted by Bush. An ambitious program for entitlement reform projected mammoth savings of $233 billion, more than half coming from Medicare and Medicaid. Revenue initiatives were to yield $50 billion from the removal of subsidies and tax favors, $73 billion from the elimination of tax deductions that favored the rich, and $33 billion from raising the top rate of income tax from 31 percent to 33 percent. In addition, a 10 cent increase in gasoline tax was to generate $158 billion, and higher duties on tobacco were to produce a further $18 billion, a portion of which was to be used to fund research into finding cures for smoking-related diseases. Upgrading of IRS computer systems to improve tax collection efficiency, higher taxes on foreign companies operating in the United States, and tax code simplifications were to produce a further $31 billion.[146]

On paper at least, this plan was the very opposite of the smoke-and-mirrors formulas beloved in Washington. Even though the wealthy were targeted for big hits, everyone had to share the burden of resolving the budget crisis. Perot therefore avoided charges not only of bias toward his own class but also of being a populist demagogue in the manner of Huey Long in the 1930s. The Texan's popular appeal lay mainly in his simple prescriptions for the supposedly interconnected problems of politics-as-usual, public debt, and economic stagnation. Had Perot been elected president, it was highly unlikely that he would have triumphed over the gridlock of divided government to get his program enacted. Nor was it clear that his five-year plan could have delivered the benefits that he claimed if the financial markets had doubts about its viability.

Despite his erratic conduct in withdrawing from the race in June and reentering it in October, Perot ended up with 19 percent of the popular vote. This was the best showing by a third-party candidate since Theodore Roosevelt's Bull Moose campaign of 1912. Whether Bush could have won without him on the ballot is unclear. Exit polls suggested that Perot took votes in equal proportions from the two main-party candidates. They also indicated that "economy/jobs" was the main issue that determined ballot preference. In total, 42 percent of voters mentioned this as mattering most to them, of whom 52 percent supported Democrat Bill Clinton, 25 percent backed Bush, and 24 percent went for Perot. Nevertheless, the "budget deficit" was the issue next highest in saliency. Among the 21 percent of voters citing this, the respective shares of the three candidates were 36 percent, 27 percent, and 37 percent. Perot voters had also supported Bush over Michael Dukakis by 56–17 percent in 1988. Disproportionately, therefore, they were attitudinal Republicans that left Bush not for a Democrat but for an independent who had persuaded many of them that the budget deficit signified the failure of the political class as personified by the president to lead the nation to economic renewal.[147]

Most significantly, Perot's antideficit campaign validated Clinton's claims that the economy was seriously off track. In mid-September a *Wall Street Journal*/NBC News poll found that 86 percent of respondents believed the recession was still ongoing. Just a few days before the election, a poll for *USA Today* reported that 60 percent of voters felt that economic conditions were worsening and only 28 percent thought they were improving. In this case the minority perception was correct. Economic growth over the course of 1992 had averaged an impressive 4 percent without pushing inflation above 3 percent.[148] A lag in public perception of economic reality was by no means unusual, but Perot's diatribes against the deficit probably exacerbated it. Moreover, Bush's acceptance of higher taxes in apparently unsuccessful pursuit of deficit reduction meant that he could not deploy the Reaganite argument that lower taxes were the route to prosperity in response to the independent candidate's charges that the economy was in long-term decline.

THE BUSH LEGACY

As Bush's presidency drew to a close, most analysts considered its greatest achievements to be in foreign policy, notably managing the end of the Cold War and building an international coalition to win the Gulf War. Hardly anyone ranked his budget leadership a success, not least the president himself.

The 1990 tax increases stuck in his craw as an important factor in his election defeat. Bush blamed his downfall on congressional leaders' refusal to put the national interest above their political agendas. In retirement, he reflected, "[George] Mitchell's purpose, his goal was simply to bring my presidency down, and to some degree he deserves credit for that." His other nemesis, Newt Gingrich, also came in for harsh words. "Years later," Bush wrote, "he told me that his decision [to oppose me] was one of the most difficult he had made in his life. Maybe so, but it sure hurt me. His support could have eliminated the flak I took on the tax question and on my credibility."[149]

In time, however, many analysts recognized that the budget agreement was "prematurely and unfairly pronounced a failure."[150] It came to be seen as having lain the foundations of economic and fiscal success later in the decade. Despite the focus of contemporary attention on the tax compromise, the BEA spending-control provisions played the pivotal role in holding future deficits in check. GRH had proved unworkable because it set a target for the budget deficit that was vulnerable to endogenous variables like recession, unforeseen crises, and uncontrollable entitlements. The BEA applied caps to budgetary elements that political leaders could control. In contrast to their repeated evasion of GRH targets, they could and did live by the new rules.

Bush took satisfaction from the positive reassessment of his budgetary policy. In a foreword to a book about his leadership on deficit reduction, he wrote, "We took a huge gamble then and it's nice to see it pay off."[151] The economic policy mix of tight budgets and monetary relaxation that proved so successful under his successor had its origins on his watch. Although the recession masked the initial significance of this change, the 1990 budget agreement and the interest-rate reductions that followed it constituted the first steps toward the new regime.

Notwithstanding revisionist assessment of its policy success, the political consequences of Bush's decision to prioritize resolution of the budget problem at the cost of his tax pledge remained too important to overlook. His experience underlined the difficulties of depoliticizing the deficit in the cause of the national interest. It reaffirmed that budgeting was a highly contentious domain of public policy through its embodiment of defining issues of party ideology on the size of government, taxes, and economic growth. The resolutely nonpartisan Perot campaign and the acres of printed words calling for national unity to avert the economic catastrophe from mounting public debt did next to nothing to change this. When Bush signaled his willingness to negotiate a budget agreement without preconditions, a senior Republican congressman warned him that taxes would take the place of communism as the GOP's "hate object" in the post–Cold War era.[152] Bill Clinton would discover the truth of these words as the political battles over the budget grew increasingly bitter in the final decade of the twentieth century.

CHAPTER 6

Bill Clinton:
Taming the Deficit

On January 6, 1999, Bill Clinton ran down the curtain on America's late-twentieth-century fiscal history and confidently looked forward to a new era in the new century. "Today," he declared, "I am proud to announce that we can say the era of big deficits is over." Clinton was the first president in nearly thirty years to achieve a balanced budget. A bright future of surpluses appeared to beckon. "Just as exploding deficits were the symbol of a government failing its people in the 1980s," Clinton proclaimed, "these surpluses are a symbol of a government that works in the 1990s and beyond . . . [one] more prepared than ever to meet the challenges of the 21st century."[1]

Not in his wildest dreams could Clinton have imagined making this statement when he became president. On his accession, the CBO forecast that the deficit would escalate dramatically in the late 1990s to reach $653 billion by FY2003, about 7 percent GDP, owing to rising entitlement and interest costs.[2] Instead, federal finances were in their healthiest condition for seventy years at the turn of the century. Four consecutive surpluses in FY1998–FY2001 constituted the longest unbroken run of balanced budgets since the 1920s. Having operated deficits in excess of $200 billion under Ronald Reagan and George Bush, the United States began the twenty-first century under Clinton with a huge surplus of more than $200 billion. Anticipating more to come, the White House forecast that the federal government could retire its publicly held debt by 2015.[3]

The progression from big deficits to big surpluses was not the product of new political consensus. Budget issues were at the heart of the intense partisan conflict that defined the Clinton era. Dispute centered on the means rather than the end of a balanced budget—that is, whether it was to be achieved at high or low revenue levels. Firmly committed to bringing the deficit under control, Clinton displayed boldness and tenacity in seeking to do so on his terms. His success on this score was his most significant achievement as president. However, Clinton's budget leadership was at best a triumph bookended by failures. In his first term, deficit-reduction imperatives nullified the public investment revolution that he hoped would consolidate his place in history. As his second term drew to a close, he failed to ensure that his legacy of budgetary surpluses would be used for the purposes that he advocated.

THE NEW DEMOCRAT

Born in the small town of Hope in southwest Arkansas on August 19, 1946, Bill Clinton grew to adulthood as the United States enjoyed the long postwar boom. The first president from the baby-boom generation, the huge cohort of 78 million children born in the twenty years after World War II, was "the perfect symbol of the great American meritocracy that exploded after 1945 into the creation of that profound social revolution, a mass middle class."[4] Clinton's maternal grandparents had experienced grinding poverty during their youth in rural Arkansas. His father, who was killed in a road accident before his birth, endured loss of his family's small farm near Sherman, Texas, to foreclosure in 1936. In contrast, Clinton grew up from the age of seven in modest suburban comfort in Hot Springs, Arkansas, where his mother was a nurse anesthetist and his stepfather was a car salesman.

The future president found his direction early in life when he shook hands with John F. Kennedy in the White House Rose Garden as a delegate for Boys Nation, the American Legion's national youth program, in August 1963. From that juncture, observed biographer Meredith Oakley, Clinton was "consumed by the notion of making politics his life and the presidency his goal." Benefiting from scholarships available to a student of his ability, he picked out the college education that served this ambition. He was an undergraduate in the international government program at Georgetown University, a Rhodes scholar at Oxford University, and a graduate student at Yale Law School. On returning home, he had a brief stint as a University of Arkansas law professor, taking time off to run unsuccessfully for Congress in 1974. Other than practicing as an attorney in 1981–1982, Clinton then spent his entire working life from 1977 to early 2001 in political office. Elected Arkansas attorney general in 1976, he progressed to become the nation's youngest governor in 1978 and bounced back from election defeat in 1980 to occupy the statehouse again from 1983 through 1992.[5]

Far from being a self-made politician, Clinton needed the help of others in his rise to power. Hillary Rodham Clinton, whom he married in 1975, was an equal partner in this odyssey as his foremost political and policy adviser. Clinton had also built up in college days and expanded thereafter an informal network of comrades, advisers, and promoters, the "friends of Bill." Some of these allies kept him abreast of new thinking in their fields of interest in academia, business, and public service. Clinton's engagement with them in "the Conversation" gave him access to a range of policy advice not normally available to the governor of a relatively unimportant state.[6]

Openness to new ideas defined Clinton's style of governance. Advancing seamlessly from student-academic to office holder, he retained a scholarly penchant for developing policy through study, discussion, and deliberation based on his prodigious capacity to master technical detail. An inductive thinker, Clinton drew more on data than ideology to inform his decisionmaking. In some policy areas, detailed knowledge could prevent him seeing the wood for the trees, but he displayed a sure touch in linking the specific to the general regarding economic and budgetary issues. In contrast to most politicians, he enjoyed decisionmaking in these fields and was sufficiently knowledgeable to debate policy choices with expert advisers.[7]

Engagement with economic policy reflected necessity as much as intellectual preference. Coinciding with the emerging challenges of globalization, Clinton's political career had economic renewal as its dominant theme. The core idea that shaped his outlook was absorbed from his Development of Civilization course at Georgetown. History professor Carroll Quigley implanted in him the belief that "future preference," namely a willingness to make sacrifices today for a better tomorrow, defined western civilization. Clinton saw his mission as being "to keep the American Dream alive for the next generation of Americans."[8]

Throughout his career in office, Clinton sought adaptation and change in the face of current economic challenges for the sake of future prosperity. By the end of the 1970s he was convinced that Keynesianism had lost relevance. In essence he was a "New Democrat" long before the term was invented. Addressing the Democratic National Convention for the first time in 1980, Clinton urged his party to relinquish the "symbols and accomplishments" of the past and find "creative and realistic solutions" for the interconnected problems of stagflation, huge budget deficits, and America's loss of competitive edge. Although Edward Kennedy's stirring call to restore Democratic tradition would dominate historical memory of the convention, journalist Elizabeth Drew adjudged the young Arkansas governor's speech "probably the most thoughtful . . . delivered here all week."[9]

By the time Clinton became president, he was convinced that microeconomic rather than macroeconomic policies held the solution to America's problems.[10] The challenges he faced as governor of a relatively backward state undergoing a painful transformation shaped his thinking. Clinton linked education and economic development at the core of his agenda to help Arkansas diversify from reliance on farming and declining secondary industries like clothing and furniture. He recognized that habitual southern dependence on low wages to attract new business had become outdated in the new global economy. Accordingly, his perennial theme, as expounded in 1989 economic plan, *Moving Arkansas Forward into the 21st Century,* was "either we invest more in human capital and develop our people's capacity to cooperate or we are headed for long-term decline."[11]

At the outset of the 1980s, Arkansas ranked lowest of all states in per capita education spending, many of its teachers were badly paid and lacking in qualifications, and many of its 369 school districts were too small and impoverished to fund courses in math, science, and foreign languages. A 1983 state Supreme Court ruling that funding for teachers' salaries and other educational services should be equalized across the state provided opportunity to promote change. It gave Clinton cover for a sales tax increase to boost education spending on condition that schools met new standards. Within four years, all school districts complied with these standards and delivered a full curriculum, the number of graduating seniors moving on to college increased from 38 percent to 50 percent, and teachers' salaries increased—but they remained near the bottom nationally, as did student test scores. Although aid to education increased by a greater percentage than in all but six states in 1984–1990, Arkansas needed to spend far more to close the quality gap.[12]

Without doubt, Clinton exaggerated his gubernatorial achievements in order to advance his presidential ambitions. There were limits to what a progressive governor could accomplish in a conservative state. A fair assessment of Clinton's record is that Arkansas "crept forward under him" and could have done a lot worse for itself without his leadership. Never an economy-first business Progressive in the Jimmy Carter mold, he yearned to develop an ambitious growth-oriented agenda of further education reform, employment training, work-welfare, and health-care programs, but fiscal constraints stood in his way. Clinton had charge of a state budget of only some $3 billion, less than most big cities spent annually, and had to operate under the state's constitutional balanced-budget requirement. Although he boasted in the 1992 campaign that he had balanced a budget eleven times in contrast to George Bush's tally of zero, the obligation to do so shackled his gubernatorial activism. His national preoccupations, which increasingly took him away from Arkansas in the second half of the 1980s, also distracted him from the nitty-gritty task of ensuring that the small-scale initiatives he was able to promote then worked to best effect.[13]

Clinton learned to be circumspect about redressing his funding shortages through revenue enhancement. Voter disaffection with the vehicle tax increases he promoted to finance highway infrastructure improvement was a critical factor in his 1980 election defeat. The sales tax increase that paid for educational reform only raised half the revenues he wanted. State legislators balked at proposals to increase severance taxes and reduce exemptions for businesses and utilities that funded their election campaigns. Clinton himself found it expedient to give tax breaks to agribusiness, retailing, trucking, and information technology enterprises to keep Arkansas competitive with other southern states that eroded their tax base in a desperate effort to retain or attract footloose businesses. Facing a revenue shortfall in 1985, he shifted the 1983 tax proceeds into the general fund, which resulted in about half this money being reallocated from education. Despite his constant prodding, the state legislature held out until 1991 before agreeing to raise sales and corporate income taxes to fund a new round of education and training initiatives.[14]

Running for president presented opportunities and problems of a different order to those of penny-pinching Arkansas. Clinton could envisage economic renewal on a grand scale but faced a mammoth federal deficit that had impeded program development for more than a decade. To resolve this dilemma, he campaigned for the White House on a platform that promised both to restore prosperity through a massive program of public investment and bring the deficit under control.

Strategic trade doctrine that national government should aggressively promote the international competitiveness of the home economy provided the intellectual foundations for Clinton's economic program. It gained credence in Democratic circles in the late 1980s as a more politically marketable iteration of previously in-vogue industrial policy. Clinton's initial exposure to this theory came via two of its gurus, both friends since his Oxford days. One was business consultant Ira Magaziner, but the main conduit was Harvard academic Robert Reich, probably the foremost advocate of strategic trade alongside Lester Thurow.[15] Clinton heard the same message in the Democratic Leadership Council (DLC), formed in 1985 to promote centrist policies within the national party. This group endorsed public investment as part of its New Orleans Declaration of 1990. Clinton's appointment as DLC chair in 1991 effectively anointed him as its handpicked candidate for the Democratic presidential nomination. To help him develop a program, the DLC's new think tank, the Progressive Policy Institute, supplied him with a stream of position papers that further influenced his ideas on public investment as a generator of economic growth.[16]

Strategic trade theory regarded wage stagnation, sluggish productivity, and declining competitiveness as interrelated problems. According to its proponents, national economic renewal required development of high-value, high-wage, high-tech enterprises because America could no longer compete in mass-production manufacturing with the low-wage economies of developing nations. However, U.S. workers were not sufficiently skilled or productive to compete for high-end jobs in a world that had become a seamless web for capital. To rectify this deficiency, strategic traders advocated increased investment in education, training, and infrastructure programs to develop a labor force better suited to a globalized economy. Critics charged that this posited an erroneous association between competitiveness and productivity and exaggerated the impact of globalization on the increasingly significant service sector of advanced economies. They also questioned whether the relative stagnation of median income and wages in the United States was due to international competition rather than structural changes in the domestic manufacturing base.[17]

Unmoved by the skeptics, Clinton embraced strategic trade with enthusiasm, becoming both its policy entrepreneur and political exponent. It provided a third-way formula for economic growth distinct from Reaganomics and Keynesianism. As its champion, Clinton could present himself as a New Democrat unfettered by the ideologies of the past. In his diagnosis of the nation's economic problems, antistatist conservatism had not equipped Americans "to compete and win in the new world economy," and big-government liberalism had assumed that "we can just tax and spend our way out of any problem we face." The necessary corrective was a public investment strategy that empowered workers to maximize their wealth creation.[18]

After declaring his presidential candidacy in October 1991, Clinton waxed lyrical in setting out his economic vision but remained fuzzy on deficit reduction. Like other governor-presidents, he underestimated the scale of federal fiscal problems. When reality dawned, he reportedly confessed to an aide, "I always thought, Why can't these guys in Washington get their act together and figure it out? It's not that hard." Clinton's early pronouncements on the budget also betrayed excessive optimism that economic growth from public investment would provide the cure. In a speech penned by the DLC's Bruce Reed, he trumpeted this organization's line that the 1990 budget agreement should be discarded because its tax increases deterred investment. Fortunately for him, the media had not yet paid sufficient attention to his candidacy to quiz him on how this would reduce the deficit. Clinton also got away with an impromptu and nonsensical claim on NBC's *Meet the Press* on January 5, 1992, that his public investment program would not only produce a balanced budget but also generate a debt-reducing surplus within four years.[19]

As Clinton progressed toward winning the Democratic presidential nomination, reporters showed increasing interest in how he would simultaneously pay for investments and cut the deficit. Realizing the need of a proper plan, he delegated a team of advisers to provide him with one. Coordinated by Gene Sperling, former economic adviser to Governor Mario Cuomo of New York, this group drew its membership from an eclectic mix of Wall Street bankers, DLC aides, and "friends of Bill" strategic traders. In a struggle that would spill over into the early Clinton administration, the financial faction that included Robert Rubin looked to restrain the ambitions of the public investors headed by Robert Reich. These group dynamics shaped a deficit-reduction plan that was strong on promise but soft in substance owing to the difficulty of reconciling competing priorities.[20]

The final plan estimated the four-year tab for Clinton's investments at

$220 billion, but even this was an underestimate. Unable to agree whether health-care reform would deliver efficiency savings, the Sperling group simply factored the costs at zero until these could be more rigorously computed. To pay for this largess while also halving the deficit, expenditure cuts and revenue enhancement were to deliver gross deficit reduction of $295 billion in broadly equal proportions. The most realistic proposal called for defense cuts of $37.5 billion above those planned by the Bush administration. Administrative savings, manpower cuts, and efficiency gains were to yield some $100 billion, but it was notoriously difficult to make such economies. Electoral considerations ensured that the plan was devoid of domestic program retrenchment and entitlement reform. On the revenue side, it projected some $92 billion gains from tax fairness measures, but also promised a middle-class tax cut and a higher earned income tax credit for the working poor that together cost over $22 billion. A new tax on foreign corporations doing business in America was supposed to produce $45 billion, but this was a high-end estimate in a congressional report. As Clinton advisers were well aware, the more realistic yield was just $5 billion.[21]

Clinton's campaign book, *Putting People First,* inscribed the economic plan as the centerpiece of his economic strategy to "create millions of high-wage jobs and help America compete in the global economy." It confidently forecast that the FY1996 deficit, which the CBO currently estimated at $193 billion, would decline to $141 billion if public investment generated moderate economic growth and to $75 billion if expansion was strong.[22] Nevertheless, the Clinton plan found little favor with financial analysts. The *Washington Post*'s Robert Samuelson decried it as being "patently dishonest," *Newsweek*'s Rich Thomas dismissed it as "economic fantasy," and Morgan Stanley economist Stephen Roach derided its "make believe numbers." A new CBO forecast putting the FY1996 deficit at $269 billion further damaged its credibility. Thereafter, any sign that Clinton was headed for victory caused financial markets to dip out of concern that his budget-busting program would fuel inflation.[23]

All this did not damage Clinton as it might have in normal circumstances. The three-candidate nature of the presidential race was one reason for this. Ross Perot directed his antideficit fire at George Bush, whose own fiscal record made it expedient for him to attack his Democratic rival as a tax-and-spend liberal rather than a spend-and-borrow one. To neutralize this attack, Clinton declared in the third presidential debate, on October 19, "I will not raise taxes on the middle class to pay for these [investment] programs."[24] However, the main reason why Clinton's spurious numbers did not harm his election prospects was that his core support was preoccupied more with the condition of the economy than the deficit.[25]

In line with his campaign mantra, "It's the economy, stupid," Clinton kept his attention focused on popular concerns about jobs and prosperity. In his vision the economic benefits of redressing the public investment deficit were the prerequisite for resolution of the fiscal deficit. This was the message that he established at the time of his nomination and stuck with thereafter. "Without increased investment," he intoned, "you couldn't get growth, and without growth you could never do anything on the budget deficit. . . . You could never get enough growth to balance the thing anyway." This enabled Clinton to present the budget deficit as a symbol of the misguided priorities of two Republican administrations that had squandered fiscal resources in tax cuts for the rich instead of putting them to work to renew the American Dream. To this end, he damned Bush's record as one of "wasted billions . . . exploding debt and reduced investments in our future."[26]

The crowning moment for this strategy came in the second presidential debate, which had a town meeting format. An African American woman asked the candidates, "How has the national debt personally affected each of your lives? And if it hasn't, how can you honestly find a cure for the economic problems of the common people if you have no experience of what's ailing them?" After a rote response from Perot and a waffling one from Bush, Clinton seized the opportunity to put over his explanation for the economic pain of ordinary people. "It is because America has not invested in its people," he avowed. "It is because we have not grown. It is because we have had twelve years of trickle-down economics. . . . It is because we are in the grip of a failed economic theory."[27]

Clinton consultant James Carville later commented, "I would have *paid* to have that question asked." As Carville's future wife, Republican political consultant Mary Matalin, recognized, "Beyond the Beltway, normal people mentally translated 'national debt' to 'recession.' We didn't."[28] Once Clinton became president, however, he would have to deal with political and economic actors who perceived the fiscal deficit as a substantive problem in need of speedy resolution rather than a political symbol of past mistakes. As a result, the budget moved to center stage in his governance strategy from the supporting role it had played in his electoral one.

PUTTING THE DEFICIT FIRST

Bill Clinton's priority shifted from public investment to deficit reduction between his election and inauguration. Midway through this period, Robert Reich, now heading the economic policy transition team, disconsolately noted in his diary, *"The deficit* is already framing our discussions of what we want to accomplish in the future. Getting the deficit 'under control' is becoming the most important measure of our success."[29] The transition and early weeks of the new administration saw feverish activity to produce a five-year economic plan that bore only partial resemblance to *Putting People First*. The final version combined deficit reduction on a scale matched only by the 1990 budget agreement and the greatest public investment program in American history, albeit smaller in scope than envisaged in the campaign. Congress approved the former but retrenched the latter to a shadow of presidential ambition.

Clinton's heuristic style of decisionmaking was critical to his reassessment of priorities. It alerted him to the significance of the bond market for his economic success. Whereas Jimmy Carter discovered the truth too late, Clinton became aware in the transition period that a rising deficit could undermine its confidence. This loose confederation of bankers, financiers, money managers, rich foreigners, and domestic investors was the chief source of long-term borrowing that was the lifeblood for American enterprise. Its disparate members were united in determination to ensure that their holdings of long-term debt, valued at over $10 trillion in 1993, were repaid without costly erosion by inflation.[30]

Alan Greenspan reinforced Clinton's understanding of this reality during a courtesy visit to Little Rock on December 2 that broadened into a wide-ranging policy discussion. The Fed chair warned that the inflation excesses of the 1970s still governed the inflationary expectations of the 1990s. He explained the current gap between rock-bottom short-term interest rates and the abnormally high long-term ones as an inflation premium that the bond markets levied to safeguard investments from the inflationary consequences of the anticipated growth of the deficit. If Clinton could improve expectations that the budget gap could be closed, Greenspan recalled telling him, "the latter part of the 1990s could look awfully good."[31]

The president-elect got the same message from the senior members of his new economic team. All were deficit hawks by reputation, so their selection was a clear signal that Clinton had signed up to the cause. Greenspan later commented that their appointment made Clinton "seem about as far from the classic tax-and-spend liberal as you could get and still be a Democrat."[32] Treasury Secretary Lloyd Bentsen had long demonstrated sensitivity to investor concerns about the deficit as Texas senator and Senate Finance Committee chair. OMB director Leon Panetta was a strong advocate of fiscal restraint as California congressman and House Budget Committee chair. His deputy, onetime CBO director Alice Rivlin, had been openly dismissive of the *Putting People First* numbers but found Clinton receptive to deficit concerns during her job interview. Announcing the OMB appointments, Clinton told journalists that "you should view their selection as a decision by me that we cannot grow the economy without a serious and credible long-term deficit-reduction program."[33]

Clinton's most significant appointment was Robert Rubin as National Economic Council (NEC) chair. Modeled on the National Security Council, this new body coordinated domestic and international economic policy. Its first chief was a persuasive advocate and skillful team builder for the view that fiscal responsibility was essential because of America's reliance on foreign purchase of dollar-denominated bonds in the new context of globally integrated capital markets. As CEA chair Laura Tyson commented, "At that point, it was very important that he could say that based on his own [Wall Street] experience." In essence Rubin did much to educate Clinton that globalization had financial-market consequences as well as labor-market ones. Impressed with his boss's quick grasp of this, he considered Clinton "the first American President with a deep understanding of how these issues were reshaping our economy, our country, and the world."[34]

Clinton's senior economic advisory team was distinguished by its "analytical and largely consensual approach." Even the CEA, normally the bailiwick of economic liberalism in any Democratic administration, was on message that large deficits were a threat to sustained prosperity. Tyson, a Berkeley economist, disagreed with the other principals as to how much retrenchment was possible without depriving the economy of needed stimulus in the short term. But what was more significant, she later asserted, "was our unanimous support for a multi-year, backloaded deficit reduction plan based on conservative economic assumptions."[35]

If the economic case for deficit reduction was strong, the political justification was less clear-cut. Weighing in its favor was White House concern that Ross Perot would run again in 1996 if the deficit was still seen as a symptom of a sick economy.[36] The Perot phenomenon had also shaped the composition of the new Congress. At a postelection meeting, Speaker Thomas Foley (D-WA) and Majority Leader Richard Gephardt (D-MO) informed Clinton that many in the huge class of freshman House Democrats—sixty-five in total—had signed up to the antideficit cause to win election. In their view, presidential failure to prioritize the budget problem risked losing control of the fiscal agenda to congressional deficit hawks.[37]

Nevertheless, veterans of the presidential campaign considered antideficit priorities a betrayal of election commitments. Secretary of Labor Robert Reich, NEC deputy chair Gene Sperling, and White House communications director George Stephanopoulos beat the drum for public investment spending in economic policy meetings. Pollster Stanley Greenberg warned that his focus groups of Clinton voters ranked job creation, health-care insurance, educational and training initiatives, and welfare reform above deficit reduction in importance. In support of these aides, political consultant Paul Begala circulated a memorandum to senior administration officials urging that the Clinton program should be "*an economic growth package [that] will create jobs and increase income for millions of Americans.*" To remind everyone of the campaign message, he warned, "*It's NOT the deficit, stupid.*"[38]

It was also possible that deficit reduction might not work as an economic restorative in tune with the electoral cycle. In a worst-case scenario, the fiscal drag from budgetary retrenchment could precipitate a new downturn, for which Clinton would be blamed. Alternatively, removal of stimulus from the economy could retard the growth of jobs for some years. As Clinton reportedly complained in a preinaugural meeting, "So we have to pick up the tab for the Reagan-Bush deficits. They got elected by wrecking the economy and I lose reelection by fixing it." Even if fiscal restraint produced stronger economic returns, the tax increases and spending cuts needed to reduce the deficit could alienate voters. Clinton later remarked, "There were compelling reasons for it, but the most important domestic decision of my presidency was still one big gamble."[39]

Despite his "Slick Willy" reputation for political expediency, Clinton put the long-term good of the economy uppermost in his calculations. The period of maximum danger from a rising deficit was some way off. In a White House meeting on January 29, Alan Greenspan warned that the financial crisis would hit at the end of the century. Impressed with the president's willingness to preempt future problems, the Fed chair remarked, "The hard truth was that Reagan had borrowed from Clinton, and Clinton was having to pay it back. . . . He was forcing himself to live in the real world on the economic outlook and monetary policy."[40]

Often overlooked in Clinton's conversion to deficit hawk, however, is that he did not abandon public investment. Some aides saw this as indecision that contrasted with the clear preferences of Vice President Al Gore for deficit control and of Hillary Clinton for *Putting People First* initiatives. In their view, Treasury official Larry Summers later explained, "Al had his agenda. And Hillary had her agenda. And Bill had *every* agenda."[41] However, Clinton's desire for a program combining both goals reflected his conviction that they were not mutually exclusive. Deficit reduction was what he had to do to reassure the bond market, and public investment was what he wanted to do to help ordinary Americans.

For Clinton, fixing the budget was only the means to a greater end. Despite his New Democrat identity, the president he really admired was FDR, particularly after reading Geoffrey Ward's biography on the campaign trail.[42] He aspired to join his hero in the pantheon of great presidents by promoting a bold program of public investment that transformed America's economic fortunes. "You can't turn deficit reduction into the Holy Grail of American politics," Clinton told journalist Sidney Blumenthal. "It is important as part of a strategy, but it is not the ultimate objective." The first lady similarly told journalist Joe Klein that "we couldn't have a credible activist government unless we could get the budget under control."[43]

Unveiled in broad outline to Congress on February 18, the economic plan projected deficit reduction of $473 billion over five years based on net spending cuts of $191 billion and revenue increases of $281 billion, a ratio of two to three. However, gross savings exceeded $700 billion to offset $153 billion in new investment spending and $77 billion in stimulus and investment incentive tax cuts. If the plan worked, it would reduce the FY1998 deficit from $390 billion to $241 billion. The president's message accompanying his revised budget affirmed its dual purpose in unambiguous terms: "Deficit reduction at the expense of public investment has been and will continue to be self-defeating. The Clinton plan is explicitly and emphatically aimed at reducing the deficit while increasing much-needed public investment."[44]

The key issue on deficit reduction was how much would satisfy the movers and shakers on interest rates. The administration eventually settled for a FY1997 deficit-reduction target of $140 billion, almost midway between the respective OMB and CEA preferences of $160 billion and $117 billion. This was the figure recommended by Alan Greenspan in private talks with Lloyd Bentsen as sufficient to calm the inflationary expectations of the bond market. In fact, the Fed chair believed that $130 billion would suffice to produce downward movement on long-term interest rates, but he refused to offer any assurances on keeping short-term rates low whatever figure was adopted. Nevertheless, Bentsen was confident that Greenspan would be helpful on monetary policy if the administration demonstrated its deficit-reduction resolve by adopting a target above his bottom line. The higher figure would also make a better impression on bondholders. Clinton later remarked, "Clearly economic policy making, at least in this environment, was not science, and if it was art, it had to be beautiful in the eyes of the beholders in the bond market."[45]

As further insurance, the White House maneuvered Greenspan into a public display of support. Invited to hear Clinton address a joint session of Congress on the economic plan, the Fed chair was seated in the front row of the visitors' gallery between Hillary Clinton and Tipper Gore. Television pictures of him joining in the applause for the speech offered a powerful image of his apparent endorsement. The White House had gambled on this outcome as its putative ally had only approved the deficit reduction target in outline rather than its specifics. Fortunately for Clinton, Greenspan put more emphasis on ends than means in his anxiety to see the budget problem resolved. As confirmation of this, he testified to the Senate Banking Committee that the administration plan to reduce the deficit was "serious" and "credible," remarks that made newspaper headlines.[46]

The administration proposed defense cuts amounting to $112 billion, nearly a third of gross spending retrenchment of $346 billion and a considerably larger figure than Clinton had advocated in the campaign. Further savings of $73 billion were to come from nondefense discretionary programs, mainly from efficiency reductions of 100,000 in the federal civilian workforce, crop subsidy cuts, and increases in federal-land fees for mining, lumber, and agricultural enterprises. Entitlement cuts were to yield $115 billion, primarily through Medicare cost controls that limited reimbursements to health-care providers and the states. Finally, lower debt service charges resulting from deficit control were to save $46 billion.[47]

Clinton also sought three types of tax increase. The first fell on high-income individuals by raising the top personal tax rate from 31 percent to 36 percent, placing a 10 percent surcharge on those earning over $250,000 a year, increasing the proportion of Social Security benefits taxed for the better-off, and curbing itemized deductions. The plan also featured higher business taxes, including an increase in the top corporate rate from 34 percent to 36 percent, limits on some deductions, and elimination of deductions for lobbying expenses. Finally, it included an energy tax based on heat output (BTU), an idea that Al Gore had promoted. Although the costs to the average family would not exceed $17 a month, this universal levy was intended to involve as many Americans as possible in the common cause of deficit reduction. Signaling this in his message to Congress, Clinton declared that "for the first time in more than a decade, we're all in this together."[48]

Absent from the plan was the middle-class tax cut promised in the campaign. This was not considered a great political risk because Greenberg's focus groups had not evinced strong expectation of receiving one.[49] Nevertheless, its omission would add grist to the GOP charge that Clinton was just another big-government liberal. The inclusion of a stimulus package to boost the economy in advance of deficit reduction reinforced this. It comprised $16.3 billion in new expenditure and $12 billion in business tax incentives and loan obligation authority as a supplemental appropriation to the FY1993 budget. Spread among fourteen federal agencies and departments, half the spending initiatives went into jobs and construction and the rest benefited social programs like Head Start, housing loans, and aid to the homeless.[50]

The economic plan also proposed a back-loaded public investment program that projected annually rising expenditure of $15 billion, $22 billion, $33 billion, $39 billion, and $45 billion in FY1994–FY1998. The bulk was earmarked for research in new technologies, selective subsidies to increase industrial competitiveness, job training and apprenticeships, educational initiatives, communication infrastructure improvement, and 100,000 additional police officers. A smaller portion of $26.8 billion funded expansion of the Earned Income Tax Credit (EITC) for low-income families to make work more rewarding than welfare for the poor. The plan also allocated $60 billion in additional tax breaks to stimulate business investment.

To move from blueprint to policy, the Clinton plan required enactment by a Congress that was more concerned with the political aspects of its spending and taxation proposals than its economic rationale. The new president could hardly claim a mandate for his program since his 43 percent share of the popular vote was the lowest winning tally since 1912. Lack of coattails limited his influence over his own party in Congress—all but five of the victorious House Democrats had run ahead of him in their districts. Most damagingly, partisan polarization over the budget had reached the boiling point. Shortly after the inauguration, Senate Minority Leader Bob Dole (R-KS) privately warned Clinton that the Republicans would not support a deficit-reduction plan that contained tax increases. This signaled the end of bipartisan efforts to address the budget problem that dated back to 1982.[51]

In taking the lead against Clinton, Dole looked to build support for his 1996 presidential candidacy among conservative Republicans, most of whom regarded him as a dealmaker on the deficit. White House political director Rahm Emmanuel later admitted, "We made a miscalculation. Nobody knew Bob Dole was going to start running for president within the first hundred days." If the administration expected his cooperation, it was being naïve. The Kansan was locked in by the new party orthodoxy that was the legacy of the 1990 budget imbroglio. Unified in opposition to tax increases, the GOP now had the opportunity to expose fissures in Democratic ranks over the specifics of deficit reduction. As Representative Dick Armey (R-TX) commented, "They wanted to lead, now they've got to live with the accountability. Why should we give them cover?"[52]

Denied Republican support, Clinton was entirely reliant on the cooperation of his own party. Despite his lack of coattails, congressional Democrats were anxious to work with him for fear that the public would punish them for continued gridlock in government. Testifying to this, Representative Bob Matsui (D-CA) declared, "Bill Clinton's success is our success, his failure is our failure." In turn, the centrist president was obliged to cooperate with a congressional party whose center of gravity was more "old" than "new" Democrat. This precluded inclusion of entitlement reform, the surest means of deficit control, in the economic plan. Senate Majority Leader George Mitchell (D-ME) vetoed any such initiative for fear that the Democrats would be vulnerable to the kind of demagogic attacks they had inflicted on the Republicans in the 1980s. Consequently, Clinton would not support Leon Panetta's plan to cap COLAs for Social Security recipients and increase beneficiary premiums for Medicare.[53]

Nevertheless, a significant bloc of congressional Democrats wanted to conquer the deficit rather than merely control it. Speaking for them, Senator Bill Bradley (D-NJ) insisted, "This has got to end. We're the only ones who can do it." As many as fifteen of the fifty-seven Democratic senators, mostly southerners and westerners, thought of themselves as deficit hawks but operated more as individuals pursuing personal agendas than as a group. Their counterparts in the House, who also constituted about a quarter of

Democratic ranks, were more cohesive. Some were affiliated with the Conservative Democratic Forum that represented the dwindling band of southern conservatives. Others, mainly belonging to the Democratic Budget Group organized by Tim Penny (D-MN), represented less-than-safe suburban and rural seats outside the South. Flexing their muscles in the cause of budget control in March 1992, seventy-six Democrats had joined with the Republicans to beat down the House leadership's attempt to secure more money for domestic programs by removing the caps on discretionary spending mandated by the 1990 budget deal.[54]

Despite the warning signs that enactment of the deficit-reduction package would be difficult, the White House failed to devise a legislative game plan to promote it. Preoccupation with the economics of the program made the administration neglectful of its politics. As Clinton later admitted to Rubin, this was "a crucial tactical mistake." Only belatedly was a White House "war room" established to manage the search for votes.[55] Moreover, the president never developed a communication strategy that gave equal saliency to his divergent economic goals.

Clinton's public campaign in support of his economic plan centered on its deficit-reduction component that was the focus of congressional interest and media attention. According to political scientist Dan Wood, he spoke more frequently about the deficit from February through August 1993 than any president in a comparable period before or since. Beginning with his address to Congress, however, the investment program did not receive remotely comparable emphasis, and it became progressively blurred in his rhetoric. Whether Clinton could have focused the legislative process on the differing goals of his plan with a better communication strategy must be a matter of conjecture, but the absence of one minimized his chances of doing so. The congressional Democrats had far greater interest in deficit reduction than public investment, which was fundamentally a "New" Democrat issue.[56]

In these circumstances, parts of the economic plan became casualties of the legislative process. The first to encounter difficulty was the spending element of the stimulus proposal. Senate Republicans filibustered against it as a pork-infested measure irrelevant to economic recovery. GOP ranks held firm despite Clinton's offer to trim the measure in the hope of peeling off moderates. Lacking the votes to invoke cloture, the Democratic Senate leadership abandoned the bill in late April and settled for enactment of its $4 billion provision for unemployment benefits extension as a separate measure. The economic consequences were minimal because the stimulus was too small to make much difference to recovery. In political terms, however, this was a significant defeat for Clinton that encouraged further GOP resistance to his program.[57]

Paradoxically, the president put less effort into saving his investment program, mainly because of faulty political intelligence. On March 18 the House passed a budget resolution approving his deficit-reduction proposals in broad outline but providing less than $1 billion and $6 billion respectively in the first two years for new investments and only modest increases thereafter. What triggered this retrenchment was a CBO report that the administration plan was in breach of the 1990 discretionary spending caps because it overestimated deficit reduction by some $60 billion. To stay within these limits, House Democratic leaders made savings from the investment plan. In a further indication of its low priority for them, they did not consult the White House beforehand. There was no hope of salvaging the investment program in the Senate, where some of the surviving elements also came under attack.[58]

There is some dispute as to whether the president was forewarned about the danger. According to journalist Elizabeth Drew's sources, Clinton was told at a White House meeting on March 5 that he would lose about a quarter of his investments because of the CBO projection. With some difficulty, the president's economic advisers and congressional liaison staff convinced him that this was an acceptable trade-off for getting the remainder of his budget through the House. In Bob Woodward's account, however, Clinton only learned about the caps when briefed of his investment program's devastation on April 7.[59] Until the Clinton archives are opened to researchers, assessment of what happened must remain a matter of conjecture. It is likely, however, that the president's advisers informed him about the caps at the earlier meeting but did not anticipate just how extensively the investments would be stripped to meet them.

The investment program faced further setbacks at the reconciliation stage in the Senate where the BTU tax encountered opposition from energy-state Democrats in the Finance Committee. Democratic leaders agreed to substitute it with a smaller gasoline tax of 4.3 cents a gallon, the highest level acceptable to senators from western states, where long-distance travel was a fact of life. This left a revenue shortfall of nearly $50 billion that necessitated savings elsewhere. The tax elements of Clinton's investment program were a soft target in the hunt for these. His investment credits were significantly retrenched, a surtax was put on capital gains, support for empowerment zones that targeted tax incentives at businesses in poor neighborhoods was cut by 30 percent, and the EITC increase was scaled back by a third.[60]

The House enacted its budget reconciliation bill on May 27 by a slim margin of 219–213, with every Republican and thirty-eight Democrats voting nay. The Senate vote on June 25 was even tighter, at 50–49, with Vice President Al Gore casting the deciding vote against the nays, whose ranks included every Republican and six Democrats. The conference bill produced from the different House and Senate versions faced an equally tough battle for enactment. In the House, more than thirty Democrats, mainly from rural areas where long journeys were routine, expressed opposition to the gasoline tax that now featured in the amended bill. Moreover, some legislators in both chambers wanted bigger cuts in spending, particularly for entitlements, and others held out for constituency benefits as the price of their support.[61]

With Clinton to the fore, the administration finally geared up to lobby intensively for its plan. The president met personally with almost every organized group of congressional Democrats and with many individual legislators. His primary appeal emphasized the imperative of deficit control and the need to show that the party could govern. He was also willing to make deals provided that these did not undercut his deficit reduction target, shift a greater portion of tax increases onto middle-income families, or increase Medicare cuts beyond those already approved. Having experienced eight presidents, Lloyd Bentsen had never seen one so involved in working for votes. Yet he worried that Clinton's willingness to bargain only encouraged legislators to hold out. In his view, a tougher approach that employed sticks as well as carrots would have worked better. Nevertheless, presidential lobbying firmed up Democratic support to the point that victory was in sight.[62]

Hoping to sway remaining holdouts, Clinton appealed for public support in an address to the nation on August 3. "Without deficit reduction," he warned, "we can't have sustained economic growth." Despite the superior quality of his rhetoric compared to George Bush's in 1990, Clinton had no more success in generating support for a deficit-reduction package that featured tax increases. An overnight poll by CNN showed public approval for his plan actually dropping after his Oval Office address. Moreover, constituent phone calls to legislators were preponderantly negative because the Republican message that the plan imposed substantial tax increases on everyone shaped popular perception of it.[63]

As Clinton later conceded, the opposition did a "good job" of misleading the public about his tax program. A disgusted David Stockman chastised fellow Republicans for "deceptive gibberish" that distracted from the "serious business" of deficit reduction, but the words of yesterday's man fell on deaf ears.[64] Bob Dole's response to Clinton's address on behalf of the GOP included a patently ridiculous allegation: "This plan is not just the largest tax increase in American history. It's the largest tax increase in world history." In reality, OBRA tax increases were smaller than the Reagan-Dole tax hike of 1982, which netted $268 billion in 1993 dollars over five years. Nevertheless, the Republican gospel found ready disseminators in right-wing talk-show hosts like Rush Limbaugh and grassroots groups like the Christian Coalition and Citizens for a Sound Economy. The GOP's campaign made a particular impression in the South, a region that swung decisively in its favor in 1994. Alabama State Democratic Party chair William Blount lamented that "the only message people hear is that he's [Clinton] trying to raise taxes and not cut spending."[65]

It was the partisan loyalty of some wavering Democrats that earned Clinton the last votes he needed. His huge investment of political capital in the budget bill meant that its defeat would have mortally wounded his presidency. Determined to avoid this, Democratic congressional leaders pulled out all the stops in their drive to enact it. The measure received House approval by just two votes—218 to 216—on August 5 after Pat Williams (D-MT) and Marjorie Margolies-Mezvinsky (D-PA) agreed to support it. Having promised her affluent and marginal Philadelphia district never to support tax increases, the freshman Margolies-Mezvinsky was committing political suicide to save Clinton. However, forty-one of her fellow Democrats—many from safe districts—voted against the bill in opposition to its tax hikes. The outcome in the Senate hinged on Bob Kerrey (D-NE), who considered entitlement reform essential to solve the budget problem. To get his support, Clinton agreed to establish a bipartisan commission to propose ways of controlling mandatory programs. Undecided to the end, Kerrey finally backed the measure to give Al Gore the tie-breaking vote. Knowing Clinton was watching on television, he declared from the Senate floor, "I could not and should not cast a vote that brings down your presidency."[66]

The Omnibus Budget and Reconciliation Act (OBRA) of 1993 projected net deficit reduction of $432.9 billion over five years through revenue enhancement of $240.6 billion and net spending cuts of $192.3 billion. In line with the Democratic agenda since the Reagan era, the distribution of new taxes hit the rich. Some 80 percent of costs fell on families with incomes of $200,000 or more. By 1996, millionaires contributed over twice as much to the Treasury as in 1992. Moreover, EITC expansion greatly reduced effective tax rates for low-income families to their lowest level since the 1970s. OBRA's spending provisions were also broadly consistent with Democratic priorities. Headed by Medicare cost control, entitlement cutbacks amounted in net terms to $76.9 billion (allowing for EITC expansion of $19.1 billion), but outlays on these programs were still scheduled to rise from $808 billion to $1,035 billion in FY1994–FY1998. Over the same period, annual defense outlays were to undergo a real decline of 17 percent under the combined impact of the Bush economies and OBRA savings. This huge retrenchment even permitted modest multiyear expansion of some domestic discretionary programs under OBRA without violation of spending caps.[67]

On the debit side of OBRA for Clinton was the loss of his investment program. Annual outlays for nondefense investment in physical capital, research and development, and education and training averaged $140.5 billion (FY2000$) in FY1994–FY1998, just over 10 percent higher than in the Bush budgets. Even though investment spending would rise sharply in the balanced budgets of FY1999–FY2001, it only averaged 1.7 percent GDP over the entire Clinton presidency, compared with 2.6 percent GDP in FY1965–FY1981. OBRA's failure to provide a major new source of revenue in the form of the BTU tax also hobbled Clinton's efforts to stimulate private investment through tax incentives.[68] His hopes for economic growth consequently rested on the bond market. "I have a jobs program," Robert Rubin recalled the president saying, "and my jobs program is deficit reduction."[69]

Even without his investment program, OBRA was the most important legislative achievement of Clinton's presidency. It was the crucial victory in the central budgetary conflict of the 1990s over whether the deficit was to be brought under control at a high or low level of revenue, which had significant consequences for the progressivity of the tax system and the preservation of social programs. Without this success, Clinton could not have withstood the Republican budgetary offensive of 1995. His successful defense of the OBRA settlement in this later battle laid the foundations for the bipartisan balanced-budget agreement of 1997 on terms that confirmed the principles of the 1993 legislation.

However, the president did not reap immediate political advantage from OBRA because he misinterpreted what it signified. The bond market's positive response to the measure convinced him that the deficit was resolved as an economic problem. He saw this as the green light to proceed with an activist agenda that he hoped would define his presidency but weakened it instead. His first year in office had been productive despite difficult political circumstances. In addition to OBRA, Clinton secured enactment of the Americorps national service program of exchanging community service for financial credit to attend college, family and medical leave legislation, the "Brady bill" tightening handgun control, and—most significant—ratification of the North America Free Trade Agreement. In contrast, the 1994 legislative session was among the least productive since World War II.[70]

An emboldened Clinton outlined an ambitious second-year agenda in his 1994 State of the Union address but lacked the political resources to match his vision. The minority Republicans exploited Senate procedures to obstruct most of his program. Although the president achieved four of his ten legislative priorities, his record was defined by failure to enact health-care reform and welfare reform, both key commitments of his 1992 campaign.[71] Moreover, many post-OBRA initiatives blurred his credentials as a deficit-fighter. Most damaging in this regard was the measure that he deemed essential to control budget costs in the long run.

According to Hillary Clinton, comprehensive reform of health care was "not only good public policy that would help millions of Americans, it also was inextricably tied to reducing the deficit." The United States was already spending 14 percent of its GDP on health care, more than any other industrialized nation, and every projection showed that costs would escalate massively over the next half-century. A White House task force led by Hillary Clinton and Ira Magaziner produced a plan for a complete overhaul of the nation's health-care system, with universal health insurance as its centerpiece. The consequent reduction of administrative costs and waste in Medicare and Medicaid was supposed to produce $60 billion of deficit-reducing savings over five years.[72]

Announcing the initiative to Congress on September 22, 1993, the president promised root-and-branch reform of health care founded on principles of security, simplicity, savings, choice, quality, and responsibility. From the outset, however, the Clinton plan faced widespread criticism for being hugely complex, highly bureaucratic, and very expensive. It recommended establishment of five new health-care entitlements—insurance subsidies for individuals, insurance subsidies for early retirees, payment for long-term home care, assistance to small businesses, and prescription drugs for the elderly—but without convincing demonstration of how to fund them or control costs. Instead of the large savings promised, a CBO program evaluation estimated that the proposed reform would add $70 billion to the deficit in FY1996–FY2000.[73]

Initial public support for the plan receded in the face of a huge advertising campaign mounted by health insurance companies and other hostile interests to portray it as a big-government monstrosity that would necessitate huge tax increases for middle-income families. Efforts by Democratic congressional leaders to win bipartisan support for a more modest program got nowhere. Neither the House nor the Senate brought any bill to a floor vote. More than just a failed proposal, the health-care reform fiasco was a political disaster for Clinton. It obliterated his New Democrat image that had helped to elect him in 1992 and made him look like a big-government liberal.[74]

Adding to Clinton's woes, economic recovery proceeded erratically during his first two years in office. Despite the decline in long-term interest rates, only in the final quarter of 1993 and the second quarter of 1994 was economic growth higher than in the final quarter of 1992. Unemployment remained stubbornly high, only declining from a peak of 7.6 percent in mid-1992 to 6 percent in the third quarter of 1994. The Federal Reserve bore primary responsibility for this state of affairs. Determined to ensure that recovery would not revive inflation, it nearly doubled the short-term Federal Funds rate over the course of 1994. Although Clinton wanted greater emphasis on job growth, he could not afford a public confrontation with Alan Greenspan over their different priorities. As Laura Tyson remarked, "We decided early on that the financial markets could misinterpret criticism of the Fed. And the Fed itself might react in unpredictable ways."[75]

The slow recovery kept the president's average Gallup approval rating for his job performance on the economy in 1993–1994 at a lowly 43 percent. Furthermore, it seemingly validated GOP warnings that OBRA's tax increases and failure to control spending would strangle economic growth. At the time of its enactment, Newt Gingrich had declared, "The American people have established their belief that their government is their fiscal enemy." This sentiment became a rallying cry for many GOP House candidates in the midterm elections. Echoing it, Bob Dole put out a Statement of Republican Economic Principles, whose centerpiece was a critique of OBRA written by conservative economists from the GOP's advisory network. Republican National Committee chair Haley Barbour crowed, "Clinton gave us the issue to win back our position in the country as a party of principle . . . [and] show the difference between Republicans and Democrats."[76]

The Republicans gained fifty-two seats in the House and nine in the Senate in the 1994 elections to take control of both chambers for the first time in forty years. Defying convention, their campaign had framed local choice in national terms by making taxes, big government, and the Clinton presidency the dominant issues. This generated unity among Republicans while tapping into popular resentments that had worked to Democratic advantage two years previously. In 1994, 57 percent of voters thought the economy was in bad shape, and 62 percent of these voted Republican in the House elections. In another significant indicator of anti-incumbent frustration, Perot voters went Republican by two-to-one in these contests.[77]

If the midterm ballot was more a rejection of the Democrats than endorsement of the Republicans, it demonstrated yet again that fiscal responsibility was not a vote-winner. In the House elections, twenty-eight of thirty-five defeated Democratic incumbents had voted for OBRA, the most prominent casualty being Speaker Thomas Foley. The deficit's decline from $255 billion in FY1993 to $203 billion in FY1994 did not help the losers. In fact, polls showed that some 75 percent of Americans thought it had stayed the same or was getting worse. As journalist William Greider commented, "Except for editorial writers and other elites, nobody rewards politicians for shrinking the deficit."[78] This did not bode well for Clinton's reelection, but his budgetary struggles with the Republican Congress would breathe new life into his presidency.

SHIBBOLETHS, SHOWDOWNS, AND SHUTDOWNS

Clinton's deficit-reduction initiative of 1993 was born of economic necessity. In contrast, the balanced-budget battles of 1995 were driven by competing political visions of public policy expressed in fiscal terms. Clinton's principal adversary, Speaker Newt Gingrich, declared in his first address to the House

Republican Conference, "The budget is the transformational document for this system. When you've changed the budget, you've really changed government, and until you change the budget, you've just talked about changing government."[79] The force appeared to be with the Republicans, but Clinton would trump the Gingrich transformation by appropriating its balanced-budget goal for his Democratic purposes.

During the Reagan and Bush presidencies, Gingrich was primarily concerned with preventing any Republican retreat on taxes in the name of deficit control. As Speaker, he pursued a more ambitious agenda to attain a balanced budget for the dual purpose of cutting taxes and downsizing the state. Gingrich had initially expounded the case for making government smaller in his book *Window of Opportunity*, published in 1984. The 1990 and 1993 deficit-reduction initiatives had demonstrated that large budget deficits threatened the GOP tax agenda. For Gingrich and his fellow conservatives, the only solution was a massive rollback of domestic programs as a cold-turkey cure for the federal tax-and-spend habit. In essence, deficit elimination was their instrument to defund liberalism. Pursuit of a balanced budget, Gingrich avowed, was "the only thing that gives you the moral imperative to change the whole structure of the welfare state."[80]

Everything came within the purview of the Speaker's putative revolution except Social Security reform. The Democratic National Committee had run ads in the recent campaign warning that Republicans would reduce pension benefits by 20 percent, a charge also made by Clinton in his campaign speeches. Remembrance of how the Democrats had stalled the Reagan Revolution made Gingrich wary of touching pensions for now. "In the short run," he declared, "you have to take Social Security off the table and deal with everything else. And when you finish dealing with everything else, and you've done it right, you will have earned the trust of the American people to look at Social Security." This killed off any possibility of serious national debate over the recent report of the Bipartisan Commission on Entitlement and Tax Reform that Clinton had set up under the joint chairmanship of Senators Bob Kerrey and Jack Danforth (R-MO) in return for the former's support of his 1993 deficit-reduction measure.[81]

When the budget dispute climaxed in government shutdowns, Republicans refused a compromise that would have taken a large chunk out of the deficit but left the existing framework of social welfare provision in place. As House Budget Committee chair John Kasich (R-OH) commented, "It's not about deficit reduction. I'm not particularly interested in deficit reduction. . . . I want fundamental reform of welfare; I want fundamental reform of entitlements." GOP conservatives, particularly in the House, saw themselves as fulfilling the unfinished Reagan Revolution. Aware that this had foundered after its first year, they were determined to seize the moment while midterm victory empowered them. According to Representative Christopher Cox (R-CA), formerly a Reagan White House official, "Revolutions have a very short half-life. If you don't ask for what you want early, you won't get it. The window closes on your fingers."[82]

Far sooner than his advisers, Clinton realized that he was in a battle to preserve the liberal state. In his view, one aide recalled, the Gingrich agenda was "the ugly face of Republicanism with the mask ripped off." To another confidant, he remarked, "They don't want to balance the budget; that's just an excuse. . . . What they want, what they really, really want is to end all middle-class entitlements." Clinton feared that GOP success on this score would then make it impossible to protect low-income entitlements. In more colorful language, he told Robert Reich, "Those bastards have a completely *different* view of the world. They don't think government should even *exist*, except for national defense." Accordingly, Clinton was just as unwilling as the Republicans to accept a deficit reduction agreement that compromised his core objectives. At the height of their dispute, he asserted, "I am determined to balance the budget but I won't be forced into signing a budget that violates our values, not today or tomorrow, not ever."[83]

Clinton was up against an adversary with a new concept of the Speakership. Gingrich thought of himself as a prime minister pursuing a centralized partisan agenda that aimed "to do nothing less than reshape the federal government along with the political culture of the nation." The agency of this vision was the Contract with America, the manifesto for House Republicans in the midterm elections. Exit polls suggested that fewer than one in twenty voters thought it had made them more likely to back GOP candidates, but Gingrich claimed a mandate for its enactment. The Contract with America committed House Republicans to "end . . . government that is too big, too intrusive and too easy with the people's money." At the heart of its agenda were promises to cut taxes and enact a balanced-budget constitutional amendment that would evidently necessitate huge expenditure retrenchment. As Senator Phil Gramm (R-TX) approvingly remarked, "The glue that holds the Contract with America together is cutting government spending."[84]

The embattled president turned for help to political consultant Dick Morris, who had plotted his comeback after gubernatorial defeat in 1980. The counsel he received was to renew his centrist identity through a strategy of triangulation. Morris urged him to accommodate "the needs the Republicans address but . . . in a way that is uniquely yours."[85] Nevertheless, Clinton did not heed his advice that the first step was to present a balanced-budget plan for fear that this would only legitimize GOP calls for meat-ax retrenchment. Hillary Clinton, a Morris ally in Arkansas days, and Al Gore, who wanted the Republicans to have "a rendezvous with reality," were of the same view. Accordingly, the FY1996 plan projected five-year deficits in excess of $200 billion. Aide George Stephanopoulos called it "a 'show me' budget, designed to draw clear lines in the sand and force the Republicans to specify the painful cuts it would take to pay for their popular promises."[86]

The president's involvement in the battle to defeat a balanced budget constitutional amendment further violated the triangulation concept. The House Republican leadership considered this the cornerstone of its revolution. According to John Kasich, it was the "ultimate budget hammer" because mandatory deficit elimination would compel retrenchment and provide cover against constituent anger. Approval of the amendment before introduction of the FY1996 budget resolution would also preempt potentially damaging debate about the means of balancing the budget. As Majority Leader Dick Armey admitted, "Once Members of Congress know exactly, chapter and verse, the pain . . . to get to a balanced budget, their knees will buckle." This was particularly important regarding the Senate, where the Republican center of gravity was not as conservative as in the House and procedural rules gave the Democratic minority considerable obstructive power.[87]

Clinton remained above the battle while the balanced-budget amendment was under consideration in the House of Representatives in the hope that the Republicans would fall out over its terms. With some difficulty, Gingrich persuaded his conservative supporters not to press for inclusion of the Contract with America's three-fifths supermajority requirement for future tax increases, which would have made it unacceptable to Republican moderates and Democratic deficit hawks. An amendment simply mandating balanced budgets from FY2002 onward consequently gained approval by 300 votes to 132, with support from 68 Democrats.[88] The president intervened more directly during the Senate deliberations, but this made him look more "old" than "new" Democrat. Invoking class politics, he accused Republicans of wanting to slash social programs that served ordinary Americans to fund tax cuts for the rich. The administration also publicized the amendment's dire consequences in the event of recession. Meanwhile, the White House coordinated its lobbying of Democratic senators with that of traditional party constituencies, notably labor, public employees, African Americans, and senior citizens.[89]

The Senate came up one vote short of two-thirds approval on March 2. Majority Leader Bob Dole blamed Clinton for this outcome. "If we had a real president down there," he charged, "it might be different." In fact, others had done more to engineer this defeat. New Senate Minority Leader Tom Daschle (D-SD), an amendment supporter during previous votes, decided to make its defeat a test of his authority. Others in his leadership team— Harry Reid (D-NV), Wendell Ford (D-KY), and Byron Dorgan (D-ND)— consequently switched their votes, and regional loyalties also swung Kent Conrad (D-ND) into the nays. These gains compensated for the change in the opposite direction of liberals Joseph Biden (D-DE) and Tom Harkin (D-IA) to safeguard their 1996 reelection prospects. Ultimately, Mark Hatfield (R-OR), the solitary GOP nay, cast the crucial vote. As in 1986, this moderate Republican based his opposition on the need to safeguard domestic programs from sweeping retrenchment that the amendment would generate.[90]

Without the amendment's defeat, the White House would have stood no chance of stalling the GOP drive for huge retrenchment, but victory had a cost. Though exaggerated by Dole, Clinton's role in it sent confusing signals about his position on the deficit. Morris's polling found that the president now had a credibility gap with voters. At a strategy meeting on May 16, he warned, "They believe you oppose a balanced budget. You submitted a budget in deficit, oppose the balanced-budget amendment, and attack Republican plans to balance the budget. If it talks like a duck, walks like a duck, and looks like a duck, it's a duck. Voters think Clinton is a tax-and-spend liberal." According to Morris, Clinton's reelection was at risk unless he proposed a balanced budget of his own as an alternative to the Republican one.[91]

At this juncture the Republicans were about to demonstrate that their conservative fervor transcended the habitual incrementalism of American politics. The House of Representatives approved a budget resolution containing hitherto unthinkable retrenchment of $1.04 trillion to pay for tax reduction of $353 billion and a balanced budget within seven years. Targeted for elimination to achieve this were three departments—Commerce, Education, and Energy—and nearly three hundred individual programs. More cautiously, the Senate's seven-year balanced-budget plan featured somewhat smaller but still unprecedented economies that included abolition of the Commerce Department and some one hundred programs, and made tax reduction of $170 billion contingent on revenues from economic growth.[92]

Intense negotiations between House and Senate Republican leaders produced a compromise closer to what Gingrich wanted. Dole's anxiety to placate conservatives following his failure to secure the balanced-budget amendment worked in the Speaker's favor. Accordingly, the House and Senate adopted by almost straight party votes on June 29 a budget resolution that provided $983 billion in expenditure retrenchment and unconditional tax cuts of $245 billion, mainly for capital gains relief and a $500 per child tax credit. The spending cuts fell heaviest on Medicare ($270 billion), Medicaid ($180 billion), and a range of other entitlements—including food stamps, Aid to Families with Dependent Children (AFDC), Supplementary Security Income, EITC, student loans, and unemployment benefits ($170 billion). The remaining economies hit discretionary programs, notably education, environmental protection, and highways. In a nod to Senate preferences, the plan only targeted the Commerce Department and some one hundred federal programs for actual elimination.[93]

Before the Republicans completed their budget planning, Clinton addressed the nation on June 13 to outline his own ten-year balanced-budget plan based on spending retrenchment of $1.1 trillion. Judged on the fiscal numbers, this seemed like the Republican blueprint writ slightly smaller. Clinton proposed to cut Medicare by $128 billion, Medicaid by $54 billion, and all discretionary programs—excepting defense and education—by an average of 20 percent. He also projected tax cuts of $105 billion targeted at middle-income Americans, particularly to help them pay for college education. Whereas the GOP plan employed CBO economic and fiscal forecasts to score its proposals, Clinton used more optimistic OMB assumptions that provided a fiscal margin to balance the budget without the same pain. He declared, "It took decades to run up this deficit; it's going to take a decade to wipe it out."[94]

Behind the budgetary math, however, there were significant philosophical differences between the two plans. The GOP's projected retrenchment of Medicare encapsulated its antistatist intent. It wanted seniors to take more responsibility for their health-care financial planning by capping benefits and encouraging them to opt for low-cost private health plans. Critics worried that Medicare would consequently end up with the sickest elderly, thereby increasing its deficit, which would in turn compel lower payments to health-care providers, whose likely response would be to quit the program. Gingrich fueled such concerns with his remarks about the Health Care Financing Administration that oversees Medicare funding. In a speech to the Blue Cross/ Blue Shield Association on October 24, he asserted, "We don't get rid of it in round one because we don't think that's politically smart. . . . But we believe it's going to wither on the vine because we think people are voluntarily going to leave it." The Republicans also looked to transform numerous antipoverty entitlements, including Medicaid, into block grants administered by states and localities, thereby undermining national welfare lobbies and saving money.[95]

In contrast, Clinton aimed to prove that the open-ended commitments of current entitlements for both middle- and low-income Americans were affordable within a balanced budget. Only Al Gore, domestic aide Bruce Reed, and deputy chief of staff Erskine Bowles initially supported his strategy of saving these programs by retrenching them. With the deficit steadily declining, Robert Rubin and Laura Tyson, now promoted respectively to Treasury secretary and NEC chair, thought the cuts would serve little economic purpose. New chief of staff Leon Panetta reportedly considered resigning in protest that the policy process had become beholden to poll findings. The government departments that faced economies were also up in arms.[96]

Even Hillary Clinton doubted the political wisdom of the balanced-budget plan because it was bound to alienate congressional Democrats.

Denied advance warning to prevent leaks, they responded with shock and anger on its unveiling. Representative Pat Schroeder (D-CO) typically complained, "I don't think he has even thought about Democrats over here. He's thinking about himself and presidential politics." Many worried about the consequences of cutting programs that served bedrock constituencies. Representative Donald Payne (D-NJ), chair of the Congressional Black Caucus, charged that Clinton's plan was "a quantum leap backward for social policy, and it will have long-lasting, explosive results."[97]

Without doubt, Clinton had decided after the 1994 election never again to allow his policies and political image to become estranged from mainstream opinion. Thereafter, program ideas only made it onto his agenda after being thoroughly tested for public reaction. No other president so systematically linked his policy and polling operations. According to Dick Morris, poll numbers helped Clinton get a better sense of "his shortcomings and his potential, his successes and failures." They also instilled greater consistency and focus in his political strategy to counter Republican retrenchment. Journalist Bob Woodward observed, "Ideas, language and attitudes . . . converged in the protracted budget negotiations."[98]

If polls became the reality check for Clinton's good intentions, he was still willing to buck them on matters he considered of vital importance. In early 1995, for example, he sanctioned a $20 billion loan to Mexico to keep it from defaulting on debt obligations, an action unpopular with about 80 percent of the public but one necessary to prevent the economic collapse of a North America Free Trade Agreement (NAFTA) partner. This continued a pattern of political risk-taking for the nation's economic good previously evident in the OBRA deficit reduction and his support for NAFTA ratification, which many Democrats had opposed.[99]

In presenting his own balanced-budget plan, however, Clinton thought he could do good by swimming with rather than against popular opinion. When Morris bragged that the polls showed the political wisdom of his advice, the president retorted sharply, "I did this because it's the right thing to do." Clinton had grown disenchanted with waiting for the Republicans to produce a budget that could then be attacked. "I'm president. I need to be *for* something," he told aides. "I can't just stand on the sidelines." Ultimately, his greater purpose was to safeguard social programs by drawing the line at smaller economies than the Republicans sought. Robert Rubin recalled him saying in a strategy meeting in late May, "If I'm going to be heard on anything else, I first have to show a balanced budget. Once I do that, I can talk about progressive programs. But if I don't show a balanced budget, they'll never listen to me about progressive programs." In the battle for public opinion, the Treasury secretary acknowledged, the president saw better than his advisers that the balanced budget had become a threshold issue "for getting people to listen to us and hence for doing almost everything else the administration cared about."[100]

Clinton effectively downsized the ambition of his presidency from the bold development of new programs in 1993–1994 to back-to-the-wall preservation of existing ones in 1995–1996. As two reporters put it, "Change isn't Bill Clinton's friend anymore." According to George Stephanopoulos, the president disliked "playing defense," but he was very successful at it. With his veto as his bargaining chip, Clinton was adept at holding out when possible and conceding when necessary—usually after getting a better deal than had looked likely. Having underestimated the political system's checks and balances in setting his 1994 agenda, he turned them to his advantage against adversaries whose governance strategy also failed to recognize these constraints.[101]

GOP majorities of 232–203 in the House (boosted by five southern Democrats changing party affiliation) and 54–46 in the Senate (including two Democratic crossovers) were hardly veto-proof. Nevertheless, Republican leaders thought they possessed a weapon to overpower the president. By late May, Gingrich was speaking openly of a government shutdown, a "train wreck" in Washington-speak, if Clinton did not sign budget bills. "You had to find a trump to match his trump," he declared, "and the right to pass money bills is the only trump that is equally strong." As the Speaker told *Time* magazine, the president would be faced with a choice of running "the parts of government that are left" or "he could run no government." So confident were the Republicans that Clinton would buckle, they made no contingency plans in case he proved resilient. Their disdain for him blinded them to his toughness at other critical moments in his career. As House Republican Conference chair John Boehner (R-OH) later admitted, "We just assumed that given enough pressure, Clinton would . . . cave and cut a deal."[102]

Even when Clinton acted tough, he did not come across that way to Republicans. On June 7 he cast his first-ever veto against a rescission bill that cut $16.4 billion from funds previously appropriated for public service, education, and nutrition programs. The president wanted to demonstrate that he would be no pushover on bigger budget battles to come. "I have to show them I can do it," he told aides, "and how to negotiate with me." After five weeks of intermittent talks, however, Clinton accepted a compromise that restored only $700 million for education and social programs, less than half of what he initially called for. The outcome convinced Gingrich that his adversary was not a fighter.[103]

Thanks to the ideological zeal of younger House conservatives, the Speaker experienced more problems getting Congress to deliver a budget on time than he anticipated in getting Clinton to approve it. Almost a third of the Republican complement, the 73-strong freshman class was determined to change government before it changed them. According to its vice president, Representative Mark Souder (R-IN), "We aren't going to be housebroken, period." Gingrich had been instrumental in molding the freshmen in his own image during his days as an opposition bomb-thrower. His GOPAC organization had picked out many to run for office, helped indoctrinate them through seminars and policy literature, and given them campaign advice. Seeing themselves as the GOP's ideological conscience, the House freshmen were uninterested in anything less than total victory for their cause. Their insistence on adding anti-abortion, environmental deregulation, and other riders to budget bills provoked opposition from moderate Republicans in both the House and Senate. Their determination to make even deeper spending cuts than required by the budget resolution had the same effect. The freshmen that Gingrich had placed on the Appropriations Committee to keep chair Bob Livingston (R-LA) in line were particularly troublesome in this regard. Consequently, only two minor appropriation bills had received congressional approval by the start of the fiscal year.[104]

In these circumstances Republican leaders negotiated a Continuing Resolution (CR) with the White House on September 28 to finance government operations for six weeks. This was to buy time for the congressional budget process to grind to a conclusion. The game plan was to send Clinton a more stringent CR next time as a prelude to forcing his acceptance of the budget reconciliation bill when enacted. To soften him up in the second stage, the Republicans attached a rider requiring a balanced budget by 2002 scored on CBO economic forecasts to a debt-limit extension bill enacted on November 8. The next day they passed a new CR that made deep cuts in a range of social programs, some as high as 40 percent. This measure also eliminated a scheduled reduction in Medicare premiums to avoid making the higher charges planned in the Republican budget awaiting enactment look worse than they actually were. Confident of victory over Clinton, House Republican Whip Tom DeLay (R-TX) proclaimed, "If he shuts the government down, we'll keep it shut down until he signs a bill or an agreement in writing about what he will do."[105]

The veto of both measures on November 13 not only precipitated a government shutdown at midnight but also raised the possibility of an unprecedented federal default on interest payments. Clinton was nervous about how global financial markets would react, but Robert Rubin stiffened his resolve. The Treasury secretary warned that capitulation would create a terrible precedent for future congressional use of debt financing as a blackmail weapon to weaken the presidency. He also provided the wherewithal to meet immediate government obligations by borrowing from two trust funds under his department's control, the Civil Service Retirement Fund and a federal savings plan. Significantly, he resisted borrowing from the Social Security trust fund so as not to hand Republicans an opportunity to charge that the administration was depleting retirement benefits to finance its deficit habit.[106]

The government shutdown went ahead against the preferences of the main protagonists. Clinton ran the risk of the Republicans persuading the public that he was to blame for it.[107] Normally a dealmaker, Bob Dole found himself a prisoner of his ambitions for national office. If he fell out with House conservatives, Phil Gramm would exploit the breach to boost his own presidential candidacy. The Texan informed Dole, "There is no amount of political pressure that Democrats can exert, which will induce me to hand Bill Clinton the keys of the Treasury and tell him to take what he needs." From the party's grassroots, the Republican Governors Association also urged the Senate leader to stand firm against "the impending disaster that larger and larger deficit spending portends." Nonetheless, Dole also feared being tied to the increasingly unpopular Gingrich because the White House and the Democratic National Committee were now running personalized attack ads on both as enemies of Medicare.[108]

Despite his tough talk, Gingrich himself did not welcome a shutdown with his popularity at its nadir. A Gallup poll on November 10 put his favorable and unfavorable ratings at 25 percent and 56 percent, respectively, while giving Clinton 52 percent approval, his highest in eighteen months. Gingrich knew the danger of "losing the public's understanding and approval of what we were trying to do." The Speaker was also aware that he faced a rebellion in his own ranks if he retreated. The freshman class had effectively issued an ultimatum that it would oust him as House leader if he reneged on his promises like the hated George Bush. At one juncture in their talks, Gingrich urged Clinton to show more flexibility lest he have to deal in future with hard-liner Dick Armey as Speaker.[109]

Republican insistence on defining the dispute as one over political values rather than fiscal responsibility worked to the president's advantage. In vetoing the debt extension bill, he declared, "Our country has to choose between two very different options, two very different visions and paths to the 21st century." With polls indicating that Medicare was the hot-button issue for the public, Clinton also emphasized his determination to protect seniors from Republican higher premiums. Nevertheless, he was equally committed to safeguarding Medicaid and other antipoverty programs. Meeting with Republican leaders on November 13 with the shutdown just hours away, he vowed, "I will never sign your Medicaid cuts. I don't care if I go down to five percent in the polls. If you want your budget passed, you're going to have to put someone else in this chair."[110]

Lasting six days, the shutdown resulted in 800,000 federal workers being furloughed, the closure of all but essential services, and government contracts being put on hold. Polls indicated that the public overwhelmingly blamed the Republicans for this denouement by a two-to-one majority. Anxious to recapture the high ground, Gingrich secured House enactment on November 15 of a new CR without the stringent conditions of the previous one. This simply demanded acceptance of a balanced budget within seven years based on CBO scoring as the price for reopening government. Sensitive to constituent anger over the shutdown, forty-eight House Democrats and seven Senate Democrats backed the measure. Rumors abounded that another veto would be unpopular with many more. As White House press secretary Mike McCurry acknowledged, "The Republicans lose the debate on the budget itself, but when they keep it on the continuing resolution, it's about balancing the budget."[111]

Clinton now decided on a calculated accommodation to get the budget debate back onto Democratic values. Agreeing to a four-week CR on November 20, he provided written acceptance of a CBO-scored balanced budget in seven years "if and only if" there was adequate funding for Medicare, Medicaid, education, and environmental protection. Believing that the White House had conceded their key demand, the Republican leaders took the deal. They even substituted the "if and only if" clause to "and" in the written agreement as reassurance that they were not eliminating these programs.[112] This proved a tactical error of the first order. It necessitated holding talks to discuss a budget settlement, something Gingrich had hitherto refused because Republicans had such bad memories of the 1990 summit negotiations. Clinton could now affirm his significance in the budget process as the protector of social programs. Seizing this opportunity, the White House formally reiterated to the Republican leadership the terms on which it was willing to conduct "serious negotiations to reach a balanced budget that reflects the values and priorities of the American people."[113]

Overshadowed by the shutdown, Congress on November 18 finally approved its budget reconciliation bill to reduce spending by $894 billion over seven years along similar lines to its original resolution. This was the first balanced-budget plan proposed by Congress since enactment of the Budget Control and Impoundment Act of 1974. Gingrich exulted, "It's the most decisive vote on the direction of government since 1933." Caught up in the euphoria, Dole also proclaimed, "Americans want fundamental change; we'll give them fundamental change." The measure lived up to this hype. In addition to Medicare economies of $270 billion, Medicaid was to become a block grant, thereby terminating its entitlement status, and its rate of growth was to be cut nearly in half. These and other savings, many on programs benefiting the poor, helped to pay for tax cuts of $245 billion that mostly benefited the well off. Donning the mantle of liberal conservationist, Clinton vetoed the bill on December 6 with the pen that Lyndon Johnson had used to sign Medicare into law in 1965.[114]

Meanwhile, the two sides were locked in budget negotiations that went nowhere. They moved closer on the numbers but remained as far apart as ever on philosophy. On December 7, Clinton produced a new seven-year balanced-budget plan based on OMB figures but containing $140 billion savings above his original ten-year plan. For Republicans, John Kasich furiously retorted that it was "at minimum $400 billion in the hole." On December 11, however, the CBO lowered its seven-year deficit forecast by $135 billion to take account of the economy's rapid improvement. The Republicans consequently reduced their program cuts to leave the two sides $115 billion apart in the seventh year of their plans. A White House counterproposal still depended on OMB projections and possible revocation of tax cuts to eliminate the deficit in FY2002. In view of the almost certain inaccuracy of any forecast over seven years, the obvious solution was to split the difference, but divergent political values ruled out fiscal compromise.[115]

Expiry of the second CR precipitated another government shutdown on December 15. Lasting until January 6, 1996, this caused hardship over the Christmas period to the families of 280,000 furloughed federal employees and to citizens whose government checks were not being processed. Orchestrating popular resentment, the president painted the House Republicans as unfeeling hard-liners willing to go to any lengths to get their way, a strategy also designed to drive a wedge between Dole and Gingrich. With the polls in his favor, he had no incentive to surrender his fundamental goals. Although Clinton's issuance of eight budget-related vetoes in late 1995 sustained the impasse, the public rewarded his intransigence because it perceived him as protecting popular programs and the Republicans as extreme.[116] Realizing the public relations battle was lost, a frustrated Bob Dole complained, "Our message is a balanced budget in seven years. Our message is not some government shutdown." On January 2, he unilaterally rammed a bill through the Senate to reopen the government. Rather than see Republicans hopelessly split, Gingrich used his remaining authority to force the House to follow suit on January 5.[117]

In return, the GOP leaders wanted Clinton to produce an acceptable seven-year balanced-budget plan, but to no avail. The president's new proposal of January 7 and subsequent revisions by both sides reduced their difference on gross expenditure savings to $136 billion. Clinton's final offer projected $276 billion more in spending cuts than in his first one six months earlier. He moved closer to the economies proposed by the Republicans for discretionary programs ($295 billion to $349 billion), Medicaid ($59 billion to $85 billion), and Medicare ($124 billion to $154 billion). However, the two sides still disagreed over Medicaid's continuation as an open-ended federal entitlement and on capping Medicare benefits as a way of transferring future cost growth to health-care providers and, indirectly, recipients themselves.

Equally significant, they were no closer on tax reduction. Although the Republicans scaled down their program to $203 billion, Clinton offered cuts of only $87 billion, less than in his June 1995 plan.[118]

Unable to take this deal for fear of provoking a party rebellion, Republican leaders beat an orderly retreat. To avoid giving Clinton a high-profile opportunity to declare victory, Gingrich announced that the budget negotiations were effectively dead the day after the State of the Union address. He now declared that the Republicans would seek a modest package of $40 billion spending cuts and $30 billion in tax cuts in FY1996 as a down-payment on balancing the budget at an unspecified future date. "It's not a big deal," the Speaker admitted, "but it's a start." Even this was beyond his reach. It required fourteen Continuing Resolutions before the fractious FY1996 budget was settled. All the Republicans could show for their efforts was a net $3 billion reduction in discretionary domestic outlays. The White House, meanwhile, secured restoration of $5 billion that the GOP budget reconciliation measure had cut from various education, training, and environmental programs. There was no reduction in Medicare and Medicaid, nor were there any significant tax changes.[119]

By then, there were only five months left to deal with the FY1997 budget. Seeing no purpose in another showdown with a president now riding high in the polls thanks to a buoyant economy, GOP leaders offered to negotiate an omnibus budget package in September. Dole's earlier resignation from the Senate to run for president made it easier to reach agreement than would have been the case if both rival candidates were involved in the talks. In their anxiety not to appear intransigent, however, the Republicans ended up accepting spending increases that exceeded the limits set in the congressional budget resolution. Under the settlement, there was to be a 3 percent real increase in discretionary domestic spending. Most domestic departments received substantially bigger budgets than in FY1996, with Education receiving an increase of nearly 15 percent. The Commerce Department and most of the myriad programs that the GOP had targeted for elimination in 1995 also had more funds. The solitary Republican successes over spending were the addition of $10 billion to Clinton's defense request and 10 percent to his military construction estimate. On the tax front, the only change was a miniscule cut of $10 billion over five years for small business, but even this was part of a bill that met administration demands for an increase in the minimum wage.[120]

Nevertheless, the Republicans could still make gains when they picked their fights. The Freedom to Farm Act of 1996 phased out agricultural price supports over seven years, effectively projecting an end to the New Deal subsidy system. The booming economy created the political conditions for this reform because higher commodity prices had reduced the need for what

Republicans dubbed farm welfare.[121] Enhanced prosperity also facilitated another assault on the New Deal legacy in the shape of welfare reform. In this case, the needs of triangulation boxed the president into making concessions that infuriated many Democrats.

In 1995 a Heritage Foundation report claimed that thirty-year welfare spending of $5.4 trillion in 1993 dollars had worsened dependency and out-of-wedlock births. Though the report was patently spurious in some regards, Republicans seized on its findings as justification for a complete overhaul of antipoverty programs.[122] This was what Clinton had advocated in *Putting People First,* but his plan required higher short-term costs to fund job training and child care for those in transition from welfare to work. Accordingly, he twice vetoed welfare reform bills enacted by the GOP Congress in 1996 on grounds that they were too harsh. Particularly objectionable to him was their intent to terminate entitlement to Medicaid and food stamps and reduce nutritional supplements to children by turning these supports into fixed-term block grants. The Medicaid savings in the second bill amounted to $72 billion over six years, equivalent to almost 10 percent of projected program costs.[123]

The Republicans then produced a third bill that provided more financial support for moving people to work and child-care needs and restored federal guarantees of food stamps and medical benefits. Its key provision replaced the entitlement to cash assistance under AFDC with two new block grants, Temporary Assistance for Needy Families and a child-care program. States now had considerable latitude to determine benefit levels and eligibility and to decide on which services to spend up to 30 percent of their grant. The measure projected savings of $55 billion in FY1997–FY2002, half coming from cutbacks in food stamps, eligibility for which was tightened and restricted to three months a year. A portion also came from denying welfare benefits to legal immigrants, except those having worked in the United States for more than ten years or associated with the military, and to many able-bodied childless adults aged between eighteen and fifty.[124]

Critics charged that the bill would push a million additional children into poverty in the cause of budgetary retrenchment. A CBO estimate that funding to meet work requirements and child-care provision were respectively $12 billion and a minimum of $1 billion short of need seemingly validated them. Mayors also warned that the supposed annual savings would be gobbled up by the increased costs of crime, job training, and lost purchasing power.[125] However, National Opinion Research Center surveys tracking mass opinion on government spending found that 56 percent of respondents now thought welfare spending too high, compared with only 40 percent in 1991. The strong economy engendered widespread belief that welfare recipients could find jobs if they truly wanted to work. Based on his private polling, Dick

Morris warned Clinton that further resistance to welfare reform could endanger his reelection. Unwilling to risk this for a bill that contained some acceptable features, the president decided to sign it and work to correct its flaws. He told aides, "This is a decent welfare bill wrapped in a sack of shit."[126]

The adversaries in the budget confrontations of 1995 settled their differences through compromise in 1996. Clinton had greater cause for satisfaction because he got most of what he wanted. Having promised too much, the Republicans ended up with relatively little. However, two important GOP achievements did not as yet show up in the fiscal ledger. The president had conceded that the deficit should be eliminated and had moved significantly closer to the Republican position on the budgetary numbers for doing so by the time the shutdown imbroglio ended. This established the framework for their negotiations in the next Congress.

THE DEFICIT OVERCOME

The deficit was down to 1.4 percent GDP in FY1996, the lowest in more than two decades. Looking to build on this success in his second term, Clinton told ABC's David Brinkley that if he could "accomplish only one thing . . . I would pass a balanced budget that would . . . open the doors to college to all Americans and continue the incremental progress we've made in health care reform." In their last official meeting, outgoing Secretary of Labor Robert Reich accused his old friend of misguided priorities. The deficit, he declared, "is down to almost *nothing*. The whole goddamned budget is an *accounting* number. What about the *poor?* They're bearing the brunt of deficit reduction."[127]

Reich misunderstood that Clinton now regarded deficit elimination as the best way to advance programs that helped the poor. Instead of Republican pressure forcing his hand, he embraced a balanced budget of his own volition as the instrument to win public trust for the renewal of his progressive agenda. Though less potent than four years earlier, Ross Perot's independent candidacy in the 1996 election had shown that the deficit was still a negative symbol to many Americans. The Texan's 9 percent share of the vote denied Clinton his ambition of a popular majority. Nevertheless, a far greater achievement beckoned if he could conquer the budget problem. New NEC chair Gene Sperling commented, "For the president, this will be a legacy . . . that he was able to bring down the deficit, reform welfare and still show there was a significant role for a smaller but more effective government in investing in people."[128]

Notwithstanding the deficit's current decline, OMB and CBO forecasts still projected future growth without remedial action. Both agencies calculated that the scale of savings needed to balance the budget over five years was about half what the 1990 and 1993 deficit-reduction plans had each achieved.[129] Clinton needed to work with the Republicans if he wanted to get federal finances out of the red. Confounding expectations of continued gridlock, the White House and GOP congressional leaders adapted to new circumstances to resolve the budget impasse that had dominated Washington politics since the early 1980s.[130]

Recent experience had taught Gingrich that further confrontation with Clinton over a radical agenda was futile. As he later remarked, "We decided that four years of incremental achievement in our direction are superior to four years of obstruction while we scream about values." The 1994 freshmen were also less of a problem than before. In 1996, eighteen had lost their seats and twenty-two of the victors had won with 53 percent or less of the popular vote. Many of the survivors wanted to build a record of achievement that would provide more solid foundations for their political careers. Moreover, moderate Republicans now held the balance of power in the House, where the GOP majority was down to twenty-one seats. Meanwhile, new Majority Leader Trent Lott (R-MS) was more interested in proving that Republicans could govern than fighting ideological battles. His lack of presidential ambitions also gave him more freedom to maneuver in negotiating with the White House.[131]

The 1996 election gave both sides cause to reconsider their positions. Republicans could no longer assume that the public was in their corner on tax reduction. Bob Dole's promise to slash income taxes by 15 percent and halve the capital gains tax failed to lift his campaign. Warning that his opponent's $550 billion program risked inflating the deficit, Clinton offered a much smaller tax cut of $110 billion, mainly targeted at people wanting a college education, low-income workers, and families with children. Initial polling by Dick Morris found that voters preferred this approach by a majority of almost two to one.[132] Nevertheless, the Republicans retained control of both houses of Congress for the first time since 1928. Although just one in seven voters split their tickets, Clinton interpreted the divided-government outcome as a signal of popular desire for bipartisan cooperation to build the nation's future. "America demands and deserves big things of us," he declared in his second inaugural address, "and nothing big ever came from being small."[133]

Signaling his desire for fiscal entente, the president took the lead in initiating budget talks by committing to accept the original GOP target of FY2002 for deficit elimination, now only five years hence.[134] Both sides also changed their negotiating personnel to facilitate agreement. The direct participation of the main political principals—Clinton, Gore, Gingrich, and Dole—in the shutdown talks had intensified confrontation. In 1997, devolution of negotiating responsibility to second-tier officials—chief of staff Erskine Bowles,

OMB director Franklin Raines, congressional liaison head John Hilley and Gene Sperling for the White House, and Budget Committee chairs John Kasich and Peter Domenici for the GOP—greased the wheels of conciliation. Bowles proved to be the key figure. Already a Clinton confidante, he earned Gingrich's trust as a dealmaker and a go-between to the president. His appointment proved critical in convincing both leaders of their mutual commitment to reaching a balanced budget agreement.[135]

Though never plain sailing, the negotiations produced agreement on May 1 on a five-year balanced budget plan. Republicans got gross tax reduction totaling $135 billion, far less than their 1995 target but close to the annual average tax cut ($27 billion compared to $29 billion) in their final proposal in the shutdown imbroglio. This included capital gains relief, something Democrats had long resisted. However, the agreement required offsetting tax increases of $50 billion, primarily on airline tickets and excises, in the interests of deficit reduction. In turn, the administration accepted spending cuts of $280 billion, falling evenly on discretionary and entitlement programs, with caps on the former being extended to FY2002 and four-fifths of savings on the latter coming from Medicare. This was actually well below average annual savings in its final shutdown offer ($56 billion, compared to $68.3 billion). Increasingly optimistic CBO fiscal projections made deeper cuts unnecessary. The agreement also provided $30 billion in new funding for designated presidential priorities, particularly children's health insurance, welfare benefits for disabled legal immigrants, and food stamps. In a further trade-off, the negotiators agreed that tax reduction would commence in FY1997 but some 70 percent of the spending cuts would be shoehorned into FY2001–FY2002, when Clinton was no longer in office.[136]

These terms were incorporated into the congressional budget resolution. The president made his agreement to them contingent on a majority of Democrats in both chambers voting for this, which duly occurred on June 25. At the White House's behest, the resolution also required that the spending and revenue reconciliation bills be considered separately to facilitate a veto in case of GOP backsliding on either element of the agreement. These were enacted in form acceptable to the president as the Balanced Budget Act (BBA) and the Taxpayers Relief Act (TRA) at the end of July. Both measures won a high level of bipartisan support in the Senate, but nearly 40 percent of House Democrats, including Minority Leader Dick Gephardt, voted against them for giving away too much. With deficit projections continuing to decline, the BBA required significantly smaller savings than the May agreement ($90 billion for discretionary programs and $105 billion net for entitlements). According to the CBO, the TRA provided net tax cuts of $80 billion over five years and $242 billion over ten years.[137]

Some conservative Republicans and liberal Democrats predictably accused their leaders of surrender. In response to GOP critics, John Kasich contended, "Of course, Republicans in Congress could have gone it alone, seen our plans vetoed and not accomplished anything. No tax cuts. No solvency for Medicare over the next ten years. No entitlement reform. No restraint in Washington spending. No balanced budget." To Democratic skeptics, Gene Sperling and Franklin Raines asked, "Do the critics believe that holding out for the purest position and certain gridlock is preferable to an agreement that puts the deficit on a path to zero while investing more in education, the environment and children's health?" According to Sperling the budget measures together provided $70 billion over five years for families with an income of under $30,000.[138]

As to which side gained more, the most careful academic study concludes that it "shifted budget priorities in a Republican direction." According to this assessment, the big-ticket items—the first net tax cut since 1981, the largest Medicare savings ever enacted, and real cuts in discretionary domestic spending—were GOP goals, whereas the gains for Clinton were small in comparison.[139] However, the president's achievement appears in better light if the 1995 Republican budget offensive is taken as the baseline for comparison.

With economic prosperity generating ever-shrinking projections of the deficit, the BBA only required net five-year savings of $90 billion in discretionary programs and $105 billion in entitlements. The Medicare cuts of $110 billion were primarily achieved through lower payment rates for health-care providers. The economies did not require major benefit changes nor did they affect program coverage that the GOP had once sought to transform. Moreover, the BBA contained additional money for some entitlement programs that partially offset cuts in others. Most significant, it created a new State Children's Health Insurance Program (SCHIP), financed through a $20 billion five-year block grant. The largest expansion of public health insurance coverage since 1965, this benefited more than five million children of working parents too well off for Medicaid but unable to afford private insurance. The BBA also allocated more funding for SSI, food stamps, and welfare-to-work programs and earmarked $14 billion for restoration of some of the benefits that welfare recipients had lost in the 1996 welfare reform.[140]

The 1997 tax cuts were also significantly different in size and distributional effect from those sought by the GOP in 1995. The estimated net revenue loss over five years was a mere 1 percent of annual receipts, or less than 0.3 percent GDP, because offsetting revenue increases amounted to $60 billion, 20 percent higher than in the May 1 agreement ($131 billion over ten years). The latter included a $5 billion increase in tobacco tax to help defray SCHIP costs. Moreover, $112 billion of the gross tax reductions of $141 billion went on the child tax credit ($73 billion) and postsecondary education incentives for taxpayers with adjusted gross incomes of up to $40,000 ($39 billion), both of which primarily benefited middle-income and low-income taxpayers.[141] In 1999 an estimated ten million of the fourteen million Americans eligible for the education tax breaks took advantage of them. With some justification, Clinton speechwriter Michael Waldman claimed that this represented "the biggest single federal investment in higher education" since the GI bill of 1944.[142]

Clinton firmly opposed some Republican tax proposals that contradicted his distributional preferences. Most notably he insisted that EITC recipients should benefit from the child tax credit. This almost precipitated a breakdown of the bipartisanship because Gingrich considered it a backdoor increase in welfare spending. With the onus on compromise, however, the Republicans conceded that the child credit would be partially refundable for low-income families with three children in return for White House acceptance that it should be available to families with incomes up to $110,000, nearly double Clinton's original $60,000 limit. In another trade-off, the president got $5 billion more for the education tax incentives in exchange for accepting Republican priorities on estate taxes, individual retirement accounts, and the alternative minimum tax.[143]

Though a potent demonstration that political compromise over the budget was possible, the 1997 agreement was less significant as an agency of actual deficit elimination. With the growing economy delivering bountiful revenues and previous budget agreements holding down spending, federal finances moved out of the red in one year rather than five. In FY1994–FY1997 annual revenue growth far outstripped expenditure growth in real terms by 8.1 percent to 3.2 percent. By FY1997 revenues were 19.3 percent of GDP, the third-highest level since World War II (exceeded only in inflation-affected FY1981 and the surtax-generated balanced budget of FY1969), and spending was only 19.6 percent of GDP, its lowest level since FY1974. As the budget moved into the black, the fiscal indicators repeatedly set new standards of historical significance. In FY2000 outlays constituted 18.4 percent GDP (the lowest since FY1966), revenues were 20.9 percent GDP (matching the record high of FY1944), and individual income taxes equaled 10.3 percent GDP, a new high (all the FY1998–FY2001 budgets also beat the previous record set in FY1944).[144]

More than anything else, the fiscal transformation was the product of boom times. From 1996 through 2000 annual economic growth exceeded 4 percent and added over $400 billion each year to GDP. The unemployment rate fell from 5.6 percent to 4 percent, inflation kept on its lowest track since the 1950s, and productivity growth averaged 2.7 percent a year, virtually double its level in 1973–1995. Analysts generally attributed this success to the confluence of productivity-boosting new technology, America's well-functioning venture capital markets, and the impact of globalization.[145] There was also consensus that monetary policy made a significant contribution, but the role of fiscal policy was more contentious.

Alan Greenspan conventionally received primary credit for facilitating the boom. Once reassured that inflation was under control, he reversed monetary course to keep interest rates low for a four-year period commencing in mid-1995. The Fed chair earned particular commendation for a timely series of rate cuts to sustain investor and business confidence against the spread of international financial crisis from East Asia and Russia in late 1998.[146] Although Greenspan never endorsed the concept of a nonaccelerating inflation rate of unemployment, his strategy from mid-1995 to mid-1999 implicitly operated on the assumption that monetary fine-tuning to promote economic growth was at least possible in some circumstances. Once fearful that Greenspan's interest-rate strategy was retarding economic recovery, the White House economic team thought of him as one of them by 1996 because, in Laura Tyson's words, he "wasn't running the Fed as a Republican." Clinton signaled this rapprochement by appointing Greenspan to two more terms in office.[147]

In contrast, opinion was divided even among liberal economists about Clinton's contribution to growth. Some charged that his drive for deficit reduction served only to constrain the distribution of prosperity created by monetary relaxation.[148] This rather underplayed the probability that the former was the prerequisite for the latter. With arguably better cause, Alan Blinder and Janet Yellen, both of whom served in the Clinton CEA and the Greenspan Fed, saw the 1990s economic experience as proof that *"tight government budgets and (relatively) easy monetary policy can create a pro-investment macroeconomic climate by holding down real interest rates."* In their view, Greenspan's confidence that the deficit was under control was critical to his relaxation of interest rates. In confirmation of this, the Fed chair himself acknowledged to Clinton, "If you had not turned the fiscal situation around, we couldn't have had the kind of monetary policy we've had."[149]

THE GRIDLOCK OF SURPLUS POLITICS

In a moment of optimism the *New York Times* characterized deficit elimination as "the fiscal equivalent of the fall of the Berlin Wall." In contrast to the Cold War, of course, the other red peril was merely dormant rather than dead. For a time, however, the terms of fiscal debate focused on what to do with government's abundant revenues. This did not produce a new era of consensus. Having resolved gridlock over the deficit, America's political leaders renewed it over the surplus.[150]

Seeing an opportunity to address the greatest fiscal challenge of the next century, Bill Clinton wanted to invest the surplus in strengthening the long-term solvency of Social Security and Medicare. As domestic aide Bruce Reed recalled, "Everyone had spent years thinking that real pain would be required . . . but we had the money to do it right there and then."[151] Many Republicans, in contrast, regarded the surplus as the people's money to be returned to them in the form of tax cuts. To outmaneuver them, Clinton looked to redefine the center ground of budgetary politics by converting Newt Gingrich into an ally. This was the boldest initiative of his second term, but its ultimate failure limited the scope of his fiscal legacy.

Clinton wanted to show that government could solve national problems within a balanced budget. He told an aide, "FDR's mission was to save capitalism from its own excesses. Our mission has been to save government from its own excesses so it can again be a progressive force."[152] Fixing the pension problem would be the ultimate justification of fiscal discipline as a tool of activist government. On current projections, Social Security would be paying out more in benefits than it collected in taxes within twenty years because of the retirement of the baby-boom generation. In theory, the program would then draw on its trust fund to continue paying benefits until this ran out of money in 2031. In reality, the Social Security surpluses accumulated to date had been spent, leaving the trust fund with government IOUs that taxpayers would eventually have to repay. As the FY2000 budget plan explained, they existed "only in a bookkeeping sense" rather than as "real economic assets that can be drawn down in the future to fund benefits." To put matters right, Clinton tied the fiscal surplus to the pension problem under the slogan "Save Social Security First."[153]

Learning from the health-care debacle, Clinton looked to build bipartisan support for change and educate the public about the issues before proposing a plan. In his 1998 State of the Union address he called for a national debate on Social Security. Pending reform, however, he announced that future budget surpluses should be reserved for a ten-year period for national debt reduction. The interest savings from this would then become available to replenish the Social Security trust fund. As Robert Rubin recounted, "The idea was . . . to remind the public that if the surplus was their money, the debt was their debt as well, and to connect saving the surplus with a purpose that was easy to explain." An appreciative Alan Greenspan told Gene Sperling, "You've found a way to make debt reduction politically attractive."[154]

Reform plans from think tanks, interest groups, and government advisory bodies were already circulating in Washington. Although these still manifested significant differences, there was emergent consensus over proposals that preserved the integrity of the system but allowed for structural change in the retirement age and some form of private accounts tied to stock market investment options. Support for this incremental approach was also growing among moderates in both parties. Meanwhile, Clinton pollster Mark Penn found that 73 percent of Democratic voters favored some element of privatization. Independent surveys confirmed that younger workers particularly supported change to ensure program solvency into their old age. The chief political strategist of the American Association of Retired Persons also perceived the opportunity for reform because the "stars are in alignment."[155]

With Erskine Bowles again their go-between, Clinton and Gingrich inched toward cooperation that would serve the national good and their personal ambitions. Social Security reform would ensure Clinton's reputation as the president who had strengthened America to meet the challenges of the new century. He was ready to take the heat from liberals for sanctioning partial privatization in return for Gingrich facing down the Republican right by trading tax reduction for pension reform that included some private investment. In the Speaker's calculation, a record of constructive achievement was a better foundation than partisan confrontation for his presidential ambitions and would give him a new power base among GOP moderates. According to Gingrich, the balanced budget measure of 1997 was "Act I" in his shift toward engagement with Clinton, and Social Security was to have been "Act II."[156]

The one-time adversaries were agreed on the broad outlines for Social Security reform by early 1998. As a further demonstration of rapprochement, they also collaborated to establish a National Bipartisan Commission on the Future of Medicare, chaired by Senator John Breaux (D-LA), to explore cost control. However, revelations of Clinton's illicit relationship with White House intern Monica Lewinsky and associated allegations of presidential lies and obstruction of justice put an end to emergent bipartisanship. Instead of working together for the future, Clinton and Gingrich became embroiled in an increasingly bitter partisan conflict that culminated in the attempted Republican impeachment of the president.

Reflecting on his failure to reform Social Security, Clinton told journalist Joe Klein, "I think we could have gotten it if we hadn't had that whole impeachment thing." White House officials and Republicans involved in the reform negotiations were of the same mind.[157] Others on the edges of the talks were more skeptical whether agreement on specific details was possible. According to Robert Rubin, liberal Democrats and their interest-group allies would never have accepted private accounts, which was essential for Republican support. Whether the opportunity for reform was substantial or small, the Lewinsky scandal restored the confrontational nature of Washington politics. Worried that he would otherwise lose his position as Speaker, Gingrich joined conservative Republicans in baying for Clinton's head. For his part, the president was thrown into an alliance with liberal Democrats, whose votes he needed to survive impeachment. In other words, the Lewinsky scandal empowered those groups in both parties most opposed to compromise over Social Security.[158]

Accordingly, the Social Security plan that Clinton unveiled in his 1999 State of the Union address was more adjustment than reform. It proposed allocating 60 percent of budget surpluses over fifteen years to Social Security (extending trust fund solvency to 2055) and 16 percent to Medicare (extending solvency by ten years, to 2020). Because these transfers were not required to fund current benefits, they would be used mainly to pay down the public debt in the first instance. A small portion of the Social Security money would be invested in equity purchases to extend trust fund solvency. Instead of individual accounts, Clinton recommended Universal Savings Accounts, a voluntary investment-oriented scheme that allocated 11 percent of the surplus to provide tax credits for Americans with income under $100,000 to open retirement accounts. Entirely separate from Social Security, these had no implications for an account holder's pension benefits. Clinton later claimed that this was "perhaps the largest proposal ever made to help modest-income families save and create wealth." A far cry from private accounts, this tool for retirement finance never received serious consideration from the Republicans. Plans for the remaining portion of the surplus to be spent on discretionary programs further exacerbated GOP ire.[159]

In another blow to entitlement reform, Clinton signaled opposition to the Breaux commission's majority proposal for shifting Medicare toward a defined-contribution approach. Under this, government would pay a lump sum and the beneficiary would pay the marginal dollar. This presidential stance accorded with the preference of most congressional Democrats for preservation of traditional Medicare. In late 1999 Clinton advanced a compromise proposal broadly based on Breaux plan principles but providing safeguards for program beneficiaries, particularly against higher premiums. This modest departure from liberal orthodoxy got nowhere because it went too far for most Democrats and not far enough for most Republicans. Moreover, steadily improving projections of trust fund solvency based on the boom-driven buoyancy of payroll tax receipts eased the pressure to fix Medicare.[160]

Without positive focus for bipartisanship, the White House and the congressional Republicans drew new battle lines that produced gridlock over surplus disposal. The sole exception was the agreement reached in late 1999 to place the annual Social Security surplus in a "lockbox" that could not be raided to fund other programs. More significant, the president did not gain approval for the budget plan in the administration's Mid-Session Review, released in June 1999. This proposed allocating the bulk of the on-budget surplus to the Social Security and Medicare trust funds in accordance with Clinton's State of the Union announcement. Initially the money would be used to pay down the public debt to achieve its elimination by 2015. As the scale of debt repayment diminished, actual transfers into the trust funds would begin in 2011 commensurate with the interest savings produced.[161]

In their version of surplus disposal, the Republicans enacted the Taxpayer Refund and Relief Act in August 1999. This provided for personal tax cuts, estate tax relief, capital gains reduction, alternative minimum tax relief, and other allowances at a ten-year cost of $792 billion. Clinton vetoed the measure on grounds that it disproportionately benefited upper-income groups, prevented elimination of the public debt, and delayed resolution of the funding shortfalls facing senior citizens' entitlements. "This legislation," he declared, "would reverse the fiscal discipline that has helped make the American economy the strongest it has been in generations."[162]

The surplus deadlock did not prevent the president from winning smaller fiscal battles with the Republicans as part of his strategy to consolidate liberal Democratic support in the Lewinsky scandal. Unable to complete the appropriations process on time, GOP leaders sought to roll outstanding FY1999 spending bills into an omnibus measure. Seizing his opportunity to dictate terms, Clinton threatened to veto any legislation not providing additional funds for domestic programs. After a White House meeting on October 9, the president and Democratic congressional leaders went before the television cameras to avow determination to fight for their common priorities. Although impeachment proceedings had already commenced, the Republicans agreed to budget negotiations to avoid another government shutdown. The president consequently secured an extra $1.1 billion to help school districts hire 100,000 additional elementary teachers, more money for subsidized housing, environmental protection and highway construction, and a major increase in America's contribution to the International Monetary Fund.[163] With the Republicans also winning additional military spending, discretionary outlays exceeded the 1997 caps by $20 billion. Accordingly, the GOP leadership arranged for the overshoot to be designated "emergency spending." Enjoying his adversaries' discomfiture, Clinton joked with aides that they were "basically bringing money to us in a wheelbarrow."[164]

The terms of the settlement sewed disillusion and discord in GOP ranks. Conservatives lambasted Gingrich for a surrender over spending that diverted funds from tax reduction. Conversely buoyed by Clinton's success, many Democrats ran in the midterm elections on a platform of Save Social Security First, educational investment, and opposition to impeachment. Their reward was a five-seat gain in the House and no aggregate loss in the Senate, the first time since 1822 that a president's party had increased its congressional representation during his second term. After this setback, Gingrich announced his intention to quit Congress altogether in January.[165]

The president continued to win the budget skirmishes during his final years in office. Discretionary spending exceeded the 1997 caps by more than $50 billion in FY2000 and nearly $80 billion in FY2001, with Clinton's priorities the main beneficiaries as before. Domestic programs received two-thirds of total discretionary spending increases in his four surplus budgets. The president also maneuvered around PAYGO limits on entitlements. Although curbed by the 1997 agreement, Medicare reimbursements for health-care providers rose more than $50 billion in FY1999–FY2000. Health-care entitlement for military retirees, veterans' benefits, and children's health insurance also got bigger increases than budget rules allowed.[166]

Impressive though Clinton's budget victories were, they killed off fading hopes of bipartisan agreement over surplus disposal. Republicans grew increasingly resentful of the president's stealthy ratcheting up of spending under cover of fiscal discipline. Claiming to be "a balanced budget with a balanced approach to national problems," his FY2001 plan projected sizeable multiyear increases for education, health care, environmental protection, and other domestic programs. "How can the era of big government be over," asked Speaker Dennis Hastert (R-IL), "when this budget would create close to $350 billion in new government programs?" Meanwhile, Clinton used the specter of renewed deficits to thwart modest Republican initiatives for tax reduction. The Marriage Tax Relief Reconciliation Act of 2000 incurred his veto on grounds that it was skewed toward the affluent and would "plunge America back into deficit." It was small wonder that many Republicans increasingly saw the surplus as a threat to their agenda. Voicing their concerns, Governor George W. Bush of Texas declared that "surpluses will be spent if we don't have a leader who's willing to cut taxes."[167]

THE CLINTON LEGACY

Bill Clinton's effort to blend fiscal discipline and government activism found little favor with traditional Democrats. To some of these, the tension between these ends resulted in the former taking precedence over the latter. Liberal doyen James MacGregor Burns charged that Clinton's historical epitaph would be that of "deficit buster," thereby casting him as the legatee of Dwight Eisenhower rather than Franklin Roosevelt. For other liberals, Clinton's linkage of balanced budgets and progressive intent meant that he fed on scraps in pursuit of ad hoc gains rather than a grand vision. Voicing this concern, Richard Gephardt complained that the president "was enamored of small ideas that nibble round the edges of big problems."[168]

Such judgments do less than justice to Clinton's achievements if allowance is made for the political context of divided party control of government. Having turned back the Republican onslaught against social programs in the

104th Congress, Clinton was effective in manipulating the budget process to promote their expansion during his second term. If not amounting to a public investment revolution, the college tax credits of 1997, SCHIP, EITC expansion, health-care initiatives, and the additional money for education and related programs in his later budgets were tangible achievements that made a difference to millions of people. Liberal critics also underestimated the significance of balancing the budget after twenty years of red ink. Clinton's most important political legacy was to demonstrate that Democrats could again be trusted to use government to solve problems without blowing a hole in the public purse. In his wake, Republicans would find it more difficult to saddle their opponents with paternity for the illegitimate twins of big government and big deficits.

The best case for the fiscal legacy of the last Democratic president of the twentieth century was made by the first one of the new century. In Barack Obama's estimate, Clinton "instinctively understood the falseness of the choices" in the Republican agenda and "saw that government spending and regulation could, if properly designed, serve as vital ingredients and not inhibitors to economic growth, and how markets and fiscal discipline could help promote social justice."[169]

Clinton himself also claimed a legacy of prosperity from his deficit reduction success. At a reunion of OBRA supporters in 1998, he declared that "the economic plan worked, and it worked for reasons we said it would. . . . [We] actually enacted a law of intended consequences in American public life."[170] Though an accurate statement of the initiative's significance, this underplayed the unintended consequences of its success. The reduction in long-term interest rates encouraged by OBRA helped to make the stock market more attractive than the bond market to many investors. Economic growth, low short-term interest rates, and the prospect of a killing in the new high-tech sector all combined to turn a boom into a bubble. As Clinton's presidency drew to a close, the stock market was showing worrying signs of volatility because of concerns that "new economy" company shares had become overvalued.[171] The resultant shakeout precipitated the onset of recession in early 2001. If Clinton's fiscal policy cannot be held responsible for this, the experience of the late 1990s indicated that the psychological benefits of balanced budgets for investor behavior were not always predictable.

Nevertheless, the Clinton administration's reliance on the interaction of tight budgets and low interest rates to generate economic growth did not provide an enduring model for Democratic political economy. "If the Democratic party stands for anything," Robert Reich declared, "it's the simple proposition that prosperity should be shared." Measured on this criterion, Clintonomics was not particularly successful. Real median family income, which did not exceed its 1989 level until 1998, stagnated for most of the

Clinton era. Workers with only a high school education or less benefited least from the boom. Moreover, the unemployment rate of 8.2 percent among African American males was more than double that of 3.6 percent among white men in 1999. Although the poverty rate declined steadily from 15.1 percent of the population in 1993 to 11.8 percent in 1999—the lowest since 1979—this was not significantly better than the 12.8 percent level at the end of the Reagan era. Even Greenspan admitted that the fruits of economic success had fallen unevenly. "Expansion of income and wealth have been truly impressive," he declared in his Harvard commencement address in 1999, "though regrettably the gains have not been as evenly spread across households as I would like."[172]

Even judged on Clinton's aspirations to lay the foundations for long-term economic growth, his legacy did not look as impressive a decade later as it had when he left office. The turnaround in the budgetary situation improved but did not resolve the problem of low national saving inherited from the Reagan era. A remarkable surge in real annual investment of more than 10 percent between 1990 and 2000, particularly in business equipment and software, generated productivity improvements and low inflation. Strong output growth, high profits, and rapid technological progress were all instrumental in spurring investment. Also significant was the decline of federal borrowing that left more national saving available for private use. Nevertheless, this masked the decline in personal saving from 7.7 percent to 2.3 percent of disposable income from 1992 to 2000. The surge in domestic investment consequently overwhelmed the modest net increase in domestic saving to require an increase in the supply of funds from abroad. The effect was to perpetuate large trade deficits through which foreigners directed their saving to the United States. Paradoxically, the attainment of balanced budgets coincided with the period of sharpest decline in private saving, which most economists attributed "primarily to the dramatic runup in stock prices."[173]

The stock market boom of the late twentieth century and the bust of early 2001 offered warning signs of what could happen under a monetary regime that did not restrain credit excess. Greenspan could have pricked the stock market bubble at an early stage by utilizing the Federal Reserve's power to raise margin requirements governing how much stock could be bought with borrowed money. However, he told the open market committee on September 24, 1996, that this action might drag down the broader economy in addition to dousing speculation.[174]

The architects of Clinton-Greenspan economics also proved shortsighted in their advocacy of financial market liberalization as an instrument of economic growth. The Fed chair's enthusiasm for derivatives as a means to spread debt risk made him resistant to calls for stronger regulation of their use in the 1990s, a stand supported by the Clinton administration. In time, these would become, in the words of America's most successful money manager, Warren Buffet, the "financial weapons of mass destruction" that were instrumental in laying the economy low in 2008. The Clinton administration, with Treasury Secretary Larry Summers to the fore, also joined with Greenspan to promote the Financial Services Modernization Act of 1999. This repealed the Glass-Steagall Act of 1933, which limited the ability of banks, investment firms, and insurance companies to enter each other's markets. Supporters regarded this reform as providing necessary flexibility for U.S. financial services to compete in a globalized market. In Greenspan's opinion, Glass-Steagall was based on "faulty history" that banks had made inappropriate use of their security affiliates in advance of the 1929 crash, but the subprime crisis would soon prove the historical wisdom of Depression-era legislators.[175]

Finally, Clinton was denied his ambition to go down in history as the president who had fixed the Social Security problem. With hindsight, of course, the inclusion of private accounts tied to investment options as the price of striking a deal with the Republicans looked less alluring in the wake of the stock market's performance in the first decade of the twenty-first century. Nevertheless, the failure to win bipartisan agreement for Social Security reform and the associated commitment of the budget surplus to this end denied Clinton a fiscal legacy of historic significance. Instead, he had to make do with passing on a more limited and transitory bequest. As Bruce Reed observed, "Bill Clinton may be the only leader in all of history to leave a budget surplus of such magnitude for his successor to figure out how to use."[176] Unfortunately for the forty-second president, the forty-third president would have very different ideas about what he wanted to do with this legacy.

CHAPTER 7

George W. Bush:
Resurrecting the Deficit

Hopes that the age of deficits would give way to a new era of surpluses in the twenty-first century were short-lived. Federal finances again sank deep into the red during George Bush's first term. Abetted by a predominantly Republican Congress, the forty-third president abandoned the fiscal sobriety of the 1990s to binge on an expensive budgetary cocktail of tax cuts, defense expansion, and domestic program growth. Promising signs of deficit reduction in his second term were ultimately blown away by the worst economic crisis since the 1930s. As Bush's presidency drew to a close, it was evident that the fiscal future was colored a deeper red than ever before in peacetime. In light of the massive costs of repairing the financial system and generating economic expansion, former CBO director Rudolph Penner observed, "We're going to make Ronald Reagan look like a piker in terms of deficit creation."[1]

At the outset of his presidency, Bush predicted that budget surpluses would be even greater than the CBO and other agencies were currently forecasting. "We can do better than that in America," he declared. "We've just got some unbelievable productivity gains to be achieved in our economy." Tax cuts that could be delivered "without fear of budget deficits" were to be the instrument of this expansion. When the surplus vanished, Bush presented himself as the victim of exceptional circumstances. He often recalled saying during the 2000 election that deficits were acceptable in conditions of war, national emergency, or recession. "Little did I realize," he would add, "we'd get the trifecta."[2]

The lack of any record of this campaign statement does not preclude recognition that the recession of 2001, the needs of homeland security after the September 11 terrorist attacks, and the prolonged military interventions in Afghanistan and Iraq put new pressures on the budget. Nevertheless, Bush's stewardship of federal finances was anything but prudent and contributed substantially to the resurrection of the deficit problem. As such, he confirmed the lesson of the late twentieth century that presidential leadership was fundamental in determining the nation's fiscal course.

TEXAN FIRST SON

Born in New Haven, Connecticut, on July 6, 1946, and raised in Texas from the age of two, George W. Bush had an undistinguished career until well into his forties. In 1990 hardly anyone would have thought him capable of becoming president ten years later. At that juncture, Bush bore all the hallmarks of being "the under-achieving son of a super-achieving father."[3]

An indifferent student at Phillips Academy and then Yale from 1964 to 1968, Bush redeemed himself somewhat by gaining an MBA from Harvard Business School in 1975. Ducking paternal example of active duty overseas, he performed his Vietnam-era military service in the home-based Texas Air National Guard in 1968–1970. After Harvard, however, Bush did follow fatherly precedent by taking an entry-level appointment in the Texas oil industry. Shortly afterward, he established his own oil exploration firm, Arbusto Energy (renamed Bush Exploration in 1982), but financial success proved elusive. In 1984 he accepted a takeover in return for becoming chairman of the merged company, which soon hit financial difficulties because of collapsing oil prices. In 1986 it was bought up by Harken Energy Corporation, which gave Bush a seat on its board and a generous chunk of stock. What had twice saved him from sinking along with his companies was being the vice president's son. Harken co-owner George Soros later commented, "We were buying political influence. . . . He was not much of a businessman."[4]

The sale of two-thirds of his Harken shares in 1990 for more than twice their original value financed Bush's stake in an investment group that bought the Texas Rangers, a second-tier baseball team. This marked the upward turn in his career that led eventually to the White House. With a new stadium in Arlington and the resources to purchase star players, the baseball franchise proved a gold mine. When it was sold in 1998, Bush made $14.9 million from his original investment of $606,000, thereby guaranteeing his financial well-being. His role as the public face of the Texas Rangers ownership group also paved the way for a new career in politics. As well as making him a state celebrity, it constituted a solid achievement after a succession of false starts. On announcing his gubernatorial candidacy in 1993, Bush declared of the new ball park, "Here is visible evidence that I can think big thoughts, dream big dreams, and get something done."[5]

Bush defeated popular Democratic incumbent Ann Richards to become Republican governor of Texas in 1994. His reelection four years later with a record 69 percent of the popular vote made him the frontrunner for the GOP presidential nomination in 2000. Bush's name recognition, huge war chest, and strong partisan appeal swept him to victory over his main challenger, Senator John McCain (R-AZ).[6] He went on to defeat his Democratic opponent, Vice President Al Gore, in controversial circumstances in the presidential election. Not only did Bush fail to win a popular-vote plurality but also his electoral-college victory hinged on narrowly carrying Florida amid allegations of vote miscounting.

Bush's prepresidential background offers clues to the substance and style of his budget leadership as president. Three fundamental influences stand out—the values inculcated from his Texas business experience, his absorption of the Bush family ethos of duty, and his determination not to repeat his father's political mistakes as president. These shaped a fiscal outlook that never saw the deficit as a threat in the way that his predecessors had done.

More than anything, Bush's budget policy bore the stamp of the no-limits, growth-oriented, quasi-frontier mindset of Lone Star state entrepreneurs.[7] Far more than his father, he was Texan to the core and saw his home state as the land of individual opportunity. Reflecting on his Harvard experience, he once declared, "People there don't realize horizons can be broadened. There is no growth potential there. West Texas is a doer environment. People can do things."[8] After an unsuccessful run for Congress in 1978, what Bush wanted to do was make money from oil.

Texan entrepreneurs looking to make their fortune through a big strike were not prone to obsess about the short-term bottom-line of company accounts. Even in their never-say-die world, however, Bush's capacity to prosper in spite of prolonged association with indebted ventures was unusual. As Charles Lewis of the nonpartisan Center for Public Integrity later remarked, "It's Forrest Gump does finance. Every time he seemed to be in trouble, he would end up with a box of chocolates."[9] Harry Truman's preference as president for pay-as-you-go budgeting owed something to his painful experience of repaying debts over many years after the failure of his Kansas City haberdashery business in 1922. Bush never experienced the same discipline of having to pay down losses on a failed venture. Investors, mostly family and friends, took the big hits from his first company's lack of profitability. Bush also escaped the consequences of borrowing $180,375 at 5 percent interest from Harken in 1989 (when the prime rate was more than double this) to buy additional stock in the firm. Because the loans were nonrecourse notes that carried no liability to the borrower in the event of default, the Harken board voted to "forgive" them after the company's value collapsed the following year.[10]

Given that his background did not incline him to financial caution, it was hardly surprising that Bush was not deeply troubled when federal finances took a sharp turn for the worse during his presidency. His borrower's luck stayed good because East Asian central banks lined up to buy U.S. Treasury securities, thereby gaining currency exchange-value advantages for their countries' trade with America. The resultant capital glut enabled the Federal Reserve to keep interest rates low despite steeply rising government demand for loan finance during Bush's first term.[11]

Having always escaped from his personal financial holes, Bush remained optimistic that the fiscal future was bright. His FY2009 budget message offered assurance that federal finances were on course to balance by FY2012 thanks to "the hard work of the American people and spending discipline in

Washington." This had all the hallmarks of being another of his dry wells even before economic crisis necessitated drastic reconsideration of the budgetary future. Bush's forecast did not include costs of military operations in Iraq and Afghanistan beyond 2009 and revenue losses if tax cuts were extended beyond their scheduled expiry in 2010.[12]

Bush's Texan entrepreneurial background also shaped his outlook on taxation as president. He was not hostile in Ronald Reagan's manner to taxes as a threat to liberty. Like his father, his animus was directed at those taxes that they saw as discouraging saving and investment, the lifeblood of the entrepreneurial class. In Bush's purview, these included taxes on dividend, interest, capital gains, estates and gifts, and corporate profits. As Texas governor, he established a committee, on which corporate supporters of his election campaign were well represented, to recommend a major overhaul of state taxes. Bush backed its proposal for a $3 billion easing of property taxes, but this did not get the Democrat-controlled legislature's approval. Bush eventually settled for a $1 billion reduction in taxes, which was still the largest tax cut in Texas history. In addition, he promoted enactment in 1999 of tax breaks to small oil and gas producers.[13]

As constitutionally required, the state budget was always in balance under Bush, but his tax cuts prevented accumulation of large surpluses on the back of the Texas high-tech boom of the late 1990s. The alternative would have been to bank the revenue in the state's contingency fund as cover against a future economic downturn. Lack of adequate reserves became a problem when the stock market collapse and consequent recession of 2001 ended the boom times. The state government had to slash spending to balance its budget, which further diminished its already low provision for social and education programs.[14]

Bush's outlook on taxes as governor and president derived intellectual legitimacy from the work of a new generation of supply-side theorists, dubbed "neoconomists" by financial journalist Daniel Altman. Seeing labor force expansion and technological innovation as fixed elements in the economy, the first-wave proponents of this doctrine had pinned their hopes for long-term growth on boosting capital expenditure to expand productive capacity. In their estimate, a taxation system that diminished virtually every type of return on the individual saving that financed investment simply encouraged people to spend their money to keep it from government's grasp. These early supply-siders anticipated that the economy would experience a growth spurt from investment-boosting tax cuts before settling back to its normal rate of expansion, but now from a higher base that allowed for permanent improvement in living standards. Taking this theory a stage further amid the 1990s boom, their successors believed that tax cuts could also generate technological change, whose economic potential outstripped what was possible through capital expenditure growth alone. According to the new logic, if more money were available to invest in research and development, it would produce a constant flow of technological innovation that would continuously boost economic growth.[15]

Instinct and experience were sufficient to make Bush "a neoconomist in the flesh," but two gurus honed his understanding of the message.[16] As governor, he found a ready source of guidance on the investment benefits of low taxes in former Reagan adviser Charls Walker, a director of the Enron energy corporation and chair of the American Council for Capital Formation.[17] Once his presidential ambitions took shape, Bush sought advice from Harvard economist Martin Feldstein, who visited him in Austin to impart the gospel that high taxes were the chief cause of low saving.[18]

During Feldstein's tenure as CEA chair in 1982–1984, his jeremiads about the budget deficit's effect on national saving had angered Ronald Reagan. A decade later, he condemned the marginal tax rate hikes in Bill Clinton's deficit reduction program because they "substantially exacerbated the inefficiency—that is, the deadweight loss—of the income tax system." In his opinion, the real cause of the revenue surge that eventually balanced the budget was "the increase in economic growth driven by the new technology that raised taxable personal incomes, corporate profits, and capital gains."[19] Feldstein authored the tax reduction plan on which Bob Dole campaigned for president in 1996. His influence with Bush was manifest in the appointment of his former graduate students, Larry Lindsey and Glenn Hubbard, as chairs respectively of the National Economic Council and the CEA in the new Republican administration.[20]

Finally, Bush's entrepreneurial background was reflected in his less-than-respectful attitude as president to budget rules and conventions. In Texas he rubbed shoulders with men who showed scant regard for accounting rules in pursuit of profit. Among them was Kenneth Lay, head of Enron and one of Bush's chief political backers, who became a major embarrassment when his company collapsed into bankruptcy in 2002 amid revelations of systematic accounting malpractice. Bush himself did not have a spotless record in this regard. According to Charles Lewis, he had "more familiarity with . . . accounting irregularities" than probably any previous president.[21]

Allegations of insider trading in selling his Harken shares just before a fall in their value dogged Bush for years. An internal Securities and Exchange Commission report concluded that he had broken the law requiring prompt disclosure of insider sales. The agency's decision not to file charges prompted suspicion that Bush's status as the president's son had been his salvation. In another questionable transaction, he was privy as director to Harken's sale in 1989 of its Aloha Petroleum subsidiary to company insiders as a way of overstating profits.[22] Excusing this lapse when president, Bush claimed, "In the corporate world, sometimes things aren't exactly black and white when it comes to accounting."[23]

The same could be said of the Bush administration's approach to budgeting. In presenting the 2001 tax cut as a case of handing back the people's money, the president obscured the reality that it was predicated on revenue forecasts that were vulnerable to changing economic conditions rather than on return of funds actually sitting in federal coffers. Bush's insistence that his largess on this score particularly benefited nonwealthy taxpayers was also disingenuous. The 2001 tax cut was deliberately crafted to create that impression in its first year of operation, after which the distributional effects swung sharply in favor of the top fifth of income earners. According to independent tax expert Martin Sullivan, the Treasury Office of Tax Policy deserved to be renamed the Office of Tax Propaganda because its analyses of the measure's benefits were "so embarrassingly poor and so biased."[24] The Bush administration's practice of funding foreign military operations through emergency appropriations also undermined the transparency of budgetary planning. According to one estimate, supplemental spending averaged $120 billion a year in FY2002–FY2005, compared with only $14 billion from FY1975 through FY2001.[25]

Next to his Texan business values, family tradition had the most significant influence on Bush's approach to budget leadership. Early in his presidency, some dubbed him the political heir of Ronald Reagan rather than his own father, but the reality was more complex.[26] Bush shared Reagan's free-market ethos, dedication to limit government involvement in the economy, and belief that low taxes were the drivers of economic growth. Nevertheless, his self-identity as a "compassionate conservative" traced its pedigree to his father's politics. Appearing to distance himself from Reagan prior to launching his presidential bid, Bush condemned "the destructive mindset . . . that [believes] if government would only get out of our way, all our problems would be solved." As exemplified by his address to the Republican national convention in 2004, his presidential rhetoric consistently portrayed government as having an obligation to "help people improve their lives."[27] This did not mean that he embraced the collective purpose of the liberal state. Many of his administration's initiatives—notably the No Child Left Behind Act, the prescription drug entitlement, and the failed Social Security reform—aimed to enhance individual choice or facilitate individual capacity to contract with private-sector institutions.

Unsurprisingly, there was considerable disagreement about what Bush really stood for. Reviving suspicions once harbored against Reagan, some liberals feared that his seemingly inchoate fiscal agenda of tax cuts, defense growth, and domestic spending expansion was intended to drain the Treasury as a way of ultimately forcing massive elimination of government programs.[28]

The decline of the deficit in the middle years of his presidency put to rest this theory, however. Meanwhile, many on the right came to regard Bush as an exemplar of a new political phenomenon of "big-government conservatism." To critics, his administration had engaged in a moral and spiritual betrayal of Reaganism through its "appetite for an ever-enlarging, all-powerful government, a post-9/11 version of statism."[29] In their view, tax cuts to boost private savings and investment were incompatible with the growth of domestic programs that "drain resources from the private sector and put them to less efficient use."[30] To Bush's conservative supporters, however, the attempted revolutions of Ronald Reagan and Newt Gingrich had demonstrated that massive retrenchment of government was a hopeless quest. Far better in their view to accept the reality of big government and deploy it in the interests of Republican constituencies rather than Democratic ones.[31]

As political scientist High Heclo observed, Bush family politicos were "equal opportunity disparagers" of political ideology of any stripe. Consequently, the forty-third president never got hung up over the divisions that he sparked on the right. Though more interested in ideas than his father, the essence of politics for him was about making decisions and acting on these. According to speechwriter David Frum, "getting things done *was* a principle" for Bush. Political leadership was the pinnacle of the public-service ethos that had guided three generations of his family. In their creed, action revealed character, and politics was the greatest arena in which to display this. The belief that performance motivated by duty was the noblest calling also freed them from ideological soul-searching when under conservative attack.[32]

Bush carried his family ethos to its furthest extent as one of the most executive-oriented presidents in American history. Explaining his gubernatorial leadership, he declared, "The Governor is a chief executive officer. I believe my job is to set its [government's] agenda, to articulate the vision and to lead. . . . A Governor sets a tone. . . . A strong person can make a powerful difference." Carrying this mindset into the White House, Bush was proactive, hierarchical, programmatic, and resolute in his style of presidential leadership. He also focused on the long-term in the solutions he offered to the nation's problems. In his view, "The role of the chief executive of the country, the president, is to anticipate."[33]

This approach was significant for Bush's budget policy in two ways. Defining his job in terms of what he wanted to be done rather than by the limits he faced, he was averse to prioritizing deficit control. For Bush, the long-term benefits of tax reduction for economic growth always trumped their short-term consequences for the federal balance sheet. When promoting his 2001 tax cut, he declared, "Some in Congress want America . . . to think of the present and not the future."[34] Bush also favored bold ventures over scaled-down initiatives that minimized opposition. This approach did not preclude eventual compromise but set the bar for this at a high level. With his economic advisers inclined to tailor the administration's proposal for another tax cut in 2003 to what they thought Congress would accept, Bush remonstrated: "Don't let's be negotiating with ourselves. You don't hear the word 'no' until it's spoken."[35] The administration consequently recommended an ambitious plan with an estimated five-year revenue cost of $670 billion and settled for a five-year $350 billion measure, still a significant amount of tax relief, in order to win Senate approval.

The forty-third president's executive style also reflected his determination to learn from his father's mistakes. Whereas the senior Bush had not developed a clear set of goals for his administration, he constantly trumpeted his pursuit of an agenda. Moreover, he was determined never to break an election pledge, as his father had done over taxes, regardless of changing conditions. Believing himself accountable only to voters, Bush based his agenda on his campaign commitments. For him, victory at the polls—however narrow—provided a mandate that obviated need to compromise. As he declared on being reelected by the smallest popular-vote margin of any previous incumbent, "I'll work with everyone who shares our views."[36] Convinced that a mission-accomplished mindset had transfixed his father's presidency after the Gulf War, Bush also deemed it essential to build on his achievements. As he saw it, "Dad never spent the capital he earned from the success of Desert Storm. . . . I learned that you must spend political capital when you earn it, or it withers and dies."[37]

Nothing demonstrated Bush's chief executive approach to presidential leadership better than his determination to fulfill his 2000 election pledge to enact massive tax relief of $1.6 trillion. This commitment marked his clearest policy difference from Al Gore in the campaign. The Democrat had promised a smaller tax cut of $400 billion targeted at middle-income families, but, like Bill Clinton, he wanted to put the bulk of the projected surplus into a "lockbox" that guaranteed future Social Security and Medicare funding. Many in Washington expected Bush to be cautious over taxes because of the question mark over his election. Instead, Vice President–elect Dick Cheney made it clear that his boss had run on a platform that was "very carefully developed . . . and we have no intention at all of backing off of it."[38]

Bush's executive style was also evident in his efforts to staff his administration with loyalists. This "Team Bush" approach was intended to spare him the kind of in-fighting among aides that had weakened his father's presidency. However, it proved difficult to hold a collective line over the budget once the deficit resurfaced. Treasury Secretary Paul O'Neill, a deficit hawk, received his pink slip for feuding with the Bush economists over the need for further tax cuts to boost the economy. One of his adversaries, NEC chair Larry

Lindsey, got his at the same time. It was widely assumed that he was taking the blame for the economy's poor performance, but his sacking also signaled White House anger at his public estimation that war with Iraq would cost $100 billion a year, which contradicted the lower numbers that it wanted put out.[39] New CEA chair Gregory Mankiw got into trouble on the same issue. Shortly before publication of the 2005 *Economic Report of the President,* presidential aides insisted on removal of two chapters about the economic costs of the Iraq occupation. Although Mankiw refused to comment on this censorship, he resigned office after the report's release.[40]

With dissent treated in his White House as disloyalty, Bush tended to get the advice he wanted to hear. Paul O'Neill was shocked by his new boss's lack of engagement with policy analysis compared with Richard Nixon and Gerald Ford, presidents whom he had previously served. Alan Greenspan's independent voice also carried far less weight with Bush than with Bill Clinton.[41] A top aide reportedly told journalist Ron Suskind that the Bush White House was not constrained by the limitations of "what we call the reality-based community," which believed that policy emerged "from judicious study of discernible reality." Instead, declared this insider, "we create our own reality. . . . We're history's actors."[42] If this truly was its mindset, Team Bush could never create the reality in which the deficit ceased to exist.

THE DEFICIT REDUX—AND DOWNGRADED

When Bush took office, the CBO projected a ten-year (FY2002–FY2011) baseline budget surplus of $5.6 trillion, well above its $4.6 trillion estimate just six months previously. It forecast a surplus of $313 billion in FY2002 and one exceeding $500 billion in FY2006, by when the reducible public debt (excluding securities that investors wanted to retain) was expected to be paid off. For good measure, the CBO predicted that half-a-trillion dollar surpluses would thereafter be the norm. OMB, Treasury, and Federal Reserve estimates manifested the same optimism. As Alan Greenspan remarked, a $500 billion surplus was "an almost unimaginable accumulation," equal to the total assets of the five largest American pension funds.[43]

This vision of fiscal nirvana was a short-lived mirage. In January 2002 the CBO produced a sharply reduced ten-year surplus estimate of only $1 trillion. A year later its forecast transmuted into cumulative deficits of $1.3 trillion, which grew within another twelve months to $1.9 trillion.[44] This should not have been a great surprise. From FY1981 through FY2001, the average absolute difference between the CBO's fifth-year projection and actual receipts exceeded 2 percent of GDP because revenues were extremely sensitive to economic fluctuations. Budgeting for a ten-year period therefore entailed huge fiscal risk. Acknowledging this, Bush declared in his FY2003 budget that OMB would henceforth operate on five-year budget figures because recent efforts to forecast a decade into the future had proven "unreliable and ultimately futile."[45] By then, of course, he had achieved a massive tax cut on the basis of the ten-year surplus projections.

The FY2003 deficit set a new current-dollar record of $377.6 billion, one immediately surpassed by the FY2004 deficit of $412.7 billion. The imbalances were less startling in relationship to economic output. Nevertheless, the fiscal deterioration of 6 percent GDP in the shift from a surplus of 2.4 percent GDP in FY2000 to a deficit of 3.6 percent in FY2004 was unmatched in peacetime since the decline of 6.7 percent GDP in the Depression-era budgets of FY1930–FY1934.[46] Over three-quarters of this decline resulted from the collapse of receipts from the post-1945 high of 20.9 percent GDP in FY2000 to 16.3 percent GDP in FY2004, the lowest since the recession-hit Eisenhower budget of FY1959.[47]

As the deficit grew, Bush steadfastly insisted that his budgets fulfilled his administration's "three highest priorities," which were to ensure that America prevailed in the war on terror; to strengthen homeland security after the September 11, 2001, terrorist attacks; and to restore the economy after the downturn of 2001.[48] Acknowledging that a deficit initially projected to reach $521 billion in FY2005 was "a legitimate subject of concern," the OMB deemed this "the unavoidable product" of new economic conditions and national security threats. It also expressed confidence that economic growth generated by the Bush tax cuts would shrink the fiscal gap to less than half this dollar amount over the next four years. The notion that tax reduction was the cure for rather than the cause of the budget deficit formed the core of the administration's fiscal message. The OMB insisted that even without "one dime of tax relief," the FY2002–FY2004 budgets would still have been in the red because of the revenue shortfall from the stock market decline and recession.[49]

The business-cycle decline of 2001 ranked among the mildest downturns since World War II, but its effect on tax revenues was unusually severe. The waning of the dot-com boom in the stock market in 2000 was the trigger for recession. The economy experienced three consecutive quarters of decline in 2001 before recovery in the final quarter of the year. The decline in stocks accelerated during the downturn, with the Standard & Poor 500 companies losing more than 20 percent of their total value. The recession was comparable in duration but not severity to that of 1990–1991. In 2001 GDP only declined by 0.6 percent from its prerecession peak, which it exceeded after a single quarter of recovery. In the previous recession, economic output had declined by 1.5 percent and took a year to surpass its previous peak.[50] Nevertheless, tax receipts declined in real terms by 9.3 percent in FY2002, the largest single-year fall since FY1946, compared with only 2.1 percent in FY1991.

Budget forecasters failed to anticipate how sharply revenue from capital gains, dividends, and related taxes would fall as a result of the stock market decline. By August 2002 the CBO had reduced its estimate of FY2002 receipts by $376 billion from its projection of $2.2 trillion in January 2001. It attributed $75 billion (20 percent) of this shrinkage to the 2001 tax cuts, $125 billion (33 percent) to the weakening of general economic activity, and $176 billion (47 percent) to technical changes, coded language for misestimates of revenues from stock market investments. As Alan Greenspan later observed, "Just as the bull market of the tech boom had generated the surplus, the post-dot.com bear market took it away."[51]

Explaining the vanishing surplus was not quite the same as explaining the persistence of unbalanced budgets when prosperity returned. Upon signing the 2003 tax cut bill, Bush declared, "We have taken aggressive action to strengthen the foundation of our economy so that every American who wants to work will be able to find a job." He had previously lauded the 2001 tax reduction legislation as "an important boost at an important time for our economy."[52] In reality, the complex phase-in rules of the 2001 tax cuts over ten years and the distributional skew of both measures in favor of the wealthy limited their compensatory utility, but their effect on the deficit was long-lasting. The congressional Joint Committee on Taxation put the aggregate cost of tax cuts enacted since 2001 at $251 billion (including interest on higher government borrowing necessitated by revenue loss) in FY2006, when the deficit itself amounted to $248 billion. In other words, without the tax cuts the FY2006 budget would have been in balance, even with the costs of the Iraq and Afghanistan wars and the emergency response to the Hurricane Katrina disaster.[53]

Bush claimed the surge of revenues from 16.4 percent GDP in FY2004 to 18.5 percent GDP in FY2006 as vindication for his tax program. The growth of receipts in real terms by 10.1 percent in FY2005 and 8.1 percent in FY2006 constituted the largest and second-largest annual expansions since FY1969.[54] With the deficit undergoing parallel decline from $412 billion (3.6 percent GDP) in FY2004 to $162 billion (1.9 percent GDP) in FY2007, Bush had seemingly made good on his promise to reduce it by half in his second term. Buoyed by this success, he declared in July 2006, "Some in Washington say we had to choose between cutting taxes and cutting the deficit. . . . [These budget] numbers show that that was a false choice. The economic growth fueled by tax relief has helped to send our tax revenues soaring."[55]

The president sought to make the 2006 elections a referendum on the extension of his tax cuts beyond their scheduled expiry. The nation had "a choice to make," he told a fundraising event: "Do we keep taxes low so we can keep this economy growing, or do we let the Democrats in Washington raise taxes and hurt the economic vitality of this country?"[56] His rhetoric was reminiscent of Ronald Reagan's "Laffer curve" rationale for tax reduction and just as spurious. According to Treasury Department data, extending the tax cuts would at best only increase annual economic output by 0.7 percent over ten years. Meanwhile, the CBO calculated that the total cost of doing so would add $143 billion to the aggregate deficit through FY2010 and $1.5 trillion in FY2011–FY2015.[57]

The bounce in receipts may have been impressive, but it came off a historically low floor. If measured in constant dollars, revenues did not surpass their FY2000 level until FY2006, and then only by a meager 0.7 percent. Moreover, the gains were concentrated in corporate tax receipts, upper personal-income bands, and nonwage income from stocks that reflected growing profits, higher salaries and bonuses, and rising share values for the wealthy rather than a widely shared expansion of prosperity.[58] As Brookings Institution analyst Isabel Sawhill commented, "When the distribution of income shifts upwards . . . you get a revenue kicker from that." There were also plenty of skeptics about the Bush fiscal miracle on the right. Alan Viard of the American Enterprise Institute saw no evidence that the tax cuts "come anywhere close" to being self-funding. According to conservative economist Bruce Bartlett, interest-rate reductions were far more significant in generating the business-cycle recovery. In his view, "Much revenue was sacrificed to achieve not very much in terms of improving the tax code or stimulating economic growth."[59]

Among the critics of Bush's fiscal record was Alan Greenspan. This would have given previous occupants of the White House considerable cause for concern. The Federal Reserve habitually tightened credit as a safeguard against the inflationary consequences of budgetary red ink. Bush's three predecessors had sanctioned tax increases in the hope that the central bank would relax interest rates, but he did not have to follow their example. Greenspan did not tighten the monetary screws because there was no sign that the return of the deficit was overheating the economy. Nevertheless, he worried that the loss of fiscal discipline would have serious consequences in the near future.

The Fed chair initially supported tax reduction in 2001 out of concern that "chronic surpluses could be almost as destabilizing as chronic deficits." With the elimination of the public debt seemingly within reach, he feared that politicians in both parties would fall back into old spending habits that would be difficult to rein in if budgetary circumstances changed again for the worse. To preempt this danger, Greenspan wanted the budget put on a "glide path" toward equilibrium between revenues and outlays. This entailed paying off the public debt while simultaneously cutting taxes and shoring up Social Security funding as the basis for partial program privatization in order to leave little or no additional surplus once the debt reached zero. Even so, Greenspan was not blind to the possibility that the projected surpluses might never materialize. Consequently, he supported the inclusion of "trigger" provisions in the tax bill to rescind or reduce the tax cuts automatically in that eventuality, but the White House refused to countenance such a proposal.[60]

When the budgetary situation deteriorated, Greenspan grew increasingly critical that Bush's fiscal program was making matters worse. The expansion of new domestic spending commitments initially aroused his ire, but he reserved his strongest condemnation for the huge tax cut that the administration proposed in 2003. Testifying before the Senate Banking Committee on February 11, he warned that "faster economic growth alone is not likely to be the full solution to the currently projected long-term deficits." Unless tough choices were made to restore fiscal discipline, Greenspan worried that federal finances would be in a dangerously weak condition by the time that an aging population put new pressures on fiscal resources. "We should be preparing ourselves," he declared, "for the retirement of the baby boomers with balanced budgets or surpluses for the difficult years ahead."[61]

Despite concern about the future, Greenspan had his hands full dealing with the present state of the American economy. The Federal Reserve aggressively lowered the Federal Funds short-term interest rate from 6.5 percent in late 2000 to a historic low of 1 percent in mid-2003 to counter uncertainty from the stock market decline, recession, and the September 11 attacks. To the detriment of his 1990s reputation of monetary maestro, Greenspan mitigated the consequences of one bubble bursting by creating an even bigger one that would eventually implode even more spectacularly. Cheap credit fueled a boom in residential real estate and home improvement that drove the recovery of the entire economy. The central bank eventually changed course in mid-2004 for fear that house-price inflation, now running at a twenty-five-year high, would feed into the rest of the economy. First under Greenspan and then Ben Bernanke, it steadily raised the Federal Fund rate over the next two years to a peak of 5.25 percent. Even so, this was hardly tight money if measured by the recent past. The Fed had held its short-term rate at or above this level for all but some thirty-four months of Clinton's presidency but only kept it there for twelve months of Bush's.[62]

While fiscal deficits pushed up public borrowing, cheap credit encouraged homeowners and consumers to go on a binge of private borrowing. As a result, the net national savings rate fell from 6 percent of national income in 2000 to 1.8 percent in 2004 and turned negative for the first time since 1933 in 2005.[63] Accordingly, the only way the United States could meet its capital needs was by importing savings from abroad and running external imbalances of historically unprecedented magnitude to attract foreign capital. By 2006 its current account deficit (comprising the trade deficit, net interest payments to foreign holders of national assets, and transfer programs like foreign aid) stood at $856.7 billion (6.5 percent GDP). America was effectively borrowing $2.3 billion a day from abroad, which added up in annual terms to some 80 percent of the rest of the world's surplus saving.[64]

In these circumstances the savings-starved United States entered into a symbiotic economic relationship with the high-saving, export-led countries of Asia. With Japan and the People's Republic of China in the lead, these nations doubled their U.S. currency holdings between early 2000 and mid-2004. Asian central banks then recycled this cash back into the United States by purchasing business shares, real estate, and, above all, Treasury securities. The twofold effect was to keep the dollar's value high in relation to their own currencies, thus securing price advantage for their countries' goods in the giant U.S. market, and to underwrite a glut of cheap credit for America's government, corporations, and consumers.[65]

To some analysts, including Bush's economic advisers, the world's appetite for U.S. assets was a sign of America's strength rather than weakness. In their assessment, global capital flowed to those countries that could turn it to most productive use and provide the best combination of investment return and security.[66] Pessimistic commentators worried, in contrast, that the United States was growing vulnerable to financial crisis in the event of a slowing down or reversal of capital inflows from abroad.[67] In fact, this particular day of reckoning never dawned in the Bush years. Consistently high foreign demand for American assets meant that any problems of readjustment were stored for the future.

With the Bush administration free of the monetary constraints faced by its predecessors, the last chance that it might revert to balanced-budget orthodoxy vanished with the elections of 2002. GOP success in regaining control of the Senate and increasing its majority in the House of Representatives in defiance of historical midterm trends encouraged the White House to move ahead with plans for further tax cuts. When Paul O'Neill privately cautioned Dick Cheney that this could undermine "our economic and fiscal soundness," he received a curt response: "Reagan proved deficits don't matter. . . . We won the midterms. This is our due."[68] This assessment was questionable on both counts. The fiscal lesson of the 1980s was that unbalanced budgets had problematic political and economic consequences. Moreover, the 2002 elections constituted a vote of confidence in Bush's leadership in the war on terror rather than a mandate for further tax reduction.

Other administration officials dismissed concerns that a growing deficit would lead to higher interest rates. "That's Rubinomics," scoffed Glenn Hubbard, "and we think it's completely wrong." This was directly at variance with his assertion about the beneficial consequences of deficit reduction for monetary relaxation in the 1990s in the latest edition of his best-selling economics textbook.[69] OMB director Mitch Daniels similarly asserted, "We've gone from surplus to deficit and interest rates have gone down. So I do not see the correlation." John Snow, O'Neill's replacement as Treasury secretary, read from the same script. As chair of giant railroad corporation CSX in 1995, he had co-signed a letter from business leaders to the *New York Times* urging a balanced budget within seven years as essential for sustained economic growth. As salesman for the 2003 tax cut, he no longer advocated a deadline for erasing a deficit that he assured the House Ways and Means Committee was "entirely manageable."[70]

Statements of this ilk brought condemnation from some quarters that the administration simply did not care about the deficit. "As a drunk is to alcohol," declared Princeton economist and *New York Times* columnist Paul Krugman, "the Bush administration is to budget deficits." Seeing no end to deficits, he feared that things would get much worse when the baby-boomers retired. "We're going to miss Rubinomics," Krugman warned. "Maybe not today, and maybe not tomorrow, but soon, and for the rest of our lives." In an acerbic *Los Angeles Times* column, Ronald Brownstein damned Bush for breaking the tradition initiated by Abraham Lincoln that wartime presidents called for national sacrifice in the shape of tax increases. In his view, proposing a deficit-financed tax cut amid the war on terror was tantamount to "shifting the cost of defending our nation onto our children." The fact that the wealthy would be the main beneficiaries only added insult to injury. "Forget guns and butter," trumpeted Brownstein. "Bush is now offering bombs and caviar."[71]

With Alan Greenspan also snapping at its heels, the White House recognized that its insouciant rhetoric on the deficit was in danger of sounding extreme and irresponsible. Accordingly, the president and his advisers offered reassurance that he would not tolerate huge fiscal imbalances indefinitely. In his FY2004 budget message, Bush avowed, "My administration firmly believes in controlling the deficit and reducing it as the economy strengthens and our national security needs are met."[72] At the same time, he proposed new tax cuts that cost huge quantities of deficit-reducing revenues. This set the pattern for the next three years. Every Bush budget from 2003 through 2006 promised deficit reduction while calling for further tax relief. This was a case of wanting to be fiscally virtuous but not yet. Bush ducked the tough choices to repair government finances when he had the window of opportunity to do so. Judged on his record, he was the least deficit-conscious president since the Budget and Accounting Act of 1921 endowed the office with budgetary responsibility.

THE POLITICS OF UNTAXING TIMES

Bush ran for president on the banner promise of across-the-board tax relief. Devised by a team of economic advisers headed by Larry Lindsey, his tax plan featured significant cuts in the marginal rates of personal income tax. Most notably, it proposed to cut the rate from 15 percent to 10 percent on the first $6,000 of income ($12,000 for families) and from 39.6 percent to 35 percent on income in excess of $297,350. In addition, it made provision for child tax credits, increased deductions for married couples, retirement savings and education expenses, and the phasing out of the estate tax. The initial program, unveiled on December 1, 1999, cost only $468 billion and drew widespread derision from conservatives for lacking boldness. Millionaire publisher Steve Forbes, a presidential rival, denounced it as a "Mini-Me" pale shadow of his flat-tax plan. As the surplus estimate grew, however, the Bush plan expanded with it to cost $1.6 trillion by the time of the election.[73]

The controversial circumstances of his election made Bush all the more determined to cut taxes. Fulfilling his most important campaign pledge was a way of demonstrating the legitimacy of his presidency. It also signaled to his party that he would not compromise its core belief as his father had done. Finally, success on this score would give him the political momentum to pursue the rest of his agenda. At the end of his first hundred days in office, the president told reporters, "You spend [political] capital on what you campaigned on . . . and you earn capital by doing that." In his calculation, a win on taxes would lead to a win on education reform that would lead in turn to other legislative successes. As the tax bill approached enactment, Mitch Daniels predicted, "It's not going to be a presidency of miniature gestures."[74]

Despite presidential determination to press ahead, the political climate was not favorable to tax reduction. In the 2000 campaign Bush had presented his tax cut as a populist measure to give taxpayers their due. "See, I don't think the surplus is the government's money," he declared in the third presidential debate. "I think it's the people's money." Even aside from its questionable nature, his victory hardly constituted a mandate for this initiative. A scholarly analysis of election survey data found a low level of issue-voting on the tax cut/Social Security lockbox choice in support of either Bush or Gore because only a small segment of the public understood the trade-off.[75] Moreover, the election had left the congressional GOP in a weakened condition. Its House majority had dwindled to nine seats, and it was effectively tied with the Democrats in the Senate, where the vice president's casting vote constituted its margin of majority.

Opinion polls taken early in 2001 confirmed that the new president's tax agenda lacked strong support. These generally found that between 50 and 60 percent of respondents voiced approval when asked if they favored "the Bush tax cuts." Given a choice between tax cuts and higher spending on specified domestic programs, however, the public generally opted for the latter by two to one or better. This preference did not simply extend to popular entitlements like Social Security and Medicare. One survey found that 69 percent of respondents wanted more for "education, the environment, health care,

crime-fighting, and military defense," but only 22 percent prioritized tax reduction. Polls also indicated overwhelming popular sentiment that middle-
income families should be the main beneficiaries of tax relief.[76]

The public's less than hearty appetite for income tax reduction reflected
the changing nature of the federal tax bite. The personal income tax obligations of most Americans had been in steady decline for twenty years thanks
to the reduction of marginal tax rates in 1981, the automatic indexing of tax
relief to inflation from 1985 onward, and the progressive orientation of tax
law adjustments enacted in 1986, 1990, 1993, and 1997. Meanwhile, social
insurance tax burdens had moved in the opposite direction since the Social
Security reform of 1983. By 2001 some 80 percent of working Americans
paid more in payroll taxes than in income taxes and over a quarter of personal
tax returns (some 45 million) actually showed no payments owed because the
individual's income was under the floor at which obligations commenced.[77]

Liberated from the constituency pressures that their precursors had experienced during the debate over the Reagan tax cuts, congressional Democrats were almost unanimous in condemning the Bush plan on grounds of
affordability, economic soundness, and equity. Even "Blue Dog" conservatives in the House of Representatives preferred to reduce the public debt
than support income tax cuts.[78] Nor could Bush count on Republican unity
in the Senate, where some moderates shared Democratic concerns about
his tax program. Nevertheless, the White House outmaneuvered its opponents through a legislative strategy that combined boldness, compromise,
and stealth.

Senator Phil Gramm (R-TX) and Senator Zell Miller (D-GA) introduced
a version of Bush's tax plan on the first day of the new Congress. Guided
by Reagan's strategy of securing bipartisan sponsorship for his tax cut, the
president had personally enlisted the renegade Democrat's support and got
Gramm, once a renegade Democrat himself, to work with him.[79] The administration's speed of action enabled it to dictate the terms of the congressional
tax debate. Abandoning Gore's idea of targeted tax relief, the Senate Democratic leadership quickly countered with a proposal for $700 billion of across-
the-board tax cuts. Bush's initiative also paid dividends in bringing forward
legislative consideration of tax reduction. Had he followed a more measured
schedule, the Democrats would have been better placed to determine the
outcome after gaining control of the Senate in late May when James Jeffords
(R-VT) assumed independent status. Moreover, Alan Greenspan would not
have intervened to such significant effect if early consideration of Bush's program had not coincided with peak optimism about the projected surplus.

The Fed chair voiced support for tax reduction to run down the surplus
before the Senate Budget Committee on January 25, 2001. He later claimed
that he would have given the same statement had Al Gore been president.

There was certainly no hint of bias in favor of either tax plan currently before Congress in his testimony. Greenspan also advocated trigger provisions that would retract tax cuts if the rosy fiscal scenario proved false. Nevertheless, he did not recommend any restriction on the size of tax reduction and affirmed that tax cuts were preferable to spending increases as a way of bringing down the surplus. As Democrats like Robert Rubin had forewarned, the media was unanimous in interpreting his words as endorsing the administration's proposal. GOP leaders also spun them to their party's advantage. Senate Finance Committee chair Charles Grassley (R-IA) claimed on the basis of Greenspan's testimony that the Bush tax cut "is doable and it's important to do it."[80]

Working closely with GOP leaders in the House of Representatives, Bush accepted their advice to submit his program as individual bills rather than an omnibus package that stood less chance of winning some Democratic support. To facilitate later Senate enactment, presidential aides also worked behind the scenes to resist calls from House conservatives for bigger tax cuts and persuaded business leaders not to press for corporate tax cuts. With the benefit of a special rule waiving the normal requirement that approval of a budget resolution should precede consideration of specific budget measures, the GOP leadership secured House approval of the Bush tax plan more or less in its entirety. As expected, only ten Democrats voted for the income tax cuts, which accounted for some two-thirds of program costs, but other provisions received considerably larger cross-party support.[81]

As the battle shifted to the Senate, Bush campaigned for his tax plan in the states of electorally vulnerable Democrats but did not create a groundswell of support. Meanwhile, the GOP leadership failed to protect his program from significant change. The Senate's different institutional rules meant that a budget resolution was necessary to safeguard fiscal legislation against filibuster during floor deliberations. With the Senate Budget Committee unable to agree on one, Majority Leader Trent Lott (R-MS) brought it directly to a floor vote. The outcome was a series of amendments that significantly reduced the scale of tax relief and moved the savings to education and other spending programs. With the White House stiffening their resolve, GOP conference negotiators eliminated most of these changes in talks from which the Democrats were excluded. Senate Budget Committee chair Pete Domenici (R-NM) bluntly informed them, "We don't expect you to sign [the conference report], so we don't expect you to be needed." With Democratic defections compensating for two GOP nays, the Senate consequently approved the conference resolution that provided for ten-year tax cuts.[82]

One of the most remarkable aspects of the maneuvering over the budget resolution was the role of Paul O'Neill. Although the Treasury secretary never made his dissent open, no senior member of any previous administration had actively encouraged legislators to challenge a president's key economic objective. O'Neill was an old-fashioned balanced-budget Republican of the same school as Gerald Ford, during whose administration he served in the OMB and struck up a lifelong friendship with then CEA chair Alan Greenspan. He had encouraged George H. W. Bush, another friend from the 1970s, to break his tax pledge in the interests of deficit reduction. In response to U.S. Chamber of Commerce criticism of the president, he had summarily withdrawn Alcoa, the corporation he served as CEO, from this organization. O'Neill's experience in government convinced him that presidential commitment to fiscal discipline was essential for budgetary control. In his opinion, George W. Bush's promotion of huge tax relief without some mechanism of conditionality pertaining to the surplus was the height of fiscal irresponsibility.[83]

The author of the trigger provision idea, O'Neill hatched a plan with Greenspan to promote its enactment. The Fed chair became the public advocate of the initiative while the Treasury secretary worked behind the scenes encouraging a bipartisan group of centrist senators to press its inclusion in the tax bill. Bush's response was to insist that the best safeguard for the surplus was unconditional tax relief to sustain economic growth. Accordingly, Republican Senate leaders strongly resisted the trigger's adoption. Meanwhile, their Democratic counterparts sought to limit the cost of the tax cut as the best insurance for fiscal discipline. Only on the eve of the final Senate vote did they unequivocally back the proposal, but an amendment offered by Olympia Snowe (R-ME) and Evan Bayh (D-IN) went down to defeat by a vote of 50–49 on May 21. Even had this passed, it stood no chance in the House, where the GOP leadership prevented it from even reaching the floor.[84]

O'Neill also got his congressional allies to demand a tax rebate for FY2001 to dispose of most of the $125 billion surplus in the Treasury's checking account. His aim was to undercut Bush's newfound justification for his ten-year tax cut as a stimulus to prevent recession. The gathering momentum in favor of the rebate forced the president to change tack. In a speech in Kalamazoo, Michigan, on March 27, he warned against passing it as a substitute for his tax plan that would encourage economic activity for years to come. "Our economy needs more than a pick-me-up," declared Bush, "more than a one-time boost." However, the White House recognized that the best way to preempt the rebate taking precedence was to incorporate it within the president's plan. Costing $100 billion (including $15 billion for a refundable child credit that was charged to budgetary outlays), this initiative returned up to $600 to each working household ($300 to individual filers), depending on the amount of income taxes paid in FY2000.[85]

The White House further agreed to a compromise on the scale of tax reduction brokered by Charles Grassley and Max Baucus (D-MT) in the Senate

Finance Committee. This allowed for only $1.25 billion relief and scaled back the top-band marginal rate to 35 percent instead of 33 percent as Bush wanted. It gained support from twelve moderate and conservative Democrats and every Republican in the floor vote. Despite protests from House GOP conservatives that the Senate bill was inadequate, the White House pressurized Republican conference members to adopt it. Both chambers then approved the Economic Growth and Tax Relief Reconciliation Act (EGTRRA) with its $1.35 trillion tag (including the rebate) on May 26, two months earlier in the legislative calendar than enactment of the 1981 tax cut.[86]

Bush promoted EGTRRA as a something-for-everyone measure that would underwrite the continuation of the American Dream in the twenty-first century. "No one is targeted in or out," he told a joint session of Congress. According to the president, the top-rate marginal tax cut would encourage a plethora of small business formation, and the bottom-rate one would furnish greater opportunity for upward economic mobility.[87] Keen to publicize EGTRRA as helping ordinary Americans, GOP congressional leadership staff asked business lobbyists to don hard hats when appearing at a rally in its support. The Democrats were correspondingly intent on putting across the message that it was a rich man's bill.[88]

EGTRRA spread its benefits more widely than the original Bush proposal. The CBO calculated that the new 10 percent bracket accounted for one-third of its revenue costs. Nevertheless, this estimate implicitly inflated the progressive nature of a measure that significantly widened the disparity of income. Under EGTRRA, individual taxpayers would gain in after-tax income over the course of calendar 2001–2010 in descending order of income quintiles: $46,243; $10,453; $6,516; $4,037; and $827. It was true that the biggest cuts in percentage of tax relief went to taxpayers with the lowest incomes. However, the rich benefited more in aggregate terms because they had far greater income on which they paid taxes. Even this set of statistics understated the bias toward the wealthy because of its disregard of those not paying income tax. Measuring EGTRRA's benefits across the whole of American society, the Citizens for Tax Justice calculated that 40 percent flowed to the richest 1 percent, virtually the same share as the bottom 80 percent on the income ladder received.[89]

The White House and the GOP congressional leadership crafted the tax cuts to mask their distributional skew. Complex phase-in rules meant that relief for top-band taxpayers was concentrated in the latter half of EGTRRA's ten-year duration. This made little economic sense because it minimized the stimulus effects of tax reduction during the recovery from recession. Bush's onetime economic mentor, Martin Feldstein, contended that immediately cutting the top rate to 33 percent or even 28 percent would have had greater effect for relatively little revenue loss. Other analysts claimed that the economy would have grown faster without the tax cuts because the phase-ins induced wealthier taxpayers to defer income accumulation until it was taxed less.[90] In political terms, however, the phase-ins made EGTRRA appear more progressive than it actually was and blurred the long-term costs.

The sunset rules also created, in the words of two analysts, "an unprecedented new political environment—one that is highly favorable to the tax-cutters' core goals." Whereas Reagan had spent much of his time defending his tax cuts against reversal, Bush was constantly on the offensive to extend his fixed-term measures beyond their scheduled expiry.[91] Moreover, EGTRRA's credit and deduction provisions had significant implications for Alternative Minimum Tax (AMT) obligations. Initially designed to penalize use of tax shelters by the wealthy, this levy was not indexed to inflation in the manner of personal income taxes. According to some estimates, the proportion of taxpayers liable to AMT payment would mushroom from 2 percent in 2002 to about a third by 2010, making it likely that further tax relief would be required to compensate for this at a ten-year revenue cost of some $800 billion.[92]

The Bush administration followed up EGTRRA with the Job Creation and Worker Assistance Act of 2002. The smallest of its various tax cuts with a cost of just $29 billion, this targeted incentives and benefits at businesses and workers affected by the recession and the September 11 attacks. Looking to boost economic recovery, Bush proposed a much larger tax cut in 2003 at a ten-year cost estimated by the White House at $670 billion but put higher at $726 billion by the CBO. Its provisions included immediate phase-in of tax cuts previously scheduled to begin in 2004 and 2006 ($64 billion), reduction in the marriage penalty ($58 billion), and an increase in child credit ($91 billion). However, the core of the plan was the elimination of the tax on stock dividends at a cost of $364 billion.[93]

Glenn Hubbard authored the proposal to eliminate double taxation of investors' dividends. The CEA chair had previously written papers surmising that this would raise stock prices by 10–20 percent. Other analysts contended that the benefits would be much smaller because half the dividends eligible for this break went to non-taxpaying entities such as pension funds and retirement accounts, for which the tax cut would be irrelevant. In their view, the president was risking $500 billion (including interest costs) on a questionable academic theory. "This is beyond Voodoo Economics," declared *Newsweek* Wall Street editor Allan Sloan. "It's just a mistake. Call it Booboo Economics." Some commentators thought that directly reducing dividend taxes on corporations rather than eliminating them for investors would have far greater benefit. The huge loss of revenues almost certainly ruled out this option. A White House source also indicated that recent corporate scandals affecting Enron, WorldCom, and Tyco made it politically impossible.

According to Dan Mitchell of the Heritage Foundation, "George Bush is the biggest supply-sider in the White House, [but] Karl Rove wants to see him reelected."[94]

The administration plan broke new ground for presidential tax policy in at least three ways. No president had hitherto asked for such a large tax cut in quick succession to another. Having just promoted the second-largest tax cut in America's history, Bush was now seeking the third largest. No president had ever proposed tax relief on this scale in the face of a rising deficit. Finally, no president had looked to cut taxes on the eve of foreign war. Unsurprisingly, therefore, the 2003 tax reduction was the most controversial element of Bush's tax program.

Ten Nobel laureates, including Joseph Stiglitz, Franco Modigliani, and Lawrence Klein, joined 450 predominantly liberal economists to take out a full-page ad in the *New York Times* in opposition to the president's initiative. In their assessment, it would not help the economy in the short-term because its supply-side orientation did not stimulate demand and would hurt it in the long run by fueling runaway deficits that would eventually drive up interest rates. They also warned that the resultant fiscal deterioration would seriously undermine government capacity to fund not only Social Security and Medicare but also education, health, infrastructure, and basic research programs that represented a vital investment in the nation's future.[95] Business groups conversely threw their weight in support of the proposal as an overdue correction of the excessive taxation of dividends since New Deal days. They had no truck with the opposing view that the Bush plan would blow a hole in government finances. "If it stimulates economic growth both in the short term and long term," declared Business Roundtable president John Castellani, "then it'll produce the kind of economy that'll produce revenues that'll cause the deficit to disappear."[96]

Bush's bill ran into problems in both the House and Senate because of concerns about the already escalating deficit and the imminent invasion of Iraq. In contrast to 2001, this was an intra-Republican rather than an interparty squabble. The results of the 2002 elections had largely relegated the Democrats to the sidelines of the debate. The GOP now held majorities of twenty-four seats in the House of Representatives and two in the Senate. Despite White House criticism that he was hijacking the president's plan, Representative Bill Thomas (R-CA), chair of the Ways and Means Committee, made an alternative proposal for a five-year cut in both the capital gains and dividend taxes to 15 percent from 20 percent and 38.6 percent respectively. In the estimate of several conservative analysts, this would have just as much economic benefit as the complete elimination of the dividend tax while costing less revenue. It became the cardinal feature of a $550 billion tax bill approved by the House. Meanwhile, under pressure from moderates, the GOP

Senate leadership agreed to set a $350 billion cap on the president's tax-cut proposals by sunsetting them to last three to six years instead of ten.[97]

Faced with two measures different from each other and from his, Bush set a Memorial Day deadline for signing a bill. Once it became evident that his continued lobbying for dividend tax elimination jeopardized enactment of any legislation, he changed tack to accept the House proposal in broad outline and the Senate's in terms of duration. Bush delegated Dick Cheney to win House leaders' acceptance of the smaller Senate tax cut that he had initially derided as "little bitty." It still required the vice president's tie-breaking vote to get the conference bill agreed in the Senate. Two Democrats—Zel Miller and Ben Nelson (NE)—joined the ayes, but three Republicans—Lincoln Chafee (R-RI), John McCain, and Olympia Snowe—voted against. Bush's acceptance of a last-minute addition of $20 billion to rescue recession-hit state and local governments from financial difficulty was crucial in winning the votes of the hitherto undecided Nelson and George Voinovich (R-OH). Only Jim Leach (R-IA) broke Republican ranks to vote nay in the House.[98]

Pressure from the Club for Growth and Americans for Tax Reform, antitax groups headed by Stephen Moore and Grover Norquist, respectively, helped to minimize GOP defections. Flush with funds from wealthy donors, the former ran ads against recalcitrant Republicans and threatened to finance primary challenges against them. As Representative Jeff Flake (R-AZ) admitted, "When you have 100 percent of Republicans voting for the Bush tax cut, you know that they are looking over their shoulder and not wanting to have Steve Moore recruiting candidates in their district."[99]

Although the Jobs and Growth Tax Relief Reconciliation Act (JGTRRA) of 2003 differed from his original proposal, its enactment was still a personal victory for Bush. According to Senator Robert Bennett (R-UT), "By force of his personality, he stepped into the squabble between the House and Senate . . . and said 'You're going to get this done by Memorial Day.'" Though somewhat effusive, this judgment testified to a widespread sense that Bush had proved an effective party leader over the issue. Despite differences of detail, JGTRAA was consistent with his supply-side convictions that the "best way to have more jobs is to help the people who create new jobs." An estimated 46 percent of its capital gains and dividend tax cuts flowed to the 0.2 percent of households with annual incomes over $1 million, and nearly three-quarters went to the 3.1 percent making more than $200,000 a year. JGTRAA also provided $58 billion more tax relief in its first two years than Bush's plan and carried a larger cost of $800 billion if prorated over ten years.[100]

Following enactment of this huge tax cut, House Majority Leader Tom DeLay (R-TX) promised, "This ain't the end of it—we're coming back for more."[101] Further deficit-financed tax relief duly followed. The Working Families Tax Relief Act (WFTRA) of 2004 renewed EGTRRA benefits scheduled for expiry at the end of the year. It extended the $1,000 child tax credit to 2009, the $6,000 income level for the 10 percent tax rate to the end of 2010, and the tax break for married couples to 2008. Other provisions included postponement of application of the AMT to new taxpayers for one year. Excluding associated interest costs on the public debt, WFTRA carried a revenue tab of $146 billion. In contrast to the tax cuts of 2001 and 2003, however, it sailed though the House by 339–65 votes and the Senate by 92–3 votes on September 23. The only senators to oppose it were the retiring Ernest Hollings (D-SC) and GOP deficit hawks Olympia Snowe and Lincoln Chafee.

Representative Jim McCrery (R-LA) set the terms of debate in warning, "Anyone voting 'no' is voting for a tax increase for the American people, especially the middle class." With elections upcoming, most Democrats deemed it expedient to support renewal of the EGTRRA provisions that provided most benefit to nonaffluent taxpayers. Presidential candidate Senator John Kerry (D-MA) declared, "Millions of American families are being squeezed by the weak Bush economy, falling incomes and rising health costs, and we should extend middle-class tax breaks to help them." In reality, the wealthy were again the main beneficiaries. According to one estimate, households in the top income quintile received 70 percent of WFTRA cuts, and the middle-income quintile got 9 percent.[102] Exploiting its nomenclature, Bush lauded the bill as a bounty to hard-working ordinary families when signing it in the American heartland of Des Moines, Iowa, on October 7. Shortly afterward and with considerably less fanfare, the president put his name to another measure providing corporate tax breaks to manufacturers, energy producers, and agricultural producers at a five-year cost of $136 billion.[103]

The pace of tax reduction slowed in Bush's second term but did not stop. With deficit concerns on the rise in Congress, his hopes of getting his first-term tax cuts made permanent fell by the way. Accordingly, he settled for extending the capital gains and dividend tax cuts of 2003 beyond their 2008 expiry date. Conservative Republican demands for cutbacks in entitlements and discretionary programs to pay for this provoked bitter Democratic criticisms that lower-income citizens were being made to finance handouts to the rich. "The spenders are fighting back," warned Grover Norquist. "The deficit is the word they use because they think it sounds more acceptable than saying they want to spend more money." Though House right-wingers like Rules Committee chair David Dreier (R-CA) could dismiss Democratic charges as "nothing but the ideological baggage of the past," the attacks discomfited many Senate Republicans, particularly those facing reelection in 2006.[104]

By the end of 2005 the House had passed four separate measures with an aggregate cost of $94.5 billion over five years, including $56 billion for extending the capital gains and dividend tax cuts and $31 billion to slow AMT expansion. In contrast, the Senate approved $70 billion of tax relief, mainly to save 15 million taxpayers from AMT obligations but also to renew $20 billion of expiring tax breaks targeted at middle- and lower-income groups, including deductions for college tuition and a savings credit. Speedy reconciliation proved impossible because of Senate insistence that broad-based tax relief was more important than renewing investor benefits not scheduled to expire for another three years.[105]

The White House only got the House and Senate GOP leaderships to resolve their differences in the following spring. Administration officials broadcast the message that the 2003 tax cuts had sparked the current stock market revival to the consequent benefit of budget revenues. "It was as if a light switch had been thrown on," declared John Snow. "Rarely has a piece of policy been so effective, with the effects so evident and immediate." Adding grist to this case, a report by the Republican staff of Congress's Joint Economic Committee showed that nonresidential business investment, having declined annually at 5.6 percent from mid-2000 through mid-2003, had grown by 9.2 percent over the next three years.[106]

The Tax Increase Prevention and Reconciliation Act (TIPRA) of 2005, enacted on May 11, 2006, but dated for the previous year as a carryover from budget reconciliation, extended the capital gains and dividend tax cuts for two years and provided retroactive AMT relief for 2006. Despite the diminishing deficit, the Senate insisted on keeping the five-year costs below $70 billion by sacrificing the low-income tax breaks it had previously approved and raising $21 billion in new revenue through loophole closures affecting business and high-income savers. Another significant victory against the odds for the White House, TIPRA locked in the 2003 tax cuts to the same expiry date at the end of 2010 as the other major Bush tax cuts.[107]

In conjunction with EGTRRA and JGTRRA, TIPRA reasserted Bush's determination to make supply-side tax cuts that benefited investors and high earners a party-defining issue. The economic rationale for this core element of his tax program clearly reflected ideas derived from his family's financial background and reinforced by his economic advisers. Supply-side tax cuts also had an important political rationale to promote his reelection and build a new Republican majority that would safeguard his legacy beyond his time in office.

According to Jacob Hacker and Paul Pierson, a tax program skewed toward the wealthy fitted the highly competitive electoral environment in which parties had to mobilize their base to maximum effect in the quest of power. In their view, the GOP leadership in both the White House and Congress saw it as a way to please "the partisans, activists, and moneyed interests that are their first line of support."[108] Other analysts, in contrast, regarded Bush's tax program as part of a base-broadening strategy for the GOP's long-term benefit. In Grover Norquist's opinion, "The President got out ahead and laid claim to the growing investor class." For this school of thought, the administration's tax program paralleled its efforts to promote Individual Retirement Accounts and create private Social Security Accounts in seeking to increase the number of people with a pool of private capital. In its view, this was part of a grand strategy to expand the "ownership society" that had more interest in the services provided by the private sector rather than government.[109]

The latter theory conformed better with Bush's stated ambition to create a lasting GOP majority.[110] Demographic and economic changes seemingly indicated that the pro-Republican shift of the electorate since 1980 might finally be consolidated to produce a dominant partisan regime. As pollster Scott Rasmussen observed, "The workforce today is a lot closer to George W. Bush's goal of an 'ownership society' than it is to Franklin D. Roosevelt's New Deal." Fellow pollster John Zogby saw immediate payoff to the base-broadening strategy in the 2004 presidential election. According to his data, 46 percent of voters were self-identified investors, and this group went for Bush by 61–39 percent, whereas noninvestors backed John Kerry by 57–42 percent. In Norquist's opinion, the defining characteristic of the investor class was that it did not need anything from government, hence its natural tendency to be Republican. However, the advent of the most serious economic crisis since the Great Depression in 2008 changed the political landscape. Many Americans in the "ownership society" now saw renewed cause for activist government to safeguard their jobs, homes, and futures.[111]

BIG SPENDER

Reversing "tax and spend" liberalism had been a Republican goal since the New Deal. In the Bush era, a GOP president and Congress cooperated to deliver the first half of this mission but found partisan cause to expand domestic spending at the very moment that they also reversed post–Cold War defense retrenchment. Significantly, the balanced-budget constitutional amendment that Republicans had supported as the instrument of spending control throughout the 1980s and 1990s had no place in their agenda. Nor did Bush lift a finger to save the Budget Enforcement Act, whose PAYGO rules the Republican House and Democratic Senate allowed to expire on September 30, 2002. Moreover, the president desisted from using his veto to constrain spending until facing a Democrat-controlled Congress in his seventh year in office.

Representative Mike Pence (R-IN), chair of the conservative Republican Study Group, had no doubt where blame lay for GOP loss of expenditure restraint. "The Republican majority," he declared, "left to its own devices from

1995 to 2000, was a party committed to limited government and restoring the balances of federalism with the states. Clearly, President Bush has had a different vision, . . . [resulting] in education and welfare policies that have increased the size and scope of government." In Pence's opinion, the entire Republican slate would have paid the price for Bush's profligacy had the Democrats run a credible deficit hawk for president in 2004.[112]

This judgment wrongly absolved GOP legislators of responsibility for loss of fiscal discipline. Many now engaged in the kind of constituency-oriented and party-building expenditure for which they had once damned the Democrats. Needing to hold small GOP majorities together, the House and Senate leaderships increasingly used budget funds as their glue. Now retired from Congress, Contract with America architect Dick Armey lamented, "Excessive spending under the Republican Congress is one of the most pressing concerns for those who support limited government." According to former Clinton speechwriter Jacob Weisberg, the GOP now manifested "the curious governing philosophy of interest-group conservatism: the expansion and exploitation of government by people who profess to dislike it."[113]

Bush may not have led the congressional GOP into spending temptation, but he set it a bad example. Although the president made half-hearted pleas for domestic economies to mitigate defense and homeland security expansion after the September 11 terrorist attacks, he did not exploit his sky-high ratings in support of this cause. Far from implementing his threat to veto budget-busting legislation, Bush was soon out in front of the GOP charge to expand domestic programs. The FY2003 budget set the pattern for most of the Bush years. Defense outlays amounted to 3.7 percent GDP, the highest since FY1995, and discretionary domestic spending reached 3.6 percent GDP, the highest since FY1983. This amounted to a 10 percent real increase in discretionary spending, the biggest single-year growth since FY1968, and almost twice what Bush had requested.[114] Speaking for many disillusioned conservatives, economist Bruce Bartlett voiced a hitherto unthinkable sentiment: "On the budget, Clinton was better." AEI economist Kevin Hassett similarly expostulated, "Bring back the Clinton administration. Well, maybe not all of it, but at least its spending habits."[115]

Particularly shocking to many on the right was Bush's support for the Farm Security Act of 2002. Initially promoted by farm-state legislators and agricultural lobbyists, this expanded subsidies that the Freedom to Farm Act of 1996 had cut and created new ones at a total ten-year cost of $190 billion, an increase of $83 billion over scheduled payments. Bush had initially proposed farm economies in his FY2002 budget revisions in line with his election promise of a market-oriented agricultural program, but he reversed course in his FY2003 plan. Over the objections of OMB director Mitch Daniels, the president accepted Karl Rove's advice that the farm bill would boost party support in rural states crucial to GOP hopes of recapturing the

Senate in 2002. Bush now justified agricultural subsidies on the spurious grounds of their necessity to safeguard food supplies in the post–September 11 environment.[116]

Bush also had no qualms about promoting expensive measures to help his own reelection. Without doubt, the No Child Left Behind Act of 2001 embodied a personal commitment to educational reform. However, it was also intended to win votes from the "soccer mom" target group on an issue that usually favored the Democrats. Once a Republican target for elimination, the Department of Education budget doubled in five years under the aegis of this legislation, its largest increase since the 1960s.[117] Conservative dismay at this measure was as nothing compared to the outcry against a new prescription entitlement. "Every spending binge before this was just practice," declared Stephen Slivinski of the Cato Institute. "The Medicare drug vote was the coming-out party."[118]

Bush's costliest domestic initiative honored his 2000 campaign commitment to provide prescription benefits for senior citizens as an extension of Medicare. His initial proposal carried a price tag of only $48 billion in temporary block grants to the states over four years, targeted benefits toward the neediest elderly, and made them conditional on allowing competition from private-sector insurance providers. However, Representative Bill Thomas and Senator Charles Grassley, whose committees had jurisdiction over the measure, wanted a more comprehensive proposal. The administration responded with a plan providing broader benefits to seniors at a ten-year cost of $400 billion but still containing market reforms. The House approved a version of this in 2002, but the Senate rejected four different bills under its consideration. With prescription benefits a legislative priority for the American Association of Retired Persons and its 35 million members, Bush wanted a bill in time for his reelection. When the issue came before the next Congress, White House Press Secretary Ari Fleischer told journalists that the president would support any measure it approved.[119]

In late 2003 the legislature enacted a $400 billion measure that lacked any reform component, a sticking point for moderate Republicans in the Senate. With Democrats holding out for a still-more-generous provision, the bill relied wholly on GOP support for House enactment. Facing a rebellion from conservative backbenchers demanding market reforms, Republican leaders browbeat most of them into submission by threatening to put the even more objectionable Senate version of the bill directly to a floor vote if the compromise measure was rejected. Even so, it won only narrow approval, by 220–215 votes, with sixteen Republicans among the nays, before progressing to easier Senate passage by 55–44 votes.[120]

While the legislative drama was being played out, the administration prevented revelation of new Department of Health and Human Services (DHHS) forecasts showing that the program would be even more expensive than projected. It later transpired that Medicare chief administrator Thomas Scully, a Bush appointee, threatened to fire chief actuary Richard Foster if he released numbers showing that the ten-year cost would be $534 billion rather than $400 billion as the CBO estimated. Many Republicans claimed that they would not have supported the bill had they known the real cost. According to Senator Lindsey Graham (R-SC), "There is buyers' remorse among many who voted for it." A DHHS investigation eventually concluded that Scully, by now a private lobbyist and so a convenient fall guy, had been guilty of withholding information, but made no effort to track White House involvement in the cover-up. However, new forecasts soon overtook the hidden ones to put ten-year costs in excess of $700 billion.[121]

In adding an estimated $8 trillion to Medicare's seventy-five-year unfunded liability, the prescription drug plan contradicted the necessity to bring entitlement costs under control. Bush appeared to move in this direction in his attempted promotion of Social Security reform at the outset of his second term. Nevertheless, his primary inspiration was to promote the Republican "opportunity society" through partial privatization of the program rather than ensure trust fund solvency.

The plan that the president introduced after his reelection envisaged workers diverting some of their Social Security contributions into private investment accounts that would tie a portion of their benefits to stock market performance. It came under immediate attack from a host of economists and budget watchdogs. Critics warned that its estimate of investment returns was excessively optimistic and that program solvency required a combination of benefit reductions and higher payroll taxes. There was also strong condemnation of the immense ten-year transitional costs of $1.4 trillion to fund a larger program bureaucracy and cover shortfalls in initial investment payouts.[122] Clinton political consultant Dick Morris warned, "Americans won't buy it and Bush will be accused of borrowing his way into disaster if he diverts Social Security revenues without any offset in cuts." Seeking to generate grassroots support, the administration mounted a public campaign that included some 200 "town hall" events attended by prescreened participants, but this proved wholly unsuccessful. With congressional Republicans at best ambivalent and the Democrats downright hostile, the White House quietly abandoned Social Security reform during the summer recess.[123]

Meanwhile, the defense budget was increasing at a faster rate than at any time since the early 1980s. The Bush administration largely funded military operations in Iraq and Afghanistan through emergency supplemental appropriations, which regularly accounted for one-fifth or more of total defense spending. Supplementals were not uncommon instruments of funding American wars in their early stages when full costs were not sufficiently predictable to be included in the budget baseline. However, the Bush administration not only continued their use but also increased their volume as the Iraq and Afghan conflicts progressed.

According to the Center for Arms Control and Non-Proliferation, Iraq war annual supplementals (current dollars) grew steadily every year, from $53 billion in FY2003 to $158 billion in FY2008. Emergency spending also funded the Afghan conflict but rose more steadily from $20.8 billion in FY2001–FY2002 to $36.5 billion in FY2008. The Bush administration's reliance on this instrument drew criticism from the bipartisan Iraq Study Group for "making it difficult for both the general public and members of Congress to . . . answer what should be a simple question: How much money is the President requesting for the war in Iraq?"[124]

Even when the Bush administration put war cost estimates into baseline budgets, these were neither realistic nor multiyear in nature. This did not make for efficient and transparent budget planning because it circumvented the requirement for five-year cost estimates under budget resolution rules. According to critics, the administration's approach to war funding was a smokescreen to hide the true scale of its military expansion from proper scrutiny. Emergency spending also mitigated pressure for domestic economies that likely would have been greater had the conventional appropriations process more fully governed war outlays.[125]

Leaving aside other criticisms of its Iraq policy, the Bush administration grossly underestimated the fiscal cost of occupying and reconstructing that country. Defense Secretary Donald Rumsfeld predicted that this would amount to a mere $50–60 billion, part of which would be financed by other nations. Even more unrealistically, his deputy, Paul Wolfowitz, claimed that postwar reconstruction would pay for itself from Iraq's increased oil revenues. According to reliable calculations, however, the aggregate cost of Iraq operations to American taxpayers through the end of 2007 was $473 billion, alongside $173 billion for Afghanistan. With the troop surge pushing up costs, monthly outlays on Iraq were projected to exceed $12.5 billion in 2008, compared with $4.4 billion in 2003.[126]

Three factors drove the rising costs of Iraq operations since their inception. Most important was the need to replenish and improve weapons and equipment.[127] In conjunction with this, the United States incurred considerable unforeseen expense in equipping and training indigenous security forces. Second, personnel costs skyrocketed beyond anything foreseen in 2003. Recruitment benefits, combat pay, hardship benefits, and reenlistment bonuses (which could reach $150,000) all rose dramatically. Increasing reliance on Reservists and the National Guard also obliged the Department of Defense to defray a portion of their civilian salary. Growing use of contractors further jacked up costs. In 2007 private security guards employed by companies like Blackwater and Dynacorp earned up to $1,222 a day, compared to

$190 maximum in pay and benefits for an army sergeant. According to critics, bad contracting practices and inadequate government monitoring resulted in considerable waste and questionable billing by private firms.[128] Last, the quintupling of the world price of a barrel of oil in the five years between the invasion of Iraq and the oil deflation of late 2008 pumped up occupation costs.[129]

In the absence of credible administration estimates, other analysts tried to calculate the costs of its military operations, but their assessments varied enormously. In 2008 former Clinton CEA chair Joseph Stiglitz and Harvard scholar Linda Bilmes produced a top-end forecast by taking into account not only military outlays but also veterans' benefits (including health and disability costs), other hidden extras, and interest payments on government borrowing. In their estimate, the Bush-initiated interventions could amount to $1.68 trillion on a best-case scenario and to $2.85 trillion on a "realistic-moderate" (i.e., still conservative) one over FY2008–FY2017. A more conservative estimate by the CBO predicted that five-year costs of Iraq and Afghanistan operations from FY2009 onward could amount to $268 billion if troop levels declined to 30,000 in 2010 and $616 billion if they fell more slowly to 75,000 by 2013.[130]

With defense outlays growing, Bush manifested new determination to control domestic spending at the outset of his second term in order to fulfill his 2004 pledge to cut the deficit in half by the time he left office. His FY2006 plan proposed aggregate five-year reductions of $188 billion in discretionary programs and $62 billion in entitlements. Described by Dick Cheney as "the tightest budget that has been submitted since we got here," it provoked outrage from representatives of low-income constituencies. Baltimore Democratic mayor Martin O'Malley called it an attack on America's cities. Representative John E. Peterson (R-PA), cochair of the Congressional Rural Caucus, angrily declared, "The cuts disproportionately target essential programs in rural communities while turning a blind eye to the wasteful spending that is rampant in many big cities across the country."[131]

With the assistance of intensive administration lobbying, GOP congressional leaders got a budget resolution approved after prolonged maneuvering. The House was willing to make deep cuts in domestic spending, even on entitlements, but the Senate wanted far smaller reductions, especially in programs that helped low-income Americans. In the end the White House settled for a compromise resolution that reduced discretionary outlays by $143 billion and entitlements by $30.5 billion over five years. With his Social Security reform patently in trouble, Bush cited the settlement as proof of his ability to get things done on Capitol Hill. However, the more important test of his leadership would be to get Congress to make the cuts.[132]

Instead of economizing, legislators stuck their hands deeper into the pork barrel. There were over 15,000 "earmarks" directing spending toward pet projects in FY2006 appropriations, compared to 1,439 in the last Democrat-led Congress. The defense appropriations bill ended up with 2,847 at a cost of $9.3 billion for projects ranging from dog mushers' grants in Alaska to cranberry farming in Wisconsin.[133] Even this looked modest in comparison to the Highway Act of 2005, which approved expenditure of $295 billion on transportation programs. The National Taxpayers Union estimated that it contained approximately 6,500 earmarks, a record for a single bill. Among them was Alaska's notorious "bridge to nowhere" that required a span nearly as long as San Francisco's Golden Gate Bridge to connect the city of Ketchikan to Gravina Island (population 50) at a cost of $231 million.[134] An accounting gimmick requiring Congress to defer spending $8.5 billion until after the bill expired on September 30, 2009, kept the measure within budget resolution limits. Seizing on this fiction, Bush declared the bill "fiscally responsible" in a signing ceremony in the suburban Chicago constituency of Speaker Dennis Hastert (R-IL) that benefited from earmarks within it worth $500 million.[135]

The need for emergency spending in response to the Hurricane Katrina disaster that devastated New Orleans and the Gulf Coast in August 2005 blew an even bigger hole in the administration's hopes for discretionary cutbacks. Prompted by Bush, Congress quickly passed two measures costing $62 billion as a first installment for relief and reconstruction without making provision for how this aid was to be financed. This was by far the largest sum ever appropriated for disaster relief, but it was widely anticipated that the final bill would go far higher.[136]

Hoping to prevent the costs being passed to future generations, the Republican Study Group (RSG) demanded offsetting economies in other programs. It came up with a plan for first-year savings of $100 billion, notably by removing $25 billion of earmarks from the highway bill, delaying the start of prescription benefits, and terminating programs slated for abolition in the Contract with America. Medicare and Medicaid economies were to cover the bulk of additional costs in later years. Although the RSG plan gained support from GOP deficit hawks in the Senate, it had no chance of enactment because of opposition from the White House and the congressional leadership. The tide of bad publicity did sink the "bridge to nowhere," but the prerogatives of pork dictated that the money saved went to another Alaska project rather than to help Katrina victims.[137]

Nevertheless, the RSG initiative gave Bush an opening to press for the entitlement savings contained in his original budget plan under the guise of offsetting some Katrina costs. The resultant Deficit Reduction Act (DRA) of 2005, enacted in February 2006, provided nearly $40 billion savings over five years, mainly from the Medicaid, student loans, federal child support, and federal pension insurance programs. The package omitted cuts that the White House had requested in the farm program and food stamps. Although this was the first time that Congress had economized on entitlements since the Balanced Budget Act of 1997, the savings had only marginal effect in slowing their overall growth. Even so, the DRA imposed real costs on many Americans in the bottom half of the income distribution. The CBO calculated that the Medicaid economies would increase the medical expenses of thirteen million program beneficiaries and end insurance coverage for 65,000 individuals. The Democrats consequently blasted the administration for cutting social programs that helped low-income Americans in the name of deficit control when it also sought new tax cuts for the affluent that would enlarge the deficit.[138]

Bush's FY2007 budget maintained his drive for domestic retrenchment, which extended to slowing down Medicare growth to achieve five-year savings of $35 billion.[139] However, the plan also contained the usual dose of fiscal snake oil. "This seems familiar," commented former CBO director Douglas Holtz-Eakin, "because it is familiar." It may have been the first Bush budget to request funding for operations in Iraq and Afghanistan, but its $50 billion estimate was utterly unrealistic. Furthermore, projected deficit reduction assumed a growing revenue windfall from the AMT despite likely provision of relief from this levy. "The budget does not signal a willingness to make trade-offs by putting everything on the table," declared Concord Coalition director Ed Lorenzen. "The President must . . . demonstrate a willingness to compromise by applying fiscal discipline to his priorities in order to reach a bipartisan solution to our long-term fiscal challenges."[140]

In fact, the FY2007 budget was the high-water mark for Bush so far as deficit control was concerned. Thanks to higher-than-anticipated revenues and a limited degree of spending control, the budgetary gap diminished to 1.2 percent GDP, the smallest since FY1996. Lower-than-expected post-Katrina spending and retrenchment of other outlays produced a real decline of 2.8 percent in domestic discretionary expenditure, a first for a Bush budget. Many of the cuts were made by the incoming Democratic-led 110th Congress because its GOP-led predecessor had been unable to agree a budget. However, the escalating costs for Iraq War operations, which largely accounted for the real increase of 3.1 percent in defense spending, obliterated the benefits of domestic savings for deficit reduction. In no way, therefore, did the FY2007 budget have any parallel with those of the mid-1990s in which a diminishing deficit was the precursor to balanced budgets. In fact, it turned out to be nothing more than the calm before a new fiscal storm.

FACE-OFF AND BLOW-OUT

As the highway bill of 2005 rolled toward enactment, Jeff Flake commented, "Bipartisan porkfests like this make me long for the days of gridlock." In line with this sentiment, a number of influential conservative commentators contended that divided government now offered the best hope of fiscal restraint.[141] Democratic success in the 2006 midterm elections to win working majorities of thirty-one seats in the House and two in the Senate created the conditions to test this theory. Its proponents could take some comfort from Bush's interactions with the 110th Congress in 2007. However, the same political actors engaged in fiscal expansion on an unprecedented scale in 2008 to prevent economic collapse.

In what would soon look like fantasy, political dispute over the budget in 2007 centered on how to bring about its return to the black within five years. Declaring "mission accomplished" two years early on his promise to halve the deficit, Bush projected its elimination by FY2012 in the first budget that he sent the opposition-controlled legislature. Formally renewing commitment to PAYGO principles, the Democrats set the same timetable for balancing the budget but projected its achievement through quite different means.

The Bush budget put the burden of deficit elimination on five-year domestic expenditure savings of $24.7 billion in Medicaid, $66 billion in Medicare, and $114 billion in discretionary programs spending. It also contained the president's standard request for extension of the 2001 and 2003 tax cuts beyond their 2010 expiry date to sustain economic growth. However, White House projections implicitly assumed that greatly swollen AMT receipts would partially defray any revenue loss.[142] Conversely, the Democrats proposed a 2 percent increase of $29 billion in discretionary domestic spending for FY2008, mainly for education, children's health care, and veterans' services, and continuing but smaller increases thereafter. To fund this expansion on a PAYGO basis, the congressional budget resolution implicitly assumed expiry of the Bush tax cuts to produce a balanced budget in FY2012 at around 19 percent GDP. Because its revenue projections fell $175 billion below what would be collected if PAYGO were fully applied, this seemingly provided some margin for AMT relief, for which there was no explicit allowance.[143]

Each side poured scorn on the other's fiscal plan as a false route to the promised land. For the Democrats, Senate Budget Committee chair Kent Conrad charged, "The president's budget is filled with debt and deception . . . and continues to move America in the wrong direction. This administration has the worst fiscal record in history and this budget does nothing to change that." In response to the congressional budget resolution, OMB director Rob Portman sent Democratic leaders a public letter warning that the president would veto any budget-busting appropriation. In a Saturday radio address, Bush himself asserted, "They've passed a budget that would mean higher taxes for American families and job creators, ignore the need for entitlement reform, and pile on hundreds of billions of dollars in new government spending over the next five years."[144]

The opening shots in the battle of the budget were fired over Iraq. The presidential and congressional blueprints set the same funding levels to support military operations through FY2009 but made no provision for future years. The lack of multiyear expenditure projections was standard for the administration. However, the Democrats believed that voters had given them a mandate in the midterm elections to end an unpopular and costly war. The congressional power of the purse was their intended instrument to compel presidential acceptance of a timetable for U.S. withdrawal. Bush's first request to the new Congress for supplemental FY2007 war funds became a test of wills on this score. Democratic leaders not only inserted $21 billion for domestic outlays in the $124 billion appropriation bill but also attached a rider requiring that American forces commence withdrawal by October 1, 2007. They delayed sending the measure to Bush until the fourth anniversary of his speech on the USS *Abraham Lincoln* proclaiming the end of "major combat" in Iraq. "Since the president claimed 'mission accomplished' in Iraq," declared House Democratic Caucus chair Rahm Emmanuel (D-IL), "America has lost thousands of young lives and spent hundreds of billions of dollars."[145]

Bush immediately vetoed the bill on grounds that it set arbitrary deadlines for withdrawal without regard to conditions on the ground, contained billions of dollars of unjustified domestic spending as a way of circumventing the legislature's own PAYGO rules, and infringed the president's constitutional powers as commander-in-chief. "Precipitous withdrawal from Iraq," he warned, "is not a plan to bring peace to the region or to make our people safer here at home." Congressional Republicans united in Bush's support to uphold his first veto of a spending bill. Even critics of his war policy considered efforts to set a deadline for withdrawal as utterly misguided.[146]

As a compromise, Senate leaders proposed a new appropriations bill that substituted the timeline requirement with benchmark provisions authored by Senator John Warner (R-VA). This made continued war funding dependent on Iraqi government progress in meeting eighteen benchmarks and obliged the president to make regular reports on this to Congress beginning on July 1, 2007. In theory, the benchmark requirement was an unprecedented assertion of congressional authority to determine war policy, but many antiwar Democrats considered it a fig leaf for political surrender.[147] The congressional party was badly divided over the measure, which needed Republican support for enactment on May 24. House Democrats voted 140–86 against the bill, with Speaker Nancy Pelosi (D-CA) among the nays and the rest of the leadership supporting it. Wanting to avoid another veto, Senate Democrats voted 37–10 for the measure. One of the yeas, Majority Whip and long-time war opponent Richard Durbin (D-IL), commented, "We do not have it within our power to make the will of America the law of the land." Speaking for the nays, presidential aspirant Barack Obama (D-IL) contended, "This vote is a choice between validating the same failed policy in Iraq that has cost so many lives and demanding a new one."[148]

Despite Bush's low poll ratings, this outcome demonstrated that he still had clout in Washington. Having thwarted the opposition on the timeline issue, he signed the $120 billion bill, even though it included $17 billion for domestic ends, notably for post-Katrina recovery assistance, drought relief, and conversion of military bases due for closure. Nevertheless, budget conflict over Iraq was far from over. Representative John Murtha (D-PA), chair of the House Appropriations subcommittee on defense, removed the war funding requested in the president's budget from the 2008 Pentagon spending bill. This ensured that Bush would have to seek a new supplemental for the counteroffensive troop surge in Iraq that boosted U.S. force levels by 28,000 to 160,000.[149]

On November 14, House Democrats approved a $50 billion supplemental conditional on troop withdrawal beginning thirty days after enactment and being completed by December 15, 2008. In the Senate, however, Republicans threatened to filibuster any omnibus budget bill not containing stringless funds for Iraq. Lacking the sixty votes required to overcome this, the Democrats were in danger of ending the session without securing domestic appropriations. To avoid this, twenty-one of them broke ranks to join forty-eight Republicans—Gordon Smith (R-OR) was the only GOP nay—to approve on December 18 an omnibus measure that included $70 billion unconditional funding for military operations in Iraq and Afghanistan. House leaders saw no purpose in prolonging the fight but needed GOP support to get the Senate measure adopted by a vote of 272–142, with their fellow Democrats voting 141–78 against. One of the latter, Representative Jim McGovern (D-MA), complained, "This is a blank check. . . . It is an endorsement of George Bush's policy of endless war."[150]

The Iraq funding dispute took place alongside confrontation over domestic outlays. For the first time, Bush honored his pledge to reject bills that exceeded spending limits set in his budget by vetoing a five-year $35 billion expansion of the State Children's Health Insurance Program (SCHIP), a $23 billion water resource authorization, and the $603 billion education, health, and labor omnibus bill. The president supported his pen-and-blade strategy with tough talk from the bully pulpit. Taking a leaf from Ronald Reagan's book, he compared the Democrats with spendthrift children. "The majority," he declared, "was elected on a pledge of fiscal responsibility, but so far it's acting like a teenager with a new credit card."[151]

Bush's stand on SCHIP reflected his preference for a bill that expanded health insurance coverage through tax breaks. Believing that he would never reject a health-care bill for children, Democratic leaders had scheduled it to reach his desk first in the hope of undermining his veto strategy, but to no avail. Bush's subsequent veto of the education, health, and labor bill was his first against one of the annual spending measures needed to keep government operating. The president showed boldness in striking down an appropriation that included Medicare funds. His objection focused on its provision of $9.8 billion more for discretionary spending than requested in his budget, an increase of just 4.3 percent. Bush also indicated that he would not sign the transport, housing, and urban development bill if it contained the House-approved appropriation that was $3 billion in excess of his request. All this was small potatoes compared to what he had tolerated from a Republican Congress.[152]

Some Republicans hoped Bush could resurrect his poll standing by facing down an opposition Congress just like Bill Clinton had, but this was wishful thinking. Clinton pursued a triangulation strategy that co-opted the most popular issues of both parties to position himself in the center. Bush, in contrast, was pursuing a strategy of polarization in pursuit of an agenda far distant from the middle ground. Opinion polls clearly indicated that it was unpopular with the American public. A *Washington Post*/ABC survey found that the Democrats had a twenty-three-point lead over the Republicans as the party more trusted to handle budget issues. In SCHIP's case, some 70 percent of respondents supported the higher spending in the bill that Bush vetoed. The same proportion wanted Congress to retrench presidential requests for Iraq military operations. Seizing on this, Senator Edward Kennedy (D-MA) charged that "urgent priorities have . . . fallen victim to a president who squanders billions of dollars in Iraq but is unwilling to invest in America's future."[153]

The president's attacks on the Democrats were most effective when focused on their failure to honor pledges to control earmark spending. Having stripped pork-barrel projects from unfinished FY2007 budget legislation, they soon fell back into old habits. Bush could point to over 2,200 earmarks in the health, education, and labor appropriations bill that he vetoed. According to the nonpartisan Taxpayers for Common Sense, the total number in FY2008 legislation that eventually received presidential signature amounted to 12,881 at a cost of $18.3 billion.[154]

Ultimately the president's pen rather than his rhetoric frustrated the Democrats because his veto was virtually unassailable. His only override was on the water project authorization that had bipartisan support because of its earmarks. The Democrats eventually resorted to an accounting gimmick to circumvent Bush's domestic spending limit. They reduced the excess funding to $11 billion and designated the extra money as emergency provision for border security, veterans' care, and nutrition assistance in the omnibus bill that included the Iraq supplemental.[155]

This outcome enabled both sides to declare a victory of sorts. Republican votes had been essential to pass a bill that breached the president's spending limits because most Democrats would not support its Iraq funding. Nevertheless, Bush could still claim to have reined in the worst of Democratic extravagance. Echoing this, Minority Leader John Boehner (R-OH) enthused, "Our work on holding the line on spending gave us an omnibus that is better than I've seen in my 17 years here." Such mutual congratulation was implicit acknowledgment that it was easier for Bush to stand up to a Democratic Congress on domestic restraint than a Republican one. Conversely, the Democrats found some comfort from reversing the domestic retrenchment of the past two Bush budgets and staking out their priorities for the next election. The message to voters wanting change, declared Senator Charles E. Schumer (D-NY), was "elect more Democrats."[156]

Bush and the Republicans also thwarted Democratic efforts to pay for middle-class AMT relief with offsetting tax increases on the rich. After a tense debate that manifested bitter partisanship, the House of Representatives enacted a $73.8 billion tax bill by 216–193 votes on November 9. This protected some twenty-three million households from the AMT, offered a mortgage interest deduction to families that did not itemize their deductions, and expanded tax rebates to working parents too poor to pay income tax. Under PAYGO rules, it offset the cost by closing tax loopholes that allowed super-rich private-equity "buyout" and hedge fund managers to count their earnings as capital gains, subject to 15 percent tax, rather than income, subject to 35 percent tax. The House Democrats, claimed Nancy Pelosi, "had planted the flag for fiscal responsibility . . . as we gave a tax cut to the middle class." This posed a dilemma for Blue Dog Democrats, who had promised voters to resist tax increases, but most supported the party line. Speaking for them, Representative Baron Hill (D-IN) declared, "If we're going to lead on paygo, we need to practice what we preach."[157]

In the Senate, however, Democrats accepted a substitute measure providing $50 billion in AMT relief without PAYGO revenue enhancement to avoid a GOP filibuster that would hold up spending bills. Wall Street lobbying to prevent adoption of the House measure was almost redundant. Republicans needed no second invitation to torpedo Democratic claims to be the party of fiscal rectitude and block a tax increase into the bargain. Senator John Thune (R-SD) crowed, "That's a huge concession on their part, completely repudiating one of their principles." The House leadership had to follow suit if AMT relief was to be enacted before the end of session. Needing two-thirds approval to pass under the lower chamber's fast-track rules, the Senate bill won easy passage by a vote of 352–64 with massive Republican support. The nays were mostly Blue Dog Democrats who refused to sacrifice PAYGO principles. "The politics have been very bad," declared Representative John Tanner (D-TN). "Politicians giving the voters everything they want without paying for it . . . that's how you become a Third World country."[158]

It was widely expected that Bush's final year in office would see a rerun of the budget battles of 2007, but the onset of the worst economic problems since the 1930s changed the context of fiscal politics. Although not officially recognized for another twelve months, the recession that began in December 2007 set new records for the length and depth of a post-1945 downturn. In its first year, 1.9 million jobs were lost, two-thirds of them in September–November 2008. The disappearance of 533,000 jobs in November was the largest monthly loss since December 1974, but this occurred as the downswing appeared to be just gathering momentum rather than at its trough as before. Intertwined with this development was a financial crisis that threatened meltdown of the banking system. The economy was in a downward spiral with employment, incomes, spending, and credit all collapsing together.[159]

The implosion of the subprime mortgage market in August 2007 set off the downturn. A combination of cheap credit, financial institution competitive pressures, and lax government regulation had generated massive lending with minimal or no down-payment requirements to borrowers with low incomes, limited assets, and troubled credit histories. As interest rates rose to cool house-price inflation, however, many homeowners experienced difficulty making their monthly payments. By September 2008 one in ten of all mortgage holders was either delinquent on loans or in foreclosure. Financial institutions, many holding mountains of bad debt in the form of mortgage-backed securities, now became reluctant to lend money to individuals, businesses, and each other. The credit crunch led to an equity crisis as worried investors liquidated stock portfolios, wiping more than two-fifths off their aggregate value in 2008. The combination of declining real estate values that resulted from the subprime collapse, the loss of wealth from the free-fall of stocks, and rising unemployment undermined consumer confidence. By the end of 2008 this was lower than at any time since the Reuters/University of Michigan Survey of Consumers began polling in the 1950s.[160]

The Federal Reserve's speedy reduction of short-term interest rates from 5.25 percent in September 2007 to 2 percent by the end of April 2008 slowed but did not stop the downturn. Fiscal stimulus consequently made an unexpected return as a tool of economic management. Hoping to avert a serious recession, Treasury Secretary Henry Paulson, John Boehner, and Nancy

Pelosi worked together in early 2008 to craft a proposal for an immediate rebate for taxpayers scaled according to income (maximum $600 for individuals and $1,200 for joint filers). To reach a deal, the White House allowed income caps on full rebates to be set at $75,000 for individuals ($150,000 for joint filers) and did not press for the package to include renewal of the 2001 and 2003 tax cuts. In turn, Pelosi accepted tax breaks to encourage business spending and did not demand extension of unemployment benefits and increases in food stamps.[161]

Enacted without offsetting savings, the Economic Stimulus Act put $152 billion into the economy in 2008—equivalent to 1 percent GDP—and $168 billion in total. Its centerpiece was a $100 billion tax rebate for 130 million households in the hope of encouraging retail spending. Financial experts were divided over its economic benefit because recipients were estimated to have spent only between 15 percent and 25 percent of the money and either saved the rest or used it to pay off debt. The injection of money generated a slight expansion of consumer spending in mid-2008, but this was an artificial boost. Payroll employment continued a steady decline throughout the first half of the year, and personal income headed the same way in the second half. The combined effect of the stimulus, the one-third increase in unemployment insurance outlays, growing demand for food stamps and other welfare benefits, and declining revenue from taxes on high earners and business profits sent the FY2008 deficit soaring to $458 billion (3.2 percent GDP), double the administration's initial forecast of $239 billion (1.6 percent GDP).[162] However, this soon looked small in comparison with what followed in FY2009.

The landscape of the American financial system changed forever as the fall-out from the subprime collapse reached a critical stage. Commercial banks that loaned money to trusted clients and held the debt on their books were still in good shape. However, the so-called shadow banking system of finance companies, investment banks, hedge funds, and government-sponsored mortgage agencies were more vulnerable to the toxic effect of bad debts. Subject to lighter regulation than traditional banks, these institutions had increasingly engaged in the buying and selling of pooled securities known as derivatives for everything from mortgages to car loans to credit default swaps. Having grown from a negligible level in the mid-1980s to $106 trillion in 2002, the derivative market then spiraled to $531 trillion in 2008. In 2001 the value of debt securitization overtook the value of outstanding banks loans. Thereafter, the scale and complexity of debt repackaging increased enormously as a result of the housing boom. When home prices fell, however, massive losses from their overexposure to the subprime market brought some eminent financial institutions to the verge of bankruptcy. Wall Street investment banks that relied on high leverage and wholesale funding were the hardest hit. In September 2008 Lehman Brothers went bust, Merrill Lynch was swallowed up by a commercial bank, and Goldman Sachs and Morgan Stanley became commercial banks themselves.[163]

The scale of the debt crisis threatened to destabilize the entire global financial system. The only cure appeared to be an injection of capital to prop up ailing institutions. With commercial banks reluctant to make such high-risk loans, the federal government made its most dramatic intervention in financial markets since the early New Deal. In rapid succession between September 7 and October 3, it nationalized the two government-created secondary-mortgage giants, Freddie Mac and Fannie Mae, providing each with $100 billion additional capital; effectively took over AIG, the world's largest insurer; and enacted the Troubled Assets Recovery Program (TARP), which committed the Treasury to take up to $700 billion of private mortgage-related assets onto its books. What this meant in budgetary terms was that the federal government in less than a month had expanded its gross liabilities by more than $1 trillion, which was almost twice the cost to date of the Iraq war.[164]

The House of Representatives rejected the initial version of TARP on September 29 by a 228–205 majority, with some two-thirds of Republicans and two-fifths of Democrats voting against it. Most of the nays on both sides of the aisle objected that the measure amounted to public compensation for the reckless behavior of rich bankers. Opinion polls and constituent telephone calls indicated that the public saw it this way too. Nevertheless, the consequent stock market crash that in one day wiped out a trillion dollars in paper wealth, including a large chunk of retirement savings, prompted congressional reconsideration. Enactment of an amended TARP on October 3 signified recognition that the financial crisis had repercussions for Main Street as well as Wall Street.[165]

The TARP bailout averted financial catastrophe but did little to revive consumer spending, on which economic recovery depended. The flow of credit on which many Americans depended to fund their shopping habit had slowed dramatically. Most of the big credit card companies were parts of banks that had billions on deposit but were averse to taking on more risk of bad debt. These lenders now wanted much better credit scores from consumers at the very time that millions of Americans were far less creditworthy than ever before because of missed or late payments on mortgages or other borrowings. Reflecting this new caution, capital-market investors were no longer interested in credit-card-backed securities, whose issuance was zero in October 2008 compared with the monthly average of $8 billion in 2007. In an effort to revive credit flows, the Treasury announced plans on November 25 to pump $200 billion loan funds into credit markets to encourage private investor purchase of securities backed by student and auto loans, credit card debt, and small-business loans. However, surveys showed that many

Americans were now keener to save than take on more debt because of job insecurity and declining property values.[166]

In these circumstances, Democrats contended that only fiscal stimulus could restore consumer demand wiped out by the credit crunch. During his victorious campaign for president, Barack Obama had promised tax cuts and job-creating measures costing at least $175 billion over two years. At a meeting with his economic policy transition team in Chicago on December 16, 2008, the president-elect was told the recovery program had to be four to five times bigger than this to turn round an economy contracting at an annual rate of 6.5 percent. According to Lawrence Summers, appointed National Economic Council chair in the incoming administration, the fiscal boost had to be "speedy, substantial and sustained over a several-year interval."[167]

THE BUSH LEGACY

"I inherited a recession, I'm ending on a recession," George W. Bush noted in his last press conference. This was a disclaimer of responsibility for both downturns and a plea for his economic and budgetary record to be judged on what happened in the interim, but there was little to recommend it therein. His fiscal policies did much to keep the budget in the red after the economy recovered from the 2001 recession; the financial hole in America's retiree programs had grown hugely during his stewardship; the tax system he bequeathed to his successor was an unstable, patched-up mess; and the transparency of the budget process had been undermined. The Bush legacy, according to a critical assessment that did not come from left field, "is littered with wasted opportunity, bad judgments and politicized policy."[168]

Bush had hoped through his economic and budget policy to build an enduring Republican majority to complete the process of political transformation started by Ronald Reagan, but his presidency looked instead to have marked the end of the Age of Reagan. The Reaganite formula for economic growth had not delivered the goods for Bush's America, and the renewal of massive budget deficits had exacerbated the structural economic problems associated with low national saving that had first become manifest in the 1980s.

As he departed the White House, Bush trumpeted enduring belief in the core element of his fiscal strategy: "Sound economic policy begins with keeping taxes low." Nevertheless, Mark Zandi, a Wall Street economist and McCain campaign adviser, characterized the forty-third president's period in office as "almost a lost decade," a term conventionally used to describe Japan's economic experience in the 1990s. Bush's promotion of the largest tax cuts since 1981 generated meager economic returns. Far from the economy turning into a dynamic engine of growth from their thrust, GDP rose at an anemic annual average rate of 2.6 percent during the twenty-four quarters of consecutive expansion between the recession of 2001 and the downturn that began in late 2007. This compared with 3.7 percent in the previous expansion cycle that lasted thirty-eight quarters from mid-1991 through 2000. Moreover, despite a record fifty-two months of consecutive job creation in the middle years of his presidency and factoring out the effect of recession, total civilian employment growth under Bush amounted to just 6.6 percent, a lower level than any eight-year period since 1945 and far below the expansion of 15.5 percent under Clinton.[169]

The interrelated booms in housing, consumer spending, and financial markets drove much of the economic growth that did occur during Bush's presidency. What underwrote buoyancy in all three was reliance on borrowing. Private-sector debt spiraled from $22 trillion in 2000 (222 percent GDP) to $41 trillion (294 percent GDP) in 2007. Though financial-sector borrowing accounted for the bulk of increased indebtedness, virtually all the rise in nonfinancial debt was among households. This marked one of the major differences between the U.S. financial crisis that began in 2007 and the earlier one experienced by Japan that resulted in prolonged stagnation for its economy in the 1990s. With a healthy saving rate going into the crisis, Japanese households could partially counter corporate debt redemption and balance-sheet adjustment through a reduction in their own saving. In contrast, U.S. household saving was negative in 2007 but rose to 3.6 percent of disposable income in 2008 because of pessimism about the economy. The effect of this may be to necessitate more persistent and larger federal budget deficits than in Japan's case to prop up demand.[170]

If deficits were an important part of the solution to the economic crisis, they had also been a contributory factor in its development. In the 1980s the absorption of a large portion of national saving by the Reagan deficits had necessitated high real interest rates to attract foreign capital for new investment. In the 1990s the Clinton administration and the Greenspan Fed had pursued the reverse mix of tight budgets and monetary easing to grow the economy, but the decline of private saving had still necessitated U.S. reliance on foreign capital to meet rising investment demand. In the Bush era the White House and the Federal Reserve developed yet another variation of the economic mix, in which fiscal and monetary policy both moved in the same direction of ease. The willingness of East Asian central banks, particularly that of the People's Republic of China, to fund the Bush deficits eschewed necessity for interest-rate adjustments to compensate for federal dissaving. This was a critical factor in the availability of easy credit that fueled unsustainable booms in the housing and financial sectors and in consumer spending on cheap foreign imports.

The experience of the early twenty-first century holds important lessons not only for the United States but also the rest of the world about the problems of an imbalance of international trade and capital flows. The growth of the entire global economy became overdependent on China's capacity to save and export and America's propensity to borrow and consume. The rebalancing of the global economy may well require closer international cooperation to limit exchange rate deviations beyond their equilibrium value and to coordinate fiscal and monetary policies in a way to encourage production and exports in some countries, notably the United States, and demand and imports in others, notably China.[171] The restoration of balanced budgets would be an important part of the policy mix underwriting America's involvement in such a process.

More immediately, the economic crisis that engulfed America at the end of the Bush presidency raised fundamental questions about the role of government in the economy and the relationship of budget deficits to this. In his inaugural address during an era of unprecedented stagflation, Ronald Reagan had proclaimed, "In the present crisis, government is not the solution to our problems; government is the problem." In his final *Economic Report* as president, Bush appeared to repudiate this antistatist credo by acknowledging that in the current "extraordinary circumstances . . . a systemic, aggressive, and unprecedented Government response was the only responsible policy action." Nevertheless, he was not throwing in the towel to declare the Age of Reagan dead. Insisting that federal antirecession initiatives should be a temporary response to crisis, he also called for his tax cuts to be made permanent as the best way to strengthen recovery and lay the foundations for sustained growth.[172]

The tax cuts that Bush had promoted in his first six years as president were instrumental in keeping the budget in the red long after recovery from the 2001 recession, but he considered their long-term benefits vastly more important than their short-term effect on federal finances. With his departure from office, however, America's fiscal history was about to take a new turn. The Age of Deficits looked set to continue for some time to come, but it had entered a new phase. No longer the price for conservative tax reduction, unbalanced budgets were to become once more an instrument of liberal purpose. Signaling this, Bush's successor repudiated the ethos of his political economy and its Reaganite inspiration in avowing, "As we've learned very clearly and conclusively over the last eight years, tax cuts alone can't solve all of our economic problems—especially tax cuts that are targeted to the wealthiest few Americans. We have tried that strategy, time and time again. And it's only helped lead us to the crisis we face right now."[173]

Barack Obama:
Dealing with Deficits and Debt
in the Short Term and Long Term

In the transition period between his election and inauguration as president, Barack Obama declared,

> We are inheriting an enormous budget deficit . . . [of] over a trillion dollars. That's before we do anything. And so we understand that we've got to provide a blood infusion into the patient right now, to make sure that the patient is stabilized, and that means that we can't worry short-term about the deficit. We've got to make sure the stimulus is large enough to get the economy moving.[1]

A few days earlier, however, Obama had announced that "as soon as the recovery is well underway, then we've got to set up a long-term plan to reduce the structural deficit and make sure we're not leaving a mountain of debt for the next generation."[2]

These two statements encapsulated the budgetary challenge facing America's forty-fourth president. In the short-term the deficit could be an instrument of economic salvation. In the longer term, the United States is faced with a crisis of fiscal sustainability pertaining to rising entitlement costs that could undermine its prosperity at some juncture in the mid-twenty-first century. In the eyes of history, therefore, Obama's success as budget leader is likely to depend on his ability to develop a fiscal agenda that balances the immediate requirement for economic stimulus with the need to improve the future budget outlook.

Recovery from the economic catastrophe that engulfed America at the end of the first decade of the twenty-first century is necessary before its leaders can move on to deal with the less immediate but still crucial problem of growing public debt. Provided the downturn does not become a prolonged slump, the costs of the measures to bring it under control are unlikely to have much effect on the future deficit problem. Temporary costs, even if very large in the short run, add much less to the long-term fiscal gap than permanent costs because the expense is small relative to the size of the economy over time. Conversely, the measures necessary to fix the budget in the long term will make little contribution to deficit reduction in the short term because their fiscal benefits will come much later.

Obama's accession to the presidency coincided with the restoration of fiscal policy, the presidential domain of economic policy, as the primary instrument of economic management. The ascendancy of monetary policy since the late 1970s had effectively made the Federal Reserve chair the chief manager of prosperity. However, the incapacity of interest-rate cuts and other monetary actions to get credit flowing freely put the onus on fiscal activism to rescue the economy. To all intents and purposes, even if it did not explicitly use the K-word, the new administration turned to Keynesianism to provide a solution to the economic crisis. Signaling this in remarks at his first press conference as president, Obama proclaimed that "at this particular moment, with the private sector so weakened by this recession, the federal government is the only entity left with the resources to jolt our economy back into life."[3] The stimulus program therefore marked the "reintegration" of fiscal policy after its prolonged "disintegration" since the 1970s.

The American Recovery and Reinvestment Act (ARRA) that the Obama administration promoted in conjunction with Democratic congressional leaders ran counter to the antistatist impulse of the Age of Reagan. It looked to save or create some 3.6 million jobs at a fiscal cost of $787 billion over three years. Composed of spending initiatives (63.4 percent) and tax cuts (36.6 percent) in a ratio of approximately two to one, ARRA constituted the largest stimulus program in America's history. Not even the New Deal at its most expansive had undertaken fiscal action on this scale.

The centerpiece of the recovery plan was a massive program of public investment that was hugely expensive in the short run but could yield important benefits for economic growth and expenditure savings in the medium term. This included the most expensive public works program since the construction of the interstate highway system to rebuild the nation's crumbling road, bridge, and flood control infrastructure; the upgrading of schools to modernize classrooms, libraries, and laboratories; computerization of the health-care records of every American within five years; green initiatives to double national capacity to generate alternative energy sources within three years; energy-efficiency improvements for some two million homes and 75 percent of federal buildings; extension of broadband Internet service to rural areas; and development of a more efficient national electric grid. Additionally, it addressed immediate needs in providing fiscal assistance to help state governments continue operations threatened by the recession's erosion of their tax revenues and supporting laid-off workers through extension of their unemployment benefits. The stimulus also featured a number of tax initiatives, including a tax credit for working- and middle-class families, an AMT patch, and a college tax credit.[4]

Even though ARRA was a response to the worst economic crisis since the 1930s, the political reaction to it was a familiar one in the Age of Deficits.

Republicans and conservative think tanks condemned the recovery program as a stratagem to restore big government under cover of recession on grounds that less than half its spending provisions would be implemented in FY2009–FY2010. They also criticized the earmarks that Democratic legislators had smuggled into the legislation to benefit their home states and favored special interests. With Rush Limbaugh to the fore, conservative radio talk show presenters similarly derided it as a "porculus" bill.[5]

Independent analysts also disapproved of specific items in the ARRA. The AMT patch, a sop to ensure Senate enactment, came in for particular censure as having no place in the recovery program on grounds that this was a continuation of current policy and principally benefited higher-income taxpayers likely to save rather than spend the money it allowed them to keep. There was also disappointment that the final bill provided $25 billion less fiscal relief to the states than the House version to appease conservative Democrats and win some GOP votes in the Senate. With state governments facing an aggregate $350 billion in budget shortfalls through 2011, many had begun raising taxes, cutting social programs, and laying off workers in a way that ran counter to the goals of the federal stimulus.[6]

Some of these criticisms appeared justified, but others did not. According to Congressional Budget Office estimates, more than 80 percent of ARRA's spending and taxation provisions would be operational in 2009–2011, with about a third of the total stimulus occurring in 2011. With the downturn expected to be longer and deeper and the recovery slower than usual in post-1945 recessions, providing a fiscal boost over a longer period was arguably sound policy. According to CBO director Douglas Elmendorf, a program of short duration "runs the risk of exacerbating economic weakness when the stimulus ends." Acknowledging that ARRA was "far from perfect," the Center on Budget Policy and Priorities (CBPP) still judged its schedule of fiscal assistance "quite well designed."[7]

In signing the bill into law on February 18, 2009, Obama recognized that the stimulus by itself would not be enough to bring about recovery. Economist Mark Zandi estimated that three million more jobs would be lost despite the stimulus, but the benchmark of its success would be whether monthly unemployment growth would have come down from 600,000 in January to 250,000 by the end of the year. Further initiatives under consideration to improve matters included overhaul of the Troubled Asset Relief Program to coax private lending and investment and provision of mortgage assistance to turn back the tide of home foreclosures. Meanwhile, the troubled Detroit-based automobile companies had requested further loans beyond those awarded them at the end of 2008 in order to avoid bankruptcy. Though denying that there were any plans for a second stimulus package, the White House also refused to rule this out if necessary for economic recovery.[8]

Even without any further action to boost the economy, the federal government had already entered uncharted fiscal waters. The combined costs of the stimulus, the financial bailout, and the automatic stabilizers that operate in recession drove the deficit to a record peacetime level in FY2009. Early forecasts suggested that it would exceed $1.4 trillion, around 10 percent GDP. This was far above the previous post-1945 high of 6 percent in FY1983. Following enactment of ARRA, however, the CBO estimated that the deficit would amount to some $1.7 trillion (11.9 percent GDP) and could go as high as $1.85 trillion (13.1 percent GDP). The effect would be a massive increase in the public debt–GDP ratio from 40.8 percent in FY2008 to 56.8 percent in FY 2009. Another trillion-dollar imbalance also looked likely in FY2010. Trying to adjust to this, new Senate Appropriations Committee chair Daniel Inouye (D-HI) commented, "We're a country that's used to saying a 'million' or 'billion.' 'Trillion' is something that's very seldom used."[9]

The deficit was likely to fall from the high peaks of FY2009–FY2010, but how far was unclear. Obama's first budget plan projected that it would decline to $533 billion (about 3 percent GDP) in FY2013 through reduction of military operation costs in Iraq and Afghanistan and higher taxes on high earners and corporations after the expiry of the Bush tax cuts in 2010. Even under this scenario, the public debt was set to double in dollar size in FY2009–FY2013. Based on differing projections of baseline revenues and outlays, however, the CBO put the tab much higher in its analysis of the president's budget. This estimated that the Obama plan would keep the deficit abnormally high in both the short and medium term to average 5.6 percent GDP in FY2010–FY2014 and 5.3 percent in FY2010–FY2019. According to CBO calculations, the ten-year deficit accruing from the Obama plan would amount to $9.3 trillion, rather than $7.2 trillion as the White House had forecast. The outcome would be a doubling of the FY 2008 debt-GDP of 40.8 percent by FY2019 (See Epilogue Table 1).[10]

Friends and foes alike were in agreement that the Obama budget plan constituted the greatest ideological shift in Washington since Ronald Reagan's coming to power. It permanently extended many of the provisions of the 2001 and 2003 tax cuts for married taxpayers earning under $250,000 a year (and single ones earning $200,000) at a ten-year cost of $1.9 trillion (1.1 percent GDP). More contentiously, it envisaged huge investment in alternative energy, education, and health care while raising taxes on top income earners and oil and gas companies. The new president sought to increase federal domestic outlays by at least $500 billion over the course of the next decade, a figure likely to go higher once the details of health-care reform were finalized.

Obama trumpeted his budget as a fundamental reordering of national priorities to deliver "the sweeping change that this country demanded when

Epilogue Table 1. The Congressional Budget Office Analysis of the 10-Year Fiscal Effects (Percentage GDP) of the President's FY2010 Budget Plan

Fiscal Year	Revenues	Outlays	Net Interest	Surplus/Deficit	Public Debt
2010	15.9	25.5	1.2	–9.6	64.7
2014	18.7	23.1	2.7	–4.3	73.2
2019	18.8	24.5	3.8	–5.7	82.4

Source: Congressional Budget Office, *A Preliminary Analysis of the President's Budget and an Update of CBO's Budget and Economic Outlook* (Washington, DC: CBO, March 2009).

it went to the polls in November." In like vein, White House chief of staff Rahm Emmanuel declared that the president's fiscal plan "rejects the past and says we are going to be a culture and a society that invests and saves." In contrast, House Minority Leader John Boehner (R-OH) called the Obama budget an "audacious move to a big socialist government" that piles "debt on the backs of our kids and grandkids." Similarly, Senate Minority Leader Mitch McConnell (R-KY) warned that it "calls for a dramatic and potentially irreversible shift of our nation to the left."[11]

A nonbinding budget resolution that largely embodied Obama's plan received approval from the House of Representatives by a vote of 233–193 and from the Senate by a vote of 53–43 without any Republican support on April 29, coincidentally Obama's one-hundredth day in office. This represented a huge victory for the president, even though legislators trimmed his proposals in refusing to extend the tax credit for families beyond 2010 unless offset by savings elsewhere and cutting $10 billion from his domestic program request. In addition, they approved the use of reconciliation procedure to deal with his forthcoming proposal to expand health coverage for the uninsured, thereby limiting the danger of it being filibustered to death, but refused to do the same for the White House plan to cap greenhouse gas emissions.[12]

This success did not eradicate doubts about the affordability of Obama's programs, even among Democrats. When asked by reporters how healthcare reform would be funded, House Ways and Means Committee chair Charles Rangel (D-NY) responded, "With great difficulty." The administration showed no inclination to grasp the nettle of higher taxes across the board to pay for its initiatives. In an address marking tax day on April 15, Obama repeated his election pledge not to raise taxes on families earning less than $250,000 a year. Republicans and their supporters were openly skeptical that he could honor this. On the same day, FreedomWorks, a conservative group led by onetime Republican congressional leader Dick Armey, organized thousands of antitax "tea parties" across the nation. Though satisfied with current tax rates, Obama's critics were fearful that these would soon have to rise to fund his expansion of government. "There's no way he can do the spending he does and cut taxes for most people," warned Armey. "People know that spending inevitably means more taxes."[13]

Whether or not large tax increases are eventually sought to pay for the Obama program, this will not solve the long-term fiscal problem confronting the United States. The drivers of future budgetary unsustainability are the inherited policy commitments pertaining to the three largest entitlements: Social Security, Medicare, and Medicaid. The danger of a fiscal tsunami generated by their rising costs has long been evident. The failure hitherto of political leaders to take action to avert this future crisis may be understandable in view of the difficulty of resolving immediate issues pertaining to taxation and spending, but it only added to the scale of the fix that will eventually be needed. As financial columnist Robert Samuelson observed in 1995, "We are a nation in deep denial. There's a sanctioned avoidance of problems that almost everyone knows will worsen with time." Nearly a decade later, three Brookings Institution analysts expressed a similar sentiment. "If the current budget problem is a gale," they warned, "the long-term problem is a hurricane." The growing dimensions of the coming storm over the course of the Bush presidency showed the dangers of delaying action to avoid it. The long-term (FY2075) unfunded cost of America's programs for the elderly rose from $13 trillion, or 3 percent of future wages, in 2000 to $43 trillion, or 5 percent of future wages, in 2007.[14]

A host of governmental and nongovernmental organizations are in agreement that the United States must act to preempt a future of overwhelming public deficits and debt. They include the CBO, the Government Accountability Office (GAO), the Concord Coalition, the Committee for a Responsible Federal Budget (CRFB), and the CBPP. Despite their philosophical differences on many other issues of public policy, the Brookings Institution and the Heritage Foundation collaborated to produce a series of recommendations for long-term fiscal salvation.[15]

So concerned was David M. Walker about the debt-ridden future that he resigned as GAO comptroller-general in early 2008 to campaign for corrective action as president of the Peter G. Peterson Foundation, an organization dedicated to promoting fiscal sustainability. To raise awareness among ordinary citizens, he crisscrossed the country explaining the gravity of the problem in a host of public forums. His activities became the subject of a documentary movie, *I.O.U.S.A.,* modeled on Al Gore's efforts to arouse popular concern about climate change through his film, *An Inconvenient Truth.*[16]

The long-term estimates of deficits and debt put forward by various organizations are necessarily inexact but convey a broadly similar assessment of the magnitude of future budget problems. The projections of the CBPP, a liberal budget watchdog, are reproduced in Epilogue Table 2. Released in late 2008, these are by no means the bleakest set of figures of the many in the public domain. Moreover, while anticipating the extension of most Bush tax cuts, the CBPP analysis does not allow for the costs of the Obama spending program that will accelerate the deterioration of the debt-GDP ratio. According to its calculations, the deficit and the public debt will grow respectively to 21 percent GDP and 279 percent GDP by FY2050 on the basis of current policy commitments. In this scenario, outlays on Social Security, Medicare, Medicaid, and defense will consume all federal revenues by 2031. Spending on all other programs (including net interest) that constituted just over a third of total outlays in FY2008 would then have to be funded from the deficit. Owing to the consequent mushrooming of the public debt and the mathematics of compound interest, annual interest payments would cost nearly 80 percent of total revenues by FY2050.

Another way of measuring the scale of the problem is to examine the long-term fiscal gap, namely the average amount of budgetary adjustments needed to stabilize the public debt–GDP ratio in 2050 at its share of the economy at the end of 2009. According to CBPP projections (based on a low estimate of the debt at 46 percent GDP, compared with the later CBO figure of 57 percent), this would add up to 4.2 percent GDP annually. It would be achievable through an immediate and permanent 24 percent increase in tax revenues or an immediate and permanent 20 percent reduction in outlays for all federal programs—or some combination of both. To put matters in perspective, savings of some $650 billion annually would be needed to commence this task of fiscal restoration in FY2010. If some programs were held at current levels, even deeper compensatory cuts would be required elsewhere. Should defense, for example, remain at its FY2004–FY2007 average of 4.0 percent GDP without offsetting savings, the fiscal gap through FY2050 would increase by a quarter to 5.3 percent GDP.[17]

Deficit reduction of this magnitude is not only politically impossible but also utter folly in terms of its impact on the economy. However, the longer the current cycle of unbalanced budgets continues, the more the long-term fiscal gap will widen because of the compound-interest effect of continuing deficits. Restoration of fiscal responsibility, in contrast, will ease the burden of annual debt servicing through the reverse benefits of compound interest.

It is difficult to envision the fiscal gap being closed without some enhancement of tax receipts. High revenue levels of 19.7 percent GDP in FY1969 and 20.2 GDP on average in FY1998–FY2001 underwrote the only balanced budgets since FY1960. Average revenue levels of 18.3 percent GDP in the forty-year period since FY1969 have been associated with chronic deficits. The surest way of boosting receipts would have been to allow the Bush tax cuts of 2001 and 2003 to expire on schedule on December 31, 2010—or to make full offsets for any that were extended. The resultant annual increase of

Epilogue Table 2. The Budget, the Deficit, and the Public Debt as Shares (Percent) of GDP, FY2000–FY2050

Fiscal Year	Revenues	Outlays	Interest	Surplus (+) / Deficit (–)	Debt Held by the Public
2000	20.9	16.1	2.3	+2.4	35
2010	16.9	21.3	2.4	–6.8	51
2020	17.7	19.2	3.2	–4.6	67
2030	17.8	21.8	5.4	–9.4	108
2040	17.4	23.4	8.7	–14.7	179
2050	17.2	24.6	13.7	–21.1	279

Source: Richard Kogan, Kris Cox, and James Horney, *The Long-Term Fiscal Outlook Is Bleak: Restoring Fiscal Sustainability Will Require Major Changes to Programs, Revenues, and the Nation's Health Care System* (Washington, DC: CBPP, December 2008), 14.

2 percent GDP in revenues would have generated immediate improvement in the budget outlook, and its compounding effect would close the long-term fiscal gap to 2.3 percent GDP by FY2050. Even with forty years of additional revenues, however, the public debt would still amount to 171 percent GDP in 2050, far above its level of 109 percent GDP at the end of World War II. Offsetting any Alternative Minimum Tax fix and other tax adjustments would only bring it down further to 117 percent GDP.[18]

Accordingly, reform of the three largest entitlements is essential. Even under moderate assumptions, the aggregate costs of Social Security, Medicare, and Medicaid are forecast to rise from around 9 percent of GDP in FY2008 to 19 percent GDP in FY2050. Even though it has received greater public attention because of the imminent retirement of the baby boomers, Social Security may be the least problematic to fix in policy terms.

The Social Security trust fund shows a positive balance through 2040, but this is simply an accounting device that keeps track of program claims on general revenues with assets that in reality consist of Treasury IOUs. What matters fiscally and economically is Social Security's cash balance that represents the annual difference between outlays and earmarked tax revenues. This is projected to be in deficit from 2017 onward.[19] Nevertheless, a number of straightforward policy reforms could significantly reduce Social Security outlays once the baby-boom retirement bulge wanes after 2030. These include COLA reductions, further adjustments in the retirement age to take account of greater life expectancy, and substitution of price indexing for wage indexing in determining initial benefits for future retirees. By itself the latter measure would reduce Social Security costs from 6 percent GDP in 2030 to approximately its current level of 4.3 percent GDP in 2050. However, this change would significantly lower lifetime benefits by 20 percent for workers retiring in 2030 and by 40 percent for those doing so in 2050. Retention of wage indexation for low-income retirees would offer a progressive compromise that traded off smaller savings for greater equity in the distributive effects of reform.[20]

Far more significant in the development of the fiscal gap are the health-care entitlements. According to the CBO, "The rate of growth of spending on health care is the single greatest threat to budget balance over the long run, and such spending will have to be controlled in order for the fiscal situation to be sustainable in future decades."[21] The primary factor in Medicare and Medicaid outlay growth has not been rising beneficiary numbers but rising costs per beneficiary, which have increased on annual average by 2.5 percent more than per capita GDP since the 1970s. If costs continue to grow at this rate, combined program spending will exceed 8 percent GDP in 2020 and then rise to nearly 22 percent GDP by 2050. A 1 percent rate of excess cost growth for these programs would contain their combined outlays to 12.5 percent GDP in 2050 and reduce the fiscal gap to 2.7 percent GDP. If health-care costs grew only at the same rate as per capita GDP—a highly unlikely scenario—Medicare and Medicaid expenditure would amount to 6 percent GDP, leaving a fiscal gap of only 1.2 percent GDP.[22]

If the need for health-care cost control is not in doubt, the solutions are less evident than for Social Security. The most obvious initiative is to control Medicare fees paid for physicians' services from 2010 onward by the rate-setting system (the "sustainable growth rate") that is provided for in current law. Congress has annually enacted legislation to override these reductions in every year since 2003, but permitting their operation would effect ten-year savings of $324 billion.[23] Nevertheless, the growing expense of Medicare and Medicaid more than anything else reflects medical advances that have improved health and life expectancy.

Efficiency gains can be made from modernization of health information technology contained in the ARRA stimulus, greater incentives to medical providers to use cost-effective treatments, elimination of large overpayments to medical insurers, and targeting health-care cost transfers on high-income Medicare beneficiaries. However, these strategies are largely untested, and there is no consensus about the savings that they would yield.[24] An increasing number of health-care policy experts also insist that universal insurance is an essential component of cost control because lack of coverage results in the sick getting expensive emergency-room treatment if their untreated conditions worsen. According to one estimate, the tab for potentially preventable hospitalizations in 2004 was $29 billion in hospital costs. Others put the bill for "uncompensated care" even higher, at $43 billion in 2005, with one-third of the cost paid by Medicare and other government programs and the rest through higher premiums for private health insurance.[25]

In line with these findings, some analysts insist that health-care reform must also address the expense of private health care that is growing at a comparable rate to entitlement care. In their view, which the Obama administration broadly supports, constraining only Medicare and Medicaid ignored the broader problem pertaining to medical costs. It would produce a two-tier health system that was not only inequitable but also inefficient because continued growth of private health-care spending, a substantial portion of which is nontaxable, ultimately results in federal revenue loss.[26]

Hitherto, the United States has been able to cover its twenty-first-century budget deficits through massive borrowing on relatively easy terms. Ironically, unprecedented interest-rate reductions intended to counteract economic decline helped to reduce federal net interest payments from 1.8 percent GDP in FY2008 to an estimated 1.2 percent GDP in FY2009 despite the parallel 40 percent increase in the public debt–GDP ratio. Nevertheless, interest rates will not remain at historically low levels once the economy recovers, so debt servicing is projected to become more costly from FY2011 onward.[27]

Some analysts have also expressed concern that much of this cheap credit comes from abroad. In the first five years of George W. Bush's presidency, foreign ownership of U.S. Treasuries increased by $1.2 trillion after falling more than $200 billion in the last thirty months of Clinton's administration. Over Bush's entire tenure, about 70 cents of every additional dollar of federal debt was borrowed from abroad. By the end of 2008 foreigners held about half of the outstanding public debt. It is highly unlikely that they will continue supporting the American government's expanding indebtedness over the long term if its scale raises concern that the United States will one day inflate its way out of the problem through the expediency of printing more dollars or even, in extreme circumstances, default.[28]

The People's Republic of China, whose central bank holds some $1.4 trillion of U.S. dollar reserves, has increasingly voiced concerns about America's continuing debt habit. "We have lent a huge amount of money to the U.S.," Chinese premier Wen Jinbao declared in early 2009. "Of course we are concerned about the safety of our assets." America will face an unpleasant reality should lenders from abroad become wary of funding its massive debt. "At some point," warned Barack Obama in 2006, "foreigners will stop lending us money, interest rates will go up, and we will spend most of our nation's output paying them back." In his assessment, the restoration of fiscal responsibility was the only way to avoid such a future.[29]

Obama penned these words before severe recession necessitated immediate expansion of the deficit ahead of any effort to avert long-term crisis of public finance, but he had evidently not forgotten them as president. Warning of "trillion-dollar deficits for years to come" without a change of fiscal course, he avowed shortly before his inauguration, "We're going to have to stop talking about budget reform. We're going to have to totally embrace it. It's an absolute necessity." Obama issued an even more explicit admonition in his first presidential press conference. "Unless we deal with entitlements in a serious way," he declared, "the problems we have, with this year's deficit and next year's deficit, pale in comparison with what we're going to be seeing 10 or 15 or 20 years down the road."[30]

The forty-fourth president had to deal with economic and fiscal problems that were larger and more complex than any of his post-1945 predecessors had faced. Only Franklin D. Roosevelt had confronted a comparable challenge with regard to promoting economic recovery, but his reform task was one of liberal state-building in contrast to Obama's need to rein in the costs of entitlements created under the New Deal–Great Society political order. Nevertheless, the experience of the presidents under review in this study still has relevance for the leadership challenge he faced. The following conclusions appear most pertinent in this regard.

Conclusion 1. The president's capacity to set the agenda for the legislature's fiscal deliberations is his most important budgetary power, and this authority is most effective when deployed cogently and consistently in pursuit of clear goals established at the outset of an administration.

Obama appeared to have taken this lesson to heart by focusing attention both on America's immediate and future problems at the outset of his presidency. He delivered a cogent and simple message regarding the necessity for huge fiscal stimulus to boost economic recovery: America was in a terrible crisis; only government could break the vicious cycle of decline; things would get much worse unless it acted swiftly. However, he also warned that entitlement reform could no longer be deferred if future crisis was to be averted: "What we have done is kicked this down the road. We are now at the end of the road and are not in a position to kick it any further. We have to signal seriousness in this by making sure that some of the hard decisions are made under my watch, not someone else's."[31]

The administration saw health-care reform, including universal insurance coverage, as the key to long-term budgetary sustainability. "Health-care reform is entitlement reform," declared OMB director Peter Orszag. "The path to fiscal responsibility must run directly through health care." Following ARRA's enactment, Obama moved quickly to put it at the heart of his governing agenda. Although lacking a detailed proposal, his FY2010 budget plan paved the way for the introduction of one in mid-2009. In support of this, the president hosted a bipartisan White House forum on health reform on March 5 to discuss options for comprehensive reform. In his opening remarks, he declared, "Medicare costs are consuming our federal budget. Medicaid is overwhelming our state budgets. . . . The greatest threat to America's fiscal health . . . is the skyrocketing cost of health care."[32]

Conclusion 2. Recent presidents have found it increasingly difficult to win bipartisan support on budget issues in Congress, but its attainment was not impossible and proved significant for deficit control in the late twentieth century.

Obama promised in the 2008 presidential campaign to reach out across the party divide in order to govern. He had previously written that ordinary Americans were "waiting for a politics with the maturity to balance idealism and realism, to distinguish between what can and cannot be compromised, to admit the possibility that the other side might sometimes have a point."[33] However, the process of enacting the stimulus bill appeared to run contrary to bipartisanship.

Although Obama made personal efforts to secure bipartisan support for ARRA, he delegated responsibility for writing the bill to Democratic congressional leaders, who remained in thrall to the old politics. One reason that the bill received no GOP votes in the House and only three in the Senate was that Republicans played no part in its formulation. Obama may have secured more cross-party support by sending a White House–authored pork-free stimulus proposal to Congress. Nevertheless, Republican dedication to cutting taxes as a way out of recession could well have proved an insuperable obstacle to cooperation. Any further concessions beyond those made to win the necessary margin of GOP support in the Senate might have sparked serious dissent in Democratic ranks. Some in Obama's party complained that too much had been already surrendered, notably in scaling down aid to the states, school construction, and health-care for the unemployed. As Representative Jerrold Nadler (D-NY) commented, "I'd rather forgo Republican votes and prevent a depression than get Republican votes at the cost of slowing the depression but not stopping it."[34]

Nevertheless, the White House saw bipartisan outreach as important to promote a new atmosphere of civility and break down the polarization that had developed in Congress over the previous twenty years. It was Obama's hope that "over time some of these habits of consultation and mutual respect will take over."[35] Such a change may never happen, but it was worth pursuing. The Democrats had the votes to enact the stimulus with minimal Republican support, but bipartisan cover would be important when it came to asking Americans to accept the sacrifices necessary to reform entitlements.

Despite not picking up GOP votes, Obama gained credit with the public for trying. One poll found that 61 percent of respondents blamed the Republicans for not working with him on the stimulus, compared to 16 percent holding the president responsible. With Obama's approval rating solidly in the midsixties, a level maintained over the first hundred days of his presidency, the same survey found that only 34 percent approved of the job that GOP congressional leaders were doing and that 51 percent expressed disapproval.[36] Such findings suggested that the Republicans could not long engage in the politics of negativity. With the Obama administration contemplating far-reaching reforms of entitlements, they risked having not much of a voice in the debate and no seat at the table where policy would be decided.

Conclusion 3. Presidents have attempted to depoliticize budget problems through creation of a special commission to make policy recommendations but have rarely demonstrated political will to make effective use of such a body.

The Social Security Commission of the early 1980s was the only successful body of this kind because the Reagan administration and the Democratic congressional leaders had a common interest in making it work. Other bodies either did not produce findings with bipartisan credibility or their recommendations fell afoul of renewed partisan conflict. As Obama took office, congressional budget hawks in both parties and a number of budget watchdog groups urged the creation of a bipartisan task force to propose entitlement reform and tax code reform as a solution to long-term budget problems. Prominent supporters included Senator Kent Conrad (D-ND) and Senator Judd Gregg (R-NH), respectively Senate Budget Committee chair and ranking Republican. Their proposal for establishing such a body required that its recommendations should be subject to an up or down congressional vote without possibility of amendment, similar to the process used to close military bases. The refusal of House Speaker Nancy Pelosi (D-CA) to surrender congressional authority over Social Security reform put paid to this idea for the time being. Seeking a middle-way approach, the Obama administration held a bipartisan "fiscal responsibility summit" at the White House to establish an agenda for long-term budget reform, but this did not produce substantive recommendations.[37]

Whatever the process of bipartisan deliberation, if established, a successful outcome would necessarily depend on both parties being willing to compromise on their historic commitments to avert the future crisis of fiscal sustainability. The challenge for the president would be to keep it on track to make a grand bargain whereby Democrats accept the necessity to scale back entitlement benefits and Republicans accept universal health-care insurance, control of private health-care costs, and nonprivatization of Social Security.

Conclusion 4. Presidents have an inconsistent record in promoting transparency and accountability in the budget process, but procedural reform and openness has had an important role in facilitating deficit control.

The 1990s stand out as the golden age of procedural effectiveness and transparency in deficit control. In contrast to the fiscal legerdemain that characterized Reagan-era efforts at budget restraint, the PAYGO requirements and discretionary spending caps mandated by the Budget Enforcement Act

(BEA) of 1990 were effective in constraining programs that caused deficits. Its expiry in 2002 led to a new era of budget opacity that worked against fiscal planning and deficit control. As Barack Obama took office, the Concord Coalition declared, "The federal budget is suffering from a lack of transparency and accountability similar to the private sector institutions the government has been forced to rescue. . . . It is becoming increasingly difficult to know where the budget is headed, even in the short-term, by looking at official documents."[38]

Needing to reassure Blue Dog Democrats that the stimulus was "an extraordinary response to an extraordinary situation," the White House signified its intent to promote new budget rules based on the BEA principles that "helped create the surpluses of a decade ago." How quickly it would follow up on this remained to be seen. Nevertheless, a number of Obama's early initiatives signified substantive rather than merely rhetorical commitment to budgetary accountability and transparency. The establishment of the recovery.gov Web portal enabled the public to track that ARRA funds were being expended in a "timely, targeted and transparent manner." More significant, in contrast to his predecessor's practice, Obama's first budget included substantive projections of Afghan and Iraqi military operation costs, did not count legislated savings from lower Medicare payments to doctors that were habitually overridden, and excluded AMT payments from which taxpayers were routinely given relief.[39]

Conclusion 5. Presidents can go public to promote popular approval of their budget policies but have rarely done so to educate Americans about fiscal problems.

Obama's rhetorical skills were instrumental in catapulting him from relative political obscurity to the presidency in a short span of time, and he may well establish himself as one of the most inspiring public speakers ever to occupy the White House. Among his predecessors only George W. Bush got away with being "the 'unrhetorical president' operating in the age of the rhetorical presidency."[40] The inability of Jimmy Carter and George H. W. Bush to find their public voice was a factor in their presidencies being political failures. In contrast, the political communication skills of Ronald Reagan and Bill Clinton were an important element in their presidential leadership. Nevertheless, even they found that words were not always an effective instrument to promote their policies. Similarly, Obama's intensive public campaign in support of the stimulus could not prevent public support for it slipping over the course of the enactment process.[41]

Whether accomplished wordsmiths or not, Obama's predecessors engaged in public campaigning in order to seek approval of their budget policies rather than to educate Americans about budget problems. According to political scientist Erwin Hargrove, presidents engaged in "the teaching of reality" do so through rhetoric that "is informative and concrete, recognizes contingencies and uncertainties, and appears generally designed to educate." In his estimate, FDR's fireside chats offered the best model for this in the sense that they described problems in solid fashion, explained the proposed solution, and admitted uncertainties that could be faced. Roosevelt's rhetoric did not substitute abstract creeds for policy ideas, and it appealed to collective purpose rather than self-interest.[42]

Obama's public campaign for the ARRA seemed more intent on frightening than educating Americans. "If we don't act immediately," the president declared on a visit to Elkhart, Indiana, "our nation will sink into a crisis that, at some point, we may be unable to reverse."[43] He made little effort to engage in dialogue over the respective merits of a stimulus plan based on spending or tax cuts. The urgency of the economic situation arguably justified this peremptory approach, but the task of promoting entitlement reform calls for a different style of leadership that emulates FDR's skill in teaching reality.

The new president moved somewhat closer to the Rooseveltian model to promote acceptance of his first budget. Stung by Republican opposition to ARRA, he did not lobby for bipartisan support of his fiscal proposals. Instead, taking his case to the country through prime-time news conferences, appearances on late-night talk shows, and convening town-hall meetings outside Washington, Obama sought to frame the way he wants Americans to engage with the opportunities and problems of the future.

Educating Americans about fiscal sustainability is likely to be a permanent campaign for the forty-fourth president. Widespread agreement that the nation has to face up to its problem of public debt is not matched by consensus on the solutions. At issue in entitlement reform is how to ensure that the commitments of the past do not constrain government's capacity to address the needs of the future. It entails rewriting the New Deal–Great Society compact to bring about a more equitable distribution of public benefits and burdens between generations. In essence, Americans have to revisit the questions that have recurred throughout their history regarding their expectations of what government should do and how this should be paid for. Perhaps no one has put the case for such a dialogue better than Obama himself. Politicians who believed in government as a positive force, he wrote in 2006, had an obligation to reengage Americans in the project of national renewal that would require them to accept tough choices based on understanding of "their own self-interest as inextricably linked to the interest of others."[44]

Shortly before Obama's election the U.S. debt clock near New York City's Times Square provided a symbolic warning of America's need to change fiscal course. In September 2008 it ran out of digits to record the growth of national indebtedness above $10 trillion. The dollar sign on the display was temporarily removed to make room for the extra figure. Originally erected to highlight the $2.7 trillion level of debt in 1989, the clock had been switched off in September 2000 in anticipation that surpluses as far as the eye could see would result in elimination of the public debt. The red hues that once more colored the fiscal future caused it to be turned back on in July 2002. To ensure that the clock could keep doing its dismal task, the owner announced that two new zeros would be added in 2009 so that it had the capacity to record a quadrillion dollars of debt.[45]

The leaders of the United States will hopefully display the will, ingenuity, and perseverance to close the fiscal gap long before such a debt marker is reached. Optimists can find comfort in America's repeated ability to renew and strengthen itself in the face of crisis since the birth of the republic. The challenges confronting the current generation of leaders are different from those of the past, however. They must not only restore prosperity to the benefit of today's Americans but also lay foundations for fiscal recovery to the benefit of generations to come. Barack Obama faces a formidable task of presidential leadership to address these issues, but he has the historic opportunity to put America's economy and its government on sound and sustainable foundations. If he succeeds in this, it will truly represent the triumph of "the audacity of hope."

Presidential Fiscal Profiles: Description

FISCAL YEARS

Data for each president is presented from the fiscal year (FY) budget that commenced during his first October in office to the fiscal year budget that started during his final October in office. In other words, the budget in operation during each president's first eight months in office is treated as his predecessor's, whereas the one in operation for his successor's first eight months in office is treated as his. This does not capture each president's fiscal record perfectly because supplemental additions can change the composition of inherited budgets. For example, George W. Bush's tax rebate reduced the deficit in Bill Clinton's FY2001 budget by $100 billion. (Bush's own profile below excludes figures for FY2009 because not only was data unavailable other in estimated form for this budget at time of writing but also Barack Obama's stimulus program and other initiatives made substantial supplementary adjustments to it.) The final details of every budget, it should be reaffirmed, are the work of Congress. Nevertheless, what follows is a useful index of the fiscal record of each president under review in this study.

INCOME SECURITY

Mandatory outlays in this category include unemployment compensation, Supplemental Security Income, the refundable portion of the earned income and child tax credits, food stamps, family support, child nutrition, and foster care.

PUBLIC DEBT

This refers to the total debt held by the Federal Reserve System and other lenders at the end of the fiscal year (i.e., it excludes debt held by federal government accounts).

SOURCES

The tables are based on data drawn from *Budget of the United States Government FY2009: Historical Tables*; and Congressional Budget Office, *The Budget and Economic Outlook: Fiscal Years 2005 to 2014* and *Fiscal Years 2009 to 2018*.

STRUCTURAL DEFICIT/SURPLUS

The structural deficit/surplus (also known as the standardized-budget deficit/surplus) indicates the "policy gap" between spending and revenues that emanates from budget appropriations and entitlement outlays. Its calculation excludes (1) the effects of cyclical fluctuations in output and unemployment on federal receipts and expenditure, and (2) other adjustments like deposit insurance or contributions from allied nations in FY1991–FY1992 for Operation Desert Storm. In essence, this index measures the deficit (or surplus) that would have accrued had the economy been operating at maximum capacity.

Presidential Fiscal Profile: Jimmy Carter

Table B.1. Aggregate Deficits

FY	Deficit Current $ (billions)	Deficit FY2000 $ (billions)	Deficit-GDP (percent)	Structural Deficit– GDP (percent)
1978	–59.2	–141.1	–2.7	–1.5
1979	–40.7	–89.5	–1.6	–0.7
1980	–73.8	–146.8	–2.7	–0.4
1981	–79.0	–142.0	–2.6	–0.4

Table B.2. Outlays and Receipts as a Percentage of GDP

FY	Outlays	Receipts
1978	20.7	18.0
1979	20.1	18.5
1980	21.7	19.0
1981	22.2	19.6

Table B.3. Net Interest and Public Debt as a Percentage of GDP

FY	Net Interest	Public Debt
1978	1.6	27.4
1979	1.7	25.6
1980	1.9	26.1
1981	2.2	25.8

270   Appendix B

Table B.4. Entitlement and Other Mandatory Outlays as a Percentage of GDP

FY	Social Security	Medicare	Medicaid	Income Security	Other Programs	Total (adjusted for offsetting receipts)
1978	4.2	1.1	0.5	1.4	3.0	9.2
1979	4.1	1.1	0.5	1.3	2.8	8.8
1980	4.3	1.2	0.5	1.6	3.0	9.6
1981	4.5	1.4	0.6	1.6	3.1	9.9

Table B.5. Discretionary Outlays as a Percentage of GDP

FY	Defense	International	Domestic	Total
1978	4.7	0.4	4.8	9.9
1979	4.7	0.4	4.6	9.6
1980	4.9	0.5	4.7	10.1
1981	5.2	0.4	4.5	10.1

Table B.6. Revenues as a Percentage of GDP

FY	Individual Income Taxes	Corporation Income Taxes	Social Insurance and Retirement Receipts	Others
1978	8.2	2.7	5.5	1.7
1979	8.7	2.6	5.6	1.6
1980	9.0	2.4	5.8	1.9
1981	9.3	2.0	6.0	2.2

Presidential Fiscal Profile: Ronald Reagan

Table C.1. Aggregate Deficits

FY	Deficit Current $ (billions)	Deficit FY2000 $ (billions)	Deficit-GDP (percent)	Structural Deficit–GDP (percent)
1982	–128.0	–214.8	–4.0	–1.1
1983	–207.8	–332.7	–6.0	–3.0
1984	–185.4	–282.8	–4.8	–3.6
1985	–212.3	–313.1	–5.1	–4.3
1986	–221.2	–318.4	–5.0	–4.8
1987	–149.7	–209.6	–3.2	–3.4
1988	–155.2	–210.8	–3.1	–2.6
1989	–152.5	–199.8	–2.8	–2.3

Table C.2. Outlays and Receipts as a Percentage of GDP

FY	Outlays	Receipts
1982	23.1	19.2
1983	23.5	17.4
1984	22.1	17.3
1985	22.8	17.7
1986	22.5	17.5
1987	21.6	18.4
1988	21.2	18.1
1989	21.2	18.3

Table C.3. Net Interest and Public Debt as a Percentage of GDP

FY	Net Interest	Public Debt
1982	2.6	28.7
1983	2.6	33.0
1984	2.9	34.0
1985	3.1	36.3
1986	3.1	39.5
1987	3.0	40.6
1988	3.0	40.9
1989	3.1	40.6

Table C.4. Entitlement and Other Mandatory Outlays as a Percentage of GDP

FY	Social Security	Medicare	Medicaid	Income Security	Other Programs	Total (adjusted for offsetting receipts)
1982	4.8	1.5	0.5	1.6	3.0	10.4
1983	4.9	1.6	0.6	1.9	3.0	10.6
1984	4.6	1.6	0.5	1.3	2.6	9.4
1985	4.5	1.7	0.5	1.3	2.9	9.7
1986	4.5	1.7	0.6	1.2	2.5	9.4
1987	4.4	1.7	0.6	1.2	2.3	9.1
1988	4.3	1.7	0.6	1.1	2.3	8.9
1989	4.3	1.7	0.6	1.1	2.4	9.0

Table C.5. Discretionary Outlays as a Percentage of GDP

FY	Defense	International	Domestic	Total
1982	5.8	0.4	3.9	10.1
1983	6.1	0.4	3.8	10.3
1984	5.9	0.4	3.5	9.9
1985	6.1	0.4	3.5	10.0
1986	6.2	0.4	3.3	10.0
1987	6.1	0.3	3.1	9.5
1988	5.8	0.3	3.1	9.3
1989	5.6	0.3	3.1	9.0

Table C.6. Revenues as a Percentage of GDP

FY	Individual Income Taxes	Corporation Income Taxes	Social Insurance and Retirement Receipts	Others
1982	9.2	1.5	6.2	2.1
1983	8.4	1.1	6.1	1.9
1984	7.8	1.5	6.2	1.9
1985	8.1	1.5	6.4	1.8
1986	7.9	1.4	6.4	1.6
1987	8.4	1.8	6.5	1.6
1988	8.0	1.9	6.7	1.6
1989	8.3	1.9	6.7	1.5

Presidential Fiscal Profile: George H. W. Bush

Table D.1. Aggregate Deficits

FY	Deficit Current $ (billions)	Deficit FY2000 $ (billions)	Deficit-GDP (percent)	Structural Deficit– GDP (percent)
1990	−221.2	−280.6	−3.9	−2.2
1991	−269.3	−327.4	−4.5	−2.4
1992	−290.4	−341.3	−4.7	−2.9
1993	−255.1	−292.4	−3.9	−2.8

Table D.2. Outlays and Receipts as a Percentage of GDP

FY	Outlays	Receipts
1990	21.8	18.0
1991	22.3	17.8
1992	22.1	17.5
1993	21.4	17.5

Table D.3. Net Interest and Public Debt as a Percentage of GDP

FY	Net Interest	Public Debt
1990	3.2	42.0
1991	3.3	45.3
1992	3.2	48.1
1993	3.0	49.4

Table D.4. Entitlement and other Mandatory Outlays as a Percentage of GDP

FY	Social Security	Medicare	Medicaid	Income Security	Other Programs	Total (adjusted for offsetting receipts)
1990	4.3	1.9	0.7	1.2	2.8	9.9
1991	4.5	1.9	0.9	1.5	3.1	10.1
1992	4.6	2.1	1.1	1.8	2.0	10.4
1993	4.6	2.2	1.2	1.8	1.5	10.2

Table D.5. Discretionary Outlays as a Percentage of GDP

FY	Defense	International	Domestic	Total
1990	5.2	0.3	3.2	8.7
1991	5.4	0.3	3.3	9.0
1992	4.8	0.3	3.4	8.6
1993	4.4	0.3	3.4	8.2

Table D.6. Revenues as a Percentage of GDP

FY	Individual Income Taxes	Corporation Income Taxes	Social Insurance and Retirement Receipts	Others
1990	8.1	1.6	6.6	1.6
1991	7.9	1.7	6.7	1.6
1992	7.6	1.6	6.6	1.6
1993	7.7	1.8	6.5	1.5

Presidential Fiscal Profile: Bill Clinton

Table E.1. Aggregate Deficits/Surpluses

FY	Deficit/Surplus Current $ (billions)	Deficit/Surplus FY2000 $ (billions)	Deficit/Surplus-GDP (percent)	Structural Deficit/ Surplus-GDP (percent)
1994	–203.2	–228.3	–2.9	–2.0
1995	–164.0	–179.8	–2.2	–2.0
1996	–107.5	–115.2	–1.4	–1.2
1997	–22.0	–23.1	–0.3	–1.0
1998	+69.2	+72.1	+0.8	–0.4
1999	+125.6	+128.8	+1.4	+0.1
2000	+236.4	+236.4	+2.4	+1.1
2001	+127.4	+124.5	+1.3	+1.0

Table E.2. Outlays and Receipts as a Percentage of GDP

FY	Outlays	Receipts
1994	21.0	18.1
1995	20.7	18.5
1996	20.3	18.9
1997	19.6	19.3
1998	19.2	20.0
1999	18.6	20.0
2000	18.4	20.9
2001	18.6	19.8

Table E.3. Net Interest and Public Debt as a Percentage of GDP

FY	Net Interest	Public Debt
1994	2.9 ·	49.3
1995	3.2	49.2
1996	3.1	48.5
1997	3.0	46.1
1998	2.8	43.1
1999	2.5	39.8
2000	2.3	35.1
2001	2.1	33.1

Table E.4. Entitlement and Other Mandatory Outlays as a Percentage of GDP

FY	Social Security	Medicare	Medicaid	Income Security	Other Programs	Total (adjusted for offsetting receipts)
1994	4.6	2.3	1.2	1.7	1.6	10.3
1995	4.5	2.4	1.2	1.6	1.4	10.1
1996	4.5	2.5	1.2	1.6	1.4	10.2
1997	4.4	2.5	1.2	1.5	1.3	9.9
1998	4.4	2.4	1.2	1.4	1.5	9.9
1999	4.2	2.3	1.2	1.4	1.5	9.8
2000	4.2	2.2	1.2	1.4	1.6	9.8
2001	4.3	2.4	1.3	1.4	1.6	10.1

Table E.5. Discretionary Outlays as a Percentage of GDP

FY	Defense	International	Domestic	Total
1994	4.1	0.3	3.4	7.8
1995	3.7	0.3	3.4	7.4
1996	3.5	0.2	3.2	6.9
1997	3.3	0.2	3.1	6.7
1998	3.1	0.2	3.1	6.4
1999	3.0	0.2	3.0	6.3
2000	3.0	0.2	3.1	6.3
2001	3.0	0.2	3.2	6.5

Table E.6. Revenues as a Percentage of GDP

FY	Individual Income Taxes	Corporation Income Taxes	Social Insurance and Retirement Receipts	Others
1994	7.8	2.0	6.6	1.6
1995	8.1	2.1	6.6	1.7
1996	8.5	2.2	6.6	1.5
1997	9.0	2.2	6.6	1.5
1998	9.6	2.2	6.6	1.6
1999	9.6	2.0	6.7	1.7
2000	10.3	2.1	6.7	1.6
2001	9.9	1.5	6.9	1.6

Presidential Fiscal Profile:
George W. Bush

Table F.1. Aggregate Deficits

FY	Deficit Current $ (billions)	Deficit FY2000 $ (billions)	Deficit-GDP (percent)	Structural Deficit–GDP (percent)
2002	–157.8	–151.3	–1.5	–1.6
2003	–377.6	–352.8	–3.5	–2.6
2004	–412.7	–374.7	–3.6	–2.4
2005	–318.3	–278.8	–2.6	–1.9
2006	–248.2	–210.2	–1.9	–1.8
2007	–162.0	–134.3	–1.2	–1.1
2008	–458.6	–364.4	–3.2	–2.5

Table F.2. Outlays and Receipts as a Percentage of GDP

FY	Outlays	Receipts
2002	19.4	17.9
2003	20.0	16.5
2004	19.9	16.4
2005	20.2	17.6
2006	20.4	18.5
2007	20.0	18.8
2008	20.9	17.7

Table F.3. Net Interest and Public Debt as a Percentage of GDP

FY	Net Interest	Public Debt
2002	1.6	34.1
2003	1.4	36.2
2004	1.4	37.4
2005	1.5	37.5
2006	1.7	37.1
2007	1.7	36.8
2008	1.7	40.8

Table F.4. Entitlement and other Mandatory Outlays as a Percentage of GDP

FY	Social Security	Medicare	Medicaid	Income Security	Other Programs	Total (adjusted for offsetting receipts)
2002	4.4	2.4	1.4	1.7	1.6	10.7
2003	4.4	2.5	1.5	1.8	1.7	10.9
2004	4.3	2.6	1.5	1.7	1.7	10.8
2005	4.2	2.7	1.5	1.6	1.8	10.8
2006	4.2	2.9	1.4	1.5	1.9	10.8
2007	4.3	3.2	1.4	1.5	1.6	10.6
2008	4.3	3.2	1.6	1.6	2.0	11.2

Table F.5. Discretionary Outlays as a Percentage of GDP

FY	Defense	International	Domestic	Total
2002	3.4	0.3	3.5	7.1
2003	3.7	0.3	3.6	7.6
2004	3.9	0.3	3.5	7.8
2005	4.0	0.3	3.6	7.9
2006	4.0	0.3	3.5	7.8
2007	4.0	0.3	3.4	7.6
2008	4.3	0.3	3.4	8.0

Table F. 6. Revenues as a Percentage of GDP

FY	Individual Income Taxes	Corporation Income Taxes	Social Insurance and Retirement Receipts	Others
2002	8.3	1.4	6.8	1.4
2003	7.3	1.2	6.6	1.3
2004	7.0	1.6	6.4	1.3
2005	7.6	2.3	6.5	1.3
2006	8.0	2.7	6.4	1.4
2007	8.5	2.7	6.4	1.2
2008	8.1	2.1	6.3	1.2

Notes

Chapter 1. Presidents and the Other Red Peril

1. Joseph White and Aaron Wildavsky, *The Deficit and the Public Interest: The Search for Responsible Budgeting in the 1980s* (Berkeley: University of California Press, 1989), xv.

2. Daniel Patrick Moynihan, *Miles to Go: A Personal History of Social Policy* (Cambridge, MA: Harvard University Press, 1996), 95.

3. "Anti-Inflation Program Address to the Nation," October 24, 1978, in John T. Woolley and Gerhard Peters, American Presidency Project (Santa Barbara: University of California [host]; Gerard Peters [data base] available online at www.american presidency.org [hereafter, APP]).

4. "Address before a Joint Session of the Congress on the State of the Union," January 25, 1983, APP.

5. "Address to the Nation on the Federal Budget Agreement," October 2, 1990, APP.

6. "Address before a Joint Session of Congress on Administration Goals," February 17, 1993, APP.

7. "Address before a Joint Session of Congress on the State of the Union," January 20, 2004, APP.

8. Quoted in Louis Uchitelle and Robert Pear, "Deficit Rises, and Consensus Is to Let It Grow," *New York Times*, October 20, 2008, A1.

9. Allen Schick, *The Federal Budget: Politics, Policy, Process*, rev. ed. (Washington, DC: Brookings Institution, 2000), 90.

10. Howard E. Shuman, *Politics and the Budget: The Struggle between the President and the Congress*, 3rd ed. (Englewood Cliffs, NJ: Prentice Hall, 1992), 7; James L. Sundquist, *The Decline and Resurgence of Congress* (Washington, DC: Brookings Institution, 1981), 39.

11. Larry J. Berman, *The Office of Management and Budget and the Presidency, 1921–1979* (Princeton, NJ: Princeton University Press, 1979); Hugh Heclo, "OMB and the Presidency—The Problem of Neutral Competence," *Public Interest* 38 (Winter 1975), 87; John P. Frendreis and Raymond Tatalovich, *The Modern Presidency and Economic Policy* (Itasca, IL: F. E. Peacock, 1994), 57–60.

12. Paul C. Light, *The President's Agenda* (Baltimore: Johns Hopkins University Press, 1983); John Kingdon, *Agendas, Alternatives, and Public Policies* (Boston: Little, Brown, 1984).

13. Richard Neustadt, *Presidential Power and the Modern Presidents: The Politics of Leadership from Roosevelt to Reagan* (New York: Free Press, 1990).

14. Jeffrey Tulis, *The Rhetorical Presidency* (Princeton, NJ: Princeton University Press, 1987); Samuel Kernell, *Going Public: New Strategies of Presidential Leadership*, 3rd ed. (Washington, DC: Congressional Quarterly, 1997); George C. Edwards III, *On Deaf Ears: The Limits of the Bully Pulpit* (New Haven, CT: Yale University Press, 2003).

15. See, in particular, B. Dan Wood, *The Politics of Economic Leadership: The Causes and Consequences of Presidential Rhetoric* (Princeton, NJ: Princeton University Press, 2007), 20–26, 28–29. According to Wood's calculations, presidents from Jimmy Carter to Bill Clinton spoke an average of 22.93 sentences a month on the deficit, compared with the average of 4.87 for their predecessors from Harry Truman to Gerald Ford. George W. Bush's downplaying of the deficit problem was reflected in its relative insignificance in his rhetoric (5.79 sentences a month in his first term).

16. Donald Kettl, *Deficit Politics: Public Budgeting in Institutional and Historical Context* (New York: MacMillan, 1992), 124–139; and Schick, *The Federal Budget*, 8–35.

17. Louis Fisher, *The Politics of Shared Power: Congress and the Executive*, 2nd ed. (Washington, DC: Congressional Quarterly, 1988), 215.

18. Dennis S. Ippolito, *Congressional Spending* (Ithaca, NY: Cornell University Press, 1981); Sundquist, *The Decline and Resurgence of Congress*, 199–237.

19. Stephen Schier, *A Decade of Deficits: Congressional Thought and Fiscal Action* (Albany: State University Press of New York, 1992); Jasmine Farrier, *Passing the Buck: Congress, the Budget, and Deficits* (Lexington: University Press of Kentucky, 2004); Lance T. LeLoup, *Parties, Rules, and the Evolution of Congressional Budgeting* (Columbus: Ohio State University Press, 2005).

20. One analyst calculated that Congress stayed within 2 percent of presidential aggregates in setting its resolution until the advent of surplus budgets in 1999–2000. See Patrick Fisher, *Congressional Budgeting: A Representational Perspective* (Lanham, MD: University Press of America, 2005), 80–81.

21. Harrison Donnelly, "Uncontrollable U.S. Spending Limits Hill Power of the Purse," *Congressional Quarterly Weekly Report* [henceforth *CQWR*], January 19, 1980, 117–124; R. Kent Weaver, *Automatic Government: The Politics of Indexation* (Washington, DC: Brookings Institution, 1988); Allen Schick, *The Capacity to Budget* (Washington, DC: Urban Institute Press, 1990), 42–44, 120–126.

22. Herbert Stein, *Governing the $5 Trillion Economy* (New York: Oxford University Press, 1989), 18.

23. Clinton Rossiter, *The American President* (New York: Harcourt, Brace, 1956), 17–19.

24. Ronald Reagan, "Address to the Nation on the Federal Budget and Deficit Reduction," April 24, 1985, APP; Ronald Reagan, "Remarks at the Annual Meeting of the National Association of Manufacturers," May 24, 1985, APP; Ronald Reagan, *An American Life: The Autobiography* (London: Hutchison, 1990), 336.

25. William J. Clinton, "Address to the Nation on the Plan to Balance the Budget," June 13, 1995, APP; Bill Clinton, *My Life* (New York: Knopf, 2004), 693.

26. *Congressional Record*, 101st Congress, 2nd Session, 1990, 135, Part 150: S17568, and 104th Congress, 2nd session, 1996, 142, Part 44: S2963. See also Farrier, *Passing the Buck*, esp. 215–224.

27. For data, see *Gallup Report* 18 (May 1981), 31; and *Gallup Poll Monthly* 296 (May 1990), 27; Adam Clymer, "Carter Budget Gets Support in Survey," *New York Times*, January 31, 1979, A1.

28. In 1978–1979 and 1981, Gallup polls surveying popular estimates of each tax dollar wasted by Washington elicited a median response of 48 cents (compared with 30 and 24 cents respectively for state and local government). In 1995 a poll found that popular estimation of federal waste was 50 cents of each tax dollar. See Seymour M. Lipsett and William Schneider, "The Decline of Confidence in American Institutions," *Political Science Quarterly* 98 (Fall 1983), 83–84; Karlyn Bowman, "Flat Tax Fever? Depends on What Question the Pollsters Ask," *Roll Call*, February 5, 1996.

29. White and Wildavsky, *The Deficit and the Public Interest*, 423–426; Fisher, *Congressional Budgeting*, 133–168.

30. Robert Samuelson, "Avoidance Anxiety," *Washington Post National Weekly Edition*, August 8–14, 1994, 4.

31. Hearing before the Senate Committee on the Budget, *Concurrent Resolution on the Budget for FY96, Volume II* (Washington, DC: Government Printing Office, 1995), 55.

32. Alexander Hamilton, "Federalist Number 30," in Alexander Hamilton, James Madison, and John Jay, *The Federalist Papers*, edited with an introduction by Max Beloff (Oxford: Basil Blackwell, 1948), 142–143.

33. Aaron Wildavsky, *The Politics of the Budgetary Process* (Boston: Little, Brown, 1964), 4.

34. "Remarks at a Rally Supporting the Proposed Constitutional Amendment for a Balanced Federal Budget," July 19, 1982, APP; "Interview with Reporters from the *Los Angeles Times*," January 20, 1982, APP. Reagan's recollection of Friedman's opinion was fundamentally accurate, if faulty on the numbers. The economist had actually written, "I would far rather have total spending at $200 billion with a deficit of $100 billion than a balanced budget of $500 billion." See Milton Friedman, "The Limitations of Tax Reform," *Policy Review* (Summer 1978), 11–12.

Chapter 2. Presidents and Balanced Budgets: A Historical Perspective

1. Michael Foley, *American Credo: The Place of Ideas in U.S. Politics* (New York: Oxford University Press, 2007), 15.

2. Herbert Stein, *The Fiscal Revolution in America: Policy in Pursuit of Reality*, 2nd ed. (Washington, DC: AEI Press, 1996), 16; James Savage, *Balanced Budgets and American Politics* (Ithaca, NY: Cornell University Press, 1988), 3–4.

3. For historical budgetary trends, see Dennis S. Ippolito, *Why Budgets Matter: Budget Policy and American Politics* (University Park: Pennsylvania State University Press, 2003).

4. Allen Schick, *The Federal Budget: Politics, Policy, Process*, rev. ed. (Washington, DC: Brookings Institution, 2000), 9–14 (quotation p. 13); Ippolito, *Why Budgets Matter*, 21–60.

5. Lewis H. Kimmel, *Federal Budget and Fiscal Policy, 1789–1958* (Washington, DC: Brookings Institution, 1959), 14.

6. Savage, *Balanced Budgets and American Politics*, 5.

7. Forrest McDonald, *Alexander Hamilton: A Biography* (New York: Norton, 1979); John Steele Gordon, *Hamilton's Blessing* (New York: Wallace, 1997), esp. 22–41.

8. Quoted in Kimmel, *Federal Budget and Fiscal Policy, 1789–1958*, 14.

9. See, in particular, Drew McCoy, *The Elusive Republic: Political Economy in Jeffersonian America* (Chapel Hill: University of North Carolina Press, 1980); Herbert Sloan, *Principle and Interest: Thomas Jefferson and the Problem of Debt* (Charlottesville: University of Virginia Press, 2001); and Robert E. Wright, *One Nation Under Debt: Hamilton, Jefferson, and the History of What We Owe* (New York: McGraw-Hill, 2008).

10. Ippolito, *Why Budgets Matter*, 42–47; McCoy, *The Elusive Republic*, chapter 8.

11. "Third Annual Message," December 8, 1831, APP.

12. Louis Fisher, *Presidential Spending Power* (Princeton, NJ: Princeton University Press, 1975), 15–19; Kimmel, *Federal Budget and Fiscal Policy, 1789–1958*, 16–37.

13. Savage, *Balanced Budgets and American Politics*, 131–143.

14. W. Elliot Brownlee, *Federal Taxation in America: A Short History* (New York: Cambridge University Press, 1996), 23–30; Robert T. Patterson, *Federal Debt-Management Policies, 1865–1879* (Durham, NC: Duke University Press, 1954).

15. Morton Keller, *Affairs of State: Public Life in Late Nineteenth Century America* (New York: Cambridge University Press, 1977), 309–310; Tom E. Terrill, *The Tariff, Politics, and American Foreign Policy, 1874–1901* (Westport, CT: Greenwood Press, 1973), 210–217; Joanne Reitano, *The Tariff Question in the Gilded Age: The Great Debate of 1888* (University Park: Pennsylvania State University Press, 1994).

16. Fisher, *Presidential Spending Power*, 21–24; Charles H. Stewart III, *Budget Reform Politics: The Design of the Appropriations Process in the House of Representatives, 1865–1921* (New York: Cambridge University Press, 1989).

17. *Historical Statistics of the United States, Colonial Times to 1970* (Washington, DC: U.S. Bureau of the Census, 1975), 1114 [henceforth *Historical Statistics*]. For the "Billion Dollar Congress," see Matthew Josephson, *The Politicos, 1865–1896* (New York: Harcourt, Brace, & World, 1966), 460–461.

18. Kimmel, *Federal Budget and Fiscal Policy, 1789–1958*, 70–82; Fisher, *Presidential Spending Power*, 20–21, 25–27; Ippolito, *Why Budgets Matter*, 75–80. See also Richard E. Welch, *The Presidencies of Grover Cleveland* (Lawrence: University Press of Kansas, 2000), 83–89.

19. For contemporary opinion, see Rollo Ogden, "The Rationale of Congressional Extravagance," 6 *Yale Review* 37 (May 1897); George Cortelyou, "Regulation of the National Budget," *North American Review* 189, No. 4 (1909); and Allen Johnson, "American Budget Making," 18 *Yale Review* 363 (1909).

20. *Historical Statistics*, 224, 1114–1115.

21. Stephen Graubard, *The Presidents: The Transformation of the American Presidency from Theodore Roosevelt to George W. Bush* (London: Penguin Books, 2006), 109. For canal costs, see Davis Rich Dewey, *Financial History of the United States* (London: Longmans, Green, 1920), 243–246.

22. Quoted in Kimmel, *Federal Budget and Fiscal Policy, 1789–1958*, 84.

23. "Second Annual Message," December 8, 1914, APP.

24. John F. Witte, *The Politics and Development of the Federal Income Tax* (Madison: University of Wisconsin Press, 1985), 75–76; Joseph A. Pechman, *Federal Tax Policy,* 5th ed. (Washington, DC: Brookings Institution, 1987), 135.

25. Brownlee, *Federal Taxation in America,* 43–46.

26. For data, see Witte, *The Politics and Development of the Federal Income Tax,* 79–87. For contrasting "redistributive" and "pluralist" explanations of wartime taxation, see, respectively, Brownlee, *Federal Taxation in America,* 48–58, and Gilbert C. Fite, *American Financing of World War I* (Westport, CT: Greenwood Press, 1970).

27. Fisher, *Presidential Spending Power,* 27–35; Stephen Skowronek, *Building a New American State: The Expansion of National Administrative Capacities, 1877–1920* (New York: Cambridge University Press, 1982), 187–188, 192–193, 206–207. For a contemporary analysis by a member of the Taft Commission who wrote the original draft of the 1921 legislation, see W. F. Willoughby, *The Problem of the National Budget* (New York: Appleton, 1918).

28. "Inaugural Address," March 4, 1925, APP; Ronald Reagan, *An American Life* (London: Hutchison, 1990), 244.

29. Ippolito, *Why Budgets Matter,* 115–123; Brownlee, *Federal Taxation in America,* 65–73; Savage, *Balanced Budgets and American Politics,* 147–150.

30. Robert Lekachman, *The Age of Keynes* (London: Allen Lane, 1967), 104.

31. Stein, *The Fiscal Revolution in America,* 6–38; Brownlee, *Federal Taxation in America,* 66–68.

32. *Annual Report of the Secretary of the Treasury on the State of the Finances for the Fiscal Year Ended June 30, 1940* (Washington, DC: Government Printing Office, 1940), 22–36; Stein, *The Fiscal Revolution in America,* 43–72. For spending restraint, see Julian E. Zelizer, "The Forgotten Legacy of the New Deal: Fiscal Conservatism and the Roosevelt Administration, 1933–1938," *Presidential Studies Quarterly* 30 (June 2000), 331–357.

33. Stein, *The Fiscal Revolution in America,* 91–130; Dean L. May, *From New Deal to New Economics: The American Liberal Response to the Recession of 1937* (New York: Garland, 1981); Alan Brinkley, *The End of Reform: New Deal Liberalism in Recession and War* (New York: Knopf, 1995), 65–105.

34. Lekachman, *The Age of Keynes,* 105–119; James MacGregor Burns, *Roosevelt: The Lion and the Fox* (New York: Harcourt, Brace, 1956), 335.

35. "Annual Budget Message," January 5, 1939, APP.

36. James T. Patterson, *Congressional Conservatism and the New Deal: The Growth of the Conservative Coalition in Congress, 1933–1939* (Lexington: University of Kentucky Press, 1967); Savage, *Balanced Budgets and American Politics,* 172–174; Stein, *The Fiscal Revolution in America,* 120–123.

37. See, in particular, Brinkley, *The End of Reform,* chapters 1–6 (quotation p. 10).

38. Alvin M. Hansen, *Fiscal Policy and Business Cycles* (New York: Norton, 1941), 84.

39. E. Carey Brown, "Fiscal Policy in the Thirties: A Reappraisal," *American Economic Review* 46 (December 1956), 866–887.

40. For Roosevelt's tax program, see Mark H. Leff, *The Limits of Symbolic Reform: The New Deal and Taxation, 1933–1939* (New York: Cambridge University

Press, 1984); and Witte, *The Politics and Development of the Federal Income Tax*, 96–109.

41. Robert M. Collins, *The Business Response to Keynes, 1929–1964* (New York: Columbia University Press, 1981), 44–49 (quotation p. 45).

42. Robert M. Collins, *More: The Politics of Economic Growth in Postwar America* (New York: Oxford University Press, 2000), 10–16. On the war as a "laboratory" for Keynesianism, see A. E. Holmans, *United States Fiscal Policy, 1945–1959: Its Contribution to Economic Stability* (London: Oxford University Press, 1961), 30–44; Lekachman, *The Age of Keynes*, 123–148; and Byrd L. Jones, "The Role of Keynesians in Wartime Policy and Postwar Planning, 1940–1946," *American Economic Review* 62 (May 1972), 125–133.

43. Brinkley, *The End of Reform*, 227–264; Collins, *The Business Response to Keynes, 1929–1964*, 99–112; Hugh Norton, *The Employment Act and the Council of Economic Advisers* (Columbia: University of South Carolina Press, 1977).

44. For the postwar "domestication" of Keynesianism, see Stein, *The Fiscal Revolution in America*, 197–240; and Collins, *The Business Response to Keynes, 1929–1964*, 142–172.

45. See, in particular, Alonzo Hamby, *Beyond the New Deal: Harry S. Truman and American Liberalism* (New York: Columbia University Press, 1973); and Iwan W. Morgan, *Eisenhower versus "The Spenders:" The Eisenhower Administration, the Democrats, and the Budget, 1953–60* (New York: St. Martin's Press, 1990).

46. Quoted in Iwan Morgan, *Deficit Government: Taxes and Spending in Modern America* (Chicago: Ivan Dee, 1995), 57–58. See also "Radio and Television Address to the American People Following the Signing of the Defense Production Act," September 9, 1950, APP.

47. Eisenhower to Edgar Eisenhower, October 23, 1958, Ann Whitman File [hereafter, AWF], Name Series, Box 11, Eisenhower to General Alfred Gruenther, May 4, 1953, AWF, Diary Series [hereafter, DS], Box 3, and "Paraphrase of Remarks by the President on Future Budget and Program at the Cabinet Meeting of November 27, 1959," AWF, DS, Box 45, all in Dwight D. Eisenhower Presidential Papers [hereafter, EPP], Dwight D. Eisenhower Library [hereafter, DDEL].

48. "Special Message to the Congress: The President's Midyear Economic Report," July 11, 1949, APP; Eisenhower to Russell C. Leffingwell, February 16, 1954, AWF, DS, Box 5, EPP, DDEL.

49. Committee for Economic Development, Research and Policy Committee, *Taxes and the Budget: A Program for Prosperity in a Free Economy* (New York: Committee for Economic Development, 1947); Herbert Stein, *Presidential Economics: The Making of Economic Policy from Roosevelt to Clinton*, 3rd ed. (Washington, DC: AEI Press, 1994), 80.

50. "The President's News Conference of October 8, 1953," APP; The President's Cabinet Committee on Price Stability for Economic Growth, *Managing Our Money, Our Budget, and Our Debt* (Washington, DC: Government Printing Office, 1959), 5–6. See also *Economic Report of the President 1960* (Washington, DC: Government Printing Office, 1960), 5–7.

51. Brownlee, *Federal Taxation in America*, 89–100; Carolyn C. Jones, "Mass-Based Income Taxation: Creating a Taxpaying Culture, 1940–1952," in W. Elliot

Brownlee, ed., *Funding the Modern American State, 1941–1995: The Era of Easy Finance* (Washington, DC: Woodrow Wilson Center Press/Cambridge University Press, 1995), 104–148.

52. Holmans, *United States Fiscal Policy, 1945–1959*; Wilfred Lewis Jr., *Federal Fiscal Policy in the Postwar Recessions* (Washington, DC: Brookings Institution, 1962); and John Sloan, *Eisenhower and the Management of Prosperity* (Lawrence: University Press of Kansas, 1991), 133–151.

53. Cathy Jo Martin, *Shifting the Burden: The Struggle over Growth and Corporate Taxation* (Chicago: University of Chicago Press, 1991), and "American Business and the Taxing State: Alliances for Growth in the Postwar Period," in Brownlee, ed., *Funding the Modern American State*, 354–407; Witte, *The Politics and Development of the Federal Income Tax*, 121–154; Jones, "Mass-Based Income Taxation."

54. Calculations based on *Budget of the United States Government Fiscal Year 2009: Historical Tables*, 25–26, 45–47, 110–112 [hereafter, *Historical Tables*].

55. Hamby, *Beyond the New Deal*; Morgan, *Eisenhower versus "The Spenders"*; Edward D. Berkowitz, "Social Security and the Financing of the American State," in Brownlee, ed., *Funding the Modern American State*, 149–194.

56. Witte, *The Politics and Development of the Federal Income Tax*, 131–144; James L. Sundquist, *The Decline and Resurgence of Congress* (Washington, DC: Brookings Institution, 1981), 69–73; Ippolito, *Why Budgets Matter*, 155–156.

57. Stein, *The Fiscal Revolution in America*, 284–345; Witte, *The Politics and Development of the Income Tax*, 144–153; Dwight D. Eisenhower, "Annual Message to Congress on the State of the Union," January 7, 1960, APP.

58. Douglas Kinnard, *President Eisenhower and Strategy Management: A Study in Defense Politics* (Lexington: University Press of Kentucky, 1977); Stephen E. Ambrose, *Eisenhower the President, 1953–1969* (New York: Simon & Schuster, 1984); Saki Dockrill, *Eisenhower's New-Look National Security Policy, 1953–1961* (London: Routledge, 1996). For recession politics, see Morgan, *Eisenhower versus "The Spenders,"* chapter 5.

59. Dwight D. Eisenhower, *The White House Years: Waging Peace, 1956–61* (Garden City, NY: Doubleday, 1966), 460–462; Stein, *The Fiscal Revolution in America*, 346–354; Sloan, *Eisenhower and the Management of Prosperity*, 125–130. For assessment by Eisenhower's Treasury secretary, see Robert Anderson, "The Balance of Payments Problem," *Foreign Affairs* 38 (April 1960), 419–432, and "Financial Policies for Sustainable Growth," *Journal of Finance* 15 (May 1960), 127–139.

60. Morgan, *Eisenhower versus "The Spenders,"* 127–151; T. R. B., "Washington Wire," *New Republic*, June 8, 1959, 2.

61. Stein, *The Fiscal Revolution in America*, 364–371; Sloan, *Eisenhower and the Management of Prosperity*, 49–52, 154–155; Collins, *More*, 45–51.

62. Walter Heller, *New Dimensions of Political Economy* (Cambridge, MA: Harvard University Press, 1966), 58–116 (quotation p. 70); Statement of the Council of Economic Advisers before the Joint Economic Committee, March 6, 1961, "The American Economy in 1961: Problems and Policies," reproduced in James Tobin and Murray Weidenbaum, eds., *Two Revolutions in Economic Policy: The First Economic Reports of Presidents Kennedy and Reagan* (Cambridge, MA: MIT Press, 1988), 17–86.

63. *Annual Report of the Council of Economic Advisers, 1962* (Washington, DC: Government Printing Office, 1962), 44–56, 78–82 (reproduced in Tobin and Weiden-baum, eds., *Two Revolutions in Economic Policy*). For new economists' endorsement of the "Phillips curve," see Paul Samuelson and Robert Solow, "Analytic Aspects of Anti-Inflation Policy," *American Economic Review* 50 (May 1960), 177–194.

64. *Economic Report of the President, 1963* (Washington, DC: Government Printing Office, 1963), 74; Heller, *New Dimensions of Political Economy*, 27.

65. Walter Heller interview in Erwin C. Hargrove and Samuel A. Morley, eds., *The President and the Council of Economic Advisers: Interviews with CEA Chairmen* (Boulder, CO: Westview Press, 1984), 195–202.

66. Allen J. Matusow, *The Unraveling of America: A History of Liberalism in the 1960s* (New York: Harper & Row, 1984), 30–59; Irving Bernstein, *Promises Kept: John F. Kennedy's New Frontier* (New York: Oxford University Press, 1991), 118–159.

67. Irving Bernstein, *Guns or Butter: The Presidency of Lyndon Johnson* (New York: Oxford University Press, 1996), 27–38; Arthur M. Okun, *The Political Economy of Prosperity* (New York: Norton, 1970), 39; Ippolito, *Uncertain Legacies*, 40–43.

68. Arthur M. Okun, "Measuring the Impact of the 1964 Tax Reduction," in Joseph A. Pechman, ed., *Economics for Policymaking: Selected Essays of Arthur M. Okun* (Cambridge, MA: MIT Press, 1983), 405–423; James Tobin, "The Political Economy of the 1960s," in David C. Warner, ed., *Towards New Human Rights: The Social Policies of the Kennedy and Johnson Administrations* (Austin: University of Texas Press, 1977), 35.

69. "Commencement Address at Yale University," June 11, 1962, APP.

70. Collins, *More*, 52–61; Schick, *The Capacity to Budget*, 20–23, 26–29; Stein, *Presidential Economics*, 113–118.

71. Economic data calculated from *Economic Report of the President, 2008*, tables B-35 and B-63.

72. "Special Message to Congress on the State of the Budget and the Economy," August 3, 1967, APP. For the inflationary consequences of the war, see Matusow, *The Unraveling of America*, 155–162, 169–175; and Bernstein, *Guns or Butter*, 358–378.

73. Collins, *More*, 68–97, provides cogent analysis of the gold crisis and its reverberations.

74. Arthur M. Okun, *The Political Economy of Prosperity* (New York: Norton, 1970), 130.

75. Economic data based on *Economic Report of the President, 2008*, table B-63. For contemporary discussion, see Dale E. Hathaway, "Food Prices and Inflation," *Brookings Papers on Economic Activity*, No. 1 (1974), 65–107; George L. Perry, "The United States," in Edward R. Fried and Charles L. Schultze, eds., *Higher Oil Prices and the World Economy: The Adjustment Problem* (Washington, DC: Brookings Institution, 1975), 71–104; and Alan Blinder, *Economic Policy and the Great Stagflation* (New York: Academic Press, 1979).

76. Allen J. Matusow, *Nixon's Economy: Booms, Busts, Dollars & Votes* (Lawrence: University Press of Kansas, 1998), 303–308 (quotation p. 306).

77. Joanne S. Gowa, *Closing the Gold Window: Domestic Politics and the End of Bretton Woods* (Ithaca, NY: Cornell University Press, 1983); Matusow, *Nixon's Economy*, chapter 5; and Collins, *More*, 117–121.

78. Herbert Stein, "The Disintegration of Fiscal Policy," in Stein, *On the Other Hand...: Essays on Economics, Economists, and Politics* (Washington, DC: AEI Press, 1995), 155–163 (quotation p. 157); and Stein, "The Fiscal Revolution in America, 1964–1994," in Stein, *The Fiscal Revolution in America*, 521–523.

79. Ippolito, *Why Budgets Matter*, 198–203; Sundquist, *The Decline and Resurgence of Congress*, 201–215; Stein, *Presidential Economics*, 197–200.

80. The published version is Milton Friedman, "The Role of Monetary Policy," *American Economic Review* 58 (March 1968), 1–17. For a critical but still admiring assessment, see Paul Krugman, *Peddling Prosperity: Economic Sense and Nonsense in the Age of Diminished Expectations* (New York: Norton, 1994), 34–47.

81. A. James Reichley, *Conservatives in an Age of Change: The Nixon-Ford Administrations* (Washington, DC: Brookings Institution, 1981), 205–231; Matusow, *Nixon's Economy*, 7–33, 58–62, 98–102, 110–112, 292–295; Wyatt C. Wells, *Economist in an Uncertain World: Arthur F. Burns and the Federal Reserve, 1970–1978* (New York: Columbia University Press, 1994).

82. Hargrove and Morley, *The President and the Council of Economic Advisers*, 443. See also Alan Greenspan, *The Age of Turbulence: Adventures in a New World* (New York: Penguin Press, 2007), 67–73.

83. Reichley, *Conservatives in an Age of Change*, 382–406; Andrew D. Moran, "American Political Economy in the Age of Limits, 1974–76: Gerald Ford, the Democrats, and the Great Stagflation," Ph.D. dissertation, London Guildhall University, 2002; Yanek Mieczkowski, *Gerald Ford and the Challenges of the 1970s* (Lexington: University Press of Kentucky, 2005), 95–194. Muskie quotation in Morgan, *Deficit Government*, 127.

Chapter 3. Jimmy Carter: Confronting the Deficit

1. Robert Gates, *From the Shadows: The Ultimate Insider's Story of Five Presidents and How They Won the Cold War* (New York: Simon & Schuster, 1996), 572.

2. Thomas P. O'Neill, *Man of the House: The Life and Political Memoirs of Speaker Tip O'Neill* (New York: Random House, 1987), 313.

3. Jimmy Carter, *Keeping Faith: Memoirs of a President* (New York: Bantam Books, 1982), 78. For analysis of Carter's economic policy, see Bruce J. Schulman, "Slouching Towards the Supply Side: Jimmy Carter and the New American Political Economy," in Gary M. Fink and Hugh Davis Graham, *The Carter Presidency: Policy Choices in the Post–New Deal Era* (Lawrence: University Press of Kansas, 1997), 51–71; W. Carl Biven, *Jimmy Carter's Political Economy: Policy in an Age of Limits* (Chapel Hill: University of North Carolina Press, 2002); and Iwan Morgan, "Jimmy Carter, Bill Clinton, and the New Democratic Economics," *Historical Journal* 47 (December 2004), 1015–1039.

4. For biographical detail, see James Wooten, *Dasher: The Roots and Rising of Jimmy Carter* (New York: Basic Books, 1978); Betty Glad, *Jimmy Carter: In Search of the Great White House* (New York: Norton, 1980); Kenneth E. Morris, *Jimmy Carter: American Moralist* (Athens: University of Georgia Press, 1996); and Peter Bourne, *Jimmy Carter: A Comprehensive Biography from Plains to Postpresidency* (New York: Scribner, 1997).

5. Bourne, *Jimmy Carter*, 369.

6. Bert Lance with Bill Gilbert, *The Truth of the Matter: My Life In and Out of Politics* (New York: Summit Books, 1991), 127–128.

7. Jimmy Carter, *Why Not the Best?* (Nashville, TN: Broadman, 1975), vii; Bill Moyers, "A Talk with Carter," *Los Angeles Times*, May 16, 1976, in Don Richardson, ed., *Conversations with Carter* (Boulder, CO: Lynne Rienner, 1998), 13; Carter, *Keeping Faith*, 88. See also Gary M. Fink, *Prelude to the Presidency: The Political Character and Legislative Leadership Style of Jimmy Carter* (Westport, CT: Greenwood Press, 1980), 16–17; and Charles O. Jones, *The Trusteeship Presidency: Jimmy Carter and the United States Congress* (Baton Rouge: Louisiana State University Press, 1988), 10.

8. Fink, *Prelude to the Presidency*, 4; Bourne, *Jimmy Carter*, 238; Carter, *Keeping Faith*, 73–74.

9. Arthur Schlesinger Jr., "The Great Carter Mystery," *New Republic*, April 12, 1980, 21.

10. Steven M. Gillon, *The Democrats' Dilemma: Walter F. Mondale and the Liberal Legacy* (New York: Columbia University Press, 1992), 161. For another critique of Carter's lack of coherent vision, see Burton I. Kaufman and Scott Kaufman, *The Presidency of James Earl Carter Jr.*, 2nd ed. (Lawrence: University Press of Kansas, 2006).

11. John Shelton Reed, *One South: An Ethnic Approach to Regional Culture* (Baton Rouge: Louisiana State University Press, 1982), 124; Robert Shogan, *Promises to Keep: Carter's First Hundred Days* (New York: Thomas Y. Cromwell, 1977), 33. See also William J. Cooper Jr. and Thomas E. Terrill, *The American South: A History* (New York: Knopf, 1990), 740–744.

12. Robert J. McMath, "Jimmy Carter: A Southerner in the White House?" in Elizabeth Jacoway and Dan Carter, eds., *The Adaptable South* (Baton Rouge: Louisiana State University Press, 1991), 237–263. Carter claimed to be influenced by the beliefs of Southern populism and often labeled himself a populist in the 1976 presidential campaign to capitalize on the anti-Washington national mood generated by Watergate. However, scholars have noted that his description of Southern populist values more accurately fit those of Southern progressivism. See Carter, *Keeping Faith*, 74; Erwin Hargrove, *Jimmy Carter as President: Leadership and the Politics of the Public Good* (Baton Rouge: Louisiana State University Press, 1988), 6–7; Kaufman and Kaufman, *The Presidency of James Earl Carter Jr.*, 32.

13. George Tindall, *The Persistent Tradition in New South Politics* (Baton Rouge: Louisiana State University Press, 1975); Dewey W. Grantham, *Southern Progressivism: The Reconciliation of Progress and Tradition* (Knoxville: University of Tennessee Press, 1983), chapter 9; Larry Sabato, "New South Governors and the Governorship," in James F. Lea, ed., *Contemporary Southern Politics* (Baton Rouge: Louisiana State University Press, 1988), 194–213; Numan V. Bartley, *The New South, 1945–1980* (Baton Rouge: Louisiana State University Press, 1995), 398–404.

14. James C. Cobb, *The Selling of the South: The Southern Crusade for Industrial Development, 1936–1990*, 2nd ed. (Urbana: University of Illinois Press, 1991); and Bruce J. Schulman, *From Cotton Belt to Sunbelt: Federal Policy, Economic*

Development, and the Transformation of the South, 1938–1980 (New York: Oxford University Press, 1991).

15. Fink, *Prelude to the Presidency*, 114–116; Glad, *Jimmy Carter*, 176–178; Kandy Stroud, *How Jimmy Won: The Victory Campaign from Plains to the White House* (New York: Morrow, 1977), 292.

16. Glad, *Jimmy Carter*, 179–180; Aaron Wildavsky and Jack Knott, "Jimmy Carter's Theory of Governing," in Walter Dean Burnham and Martha Wagner Weinberg, eds., *American Politics and Public Policy* (Cambridge, MA: MIT Press, 1978), 65–66; George S. Nimier and Roger H. Hermanson, "A Look at Zero-Base Budgeting—The Georgia Experience," *Atlanta Economic Review*, July-August 1976, 5–12.

17. Charles Schultze interview, Project on the Carter Presidency, White Burkett Miller Center of Public Affairs, University of Virginia [hereafter, PCP-MC]; Erwin Hargrove and Samuel Morley, eds., *The President and the Council of Economic Advisers: Interviews with CEA Chairmen* (Boulder, CO: Westview Press, 1984), 465. For Keynes quotation, see John Maynard Keynes, *The General Theory of Employment, Interest, and Money* (New York: Harcourt Brace Jovanovich, 1964), 127.

18. Herbert Rowen, "The Tax-Cut Dilemma," *Washington Post*, May 11, 1978, A1. See also Biven, *Jimmy Carter's Economy*, 54–55.

19. Fink, *Prelude to the Presidency*, 10, 14; Jimmy Carter, *A Government as Good as Its People* (New York: Simon & Schuster, 1977), 23.

20. "Presidential Campaign Debate," September 23, 1976, APP.

21. Bourne, *Jimmy Carter*, 238; Carter, *Why Not the Best?* 134; Shogan, *Promises to Keep*, 33.

22. Shogan, *Promises to Keep*, 50. For the Democratic platform, see "Peace Prevails as Democrats Write Platform," *CQWR*, June 19, 1976, 1551–1554; and Henry Plotkin, "Issues in the 1976 Presidential Campaign," in Gerald Pomper with Colleagues, *The Election of 1976: Reports and Interpretations* (New York: Longman, 1977), esp. 36–41.

23. Jimmy Carter, "An Economic Position Paper for Now and Tomorrow," in *The Presidential Campaign, 1976*, Vol. 1, Part 1, *Jimmy Carter* (Washington, DC: Government Printing Office, 1978), 146.

24. *The Presidential Campaign, 1976*, Vol. 1, Part 2, *Jimmy Carter* (Washington, DC: Government Printing Office, 1978), 755.

25. "Presidential Campaign Debate," September 23, 1976, APP; Pat Caddell, "Initial Working Paper on Political Strategy," December 10, 1976, Jody Powell Papers [hereafter, JPP], Box 4, Jimmy Carter Library [hereafter, JCL]; A. James Reichley, *Conservatives in an Age of Change: The Nixon-Ford Administrations* (Washington, DC: Brookings Institution, 1981), 406.

26. Biven, *Jimmy Carter's Economy*, 27–36; *The Presidential Campaign, 1976*, Vol. 1, Part 2, 703; Reichley, *Conservatives in An Age of Change*, 403–404; Gerald Pomper, "The Presidential Election," in Pomper with Colleagues, *The Election of 1976*, 71, 74–75.

27. For voting data, see *New York Times*, November 4, 1976, 25.

28. Caddell, "Initial Working Paper on Political Strategy," December 10, 1976, and Memorandum to Governor Carter, "Additions to Dec. 10 Working Paper," December 21, 1976, JPP, Box 4, JCL.

29. Matthew D. Lassiter, *The Silent Majority: Suburban Politics in the Sunbelt South* (Princeton, NJ: Princeton University Press, 2006), 3.

30. See, in particular, Lassiter, *The Silent Majority*; William Schneider, "The Suburban Century Begins," *Atlantic Monthly* (July 1992), 33–44; and Stanley Greenberg, *Middle Class Dreams: The Politics and Power of the New American Majority*, rev. ed. (New Haven, CT: Yale University Press, 1996). For middle-class concern about inflation, see "The Inflation Surge," *Newsweek*, May 29, 1978, 26–28; Paul Blumberg, "White-Collar Status Panic," *New Republic*, December 1, 1979, 21–23; and Douglas Hibbs, *The American Political Economy* (Cambridge, MA: Harvard University Press, 1987), 19–26.

31. Jody Powell Interview, PCP-MC, 33.

32. Carter, *Keeping Faith*, 77; Jody Powell Interview, PCP-MC, 91. For similar comments, see Stuart Eizenstat Interview, PCP-MC, 62–63.

33. Jody Powell Interview, PCP-MC, 94–95.

34. "Economic Recovery Program: Message to the Congress," January 31, 1977, APP.

35. Moe quoted in Bourne, *Jimmy Carter*, 417; Walter Mondale, Memorandum for the President, "Review of My Vice Presidency," September 6, 1977, Staff Office Files [hereafter, SOF]–Chief of Staff: Hamilton Jordan [hereafter, Jordan], Box 37, JCL. See also Gillon, *The Democrats' Dilemma*, 123–179.

36. George McGovern, "Memo to the White House," *Harper's*, October 1977, 33–35.

37. John A. Farrell, *Tip O'Neill and the Democratic Century* (Boston: Little, Brown, 2001), 7 (quotation), 448–449; O'Neill, *Man of the House*, 313.

38. Jimmy Carter Interview, PCP-MC, 69.

39. Frank Moore, Memorandum for the President, "Weekly Legislative Report," December 7, 1978, Staff Secretary File–Presidential Handwriting File [hereafter, SSF-PHF], Box 111, JCL.

40. Representative John Brademas (D-IN), Memorandum, "Meeting at White House, Monday, May 2, 1977," Tim Barnicle to Hubert Humphrey, "White House Leadership Breakfast," May 2, 1977, Hubert Humphrey Papers, Senatorial File 1971–1978 [hereafter, HP-SF], VIP Correspondence [hereafter, VIPC], Box 1, Minnesota State Historical Society [hereafter, MSHS]; Haynes Johnson, *In The Absence of Power: Governing America* (New York: Viking Press, 1980), 162–163.

41. Farrell, *Tip O'Neill and the American Century*, 460; Hubert Humphrey to David Broder, November 25, 1974, HP-SF, Correspondence Files–Administrative 1974, Box 6, MSHS; Johnson, *In the Absence of Power*, 163–164. For Carter's diary comments on this meeting, see *Keeping Faith*, 77.

42. Katherine Schirmer to Stuart Eizenstat, December 3 and 4, 1976, Domestic Policy Staff [hereafter, DPS]–Al Stern's Files, Box 5, JCL; Eizenstat to Carter, February 15, 1977, DPS-Eizenstat, Box 315, JCL; "Water Resource Projects Message to Congress," February 21, 1977, APP.

43. Cecil Andrus to Carter, February 14, 1977, White House Central Files [hereafter, WHCF], Box NR14, JCL; Lance, *The Heart of the Matter*, 114 (quotation), 117–118.

44. Senator William Proxmire (D-WI) and others to Carter, February 14, 1977, Box 315, DPS-Eizenstat, JCL; Carter, *Keeping Faith*, 78–79.

45. Cabinet Minutes, October 3, 1978, James McIntyre Records, Box 2, JCL; "Veto of Energy and Water Development Appropriations Bill," October 5, 1978, APP.

46. Biven, *Jimmy Carter's Economy*, 69–70. See also Congressional Budget Office [hereafter, CBO], *The Disappointing Recovery* (Washington, DC: Government Printing Office, 1977).

47. Economic Policy Group, Memorandum to the President, "Economic Recovery Program," January 22, 1977, SSF-PHF, Box 4, JCL; "Economic Recovery Program Message to Congress," January 31, 1977, APP.

48. Charles Schultze, Memorandum to the President, "Economic Stimulus Package-Program Taxes," March 7, 1977, DPS-Eizenstat, Box 193, JCL; Schultze testimony, House Committee on the Budget, *Hearings on the Economy and the Stimulus Proposal*, 211.

49. Larry Klein to Stuart Eizenstat and Jerry Jasinowski, "Contemporary Economic Outlook," November 18, 1976, DPS-Eizenstat, Box 194, JCL; Walter Heller to Hubert Humphrey, January 3, 1977, and Humphrey to Heller, 23 January 1977, HP-SF, Correspondence Files-Legislative [hereafter, CF-L], 1977–1978, Box 3.

50. Stuart Eizenstat to Jimmy Carter, November 14, 1976, Box 4, JPP, JCL; Kaufman and Kaufman, *The Presidency of James Earl Carter Jr.*, 33–34; Biven, *Jimmy Carter's Economy*, 72; Gillon, *The Democrats' Dilemma*, 189–190.

51. Lance, *The Truth of the Matter*, 121; Jody Powell, "Notes for the Rebate Question," undated, SSF-PHF, Box 17, JCL; Walter Mondale to Carter, "Cranston Conversation," April 17, 1977, Box 17, SSF-PHF, JCL; "Interview with Jimmy Carter," November 29, 1982 [abbreviated version of Jimmy Carter Interview, CPP-MC] in Richardson, ed., *Conversations With Carter*, 245–246.

52. Christina D. Romer and David H. Romer, "What Ends Recessions?" in Stanley Fischer and Julio Rotemberg, eds., *NBER Macroeconomics Annual 1994* (Cambridge, MA: MIT Press, 1994), 35; "Remarks at the United Auto Workers' Convention in Los Angeles," May 17, 1977, APP.

53. Cabinet meeting minutes, February 14, 1977, SSF-PHF, Box 8, JCL; Farrell, *Tip O'Neill and the American Century*, Farrell, 459; Jimmy Carter to John McClellan, May 25, 1977, copy in HHSP, VIPC, Box 1, MSHS.

54. Bourne, *Jimmy Carter*, 432–433.

55. Eizenstat, Memorandum for the President, June 14, 1978, DPS-Eizenstat, Box 242, JCL.

56. Bourne, *Jimmy Carter*, 433–434; "Remarks at the United Auto Workers' Convention in Los Angeles," May 17, 1977, APP; Joseph A. Califano Jr., *Governing America: An Insider's Report from the White House and the Cabinet* (New York: Simon & Schuster, 1981), 142–144.

57. Kaufman and Kaufman, *The Presidency of James Earl Carter Jr.*, 102–105; Califano, *Governing America*, 89–119, 147–153; Califano to the President, May 15, 1978, SSF-PHF, Box 85, JCL.

58. Carter, *Keeping Faith*, 86–87; Califano, *Governing America*, 113–117.

59. Stuart Eizenstat and Joe Onek, Memorandum for the President, March 20, 1979, DPS-Eizenstat, Box 241, JCL; Califano, *Governing America*, 127–135; "National Health Plan: Message to Congress on Proposed Legislation," June 12, 1979,

APP; *Congress and the Nation, 1977–1980* (Washington, DC: Congressional Quarterly, 1981), 637.

60. Califano, *Governing America*, 320–354 (quote p. 334); Califano to Carter, April 11, 1977, DPS-Eizenstat, Box 314, JCL; Hamilton Jordan to Carter, April 11, 1977, SOF-Jordan, Box 37, JCL.

61. Laurence Lynn Jr. and David Whitman, *The President as Policymaker: Jimmy Carter and Welfare Reform* (Philadelphia: Temple University Press, 1981); James T. Patterson, "Jimmy Carter and Welfare Reform," in Fink and Graham, *The Carter Presidency*, 117–136.

62. Lynn Daft, Memorandum to Stuart Eizenstat, "OMB 1980 Food Stamp Budget Proposal," November 27, 1978, DPS-Eizenstat, Box 152, JCL; Christopher Edley to Stuart Eizenstat and Bert Carp, "Food and Nutrition Service (USDA) Budget Issues," November 20, 1978, DPS-Eizenstat, Box 152, JCL.

63. "The 'Welfare Reform' Charade," *Progressive*, August 1977, 6–7; "A Very Modest Proposal," *Nation*, August 20, 1977, 131–132; Lynn and Whitman, *The President as Policymaker*, 234–237; Frank Moore, Memorandum for the President, March 9, 1978, DPS-Eizenstat, Box 318, JCL.

64. Califano, *Governing America*, 336, 363; James McIntyre to Carter, "Incremental Welfare Reform: Administration Strategy," June 9, 1978, SSF-PHF, Box 92, JCL.

65. Carter, handwritten comment on Christopher Edley and Bill Spring to Eizenstat, May 23, 1979, DPS-Eizenstat, Box 317, JCL.

66. Margaret Weir, *Politics and Jobs: The Boundaries of Employment Policy in the United States* (Princeton, NJ: Princeton University Press, 1992), 134–140; Timothy Thurber, *The Politics of Equality: Hubert H. Humphrey and the African American Freedom Struggle* (New York: Columbia University Press, 1999), 233–247.

67. Charles Schultze to the President, May 23, 1977; Stuart Eizenstat to the President, May 24, 1977; Bert Lance to the President, May 31, 1977, SSF-PHF, Box 24, JCL.

68. Humphrey to Gus Hawkins, August 20, 1977, HHSP, Box 3, CF-L 1977–1978; Stuart Eizenstat and Charles Schultze to the President, "Negotiations on the Humphrey-Hawkins Bill," October 6, 1977, "Humphrey/Hawkins: Final Round," October 19, 1977, and "Final Steps on Humphrey-Hawkins," October 26, 1977, DPS-Eizenstat, Box 221, JCL; Schultze to the President, "CEA Weekly Report," March 18, 1978, SSF-PHF, Box 77, JCL; Frank Moore to the President, "Weekly Legislative Report," October 7, 1978, SSF-PHF, Box 105, JCL.

69. Stuart Eizenstat to the President, "The Full Employment and Balanced Growth Act of 1978," October 27, 1978, SSF-PHF, Box 105, JCL; "Remarks on Signing the Full Employment and Comprehensive Employment and Training Act Bills into Law," October 27, 1978, APP; Robert M. Collins, *More: The Politics of Economic Growth in Postwar America* (New York: Oxford University Press, 2000), 170–171.

70. Califano, *Governing America*, 368–383; "Remarks at the Social Security Amendments of 1977 Bill Signing Ceremony," December 20, 1977, APP.

71. Stuart Eizenstat and Frank Raines, Memorandum for the President, March 21, 1978, SSF-PHF, Box 77, JCL; Califano, *Governing America*, 386–389.

72. Robert Ball, Wilbur Cohen, and Nelson Cruikshank, Memorandum for the President, "Analysis of HEW/OMB Budget Proposals for FY'80 as they relate to Social Security Trust Fund Expenditures," December 19, 1978, Box 113, SSF-PHF, JCL; Stuart Eizenstat, Memorandum for the President, "Meeting with Nelson Cruikshank," January 15, 1979, Box 115, SSF-PHF, Box 115, JCL; Califano, *Governing America*, 391–397.

73. Califano, *Governing America*, 395.

74. Herbert Stein, *Presidential Economics: The Making of Economic Policy from Roosevelt to Clinton*, 3rd ed. (Washington, DC: AEI Press, 1994), 117.

75. Walter Mondale, Memorandum for the President, "Tax Reform," May 13, 1977, and Stuart Eizenstat and Bob Ginsburg, Memorandum for the President, "Assessment of Senator Kennedy's Tax Reform Package," July 14, 1977, DPS-Eizenstat, Box 287, JCL; Edward Kennedy, Memorandum for President Carter, "Politics of Tax Reform," September 22, 1977; DPS-Eizenstat, Box 288, JCL; Kennedy to Stuart Eizenstat, January 23, 1978, with attachment "Statement of Senator Edward M. Kennedy on the President's 1978 Tax Reform Program," January 21, 1978, DPS-Eizenstat, Box 289, JCL.

76. Stuart Eizenstat, Memorandum for the President, "Blumenthal/EPG Memo on Tax Bill," April 24, 1978, SSF-PHF, Box 82, JCL; Bob Ginsburg to Eizenstat, "Campaign against Steiger Proposal," June 27, 1978, and Michael Blumenthal, Memorandum for the President, "Status of the Tax Bill," September 20, 1978, DPS-Eizenstat, Box 289, JCL; Robert L. Bartley, *The Seven Fat Years and How To Do It Again* (New York: Free Press, 1995), 61–62.

77. Charles Schultze, Memorandum for the President, "Tax Meeting with Long and Ullman," October 11, 1978, SSF-PHF, Box 106, JCL; Jimmy Carter to Russell Long and Al Ullman, undated handwritten note, JPP, Box 40, JCL.

78. Edward Kennedy, "Memorandum for the President on the Revenue Act of 1978," October 11, 1978, SSF-PHF, Box 106, JCL; "Statement of Senator Edward M. Kennedy Calling for a Veto of the Tax Bill," October 18, 1978; George Meany to the President, October 20, 1978, SSF-PHF, Box 107, JCL; Charles Schultze, Memorandum for the President, "The Tax Bill," September 27, 1978, Stuart Eizenstat and Bob Ginsburg, Memorandum for the President, "Tax Strategy," October 10, 1978, DPS-Eizenstat, Box 289, JCL.

79. James McIntyre and Frank Moore, Memorandum to the President, "White House Budget Task Force," December 6, 1978, SSF-PHF, Box 111, JCL.

80. Charles Schultze, Memorandum for the President, "Friday Morning Meeting with Your Economic Advisers," December 7, 1977, SSF-PHF, Box 63, JCL; Michael Blumenthal and Charles Schultze, Memorandum for the President, July 24, 1978, SSF-PHF, Box 95, JCL.

81. James McIntyre interview, PCP-MC, 6, 59; Treasury Secretary Michael Blumenthal to the President, "Possible Further Cut in FY'79 Budget," undated, PHF-SSF, box 87, JCL; Ray Marshall, Memorandum to the President, "Economic Policy Decisions," October 25, 1977, Box 57, PHF-SSF, JCL; Mondale and Eizenstat to Carter, "U.S. Economic Recovery and Administration Economic Policies," May 4, 1977, DPS-Eizenstat, JCL, Box 197; Eizenstat and Bob Ginsburg to Carter, "Secretary Marshall's Memorandum on Economic Policy Decisions," November 2, 1977,

SSF-PHF, Box 57, JCL. In the spring of 1977, Hamilton Jordan advised Carter that the EPG was not an effective mechanism because it negotiated recommendations on the basis of its principals' different outlooks and constituencies. See Jordan to the President, untitled and undated (but about March 1977), SOF-Jordan, Box 34, JCL.

82. Charles Schultze, Memorandum to the President, "Economic and Budgetary Outlook for Fiscal Years 1979–1981," July 7, 1977, DPS-Eizenstat, Box 191, JCL.

83. Charles Schultze, Memorandum to the President, "Some Disturbing Thoughts about the Economic Outlook," May 6, 1978, SSF-PHF, Box 84, JCL. For further CEA reflections on the productivity slowdown, see two memoranda from Schultze to the president: "Economic and Fiscal Policy for FY 1980, and Implications for FY 1979," May 9, 1978, SSF-PHF, Box 85, JCL; and "Our Past Forecasts," December 14, 1979, SSF-PHF, Box 159, JCL.

84. Charles Schultze, Memorandum to the President, "An Outline of Short and Long Run Anti-inflation Strategy," October 17, 1979, SSF-PHF, Box 152, JCL.

85. "Anti-Inflation Program Address to the Nation," October 24, 1978, APP. For discussion of anti-inflation rationale of fiscal policy, see James McIntyre to Carter, "Talking Points for the President—Meeting with Cabinet and Major Agency Heads, May 25, 1978," May 24, 1978, SSF-PHF, Box 87, JCL (Carter underscored numerous parts of this briefing, including the statement "Unless we act very, very strongly to curb expenditures, the 1980 budget will be inflationary."); Carter Remarks, Minutes of Cabinet Meeting, October 3, 1978, James T. McIntyre Records, Box 2, JCL.

86. Michael Blumenthal to the President, September 27, 1978, Charles Schultze, "Anti-Inflation Program: Decision Memo," September 26, 1978, Stuart Eizenstat and Bob Ginsberg to the President, "Schultze Decision Memo on the Anti-Inflation Program," September 29, 1978, DPS-Eizenstat, Box 145, JCL. For media commentary on inflation, see "The Great Government Inflation Machine," *Business Week*, May 22, 1978, 106–119; "Inflation: Where Do We Go from Here?" *U.S. News and World Report*, October 2, 1978, 30–35, 50–51.

87. James McIntyre, "A 1980 Budget with No Real Growth," October 16, 1978, James McIntyre Records, Box 1, JCL; McIntyre, "The Economic and Budgetary Outlook for 1979 and 1980," October 25, 1978, SSF-PHF, Box 107, JCL; Rick Hutcheson to Carter, December 21, 1978 (outlining Stuart Eizenstat's views on McIntyre and Schultze, Memorandum for the President, "Projections of Interest Rates for the 1980 Budget"), SSF-PHF, Box 113, JCL; Eizenstat, Memorandum for Jim McIntyre, John White, Bo Cutter, "Budget Meeting with President," undated, DPS-Eizenstat, Box 152, JLC.

88. Anne Wexler to Hamilton Jordan, "Political Planning," May 30, 1978, SOF-Jordan, Box 40, JCL; Califano, Memorandum to the President, "Inflation and the Budget Strategy for Fiscal 1980," September 18, 1978, SSF-PHF, Box 105, JCL; Gillon, *The Democrats' Dilemma*, 256–259.

89. "Congressional Black Caucus Statement on Economic Policy," January 19, 1979, SOF-Louis Martin, Box 15, JCL. For the midterm convention, see Timothy Stanley, "Jimmy Carter and the Democratic Party, 1977–1981," Ph.D. dissertation, Cambridge University, 2007, 159–165.

90. Stuart Eizenstat, Memorandum for the President, "Defense Budget,"

December 18, Box 112, SSF-PHF, JCL; Eizenstat, Memorandum for the President, "Budget Deficit," January 2, 1979, SSF-PHF, JCL, Box 113.

91. Jimmy Carter to Congressman George Mahon, August 1, 1978, SSF-PHF, Box 97, JCL; James McIntyre to the President, "Defense Authorization Bill (H.R. 10929)," August 16, 1978, SSF-PHF, Box 99, JCL. See also Dennis S. Ippolito, *Uncertain Legacies: Federal Budget Policy from Roosevelt through Reagan* (Charlottesville: University Press of Virginia, 1990), 127–134.

92. U.S. Senate, Committee on Armed Services, *United States/Soviet Military Balance: A Frame of Reference for Congress* (Washington, DC: Government Printing Office, 1976), quotation p. 32; Central Intelligence Agency, *A Dollar Comparison of Soviet and U.S. Defense Activities, 1965–1975* (Washington, DC: CIA, 1976), 2, 5; *Department of Defense Annual Report, Fiscal Year 1980* (Washington, DC: Government Printing Office, 1979), 5. See also Charles W. Ostrom and Robin F. Marra, "U.S. Defense Spending and the Soviet Estimate," *American Political Science Review* 80 (September 1986), 819–842.

93. Sam Nunn, John Tower, and Henry Jackson to the President, August 2, 1979, WHCF, Box FO40 and FO42, JCL; Harold Brown and Jim McIntyre, Memorandum for the President, "The Defense Budget," September 10, 1979, and Frank Moore to the President, September 12, 1979, SSF-PHF, Box 146, JCL; McIntyre, Memorandum for the President, "SALT Testimony and the FY1981 Defense Budget," undated, James McIntyre Records, Box 1, JCL.

94. Christopher Conte, "Budget: Liberals Force Social Spending Hike," *CQWR*, May 26, 1979, 995–96; Steven Roberts, "Conferees Agree $29.9 Billion Deficit in Budget for 1980," *New York Times*, November 1, 1979, A1; Steven Roberts, "U.S. Budget for '80 Clears Congress after House Rejects Cuts by G.O.P.," *New York Times*, November 29, 1979, B21.

95. Stuart Eizenstat, Memorandum for the President, "Economic Decisions," March 1, 1980, SSF-PHF, Box 173, JCL; James McIntyre, Memorandum for the President, "1980 Supplemental Requests," April 28, 1980, James McIntyre Records, Box 39, JCL; *Budget of the United States Government Fiscal Year 2009: Historical Tables*, 124.

96. Calculations based on data in *Budget of the United States Government Fiscal Year 2009: Historical Tables*, table 8.8

97. Carrie Johnson, "How a Small Crusade Grew," *Washington Post*, February 14, 1979, A4; Alan Berlow, "Group Wants to Balance Nation's Checkbook," *CQWR*, February 17, 1979, 277–279. See also Iwan Morgan, "Unconventional Politics: The Campaign for a Balanced Budget Constitutional Amendment in the 1970s," *British Journal of American Studies* 32 (December 1998), 421–446; and Russell Caplan, *Constitutional Brinkmanship: Amending the Constitution by National Convention* (New York: Oxford University Press, 1988), 78–80.

98. Charles Schultze, "Some Social and Economic Effects of a Constitutional Amendment Mandating a Balanced Budget," February 15, 1979, James McIntyre Records, Box 1, JCL; "Balance-the-Budget Boom," *Newsweek*, February 12, 1979, 34 (includes Greenspan quote); Carter to [Attorney General] Griffin Bell, undated comment on Lawrence Tribe, "A 'Balanced Budget' Constitutional Convention," February 17, 1979, SSF-PHF, Box 120, JCL. See also Bruce Ackerman, "Unconstitutional

Convention," *New Republic*, March 3, 1979, 8; "Brown vs. the Board," *Time*, March 5, 1979, 39; Marvin Stone, "A Constitutional Convention?" *U.S. News and World Report*, March 12, 1979, 96.

99.   Morgan, "Unconventional Politics," 437–438; Senior Staff, Memorandum to the President, "Constitutional Convention/Balanced Budget Amendment," February 17, 1979, p. 21, SSF-PHF, Box 120, JCL [hereafter, Senior Staff, "Constitutional Convention"].

100.   Senior Staff, "Constitutional Convention," 22–23.

101.   Richard Moe, Memorandum to the President, "Constitutional Convention/Balanced Budget Amendment," February 17, 1979, SSF-PHF, Box 120, JCL; Senior Staff, "Constitutional Convention," 18–20.

102.   Lou Cannon, "Governor Brown Loses Battle for Budget Amendment," *Washington Post*, February 23, 1979, A1; T. R. Reid, "Balanced Budget Campaign Falters," *Washington Post*, May 29, 1979, A2; Morgan "Unconventional Politics," 427, 442–443.

103.   "Senator Muskie Criticizes States on Budget-Balancing Moves," *Washington Post*, February 14, 1979, A2; "Constitutional Convention May Not Reach Finish Line," *Washington Post*, February 25, 1979, A2.

104.   Richard Moe, Memorandum to the President, "Status Report on Constitutional Convention Effort," May 30, 1979, SSF-PHF, Box 134, JCL; "The President's News Conference of January 17, 1979," and "Remarks and a Question-and-Answer Session with American Press Institute Editors," March 30, 1979, APP.

105.   Charles Schultze, Memorandum to the President, "The Effect of Energy Prices on Overall Inflation," September 10, 1979, SSF-PHF, Box 146, JCL; Alfred Kahn, Memorandum to the President, "The Wage and Price Standards, First and Second Years," October 24, 1979, SSF-PHF, Box 153, JCL.

106.   Paul Volcker and Toyoa Gyohten, *Changing Fortunes: The World's Money and the Threat to America's Leadership* (New York: Times Books, 1992), 64; Biven, *Jimmy Carter's Economy*, 237–246.

107.   Alfred Khan, Memorandum to the President, "Taking Stock of Anti-Inflationary Policy," November 5, 1979, SSF-PHF, Box 155, JCL. For trenchant criticism of the lack of empirical evidence for "inflationary expectations" theory, see James Savage, *Balanced Budgets and American Politics* (Ithaca, NY: Cornell University Press, 1988), 42–47.

108.   Charles Schultze to the Economic Policy Group, December 13, 1979, James McIntyre, Memorandum to the President, "Implications of the Economic Outlook for the 1981 Budget Policy," December 14, 1979, Schultze, Memorandum to the President, "The Economic Assumptions to be Published in the Budget," December 17, 1979, all in SSF-PHF, Box 160, JCL.

109.   Eizenstat to Carter, December 21, 1979, and Carter's handwritten note on Eizenstat to the President, December 26, 1979, SSF-PHF, Box 161, JCL; Eizenstat, Memorandum to the President, "Defense Budget," December 5, 1979, SSF-PHF, Box 159, JCL.

110.   "The Peashooter War on Inflation," *New York Times*, January 31, 1980, A18; Martin Tolchin, "Reaction on Capitol Hill Splits along Party Lines," *New York Times*, January 29, 1980, A1; "Statement of Senator Edward M. Kennedy on the Carter

Administration Budget for Fiscal Year 1981," February 12, 1980, copy in SOF-Louis Martin, Box 79, JCL.

111. Lindley B. Richert, "Yields for Long-Term Obligations of U.S. Rise Decidedly Above 11% for the First Time," *Wall Street Journal*, January 30, 1980, 33; "The World Feels Worse after Doctor Volcker's Medicine," *Economist*, February 23, 1980, 89; "America's Bond Market Crash," *Economist*, March 8, 1980, 12–13. See also Aaron Wildavsky and Joseph White, *The Deficit and the Public Interest: The Search for Responsible Budgeting in the 1980s* (Berkeley and New York: University of California Press and Russell Sage Foundation, 1989), 28–30.

112. Daniel Hertzberg, "Troubled Houses," *Wall Street Journal*, February 22, 1980, 1; Olsen and other bankers' comments in Harry Anderson and others, "Fighting the Inflation 'Crisis,'" *Newsweek*, March 10, 1980, 24–26; Volcker quoted in Art Pine, "White House Aides Debate Budget Cuts in War on Inflation," *Washington Post*, February 24, 1980, A5. For editorial comment, see "A Lever against Inflation," *Washington Post*, February 24, 1980, B6; and "The Case for a New, and Balanced, Budget," *New York Times*, February 28, 1980, A22.

113. Art Pine and John Berry, "Carter's Economists Seeking to Balance the Budget for 1981," *Washington Post*, March 4, 1980, A1; Richard Levine and Robert Merry, "Carter's Plan May Calm Markets but Won't Be Quick Fix for Inflation," *Wall Street Journal*, March 10, 1980, 1; Eizenstat, Memorandum to the President, "Economic Decisions," March 1, 1980, SSF-PHF, Box 173, JCL.

114. "Message to Congress Transmitting Revisions to the Fiscal Year 1981 Budget," March 31, 1980, APP; Al From to Alfred Kahn, "Our 'New' Program," March 7, 1980, SSF-PHF, Box 174, JCL.

115. Gene Godley to William Miller and Frank Moore, "Economic Consultations," March 4, 1980, and Frank Moore to Economic Policy Group, "Summary of Economic Consultations with Members of Congress," March 5, 1980, SSF-PHF, Box 174, JCL; Stuart Eizenstat, Memorandum to the President, "Anti-Inflation Program," March 6, 1980, SSF-PHF, Box 173, JCL; Eizenstat, Memorandum to the President, "Congressional Budget Resolution," May 23, 1980, SSF-PHF, Box 188, JCL.

116. Wildavsky and White, *The Budget and the Public Interest*, 40–54; Ralph Schlosstein to Eizenstat, "General Purpose Fiscal Assistance Programs," March 11, 1980, DPS-Eizenstat, Box 153, JCL; Stuart Eizenstat to the President, May 26, 1980, SSF-PHF, Box 188, JCL.

117. Carter, *Keeping Faith*, 529–530.

118. Paul Abramson, John Aldrich, and David Rohde, *Change and Continuity in the 1980 Elections* (Washington, DC: Congressional Quarterly Press, 1982), 19–25; Andrew E. Busch, *Reagan's Victory: The Presidential Election of 1980 and the Rise of the Right* (Lawrence: University Press of Kansas, 2005), chapter 3; Stanley, "Jimmy Carter and the Democratic Party," 222–242.

119. James McIntyre, Memorandum to the President, "Current Status of the Budget Resolution," June 18, 1980, SSF-PHF, Box 193, JCL; Stuart Eizenstat, Memorandum to the President, "Our Economic Program and the Poor," July 9, 1980, SSF-PHF, Box 195, JCL.

120. Stuart Eizenstat and David Rubenstein, Memorandum to the President, "1980 Democratic Platform," June 17, 1980, SSF-PHF, Box 194, JCL; Eizenstat,

Memorandum to the President, "Platform Compromises," July 31 and August 5, 1980, SOF-Susan Clough, Box 38, JCL.

121.   Leonard Silk, "Carter, Jobs, and $12 Billion," *New York Times*, August 15, 1980, IV: 2; Elizabeth Drew, *Portrait of an Election: The 1980 Presidential Campaign* (New York: Simon & Schuster, 1981), 245–252, 253 (Carter quotation).

122.   Allan Mayer and others, "Reagan's Tax-Cut Ploy," *Newsweek*, July 7, 1980, 20; "Remarks at the Democratic Congressional Campaign Victory Luncheon," August 14, 1980, and "Remarks Accepting the Presidential Nomination at the 1980 Democratic National Convention," August 14, 1980, APP.

123.   Judith Stein, "The Locomotive Loses Power: The Trade and Industrial Policies of Jimmy Carter," in Fink and Graham, *The Carter Presidency*, 85.

124.   William Miller, Memorandum to the President, "Background for Meeting with Economic Advisers," July 30, 1980, SSF-PHF, Box 197, JCL; Steven Rattner, "Carter Seeks Recovery Plan to Help Business and Jobless; Revitalization Panel Named," *New York Times*, August 29, 1980, A1.

125.   "Remarks Announcing the Economic Renewal Program," August 28, 1980, APP; "White House Fact Sheet on Carter's Economic Program for 80's," *New York Times*, August 29, 1980, D12.

126.   Drew, *Portrait of an Election*, 319.

127.   Eizenstat to Carter, May 24, 1980, WHCF, Box BE-13, JCL; Clinton quoted in William Leuchtenburg, "Jimmy Carter and the Post–New Deal Presidency," in Davis and Graham, *The Carter Presidency*, 21.

128.   Poll data in William Schneider, "The November 4 Vote for President: What Did It Mean?" in Austin Ranney, ed., *The American Elections of 1980* (Washington, DC: American Enterprise Institute, 1981), 237–238. For the economic context of the election, see Hibbs, *The American Political Economy*, 191–195.

129.   William Leuchtenburg, *In the Shadow of FDR: From Harry Truman to Bill Clinton* (Ithaca, NY: Cornell University Press, 1993), 203.

130.   Seymour Melman, "Jimmy Hoover?" *New York Times*, February 7, 1979, A21; Sidney Weintraub, "Carter's Hoover Syndrome," *New Leader*, March 24, 1980, 18.

131.   O'Neill, *Man of the House*, 314.

Chapter 4. Ronald Reagan: Coexisting with the Deficit

1.   "Transcript of Reagan Speech Outlining Five-Year Economic Program for U.S.," *New York Times*, September 10, 1980, B4.

2.   "Address Before a Joint Session of Congress on the State of the Union," January 25, 1983, APP.

3.   Lou Cannon's three biographies offer the most authoritative assessment of Reagan's life: *Reagan* (New York: Putnam, 1982); *Governor Reagan: His Rise to Power* (New York: Public Affairs, 2003); and *President Reagan: The Role of a Lifetime* (New York: Simon & Schuster, 1991). The most valuable revisionist biography is John P. Diggins, *Ronald Reagan: Fate, Freedom, and the Making of History* (New York: Norton, 2007). Reagan's two volumes of memoirs are also essential sources: (with Richard Hubler) *My Early Life: or Where's the Rest of Me?* (London: Sidgwick & Jackson, 1981); and *An American Life* (London: Hutchinson, 1990).

4. Reagan, *An American Life*, 20–21, 106–115, 231–232, 129–130. See also Robert M. Collins, *Transforming America: Politics and Culture during the Reagan Years* (New York: Columbia University Press, 2007), 31–32, 53–54, 80–81, 202–203; Stephen Vaughn, *Ronald Reagan in Hollywood: Movies and Politics* (New York: Cambridge University Press, 1994); Thomas W. Evans, *The Education of Ronald Reagan: The General Electric Years and the Untold Story of his Conversion to Conservatism* (New York: Columbia University Press, 2006).

5. Sidney Blumenthal, *The Rise of the Counter-Establishment: From Conservative Ideology to Political Power* (New York: Harper & Row, 1986), 284.

6. See, in particular, Hugh Heclo, "Ronald Reagan and the American Public Philosophy," in Elliot Brownlee and Hugh Davis Graham, eds., *The Reagan Presidency: Pragmatic Conservatism and Its Legacies* (Lawrence: University Press of Kansas, 2003), 17–39; and Diggins, *Ronald Reagan*, 37–54.

7. "Reagan's first inaugural address as governor of California," January 5, 1967, www.cnn.com/SPECIALS/2004,reagan/stories/speech.archive/cal.inaug.html.

8. Reagan, *An American Life*, 66–67, 120 (quotation); "Remarks Accepting the Presidential Nomination at the Republican National Convention in Detroit," July 17, 1980, APP.

9. Robert Dallek, *Ronald Reagan: The Politics of Symbolism* (Cambridge, MA: Harvard University Press, 1984), 39–53 (quotation p. 53); Cannon, *Governor Reagan*.

10. "Revenue Control and Tax Deduction, submitted to the California Legislature by Governor Ronald Reagan," March 12, 1973, quoted in Diggins, *Ronald Reagan*, 175.

11. Cannon, *Governor Reagan*, 368–379; Robert M. Collins, *More: The Politics of Economic Growth in Postwar America* (New York: Oxford University Press, 2000), 206–207; Amos Kiewe and Davis W. Houck, *A Shining City on a Hill: Ronald Reagan's Economic Rhetoric, 1951–1989* (New York: Praeger, 1991), 94–102.

12. "Remarks at a Rally Supporting the Proposed Constitutional Amendment for a Balanced Budget," July 19, 1982, APP.

13. See Reagan radio talks, "Spending," July 6, 1977, "Government Cost," July 6, 1977, "The Golden Fleece," October 2, 1979, in Kiron K. Skinner, Annelise Anderson, and Martin Anderson, *Reagan's Path to Victory: The Shaping of Ronald Reagan's Vision: Selected Writings* [henceforth *RPtV*] (New York: Free Press, 2004), 176–179, 482–483.

14. Kiewe and Houck, *A Shining City on a Hill*, 116–117; Cannon, *Reagan*, 202–204; Richard P. Nathan, Fred C. Doolittle, and Associates, *Reagan and the States* (Princeton, NJ: Princeton University Press, 1987), 47–48. See also Reagan to Mr. and Mrs. Fitzgerald, circa November 1980, and to Mr. and Mrs. Richard A. Stetson, February 10, 1982, in Kiron K. Skinner, Annelise Anderson, and Martin Anderson, eds., *Reagan: A Life in Letters* [hereafter, *RLIL*] (New York: Free Press, 2003), 340–342.

15. "Address before a Joint Session of the Alabama State Legislature in Montgomery," March 15, 1982, APP.

16. Reagan to William H. Hoyerman, November 10, 1981, *RLIL*, 300. For a critique of debt monetization, see James Savage, *Balanced Budgets and American Politics* (Ithaca, NY: Cornell University Press, 1988), 24–33.

17. Reagan radio talks, "Indexing," June 15, 1977, and "Money," June 29, 1979, in Kieron K. Skinner, Annelise Anderson, Martin Anderson, eds., *Reagan: In His Own Hand* [hereafter, *RIHOH*] (New York: Free Press, 2001), 261–262 (quotation p. 261), 272–274; "Remarks at the 1980 Presidential Campaign Debate," October 28, 1980, APP.

18. See Reagan radio talks, "National Security," November 29, 1977, "Budget," March 13, 1978, "Brainwashing II," August 7, 1978, "Nuclear Carrier," October 31, 1978, in *RPtV*, 233–234, 276–277, 352–353, 370–371.

19. Elizabeth Drew, "Reporter at Large: 1980: Reagan," *New Yorker*, March 24, 1980, 71; "Mr. Minister," September 23, 1984, *RIHOH*, 496. See also Edmund Morris, *Dutch: A Memoir of Ronald Reagan* (New York: Harper Collins, 1999), 435–436; and Peter Schweizer, *Reagan's War: The Epic Story of His Forty-Year Struggle and Final Triumph over Communism* (New York: Random House, 2002), 138–152.

20. Martin Anderson, *Revolution* (San Diego: Harcourt Brace Jovanovich, 1987), 336.

21. Reagan, *An American Life*, 333.

22. Anderson, *Revolution*, 114–121 (quotation p. 116); Collins, *More*, 191–197.

23. For supply-side tracts, see Jude Wanniski, *The Way the World Works* (Morristown, NJ: Polyconomics, 1978); Jack Kemp, *An American Renaissance: A Strategy for the 1980s* (New York: Harper & Row, 1979); Bruce Bartlett, *Reaganomics: Supply-Side Economics in Action* (Westport, CT: Arlington House, 1981); and Paul Craig Roberts, *The Supply-Side Revolution: An Insider's Account of Policymaking in Washington* (Cambridge, MA: Harvard University Press, 1984).

24. Kemp, *American Renaissance*, 49–76; Bartlett, *Reaganomics*, 125–135; David A. Stockman, *The Triumph of Politics: How the Reagan Revolution Failed* (New York: Harper & Row, 1986), chapter 2; Anderson, *Revolution*, 161–163.

25. Reagan, *An American Life*, 231–232; Edwin Meese III, *With Reagan: The Inside Story* (Washington, DC: Regnery Gateway, 1992), 123.

26. Kemp, *American Renaissance*, 77–96 (quotation p. 96). See also Roberts, *The Supply-Side Revolution*, 95–98.

27. Reagan to Clair Burgerner, 1980 (otherwise undated), in *RLIL*, 294.

28. Collins, *More*, 177–178; U.S. Congress, Committee on the Budget, House of Representatives and Senate Budget Committee, United States Senate, *Leading Economists' Views of Kemp-Roth*, Joint Committee Print, 95: 2 (Washington, DC: Government Printing Office, 1978).

29. Wanniski, *The Way the World Works*, chapter 6; Robert L. Bartley, *The Seven Fat Years and How to Do It Again* (New York: Free Press, 1995), 57–59, 169–173; Herbert Stein, *Presidential Economics: The Making of Economic Policy from Roosevelt to Clinton*, 3rd ed. (Washington, DC: AEI Press, 1994), 246–248.

30. "Taxes," October 18, 1977, *RIHOH*, 277; "Exchange with Reporters on the Program for Economic Recovery," February 19, 1981, APP.

31. Charls Walker, "Summary of Discussion" in Martin Feldstein, ed., *American Economic Policy in the 1980s* (Chicago: University of Chicago Press, 1994), 224–225; W. Elliot Brownlee and C. Eugene Steuerle, "Taxation," in Brownlee and Graham, eds., *The Reagan Presidency*, 160–161.

32. Cannon, *President Reagan*, 236–238; Anderson, *Revolution*, 246–249.

33. James Pfiffner, *The Strategic Presidency: Hitting the Ground Running*, 2nd ed. (Lawrence: University Press of Kansas, 1996), 104.

34. Gregory B. Mills, "The Budget: A Failure of Discipline," in John L. Palmer and Isabel V. Sawhill, *The Reagan Record: An Assessment of America's Changing Domestic Priorities* (Cambridge, MA: Ballinger, 1984), 111–114; Joseph White and Aaron Wildavsky, *The Deficit and the Public Interest: The Search for Responsible Budgeting in the 1980s* (Berkeley: University of California Press, 1989), 108–110, 153–155.

35. Dennis S. Ippolito, *Uncertain Legacies: Federal Budget Policy from Roosevelt through Reagan* (Charlottesville: University Press of Virginia, 1990), 58–67.

36. White and Wildavsky, *The Deficit and the Public Interest*, 169–170; Kevin D. Hoover and Steven M. Sheffrin, "Causation, Spending, and Taxes: Sand in the Sandbox or Tax Collector for the Welfare State," *American Economic Review* 82 (March 1992), 25.

37. "America's New Beginning: A Program for Economic Recovery," in James Tobin and Murray Weidenbaum, eds., *Two Revolutions in Economic Policy: The First Economic Reports of President Kennedy and Reagan* (Cambridge, MA: MIT Press, 1988), 291–317. See also Murray L. Weidenbaum, *Confessions of a One-Armed Economist* (St. Louis: Center for the Study of American Business, Washington University, 1983), 9–11, 14–18; Stockman, *The Triumph of Politics*, 92–99; and William A. Niskanen, *Reaganomics: An Insider's Account of the Policies and the People* (New York: Oxford University Press, 1988), 4–12.

38. Data for "rosy scenario" data drawn from "America's New Beginning," 316, and *Budget of the United States Government, Fiscal Year 2009: Historical Tables*.

39. Data based on calculations in Ippolito, *Uncertain Legacies*, 59. For the revenue explanation of the deficit, see Paul Krugman, *Peddling Prosperity: Economic Sense and Nonsense in the Age of Diminished Expectations* (New York: Norton, 1994), 152–155. David Stockman offers a conservative confirmation of this in "Summary of Discussion," in Feldstein, ed., *American Economic Policy in the 1980s*, 226–227.

40. James M. Poterba, "Federal Budget Policy in the 1980s," in Feldstein, ed., *American Economic Policy in the 1980s*, 238–240; Andrew Busch, *Ronald Reagan and the Politics of Freedom* (Lanham, MD: Rowman & Littlefield, 2001), chapter 5; Lawrence Lindsey, *The Growth Experiment: How the New Tax Policy Is Transforming the U.S. Economy* (New York: Basic Books, 1990), chapter 7.

41. Data drawn from *Budget of the United States Government Fiscal Year 2009: Historical Tables*, tables 1.3, 2.2, 2.3, and 3.1.

42. John A. Farrell, *Tip O'Neill and the Democratic Century* (Boston: Little, Brown, 2001), 561; John W. Sloan, *The Reagan Effect: Economics and Presidential Leadership* (Lawrence: University Press of Kansas, 1999), 151.

43. Max Friedersdorf to Reagan, "Meetings with Selected Democratic Members of the House of Representatives, May 4, 1981," May 1, 1981, Legislative Affairs Office Records, OA13528, Ronald Reagan Presidential Library [hereafter, RRL]; White and Wildavsky, *The Deficit and the Public Interest*, 113–136; James A. Baker III with Steve Fiffer, *"Work Hard, Study … and Keep Out of Politics!" Adventures and Lessons from an Unexpected Public Life* (New York: Putnam, 2006), 177–179.

44. White and Wildavsky, *The Deficit and the Public Interest*, 138; Stuart Eizenstat, "The Hill's Budget Stampede," *Washington Post*, June 21, 1981, C1; *Congressional Quarterly Almanac 1981* (Washington, DC: Congressional Quarterly, 1981), 257–258; Richard Darman, Memorandum to the President, "Meeting with the Legislative Strategy Group, June 18, 1981," June 17, 1981, White House Staff and Office Collections [hereafter, WHSOC]-Craig Fuller Files [hereafter, CFF], OA10972, RRL.

45. Richard Darman, Note for the File, "Next Steps Re. Budget Reconciliation," June 18, 1981, WHSOC-CFF, OA10972, RRL; "Suggested Talking Points in Telephone Calls to Congressmen" (June–July 1981), Presidential Handwriting File [hereafter, PHF], Presidential Telephone Calls [hereafter, PTC], Box 1, Files 3–4, 1981, RRL; Barrett, *Gambling With History*, 161–163, 168.

46. Richard Darman, Memoranda to the President, "Meeting of Legislative Strategy Group, May 12, 1981," May 11, 1981, and "Tax Meeting with Democratic Leadership," June 1, 1981, WHSOC-CFF, OA10972, RRL; Murray Weidenbaum, "Reagan and Economic Policy-Making" in Kenneth W. Thompson, ed., *Reagan and the Economy: Nine Intimate Perspectives* (Lanham, MD: University Press of America, 1994), 7. For a view that 10:10 was the best deal possible, see Dave Gergen to Jim Baker, Mike Deaver, and Ed Meese, "The Tax Cut," May 18, 1981, WHSOC-CFF, OA10972, RRL.

47. Ken Duberstein to Max Friedersdorf, "The Tax Battle in the House," July 14, 1981, and Elizabeth Dole to James Baker, "Tax Coalition Update," WHSOC-M. B. Oglesby Files, OA8618, RRL; Suggested Talking Points in Telephone Calls to Congressmen, PHF, PTC, Box 1, Files 3–7, 1981, RRL; "Address to the Nation on Federal Tax Reduction," July 27, 1981, APP. For public reaction to Reagan's address, see Lou Cannon and Kathy Sawyer, "President's Speech Has Hill Switchboards Ablaze," *Washington Post*, July 29, 1981, A1; and Ellie McGrath, "Tracking the Great Persuader," *Time*, August 10, 1981, 14.

48. Stockman, *The Triumph of Politics*, 124–125, 132–133; Weidenbaum quoted in Howard E. Shuman, *Politics and the Budget: The Struggle between the President and Congress*, 3rd ed. (Englewood Cliffs, NJ: Prentice Hall, 1992), 271.

49. Secretary of Defense, *Annual Report to the Congress, Fiscal Year 1987* (Washington, DC: Department of Defense, 1986), 13, 18.

50. Ippolito, *Uncertain Legacies*, 134–141; Daniel Wirls, *Buildup: The Politics of Defense in the Reagan Era* (Ithaca, NY: Cornell University Press, 1992), 31–55.

51. Stockman, *The Triumph of Politics*, 107–108, 276–278; Barrett, *Gambling with History*, 176.

52. Stockman, *The Triumph of Politics*, 269–299 (quotation p. 274); Richard Darman, *Who's in Control? Polar Politics and the Sensible Center* (New York: Simon & Schuster, 1996), 93–98. Reagan's conviction that the public supported higher military spending was unshakeable. When later confronted with poll findings showing three-to-one majorities in favor of balancing the budget over expanding defense, he recalled the popularity of his 1980 campaign statements that he would always put the nation's security ahead of deficit control: "I never gave that answer to an audience that I did not get enthusiastic applause." "Interview with Reporters from the *Los Angeles Times*," January 20, 1982, APP.

53. Cannon, *President Reagan*, 244–251; Niskanen, *Reaganomics*, 37–39.

54. Stockman, *The Triumph of Politics*, 306–321 (quotation p. 319); Darman, *Who's in Control?* 98–100; Baker, "Work Hard, Study…", 179–182.

55. William Greider, "The Education of David Stockman," *Atlantic Monthly* (December 1981), 27–54; Baker, "Work Hard, Study…", 165–171; Darman, *Who's in Control?* 103–110. For discussions of a scaled-down program, see Darman's "Fall Offensive" memoranda to the Legislative Strategy Group, October 29 and 30, and November 5, 1981, WHSOC-CFF, OA10972, RRL.

56. Stockman, *The Triumph of Politics*, 9.

57. Ibid., 11.

58. Friedman quoted in *Fortune*, May 19, 1980, 79; Ronald Reagan, *The Reagan Diaries* [hereafter, *RD*], edited by Douglas Brinkley (New York: HarperCollins, 2006), 86.

59. Greider, "The Education of David Stockman," 46–47. See also John M. Berry, "'Trickle-Down' Theory Suffers from Its Name," *Washington Post*, January 10, 1982, A4.

60. Lesley Gelb, "The Mind of the President," *New York Times Magazine*, October 6, 1985, 32. For Reagan's changing position on the deficit, see "The President's News Conference," November 10, December 17, 1981, APP; Darman, *Who's in Control?* 101–102.

61. Daniel Patrick Moynihan to James Wright, January 27, 1984, James Wright Papers [hereafter, JWP], Box 724, Texas Christian University [hereafter, TCU]; Daniel Patrick Moynihan, "Reagan's Bankrupt Budget," *New Republic*, December 31, 1983, 18–21; Daniel Patrick Moynihan, *Miles To Go: A Personal History of Social Policy* (Cambridge, MA: Harvard University Press, 1996), 11.

62. James Wright Interview (by Ben Proctor) [hereafter, JWI], April 16, 1983, April 29, 1982, JWP, Series III, Box 1208, TCU; Hollings quoted in Savage, *Balanced Budgets and American Politics*, 229. On the same theme, see journalist William Raspberry, "Problem? What Problem?" *Washington Post*, July 22, 1985, A13.

63. "Address to the Nation on the Economy," February 5, 1981, APP.

64. Barrett, *Gambling with History*, 341; Martin Feldstein, "American Economic Policy in the 1980s: A Personal View," in Feldstein, ed., *American Economic Policy in the 1980s*, 59; Transcript, "Meet the Press," April 15, 1984, WHSOF-William Niskanen Files, OA10875, RRL; Darman, *Who's in Charge?* 80.

65. George E. Peterson, "Federalism and the States: An Experiment in Decentralization," in Palmer and Sawhill, eds., *The Reagan Record*, 217–259; Nathan and Doolittle, *Reagan and the States*, 61–64.

66. J. Steven Rhodes to Richard Williamson, "Local Government Problems," October 7, 1981, and Richard Williamson to James Baker and Michael Deaver, "Our Deteriorating Relations with State and Local Officials," November 16, 1981, WHSOC-Michael Deaver Files, OA7621, RRL; Richard S. Williamson, "The 1982 New Federalism Negotiations," *Publius* 13 (Spring 1983), 31.

67. *RD*, 61, 119.

68. Farrell, *Tip O'Neill and the Democratic Century*, 570–573; 581–586; JWI, September 7, 1981, Box 1208, JWP, TCU; "A Test of Wills," *U.S. News and World Report*, February 22, 1982, 19. The AFL-CIO wrote to all members of Congress on

February 25, 1982, proposing an alternative budget to "provide for job-creating anti-recession programs" by reversing the 1981 tax cuts and defense expansion. Copy in WHSCOC-M. B. Oglesby Files, OA8616, RRL.

69. White and Wildavsky, *The Deficit and the Public Interest*, 118–121, 207–208, 218–220; Richard F. Fenno Jr., *The Emergence of a Senate Leader: Pete Domenici and the Reagan Budget* (Washington, DC: CQ Press, 1991), 57–76; Jack Nelson, "GOP Fears Loss of Senate: Reagan Told Rising Deficits Pose a Threat to Majority," *Kansas City Times*, March 17, 1982, A1.

70. Stockman, *The Triumph of Politics*, 305; Interview with Bob Dole, "'This Is a Tough Budget' for Congress to Swallow," *U.S. News and World Report*, February 22, 1982, 23–24; Dole remarks on *Face the Nation*, February 28, 1982, Robert Dole Senatorial Papers [hereafter, RDSP], 329-90-143, Box 28, Robert J. Dole Institute of Politics [hereafter, RJDIP]; George Hager and Edgar Pianin, *Mirage: Why Neither Democrats nor Republicans Can Balance the Budget, End the Deficit, and Satisfy the Public* (New York: Times Books, 1997), 124–125.

71. Barrett, *Gambling with History*, 344–348; White and Wildavsky, *The Deficit and the Public Interest*, 228–231; Stockman, *The Triumph of Politics*, 353.

72. Savage, *Balanced Budgets and American* Politics, 258; *RD*, 71; Allen Schick, *The Federal Budget: Politics, Policy, Process*, rev. ed. (Washington, DC: Brookings Institution, 2000), 92.

73. White and Wildavsky, *The Deficit and the Public Interest*, 236–237.

74. "The Summit That Failed," *Time*, May 10, 1982, 11; JWI, April 29, 1982, Series III, Box 1208, TCU; *RD*, 82.

75. Cabinet Council on Economic Affairs to Reagan, "Balanced Budget-Tax Limitation Constitutional Amendment," April 19, 1982, White House Office of Records Management [hereafter, WHORM]-Cabinet Meetings, Box 3, RRL.

76. "Remarks at a Rally Supporting the Proposed Constitutional Amendment for a Balanced Federal Budget," July 19, 1982, APP; Reagan telephone calls to various senators, August 4, 1982, and to various House members, September 24, 25, and 30, PHF, Series IV, Presidential Telephone Calls, Box 3, RRL; Nadine Cohodas, "Senate Narrowly Approves Balanced Budget Amendment, But House Adoption Doubtful," *CQWR*, August 7, 1982, 1887–1888, 1890; White and Wildavsky, *The Deficit and the Public Interest*, 276–284.

77. "Making Amends," *Time*, April 12, 1982, 19; "Amendment on the Budget Still Pushed," *Wall Street Journal*, October 19, 1982.

78. White and Wildavsky, *The Deficit and the Public Interest*, 241–249; Fenno, *The Emergence of a Senate Leader*, 95–125.

79. Jake H. Thompson, *Bob Dole: The Republicans' Man for All Seasons* (New York: Primus, 1996), 123–126; "A No-Fingerprints Tax Bill," *Newsweek*, August 9, 1982, 23; Farrell, *Tip O'Neill*, 589.

80. Elizabeth Dole to Edwin Meese, James Baker, and Michael Deaver, "Tax Bill Recap," July 22, 1982, WHSOC-Michael Deaver Files, OA7621, RRL; Kenneth Duberstein to Reagan, "Meeting with the Senate/House Republican Leaders," August 3, 1982, "Meeting with Selected Republican Members of the House of Representatives," August 9, 1982, "Meeting with Selected House Democrats on the Tax Issue," August 18, 1982, WHSOC-Kenneth Duberstein Files, OA13258, RRL; "Address to

the Nation on Federal Tax and Budget Reconciliation Legislation," August 16, 1982, APP; "Calling Plays for the Gipper," *Time*, August 23, 1982, 8.

81. Dale Tate, "Congress Clears $98.3 Billion Tax Increase," *CQWR*, August 21, 1982, 2035–2046; Walter Isaacson, "Scoring on a Reverse," *Time*, August 30, 1982, 14–18.

82. Jerry Tempalski, "Revenue Effects of Major Tax Bills," Office of Tax Analysis Working Paper No. 81 (Washington, DC: U.S. Treasury, 2003).

83. Henry Reuss, "Supply-Side's Sunk," *New York Times*, August 30, 1982; Roberts, *The Supply-Side Revolution*, 226–245; Wendell Gunn to James Baker, ". . . The Last Remaining Supply-Siders," March 8, 1983, WHSOC-James Baker Files [hereafter, JBF], Box 5, RRL; Jack Kemp, "What This Fight Is About," *Washington Post*, August 12, 1982, A23; William V. Roth, "In Defense of the Tax Bill," *New York Times*, August 15, 1982, D21.

84. *RD* (April 28, 1982), 82. The tax delay had been proposed by, among others, Ernest Hollings in a letter to Reagan on March 10, 1982, copy in WHOSC-CFF, OA10972, RRL. For Reagan's no-surrender view on personal taxes, see Reagan to Dole, June 2, 1982, RDSP, 329-90-044, Box 7, RJDIP; Meese, *With Reagan*, 143–144; Reagan to Alfred Kingon, July 28, 1982, *RLIL*, 314; *RD* (April 27, 1982), 82.

85. Stockman, *Triumph of Politics*, 356; Brownlee and Steurle, "Taxation," 162–163; Reagan to Dole, February 24, 1983, RDSP, 329-90-044, Box 7, RJDIP.

86. Roberts, *The Supply-Side Revolution*, 301–304; House Republicans (61 signatories) to Reagan, July 27, 1982, WHSOC-M. B. Oglesby Files, OA8619, RRL; Reagan to John Lofton, July 30, 1982, PHF, Presidential Records, Box 3, RRL.

87. White and Wildavsky, *The Deficit and the Public Interest*, 300–309.

88. Reagan, *An American Life*, 314, and "Hurry Up and Wait," *Wall Street Journal*, July 8, 1993; Meese, *With Reagan*, 143–147; Don Regan, *For the Record: From Wall Street to Washington* (San Diego: Harcourt Brace Jovanovich, 1988), 182–184.

89. Murray Weidenbaum, Memorandum to the President, "Economic Situation and Outlook," May 12, 1981, WHORM, FG 010-01, RRL. For similar expressions of concern, see Beryl Sprinkel, Memorandum for the Cabinet Council on Economic Affairs, "Domestic Monetary Policy," April 24, 1981, WHORM-Cabinet Council on Economic Affairs, OA8637, RRL; Donald Reagan, Memorandum for the President, "Current Monetary Policy," May 12, 1981, WHORM-Cabinet Meetings, FG010-01, RRL; and Clyde Farnsworth, "Regan Expects Higher Interest Rate and Cites Harm to Budget Already," *New York Times*, May 7, 1981, A1.

90. Niskanen, *Reaganomics*, 168–169; Lawrence Kudlow, Memorandum for the Cabinet Council on Economic Affairs, "Financial and Economic Update," January 18, 1982, WHSOC-CFF, OA10972, RRL.

91. John Berry, "Banking Panel Attacks Volcker on Tight Money," *Washington Post*, July 22, 1981, E1; Albert Hunt and Dennis Farney, "GOP, Upset by High Interest Fees, Returns to Congress with Talk of Credit Controls," *Wall Street Journal*, September 10, 1981, 3; Meese, *With Reagan*, 155–156; Paul Volcker and Toyoa Gyohten, *Changing Fortunes: The World's Money and the Threat to America's Leadership* (New York: Random House, 1992), 175.

92. Lawrence Kudlow to James Baker, "Monetary Discussion," January 30, 1982, WHSOC-CFF, OA1092, RRL; Jonathan Fuerbringer, "Volcker Cautions That Big

Deficits Imperil Recovery," *New York Times*, January 27, 1982, A1; Arthur Burns to Reagan, January 7, 1982, PHF, Presidential Records, Box 2, RRL; Alan Greenspan, untitled enclosure in "Briefing Book for Long-Range Planning Meeting, Camp David, February 5, 1982," WHSOC-Richard Darman Files, Box 1, RRL.

93. Regan, *For the Record*, 172–173, 178; Reagan to Justin Dart, April 12, 1982, PHF, Presidential Records, Box 3, RRL; Reagan to Alfred Kingon, June 25, 1982, *RLIL*, 594.

94. Paul Volcker, "Commentary," 149, and Michael Mussa, "U.S. Monetary Policy in the 1980s," in Feldstein, ed., *American Economic Policy in the 1980s*, 114–117; Donald F. Kettl, *Leadership at the Fed* (New Haven, CT: Yale University Press, 1986), 183.

95. "Remarks in Billings, Montana, at a Celebration Marking the Centenary of Billings and Yellowstone County," August 11, 1982, and "Radio Address to the Nation on the Economy," August 28, 1982, APP; Darman, *Who's in Control?* 113.

96. William Poole, Lawrence Kudlow, Manuel Johnson, and Robert Dederick, Memorandum for T-1, "Forecast," December 13, 1982, WHSOF-CFF, OA10972, RRL; Martin Feldstein, Memorandum to the President, "The New Economic Forecast," December 30, 1982, and "Alternative Deficit Forecasts," January 13, 1983, WHSOC-Martin Feldstein Files [hereafter, MFF] , OA9815, RRL; Darman, *Who's in Control?* 118.

97. "Big Deficit Cut Urged by Group of U.S. Leaders," *New York Times*, January 20, 1983, A1; "The Federal Deficit," *New York Times*, January 25, 1983, A24.

98. "Address before a Joint Session of Congress on the State of the Union," January 25, 1983, APP; Darman, *Who's in Control?* 118–119; Reagan to Martin Feldstein, July 21, 1983, *RLIL*, 317.

99. Niskanen, *Reaganomics*, chapter 7; James E. Alt, "Leaning into the Wind or Ducking out of the Storm? U.S. Monetary Policy in the 1980s," in Alberto Alesina and Geoffrey Carliner, eds., *Politics and Economics in the Eighties* (Chicago: University of Chicago Press, 1991), 41–77; Sloan, *The Reagan Effect*, 229–235, 237–244.

100. Michael J. Boskin, *Reagan and the Economy: The Successes, Failures, and Unfinished Agenda* (San Francisco: ICS Press, 1987), 20–21, 152–153, 186; Benjamin M. Friedman, *Day of Reckoning: The Consequences of American Economic Policy under Reagan and After* (New York: Random House, 1988), 10, 156–158, 258–261.

101. Volcker and Gyohten, *Changing Fortunes*, 178–179, 248. For internal administration discussion, see William Poole, Memorandum for the Cabinet Council on Economic Policy, "The Real Rate of Interest," October 26, 1984, WHOSC-William Poole Files, OA10699, RRL. As David Stockman had previously foreseen, high real interest rates also increased the cost of servicing the national debt. See Minutes, Cabinet Council on Economic Affairs Meeting of September 23, 1982, WHSOC-William Poole Files, OA10699, RRL.

102. "Playing It Loose at the Summit," *Time*, May 30, 1983, 15; Martin Feldstein to Reagan, "European Concerns at Williamsburg," May 4, 1983, WHOSC-MFF, OA9815, RRL.

103. Arthur Burns to Reagan, January 20, 1984, and Reagan to Burns, February 22, 1984, PHF, Presidential Records, Box 8, RRL.

104. Martin Feldstein, Memoranda to the President, "Tax Increases and Economic

Recovery," October 18, 1983, "Deficits and Inflation," January 8, 1984, "Tax Rates and Tax Revenue," January 10, 1984, WHSOC-MFF, OA9815, RRL; Diary entry for January 9, 1984, *RD*, 210.

105. Paul Bluestein, "Reagan Economist Blames Deficit Growth on Arms Outlays, Lower Taxes, Debt Costs," *Wall Street Journal*, November 22, 1983, 3; Feldstein to Ed Meese, December 2, 1983, and Memoranda to the President, "Economic Rhetoric and Business Confidence," September 19, 1983, "*New York Times* Story," September 23, 1983, and "Taking the Offensive on the Budget Deficit," January 2, 1984, WHSOC-MFF, OA9815, RRL.

106. Richard Neustadt, *Presidential Power and the Modern Presidents: The Politics of Leadership from Roosevelt to Reagan* (New York: Free Press, 1990), 278–279.

107. Steven M. Gillon, *The Democrats' Dilemma: Walter F. Mondale and the Liberal Legacy* (New York: Columbia University Press, 1992), 308. See also Walter Mondale, "The Re-Education of Walter Mondale," *New York Times Magazine*, November 8, 1981, 67.

108. Revenue enhancement came from acceleration of scheduled payroll tax increases ($40 billion), extension of the federal income tax to the benefits of wealthier recipients ($30 billion), extending the payroll tax to new federal employees ($20 billion), and raising it on the self-employed ($18 billion). For discussion, see C. Eugene Steuerle, *The Tax Decade: How Taxes Came to Dominate the Public Agenda* (Washington, DC: Urban Institute, 1991), 61–64; and Martha Derrick and Steven M. Teles, "Riding the Third Rail: Social Security Reform," in Brownlee and Graham, eds., *The Reagan Presidency*, 196–204 (quotation p. 202).

109. Mary Jo Jacobi, Memorandum for Jim Cicconi, "Current Tax and Budget Measures," April 26, 1984, WHSOF-M.B. Oglesby Files, OA13000, RRL; American Business Conference and other groups (including American Council for Capital Formation, U.S. Chamber of Commerce, and National Association of Manufacturers) to the President, April 25, 1984 (also sent to every member of Congress) in ibid.; David Stockman, Memorandum for the President, "Enrolled Bill H.R. 4170 – Deficit Reduction Act of 1984," WHSOF-Edwin Meese Files, OA11837, RRL; Darman to Richard Wirthlin, "Tax Strategy," July 26, 1984, WHSOC-JBF, Box 7, RRL. For analysis of DEFRA, see Ippolito, *Uncertain Legacies*, 71–72, 74; and White and Wildavsky, *The Deficit and the Public Interest*, 401–405.

110. Richard Wirthlin to Edwin Meese, James Baker, and Michael Deaver, "Federal Deficits," August 30, 1983, WHOSC-Michael Deaver Files, OA11584, RRL. For other poll data, see "Survey List A1: Public Preferences on the Budget," in Gary C. Jacobson, "Meager Patrimony: The Reagan Era and Republican Representation in Congress," in Larry Berman, ed., *Looking Back on the Reagan Presidency* (Baltimore: Johns Hopkins University Press, 1989), 303–306.

111. "Do Deficits Matter?" *Fortune*, March 5, 1984, 113; Richard Wirthlin to James Baker et al., "Major Findings of the July National Survey," July 16, 1984, WHOSC-JBF, Box 9, RRL.

112. "Address Accepting the Presidential Nomination at the Democratic National Convention in San Francisco," July 19, 1984, APP.

113. Memorandum (no author), "Darman and Hopkins Tax Memos," July 30, 1984, WHOSC-JBF, Box 8, RRL; James Baker, Memorandum to the President, August 9,

1984, WHOSC-JBF, Box 9, RRL; "Statement Expressing Opposition to a Federal Tax Increase," August 12, 1984, APP; Hager and Pianin, *Mirage*, 129–130.

114. Martin Schram, "GOP Shot across Democrats' Bow Fizzles in the Barrel," *Washington Post*, August 11, 1984, A8; Hedrick Smith, *The Power Game: How Washington Works* (London: Fontana, 1989), 501, 1026 n36; "Remarks Accepting the Presidential Nomination at the Republican National Convention in Dallas, Texas," August 23, 1984, APP.

115. "Mondale Unveils Detailed Proposal to Slash Deficit," *Washington Post*, September 11, 1984, A1.

116. Margaret Tutwiler to James Baker et al., "Democratic Convention Coverage," July 20, 1984, WHOSC-JBF, Box 9, RRL; and "Statement by Secretary Donald Reagan," *Reagan-Bush '84 News*, September 4, 1984, copy in RDSP, 329-89-198, Box 94, RJDIP.

117. For Reagan campaign economic rhetoric, see Kiewe and Houck, *A Shining City on a Hill*, 169–173.

118. Reagan, *An American Life*, 325; Reagan to Charles Price, November 29, 1984, PHF, Presidential Records, RRL; Pat Towell, "Pentagon Asks $313.7 Billion for Defense Build-Up," *CQWR*, February 9, 1985, 229–235.

119. Hedrick Smith, "Bob Dole's Big Gamble," *New York Times Magazine*, June 30, 1985, 27; "Senator Dole and the Deficit 'Black Hole,'" *NBC Nightly News*, February 2, 1984, Transcript, RDSP, 329-89-198, Box 94, RJDIP.

120. Stockman, *The Triumph of Politics*, 386–389.

121. Fenno, *The Emergence of a Senate Leader*, 211–217, 241; Warren Rudman, *Combat: Twelve Years in the U.S. Senate* (New York: Random House, 1996), 75–79; Hager and Pianin, *Mirage*, 136–139 (quotation p. 139).

122. Jacqueline Calmes, "House, with Little Difficulty, Passes '86 Budget Resolution," *CQWR*, May 25, 1985, 975.

123. "Address to the Nation on the Federal Budget and Deficit Reduction," April 24, 1985, APP; White and Wildavsky, *The Deficit and the Public Interest*, 433; "Radio Address to the Nation on the Federal Budget," June 22, 1985, APP.

124. David Rogers and Jane Meyer, "Plan to End Social Security Rises for '86 Dropped by Reagan, Leaders of Congress," *Wall Street Journal*, July 10, 1985, 2; Regan, *For the Record*, 278–279; Rudman, *Combat*, 79–80; JWI, July 12, 1985, Box 1209, JWP, TCU. Although Reagan's diary entry for July 9 did not mention the bargain with O'Neill, it contained the cryptic comment with regard to the budget talks: "Made some headway but Tip was his usual pol. self." See *RD*, 341.

125. Jonathan Fuerbringer, "GOP Rift Widens as Dole Criticizes Reagan and House," *New York Times*, July 13, 1985, A1; Farrell, *Tip O'Neill*, 656–657; Fenno, *The Making of a Senate Leader*, 217–218.

126. Stockman, *The Triumph of Politics*, 390; Hager and Pianin, *Mirage*, 144.

127. Procurement contract authorization fell from a Reagan-era peak of $96.8 billion in FY1985 to $80.2 billion in FY1987, where it basically stabilized for the remaining Reagan budgets. Reagan's FY1986 appropriation request for SDI was cut by 25 percent, and his authorization request for MX deployments was capped at 50 percent. See Ippolito, *Uncertain Legacies*, 143–144.

128. *Congressional Record*, August 1, 1985, S10375-77; Elizabeth Wehr, "Congress Cuts Budget by More Than $55 Billion," *CQWR*, August 3, 1985, 1524.

129. Schuman, *Politics and the Budget*, 277–303; Steven Schier, *A Decade of Deficits: Congressional Thought and Fiscal Action* (Albany: State University of New York Press, 1992), 105–128; Jasmine Farrier, *Passing the Buck: Congress, the Budget, and Deficits* (Lexington: University Press of Kentucky, 2004), 82–128.

130. Rudman, *Combat*, 90, 98.

131. Dennis Thomas to Donald Regan, "Gramm-Rudman/Tax Reform," December 3, 1985, WHSOC-Dennis Thomas Files, Box 7, RRL; Susan Woodward to Beryl Sprinkel, "Debt Ceiling Battle," November 4, 1985, WHSOC-Beryl Sprinkel Files, OA17744, RRL.

132. James Baker, "*Work Hard, Study . . . ,*" 431; Thomas Moore to Donald Regan, "Current Fiscal Policy and the Economy," December 5, 1985, WHSOC-Beryl Sprinkel Files, OA17737, RRL. For the Plaza Accord, see Sloan, *The Reagan Effect*, 208–214.

133. "Radio Address to the Nation on the Major Legislative Achievements of 1985," December 21, 1985; James Miller to Bob Dole, April 21, 1986, RDSP, Majority Leader Records [hereafter, MLR], Box 21. For comment on Reagan's intransigence on defense, see Democratic Study Group, "The Reagan Defense Budget," March 7, 1986, copy in JWP, Box 724, TCU; and Sheila Burke to Bob Dole, "Call from Senator Domenici/Budget Resolution," May 13, 1986, RDSP, MLR, Box 21, RJDIP.

134. Shuman, *Politics and the Budget*, 294. For the accounting gimmicks, see Allen Schick, *The Capacity to Budget* (Washington, DC: Urban Institute Press, 1990), 205–206.

135. Jim Wright, Personal Taped Reflections, June 28, 1987, JWP, Series III, Box 1210, TCU. For GOP dissatisfaction, see Domenici to Dole, June 19, 1987, RDSP, MLR, Box 22, RJDIP.

136. William Gray to Jim Wright, July 29, 1987, JWP, Box 745, TCU; Bill Hoagland to Peter Domenici, July 1, 1987, copy, RDSP, MLR, Box 22, RJDIP.

137. "Radio Address to the Nation on the Federal Debt Ceiling Increase and Deficit Reduction," September 26, 1987, APP; Schick, *The Capacity to Budget*, 206.

138. For more positive assessment of GRH, see Sung Deuk Hahn, Mark Kamlet, David Mowery, and Tsai-Tsu Su, "The Influence of the Gramm-Rudman-Hollings Act on Federal Budgetary Outcomes, 1986–1989," *Journal of Policy Analysis and Management* 11, No. 2 (1992), 207–234; and James Savage and Amy Verdun, "Reforming Europe's Stability and Growth Pact: Lessons from the American Experience in Macrobudgeting," *Review of International Political Economy* 14 (December 2007), 848–852 (quotation p. 851).

139. Brownlee and Steuerle, "Taxation," 169–171; Regan to Reagan, November 27, 1984, PHF, Presidential Records, Box 10, RRL; James Baker to Reagan, "Tax Reform," May 10, 1985, PHF, Presidential Records, Box 11, RRL. See also James Baker, "*Work Hard, Study . . . ,*" 216–237; Darman, *Who's in Control?* 145–163; and Regan, *For the Record*, 192–219, 281–286.

140. For political maneuvering as TRA came for enactment, see Beryl Sprinkel, Memorandum for Donald Regan, "Tax Reform Priorities," July 9, 1986, WHSOF-

Beryl Sprinkel Files, OA17746, RRL; and Pat Buchanan, Memorandum for the President, "Tax Reform—Capital Gains," July 21, 1986, PHF, Presidential Records, Box 16, RRL. Jeffrey H. Birnbaum and Allan S. Murray, *Showdown at Gucci Gulch: Lawmakers, Lobbyists, and the Unlikely Triumph of Tax Reform* (New York: Vantage Books, 1988), is an excellent narrative by two journalists.

141. Brownlee and Steuerle, "Taxation," 168–174 (quotation p. 173); Friedman, *Day of Reckoning*, 289–293; Lawrence H. Summers, "A Fair Tax Act That's Bad for Business," *Harvard Business Review* 65 (March/April 1987), 53–58.

142. White and Wildavsky, *The Deficit and the Public Interest*, 502–505.

143. Ibid., 504.

144. Hobart Rowen, *Self-Inflicted Wounds: From LBJ's Guns and Butter to Reagan's Voodoo Economics* (New York: Times Books, 1994), 312–321; "When the Bull Turned," *Economist*, October 24, 1987, 11–12; Larry Martz and others, "After the Meltdown of '87," *Newsweek*, November 2, 1987, 10–16. For a prediction of troubles to come, see Stephen Marris, *Deficits and the Dollar: The World Economy at Risk* (Washington, DC: Institute for International Economics, 1985).

145. Alan Greenspan, *The Age of Turbulence: Adventures in a New World* (New York: Penguin Press, 2007), 105–110; Jeffrey A. Frankel, "The Making of Exchange Rate Policy in the 1980s," in Feldstein, *American Economic Policy in the 1980s*, 305–307.

146. Quoted in Schier, *A Decade of Deficits*, 126.

147. "America's Budget Mouse," *Economist*, November 28, 1987, 12; Lawrence Haas, "Chorus of Bronx Cheers for Budget Pact," *National Journal*, November 28, 1987, 3048.

148. Schick, *The Capacity to Budget*, 188–189.

149. "Address before a Joint Session of the Congress on the State of the Union, January 25, 1988, APP; Shuman, *Politics and the Budget*, 300–301.

150. Shuman, *Politics and the Budget*, 301–302; Schier, *A Decade of Deficits*, 127–128.

151. "Remarks on the Veto of the National Defense Authorization Act, Fiscal Year 1989, and a Question-and-Answer Session with Reporters," August 3, 1987, APP; Pat Towell, "Veto of Defense Bill Ups the Political Ante," *CQWR*, August 6, 1988, 2143–2145; Wirls, *Buildup*, 208–209.

152. "Inaugural Address," January 21, 1985, APP.

153. Jonathan Fuerbringer, "Budget-Balancing Amendment Loses," *New York Times*, March 26, 1986, D20; Nadine Cohodas, "Balanced-Budget Amendment Killed by One Vote," *CQWR*, March 29, 1986, 704. Reagan's efforts to persuade John Chaffee (R-RI), Hatfield, John Heinz (R-PA), Stafford, and—his only success—Jeff Bingaman (D-NM) are described in his handwritten notes on William Ball to Reagan, "Recommended Telephone Calls," March 12 and 25, 1986, PHF, Series IV, Box 8, RRL.

154. Richard Wirthlin to James Baker, "Reagan-Bush '84—Campaign Decisions," June 11, 1984, WHOSC-JBR, Box 9, RRL; "Interview with Reporters from the *Los Angeles Times*," January 20, 1982, APP.

155. Russell Caplan, *Constitutional Brinkmanship: Amending the Constitution by National Convention* (New York: Oxford University Press, 1988), 86–87.

156. "Remarks Announcing America's Economic Bill of Rights," July 3, 1987, APP. Other fiscal elements in the proposed program included a line-item veto and truth-in-spending legislation requiring the costs of every new program to be deficit-neutral by including equal amounts of offsets. Reagan also warned of the likelihood of a constitutional convention without speedy congressional enactment of an amendment proposal in a televised national statement: "Address on the Iran Arms and Contra Aid Controversy and Administration Goals," August 12, 1987, APP.

157. "A Convention That's Uncalled For," *New York Times*, August 13, 1987, A24.

158. James Davidson, "Response to Lane Kirkland and Phyllis Schlafly: Convention Best Route to a Balanced Budget," *Dollars & Sense* 16 (February 1985), 6–8; "Schlafly Aims to Block Parley on Constitution," *Washington Times*, February 23, 1987, A1.

159. *Washington Post*, May 9, 1988, D6; author's telephone interview with David Keating, NTU vice president, November 20, 1996.

160. Sean Wilentz, *The Age of Reagan: A History, 1974–2008* (New York: Harper-Collins, 2008), 3–4; Barack Obama, *The Audacity of Hope: Thoughts on Reclaiming the American Dream* (New York: Crown Publishers, 2006), 32–33.

161. Schick, *The Capacity to Budget*, 118–120. General Social Surveys conducted by the National Opinion Research Center showed respondents saying that the United States spent "too much" on welfare declined from 59 percent in 1980 to 43 percent in 1988.

162. Stein, *Presidential Economics*, 326–330; Friedman, *Day of Reckoning*, 194–196, 206–208; Krugman, *Peddling Prosperity*, 126–127. See also Iwan Morgan, "Reaganomics and Its Legacy," in Cheryl Hudson and Gareth Davies, eds., *Ronald Reagan and the 1980s: Perceptions, Policies, Legacies* (New York: Palgrave, 2008), 101–118.

163. Aaron Wildavsky, "President Reagan as Political Strategist," *Society* (May/June, 1987), 58.

164. Schick, *The Capacity to Budget*, 200.

165. JWI, February 13, 1986, JWP, Box 1209, TCU.

166. Krugman, *Peddling Prosperity*, 128, 158–161.

167. Benjamin M. Friedman, "U.S. Fiscal Policy in the 1980s: Consequences of Large Budget Deficits at Full Employment," in James M. Rock, ed., *Debt and the Twin Deficits Debate* (Mountain View, CA: Bristlecone Books, 1991), 150.

Chapter 5. George H. W. Bush: Compromising on the Deficit

1. "Acceptance Speech for the Presidency," August 18, 1988, APP; "Remarks on the Federal Budget Agreement and Exchange with Reporters in Honolulu, Hawaii," October 27, 1990, APP.

2. Richard Darman, *Who's in Control? Polar Politics and the Sensible Center* (New York: Simon & Schuster, 1996), 222–223.

3. Congressional Budget Office, *The Economic and Budget Outlook: Fiscal Years 1992–1996* (Washington, DC: CBO, 1991), 13–16, 66.

4. For biographical detail, see Herbert S. Parmet, *George Bush: Lone Star Yankee* (New York: Scribner, 1997); and George Bush with Victor Gold, *Looking Forward: An Autobiography* (New York: Doubleday, 1987).

5. See, for example, David Mervin, *George Bush and the Guardianship Presidency* (London: MacMillan, 1996), chapter 1; and John Robert Greene, *The Presidency of George Bush* (Lawrence: University Press of Kansas, 2000), chapter 10.

6. David Hoffman, "Bush Becomes Pragmatic Champion of the Reagan Revolution," *Washington Post*, March 5, 1988, A12.

7. Jack W. Germond and Jules Witcover, *Whose Broad Stripes and Bright Stars? The Trivial Pursuit of the Presidency, 1988* (New York: Warner Books, 1989), 141–142; Jake Thompson, *Bob Dole: The Republicans' Man for All Seasons* (Primus: New York, 1996), 168–171.

8. Parmet, *George Bush*, 220. For Bush's somewhat pallid definition of his political philosophy in his campaign autobiography, see *Looking Forward*, 80–81, 203–204.

9. "Remarks on the Administration's Domestic Policy" June 12, 1991, APP; Bush to Roger Porter, "The Vision Thing," March 14, 1992, and Porter, Memorandum to the President, "Response to Your Note," March 24, 1992, ID#5787 and 5786, Bush Presidential Records [hereafter, BPR], George Bush Presidential Library [hereafter, GBL].

10. Peggy Noonan, *What I Saw at the Revolution: A Political Life in the Reagan Era* (New York: Ivy Books, 1990), 298.

11. "Massachusetts Mirage: Spending," and "Massachusetts Mirage: Taxes," in Bush-Quayle Debate Book, September 17, 1988, Robert Teeter Collection, Box 54, GBL; Dick Morris, *Behind the Oval Office: Getting Reelected against the Odds* (Los Angeles: Renaissance Books, 1999), 7–8.

12. George Bush to James Martin, September 10, 1988, Office of Management and Budget [hereafter, OMB] Records, Director's Office Files FY1989, Control File 029931, Record Group [hereafter, RG] 51, National Archives.

13. Kevin Phillips, *American Dynasty: Aristocracy, Fortune, and the Politics of Deceit in the House of Bush* (New York: Penguin, 2004), 125.

14. For Bush's business career, see Bush, *Looking Forward*, 46–73; Parmet, *George Bush*, 62–86; and Phillips, *American Dynasty*, 119–125.

15. Fred Barnes, "On the Supply-Side: Bush Comes Down in Corporate Camp," *Business Month*, September 1988; John Kenneth Galbraith, *The Culture of Contentment* (Boston: Houghton Mifflin, 1992), 27.

16. Robert Bryce, *Cronies: Oil, The Bushes, and the Rise of Texas, America's Superstate* (New York: Public Affairs, 2004), 92–95; Daniel Yergin, *The Prize: The Epic Quest for Oil, Money & Power* (New York: Touchstone, 1992), 754.

17. Michael Duffy and Dan Goodgame, *Marching in Place: The Status Quo Presidency of George Bush* (New York: Simon & Schuster, 1992), 283.

18. Parmet, *George Bush*, 299–300.

19. Jeffrey H. Birnbaum and Alan S. Murray, *Showdown at Gucci Gulch: Lawmakers, Lobbyists, and the Unlikely Triumph of Tax Reform* (New York: Random House, 1987), 89–94; James Baker to Reagan, "Fundamental Tax Reform," May 23, 1985, White House Office of Records Management-Subject File, FI101-02, Ronald Reagan Presidential Library.

20. Frederick M. Reeder, to Bush, October 8, 1990; Bush to Reeder, October 20, 1990, White House Office of Records Management [hereafter, WHORM]-Subject File [hereafter, SF], FI004, ID#189059, BPR, GBL.

21. See, for example, Colin Campbell, "The White House and the Cabinet under the 'Let's Deal' Presidency," in Colin Campbell and Bert Rockman, eds., *The Bush Presidency: First Appraisals* (Chatham, NJ: Chatham House, 1991), 185–222; Kerry Mullins and Aaron Wildavsky, "The Procedural Presidency of George Bush," *Political Science Quarterly* 107, No. 1 (1992), 31–62.

22. Ruth Shalit, "What I Saw at the Devolution," *Reason*, March 9, 1993, 27–33; Dan Quayle, *Standing Firm: A Vice-Presidential Memoir* (New York: HarperCollins, 1994), 94.

23. Maureen Dowd and Thomas Friedman, "The Bush and Baker Boys," *New York Times Magazine*, May 6, 1990, 64.

24. Lawrence I. Barrett, *Gambling with History: Reagan in the White House* (New York: Doubleday, 1983), 377; Duffy and Goodgame, *Marching in Place*, 229–230; Parmet, *George Bush*, 232.

25. Gail Sheehy, *Character: America's Search for Leadership*, rev. ed. (New York: Bantam Books, 1990), 198.

26. Bush, *Looking Forward*, 204.

27. "Inaugural Address," January 20, 1989, APP.

28. Darman, *Who's in Control?* 191–192; Bob Woodward, "Origin of the Tax Pledge: In '88 Bush Camp Was Split on 'Read My Lips' Vow," *Washington Post*, October 4, 1992, A1, 22; and "No-Tax Vow Scuttled Anti-Deficit Mission," *Washington Post*, October 5, 1992, A1, 8–9.

29. Juan Williams, "A White House at War with Itself: The Budget Debacle," *Washington Post*, July 29, 1990, C4. For a vituperative attack on Darman by a conservative White House aide, see Charles Kolb, *White House Daze: The Unmaking of Domestic Policy in the Bush Years* (New York: Free Press, 1994), 51–123.

30. David Mervin, *George Bush and the Guardianship Presidency* (London: Macmillan, 1996), 129–131 (Sununu quotation p. 130); Bush to Kathleen Darman, October 17, 1990, in George Bush, *All the Best, George Bush: My Life in Letters and Other Writings* [henceforth, *ATB*] (New York: Scribner, 1999), 482.

31. Darman, *Who's in Charge?* 206–207; Quayle, *Standing Firm*, 192.

32. Michael Boskin to Bush, "Summary of Camp David Meeting," WHORM-SF, BE004, ID#00002-01, BPP, GBL. The business participants, notably Paul O'Neill of Alcoa and John Akers of IBM, were broadly supportive of a tax increase. The economists were more evenly divided. Kathryn Eikhoff, Martin Feldstein, Herbert Stein, and Paul Volcker were strongly in favor, but Arthur Laffer, Beryl Sprinkel, and Jude Wanniski were opposed.

33. Alan Greenspan, *The Age of Turbulence: Adventures in a New World* (New York: Penguin Press, 2007), 113; Darman, *Who's in Control?* 201–202.

34. Darman, *Who's in Control?* 222–223; John Berry and Barry Bluestein, "Price Rise Is Fastest since 1987: Fed Chief Finds Data 'Disturbing,'" *Washington Post*, February 23, 1989, A1; Bob Woodward, *Maestro: Greenspan's Fed and the American Boom* (New York: Simon & Schuster, 2000), 59–61.

35. Duffy and Goodgame, *Marching in Place*, especially chapter 1; Mervin, *George Bush and the Guardianship Presidency*, 218.

36. Quoted in Duffy and Goodgame, *Marching in Place*, 85.

37. Bert A. Rockman, "The Leadership Style of George Bush," in Campbell and

Rockman, *The Bush Presidency*, 18 (quotation), 27–29; and Mervin, *George Bush and the Guardianship Presidency*, 44–46, 208–210.

38. Greenspan, *The Age of Turbulence*, 113 (quotation), 118–120; Duffy and Goodgame, *Marching in Place*, 245.

39. Diary entry, October 6, 1990, in *ATB*, 480–481.

40. Woodward, "Origin of the Tax Pledge," A22 (Rollins quote); Lee Walczak and Douglas Harbrecht, "Them's Fightin' Words, George," *Business Week*, July 9, 1990, 25 (Sasser quote). For Democratic glee at forcing Bush's U-turn, see George Stephanopoulos, *All Too Human: A Political Education* (Boston: Little, Brown, 1999), 23.

41. Mervin, *George Bush and the Guardianship Presidency*, 47; B. Dan Wood, *The Politics of Economic Leadership: The Causes and Consequences of Presidential Rhetoric* (Princeton, NJ: Princeton University Press, 2007), 27, 29.

42. Fred I. Greenstein, *The Presidential Difference: Leadership Style from FDR to Clinton* (New York: Free Press, 2000), 169. Dan Quayle also lamented that the Bush White House "lost the chance to define itself through clear, focused rhetoric." See Quayle, *Standing Firm*, 94.

43. Thomas DeFrank and others, "An Interview with Bush," *Newsweek*, January 30, 1989, 32.

44. Interview transcript, Bush and Don Feder [*Boston Herald*] May 18, 1989, White House Press Office, Press Office Internal Transcripts, Box 133, BPR, GBL. See also David Demarest to John Sununu, "Budget Briefing for Conservatives," February 13, 1989, Office of Public Liaison, Kathryn Rust Files, ID#01800, BPR, GBL.

45. "Bush-Quayle 88—Issue Background," Robert Teeter Collection, Box 55, BPR, GBL; Darman, *Who's in Control?* 198–199.

46. Woodward, "No-Tax Vow Scuttled Anti-Deficit Mission," A1; Roger Porter, Assistant to the President for Economic and Domestic Policy, telephone interview with the author, July 23, 2007.

47. Woodward, "No-Tax Vow Scuttled Anti-Deficit Mission," A1; Darman, *Who's in Control?* 209.

48. Darman, *Who's in Control?* 206–210 (quotation p. 210); *ATB*, 420–421.

49. Darman, *Who's in Control?* 208.

50. Ibid., 214; David Rapp, "Bush Sets Course with a $1.16 Trillion Budget," and "Highlights of the President's Budget Proposal," *CQWR*, February 11, 1989, 247–256.

51. Rapp, "Bush Sets Course with a $1.16 Trillion Budget," and "Democrats Skeptical of Bush but Offer Cooperative Spirit," *CQWR*, February 11, 1989, 248, 280–281.

52. David Rapp, "Bipartisan Budget Lets Everyone Be a Winner—For Now," *CQWR*, April 22, 1989, 880; and "House, Senate Adopt Versions of $1.17 Trillion Plan," *CQWR*, May 6, 1989, 1026–1028.

53. Greene, *The Presidency of George Bush*, 61–78; Paul Quirk, "Domestic Policy: Divided Government and Cooperative Leadership," in Campbell and Rockman, *The Bush Presidency*, 69–91. For media comment, see Julie Rovner, Macon Morehouse, and Phil Kuntz, "Bush's Social Policy: Big Ideas, Little Money," *CQWR*, December 10, 1988, 3459–3465; and Janet Hook and Chuck Alston, "Mixed Signals, 'Agenda Gap,' Plague Bush's First Year," *CQWR*, November 4, 1989, 2921–2926.

54. William W. Kaufmann and Lawrence J. Korb, *The 1990 Defense Budget*

(Washington, DC: Brookings Institution, 1989); Daniel Wirls, *Buildup: The Politics of Defense in the Reagan Era* (Ithaca, NY: Cornell University Press, 1992), 212–217.

55. Lawrence J. Korb, "The 1991 Defense Budget," in Henry J. Aaron, ed., *Setting National Priorities: Policy for the Nineties* (Washington, DC: Brookings Institution, 1991), 121–123.

56. Korb, "The 1991 Defense Budget," 123; John D. Morrocco, "Defense Cuts May Force Trade-off between New Systems and Upgrades," *Aviation Week and Space Technology*, December 4, 1989, 22.

57. Edward J. Kane, *The S&L Insurance Mess: How Did It Happen?* (Washington, DC: Urban Institute Press, 1989); James Barth, *The Great Savings and Loans Debacle* (Washington, DC: AEI Press, 1991); L. William Seidman, *Full Faith and Credit: The Great S&L Debacle and Other Washington Sagas* (New York: Times Books, 1993).

58. U.S. House Committee on Appropriations, *Hearings before a Subcommittee of the Committee of Appropriations*, 100th Congress, 2nd Session, April 19, 1988, 1119. With 441 thrifts book-insolvent by the end of 1986, Congress created the Financing Corporation (FICO) in 1987 to provide funding to the insolvent FSLIC by issuing long-term bonds, which were to be repaid by the S&L industry. In 1996 all federally insured financial institutions (including banks) became responsible for paying off these bonds. See Timothy Curry and Lynn Shibut, "The Cost of the Savings and Loan Crisis: Truth and Consequences," *FDIC Banking Review*, No. 2 (2000), 27–28.

59. Robert Sherrill, "The Looting Decade: S&Ls, Big Banks, and Other Triumphs of Capitalism," *Nation*, November 19, 1990, 589.

60. "Bush Faces Powerful Foes as Bailout Battle Begins," *CQWR*, February 18, 1989, 303–310; Barbara Rudolph, "Special Report: The Savings and Loans Crisis," *Time*, February 20, 1989, www.time.com.

61. Catherine Yang, "Bush's S&L Plan: Full of Good Intentions—and Holes," *Business Week*, February 20, 1989, 32; Seidman, *Full Faith and Credit*, 209; Greene, *The Presidency of George Bush*, 82.

62. Richard W. Stevenson, "G.A.O. Puts Cost of S&L Bailout at Half a Trillion Dollars," *New York Times,* July 6, 1996, A34; Curry and Shibut, "The Cost of the Savings and Loan Crisis: Truth and Consequences," 26–35.

63. Larry Lindsey to John Sununu, "A Preliminary Analysis of the S&L Situation," February 23, 1990, WHORM-SF, FI002, ID#00002-001, BPR, GBL; Darman, "Big Issues Re: Budget—For Discussion 2/13/90," Staff & Office Files [hereafter, SOF]-Office of Chief of Staff [hereafter, CoS], ID#CF00374, BPR, GBL; Daniel P. Franklin, *Making Ends Meet: Congressional Budgeting in the Age of Deficits* (Washington, DC: CQ Press, 1993), 64.

64. Barbara Sinclair, "Governing Unheroically (and Sometimes Unappetizingly): Bush and the 101st Congress," in Campbell and Rockman, *The Bush Presidency*, 166; Howard E. Shuman, *Politics and the Budget: The Struggle between the President and the Congress*, 3rd ed. (Englewood Cliffs, NJ: Prentice Hall, 1992), 309.

65. Jackie Calmes with John Cranford, "Bush, Democrats Face Off on Bill to Cut Deficit," *CQWR*, October 7, 1989, 2610–2613; Ronald Elving, "Capital Gains Cut Dead for the Year," *CQWR*, November 18, 1989, 3141; George Hager and Eric

Pianin, *Mirage: Why Neither Democrats nor Republicans can Balance the Budget, End the Deficit, and Satisfy the Public* (New York: Times Books, 1997), 171 (Mitchell quotation).

66. Darman to Bush, "Final Sequester Report and Order," October 16, 1989, WHORM-SF, FI004, Box 21, BPR, GBL.

67. Jackie Calmes, "Leaders Press for Final Deal on Deficit Reduction Bill," *CQWR*, November 18, 1989, 3137–3138.

68. "Statement on Deficit Reduction in Fiscal Year 1990," November 2, 1989, APP; Jackie Calmes, "Bush, Congress Reach Deal on Deficit-Reduction Bill," and Ronald Elving, "Lawmakers Came Full Circle to Goal Set in April," *CQWR*, November 25, 1989, 3221–3225.

69. Darman, "Budget Status Overview for Discussion 11/28/89," SOF-CoS, ID#CF00374, BPR, GBL.

70. Darman, "The '91 Budget for Discussion 8/15/89," SOF-CoS, ID#CF00374, BPR, GBL.

71. Darman, *Who's in Control?* 227.

72. Diary entry, July 24, 1990, *ATB*, 475. For an insightful analysis, see Stuart Luxon, "A Question of Leadership: 'Read My Lips: No New Taxes,'" M.Sc. dissertation, University of London, 2007.

73. Richard G. Darman, "Director's Introduction to the New Budget," in *Budget of the United States Government, Fiscal Year 1991* (Washington, DC: Government Printing Office, 1990), esp. 7, 19–21.

74. Darman, *Who's in Charge?* 236–237; Kolb, *White House Daze*, 89–90; "The President's Press Conference," January 24, 1990, APP.

75. Darman, "Defense Budget for Discussion 11/7/89," SOF-CoS, ID#CF00374, BPR, GBL; Andrew Rosenthal, " Congress Is Warned by Bush Not to Cut Pentagon Budget," *New York Times*, January 13, 1990, A11; Gerald Seib, "Conservatives Argue over Best Ways to Spend a Peace Dividend and Whether There Is One," *Wall Street Journal*, January 31, 1990, 18. For the "peace dividend" debate, see William Kaufmann, *Glasnost, Perestroika, and U.S. Defense Spending* (Washington, DC: Brookings Institution, 1990); Wirls, *Buildup*, 217–223, and Bruce S. Jansson, *The Sixteen-Trillion Dollar Mistake: How the U.S. Bungled Its National Priorities from the New Deal to the Present* (New York: Columbia University Press, 2001), 273–276.

76. "Remarks and a Question and Answer Session at a Luncheon Hosted by the Commonwealth Club in San Francisco, California," February 7, 1990, APP.

77. Michael Gordon, "Military Ordered to Draft a 5% Cut in '92–'94 Spending," *New York Times*, November 20, 1989, A1.

78. CBO, *Analysis of the President's FY 1991 Budget* (March 1990), 65–83; Darman, "Budget Issues for Discussion 11/15/89," SOF-CoS, ID#CF00374, BPR, GBL; Patrick Tyler, "New Pentagon Guidance Cites Soviet Threat in Third World," *Washington Post*, February 13, 1990, A1.

79. Franklin, *Making Ends Meet*, 60–61.

80. Darman, "'BUBBA:' For Discussion 4/29/90," April 28, 1990, SOF-CoS, ID#CF000374, BPR, GBL [BUBBA stood for "Budget: Big Bipartisan Agreement"]; Congressional Budget Office, *The Economic and Budget Outlook: An Update* (Washington, DC; CBO, 1990), 56.

81. Hager and Pianin, *Mirage*, 163–164; Shuman, *Politics and the Budget*, 314.

82. Hager and Pianin, *Mirage*, 170–172 (quotation p. 172); Alan Ehrenhalt, ed., *Politics in America: The 100th Congress* (Washington, DC: CQ Press, 1987), 632–635.

83. Darman, *Who's in Control?* 254–255; Darman, "For Discussion 6/11/90: 'BUBBA' and/or 'Truman,'" SOF-CoS, ID#CF00374, BPR, GBL; Hager and Pianin, *Mirage*, 163.

84. Darman, "Conditions (for discussion 6/19/90)," SOF-CoS, ID#CF00374, BPR, GBL; Darman, *Who's in Control?* 260–265.

85. Mervin, *George Bush and the Guardianship Presidency*, 140–141; "The President's Press Conference," June 29, 1990, APP.

86. Hager and Pianin, *Mirage*, 165–166.

87. Republican Congressmen [90 signatures] to Bush, June 26, 1990, and Republican Senators [16 signatures] to Bush, June 27, 1990, SOF-CoS, ID#CF00374, BPR, GBL; Pamela Fessler, "Summit Talks Go in Circles as Partisan Tensions Rise," *CQWR*, July 21, 1990, 2276.

88. Darman, "Budget Negotiations: 'Realities' as of 6/22/90 (A.M.)" and "Issues Re.: Budget Summit for Discussion 6/25/90," SOF-CoS, ID#CF00374, BPR, GBL; "The President's News Conference, August 8, 1990," APP; Pat Towell, "Crisis May Spur Second Look at Defense Spending Cuts," *CQWR*, September 1, 1990, 2779–2785.

89. Darman, "For Discussion 5/9/90: General Characteristics of a Meaningful Bipartisan Agreement," SOF-CoS, ID#OD12314, GBL; Frederick McClure, "Meeting with Republican Congressional Leadership," July 17, 1990, SOF-Office of Legislative Affairs [hereafter, OLA], ID#08461, BPR, GBL; George Hager, "Balanced-Budget Amendment Fails in House; Act OK'd," *CQWR*, July 21, 1990.

90. Pamela Fessler, "Negotiators Go into Recess No Closer to Compromise," *CQWR*, August 4, 1990, 2484–2487; George Hager, "Outline Begins to Take Shape as Deadlines Come and Go," *CQWR*, September 15, 1990, 2895–2898.

91. Pamela Fessler, "Capital Gains Tax Cut Is Once Again Pivotal Issue in Deficit Bargaining," *CQWR*, September 22, 1990, 2996–2997; Charls Walker to Bush, September 14, 1990, Representative Vin Weber (R-MN) to Bush, September 13, 1990, SOF-CoS, ID#CF00374, BPR, GBL.

92. "Remarks on the Federal Budget Negotiations," September 25, 1990, APP; "Summary of Summit Agreement on Federal Spending, Revenues," *CQWR*, October 6, 1990, 3198–3199 (based on figures provided by the OMB; totals exceed $500 billion due to rounding of individual items).

93. Doug Holtz-Eakin to Michael Boskin, "Options on Revenue and Spending in Deficit Reduction," May 14, 1990, SOF-Council of Economic Advisers, ID#04330-011, BPR, GBL.

94. Hager and Pianin, *Mirage*, 176–178; Robert Koenig, "Gephardt 'Detests' Budget Proposal," *St. Louis Post-Dispatch*, October 3, 1990, 1.

95. For useful biographies, see Dick Williams, *NEWT! Leader of the Second American Revolution* (Marietta, GA: Longstreet, 1995); Mel Steely, *The Gentleman from Georgia: The Biography of Newt Gingrich* (Macon, GA: Mercer University Press, 2000); and Newt Gingrich, *Lessons Learned the Hard Way: A Personal Report* (New York: HarperCollins, 1998) (quotation p. 188).

96. Janet Hook, "President's Hill Troops Have Mutinied Whenever He's Issued Budget Orders," *CQWR*, September 29, 1990, 3097; Warren T. Brookes, "Gingrich to Save Bush from Carterism," *Boston Herald*, August 23, 1990, 5.

97. Darman, *Who's in Control?* 248–249, 259 (Gramm quotation); Steely, *The Gentleman from Georgia*, 223–225; Pamela Fessler, "Gingrich Calls for Tax Cuts to Help Bolster Economy," *CQWR*, August 25, 2709, and "Gingrich Plays His Own Tax Card," *CQWR*, September 8, 1990, 2821.

98. Richard Lesher, U.S. Chamber of Commerce President, to Bush, September 19, 1990, WHORM-SF, FI004, ID#189813, BPR, GBL; Heritage Foundation, "The Budget Summit Agreement: Serious Damage to the Economy, Part 1," October 1, 1990 (see also Part II, October 2, 1990); Frederick McClure, Memorandum for the President, "Call Recommended to Henry Hyde," October 2, 1990, SOF-OLA, ID#08461, BPR, GBL; Harrison Rainie with others, "Send in the Clowns," *U.S. News and World Report*, October 15, 1990, 34–37.

99. Nicholas Calio, Memorandum for John Sununu and Frederick McClure, September 30, 1990, SOF-OLA, ID#08461, BPR, GBL; "[David] Demarest Notes: Discussion Points on Budget Agreement," October 2, 1990, SOF-White House Office of Speechwriting, ID#04422, BPR, GBL; Bobby Kilberg and Jeff Vogt, "Drop by and Brief Remarks at Budget Meeting for Industry Leaders," October 2, 1990, SOF-Office of Public Liaison, ID#07148, BPR, GBL. See also Janet Hook, "Anatomy of a Budget Showdown: The Limits of Leaders' Clout," *CQWR*, October 6, 1990, 3189–3191.

100. "Address to the Nation on the Federal Budget Agreement," October 2, 1990, APP. For comments on the overwhelmingly negative calls on the agreement to the Indiana Republican congressional delegation, see Mark Morris to Senator Richard Lugar, October 4, 1990, copy in SOF-CoS, ID#180274, BPR, GBL.

101. For poll data, see George Edwards, "The Public Presidency," in Campbell and Rockman, *The Bush Presidency*, 143–144.

102. George Hager, "Defiant House Rebukes Leaders; New Round of Fights Begins," *CQWR*, October 6, 1990, 3187; Janet Hook, "Budget Ordeal Poses Question: Why Can't Congress Be Led?" *CQWR*, October 20, 1990, 3473.

103. "The President's News Conference on the Federal Budget Crisis," October 6, 1990, APP; "Statement on Signing a Resolution Providing Funding for Continued Government Operation," October 9, 1990, APP.

104. "The President's News Conference," October 9, 1990, APP; Franklin, *Making Ends Meet*, 84; "Statement by Press Secretary Fitzwater on the President's Meeting with House Republican Leaders," October 11, 1990, APP; James Thompson [former governor of Illinois] to Bush, October 10, 1990, WHORM, FI004, ID#189059, BPR, GBL.

105. Bush to Thompson, October 11, 1990, WHORM, FI-004, ID#189059, BPR, Box 29, BPR, GBL; Andy Ireland, Memorandum to the President, "Budget Strategy," October 11, 1990, SOF-CoS, ID#CF00374, BPR, GBL; Nick Calio to John Sununu and Richard Darman, "Conservative Democrats/Moderate Republicans on the Budget," October 12, 1990, SOF-OLA, ID#08461, BPR, GBL.

106. George Hager and Pamela Fessler, "Negotiators Walk Fine Line to Satisfy

Both Chambers," *CQWR*, October 20, 1990, 3476–3484; Steven E. Schier, *A Decade of Deficits: Congressional Thought and Fiscal Action* (Albany: State University of New York Press, 1992), 132–134; Franklin, *Making Ends Meet*, 85–88.

107. George Hager, "Deficit Deal Ever So Fragile as Hours Dwindle Away," *CQWR*, November 3, 1990; Julie Rovner, "Beneficiaries Spared Big Cuts in Medicare and Medicaid," *CQWR*, November 3, 1990, 3718–3719. For details, see "The Deficit-Reduction Pie," and "Major Tax Provisions Compared," *CQWR*, November 3, 1990, 3711, 3716.

108. Tax data drawn from outline of House and Senate's original positions and the conference compromise: "At a Glance," *CQWR*, October 27, 1990, 3575. For analysis of progressivity, see data from Congressional Joint Committee on Taxation reproduced in Shuman, *Politics and the Budget*, 329.

109. For analysis of the BEA, see Marvin H. Kosters, ed., *Fiscal Politics and the Budget Enforcement Act* (Washington, DC: AEI Press, 1992); and Jasmine Farrier, *Passing the Buck: Congress, the Budget, and Deficits* (Lexington: University Press of Kentucky, 2004), 129–164.

110. Shuman, *Politics and the Budget*, 336–337; Schier, *A Decade of Deficits*, 135–136; Allen Schick, "Deficit Government in the Age of Divided Government," in Kosters, *Fiscal Politics and the Budget Enforcement Act*, 24; James Savage and Amy Verdun, "Reforming Europe's Stability and Growth Pact: Lessons from the American Experience in Macrobudgeting," *Review of International Political Economy* 14 (December 2007), 852–857.

111. Parmet, *George Bush*, 469; Ed Rollins, *Bare Knuckles and Back Rooms: My Life in American Politics* (New York: Broadway Books, 1994), 199–208.

112. George Bush and Brent Scowcroft, *A World Transformed* (New York: Knopf, 1998), 380.

113. "Statement on the Federal Budget," October 16, 1990, APP; "Remarks at the Republican National Committee Election Countdown Rally," October 30, 1990, APP.

114. Steely, *The Gentleman from Georgia*, 223; Bush and Scowcroft, *A World Transformed*, 379–380.

115. Quayle, *Standing Firm*, 203. See too the views of James Cicconi and Bobbie Kilberg, cited in Mervin, *George Bush and the Guardianship Presidency*, 154–155; and Charles Kolb in *White House Daze*, 94–95.

116. Fred Steeper to Bob Teeter, "U.S. National Survey Findings," October 31, and November 1 and 14, 1990, SOF-Teeter, ID#28956, BPR, GBL.

117. Duffy and Goodgame, *Marching in Place*, 82–83; "U.S. National Survey #16, Question Result, January 29–30, 1992," SOF-Teeter, ID#28966, BPP, GBL.

118. Bush to Nicholas Brady, December 30, 1992, in *ATB*, 582.

119. Congressional Budget Office, "Budget Projections through 2001," Staff Memorandum, October 1991, in Schick, "Deficit Budgeting in the Age of Divided Government," 24.

120. Cato Institute, "Not a Single Benefit Promised by the 1990 Budget Deal Has Been Delivered, Study Says," October 15, 1992; Stephen Moore, "Crime of the Century: The 1990 Budget Deal after Two Years," *Policy Analysis*, No. 182, October 15,

1992, 14–17; Heritage Foundation, "What George Bush Is Not Being Told about Federal Spending," January 1992; Matthew B. Kibbe, "The Laffer Curve in Reverse," *Wall Street Journal,* July 22, 1991.

121. Congressional Budget Office, *The Economic and Budget Outlook* (Washington, DC: CBO, 1993), 28–29; Curry and Shibut, "The Costs of the Savings and Loan Crisis: Truth and Consequences," 29; Boskin, Memorandum for the President, "Spending, Taxes, and Deficits in the Bush Administration," March 17, 1992, SOF-CEA, ID#07916-006, BPR, GBL.

122. *Economic Report of the President, 1992* (Washington, DC: Government Printing Office, 1992); Herbert Stein, *Presidential Economics: The Making of Economic Policy from Roosevelt to Reagan,* 3rd ed. (Washington, DC: AEI Press, 1994), 431–437.

123. Calculated from Historical Budget Data section in Congressional Budget Office, *The Budget and Economic Outlook: Fiscal Years 2005–2014* (Washington, DC: CBO, 2004), 140.

124. Alan S. Blinder and Janet L. Yellen, *The Fabulous Decade: Macroeconomic Lessons from the 1990s* (New York: Century Foundation Press, 2001), 3–9; Daniel Yankelovich, "Foreign Policy after the Election," *Foreign Affairs* (March 1992), 1–12; Iwan Morgan, *Beyond the Liberal Consensus: A Political History of the United States since 1965* (New York: St. Martin's Press, 1994), 250–253 (Greenspan quote p. 252).

125. Dennis S. Ippolito, *Why Budgets Matter: Budget Policy and American Politics* (College Park: Pennsylvania State University Press, 2003), 252–254; Duffy and Goodgame, *Marching in Place,* 79–80; Greene, *The Presidency of George Bush,* 161.

126. Dennis S. Ippolito, *Budget Policy and the Future of Defense* (Washington, DC: Institute for National Strategic Studies/National Defense University Press, 1994), esp. 84–97; "Pentagon Gets Most of Its Wish List," *Congressional Quarterly Almanac 1992* (Washington, DC: Congressional Quarterly, 1993), 483.

127. Ippolito, *Why Budgets Matter,* 254–255; Duffy and Goodgame, *Marching in Time,* 254–257, 260; "Message to the House of Representatives Returning without Approval the Tax Fairness and Economic Growth Acceleration Act of 1992," March 20, 1992, APP.

128. Darman, "State of the Economy: For Discussion November 9, 1990," SOF-CoS, ID#CF00374, BPR, GBL; Woodward, *Maestro,* 71. Democratic leaders had also hoped that the budget deal would bring about lower interest rates. See Richard Gephardt and Leon Panetta to Alan Greenspan, October 31, 1990, copy in SOF-CoS, ID#CF00374, BPR, GBL.

129. Greenspan, *The Age of Turbulence,* 120; Blinder and Yellen, *The Fabulous Decade,* 11–12; Transcript, Federal Reserve Open Market Committee Meeting, November 13, 1990, 44, www.federalreserve.gov/monetarypolicy/files/FOMC19901113 meeting.pdf.

130. Woodward, *Maestro,* 78–84, 88–94, 121–122; Steven Greenhouse, "Bush Calls on Fed for Another Drop in Interest Rates," *New York Times,* June 24, 1992, A1; Greenspan, *The Age of Turbulence,* 121–122. See also Board of Governors of the Federal Reserve System, *79th Annual Report to Congress,* April 16, 1993, especially 107–108, 161.

131. Michael Boskin to Samuel Skinner, "What Was Being Said When About the Economy," December 17, 1991, SOF-CoS, ID#05826, BPR, GBL.

132. Paul Kennedy, *The Rise and Fall of the Great Powers: Economic Change and Military Conflict from 1500 to 2000* (New York: Random House, 1988), 514–535. See also Benjamin Friedman, *Day of Reckoning: The Consequences of American Economic Policy under Reagan and After* (New York: Random House, 1988); Alfred L. Malabre Jr., *Our Means: How America's Long Years of Debt, Deficits, and Reckless Borrowing Threaten to Overwhelm Us* (New York: Random House, 1987); and Ravi Batra, *The Great Depression of 1990* (New York: Simon & Schuster, 1987).

133. Donald Barlett and James B. Steele, *America: What Went Wrong?* (Kansas City: Andrews & McMeel, 1992). This was based on an article series that generated huge public interest when published in the *Philadelphia Inquirer*, in late 1991. For an academic version of this thesis, see Wallace Peterson, "The Silent Depression," *Challenge* (July–August 1991), 29–34, and the same author's *Silent Depression: The Fate of the American Dream* (New York: Norton, 1994).

134. Lester Thurow, *Head to Head: The Coming Economic Battle among Japan, Europe, and America* (New York: Morrow, 1992); Edward Luttwak, "Is America on the Way Down?" *Commentary*, March, 1992, 15–21. For a French perspective on this, see Jacques Atali, *Lignes d'Horizon* (Paris: Editions Sentinels, 1990).

135. David P. Calleo, *The Bankrupting of America: How the Federal Budget Is Impoverishing the Nation* (New York: Morrow, 1992). For a somewhat different take on this thesis from a financial analyst in the Christian broadcasting media, see Larry Burkett, *The Coming Economic Earthquake* (Chicago: Moody Press, 1991).

136. General Accounting Office, *Budget Policy: Prompt Action Necessary to Avert Long-Term Damage to the Economy* (Washington, DC: GAO, 1992).

137. Michael Williams to Michael Boskin, "GAO Report on the Budget Deficit," June 11, 1992, SOF-CEA, ID#07916-006, BPR, GBL; John B. Judis, "The Red Menace," *New Republic*, October 26, 1992, 26–29 (quotation p. 29).

138. Nicholas Brady, Memorandum for the Cabinet: "Talking Points on the Economy—Taking the Offensive and Debunking the Pessimists," June 16, 1992, SOF-Office of Public Liaison, ID#07148, BPR, GBL.

139. Buchanan Campaign Financial Request, December 9, 1991, copy in Robert Dole Senate Papers, 329-43-141, box 6, Robert J. Dole Institute of Politics [hereafter, RJDIP]; Michael Duffy, "How Bush Will Battle Buchanan," *Time*, March 2, 1992, 2; Duffy and Goodgame, *Marching in Place*, 258–259.

140. Andrew Kopkind, "Tsongas and the Democrats: Populism for the Middle Class," *Nation*, November 25, 1991, 653, 671–674.

141. Warren B. Rudman, *Combat: Twelve Years in the U.S. Senate* (New York: Random House, 1996), 257–260; Peter G. Peterson, *Facing Up: How to Rescue the Economy from Crushing Debt & Restore the American Dream* (New York: Simon & Schuster, 1993), 14.

142. Quoted in Duffy and Goodgame, *Marching in Place*, 232.

143. For biographical detail, see Tony Chiu, *Ross Perot: In His Own Words* (New York: Warner, 1992); Ken Gross, *Ross Perot: The Man behind The Myth* (New York: Random House, 1992); and Gerald Posner, *Citizen Perot: His Life & Times* (New York: Random House, 1996).

144. Posner, *Citizen Perot*, 245; Ross Perot, *United We Stand: How We Can Take Back Our Country* (New York: Hyperion, 1992), chapter 1 (quotation on 17).

145. Posner, *Citizen Perot*, 246–285; Hager and Pianin, *Mirage*, 200–202.

146. Perot, *United We Stand*, 34–56.

147. Paul J. Quirk and John K. Dalager, "The Election: A 'New Democrat' and a New Kind of Presidential Campaign," in Michael Nelson, ed., *The Elections of 1992* (Washington, DC: Congressional Quarterly, 1993), 65–67, 75–83; Everett Carl Ladd, "The 1992 Vote for President Clinton: Another Brittle Mandate," *Political Science Quarterly* 108, No. 1 (1993), esp. 21–25. For coverage of Perot's part in the campaign, see Jack W. Germond and Jules Witcover, *Mad as Hell: Revolt at the Ballot Box 1992* (New York: Warner Books, 1993).

148. Eugene Carson, "Campaign '92: While Voters Sing the Blues about the Economy, Hints of Optimism Emerge," *Wall Street Journal*, September 18, 1992, A6; Jessica Lee and Bob Minzesheimer, "Statistics Do Support What Bush Is Saying," *USA Today*, October 27, 1992, A6; Blinder and Yellen, *The Fabulous Decade*, 4.

149. Hager and Pianin, *Mirage*, 172; Bush and Scowcroft, *A World Transformed*, 380.

150. Blinder and Yellen, *The Fabulous Decade*, 5.

151. George Bush, "Foreword," in Daniel Ostrander, *Read My Lips: No New Taxes* (Oroville, CA: Butte College Press, 1999), xvi.

152. Philip Crane to Bush, May 9, 1990, WHORM-SF, FI004, ID#140220, BPR, GBL.

Chapter 6. Bill Clinton: Taming the Deficit

1. "Remarks on the Budget Surplus," January 6, 1999, APP.

2. Congressional Budget Office, *Economic and Budget Outlook: Fiscal Years 1994 to 1998* (Washington, DC: CBO, 1993), 27–39.

3. White House, *Mid-Session Review, Fiscal Year 2000* (Washington, DC: Office of Management and Budget, June 1999).

4. Martin Walker, *Clinton: The President They Deserve*, rev. ed. (Vintage: London, 1997), 48.

5. For biographical detail, see Meredith L. Oakley, *On the Make: The Rise of Bill Clinton* (Washington, DC: Regnery Press, 1994) (quotation p. 36); John Brummett, *Highwire: From the Back Roads to the Beltway—The Education of Bill Clinton* (New York: Hyperion, 1994); and David Maraniss, *First in His Class: The Biography of Bill Clinton* (New York: Touchstone, 1995).

6. Walker, *Clinton*, 13–17; Oakley, *On the Make*, 517.

7. Author's interview with Laura Tyson, August 10, 2005. See also Robert Rubin and Jacob Weisberg, *In an Uncertain World: Tough Choices from Wall Street to Washington* (New York: Random House, 2003), 121, 132–135; Alan Greenspan, *The Age of Turbulence: Adventures in a New World* (New York: Penguin Press, 2007), 144, 170–171; and Dick Morris, *Behind the Oval Office: Getting Reelected against All Odds* (Los Angeles: Renaissance Books, 1999), 163–164.

8. Oakley, *On the Make*, 45–46; Maraniss, *First in His Class*, 58–60; Bill Clinton,

My Life (New York: Alfred A. Knopf, 2004), 78; "Keynote Address of Gov. Bill Clinton to the DLC's Cleveland Convention," May 6, 1991, www.dlc.org/ndol.

9. Clinton, *My Life*, 281; Maraniss, *First in His Class*, 382–383; Elizabeth Drew, *Portrait of an Election: The 1980 Presidential Campaign* (New York: Simon & Schuster, 1981), 256–257.

10. Robert Reich, *Locked in the Cabinet* (New York: Alfred A. Knopf, 1997), 8.

11. Clinton, *My Life*, 305, 317–318, 320–322, 346 (quotation).

12. Oakley, *On the Make*, 280–292; Maraniss, *First in His Class*, 410–416; Clinton, *My Life*, 263–264, 307–313.

13. Brummett, *Highwire*, 260–261; George Hager and Eric Pianin, *Mirage: Why Neither Democrats Nor Republicans Can Balance the Budget, End the Deficit, and Satisfy the Public* (New York: Times Books, 1997), 190–191.

14. Maraniss, *First in His Class*, 361; Brummett, *Highwire*, 14; Oakley, *On the Make*, 290–291, 333–335, 425–426; Clinton, *My Life*, 264–266, 283, 361–362.

15. Robert Reich, *The Next American Frontier* (New York: Times Books, 1983), and *The Work of Nations: Preparing Ourselves for 21st-Century Capitalism* (New York: Simon & Schuster, 1991); Robert Reich and Ira Magaziner, *Minding America's Business* (New York: Harcourt, Brace, Jovanovich, 1982); and Ira Magaziner and Mark Patinkin, *The Silent Wars: Inside the Great Business Battles Shaping America's Future* (New York: Random House, 1989).

16. "The New Orleans Declaration: A Democratic Agenda for the 1990s" (Washington, DC: Democratic Leadership Council, March 1990); Kenneth S. Baer, *Reinventing Democrats: The Politics of Liberalism from Reagan to Clinton* (Lawrence: University Press of Kansas, 2000), 163–165, 177, 189–191; and James MacGregor Burns and Georgia J. Sorenson, *Dead Center: The Perils of Clinton-Gore Moderation* (New York: Scribner, 1999), 145–168.

17. For critiques of strategic trade, see Paul Krugman, *Peddling Prosperity: Economic Sense and Nonsense in the Age of Diminished Expectations* (New York: Norton, 1994), 254–280; and Robert Lawrence and Matthew Slaughter, "Trade and U.S. Wages: Great Sucking Sound or Small Hiccup?" *Brookings Papers on Economic Activity* (Washington, DC: Brookings Institution, 1993).

18. "A New Covenant for Economic Change: Remarks to Students at Georgetown University by Governor Bill Clinton," November 20, 1991, www.dlc.org/ndol.

19. Hager and Pianin, *Mirage*, 188–191 (quotation p. 190); "A New Covenant for Economic Change"; Baer, *Reinventing Democrats*, 169, 199.

20. Rubin and Weisberg, *In an Uncertain World*, 104–105; Bob Woodward, *The Agenda: Inside the Clinton White House* (New York: Simon & Schuster, 1994), 41–44, 47–50.

21. Bill Clinton and Al Gore, *Putting People First: How We Can All Change America* (New York: Times Books, 1992), 27–31; Woodward, *The Agenda*, 46–47.

22. Clinton and Gore, *Putting People First*, 3, 28.

23. Bruce Bartlett, *Impostor: How George Bush Bankrupted America and Betrayed the Reagan Legacy* (New York: Doubleday, 2006), 123–124; Hager and Pianin, *Mirage*, 197–198; Thomas T. Vogel, "Bonds Fall on Outlook for Clinton," *Wall Street Journal*, October 21, 1992, A1.

24. "Presidential Debate in East Lansing, Michigan," October 19, 1992, APP.

25. Voter Research and Survey Exit Polls, reproduced in Paul J. Quirk and Jon K. Dalager, "The Election: A 'New Democrat' and a New Kind of Presidential Campaign," in Michael Nelson, ed., *The Elections of 1992* (Washington, DC: Congressional Quarterly, 1993), 81.

26. Henry Muller and John F. Stacks, "An Interview with Clinton," *Time*, July 20, 1992, 26; "Address Accepting the Presidential Nomination at the Democratic National Convention in New York," July 16, 1992, APP.

27. "Presidential Debate in Richmond, Virginia," October 15, 1992, APP.

28. Mary Matalin and James Carville, *All's Fair: Love, War, and Running for President* (New York: Random House, 1994), 415–416.

29. Reich, *Locked in the Cabinet*, 29.

30. Jack Egan, "Clinton's New Market," *U.S. News and World Report*, March 1, 1993, 64–66; Louis Uchitelle, "Why America Won't Boom," *New York Times*, June 12, 1994, D1; Amy Waldman, "Of Inhuman Bondage: The Bondmarket Has Policymakers in Its Grip," *Washington Monthly* (January-February 1997), 17–21.

31. Woodward, *The Agenda*, 68–71; Clinton, *My Life*, 451; Greenspan, *The Age of Turbulence*, 143–145.

32. Greenspan, *The Age of Turbulence,* 145.

33. Paul Starobin and others, "Clinton's A-Team," *National Journal*, December 19, 1992, 2892–2896; George Hager and David S. Cloud, "Clinton Team's Similar Lines Focus on Deficit Reduction," *CQWR*, January 16, 1993, 120–123; George Hager, "Deficit Hawk Panetta Is Named White House Budget Director," *CQWR*, December 12, 1992, 3803.

34. Paul Starobin, "The Broker," *National Journal*, December 18, 1993, 878–883; John Judis, "Old Master: Robert Rubin's Artful Role," *New Republic*, December 13, 1993, 21; Rubin and Weisberg, *In an Uncertain World*, 121.

35. M. Stephen Weatherford and Lorraine M. McDonnell, "Clinton and the Economy: The Paradox of Policy Success and Political Mishap," *Political Science Quarterly* 111, No. 3 (1996), 420; Paul Starobin, "The World According to Tyson," *National Journal*, December 18, 1993, 2025; Laura Tyson, "A Squandered Legacy," *Prospect* (April 2004), 34–35.

36. Author's interview with Laura Tyson, August 10, 2005; Brummett, *Highwire*, 76–77.

37. Elizabeth Drew, *On the Edge: The Clinton Presidency* (New York: Simon & Schuster, 1994), 60–61; Hager and Pianin, *Mirage*, 205.

38. Drew, *On the Edge*, 64–65; Woodward, *The Agenda*, 108–116 (quotation on 116).

39. Walker, *Clinton*, 173; Clinton, *My Life*, 463.

40. Greenspan, *The Age of Turbulence*, 146–147.

41. Nigel Hamilton, *Bill Clinton: Mastering the Presidency* (New York: PublicAffairs, 2007), 64.

42. Geoffrey C. Ward, *A First Class Temperament: The Emergence of Franklin D. Roosevelt* (New York: Harper & Row, 1989).

43. Sidney Blumenthal, "The Education of a President," *New Yorker*, January 24,

1994, 42; Joe Klein, *The Natural: The Misunderstood Presidency of Bill Clinton* (New York: Broadway Books, 2002), 49.

44. Congressional Budget Office, *An Analysis of the President's February Budget Proposals* (Washington, DC: CBO, March 1993); *Budget of the United States Government, Fiscal Year 1994* (Washington, DC: Government Printing Office, 1993), 10.

45. Hager and Pianin, *Mirage*, 208–209; Woodward, *The Agenda*, 98, 120–121; Greenspan, *The Age of Turbulence*, 147; Clinton, *My Life*, 461.

46. Bob Woodward, *Maestro: Greenspan's Fed and the American Boom* (New York: Simon & Schuster, 2000), 100–101; Stephen Greenhouse, "Clinton's Program Gets Endorsement of Fed Chair," *New York Times*, February 20, 1993, A1; Eric Pianin, "Clinton Plan Gains Greenspan Praise," *Washington Post*, February 20, 1993, A1.

47. For convenient tabular presentation, see *Congressional Quarterly Almanac 1993* (Washington, DC: Congressional Quarterly, 1994), 88.

48. Clinton, *My Life*, 461; "Address to the Joint Session of Congress," February 17, 1993, APP.

49. Woodward, *The Agenda*, 97.

50. Jon Healey, "Spending Increases Come First in Rush to Pass Package," *CQWR*, February 20, 1993, 365–369.

51. Richard E. Cohen, "What Coattails?" *National Journal*, May 29, 1993, 1285; Barbara Sinclair, "Trying to Govern Positively in a Negative Era: Clinton and the 103rd Congress," in Colin Campbell and Bert Rockman, eds., *The Clinton Presidency: First Appraisals* (Chatham, NJ: Chatham House, 1996), 91–96; Hager and Pianin, *Mirage*, 209–210.

52. Jake H. Thompson, *Bob Dole: The Republicans' Man for All Seasons* (New York: Primus, 1996), 212; Robert D. Reischauer, "Budget Policy under United Government," in James L. Sundquist, ed., *Back to Gridlock: Governance in the Clinton Years* (Washington, DC: Brookings Institution, 1995), 20–29; Pamela Fessler, "If People Get Behind President, Congress Is Likely to Follow," *CQWR*, February 20, 1993, 380. For a critique of the lack of spending cuts in Clinton's plan, see David Taylor, Memorandum to the Republican Leader, "Budget Deficit Facts and Observations," January 13, 1993, Robert Dole Senatorial Papers [hereafter, RDSP], 329-96-336, Box 135, Robert J. Dole Institute of Politics [hereafter, RJDIP].

53. Fessler, "If People Get Behind the President," 380–381; Woodward, *The Agenda*, 105–106; Clinton, *My Life*, 488.

54. Gloria Borger, "To Democrats: Put Up or Shut Up," *U.S. News and World Report*, January 25, 1993, 68; Viveka Novak, "After the Boll Weevils," *National Journal*, June 26, 1993, 1630–1634; Timothy Penny and Stephen Schier, *Payment Due: A Nation in Debt, A Generation in Trouble* (Boulder, CO: Westview Press, 1996).

55. Rubin and Weisberg, *In an Uncertain World*, 127; Drew, *On the Edge*, 225–226.

56. In his first term Clinton made an average of seventy-seven remarks per month on the deficit, far more than any other president, and the peak period of rhetorical intensity was during the struggle to enact his economic plan in 1993. From May to August 1993, he also made an average of thirty more optimistic than pessimistic comments on the deficit per month. See B. Dan Wood, *The Politics of Economic Leadership: The Causes and Consequence of Presidential Rhetoric* (Princeton, NJ:

Princeton University Press, 2007), 83–91. For criticism of Clinton's rhetorical strategy, see Weatherford and McDonnell, "Clinton and the Economy," 426–427, 435.

57. Drew, *On the Edge*, 114–120; "Fiscal Stimulus Bill Killed," *1993 Congressional Quarterly Almanac* (Washington, DC: CQ Press, 1994), 706–709.

58. Woodward, *The Agenda*, 148, 154–156, 163.

59. Drew, *On the Edge*, 86–87, 166; Woodward, *The Agenda*, 160–162.

60. Woodward, *The Agenda*, 217–220, 234–235; Hamilton, *Mastering the Presidency*, 159–161; Weatherford and McDonnell, "Clinton and the Economy," 427.

61. Sinclair, "Trying to Govern Positively in a Negative Era," 106–107; Clinton, *My Life*, 534–535.

62. David Cloud and George Hager, "With New Budget Deal in Hand, Clinton Faces Longest Yard," and Janet Hook, "In Fight for Votes, White House . . . Here, There and Everywhere," *CQWR*, July 31, 1993, 203–208; Woodward, *The Agenda*, 297; Clinton, *My Life*, 525, 534.

63. "Address to the Nation on the Economic Program," August 3, 1993, APP; Wood, *The Politics of Economic Leadership*, 91; Woodward, *The Agenda*, 285; "Switchboards Swamped with Calls over Tax Plan," *New York Times*, August 5, 1993, A18.

64. Clinton, *My Life*, 537; David Stockman, "America Is Not Overspending," *New Perspectives Quarterly* 10, No. 3 (1993), 12–14. See also Rubin and Weisberg, *In an Uncertain World*, 125.

65. David Rosenbaum, "Beyond the Superlatives: Clinton-Dole Jousting over Budget Bills Shows How Assertions Can Mask the Truth," *New York Times*, August 5, 1993, A1; Hager and Pianin, *Mirage*, 215; Michael Kelly, "'New Democrats' Say Clinton Has Veered and Left Them," *New York Times*, May 23, 1993, A20.

66. David Rosenbaum, "House Passes Budget Plan, Backing Clinton 218–216 after Hectic Maneuvering," *New York Times*, August 6, 1993, A1; and "Clinton Wins Approval of His Budget Plan as Gore Votes to Break Senate Deadlock," *New York Times*, August 7, 1993, A1. For good narratives, see Woodward, *The Agenda*, 282–309, and Drew, *On the Edge*, 260–272.

67. Congressional Budget Office, *The Economic and Budget Outlook: An Update* (Washington, DC: CBO, September 1993), 28–29, 31, 38; *Budget of the United States Government FY2009: Historical Tables* (Washington, DC: Government Printing Office, 2008), 116; Allen Schick, "A Surplus, If We Can Keep It," *Brookings Review* 18 (2000), 36–39.

68. *Budget of the United States Government FY 2009: Historical Tables*, 157.

69. Quoted in Richard Stevenson, "The Wisdom to Let the Good Times Roll," *New York Times*, December 25, 2000, A1.

70. Charles O. Jones, *Clinton and Congress, 1993–1996: Risk, Restoration, and Reelection* (Norman: University of Oklahoma Press, 1999), 78–87.

71. Colin Campbell, "Management in a Sandbox: Why the Clinton White House Failed to Cope with Gridlock," in Campbell and Rockman, *The Clinton Presidency*. Clinton's successes from his "top ten" list were ratification of the General Agreement on Trade and Tariffs, Goals 2000 education reform, an anticrime package, and community development loans. In addition to his two major failures, the others were safe drinking water legislation, information superhighway development, superfund reform, and a reemployment proposal.

72. Hillary Rodham Clinton, *Living History* (New York: Simon & Schuster, 2003), 147. See also Jacob Hacker, *The Road to Nowhere: The Genesis of President Clinton's Plan for Health Care* (Princeton, NJ: Princeton University Press, 1997).

73. Clinton, *My Life*, 547–549; Congressional Budget Office, *The Administration's Health Plan* (Washington, DC: CBO, February 1994), xiii.

74. Allen Schick, "How a Bill Didn't Become a Law," in Thomas Mann and Norman Ornstein, eds., *Intensive Care: How Congress Shapes Health Policy* (Washington, DC: Brookings Institution, 1995), 240–251; Theda Skocpol, *Boomerang: Health Care Reform and the Turn against Government* (New York: Norton, 1997), esp. 133–188; Darrell West and Burdett Loomis, *The Sound of Money* (New York: Norton, 1999), 75–108.

75. Peter Passell, "Economic Scene: Why Isn't a Better Economy Helping Clinton?" *New York Times*, November 3, 1994, D2; Woodward, *Maestro*, 114–124; David E. Rosenbaum and Steve Lohr, "With a Stable Economy, Clinton Hopes for Credit," *New York Times*, August 3, 1996, 38.

76. Mel Steely, *The Gentleman from Georgia: The Biography of Newt Gingrich* (Macon, GA: Mercer University Press, 2000), 257; Michael Boskin, "Summary of Presentation at Senate Republican Leadership Breakfast, June 16, 1994," and Boskin to Bob Dole, July 11, 1994, RDSP, 329-96-336, Box 136, RJDIP; Hager and Pianin, *Mirage*, 226.

77. Harold W. Stanley, "The Parties, the President, and the 1994 Midterm Elections," in Campbell and Rockman, *The Clinton Presidency*, 193–194, 197–198; Gary Jacobson, "The 1994 House Elections in Perspective," in Philip Klinkner, ed., *Midterm: Elections of 1994 in Context* (Boulder, CO: Westview Press, 1996), 1–9; Charles O. Jones, *Clinton and Congress*, 95–115.

78. Patrick Fisher, *Congressional Budgeting: A Representational Perspective* (Lanham, MD: University Press of America, 2005), 93; William Greider, "Electoral Post-Mortem," *Rolling Stone*, December 1994, 153.

79. "Taking Speaker's Mantle, Gingrich Vows 'Profound Transformation,'" *Congressional Quarterly Almanac* (Washington, DC: CQ, 1995), 57D. For a cogent analysis, see Randall Strahan and Daniel J. Palazzolo, "The Gingrich Effect," *Political Science Quarterly* 119, No. 1 (2004): 89–115.

80. Newt Gingrich, *Window of Opportunity: A Blueprint for the Future* (New York: Tor Books, 1984), 184–204; Dick Williams, *Newt! Leader of the Second American Revolution* (Marietta, GA: Longstreet Press, 1995), 211.

81. Quoted in William Welch, "Benefit Cuts Proposal under Fire," *USA Today*, December 12, 1994, A6; Schier and Penny, *Payment Due*, 89–96.

82. Hager and Pianin, *Mirage*, 299; John Harwood, "Revolution II: Reagan-Era Politicians Are Now Determined to Revive 80s Policies," *Wall Street Journal Europe*, January 4, 1995, 1.

83. Steven M. Gillon, *The Pact: Bill Clinton, Newt Gingrich, and the Rivalry That Defined a Generation* (New York: Oxford University Press, 2008), 149; Morris, *Behind the Oval Office*, 173; Reich, *Locked in the Cabinet*, 336; "The President's Press Conference," December 20, 1995, APP.

84. Newt Gingrich, *Lessons Learned the Hard Way: A Personal Report* (New York: HarperCollins, 1998), 37; Ed Gillespie and Bob Schellhas, eds., *The Contract*

with America; The Bold Plan by Rep. Newt Gingrich, Rep. Dick Armey, and the House Republicans to Change the Nation (New York: Times Books, 1994); Steven Slivinski, *Buck Wild: How Republicans Broke the Bank and Became the Party of Big Government* (Nashville, TN: Nelson Current, 2006), 59.

85. Morris, *Behind the Oval Office*, 80. For insightful analysis of the Clinton-Morris relationship, see John F. Harris, *The Survivor: Bill Clinton in the White House* (New York: Random House, 2002), 159–170. For a critical insider perspective, see George Stephanopoulos, *All Too Human: A Political Education* (London: Hutchinson, 1999), chapters 13–15.

86. Elizabeth Drew, *Showdown: The Struggle between the Gingrich Congress and the Clinton White House* (New York: Simon & Schuster, 1996), 69–73; Rubin and Weisberg, *In an Uncertain World*, 163; Stephanopoulos, *All Too Human*, 344.

87. Hager and Pianin, *Mirage*, 22–23; Drew, *Showdown*, 120. For predictions of problems between the House and Senate over Contract with America fiscal commitments, see David Taylor, Memorandum to the Republican Leader, "Thinking about 1995—Tax Cuts and the Deficit," October 3, 1994, and "Thinking about 1995—A Look ahead at Clinton's FY1996 Budget," November 2, 1994, in RDSP, 329-96-336, Box 136, RJDIP.

88. Drew, *Showdown*, 119–125.

89. "The President's Radio Address," February 25, 1995, APP; Drew, *Showdown*, 153, 156–157; Laura Tyson, interview with the author, August 10, 2005.

90. Thompson, *Bob Dole*, 238–240; Howard Fineman and Thomas Rosentiel, "Mr. Inside Strikes Out," *Newsweek*, March 13, 1995, 34–37; Drew, *Showdown*, 153–166. Dole switched to the nays when it was apparent the amendment would fail (to make the official vote 65 to 35) to preserve his right to call for a revote in the same Congress. His next and last attempt to enact it also ended in failure, this time by 64 votes to 35, on June 6, 1996.

91. Morris, *Behind the Oval Office*, 162 (for full text of Morris memorandum, "Agenda for Meeting on Tuesday, May 16," see pp. 439–448).

92. David Maraniss and Michael Weisskopf, *"Tell Newt to Shut Up!"* (New York: Touchstone, 1996), 36–52; Slivinski, *Buck Wild*, 55–59.

93. George Hager and Alissa Rubin, "Last-Minute Maneuvers Forge a Conference Agreement," *CQWR*, June 27, 1995, 1814–1819; David Rosenbaum, "Congress Passes GOP's Budget-Balancing Plan," *New York Times*, June 30, 1995, A1; Dan Morgan and Eric Pianin, "Doing the Dirty Work of Deficit Reduction," *Washington Post*, July 9, 1995, A1. For good analysis of congressional budgeting in 1995, see Barbara Sinclair, *Unorthodox Legislation: New Legislative Processes in the U.S. Congress* (Washington, DC: Congressional Quarterly Press, 1997), chapter 11; and Richard F. Fenno, *Learning to Govern: An Institutional View of the 104th Congress* (Washington, DC: Brookings Institution, 1997), chapter 4.

94. "Address to the Nation on the Plan to Balance the Budget," June 13, 1995, APP; Clinton, *My Life*, 659; George Hager, "Clinton Shifts Tactics, Proposes Erasing Deficit in 10 Years," *CQWR*, June 17, 1995, 1715–1720.

95. Martin Gottlieb, "Battle over the Budget: Medical Care," *New York Times*, November 18, 1995, A9; Maraniss and Weisskopf, *"Tell Newt to Shut Up!"* 142–143;

Michael B. Katz, *The Price of Citizenship: Redefining the American Welfare State* (New York: Metropolitan Books, 2001), 274–275, 302–303.

96. Morris, *Behind the Oval Office*, 162; Rubin, *In an Uncertain World*, 164; Stephanopoulos, *All Too Human*, 346–355; Reich, *Locked in the Cabinet*, 260–262. See also David Wessell and Rick Wartzman, "Clinton Pursued His Own Balanced Budget Plan Despite the Objection of Top Democratic Aides," *Wall Street Journal*, June 16, 1995, A16; and Bob Woodward, *The Choice: How Clinton Won* (New York: Simon & Schuster, 1996), chapter 14.

97. Adam Clymer, "Whether Friend or Foe, Most Think Clinton Is Playing Politics on the Budget," *New York Times*, June 16, 1995, 1; Lloyd Grove, "How to Triangulate an Oval Office," *Washington Post*, November 28, 1995, C1.

98. Morris, *Behind the Oval Office*, 11; Woodward, *The Choice*, 345. See also Jones, *Clinton and Congress*, 160–165; and John Harris, "A Clouded Mirror: Bill Clinton, Polls, and the Politics of Survival," in Steven E. Schier, ed., *The Postmodern Presidency: Bill Clinton's Legacy in U.S. Politics* (Pittsburgh: University of Pittsburgh Press, 2000), 87–105.

99. Rubin, *In an Uncertain World*, 3–38; Paul Krugman, *The Great Unravelling: From Boom to Bust in Three Scandalous Years* (London: Penguin, 2003), 252.

100. Stephanopoulos, *All Too Human*, 360, 345; Rubin, *In an Uncertain World*, 164–165.

101. Jeffrey Birnbaum and Michael Frisby, "Big G.O.P. Win Leaves Clinton Scrambling to Regain Initiative," *Wall Street Journal*, November 10, 1995, A1; Stephanopoulos, *All Too Human*, 345.

102. Hager and Pianin, *Mirage*, 243–244; George Church, "Ripping up the Budget," May 22, 1995, 40–42; Karen Tumulty and others, "Getting the Edge," *Time*, June 5, 1995.

103. Drew, *Showdown*, 213–215; Maraniss and Weisskopf, *"Tell Newt to Shut Up!"* 151.

104. Jackie Koszczuk, "Freshmen: New Powerful Voice," *CQWR*, October 28, 1995, 3251–3254 (quotation p. 3254); Nicol C. Rae, *Conservative Reformers: The Republican Freshmen and the Lessons of the 104th Congress* (Armonk, NY: M. E. Sharp, 1998), 35–36; Dan Morgan, "Republicans on Key Panel Appropriate Policy Role," *Washington Post*, July 22, 1995, A8; Linda Killian, *The Freshmen* (Boulder, CO: Westview Press, 1998), 120–122.

105. Ippolito, *Why Budgets Matter*, 269–270; Drew, *Showdown*, 322.

106. Stephanopoulos, *All Too Human*, 400–402; Rubin, *In an Uncertain World*, 168–175.

107. Clinton, *My Life*, 683; Gillon, *The Pact*, 159–160.

108. Phil Gramm to Dole, November 15, 1995, and Republican Governors Association to Dole, November 19, 1995, RDSP, 329-96-336, Box 49, RJDIP; Maraniss and Weisskopf, *"Tell Newt to Shut Up!"* 140–143, 183.

109. Richard Morin, "Public Sides with Clinton over GOP in Fiscal Fight, Poll Finds," *Washington Post*, November 21, 1995, A4; Gingrich, *Lessons Learned the Hard Way*, 56 (quotation), 59–60; Hager and Pianin, *Mirage*, 254; Gillon, *The Pact*, 166–167.

110. "Remarks on Returning without Approval Temporary Public Debt Increase Legislation and an Exchange with Reporters," November 13, 1995, APP; Adam Clymer, "Americans Reject Big Medicare Cuts, a New Poll Finds," *New York Times*,

October 26, 1995, A1; Rubin and Weisberg, *In an Uncertain World*, 162–163; Klein, *The Natural*, 147–148.

111. Jackie Koszczuk, "Train Wreck Engineered by GOP . . . Batters Party and House Speaker," *CQWR*, November 18, 1995, 3506; Stephanopoulos, *All Too Human*, 405; Drew, *Showdown*, 334–335.

112. Drew, *Showdown*, 338–340; Maraniss and Weisskopf, *"Tell Newt to Shut Up!"* 155–156; Stephanopoulos, *All Too Human*, 405–406.

113. Leon Panetta to Bob Dole, November 24, 1995, RDSP, 329-96-336, Box 49, RJDIP.

114. George Hager, "Historic Votes Add Momentum as Conferees Start Work," *CQWR*, October 28, 1995, 3282.

115. Drew, *Showdown*, 345–356 (quotation p. 346); Hager and Pianin, *Mirage*, 276–283.

116. Alison Mitchell and Tod Purdum, "Clinton the Conciliator Finds His Line in Sand," *New York Times*, January 2, 1996, A1.

117. Gingrich, *Lessons Learned the Hard Way*, 47–63; David Cloud, "Dole Gambles on Budget Crisis," *CQWR*, January 6, 1996, 54; George Hager, "A Battered GOP Calls Workers Back to the Job," *CQWR*, January 6, 1996, 53.

118. Alissa Rubin and George Hager, "Chances of a Budget Deal Now Anyone's Guess," *CQWR*, January 13, 1996, 90; George Hager and Andrew Taylor, "GOP Looks for New Strategies as Talks Stall Yet Again," *CQWR*, January 20, 1996, 150.

119. Hager and Pianin, *Mirage*, 297; Jerry Gray, "Both Congress and Clinton Find Cause for Cheer in the Final Budget Deal," *New York Times*, April 26, 1996, A22.

120. David Rogers, "Spending Pact Marks Major Retreat by GOP Leaders," *Wall Street Journal*, September 30, 1996, A20; Ippolito, *Why Budgets Matter*, 272–274.

121. Slivinski, *Buck Wild*, 78–79; Michael Tanner, *Leviathan on the Right: How Big-Government Conservatism Brought Down the Republican Revolution* (Washington, DC: Cato Institute, 2007), 155–156.

122. Robert Rector and William F. Lauber, *America's Failed $5.4 Trillion War on Poverty* (Washington, DC: Heritage Foundation, 1995); Ron Haskins, "Welfare Reform: The Biggest Accomplishment of the Revolution," in Chris Edwards and John Samples, eds., *The Republican Revolution 10 Years Later: Smaller Government or Business as Usual?* (Washington, DC: Cato Institute, 2005), 99–139. For rebuttals of the Heritage report, see Sharon Parrott, "How Much Do We Spend on Welfare?" *Center on Budget Policy and Priorities*, August 4, 1995; and Katz, *The Price of Citizenship*, 317–321.

123. Clinton and Gore, *Putting People First*, 164–168; Hillary Clinton, *Living History*, 367–368.

124. Katz, *The Price of Citizenship*, 303, 324–327; Rebecca M. Blank and David T. Ellwood, "The Clinton Legacy for America's Poor," in Jeffrey Frankel and Peter Orszag, eds., *American Economic Policy in the 1990s* (Cambridge, MA: MIT Press, 2002), 761–768.

125. Reich, *Locked in the Cabinet*, 320–321; Congressional Budget Office, *The Economic and Budget Outlook: Fiscal Years 1998–2007* (Washington, DC: CBO, 1997), 21–22; Peter Edelman, "The Worst Thing Bill Clinton Has Done," *Atlantic*

Monthly, March 1997, 43–58; Michael Janofsky, "Mayors Fear Welfare Cuts May Increase Homelessness," *New York Times,* July 30, 1996, A9.

126. Todd Purdum, "Clinton Remembers Promise, Considers History, and Will Sign," *New York Times,* August 1, 1996, A1; Morris, *Behind the Oval Office,* 300–305, 595; Harris, *The Survivor,* 230–237 (quotation p. 236).

127. Peter Baker, "Clinton Calls Budget His Top Priority," *Washington Post,* November 11, 1996, A1; Reich, *Locked in the Cabinet,* 336–337.

128. Quoted in Alan Fram, "Clinton, Democrats Differ on Budget," *Associated Press,* July 7, 1997. See also Gillon, *The Pact,* 192.

129. Ippolito, *Why Budgets Matter,* 276.

130. For a "realist expectations" explanation of this, see Daniel J. Palazzolo, *Done Deal? The Politics of the 1997 Budget Agreement* (Chappaqua, NY: Chatham House, 1999).

131. Jackie Koszczuk and others, "Members Move to Claim Center as Voters Demand Moderation," *CQWR,* November 9, 1996, 3198–3199; Dan Balz, "Republicans Sound Conciliatory Tone; Hill GOP Would Defer to the Reelected President but Warns of Conflict," *Washington Post,* November 7, 1996, A1.

132. Gerald Pomper, "The Presidential Election," in Gerald Pomper and others, *The Elections of 1996: Reports and Interpretations* (Chatham, NJ: Chatham House, 1997), 187; Irene S. Rubin, *Balancing the Federal Budget: Trimming the Herds or Eating the Seed Corn?* (New York: Chatham House, 2003), 34; Morris, *Behind the Oval Office,* 312–314.

133. "The President's Inaugural Address," January 20, 1997, APP. See also John F. Harris and Peter Baker, "Clinton Urges an End to Divisions," *Washington Post,* January 21, 1997, A1; and Gillon, *The Pact,* 187.

134. *Budget of the United States Government, Fiscal Year 1998* (Washington, DC: Government Printing Office, 1997), 3, 7.

135. Gingrich, *Lessons Learned the Hard Way,* 61–62; Palazzolo, *Done Deal?* 50–54; Harris, *The Survivor,* 259–260.

136. *Congressional Quarterly Almanac 1997* (Washington, DC: Congressional Quarterly, 1998), 2–20.

137. Ibid., 24–52; Congressional Budget Office, *The Budget and Economic Outlook: An Update* (Washington, DC: CBO, September 1997), 36.

138. John Kasich, "The Budget Deal," *Washington Post,* June 1, 1997, C8; Gene Sperling and Franklin Raines, "Bogus Facts about the Budget," *Washington Post,* June 9, 1997, A19; Klein, *The Natural,* 160.

139. Palazzolo, *Done Deal?* 189.

140. Congressional Budget Office, *The Budget and Economic Outlook: An Update,* 40–41. For SCHIP, see Alex Waddan and Douglas Jaenicke, "The Politics and Policy of the State Children's Health Insurance Program" in Iwan Morgan and Philip Davies, eds., *The Federal Nation: Perspectives on American Federalism* (New York: Palgrave, 2008), 148–152.

141. Congressional Budget Office, *The Budget and Economic Outlook: An Update,* 35–36.

142. Gillon, *The Pact,* 200.

143. Clay Chandler, "Roth Tax Plan Sets up New Battle with Clinton," *Washington Post*, June 18, 1997, C11, and "Tax Cut Debate Centers on Fairness," *Washington Post*, July 21, 1997, A1; Palazzolo, *Done Deal?* 156, 162, 181–183, 185–186.

144. For explanation of changing budget projections, see Congressional Budget Office, *The Budget and Economic Outlook 2001–2010* (Washington, DC: CBO, January 2000), 52–58. Other data drawn from *Budget of the United States Government, Fiscal Year 2009: Historical Tables* (Washington, DC: Office of Management and Budget , 2008), and Congressional Research Service, *Deficit Impact of Reconciliation Legislation Enacted in 1990, 1993, and 1997* (August 30, 2005).

145. Michael Mandel and others, "How Long Can This Last," *Business Week*, May 19, 1997, 29–34; Stephen D. Oliner and Daniel Sichel, "The Resurgence of Growth in the Late 1990s: Is Information Technology the Story?" *Journal of Economic Perspectives*, 14 (2000), 3–22; Stephanie Schmidt, "Long-Run Trends in Workers' Beliefs about their Own Job Security: Evidence from the General Social Survey," *Journal of Labor Economics* 17 (October 1999), 127–141.

146. For effusive editorial comment, see "Who Needs Gold When We Have Greenspan," *New York Times*, March 3, 1999, A30; and "Another Term for Mr. Greenspan," *New York Times*, January 5, 2000, A24.

147. Greenspan, *The Age of Turbulence*, 161–163; Woodward, *Maestro*, 159; Rubin and Weisberg, *In an Uncertain World*, 191–196.

148. James Galbraith, "The Economy Doesn't Need the Third Way," *New York Times*, November 23, 1999, A25; Joseph Stiglitz, *The Roaring Nineties: Seeds of Destruction* (London: Penguin, 2003), 41–55.

149. Alan Blinder and Janet Yellen, *The Fabulous Decade: Macroeconomic Lessons from the 1990s* (New York: Century Foundation Press, 2001), 15–24, 83–85 (quotation p. 83); Woodward, *Maestro*, 221. See also Rubin and Weisberg, *In an Uncertain World*, 356–357; and Laura Tyson, "A Squandered Legacy," *Prospect,* April 2004, 34–39.

150. Harris, *The Survivor*, 261; John Harris, "It's a Brave New World Where Politicians Bicker over Surpluses," *Washington Post*, January 10, 1998, A1.

151. Klein, *The Natural*, 197.

152. Quoted in Jacob Weisberg, "The Governor-President," *New York Times Magazine*, January 17, 1999, 33.

153. *Budget of the United States Government, Fiscal Year 2000: Analytic Perspectives* (Washington, DC: Office of Management and Budget, 1999), 337. See also Peter G. Peterson, *Will America Grow Up Before It Grows Old?* (New York: Random House, 1996), esp. chapter 3; Douglas W. Elmendorf and Jeffrey B. Liebman, "Social Security Reform and National Saving in an Era of Budget Surpluses," *Brookings Papers on Economic Activity* 2 (2000), 1–71; and Douglas W. Elmendorf and Louise M. Sheiner, "Should America Save for Its Old Age? Fiscal Policy, Population Aging, and National Saving," *Journal of Economic Perspectives* 14 (2000), 57–74.

154. "State of the Union Address to a Joint Session of Congress," January 27, 1998, APP; Rubin, *In an Uncertain World*, 359; Greenspan, *The Age of Turbulence*, 186.

155. Douglas W. Elmendorf, Jeffrey Liebman, and David Wilcox, "Fiscal Policy and Social Security Policy during the 1990s," in Frankel and Orszag, *American Economic Policy in the 1990s* , 80–85. For reform plans, see Edward Gramlich, *Is It Time*

to Reform Social Security? (Ann Arbor: University of Michigan Press, 1998); and Sylvester Schieber and John B. Shoven, *The Real Deal: The History and Future of Social Security* (New Haven, CT: Yale University Press, 1999).

156. This analysis is based on Gillon, *The Pact*, chapter 13.

157. Ibid., 265–269 (quotation on 268); Klein, *The Natural*, 175–177. See also Bartlett, *Impostor* (New York: Doubleday, 2006), 167–168; Kevin Hassett and Maya McGuiness, "Fitting the Bill," *National Review*, March 16, 2005, www.national review.com.

158. Rubin, *In an Uncertain World*, 273–274; Harris, *The Survivor*, 350–351.

159. "Address to a Joint Session of Congress on the State of the Union," January 19, 1999, APP; Clinton, *My Life*, 842–843.

160. "Remarks on Departure for Palm Beach, Florida, and an Exchange with Reporters," and "Press Briefing by Joe Lockhart," March 16, 1999, APP; Joseph P. Newhouse, "Medicare Policy," in Frankel and Orszag, *American Economic Policy in the 1990s*, 938–941.

161. Elmendorf, Liebman, and Wilcox, "Fiscal Policy and Social Security During the 1990s," 109–112; Blinder and Yellen, *The Fabulous Decade*, 77–78.

162. "Message on Returning without Approval to the House of Representatives the 'Taxpayer Refund and Relief Act of 1999,'" September 23, 1999, APP.

163. Deborah Rosenberg and Lynette Clemerson, "A Quiet Brawl over Billions: The Clinton-Gingrich Budget Shutdown," *Newsweek*, October 26, 1998, 46–47; Peter Baker, "Clinton Celebrates a Victory Made Possible by Reduced Expectations," *Washington Post*, October 16, 1998, A1; John Broder, "The Budget Deal," *New York Times*, October 16, 1998, A1.

164. Congressional Budget Office, *The Budget and Economic Outlook: Fiscal Years 2000–2009* (Washington, DC: CBO, 1999), 34; Michael Waldman, *POTUS Speaks: Finding the Words That Defined the Clinton Presidency* (New York: Simon & Schuster, 2001), 241.

165. William C. Berman, *From the Center to the Edge: The Politics and Policies of the Clinton Administration* (Lanham, MD: Rowman & Littlefield, 2001), 87–88; Clinton, *My Life*, 822–824; Dan Balz, "Gingrich Says He's Leaving to Spare Turmoil in Party," *Washington Post*, November 10, 1998, A1.

166. Congressional Budget Office, *The Budget and Economic Outlook; Fiscal Years 2002–2011* (Washington, DC: CBO, 2001), 75; Ippolito, *Why Budgets Matter*, 286.

167. Richard Stevenson, "Clinton's Budget Stresses Surplus and Having It All," *New York Times*, February 8, 2000, A1; "Message to the House of Representatives Returning without Approval the 'Marriage Tax Relief Reconciliation Act' of 2000," August 5, 2000, APP.

168. Burns and Sorensen, *Dead Center*, 288; John E. Yang, "Looking Back to Theodore Roosevelt, Gephardt Calls for 'New Progressivism,'" *Washington Post*, December 3, 1997, A2.

169. Barack Obama, *The Audacity of Hope: Thoughts on Reclaiming the American Dream* (New York: Crown Books, 2006), 34.

170. "Remarks at a Reception for Supporters of the Omnibus Budget Reconciliation Act of 1993," April 23, 1998, APP.

171. Daniel Kadlec, "A $1 Trillion Plunge: The Thrill Ride Isn't Over," and John Greenwald, "Doom Stalks the Dotcoms," *Time*, April 17, 2000, 28–34. See also Robert Shiller, *Irrational Exuberance* (Princeton, NJ: Princeton University Press, 2000); and Robert Brenner, *The Boom and the Bubble: The U.S. in the World Economy* (New York: Verso, 2002).

172. Reich, *Locked in the Cabinet*, 318; *Economic Report of the President 1999*, 166; *Economic Report of the President 2000*, 342, 352, 354; Pamela Ferdinand and Michael Grunwald, "At Two Commencements, Perspective Is the Reality," *Washington Post*, June 11, 1999, A3.

173. Elmendorf, Liebman, and Wilcox, "Fiscal Policy and Social Security During the 1990s," 75–77, and "Summary of Discussion," [Martin Feldstein] in Frankel and Orszag, *American Economic Policy in the 1990s*, 747. Savings data from *Economic Report of the President 2009*, 320.

174. Minutes of the Federal Reserve Open Market Committee, September 24, 1996, 31, www.federalreserve.gov/monetarypolicy/fomchistorical1996.htm.

175. Charles Morris, *The Trillion Dollar Meltdown: Easy Money, High Rollers, and the Great Credit Crash* (New York: Public Affairs, 2008); Peter Goodman, "Taking a Hard Look at a Greenspan Legacy," *New York Times*, October 8, 2008; Greenspan, *The Age of Turbulence*, 198–199, 375–376.

176. Klein, *The Natural*, 198.

Chapter 7. George W. Bush: Resurrecting the Deficit

1. Lori Montgomery and Dan Eggen, "Spending Surge Pushing Deficit towards $1 Trillion," *Washington Post*, October 18, 2008, A1.

2. "Remarks to the National Conference of State Legislatures," March 2, 2001, APP; "Remarks at Western Michigan University in Kalamazoo, Michigan," March 27, 2001, APP; "Remarks at a Fundraiser for Senatorial Candidate Elizabeth Dole and Congressional Candidate Robin Hayes in Charlotte," February 27, 2002, APP.

3. Fred I. Greenstein, "George W. Bush: The Man and His Leadership," in John C. Fortier and Norman J. Ornstein, eds., *Second-Term Blues: How George W. Bush Has Governed* (Washington, DC: Brookings Institution Press/AEI, 2007), 42. For prepresidential biographies, see Bill Minutaglio, *First Son: George W. Bush and the Bush Family Dynasty* (New York: Times Books, 1999); Elizabeth Mitchell, *W: Revenge of the Bush Dynasty* (New York: Hyperion, 2000); and J. H. Hatfield, *Fortunate Son: George W. Bush and the Making of an American President*, 2nd ed. (New York: Soft Skull, 2001). Also useful is the campaign autobiography (largely written by aide Karen Hughes), George W. Bush, *A Charge to Keep: My Journey to the White House* (New York: William Morrow, 1999).

4. Paul Begala, *It's Still the Economy, Stupid: George W. Bush, the GOP's CEO* (New York: Simon & Schuster, 2002), 115.

5. Quoted in Hatfield, *Fortunate Son*, 118–119.

6. Harold W. Stanley, "The Nominations: The Return of Party Leaders," in Michael Nelson, ed., *The Elections of 2000* (Washington, DC: CQ Press, 2001), 29–32.

7. See, for example, Michael Lind, *Made in Texas: George W. Bush and the Southern Takeover of American Politics* (New York: Basic Books, 2003), chapter 4.

8. Quoted in Minutaglio, *First Son*, 163. See also Kevin Phillips, *American Dynasty: Aristocracy, Fortune, and the Politics of Deceit in the House of Bush* (New York: Penguin, 2004), 47–50.

9. Begala, *It's Still the Economy, Stupid*, 116.

10. Andrew Gumbel, "Profile: George W. Bush–This Charmed Man," *The Independent*, November 4, 2000, 5; Begala, *It's Still the Economy, Stupid*, 120.

11. Iwan Morgan, "The Indebted Empire: America's Current-Account Deficit Problem," *International Politics* 45 (January 2008), 92–112.

12. "The Budget Message of the President," February 4, 2008, www.whitehouse.gov/omb/budget/fy2009/message.html; Kris Cox, "Administration's Budget Does Not Reflect Administration Policies," Center on Budget Policy and Priorities [hereafter, CBPP], March 5, 2008.

13. Robert Bryce, *Cronies: Oil, the Bushes, and the Rise of Texas, America's Superstate* (New York: PublicAffairs, 2004), 183; Phillips, *American Dynasty*, 160; Minutaglio, *First Son*, 305–306.

14. Molly Ivins and Lou Dubose, *Bushwhacked: Life in George W. Bush's America* (New York: Random House, 2003), 73–74.

15. Daniel Altman, *Neoconomy: George Bush's Revolutionary Gamble with American's Future* (New York: Public Affairs, 2004), 21–30. See also Robert Barro and Xavier Sala-I-Martin, *Economic Growth* (New York: McGraw-Hill, 1995).

16. Altman, *Neoconomy*, 40.

17. Robert Bryce, *Pipe Dreams: Greed, Ego, and the Death of Enron* (New York: Public Affairs, 2002), 90.

18. Altman, *Neoconomy*, 32–34, 38–39; David Leonhardt, "Scholarly Mentor to Bush's Team," *New York Times*, December 1, 2002, www.nytimes.com.

19. Martin Feldstein, "Comments," in Jeffrey Frankel and Peter S. Orszag, eds., *American Economic Policy in the 1990s* (Cambridge, MA: MIT Press, 2002), 124–125, 136 (quotation p. 125). For other works by Feldstein, see "Clinton's Revenue Mirage," *Wall Street Journal*, April 6, 1993, A14; "Fiscal Policies, Capital Formation, and Capitalism," *European Economic Review* 39 (April 1995), 399–420; and "The Effect of Marginal Tax Rates on Taxable Income: A Panel Study of the 1986 Tax Reform Act," *Journal of Political Economy* 103 (June 1995), 551–572.

20. For their economic thinking, see Lawrence B. Lindsey, *The Growth Experiment: How the New Tax Policy Is Transforming the U.S. Economy* (New York: Basic Books, 1990); and R. Glenn Hubbard and Kevin A. Hassett, eds., *Transition Costs of Fundamental Tax Reform* (Washington, DC: AEI Press, 2000).

21. Quoted in Paul Krugman, "Everyone Is Outraged" (*New York Times*, July 2, 2002), in Paul Krugman, *The Great Unraveling: From Boom to Bust in Three Scandalous Years* (New York: Norton, 2003), 117. For Bush and Enron, see Ivins and Dubose, *Bushwhacked*, 184–213; and Kevin Phillips, *American Dynasty*, 155–170.

22. Bryce, *Cronies*, 175–178; Ivins and Dubose, *Bushwhacked*, 8–14.

23. "The President's Press Conference," July 8, 2002, APP.

24. Martin A. Sullivan, "The Decline and Fall of Distributional Analysis," *Tax Notes*, June 27, 2003, 1872. See also Paul Krugman, "Pants on Fire" (*New York Times*, August 24, 2001), in Krugman, *The Great Unraveling*, 161–163.

25. John Cranford, "The Deficit's Hard Truth," *CQ Weekly*, September 26, 2005, 2554–2561.

26. Bill Keller, "Reagan's Son," *New York Times*, January 26, 2003, A7.

27. George W. Bush, "Address to the Front Porch Alliance," Indianapolis, July 22, 1999, www.cpjustice.org/stories/storyreader$383; and "Address to 2004 Republican National Convention, New York," September 2, 2004, APP.

28. Paul Starr, "The Bush Bankruptcy Plan," *American Prospect*, June 1, 2003, www.prospect.org.

29. Sam Tanenhaus, "Is Bush Conservative Enough?" *Los Angeles Times*, July 22, 2003, B13. See also Bruce Bartlett, *Impostor: How George W. Bush Bankrupted America and Betrayed the Reagan Legacy* (New York: Doubleday, 2006); Stephen Slivinski, *Buck Wild: How Republicans Broke the Bank and Became the Party of Big Government* (Nashville, TN: Nelson Current, 2006); Peggy Noonan, "Hey, Big Spender," www.OpinionJournal.com, March 16, 2006; Richard A. Viguerie, *Conservatives Betrayed: How George W. Bush and Other Big Government Republicans Hijacked the Conservative Cause* (Los Angeles: Bonus Books, 2006); and Michael D. Tanner, *Leviathan on the Right: How Big-Government Conservatism Brought down the Republican Revolution* (Washington, DC: Cato Institute, 2007).

30. Tanner, *Leviathan on the Right*, 15.

31. Fred Barnes, "'Big Government Conservatism': George Bush Style," *Wall Street Journal*, August 15, 2003, and *Rebel-in-Chief: Inside the Bold and Controversial Presidency of George W. Bush* (New York: Crown Forum, 2006); John Podhoretz, *Bush Country: How Dubaya Became a Great President While Driving Liberals Insane* (New York: St. Martin's Press, 2004); and Dan Casse, "Is Bush a Conservative?" *Commentary*, February 2004, 19–26.

32. Hugh Heclo, "The Political Ethos of George W. Bush," in Fred I. Greenstein, ed., *The George W. Bush Presidency: First Appraisals* (Baltimore: Johns Hopkins University Press, 2003), 17–50 (quotation p. 37); David Frum, *The Right Man* (New York: Random House, 2003), 59.

33. Bush, *A Charge to Keep*, 218, 118–119; Altman, *Neoconomy*, 40. For insightful analysis, see Charles O. Jones, "Governing Executively: Bush's Paradoxical Style," in Fortier and Ornstein, *Second-Term Blues*, 109–130.

34. "Remarks at Western Michigan University in Kalamazoo, Michigan," March 27, 2001, APP.

35. Quoted in Podhoretz, *Bush Country*, 119.

36. Quoted in Dan Balz, "Ready to Govern in His Own Style," *Washington Post*, November 5, 2004, A5.

37. Bush, *A Charge to Keep*, 186.

38. Martin P. Wattenberg, "*Elections*: Tax Cut Versus Lockbox: Did the Voters Grasp the Trade-Off in 2000?" *Presidential Studies Quarterly* 34 (December 2004), 838–848; Alan Greenspan, *The Age of Turbulence: Adventures in a New World* (New York: Penguin Press, 2007), 216–217.

39. Donald Kettl, *Team Bush: Leadership Lessons from the Bush White House* (New York: McGraw-Hill, 2003); Ron Suskind, *The Price of Loyalty: George W. Bush and the Education of Paul O'Neill* (New York: Simon & Schuster, 2004), 281–310; Elizabeth Bumiller, "The President's Team Changes But Not Its Game Plan," *New York Times*, 5 January 2003, A14.

40. Jonathan Weisman, "Dropping Report's Iraq Chapter Was Unusual, Economists Say," *Washington Post*, February 23, 2005, A17; Bartlett, *Impostor*, 34–36.

41. Suskind, *The Price of Loyalty*, 165–169; Evan Thomas and Richard Wolffe, "Bush in the Bubble," *Newsweek*, December 19, 2005, 16–25; Greenspan, *The Age of Turbulence*, 238–240.

42. Ron Suskind, "Without a Doubt," *New York Times Magazine*, October 17, 2004.

43. Congressional Budget Office, *The Budget and Economic Outlook: An Update* (Washington, DC: CBO, July 2000), 1–2, and *The Budget and Economic Outlook: Fiscal Years 2002–2011* (Washington, DC: CBO, 2001), 2; Greenspan, *The Age of Turbulence*, 213–214, 217.

44. Congressional Budget Office, *The Budget and Economic Outlook: Fiscal Years 2003–2012* (Washington, DC: CBO, 2002), 2; *The Budget and Economic Outlook: Fiscal Years 2004–2013* (Washington, DC: CBO, 2003), 2; *The Budget and Economic Outlook: Fiscal Years 2005–2014* (Washington, DC: CBO, 2004), 1.

45. Congressional Budget Office, *The Budget and Economic Outlook: Fiscal Years 2003–2012*, 92–93; *Budget of the United States Government, Fiscal Year 2003* (Washington, DC: Government Printing Office, 2003), 6. See also Rudolph G. Penner, "Dealing with Uncertain Budget Forecasts," *Public Budgeting and Finance* 22 (Spring 2002), 1–18.

46. Richard Kogan and Robert Greenstein, "Official Treasury Report Shows Fourth Year of Deficit Growth, Despite Economic Recovery," CBPP, October 14, 2004.

47. *Budget of the United States Government Fiscal Year 2009: Historical Tables*, 25, 27.

48. "The Budget Message of the President," February 11, 2004, www.whitehouse.gov/omb/budget/fy2005/message.html.

49. Office of Management and Budget, "Ensuring Fiscal Responsibility," February 11, 2004, www.whitehouse.gov/omb/budget/fy2005/message.html.

50. Morton J. Marcus, "The Recession of 2001," *InContext* 3 (November–December 2002), www.incontext.indiana.edu/2002/nov-dec02/spotlight; National Bureau of Economic Research, "The Business Cycle Peak of March 2001," November 26, 2001.

51. Congressional Budget Office, *The Budget and Economic Outlook: An Update* (Washington, DC: CBO, August 2002); Greenspan, *The Age of Turbulence*, 224.

52. "Remarks on Signing the Jobs and Growth Tax Relief Reconciliation Act of 2003," May 28, 2003; "Remarks on Passage of the Economic Growth and Tax Relief Reconciliation Act of 2001," May 26, 2001, APP.

53. Richard Kogan and James Horney, "Deficit Announcement Masks Bigger Story: Long-Term Outlook Remains Bleak," CBPP, October 11, 2006.

54. Author's calculations based on *Budget of the United States Government Fiscal Year 2009: Historical Tables*, table 1.3. In contrast to FY1969, which reflected Lyndon Johnson's tax surcharge of 1968, the surge in receipts in FY2005–FY2006 had not benefited from revenue enhancement policy. Its scale in current-dollar terms was also impressive—the expansion in receipts by 14.5 percent in FY2005 and 11.8 percent in FY2006 were the highest since the rise of 15.8 percent in FY1981, when inflation had produced significant bracket-creep.

55. "Remarks on the Office of Management and Budget Mid-Session Review," July 11, 2006, APP.

56. Michael Abramowitz and Peter Baker, "Painting a Rosy Budget Picture: Bush Touts Declining Deficit, but Long-Term Outlook Is Dimmer," *Washington Post*, October 11, 2006, A6.

57. U.S. Treasury, "A Dynamic Analysis of Permanent Extension of the President's Tax Relief," July 25, 2006, www.treas.gov/press/releases/reports/treasurydynamicanal ysisreporjjuly252006.pdf; Congressional Research Service, *The Budget for FY 2006*, August 30, 2006. For commentary, see Nell Henderson, "Tax Cuts May Come at a Price, Study Says," *Washington Post*, July 26, 2006, D1; James Horney, "A Smoking Gun: President's Claim that Tax Cuts Pay for Themselves Refuted by New Treasury Analysis," CBPP, July 27, 2006.

58. Concord Coalition, "Concord Coalition Warns that Sustained Deficit Reduction Will Require More than Revenue Surprises," August 17, 2006; Congressional Budget Office, *Budget and Economic Update* (Washington, DC: CBO, August 2006).

59. Lori Montgomery, "Lower Deficits Spark Debate over Tax Cuts' Role," *Washington Post*, October 17, 2006, D1; Bartlett, *Impostor*, 62.

60. Greenspan, *The Age of Turbulence*, 218–219, 223.

61. Edmund Andrews, "Greenspan Throws Cold Water on Bush Argument for Tax Cut," *New York Times*, February 12, 2003, A1; Greenspan, *The Age of Turbulence*, 234–240 (quotation p. 239).

62. Stephen Roach, "Think Again: Alan Greenspan," *Foreign Policy* (January/ February 2005), 19–20; Ashley Seager, "Solid Foundations or Dangerous House of Cards? America Awaits Greenspan's Legacy," *Guardian* (London, UK), January 31, 2006, 25.

63. Peter Orszag and William Gale, "Budget Deficits, National Saving, and Interest Rates," *Brookings Institution Papers* (September 2004); Kevin Lansing, "Spendthrift Nation," *Federal Reserve Bank of San Francisco Economic Letter*, November 10, 2005; Martin Crutsinger, "Savings Rate Lowest Since Great Depression," January 30, 2006, www.breitbart.com.

64. Larry Summers, "America Overdrawn," *Foreign Policy* (July/August, 2004), 47–49; William Bonner and Addison Wiggin, *Empire of Debt: The Rise of an Epic Financial Crisis* (Hoboken, NJ: John Wiley, 2006).

65. Kenneth Rogoff, "The Debtor's Empire," *Washington Post*, October 20, 2003, A23; Nouriel Roubini and Brad Sester, *Will the Bretton Woods 2 Regime Unravel Soon? The Risk of a Hard Landing in 2005–2006*, February 2005, www.stern.nyu .edu/globalmacro/; Larry Elliot, "America Is Living Beyond Its Means," *Guardian* (London), October 2, 2006, 26.

66. Ben Bernanke, "The Global Saving Glut and the U.S. Current Account Deficit," Sandridge Lecture, Virginia Association of Economists, March 10, 2005, www .federalreserve.gov/; *Economic Report of the President 2006* (Washington, DC: Government Printing Office, 2006), chapter 6.

67. Christian Weller, "The U.S. Current Account Deficit: On an Unsustainable Path," *New Economy* 11 (December 2004), 243–248; Brad Sester and Nouriel Roubini, "Our Money, Our Debt, Our Problem," *Foreign Affairs* 84 (2005), 198–206.

68. Suskind, *The Price of Loyalty*, 291.

69. Hubbard quoted in Jonathan Chait, "Deficit Reduction," *New Republic*, January 13, 2003; R. Glenn Hubbard, *Money, the Financial System, and the Economy*, 4th ed. (Lebanon, IN: Addison, Wesley, 2001).

70. "Press Briefing on the Budget by OMB Director Mitch Daniels," February 3, 2003, www.whitehouse.gov/omb/speeches/daniels_04budget; Jonathan Weisman, "Past Remarks May Haunt New Economic Team," *Washington Post*, December 10, 2002, A10; Alan Ota, "Business Newly Tolerant of 'Manageable' Deficit," *CQ Weekly*, January 17, 2004, 162.

71. Paul Krugman, "Off the Wagon," *New York Times*, January 17, 2003; Ronald Brownstein, "Bush Breaks with 140 Years of History in Plan for Wartime Tax Cut," *Los Angeles Times*, January 13, 2003, A10. See also Michael Kinsley, "How Reaganomics Became Rubinomics," *Slate*, December 19, 2003, www.slate.com/?id=2075796.

72. "The President's Fiscal Year 2004 Budget Message," February 3, 2003, www.whitehouse/gov/news/releases/2003/02/20030203-7.html.

73. Suskind, *The Price of Loyalty*, 34–35; Bartlett, *Impostor*, 49–50. For criticism of the initial proposal, see Jacob Schlesinger, "Bush's Economic Guru Talks Like a Bear," *Wall Street Journal*, December 6, 1999, A9.

74. Jeff Madrick, "Plans to Cut Taxes May Be Clever Politics, But They're Not Wise Fiscal Policy," *New York Times*, February 15, 2001, A12; John Harris and Dan Balz, "First 100 Days Go By in a Blur," *Washington Post*, April 29, 2001, A1; Dan Balz, "Next on Bush's Agenda: Bigger Policy Changes," *Washington Post*, May 6, 2001, A1. See also Frum, *The Right Man*, 29.

75. "The 2000 Campaign: Exchanges between the Candidates in the Third Presidential Debate," *New York Times*, 18 October 2000, A26; Wattenberg, *"Elections:* Tax Cuts versus Lockbox: Did the Voters Grasp the Tradeoff in 2000?" 838–848.

76. Karlyn H. Bowman, *Public Opinion on Taxes* (Washington, DC: American Enterprise Institute, 2004), 10; Jacob S. Hacker and Paul Pierson, "Abandoning the Middle: The Bush Tax Cuts and the Limits of Democratic Control," *Perspectives on Politics* 3 (March 2005), 39.

77. Glen Kessler, "Payroll Tax: The Burden Untouched," *Washington Post*, February 6, 2001, A1; Altman, *Neoconomy*, 73.

78. Daniel Parks, "Bush's Sunny Budget Picture Leaves the Details Shaded," *CQ Weekly*, March 3, 2001, 450–455.

79. Karen Tumulty, "Five New Rules of the Road," *Time*, February 5, 2001, www.time.com.

80. Greenspan, *The Age of Turbulence*, 219–222; Suskind, *The Price of Loyalty*, 39–42; Robert Rubin and Jacob Weisberg, *In an Uncertain World: Tough Choices from Wall Street to Washington* (New York: Random House, 2003), 369; Richard Stevenson, "In Policy Change, Greenspan Backs a Broad Tax Cut," *New York Times*, January 26, 2001, A1.

81. Lori Nitschke, "House GOP Scores Victory for Bush with Swift Passage of Income Tax Bill," *CQ Weekly*, March 10, 2001, 529–532. See also Barbara Sinclair, "Context, Strategy, and Chance: George W. Bush and the 107th Congress," in Colin Campbell and Bert A. Rockman, eds., *The George W. Bush Presidency: Appraisals and Prospects* (Washington, DC: CQ Press, 2004), 112–113; John P. Burke, *Becoming*

President: The Bush Transition, 2000–2003 (Boulder, CO: Lynne Rienner, 2003), 136–137, 154.

82. Daniel Parks, "Bush Starts to Deal on the Budget, Only Hardening Resolve of Some," *CQ Weekly*, April 28, 2001, 903–906.

83. Suskind, *The Price of Loyalty*, 21, 268–269, 283–284.

84. "Remarks to the National Conference of State Legislatures," March 2, 2001, APP; Suskind, *The Price of Loyalty*, 131–136, 138, 162; Greenspan, *The Age of Turbulence*, 222–223.

85. "Remarks at Western Michigan University, Kalamazoo," March 27, 2001, APP; Suskind, *The Price of Loyalty*, 138, 149–150, 163–164.

86. Lori Nitschke, "Tax Cut Deal Reached Quickly as Appetite for Battle Fades," *CQ Weekly*, May 26, 2001, 1251–1255.

87. "Address before a Joint Session of the Congress on Administration Goals," February 27, 2001, "Remarks at a Leadership Forum in Atlanta," March 1, 2001, "Remarks to National Conference of State Legislatures," March 2, 2001, APP.

88. Juliet Eilperin and Dan Morgan, "Something Borrowed, Something Blue: Memo Enlists Lobbyists to Trade White Collars for Hard Hats," *Washington Post*, March 9, 2001, A16; David Rosenbaum, "Doing the Math on Bush's Tax Cut," *New York Times*, February 15, 2001, A12.

89. Congressional Budget Office, *The Budget and Economic Outlook: An Update* (Washington, DC: CBO, 2001), 8; Altman, *Neoconomy*, 237; Citizens for Tax Justice, "Year-by-Year Analysis of the Bush Tax Cuts Growing Tilt to the Very Rich," 2002, available at www.ctj.org/html/gwb0602.htm.

90. Martin Feldstein, "The 28% Solution," *Wall Street Journal*, February 28, 2001, available at www.nber.org/feldstein/wsj021601.html; Christopher House and Matthew Shapiro, "Phased-In Tax Cuts and Economic Activity," *National Bureau of Economic Research Working Paper*, No. 10415 (April 2004).

91. Jacob S. Hacker and Paul Pierson, *Off Center: The Republican Revolution and the Erosion of Democracy* (New Haven, CT: Yale University Press, 2005), 55–62 (quotation on 60). For similar criticism, see Altman, *Neoconomy*, 74–88.

92. Leonard Burman, William Gale, and Jeffrey Rohaly, "The AMT: Projections and Problems," *Tax Notes*, July 7, 2003, 105–117.

93. Richard Stevenson, "Bush Unveils Plan to Cut Tax Rates and Spur Economy," *Washington Post*, January 8, 2003, A1.

94. Elizabeth Bumiller, "A Bold Plan With Risks," *New York Times*, January 8, 2003, A1; Michel Hirsh and Tamara Lipper, "High Roller," and Allan Sloan, "This Cut Won't Pay Dividends," *Newsweek*, January 20, 2003, 25–28, 29.

95. "Nobel Laureates, 450 Other Economists Fault Bush Tax Cut Plan," *Economic Policy Institute Press Release*, February 10, 2003. Earlier, the National Taxpayers Union had organized a statement signed by 116 conservative economists, including Milton Friedman and two other Nobel Prize winners, warning that any congressional move to rescind the 2001 tax cuts or raise business taxes to correct the deficit would be economically harmful. See "116 Distinguished Economists Warn Congress: Don't Strangle Economic Recovery with Tax Hikes on Earnings, Options," *NTU Press Release*, January 14, 2003.

96. Quoted in "U.S. Economy: Bush Deficits May Raise Borrowing Costs,"

January 9, 2003, www.forexhsi.com/forexnews/news0103/news_231989.php. See too Ota, "Business Newly Tolerant of 'Manageable' Deficit," 162–164.

97. Jim VandeHei and Jonathan Weisman, "GOP Seeks to Change Score on Tax Cuts," *Washington Post*, February 6, 2003, A35; Bartlett, *Impostor*, 61–62; Podhoretz, *Bush Country*, 120–121.

98. David Rosenbaum, "A Tax Cut without End," *New York Times*, May 23, 2003, A1; Burke, *Becoming President*, 190–192, 206.

99. Matt Bai, "Fight Club," *New York Times Magazine*, August 10, 2003, 24; Americans for Tax Reform, "Questions and Answers about the National Taxpayers Pledge," www.atr.org/nationalpledge/index.html; Hacker and Pierson, *Off Center*, 53–54.

100. Rosenbaum, "A Tax Cut without End"; Joel Friedman, "Dividend and Capital Gains Tax Cuts Unlikely to Yield Touted Economic Gains," CBPP, March 10, 2003; "Remarks on Signing the Jobs and Growth Tax Relief Reconciliation Act of May 28, 2003," APP; Tod Lindberg, "The Bush Tax-Cut Record," *Washington Times*, June 10, 2003, A17.

101. David Firestone, "With Tax Bill Passed, Republicans Call for More," *New York Times*, May 24, 2003, A1.

102. Jonathan Weisman, "Congress Votes to Extend Tax Cuts," *Washington Post*, September 24, 2004, A1; Robert Greenstein, "New 'Middle-Class' Tax Cut Bill Represents Cynical Policymaking," CBPP, September 24, 2004.

103. "Remarks on Signing the Working Families Tax Relief Act in Des Moines, Iowa," October 4, 2004, APP; Associated Press, "Bush Quietly Signs Corporate Tax-Cut Bill," October 22, 2004, www.msnbc.msn.com/id/6307293/.

104. Jim VandeHei, "Tax Cuts Lose Top Spot on GOP Agenda," *Washington Post*, March 7, 2005, A1; Sheryl Gay Stolberg and David Kirkpatrick, "GOP Senators Balk at Tax Cuts in Bush's Budget," *New York Times*, March 10, 2005, A1; Jonathan Weisman, "$56 Billion in Tax Cuts Passed by House, 234–197," *Washington Post*, December 9, 2006, A6.

105. Jonathan Weisman, "House Passes 3 Tax Cuts, Plans a 4th: Cost Would Outstrip Recent Action on Deficit," *Washington Post*, December 8, 2005, A1; Jonathan Weisman, "Congress Seeks to Reconcile Divergent Bills," *Washington Post*, December 10, 2005, A5; Isaac Shapiro, Sharon Parrott, and Robert Greenstein, "Key Questions for Judging the Outcome of the House-Senate Reconciliation Negotiations," CBPP, December 8, 2005.

106. Jim VandeHei and Nell Henderson, "Economy Gained Muscle Last Year, Expanding Jobs: In Chicago Bush Rejoices and Says Policies Are Working," *Washington Post*, January 7, 2006, A3; Robin Toner, "Holding Fast to a Policy of Tax Cutting," *New York Times*, February 7, 2006, A1; Jonathan Weisman and Paul Blustein, "GOP Reaches Deal on Tax Cuts: $70 Billion Measure Would Extend Breaks," *Washington Post*, May 10, 2006, A1.

107. Edmund Andrews, "Senate Approves Extension of Bush Tax Cuts," *New York Times*, May 12, 2006, A1.

108. Hacker and Pierson, *Off Center*, 48–49.

109. Thomas B. Edsall, *Building Red America: The New Conservative Coalition and the Drive for Permanent Power* (New York: Basic Books, 2006), 43–44.

110. See, for example, Joel D. Aberbach, "The State of the Contemporary American Presidency: Or, Is Bush II Actually Ronald Reagan's Heir?" in Colin Campbell and Bert Rockman, eds., *The George W. Bush Presidency: Appraisals and Prospects* (Washington, DC: CQ Press, 2004), 46–72; Stephen E. Schier, "Introduction: George W. Bush's Project," in Stephen E. Schier, ed., *High Risks and Big Ambitions: The Presidency of George W. Bush* (Pittsburgh: University of Pittsburgh Press, 2004), 1–14; and John Owens, "American-Style Party Government: Delivering Bush's Agenda, Delivering Congress's Agenda," in Iwan Morgan and Philip Davies, eds., *Right On? Political Change and Continuity in George W. Bush's America* (London: Institute for the Study of the Americas, 2005), 131–160.

111. Edsall, *Building Red America*, 44; John Zogby, "Investors for Bush: How Social Security Reform Can Bring about a Republican Realignment," *Wall Street Journal*, March 15, 2005, A25.

112. Jim VandeHei, "Blueprint Calls for Bigger, More Powerful Government: Some Conservatives Express Concern at Agenda," *Washington Post*, February 9, 2005, A1.

113. Richard Armey, "Reflections on the Republican Revolution," in Chris Edwards and John Samples, eds., *The Republican Revolution 10 Years Later: Smaller Government or Business as Usual* (Washington, DC: Cato Institute, 2005), 10; Jacob Weisberg, "Interest-Group Conservatism," www.slate.com, May 4, 2005.

114. Glenn Kessler, "2003 Budget Completes Big Jump in Spending," *Washington Post*, April 15, 2002, A1; Brian Riedl, "The Quiet Earthquake in Spending," *Heritage Foundation Commentary*, November 23, 2003.

115. Bartlett, *Impostor*, chapter 7; Kevin Hassett, "Bring Back Clinton—Just His Spending Habits," www.bloomberg.com, 18 July 2005.

116. Mike Allen, "Bush Calls Farm Subsidies a National Security Issue," *Washington Post*, February 9, 2002, A4; Chris Edwards and Tad DeHaven, "Farm Bill Reversal," Cato Institute Tax and Budget Bulletin, No. 2, March 2002; John Boehner and Cal Dooley, "The Terrible Farm Bill," *Washington Times*, May 2, 2002.

117. Tanner, *Leviathan on the Right*, 168–169; Bartlett, *Impostor*, 131.

118. Slivinski, *Buck Wild*, 141.

119. Amy Goldstein, "Prescription Drug Plan Sent to Skeptical Congress," *Washington Post*, January 30, 2001, A1; Burke, *Becoming President*, 146–147; Robert Novak, "Any Health Bill Will Do," *Washington Post*, July 7, 2003.

120. Robert Pear and Robin Toner, "A Final Push in Congress," *New York Times*, November 23, 2003, A1; Major Garrett, *The Enduring Revolution: How the Contract with America Continues to Shape the Nation* (New York: Crown Forum, 2005), 254–264.

121. Amy Goldstein, "Higher Medicare Costs Suspected for Months," *Washington Post*, January 31, 2004, A1; Amy Goldstein and Helen Dewar, "GOP Seeking Afterglow of Vote on Drug Benefits," *Washington Post*, February 29, 2004, A7; Janet Hook, "President Putting 'Big' Back in Government," *Los Angeles Times*, February 8, 2005, A1.

122. Paul Krugman, "Privatizers Can't Explain Their Catch-22," *New York Times*, January 26, 2005; Robert Barro, "Why Private Accounts Are Bad Public Policy," *Business Week*, April 4, 2005, 26; Concord Coalition, "A Real Fix for Social Security Requires an Increase in National Saving," *Concord Coalition Social Security Briefing*, No. 5, April 13, 2005.

123. Dick Morris, "How Second Terms Fail," *New York Post*, January 19, 2005; Bartlett, *Impostor*, 202–204; Tanner, *Leviathan on the Right*, 132–135.

124. Christopher Helman and Travis Sharp, *Total Iraq and Afghanistan Supplemental War Funding to Date*, July 23, 2008 (calculations based on Congressional Research Service data), www.armscontrolcenter.org/policy/securityspending/articles/supplemental_war_funding; James A. Baker III and Lee Hamilton, *Iraq Study Group Report*, December 6, 2006, www.usip.org/isg/iraq_study_group_report/report/1206.

125. Martin Kady II, "Defense: A Deficit Driver," *CQ Weekly*, January 17, 2004, 155; Cranford, "The Deficit's Hard Truths," 2557; Jonathan Weisman, "Congress Unlikely to Embrace Bush Wish List," *Washington Post*, February 8, 2005, A6.

126. Joseph Stiglitz and Linda Bilmes, *The Three Trillion Dollar War: The True Cost of the Iraq Conflict* (New York: Penguin Press, 2008), 7–10; Amy Belasco, "The Cost of Iraq, Afghanistan, and Other Global War on Terror Operations since 9/11," *CRS Report to Congress*, [updated] July 16, 2007.

127. Jonathan Weisman, "Unforeseen Spending on Materiel Pumps up Iraq War Bill," *Washington Post*, April 20, 2006, A1.

128. In mid-2008, the largest single Pentagon contract in Iraq was divided among three companies, thereby ending the monopoly held by KBR, the Houston-based former Halliburton subsidiary that had been accused of waste and mismanagement and exploiting its ties with Dick Cheney, onetime Halliburton chair. With 40,000 employees in Iraq, KBR had collected $24 billion since the start of the war. Henceforth required to share with Fluor Corporation and DynCorp, it would still earn huge sums from a new ten-year joint contract for services in Iraq. See James Risen, "Controversial Contractor's Iraq Work Is Split Up," *New York Times*, May 24, 2008, www.nytimes.com.

129. The above is based on Stiglitz and Bilmes, *The Three Trillion Dollar War*, 10–16.

130. Ibid., 59; Kris Cox, "Administration's Budget Does Not Reflect Administration's Policies," CBPP, March 5, 2008.

131. Mike Allen and Peter Baker, "$2.5 Trillion Budget Cuts Many Programs," *Washington Post*, February 7, 2005, A1; Concord Coalition, "The President's Fiscal Year 2006 Budget: As Significant for What It Omits as for What It Includes," February 15, 2005; James Dao, "Mayors Urge Bush Not to Cut Programs," *New York Times*, January 19, 2005, A5; Dana Milbank, "From Bush Supporters, Anger over the Budget," *Washington Post*, February 14, 2005, A15.

132. Jonathan Weisman, "Senate Rejects GOP Budget Cuts," *Washington Post*, March 18, 2005, A4; Sheryl Gail Stolberg, "Congress Passes Budget with Cuts in Medicaid and Taxes," *New York Times*, April 29, 2005, A1; James Horney, "Assessing the Conference Agreement on the Budget Resolution," CBPP, April 28, 2005.

133. Slivinski, *Buck Wild*, 176; Winslow T. Wheeler, "Defense Pork: Putting Lipstick on a Pig," www.motherjones.com, March 21, 2006. For critical and sympathetic perspectives of earmarks, see (respectively) John McCain with Mark Salter, *Worth the Fighting For: A Memoir* (New York: Random House, 2002), 339–344; and John Cochran, "Budget Villain, Local Hero," *CQ Weekly*, June 12, 2006, 1606–1613.

134. Bartlett, *Impostor*, 138; Tanner, *Leviathan on the Right*, 151–155; Taxpayers for Common Sense, "The Gravina Access Project: A Bridge to Nowhere," www.taxpayer.net/Transportation/gravinabridge.htm.

135. Jonathan Weisman, "In Congress, the GOP Embraces Its Spending Side," *Washington Post*, August 4, 2005, A1; Shailagh Murray, "Some in GOP Regretting Pork-Stuffed Highway Bill," *Washington Post*, November 5, 2005, A1.

136. Tanner, *Leviathan on the Right*, 160–162; Howard Fineman, "Money, Money Everywhere," *Newsweek*, September 26, 2005, 30–35; Michael Grunwald and Susan Glasser, "Louisiana Goes after Federal Billions," *Washington Post*, September 26, 2005, A1.

137. Carl Hulse, "Lawmakers Prepare Plans to Finance Katrina Relief," *New York Times*, September 21, 2005, A1; Shailagh Murray, "Storm's Costs Threaten Hill Leaders' Pet Projects," *Washington Post*, September 22, 2005, A13; Carl Hulse, "Two 'Bridges to Nowhere' Tumble down in Congress," *New York Times*, November 17, 2005, A4.

138. Christopher Cooper, "President Seeks Entitlement Cuts to Pay for Katrina," *Wall Street Journal*, October 5, 2005, A1; E. J. Dionne, "Where's the Budget Outrage?" *Washington Post*, January 31, 2006, A17; Jonathan Weisman, "Budget Cuts Pass by a Slim Margin: Poor, Elderly and Students Feel the Pinch," *Washington Post*, February 2, 2006, A1.

139. Brian Riedl, "The President's Budget: Strong on Short-Term Spending, but Long-Term Challenges Remain," February 6, 2006, www.heritage.org/research/Budget/wm990.cfm?.

140. Jonathan Weisman, "Budget Plan Assumes Too Much, Demands Too Little," *Washington Post*, February 7, 2006, A10; "Concord Coalition Says President's Budget Does Not Make Realistic Tradeoffs," February 6, 2006; Jonathan Weisman, "Republicans on Hill Resist Party Leaders' Spending Cuts," *Washington Post*, March 1, 2006, A8.

141. Carl Hulse, "How to Unite Congress: Spend Billions on Projects for Roads," *New York Times*, March 11, 2005, A1; William A. Niskanen, "A Case for Divided Government," *Cato Institute Policy Report*, March-April 2003; Stephen Slivinski, "The Grand Old Spending Party: How Republicans Became Big Spenders," *Cato Institute Policy Analysis*, May 3, 2005.

142. Lori Montgomery and Nell Henderson, "Burden Set to Shift on Balanced Budget," *Washington Post*, January 16, 2007, A1; Lori Montgomery, "Bush Budget Projects a Surplus by 2012," *Washington Post*, February 5, 2007, A3.

143. Lori Montgomery, "Democrats Make Budget Proposal," *Washington Post*, May 17, 2007, A4; "Concord Coalition Applauds Pay-go in Budget Resolution but Warns that Projected Surplus Requires Hard Choices," May 17, 2007.

144. Ewen MacAskill, "Bush Slashes Aid to Poor to Boost Iraq War Chest," *Guardian* (London), February 6, 2007, 19; Michael Abramowitz, "Bush Cautions Democrats on Spending," *Washington Post*, June 17, 2007, A4; Lori Montgomery, "Congress Gets Warning on Budget," *Washington Post*, May 12, 2007, D1.

145. Carl Hulse, "Democrats Plan to Take Control of Iraq Spending," *New York Times*, December 14, 2006, A1; Jonathan Weisman, "Liberals Relent on Iraq War Funding," *Washington Post*, March 23, 2007, A1; David Stout and Sheryl Gay Stolberg, "Citing 'Rigid' Deadline, Bush Vetoes Iraq Bill," *New York Times*, May 2, 2007.

146. "Message to the House of Representatives Returning without Approval the

'U.S. Troop Readiness, Veterans' Care, Katrina Recovery, and Iraq Accountability Act, 2007,'" May 1, 2007, APP; Shailagh Murray and Jonathan Weisman, "Bush Derides Iraq War Measure," *Washington Post*, 29 March 2007, A1.

147. Shailagh Murray, "Congress Passes Deadline-Free War Funding Bill," *Washington Post*, May 25, 2007, A1.

148. Jonathan Weisman and Shailagh Murray, "Democrats Prepare for Another Funding Battle," *Washington Post*, May 27, 2007, A1; Murray, "Congress Passes Deadline-Free War Funding Bill."

149. Michael Abramowitz, "After Victory on Hill, President Shifts Tone on Iraq," *Washington Post*, May 25, 2007, A4; Thomas Ricks, "Bush Wants $50 Billion More for Iraq War," *Washington Post*, August 29, 2007, A1.

150. Elizabeth Williamson, "House Approves Bill Linking War Funds, Troop Withdrawals," *Washington Post*, November 15, 2007, A3; Paul Kane and Jonathan Weisman, "Iraq Funds Approved in Senate Budget Bill," December 19, 2007, A1; Jonathan Weisman and Paul Kane, "Key Setbacks Dim Luster of Democrats' Year," *Washington Post*, December 20, 2007, A1.

151. "Message to the House of Representatives Returning Without Approval the 'Departments of Labor, Health and Human Services, and Education, and Related Agencies Appropriations Act, 2008,'" November 13, 2007, APP.

152. Michael Abramowitz and Jonathan Weisman, "Bush Vetoes Health Measure," *Washington Post*, October 4, 2007, A1; "Statement of Administration Policy: H. R. 3074—'Department of Transportation, and Housing and Urban Development, and Related Agencies Appropriations Act, 2008,'" November 14, 2007, APP.

153. Jon Cohen and Dan Balz, "Most in Poll Want War Funding Cut," *Washington Post*, October 2, 2007, A1; Peter Baker, "Bush Veto Sets up Clash on Budget," *Washington Post*, November 14, 2007, A1.

154. John Solomon and Jeffrey Birnbaum, "In the Democratic Congress, Pork Still Gets Served," *Washington Post*, May 24, 2007, A1; Paul Kane, "Candidates' Earmarks Worth Millions," *Washington Post*, February 14, 2008, A1. The Democrats secured 57 percent of total earmarked funds. Presidential candidate Barack Obama received $91 million—$3.3 million for projects that he sponsored alone, and the rest for projects sponsored in collaboration with other Illinois congressmen. This relatively modest share put him in the bottom quartile of senatorial earmarks. Whatever his previous practice when there was less formal scrutiny of earmarks, Obama only requested funds for public entities like schools and hospitals. GOP presidential nominee John McCain was one of only five senators to reject earmarks entirely.

155. Jonathan Weisman, "A Bush Veto Is Overridden for the 1st Time," *Washington Post*, November 9, 2007, A4; Weisman and Kane, "Key Setbacks Dim Luster of Democrats' Year."

156. Jonathan Weisman, "Democrats Bow to Bush's Demands in House Spending Bill," *Washington Post*, December 13, 2007, A3, and "House Nears Approval of Domestic Spending Bill," *Washington Post*, December 18, 2007, A3.

157. Concord Coalition, "Paygo Rule Should Not Be Waived for Alternative Minimum Tax 'Patch,'" November 8, 2007; Jonathan Weisman, "House Passes Bill to Ease Alternative Minimum Tax," *Washington Post*, November 10, 2007, A1.

158. Jonathan Weisman and Jeffrey Birnbaum, "Senate Waives Pledge, Approves

Tax Bill," *Washington Post*, December 7, 2007, A3; Weisman and Kane, "Key Setbacks Dim Luster of Democrats' Year."

159. Edmund L. Andrews, "Officials Vow to Act Amidst Forecasts of Long Recession," *New York Times*, December 2, 2008, A1; Louis Uchitelle, Edmund L. Andrews, and Stephen Labaton, "U.S. Loses 533,000 Jobs in Biggest Drop since 1974," *New York Times*, December 6, 2008, A1.

160. For cogent early analysis of the crisis, see Charles Morris, *The Trillion Dollar Meltdown: Easy Money, High Rollers, and the Great Credit Crash* (New York: Public Affairs, 2008); Robert Shiller, *The Subprime Solution: How Today's Global Financial Crisis Happened and What to Do about It* (Princeton, NJ: Princeton University Press, 2008); Mark Zandi, *Financial Shock: A 360 Degree Look at the Subprime Mortgage Implosion, and How to Avoid the Next Financial Crisis* (Upper Saddle River, NJ: FT Press, 2009).

161. Steven Weinman, "Fed Cuts Rate but Hints about a Pause," *New York Times*, May 1, 2008, A1; David Herszenhorn, "Bush and House in Accord for $150 Billion Stimulus," *New York Times*, January 25, 2008, A1; David Herszenhorn and David Stout, "$168 Billion Stimulus Plan Clears Congress," *New York Times*, February 7, 2008, A1.

162. Andrew Clark, "U.S. Economy Awaits Stimulation from Bush's Tax Rebate," *Guardian* (London, UK), April 28, 2008, 27; Martin Feldstein, "The Tax Rebate Was a Flop. Obama's Stimulus Plan Won't Work Either," *Wall Street Journal*, August 6, 2008, available at www.feldstein\wsj080708.html; Christian Broda and Jonathan Parker, "The Impact of the 2008 Rebate," www.vocu.org/index.php?q=node/1541.

163. "The Doctors' Bill," *Economist*, September 27, 2008, 92–94.

164. Clive Crook, "Nationalization in All but Name," *Financial Times*, September 8, 2008, 6; David Teather, Larry Elliott, and Jill Treanor, "The Reckoning–Domino Effect that Reshaped Global Economy," *Guardian* (London, UK), September 20, 2008, 4–6; "When Fortune Frowned: A Special Report on the World Economy," *Economist*, October 11, 2008, 3–6.

165. David Herszenhorn, "Bailout Plan Talks Advance in Congress," *New York Times*, September 23, 2008, A1, and "Bailout Plan Wins Approval: Democrats Vow Tighter Rules," *New York Times*, October 4, 2008, A1; "The Politics of the Bail-out," *Economist*, October 4, 2008, 56–58.

166. Ron Lieber and Tara Siegel Bernard, "U.S. Consumer Loan Aid Will Trickle Only So Far," *New York Times*, November 27, 2008; Dan Milmo, "U.S. Pumps Another $800 billion into Mortgage and Credit Markets," *Guardian* (London, UK), November 26, 2008, 28.

167. Jackie Calmes, "2 Rivals' Plans on Fiscal Issue Add to Deficits," *New York Times*, October 29, 2008, www.nytimes.com; Scott Wilson, "Bruised by Stimulus Battle, Obama Changed His Approach to Washington," *Washington Post,* April 29, 2009, www.wash ingtonpost.com; "Spending and the Economy," and "Stimulus Packages," *Economist*, November 22, 2008, 53–54.

168. "The President's Press Conference," January 12, 2009, APP; "The Frat Boy Ships Out," *Economist*, January 17, 2009, 28.

169. *Economic Report of the President 2009*, 4, 285, 320, 328; Neil Irwin and Dan

Eggen, "Economy Made Few Gains in Bush Years," *Washington Post*, January 12, 2009, A1.

170. "Worse than Japan," *Economist*, February 14, 2009, 83–84.

171. Larry Summers, "The United States and the Global Adjustment Process," March 23, 2004, www.iie.com/publications/papers/summers0304htm; William Cline, *The U.S. as a Debtor Nation* (Washington, DC: Institute for International Economics, 2005).

172. *Economic Report of the President 2009*, 3.

173. "The President's News Conference," February 9, 2009, APP.

Epilogue. Barack Obama: Dealing with Deficits and Debt in the Short Term and Long Term

1. "Interview with Tom Brokaw on NBC's *Meet the Press*, December 7, 2008,"APP.

2. Quoted in Robert Bixby, "Congress in a Glass House," *Washington Post*, December 4, 2008, A21.

3. "The President's Press Conference," February 9, 2009, APP.

4. For details, see "Your Money at Work," www.recovery.gov/; and Urban Institute, *Tax Stimulus Report Card*, February 13, 2009, www.urban.org/. According to the former, the spending composition was $144 billion for state and local fiscal relief, $111 billion for infrastructure and science, $81 billion for protecting the vulnerable, $59 billion for health care, $53 billion for education and training, $43 billion for energy, and $8 billion for other purposes. The Urban Institute calculated tax benefits as $116.2 billion for the Making Work Pay tax credit, $69.8 billion for the AMT patch, $14.8 billion for increased eligibility for the refund portion of the child tax credit, $13.9 billion for the education tax credit, $6.6 billion for the homeownership tax credit, $4.7 billion for the increase in the earned income tax credit, $4.7 billion for the temporary suspension of taxation of unemployment benefits, and $1.7 billion for the automobile sale tax deduction.

5. Mimi Hall and David Jackson, "Stimulus Slammed as Dems' Agenda," *USA Today*, February 17, 2009, www.usatoday.com/news/washington/2009-02-17; Ike Brannon, "The Troubling Return of Keynesianism," *Cato Institute Tax and Budget Bulletin*, No. 52, January 2009; "The End of Innocence," *Economist*, February 21, 2009, 50.

6. Urban Institute, *Tax Stimulus Report Card*; Nicholas Johnson, Elizabeth McNichol, and Iris Lav, "Funding for States in Economic Recovery Package Will Close Less Than Half of State Deficits," Center on Budget Policy and Priorities [CBPP], February 20, 2009; Concord Coalition, *Designing a Framework for Economic Recovery and Fiscal Sustainability*, January 28, 2009. For details of the scaling down of state aid in the final ARRA bill—and the growing trend of state government layoffs in early 2009—see Alec MacGillis, "Despite Stimulus Funds, States to Cut More Jobs," *Washington Post*, May 12, 2009, www.washingtonpost.com.

7. Douglas Elmendorf, "The State of the Economy and Issues in Developing an Effective Policy Response," Testimony before the House Committee on the Budget,

January 27, 2009; "Statement by Robert Greenstein, Executive Director, on the Conference Agreement on the Recovery Package," February 12, 2009, CBPP.

8. "Remarks on Signing the American Recovery and Reinvestment Act, Denver, Colorado," February 17, 2009, APP; Jean Sahadi, "Stimulus: Now for the Hard Part," *CNN Money*, www.money.cnn.com/2009/02/17; Ewen MacAskill, "Obama Signs $787bn Bill, and It May Not Be the Last," *Guardian* (London, UK), February 18, 2009, 16.

9. Congressional Budget Office, *A Preliminary Analysis of the President's Budget and an Update of CBO's Budget and Economic Outlook* (Washington, DC: CBO, 2009), 1; Lori Montgomery, "Obama Team Assembling $850 Billion Stimulus," *Washington Post*, December 19, 2008, A1.

10. Lori Montgomery and Ceci Connolly, "Obama's First Budget to Trim Deficit," *Washington Post*, February 22, 2009. A1; Office of Management and Budget, *A New Era of Responsibility: Renewing America's Promise* (Washington, DC: OMB, February 26, 2009); CBO, *A Preliminary Analysis of the President's Budget*, 11–18. For media focus on Obama's deficit problem, see: David Leonhardt, "Sea of Red Ink was Years in the Making," *New York Times*, June 9, 2009; and Scott Wilson, "Obama's Spending Plans May Pose Political Risks," *Washington Post,* June 14, 2009.

11. "The President's Weekly Address," February 28, 2009, APP; Lori Montgomery, "Battle Lines Quickly Set Over Planned Policy Shifts," *Washington Post*, March 1, 2009, A1; Michael Fletcher, "Aides Defend President's Budget," *Washington Post*, March 2, 2009, A4; Lori Montgomery, "Congress Approves Budget: $3.5 trillion Spending Paves Way for Obama Goals," *Washington Post*, April 3, 2009, A1; Lori Montgomery, "Congress Approves Obama's $3.4 Trillion Spending Blueprint," *Washington Post*, April 30, 2009, A1.

12. Montgomery, "Congress Approves Obama's $3.4 Trillion Spending Blueprint."

13. Ibid.; "Remarks on Tax Relief," April 15, 2009, APP; Lori Montgomery, "America's Tax Burden Near Historic Low: Despite Obama's Pledge, Some Fear Future Hikes as Debt Grows," *Washington Post*, April 16, 2009, A4.

14. Robert Samuelson, "We Are a Nation in Deep Denial," *Newsweek*, March 13, 1995, 36–37; Ron Haskins, Alice M. Rivlin, and Isabel Sawhill, "Getting to Balance: Three Alternative Plans," in Alice M. Rivlin and Isabel Sawhill, eds., *Restoring Fiscal Sanity: How to Balance the Budget* (Washington, DC: Brookings Institution Press, 2004), 40; "The Frat Boy Ships Out," *Economist*, January 17, 2009.

15. Congressional Budget Office, *The Long-Term Budget Outlook* (Washington, DC: CBO, December 2007); Government Accountability Office, *The Nation's Long-Term Fiscal Outlook*, (Washington, DC: GAO, September 2008); Neil Howe and Richard Jackson, "A Report about Entitlements & the Budget from the Concord Coalition," *Facing Facts Quarterly* 4 (December 2008); "Taking Back Our Fiscal Future," *Brookings-Heritage Policy Report*, March 31, 2008.

16. "Another Inconvenient Truth," *Economist*, August 14, 2008. For the movie website, see www.iousathemovie.com.

17. Richard Kogan, Kris Cox, and James Horney, "The Long-Term Fiscal Outlook Is Bleak: Restoring Fiscal Sustainability Will Require Major Changes to Programs, Revenues, and the Nation's Health Care System," CBPP, December 16, 2008, 1–6.

18. Concord Coalition, *Fiscal Policy beyond Election Day: Nine Challenges For '09*, October 22, 2008; Kogan, Cox, and Horney, *The Long-Term Fiscal Outlook Is Bleak*, 3, 6–7.

19. Concord Coalition, *Designing a Framework for Economic Recovery and Fiscal Sustainability*, January 28, 2009, 5.

20. Congressional Budget Office, *The Long-Term Budget Outlook* (Washington, DC: CBO, 2005), 10, 22–23; Dennis Ippolito, "Fiscal Sustainability and Deficit Politics in the U.S.," in Diego Sanchez-Ancochea and Iwan Morgan, eds., *The Political Economy of the Public Budgets in the Americas* (London: Institute for the Study of the Americas, 2008), 73–75.

21. Statement of Robert A. Sunshine, Acting Director, *The Budget and Economic Outlook: Fiscal Years 2009 to 2019*, before the Committee on the Budget, U.S. Senate, January 8, 2009 (Washington, DC: Congressional Budget Office, 2009), 31.

22. Congressional Budget Office, *The Long-Term Budget Outlook* (2005), 7, 32–33.

23. Sunshine, *The Budget and Economic Outlook*, 20–21.

24. Paul N. Van de Water, *Medicare Changes Can Complement Health Reform*, CBPP, July 30, 2008; Ippolito, "Fiscal Sustainability and Deficit Politics in the U.S.," 76–78.

25. Allison Russo, Joanna Jiang, and Margueritte Barett, "Trends in Preventable Hospitalizations among Adults and Children, 1997–2004," Statistical Brief No. 36 (Rockville, MD: Agency for Healthcare Research and Quality, August 2007); January Angeles, "Insuring All Americans Is a Critical Component of an Efficient, High Quality Health Care System," CBPP, April 2009.

26. Peter Orszag, "Health Care and the Budget: Issues and Challenges for Reform," Testimony before the Committee on the Budget, U.S. Senate, June 21, 2007; Commission on a High Performance Health System, *A High Performance Health System for the United States: An Ambitious Agenda for the Next President* (New York: Commonwealth Fund, November 2007).

27. Sunshine, *The Budget and Economic Outlook*, 16, 20.

28. "The Deficit: How Big is Too Big?" *Economist*, October 25, 2008, 56–57; Leon E. Panetta and Bill Frenzel, "Who Bails out the U.S. Government?" *Christian Science Monitor*, November 5, 2008; Concord Coalition, *Designing a Framework for Economic Recovery and Fiscal Sustainability*, 4.

29. Anthony Faiola, "China Worried about U.S. Debt: Biggest Creditor Nation Demands a Guarantee," *Washington Post*, March 14, 2009, A1; Graham Bowley and Jack Healy, "Worries Rise on Size of U.S. Debt," *New York Times*, May 14, 2009; Barack Obama, *The Audacity of Hope: Thoughts on Reclaiming the American Dream* (New York: Crown Publishing, 2006), 188.

30. Lori Montgomery, "Obama Predicts Years of Deficits over $1 Trillion," *Washington Post*, January 7, 2009, A1; "The President's News Conference," February 9, 2009, APP.

31. Michael Shear, "Obama Pledges Entitlement Reform," *Washington Post*, January 16, 2009, A1.

32. Lori Montgomery and Amy Goldstein, "Health Care Reform Tops Fiscal Need List: Medical Costs Threaten the Nation with Bankruptcy, White House Says

at Summit," *Washington Post*, February 24, 2009, A5. White House Forum on Health Reform, Washington, DC, March 5, 2009, 1.

33. Obama, *The Audacity of Hope*, 42.

34. Alec MacGillis and Paul Kane, "As Obama Talks of Bipartisanship, Definitions Vary," *Washington Post*, February 2, 2009, A1; David Herzenshorne and Carl Hulse, "Deal Reached in Congress on $789 Billion Stimulus Plan," *New York Times*, February 12, 2009.

35. Quoted in MacGillis and Kane, "As Obama Talks of Bipartisanship, Definitions Vary."

36. "Support for Stimulus Plan Slips, but Obama Rides High," *Pew Research Center Publications*, February 9, 2009, www.pewresearch.org/pub/1109/.

37. Lori Montgomery, "Democrats Set High Goal of Sweeping Fiscal Reform," *Washington Post*, February 2, 2009, A1; David Broder, "Hiding a Mountain of Debt," *Washington Post,* March 29, 2009, A15.

38. Concord Coalition, *Designing a Framework for Economic Recovery and Fiscal Sustainability*, 6–7.

39. Office of Management and Budget Director Peter Orszag to David Obey, Chair of House Appropriations Committee, January 27, 2009, in Concord Coalition, ibid., 7; "Your Money at Work," www.recovery.gov; Jackie Calmes, "Obama Planning to Slash Deficit, Despite Stimulus Spending," *New York Times*, February 22, 2009.

40. Lori Cox Han, "The President over the Public: The Plebiscitary Presidency at Center Stage," in Michael Genovese and Lori Cox Hahn, *The Presidency and the Challenge of Democracy* (New York: MacMillan, 2006), 127.

41. "Support for Stimulus Plan Slips, but Obama Rides High." This Pew survey recorded 51 percent approval and 34 percent disapproval for the plan, compared with 57 percent and 22 percent respectively in early January. Reaction had also become more politicized since the earlier survey, with seven out of ten Democratic responders for the plan and six out of ten Republicans against it. Moreover, 48 percent of those polled thought tax cuts would do more for the economy whereas only 39 percent considered spending more effective.

42. Erwin Hargrove, *The President as Leader: Appealing to the Better Angels of Our Nature* (Lawrence: University Press of Kansas, 1998), 42–43.

43. "Remarks on the Economic Stabilization and a Question & Answer Session in Elkhart, Indiana," February 9, 2009, APP. See also Barack Obama, "The Actions Americans Need," *Washington Post*, February 5, 2009, A17; and "Gloom Offensive," *Economist*, February 14, 2009, 51–52.

44. Obama, *The Audacity of Hope*, 40.

45. "Debt Clock Runs Out of Digits," October 9, 2008, http://news.bbc.co.uk/1/hi/business/7660409.stm.

Index